The PURE THEORY
of INTERNATIONAL
TRADE

The PURE THEORY of INTERNATIONAL TRADE

Miltiades Chacholiades

ALDINETRANSACTION
A Division of Transaction Publishers
New Brunswick (U.S.A.) and London (U.K.)

First paperback printing 2006
Copyright © 1973 by Miltiades Chacholiades.

This book is printed on acid-free paper that meets the American National Standard for Permanence of Paper for Printed Library Materials.

Library of Congress Catalog Number: 2005046617
ISBN: 0-202-30844-8
Printed in the United States of America

Library of Congress Cataloging-in-Publication Data

Chacholiades, Miltiades.
  The pure theory of international trade / Miltiades Chacholiades.

        p. cm.
  Includes index.
  ISBN 0-202-30844-8 (alk. paper)
    1. International trade. 2. International economic relations. 3. Commercial policy. I. Title. II. Title: International trade.

HF1379.C385   2006
382.01—dc22   2005046617

To Mary, Lea, and Marina

Contents

Foreword

There has long been a need for a systematic introduction to the modern pure theory of international trade, that would take the student through a careful introduction to the tools of analysis and the main logical propositions into the application of the theory to practical problems of international economic policy. Too often, the student who has learned sophisticated analytical techniques in his price theory course is thrown back in his trade theory course into a morass of strange concepts and problems—such as absolute versus comparative advantage, or why free trade that theoretically benefits everyone should be one of the most unpopular of policy proposals—which could be understood and solved easily if only the appropriate price theory tools were applied and their use understood. Trade theory should be part and parcel of price theory, distinguished only by the fact that other countries form part of the natural opportunities—and natural constraints—that a country confronts in its efforts to bend nature to its desire to produce utility-yielding goods and services; but its exposition is often confused by the attachment of its expositors to obsolete problems and obsolete analytical techniques.

The great virtue of the present volume by Miltiades Chacholiades is that it concentrates on the analytical issues and techniques, and expounds them in a careful and straightforward fashion that should enable students to grasp them and hold them once-and-for-all in their intellectual bag of tools. The book is a workmanly exposition of what the student needs to know, pitched at a level that requires sustained application but no feats of imagination to follow. It does not attempt to deal with major issues of current economic policy, though students and their instructors using it should have little difficulty in applying its analysis to current policy problems. Nevertheless, it does deal with several issues of keen contemporary interest, such as the relation between economic growth and international trade, the effects of trade on social and individual welfare, and the effects of various taxes on international trade, all of which figure prominently in recent discussions of American international economic policy.

The book may seem a trifle abstract and austere, to those who would like easy answers to complex problems phrased in facile literary form and buttressed by the insertion of bite-sized chunks of theoretical analysis. But the purpose of any good book in economics, as Lord Keynes once remarked, is not to provide answers but to provide a way of thinking about the problem; and this objective is better served by a rigorous exposition of existing theory —at the appropriate level of difficulty and comprehension—than by a literary exposition that plays down the analytical apparatus and plays up the policy conclusions (which may well be wrong, or wrong in certain possible circumstances). Professor Chacholiades has followed the former course; he may not—in fact, does not—provide obvious answers to all the problems that society throws upon the area of international trade theory and policy; but neither does he provide soft answers that will not stand up to criticism. What he provides is the tools needed to arrive at answers that the economist can live by; and if the reader takes the trouble to master the tools, he should be able to arrive at answers that he can conscientiously defend.

Harry G. Johnson

Preface

The aim of *The Pure Theory of International Trade* is to present in a logical and sufficiently systematic manner those principles and tools of trade theory which every serious student of international economics ought to know. As Professor Harry G. Johnson notes in his foreword, "Trade theory should be part and parcel of price theory . . .." In this spirit, the present book provides a smooth transition from price theory to trade theory so that the reader who has mastered the principles and techniques of elementary price theory will not get the feeling that trade theory is a totally different and strange field. Quick reviews of relevant price-theory tools are provided where necessary. In addition, the development of the subject matter is honest, rigorous, up-to-date, and, at the same time, pitched at the appropriate level to serve the needs of advanced undergraduates and first-year graduates as well as the needs of the general economist.

The exposition does not make use of advanced mathematical techniques— a procedure making the book look elegant and impressive at the expense of communicating with the masses of students. It relies rather heavily on geometry which, in addition to being simpler, is often more flexible than mathematical analysis. Nevertheless, several appendices have been added to deal with more advanced material. These appendices may be omitted without interrupting the continuity of the book. Hopefully, this will insure maximum flexibility in the book's use. All theorems are proved with great care, and all assumptions are stated and explained clearly. Although it is presumed that the student has some acquaintance with the tools and principles of elementary price theory, acquaintance with elementary calculus, though desirable, is not absolutely necessary.

This book deals mainly with the tools and principles of international economic analysis. But students and instructors can easily supplement it with other readings on current policy problems. The book is divided into seven parts. Part I is a simple overview of the book. Part II (chaps. 2 and 3), dealing with the classical theory, is the simplest. It is nevertheless an important part of the book and should not be ignored, for in addition to providing an explanation of what the classical theory really is, it serves as a general introduction to the pure theory of trade and thus facilitates the understanding of the rest of the book. Parts III and IV cover essential material which should be read before V through VII are read. Nevertheless, chapter 4, "Opportunity Cost," which offers a quick review of some of the tools and principles of price theory, may be omitted by those whose background in price theory is rather strong. In addition, chapter 7, "Increasing Returns," may be omitted on a first reading without interrupting the continuity of the book. After parts II through IV are read, part V, "Growth and Trade," can be taken up either before or after parts VI and VII. Chapter 14, "Growth in a Simple Open Economy," which is more advanced than the rest of the book, can be omitted without interrupting the continuity of the book. Finally, although parts VI and VII can be taken up in any order after parts II through IV are read, it is recommended that part VI be read before part VII.

Selected bibliographies are provided at the end of each chapter. No attempt was made to provide exhaustive bibliographies.

It should be noted that the last section of chapter 5, "Neoclassical Demonstration of Comparative Advantage," is a revised version of the author's *Metroeconomica* paper "Multiple Pre-Trade Equilibria and the Theory of Comparative Advantage." Similarly, chapter 7, "Increasing Returns," is an expanded version of the author's *Southern Economic Journal* paper "Increasing Returns and Comparative Advantage." I wish to thank the editors of both *Metroeconomica* and *The Southern Economic Journal* for their permission to reproduce the above papers.

This book does not aim to push forward the frontiers of international economic analysis. Any new results which may be noticed are mere byproducts of the more important aim of careful and systematic exposition.

My indebtedness to other economists is very great. To my former teachers, Robert L. Bishop, Charles P. Kindleberger, Paul A. Samuelson, and Robert M. Solow, I owe a special debt of gratitude for the knowledge and inspiration they gave me during my graduate years (1962–65) at M.I.T. Also, I am happy to acknowledge the influence of numerous authors of books and journal articles. Unfortunately, I cannot make specific acknowledgments, partly because the list would be too long and partly because I find it difficult to identify each idea I have with the source from which it came. Above all I am infinitely indebted and grateful to Professor Harry G. Johnson, the editor of Aldine Treatises in Modern Economics, who took time from his busy schedule to read a lengthy and technical manuscript and to make numerous invaluable suggestions and criticisms which enabled me to greatly improve my presentation. Further, I am grateful to my colleague John S. Henderson who cheerfully let me try some of my ideas on him from time to time. Of course, any remaining deficiencies are mine. Finally, I would like to thank Janet Benham, Wanda Botelho, Helen Gatlin, Marilyn King, Cathy Ridings, and Sherry Walker for their efficient typing of my many drafts.

I

Introduction

1

Introduction

This chapter deals briefly with the relationship between international economics and general economic theory, the role of international trade in raising the standards of living of all countries of the world, and the overall organizational structure of the book.

1. The Main Branches of Economic Theory

Economics is a social science. Broadly speaking, it is concerned with the use of scarce resources (e.g., labor and skills of all kinds, land of various qualities, and the innumerable capital goods that modern technology requires) for the satisfaction of human wants.

Like most other disciplines, economics is divided into several branches and subbranches; the two major branches, are *microeconomics* and *macroeconomics*. Microeconomics is the study of the behavior of individuals and well-defined groups of individuals in the society, such as households, firms, and industries. On the other hand, macroeconomics is the study of broad aggregates, such as national income, employment, consumption, and investment. In a sense, the micro-macro distinction is artificial because the actual decisions about production, consumption, employment, investment, and so on, are made by the microunits of the economy. Therefore, the basic principles of economic theory are those which explain the behavior of these microunits. However, the distinction is justified by the basic differences in the objectives and methods of the two branches.

Microeconomics deals primarily with the analysis of price determination and the allocation of specific resources to particular uses. On the other hand, macroeconomics deals with the determination of the levels of national income and aggregate resource employment. While microeconomics deals

3

with individual prices and their relations to one another, macroeconomics deals only with aggregate price indices. As a result, the relationship between individual units and aggregates is not clear in macroeconomics. Nevertheless, the simplifications introduced by aggregation are quite useful. Despite the great usefulness of microeconomics (and, in particular, the general-equilibrium theory) to an understanding of the way in which the individual decision-making units of the economy fit together to form a coherent whole, its practical use in explaining aggregate behavior is severely limited by its enormous complexity. A more practical approach is offered by macroeconomics, which attempts to describe the behavior of the economic system in terms of a few simple aggregates and aims explicitly at influencing public policy.

When properly understood, microeconomics and macroeconomics become complementary rather than competitive branches of economic theory. Thus, macroeconomics can enable the policy makers to pursue appropriate economic policies to ensure an economic environment which will validate the verities of microeconomics. Microeconomics, on the other hand, can often be a fruitful source of hypotheses which can be used, with suitable modifications, to explain aggregate behavior.

Microeconomics is further subdivided into *positive economics* and *welfare economics*. The former is the study of what actually *is*. That is, positive economics deals with the problem of how the economic system actually functions, why it produces the results it does, and how changes in the fundamental data of the economy (such as factor endowments, factor ownership, tastes, and technology) affect the solution of the economic problem. It is important to observe that positive economics is, in principle, independent of ethical judgments, and its propositions can be tested against the facts of the real world which they purport to explain.

Welfare economics, on the other hand, is the study of what *ought* to be. It deals with propositions which are themselves logical deductions from a set of assumptions which may or may not be ethical in nature. In contrast with positive economics, the propositions of welfare economics cannot be tested against the facts of the real world for the simple reason that welfare is not an observable quantity. Usually, welfare propositions are tested indirectly by testing the assumptions from which they have been derived—and this is an extremely delicate task. The conclusions of welfare economics depend crucially on ethical judgments.

Perhaps an example might make clearer the distinction between positive and welfare economics. Consider an economy which is contemplating the removal of a tariff on an imported commodity, M. What effects would the removal of the tariff have on the domestic production, consumption, imports, and price of commodity M and of each and every other commodity? Would the removal of the tariff tend to raise or lower real wages and other factor rewards? These questions belong to the realm of positive economics. Notice that the accuracy of the answers given to the above questions (i.e., the conclusions of positive economics) can be tested directly against the actual events which will take place after the removal of the tariff.

Consider the following questions. (*a*) Will the removal of the tariff make the workers (of the economy contemplating the removal of the tariff) better off or worse off? (*b*) What about the effects of the removal of the tariff on the welfare of the owners of land and capital? (*c*) Should the tariff be removed or not? These questions belong to the realm of welfare economics. They all involve a comparison between two situations: the situation which actually exists before and that which will exist after the removal of the tariff. Therefore, any answers that welfare economics has to offer necessarily rest on a prediction about the consequences of doing one thing rather than another, a prediction that must be based on positive economics.

What ethical judgments are involved in answering questions (*a*)–(*c*)? Questions (*a*) and (*b*) can be handled simultaneously. Consider the case of a single individual, whether worker, landlord, or capitalist. Positive analysis can show whether, after the removal of the tariff, he moves to a higher or lower indifference curve. To be specific, assume that he moves to a higher indifference curve. Does this mean that this particular individual is better off after the removal of the tariff? Not unless we make the ethical judgment that no one else but the individual himself is the best judge of his well-being. Without this ethical judgment, we may say that he moves to a higher indifference curve, but we are then only describing how he acts—we are not judging his welfare.

Consider now question (*c*): Should the tariff be removed or not? If social welfare increases with the removal of the tariff, the tariff should be removed; if social welfare decreases, it should not be removed; and if social welfare remains constant, it makes no difference. But what is social welfare? And how can we find out whether it increases or decreases with the removal of the tariff? To answer these questions, additional ethical judgments are required. For instance, we can postulate that social welfare depends on the welfare of the individuals comprising the society, and on nothing else. The mathematical expression of this statement is the Bergson–Samuelson social welfare function in its general form, discussed in chapters 5 and 16. This function is usually made a little more specific by attributing to it an ethical property, namely, that social welfare increases when one individual becomes better off, with no one else being worse off. Now, if the removal of the tariff were to make everybody better off, we could immediately conclude, on the basis of the ethical judgments made so far, that the tariff should be removed. But this is a big *if*. What if the removal of the tariff made some people better off and others worse off? In this more likely case, several alternatives are open to us, and they will be considered in detail in chapter 16. What is important right now, however, is that the propositions of welfare economics depend on ethical judgments whereas the propositions of positive economics do not.

2. *The Scope of International Economics*

While general economic theory deals with the problems of a single, closed economy, international economics deals with the problems of two or more open economies. In particular, international economics deals with the same economic problems as those studied by general economic theory, but it deals with these problems in their international setting. Thus, international economics studies how a number of distinct economies interact upon each other in the process of allocating scarce resources to satisfy human wants. Clearly, international economics is more general than the economics of a closed economy, the latter being a special case of international economics where the number of trading countries has been reduced to one. Further, the study of general economic theory dealing with the problems of a closed economy is only a first (but necessary) step toward the study of the behavior of a real economy, because there is actually no closed economy except the world economy.

Parallel to the division of economic theory into microeconomics and macroeconomics is the breakdown of international economics into two major branches, international trade theory (or the pure theory of trade) and international monetary economics. The latter is centered upon the monetary aspects of international monetary relations. Its approach is mainly macroeconomic in nature, and it particularly deals with the short-run problems of balance-of-payments disequilibrium and adjustment.

The subject matter of this book is the pure theory of trade, which, in contrast to international monetary economics, is a long-run, static-equilibrium theory of barter. Here the short-run monetary adjustment process is assumed completed, with money having no influence whatsoever on the nature or position of long-run equilibrium. Its approach is basically microeconomic in nature. Like microeconomics, the pure theory of trade can be divided into two main branches: one branch dealing with problems of positive economics and the other dealing with problems of welfare economics. Thus, the analysis of the effects of free trade on domestic consumption, production, commodity prices, factor rewards, and so on belongs to what might be called international positive economics. On the other hand, the question of whether free trade is better than restricted or no trade is clearly an issue which belongs to the realm of (international) welfare economics.

3. *The Role of Trade*

The importance of trade springs from the extensive degree of specialization observed in our society. Even in the most primitive societies people cooperate in the use of their scarce resources, because through such cooperation more goods and services are produced than if everyone tried to do many different jobs at once.

The high degree of specialization in our society increases the standard of living of all by making more goods and services available. *But specialization necessarily implies trade and cannot occur without it.* This follows from the fact that people usually want to have a "balanced diet." The specialized producer uses only a small part—maybe none—of his own product for his personal consumption, and he exchanges his surplus for the goods and services of other specialized producers. For instance, a shoemaker does not and cannot consume only shoes. He needs, in addition, food, clothing, shelter, transportation, and so on. Therefore, he exchanges his surplus production of shoes (which, for practical purposes, may be identified with his total output of shoes) for the specialized outputs of farmers, supermarkets, auto producers, physicians, tailors, and the like. Such exchange of goods and services among specialized producers is exactly what is meant by trade.

The exchange of goods and services among residents of the same country is usually called *domestic trade*. The present book is, however, concerned with *international trade*, that is, the exchange of goods and services among residents of different countries. Countries cannot live alone any more effectively than individuals can. Thus, each country tends to specialize in the production of those commodities which it can produce relatively more cheaply than other countries, exchanging its surplus for the surplus of other countries of goods and services which they produce relatively more cheaply, or which the first country cannot produce at all. This process brings about an international division of labor which makes it possible to make more goods and services available to all countries. Therefore, the international division of labor and specialization increases the standard of living in all countries in the same way that the division of labor and specialization within a single, closed economy increases the standard of living of all of its residents. In the same way that the division of labor and specialization within a single, closed economy necessarily implies domestic trade and cannot occur without it, the international division of labor and specialization necessarily implies international trade and cannot occur without it.

4. Plan of the Book

This book is mainly concerned with the basic theoretical principles that govern international trade. In particular, chapters 2 and 3 deal with the classical theory of comparative advantage associated with Robert Torrens, David Ricardo, and John Stuart Mill. But chapters 2 and 3 actually do more than this. Because of the inherent complexity of the pure theory of trade due mainly to its general-equilibrium character, it was considered useful to introduce, within the context of the simple labor theory of value, most of the tools which are used later in the book. Hence, chapters 2 and 3 can also be considered as a general introduction to the pure theory of trade. Familiarity with the contents of the chapters will definitely improve the student's chances of understanding the rest of the book. The appendix to chapter 3 extends the analysis to many countries and many commodities. This appendix can be omitted without interrupting the continuity of the book.

Chapters 4–7 cover the neoclassical theory of international trade associated with Alfred Marshall, Jacob Viner, Gottfried Haberler, F. Y. Edgeworth, Abba P. Lerner, Wassily W. Leontief, and James E. Meade. In particular, chapter 4 deals with the theory of production and cost minimization, the concept of the production-possibilities frontier and opportunity cost. Chapter 5 deals with the concept of social indifference, and the problem of general equilibrium and comparative advantage. Chapter 6 deals with Meade's ingenious geometric technique and the stability of international equilibrium. Finally, chapter 7 deals with the problem of increasing returns to scale. Because of its more technical character, chapter 7 may be omitted without interrupting the continuity of the book. In addition, all appendices to chapters 4–7 may be omitted.

Chapters 8–11 deal with the modern theory of trade associated with Eli F. Heckscher, Bertil Ohlin, Paul A. Samuelson, and Abba P. Lerner. In particular, chapter 8 deals with the concepts of factor intensity and factor abundance; chapter 9 deals with the Heckscher-Ohlin theorem, namely, that the cause of trade is to be found largely in differences between the factor endowments of different countries; chapter 10 deals with the relationship among factor proportions, factor prices, and commodity prices; and finally chapter 11 deals with the factor-price equalization theorem, namely, that the effect of trade is to tend to equalize factor prices between countries, thus serving to some extent as a substitute for factor mobility.

Chapters 12–14 deal with the effects of economic growth due either to growth of factor endowments or to technical progress. Chapters 12–13 are largely based on Harry G. Johnson's comparative-statics model of growth. Chapter 14, on the other hand, is a dynamic model which could be considered an integration of the growth models of Robert M. Solow and Hirofumi Uzawa. Chapter 14 can easily be omitted.

Chapters 15–16 deal with the effects of international trade on economic welfare. In particular, chapter 15 discusses the effects of international trade on the welfare of the citizens of the trading countries; and chapter 16 covers the evaluation of the effects of international trade on social welfare.

Chapters 17–20 deal with international trade policy. In particular, chapter 17 deals with the forms of trade control; chapter 18, with the effects of import and export taxes when the tax-imposing country is small (i.e., a price taker in the international market); chapter 19 deals with the effects of import and export taxes when the tax-imposing country is large; and chapter 20, with the welfare effects of trade taxes, the effects of import and export subsidies, and the effects of quantitative restrictions.

SELECTED BIBLIOGRAPHY

Listed below are several selected readings in the areas of mathematical economics, microeconomics, and international economics. This list is neither exhaustive nor required for the understanding of the different aspects of the pure theory of international trade presented in this study. However, it was considered useful to provide a convenient guide to the literature relevant to the present study. More specific references will be found at the end of each chapter.

MATHEMATICS AND MATHEMATICAL ECONOMICS

Allen, R. G. D. 1959. *Mathematical Economics*. London: Macmillan & Co.
———. 1960. *Mathematical Analysis for Economists*. London: Macmillan & Co.
Apostol, T. M. 1960. *Mathematical Analysis*. Reading, Mass.: Addison-Wesley Publishing Co.
———. 1964. *Calculus*, 2 vols. New York: Blaisdell Publishing Co.
Chiang, A. C. 1967. *Fundamental Methods of Mathematical Economics*. New York: McGraw-Hill Book Co.
Courant, R. 1936. *Differential and Integral Calculus*, 2 vols. London: Blackie & Son, Ltd.
Courant, R., and H. Robbins. 1963. *What Is Mathematics?* Oxford: Oxford University Press.
Samuelson, P. A. 1947. *Foundations of Economic Analysis*. Cambridge, Mass.: Harvard University Press.
Yamane, T. 1968. *Mathematics for Economists*, 2nd ed. Englewood Cliffs, N.J.: Prentice-Hall, Inc.

MICROECONOMICS

Becker, G. S. 1971. *Economic Theory*. New York: Alfred A. Knopf, Inc.
Ferguson, C. E. 1972. *Microeconomic Theory*, 3rd ed. Homewood, Ill.: Richard D. Irwin, Inc.
Friedman, M. 1962. *Price Theory: A Provisional Text*. Chicago, Ill.: Aldine Publishing Co.
Henderson, J. M., and R. E. Quandt. 1971. *Microeconomic Theory*, 2nd ed. New York: McGraw-Hill Book Co.
Hicks, J. R. 1946. *Value and Capital*, 2nd ed. Oxford: Clarendon Press.
Lancaster, K. 1969. *Introduction to Modern Microeconomics*. Chicago: Rand McNally & Co.
Quirk, J., and R. Saposnik. 1968. *Introduction to General Equilibrium Theory and Welfare Economics*. New York: McGraw-Hill Book Co.

INTERNATIONAL ECONOMICS

American Economic Association. 1950. *Readings in the Theory of International Trade*. Homewood, Ill.: R. D. Irwin, Inc.
———. 1968. *Readings in International Economics*. Homewood, Ill.: R. D. Irwin, Inc.
Balassa, B. 1961. *The Theory of Economic Integration*. Homewood, Ill.: R. D. Irwin, Inc.
Bhagwati, J. 1964. The pure theory of international trade. *Economic Journal*, 74: 1–78.
Caves, R. 1960. *Trade and Economic Structure*. Cambridge, Mass.: Harvard University Press.

Chipman, J. S. 1965. A survey of the theory of international trade: part 1, the classical theory. *Econometrica* 33: 477–519.

———. 1965. A survey of the theory of international trade: part 2, the neo-classical theory. *Econometrica* 33: 685–760.

———. 1966. A survey of the theory of international trade: part 3, the modern theory. *Econometrica* 34: 18–76.

Clement, M. O., R. L. Pfister, and K. J. Rothwell. 1967. *Theoretical Issues in International Economics*. Boston: Houghton-Mifflin Co.

Corden, W. M. 1965. *Recent Developments in the Theory of International Trade*. Princeton University Special Papers in International Economics, No. 7.

Ellsworth, P. T. 1969. *The International Economy*, 4th ed. New York: Macmillan Co.

Enke, S., and V. Salera. 1957. *International Economics*. Englewood Cliffs, N.J.: Prentice-Hall, Inc.

Haberler, G. 1936. *The Theory of International Trade*. London: William Hodge & Co.

———. 1961. *A Survey of International Trade Theory*. Princeton University Special Papers in International Economics, No. 1, 2nd ed.

Harrod, R. 1958. *International Economics*. Chicago: University of Chicago Press.

Heller, H. R. 1968. *International Trade*. Englewood Cliffs, N.J.: Prentice-Hall, Inc.

Johnson, H. G. 1958. *International Trade and Economic Growth*. London: George Allen & Unwin, Ltd.

———. 1962. *Money, Trade and Economic Growth*. Cambridge, Mass.: Harvard University Press.

Kemp, M. C. 1964. *The Pure Theory of International Trade*. Englewood Cliffs, N.J.: Prentice-Hall, Inc.

———. 1969. *The Pure Theory of International Trade and Investment*. Englewood Cliffs, N.J.: Prentice-Hall, Inc.

Kindleberger, C. P. 1968. *International Economics*, 4th ed. Homewood, Ill.: R. D. Irwin, Inc.

Lerner, A. P. 1953. *Essays in Economic Analysis*. London: Macmillan & Co.

Meade, J. E. 1952. *A Geometry of International Trade*. London: George Allen & Unwin, Ltd.

———. 1955. *The Theory of International Economic Policy*. Vol. 2: *Trade and Welfare*. Oxford: Oxford University Press.

Meier, G. M. 1963. *International Trade and Development*. New York: Harper and Row.

Metzler, L. A. 1948. The theory of international trade. In H. S. Ellis (Editor). *A Survey of Contemporary Economics*. Philadelphia: Blackiston Co.

Mookerjee, S. 1958. *Factor Endowment and International Trade: A study and appraisal of the Heckscher-Ohlin theory*. Bombay: Asia Publishing House.

Mosak, J. L. 1944. *General Equilibrium Theory in International Trade*. Bloomington, Ind.: Principia Press.

Mundell, R. A. 1960. The pure theory of international trade. *American Economic Review*, 40: 301–22.

———. 1968. *International Economics*. New York: Macmillan Co.

Ohlin, B. 1933. *Interregional and International Trade*. Cambridge, Mass.: Harvard University Press.

Vanek, J. 1962. *International Trade: Theory and Economic Policy*. Homewood, Ill.: R. D. Irwin, Inc.

Viner, J. 1965. *Studies in the Theory of International Trade*. New York: Augustus M. Kelly, Publishers.

Walter, I. 1968. *International Economics: Theory and Policy*. New York: Ronald Press.

Yntema, T. O. 1932. *A Mathematical Reformulation of the General Theory of International Trade*. Chicago: University of Chicago Press.

II

The Classical Theory

2

Supply

1. The Problem

The pure theory of trade, as expounded by the classical economists Torrens, Ricardo, and Mill, is mainly concerned with the following three questions:

1. Which goods are exported and imported; that is, what is the direction or pattern of trade in commodities and services among the nations of the world?

2. What are the terms of trade; that is, at what prices are the exported and imported goods exchanged internationally?

3. What are the gains from trade; that is, is trade profitable from the point of view of the world as a whole, on the one hand, as well as from the point of view of each country separately, on the other? If so, how are these gains or profits divided among the participating countries?

The first two questions belong to the realm of positive economics, while the third belongs to the realm of welfare economics. However, in a presentation of the pure theory, the three questions cannot be considered apart from each other. This follows from the fact that the pattern of trade of a country; that is, which commodities it exports and which it imports, depends on the terms of trade; further, the division of the gains from trade among the trading partners also depends on the terms of trade; and finally, the gains from trade form the motivating force of all trade.

Despite the strong interdependence that exists among the three questions raised by the classical economists, for pedagogical reasons each question is dealt with separately. Before getting down to specifics, however, let us see how the classical theory answers the three questions in a rather general fashion.

To the first question (Which goods are exported and which are imported by a country?), the classical theory gives the following simple answer. Each country will concentrate on the production of those goods that it can produce relatively more cheaply than other countries and exchange the surplus; that is, whatever it produces above the requirements for its own needs, *against the surplus goods other countries produce relatively more cheaply*, or goods which the first country cannot produce at all. From this point, it is easy to derive the answer to the third question (What are the gains from trade?), because the preceding process brings about an international division of labor that makes it possible to produce more of every commodity on a worldwide basis, with the surplus production representing the gains from trade to be distributed among the trading partners. Finally, as far as the second question is concerned, the classical theory shows that the equilibrium terms of trade will be determined by international supply and demand relations and that they (i.e., the terms of trade) will provide the basis for the division of the gains from trade among the participating nations. This is the classical theory in a nutshell.

2. The Labor Theory of Value

The classical economists adopted the simplifying assumption of the labor theory of value. This theory asserts that labor is the only factor of production and that in a closed economy the prices of all commodities are determined by their labor content. In particular, since our interest lies mainly in relative as opposed to absolute prices with regard to the pure theory of trade, according to the labor theory of value, goods are exchanged against one another according to the relative amounts of labor they represent. For example, assume that there are two commodities, X and Y. Let the symbol a_x denote the amount of labor that is required for the production of 1 unit of commodity X; and the symbol a_y, the amount of labor that is required for the production of 1 unit of commodity Y. If w is used to denote the money wage rate, then the long-run average cost of production of the two commodities is given by the following equations:[1]

$$\text{average cost of } X = wa_x,$$
$$\text{average cost of } Y = wa_y.$$

Note that a common wage rate is used for both commodities because of the implicitly assumed mobility of labor between the two industries.

The coefficients of production a_x and a_y were assumed by the classical economists to be constant in the sense that they were independent of the level of output of each industry. In other words, the coefficients a_x and a_y are assumed to remain the same whether 10 or 1,000 or any other number of units of X and Y are produced. Under these circumstances, it follows that the supply curves of X and Y are horizontal at the levels wa_x and wa_y, respectively.

1. Here and elsewhere the symbols X and Y stand both for names and for quantities.

Consequently, the long-run equilibrium prices of X and Y (p_x and p_y, respectively) must necessarily be given by the equations

$$p_x = wa_x, \qquad p_y = wa_y, \tag{2.1}$$

provided that both commodities are produced.

The requirement that both commodities be produced for the validity of equations (2.1) is seen from the fact that the price of a commodity that is not produced—in the sense of the maximum price that the consumers might be willing to pay if they were to consume a positive amount of the said commodity—is usually less than the average cost of production, except in the limiting case where the market supply and demand curves happen to have a common price-axis intercept. From equation (2.1) it follows that relative prices (p) are entirely determined by relative labor requirements; that is,

$$p \equiv p_x/p_y = a_x/a_y. \tag{2.2}$$

The constancy of the coefficients a_x and a_y does not necessarily imply that the average cost of production of each firm, as opposed to each industry, is horizontal, with the optimum size of each firm being indeterminate. It may very well be that the production function of each firm is characterized successively by increasing, constant, and decreasing returns. In other words, as X and Y increase from zero, their respective coefficients a_x and a_y decrease continuously (increasing returns) until they reach their respective minima (momentary constant returns), and then they increase (decreasing returns). Under these circumstances, the average cost curve of each firm will be U-shaped, as usually assumed. However, if the production functions of all producers in each industry separately are the same, then each long-run industry supply curve will still be horizontal at the level of minimum average cost of each producer in each individual industry, as the reader should be able to verify. What this means is that, despite the fact that the coefficients a_x and a_y are actually variable, we can rest assured that Adam Smith's invisible hand will guide industries to choose their minimum values which are uniquely determined. Thus, the analysis presented earlier is more general than what it appears to be. In fact, the perfect identity of production functions of firms producing the same commodity is not actually needed. The only requirement for our conclusion is that the production functions of all firms in the same industry give rise to the same minimum value of the labor coefficient—and this may very well occur at varying levels of production among the various firms.

That the labor theory of value is an oversimplification of reality is well known. Broadly speaking, it is valid under the assumptions that labor is the only factor of production, that it is homogeneous (i.e., all labor is of the same quality), that every occupation is open to all, and that perfect competition rules everywhere. These assumptions are too restrictive; in reality, some of them are never true and some are not always true. In particular, the element of time is a difficulty the theory cannot surmount. Thus, with a positive rate of interest, the average cost of a commodity, and hence its price, is influenced not merely by the amount of labor required to produce it but also by the length of time for which it is embodied in production. For instance, if one worker can produce 1 unit of X in one year while it requires one worker two years to produce 1 unit of Y, the relative price of X in terms of Y will be smaller than one-half—that is, the price predicted by the simple labor theory of value—because the producers of Y will necessarily incur a certain amount of interest expense over and above their wage bill. In particular, assume that each worker is paid \$$w$ at the end of each year. Then

$$p_x = \$w,$$
$$p_y = \$[w(1 + i) + w],$$
$$\frac{p_x}{p_y} = \frac{w}{w(1 + i) + w} = \frac{1}{2 + i} < \frac{1}{2},$$

where $i \equiv$ the rate of interest. Thus, relative prices do not depend only on the relative amounts of labor required for the production of the two commodities; they also depend on the rate of interest.

Despite the obvious shortcomings of the labor theory of value, we shall adopt it as our point of departure for three reasons. First, it will enable us, with relatively little effort, to bring out quite sharply the nature of the problem of international specialization and the gains from trade. Second, if the interest rate remains constant, the relative price structure will be fixed. Third, it will enable us to construct a fairly simple model of international equilibrium that will serve as an introduction to the more complicated models of the neoclassical and modern writers. As noted in the introductory chapter, the pure theory of trade is a general-equilibrium theory which is inherently more difficult than the Marshallian approach of partial equilibrium. Thus, students lacking a fairly good background in general-equilibrium theory would probably give the subject up if we were to start directly with the neoclassical and modern theories. However, a student who understands well the analysis of chapters 2–3—which is fairly elementary—will be at an advantage in understanding the more complex theories in later chapters.

3. Absolute Advantage

Adam Smith emphasized the importance of free trade in increasing the wealth of all trading nations. He stated that "it is a maxim of every prudent master of a family never to attempt to make at home what it will cost him more to make than to buy." He later continued that

> What is prudence in the conduct of every private family, can scarce be folly in that of a great kingdom. If a foreign country can supply us with a commodity cheaper than we ourselves make it, better buy it of them with some part of the

produce of our own industry employed in a way in which we have some advantage. . . . By means of glasses, hotbeds, and hotwalls, very good grapes can be raised in Scotland, and very good wine too can be made of them at about thirty times the expense for which at least equally good can be bought from foreign countries. Would it be a reasonable law to prohibit the importation of all foreign wines, merely to encourage the making of claret and burgundy in Scotland? . . . As long as the one country has those advantages, and the other wants them, it will always be more advantageous for the latter, rather to buy of the former than to make.[2]

This can best be understood with a simple illustration. Let there be two countries, A and B, endowed with labor alone and producing two commodities, X and Y. In particular, assume that country A can produce a unit of commodity X with 4 units of labor and a unit of commodity Y with 2 units of labor, and that in country B the corresponding costs (in labor units) of X and Y are 2 and 4, respectively. This state of affairs is usually expressed by saying that A has an *absolute advantage* in the production of Y, because 1 unit of Y requires more units of labor in B than in A. Similarly, B has an absolute advantage in the production of X because 1 unit of X requires more units of labor in A than in B. Notice that we speak of an *absolute* advantage because each country can produce one commodity at an absolutely lower cost— measured in labor units—than the other country.

Assuming that labor is immobile between the two countries, is profitable trade in commodities possible between them? Adam Smith would say yes. He would also go on to say that it would be to the advantage of both countries if A specialized in (or confined itself to) the production of Y, and B in the production of X.

Before going any further, it can be shown quite explicitly that the international division of labor postulated by Smith will indeed increase the total world output of every commodity.

Assume that, up to this moment in time, the two countries have been isolated by prohibitive trade barriers. In their isolated general-equilibrium states, they have been producing and consuming the following quantities of X and Y per unit of time: X_A, Y_A (country A), and X_B, Y_B (country B), where the subscripts A and B indicate the country. Thus, up to now, the total world production of X (denoted by X_W) and Y (denoted by Y_W) per unit of time has been

$$X_W = X_A + X_B, \qquad Y_W = Y_A + Y_B. \qquad (2.3)$$

As long as A produces a positive amount of X and B a positive amount of Y (i.e., as long as $X_A > 0$, $Y_B > 0$) in their isolated general equilibrium states, it can be shown that it is possible to increase the total world production of every commodity if A specializes in the production of Y and B in X. Thus, suppose that, starting from the isolated general-equilibrium states,

2. Smith 1937, pp. 424–26.

country A transfers 4 units of labor from the production of X to the production of Y, and B transfers 4 units of labor from Y to X. On the basis of the assumed labor coefficients of production, the outputs of X and Y in the two countries, and the world as a whole, will change as follows:

$$\Delta X_A = -1, \qquad \Delta X_B = +2, \qquad \Delta X_W \equiv \Delta X_A + \Delta X_B = +1,$$
$$\Delta Y_A = +2, \qquad \Delta Y_B = -1, \qquad \Delta Y_W \equiv \Delta Y_A + \Delta Y_B = +1. \qquad (2.4)$$

This process can continue for as long as $X_A > 0$ and $Y_B > 0$.

Observe that, in the above illustration of absolute advantage, labor will not necessarily migrate from one country to another, even if it were perfectly mobile between countries, for after the removal of trade barriers, each country will continue to produce one product because it is more efficient than the other (in that product) in an absolute sense. Thus, the optimum distribution of labor in the sense of maximizing world output would depend ultimately on the strength of the demand for each commodity. For instance, suppose that all consumers in both countries consume the two commodities in the fixed proportion $1X:1Y$. Then, in equilibrium, the total number of units of X produced (and consumed) must be equal to the total number of units of Y produced (and consumed). Now, since with perfect labor mobility A will be producing all units of Y and B all units of X, it follows that half of the total world labor force must be working in A and the other half in B. (Remember that the labor coefficient of X in B is by assumption equal to the labor coefficient of Y in A.) This is the optimum distribution of labor between the two countries. If it existed to begin with, labor would not move internationally even if it were perfectly mobile. On the other hand, if the actual distribution of labor were different from the optimal, a limited migration would be required from the more heavily populated country to the less heavily populated country until the optimum distribution was established. Further, on the assumption that labor is perfectly mobile internationally, relative prices under conditions of free trade will be determined by the relative amounts of labor embodied in the two commodities, as in the case of a closed economy. The best way to see this is to observe that the present case does not differ at all from the case where A and B are simply two different regions of the same country, instead of being two independent countries. In this case, of course, it is obvious that relative prices are indeed determined according to the labor theory of value. However, if labor is completely immobile between countries, relative prices cannot be determined so easily. This topic will be taken up in a later section of this chapter.

Finally, the conclusion that the world output of both commodities can increase if A specializes in Y and B in X does not necessarily imply that the world output of every commodity will actually increase with free trade. The outcome, as is shown later, will depend on tastes.

What is the fundamental reason why the international division of labor postulated by Adam Smith does indeed result in an increased output of both

2. *Supply*   19

commodities? Some, including Smith himself, would hasten to point out that this is so because A has an absolute advantage in Y and B in X. But this is a superficial answer and does not really get to the crux of the matter. Suppose that A had an absolute advantage in both X and Y. What should we conclude then? That A should produce both X and Y and B nothing? This would make sense only if A and B were two regions of the same country, or if labor was free to migrate from country B to country A. But what if A and B are indeed separate countries and labor cannot move from B to A? Is it not then reasonable to conclude that even the more inefficient country B must produce something? It appears then that the fundamental reason for profitable trade is not to be found in the absolute differences in labor cost between the two countries. In other words, it appears that *profitable international trade does not necessarily require an exporter to have an absolute advantage over his foreign rivals*. But if this is so, then what is the *raison d'être* for profitable international trade? This particular question will be taken up below in sections 4 and 5, where it will be shown that absolute labor cost differences are not necessary for profitable trade.

4. *Comparative Advantage*

To gain further insight into the problem of international specialization, consider the following illustration. Assume again two countries, A and B, two commodities, X and Y, and a single homogeneous factor of production, labor. As before, assume that A's labor requirements in the production of X and Y are 4 and 2 units of labor, respectively. However, in complete contrast to the preceding illustration of absolute advantage, assume that B's labor requirements in the production of X and Y are 6 and 12 units of labor, respectively—that is, three times as much as those assumed in the preceding illustration of absolute advantage. In the present illustration, which Ricardo considered as the typical state of affairs, one of the two countries (i.e., A) can produce both goods with a smaller expenditure (cost) of labor than the other (i.e., B). It should be obvious that if A and B were two regions of the same country, or if labor were perfectly mobile among countries, all goods would eventually end up being produced in that region (or country) where costs are lower in an absolute sense. But what would happen in the presence of labor immobility among countries?

It is interesting to note some of the arguments against free trade that could be advanced in each of the two countries. Thus, in B, some politicians might argue that A's efficiency is so great that it would undersell B's producers in every line of production. Therefore, import tariffs are needed to protect B's (honest) workers from ruinous foreign competition. On the other hand, in country A, some politicians might argue that B's wage rate will definitely be lower than that of A, since the latter is more productive than the former. Therefore, it might be argued, if A's workers are subjected to the competition of B's cheap labor, the real wage of A's workers will drastically fall; hence, protective tariffs are needed. Thus, both countries could provide pseudoarguments against free trade. The greatest contribution of Ricardo and Torrens[3] was to show that both of these arguments are wrong. The workers of both countries can indeed benefit from international trade. Table 2.1 summarizes the data.

TABLE 2.1

	Country A	Country B
Labor requirements per unit of output of:		
Commodity X	4	6
Commodity Y	2	12
Relative price (or cost) of X in terms of Y	2	$\frac{1}{2}$
Relative price (or cost) of Y in terms of X	$\frac{1}{2}$	2

In table 2.1, country A has an absolute advantage in the production of both X and Y because $4 < 6$ and $2 < 12$, respectively. However, its absolute advantage is greater in the production of Y than in X because $\frac{2}{12} < \frac{4}{6}$. In other words, A requires 2 and B 12 units of labor for the production of 1 unit of Y. Or A requires $\frac{2}{12}$ (approximately 17 percent) of the amount of labor that B requires for the production of the same amount of output of Y. On the other hand, A requires $\frac{4}{6}$, or approximately 67 percent, of the amount of labor that B requires for the production of the same amount of output of X. Hence, A's advantage is greater in the production of Y than in X. It can be said that A has a *comparative advantage* in the production of Y and a *comparative disadvantage* in the production of X.

Similarly, country B has an *absolute disadvantage* in the production of both X and Y for the same reasons that A has an absolute advantage in both commodities. However, its disadvantage is smaller in the production of X than in Y, since $\frac{6}{4} < \frac{12}{2}$. This is expressed by saying that B has a comparative *advantage* in the production of X and necessarily a comparative *disadvantage* in the production of Y.

Note that comparative advantage, as opposed to absolute advantage, is a relative term. Essentially, the same inequality was used to determine the commodity in whose production each of the two countries has a comparative advantage. In other words, the inequalities $\frac{2}{12} < \frac{4}{6}$ and $\frac{6}{4} < \frac{12}{2}$ are equivalent. Therefore, in a two-country, two-commodity model, once it is determined that, for instance, A has a comparative advantage in Y, the rest (i.e., that A has a comparative disadvantage in X and that B has a comparative advantage in X and a comparative disadvantage in Y) follows automatically.

3. The theory of *comparative advantage* is usually associated with Ricardo. However, an increasing number of economists tend to believe that we owe the theory to Torrens. Therefore, it seems reasonable to call it the *Ricardo–Torrens theory*.

Can international trade be profitable even when one country has an absolute advantage in the production of every commodity? The great classical achievement was to demonstrate that, even under the present circumstances where one country is more efficient than the other in every line of production, an international division of labor would also take place that could (potentially) increase the world output of every commodity. What is even more surprising is that the truth of this theorem can be demonstrated in exactly the same way as in the simple case where each country has an absolute advantage in the production of only one commodity— Adam Smith's case. In fact, for the proof of the theorem, the same equations can be used (i.e., eq. [2.4]) that were used in Adam Smith's case. The equations are reproduced below for convenience:

$$\Delta X_A = -1, \quad \Delta X_B = +2, \quad \Delta X_W \equiv \Delta X_A + \Delta X_B = +1,$$
$$\Delta Y_A = +2, \quad \Delta Y_B = -1, \quad \Delta Y_W \equiv \Delta Y_A + \Delta Y_B = +1. \tag{2.4}$$

Starting again from the isolated general-equilibrium states of the two countries, let country A transfer 4 units of labor from the production of X to the production of Y—as before—and let country B transfer 12 units of labor from Y to X—that is, three times as many as before, since B is assumed to be three times less efficient now than before. With the qualifications made earlier, it is clear that the resulting changes in the world outputs of both commodities will again be given by equations (2.4). The proof is complete.

The general conclusion that can be derived from the preceding analysis is that, if each country specializes in the production of that commodity in which it has a comparative advantage, the total world output of every commodity necessarily increases potentially (*the law of comparative advantage*). However, it should be noted that specialization according to comparative advantage does not enable the world to produce the maximum output that could be produced if all labor were free to migrate to the most efficient country. Free commodity trade will, nevertheless, enable the world to produce more of everything, as compared with the case where each country is a closed economy with no international trade relations. Finally, free international trade is profitable (i.e., it increases potentially the world output of every commodity) if, and only if, there exists a difference in the relative labor requirements between countries. That is, if country A is more efficient than B in the production of every commodity but the degree of its superiority is the same everywhere, then there will be no basis for trade.

The principle of comparative advantage has general validity: it applies to the division of labor between individual persons. Examples are not difficult to find. A business manager, though a great typist himself, employs somebody else to do his typing because it pays him to concentrate upon those tasks in which his superiority, and thus his comparative advantage, is greatest. The same is true of the doctor who employs a gardener, or the teacher who employs an assistant to grade his papers.

5. Opportunity Cost

So far, it has been demonstrated that international trade does not require offsetting absolute advantages but is possible—and profitable to both trading countries in general—where a comparative advantage exists. However, the analysis and conclusions seem to depend on the restrictive assumption of the labor theory of value. As noted earlier, the labor theory of value is not generally accepted as valid, because labor is neither homogeneous nor the sole factor of production. Labor consists of numerous qualitatively different subgroups known as "noncompeting" groups. For instance, if the demand for medical services increases while the demand for servicing automobiles decreases, it would hardly be conceivable to expect auto mechanics to assume the role of physicians; the wage rate of the two groups would, in at least the short run, tend to move in opposite directions. But even if labor were indeed homogeneous and commanded a single wage rate in a perfectly competitive market, there remains the more fundamental objection that labor is not the only factor of production: goods are usually produced by various combinations of land, labor, and capital.[4] This makes it impossible to use the labor theory of value, however qualified. But if we shall have to discard eventually the labor theory of value as invalid, do we also have to discard the important classical conclusion that specialization according to comparative advantage increases potentially the total world output of every commodity? Fortunately, this is not the case. Gottfried Haberler (1936) succeeded in developing his *theory of opportunity costs*, which actually frees the classical theory from the restrictive assumption of the labor theory of value.

Consider again the example summarized in table 2.1. Country A's labor coefficients for X and Y are 4 and 2, respectively, and B's corresponding labor coefficients are 6 and 12. In the preceding section, the inequality $\frac{2}{12} < \frac{4}{6}$ was used to determine that A has a comparative advantage in Y and B in X. But this inequality can also be written as $\frac{2}{4} < \frac{12}{6}$. Clearly, the two inequalities are equivalent, but the interpretation of the latter is much more interesting and useful.

Consider the ratio $\frac{2}{4}$, keeping in mind that 4 and 2 are A's labor coefficients of X and Y, respectively. What is the meaning of the ratio $\frac{2}{4}$? Suppose that country A is currently employing all of its labor in the production of some positive amounts of X and Y. How much X would country A have to give up if it wished to increase the output of Y by 1 unit by transferring sufficient amounts of labor from X to Y? Since, for the production of an additional unit of Y, 2 units of labor are required, and since, as the output of X falls, labor is being released at the rate of 4 units per unit of X

4. Frank Taussig attempted to circumvent this objection by his belief that the proportion in which labor was used with other factors was the same in all industries. This seems to amount to what Marx called "equal organic composition of capital."

given up, it follows that only $\frac{2}{4}$, or half a unit, of X must be given up for the production of an additional unit of Y. *This minimum amount of X (i.e., $\frac{2}{4}$) which A has to give up in order to produce an additional unit of Y is called the opportunity cost of Y in terms of X in country A.*

Similarly, the ratio $\frac{12}{6}$ shows B's opportunity cost of Y in terms of X, since 6 and 12 are B's labor coefficients of X and Y. Therefore, the inequality $\frac{2}{4} < \frac{12}{6}$ simply tells us that A's opportunity cost of Y in terms of X is lower than B's.

It follows that, if a country, A, has a comparative advantage (in the sense of sec. 4) in the production of a commodity, Y, the opportunity cost of Y in terms of X must be lower in A than in B. Conversely, if the opportunity cost of a commodity, Y, is lower in A than in B, then A necessarily has a comparative advantage (in the sense of sec. 4) in the production of Y. Accordingly, it must be obvious that comparative advantage can be defined in terms of opportunity costs directly. Therefore, given two countries (A and B) and two commodities (X and Y), we say that a country, A, has a comparative advantage in the production of a certain commodity, Y, if, and only if, the opportunity cost of Y in terms of X is lower in A than in B. This is verified by the example of table 2.1. Thus, the third row of table 2.1 shows that the opportunity cost of X in terms of Y is 2 in A and $\frac{1}{2}$ in B; this confirms our earlier conclusion that B has a comparative advantage in X. Further, in the last row of table 2.1, the opportunity cost of Y in terms of X is seen to be $\frac{1}{2}$ in A and 2 in B; this again confirms our conclusion that A has a comparative advantage in Y.

It should be noted that the opportunity cost of X in terms of Y is nothing but the reciprocal of the opportunity cost of Y in terms of X. Thus, in the example of table 2.1, A's opportunity cost of X in terms of Y is 2 and its opportunity cost of Y in terms of X is $\frac{1}{2}$. The same relationship can be verified in the case of country B. Thus, referring back to the example of table 2.1, it is obvious that the information given in only one of the last two rows is sufficient for our purposes.

Our main conclusion is: where two countries are producing two different commodities, one country should specialize in the production of that commodity in which the country's opportunity cost is lower than the second country's opportunity cost of the same commodity. Thus, if A's opportunity cost of Y in terms of X is $\frac{1}{2}$ while B's is 2, A should specialize in Y and B in X. That this pattern of specialization necessarily increases the total world output of every commodity must be obvious by now. Thus, for every additional unit of Y produced in A, half a unit of X must be given up (because A's opportunity cost of Y in terms of X is $\frac{1}{2}$). However, the production of half a unit of X in B (to restore the total world output of X to its original level) requires the sacrifice of only $\frac{1}{2} \times \frac{1}{2} = \frac{1}{4}$ of Y (because B's opportunity cost of X in terms of Y is $\frac{1}{2}$). Hence, while the total world output of X remains constant, the output of Y increases by $1 - \frac{1}{4} = \frac{3}{4}$. Note that instead of increasing B's output of X by $\frac{1}{2}$, we could have increased it by ΔX_B, where $\frac{1}{2} < \Delta X_B < 2$. The outputs of both commodities would then increase.

What is the significance of this analysis? Is it more than a mere restatement of the conclusions of the preceding section on comparative advantage? To begin with, in the preceding discussion it is immaterial whether A produces Y with less labor than B, or B produces X with less labor than A. What this means is that offsetting absolute advantages are not required for the existence of profitable trade. This is no doubt an important conclusion, but we can go beyond it. Once comparative advantage is defined in terms of opportunity cost reflecting forgone production of other commodities, *it makes no difference whether commodities are actually produced by labor alone*. This accounts for the superiority of the theory of opportunity costs which, like the *deus ex machina*, saves the classical conclusions. What is important, in other words, is only the opportunity cost of one commodity in terms of the other in each of the two countries, and nothing else. Once these opportunity costs are given, we can determine the desirable pattern of international specialization, irrespective of what theory of production is being adopted. It is, therefore, important to realize labor cost is only a transitional consideration in the previous analysis. As Haberler repeatedly emphasized, the sole purpose of the labor theory of value is to determine the opportunity cost of one commodity in terms of the other in each of two countries.

Note that within the context of the labor theory of value, the opportunity cost of X in terms of Y in a country coincides with that country's pretrade relative price of X in terms of Y. For instance, given that A's labor coefficients of X and Y are 4 and 2, respectively, A's pretrade price ratio, p_x/p_y, and A's opportunity cost of X in terms of Y are both given by the ratio $\frac{4}{2}$. Therefore, within the context of the labor theory of value, comparative advantage can be defined alternatively in terms of pretrade relative prices instead of opportunity costs. Thus, we can say that a country, A, has a comparative advantage in X (and should specialize in the production of X) if, and only if, A's relative price of X, before trade, is smaller than B's. Does it follow, then, that comparative advantage can in general be defined in terms of pretrade prices? This can be done only under the proviso that relative prices do reflect opportunity costs.

6. Limits of the Terms of Trade and Wage Rates

The analysis so far has shown that, if each country specializes in that commodity in whose production it is relatively more efficient, the world output of every commodity increases (potentially). It is shown in this section that the introduction of free international trade will necessarily generate forces which cause this to happen.

The rest of the analysis of this chapter applies both to Adam Smith's case of absolute advantage and to the Ricardo-Torrens case of comparative advantage. Therefore, no sharp distinction needs to be drawn between the two cases for the rest of this chapter.

The main distinguishing feature of international trade singled out by Ricardo was the international immobility of labor coupled with its perfect mobility within countries. On the other hand, goods were regarded as perfectly mobile within and among countries (at zero transport cost). Now the perfect mobility of labor within a country causes, in the absence of international trade (in commodities), an allocation of labor among the various branches of production that ensures everywhere the equality between its marginal productivity and the wage rate—which is another way of saying that equations (2.1) above are satisfied, since the marginal physical product of labor in the ith industry is equal to $1/a_i$ and thus

$$p_x(1/a_x) = p_y(1/a_y) = w. \tag{2.5}$$

Therefore, the perfect mobility of labor is a necessary condition for the validity of the labor theory of value.

In our two-country, two-commodity model, before trade starts, one distinct domestic price ratio exists for each of the two countries. These pretrade price ratios are, of course, determined by the labor requirements in the production of each of the two commodities. With the opening up of trade relations, these two (in general) different price ratios will necessarily be replaced by a single ratio—the "law of one price." This international price ratio is generally referred to as the *terms of trade*. What the following analysis shows is that the actual pattern of specialization in each of the two countries (considered separately) depends on the value of the international terms of trade; further, the equilibrium value of the terms of trade will be such as to cause each country to specialize in that commodity in whose production it is relatively more efficient, that is, the commodity in whose production it has a comparative advantage.

Given the data summarized in table 2.1, the pretrade price ratios in each of the two countries can be determined as follows:

$$(p_x/p_y)_A \equiv A\text{'s price ratio} = \tfrac{4}{2} = 2,$$
$$(p_x/p_y)_B \equiv B\text{'s price ratio} = \tfrac{6}{12} = 0.5.$$

In other words, in A, 1 unit of X exchanges for 2 units of Y (or the price of X is twice as high as the price of Y), whereas in B, 1 unit of X exchanges for only 0.5 units of Y (or the price of X is one-half the price of Y).

Consider now country A by itself and assume that it has access to a huge international market where it can buy and sell unlimited quantities of X and Y at prices that are fixed internationally and cannot be substantially influenced by the purchases and sales of country A. This case can be compared with the case of a purely competitive firm that faces an infinitely elastic demand curve for its products, or with the case of a consumer who faces fixed prices. Suppose for the moment that the international price ratio

(p_x/p_y) is higher than 2 (i.e., A's domestic price ratio). Assume that the international price ratio is 10. What does the possibility of international trade imply for country A, and how will country A react to this new opportunity? This new opportunity to trade is similar to the discovery of two new production techniques, one for producing X and another one for producing Y. Thus, country A can obtain each commodity through the application of labor in either of the following two ways: (*a*) it can directly produce the commodity as it did before the opportunity to trade was available, or (*b*) it can produce the other commodity directly and then exchange it in the international market for the desired commodity. It will be to the advantage of country A to choose that production technique which requires less expenditure of labor; in fact, this will necessarily be dictated by the forces of competition.

TABLE 2.2

	A's Labor Coefficients	
	direct production	*acquisition through trade*
Commodity X	4	$(10 \times 2 =)\ 20$
Commodity Y	2	$(\frac{1}{10} \times 4 =)\ \frac{2}{5}$

Table 2.2 shows the labor requirements of each commodity both for the case of direct domestic production and for the case where each commodity is indirectly obtained through trade. The first column of table 2.2 simply repeats the first column of table 2.1. The entries in the second column ("acquisition through trade") have been determined as follows. First consider commodity X. To obtain 1 unit of X from the international market, country A has to surrender 10 units of Y, the direct domestic production of which requires $10 \times 2 = 20$ units of labor. On the other hand, in order to obtain 1 unit of Y from the international market, country A has to surrender only $\frac{1}{10}$ of a unit of X, the direct domestic production of which requires $\frac{1}{10} \times 4 = \frac{2}{5}$ of a unit of labor. From these results, it follows that country A will find it cheaper to import commodity Y and produce domestically commodity X only. This conclusion will continue to hold for as long as the international price ratio is higher than A's pretrade domestic price ratio. However, when the international price ratio falls below A's pretrade price ratio, the conclusion is reversed; that is, A will find it cheaper to import commodity X and produce domestically commodity Y only. This is illustrated in table 2.3 (which is similar to table 2.2) where it is assumed that the international price ratio is $\frac{1}{4}$. Finally, note that if the international price ratio happens to coincide with A's pretrade price ratio, the labor coefficients of both commodities for their direct production will necessarily be equal to the corresponding expenditure of labor for obtaining each commodity

TABLE 2.3

	A's Labor Coefficients	
	direct production	acquisition through trade
Commodity X	4	($\frac{1}{4} \times 2 =$) $\frac{1}{2}$
Commodity Y	2	($4 \times 4 =$) 16

through trade. In other words, country A will be indifferent between producing a commodity directly and obtaining it indirectly through trade. For this reason, its structure of production is indeterminate in this case.

Observe that A will always find it cheaper to import one commodity and export another. In other words, it is impossible for acquisition through trade to be cheaper than direct production for all goods. This can be seen as follows. Let a_x and a_y stand for the labor requirements of X and Y, respectively, and let p stand for the international price ratio. Then, from the preceding analysis it follows that the labor requirements for X and Y, if they were to be obtained indirectly through trade, are pa_y and $(1/p)a_x$, respectively. Now if X is cheaper to produce domestically, $a_x < pa_y$. But this inequality can also be written as follows: $(1/p)a_x < a_y$, which implies that Y is cheaper to obtain indirectly through trade. Thus, given the first inequality, we can derive the second, and vice versa.

When the international price ratio is different from A's pretrade price ratio, free trade will enable country A to increase (potentially) its consumption of every commodity because country A can obtain one commodity indirectly through trade with less labor than it otherwise would have to use while it can continue to produce the other commodity with the same labor as in the pretrade state.

Figure 2.1 summarizes the pattern of specialization of country A. The international terms of trade are measured along the horizontal line of figure 2.1. The vertical rule at the point α indicates where the international terms of trade are equal to A's pretrade price ratio. To the right of point α, the international price ratio is higher than A's pretrade price ratio and A specializes in the production of X; it exports X and imports Y. To the left of

A's PATTERN OF SPECIALIZATION

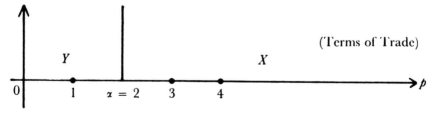

FIGURE 2.1

α, the international price ratio is smaller than A's pretrade price ratio and A specializes in the production of Y; it exports Y and imports X.

A similar analysis holds for country B, so there is no need for repetition. Figure 2.2 summarizes the conclusions for both countries. It is similar to figure 2.1 except that above the terms-of-trade line, A's pattern of specialization is indicated, whereas below it, B's pattern of specialization is shown.

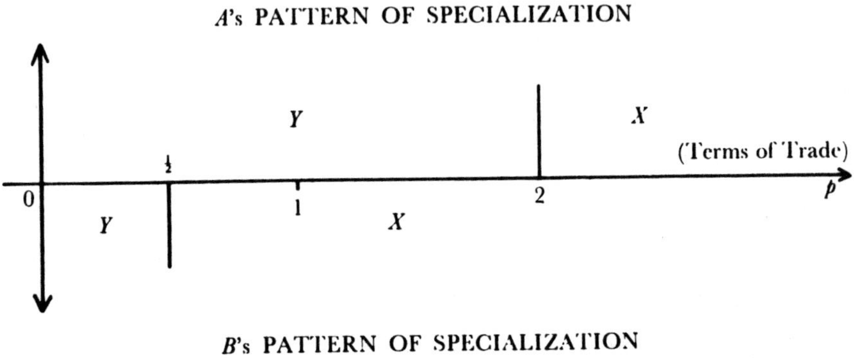

A's PATTERN OF SPECIALIZATION

B's PATTERN OF SPECIALIZATION

FIGURE 2.2

Figure 2.2 is important because it will enable us to answer the question with which we began the discussion of this section: Will free international trade generate forces that will make it profitable for each country to specialize in that commodity in whose production it has a comparative advantage? For this purpose, it is necessary to introduce one additional assumption about demand, namely, that both commodities are consumed somewhere in the world for all values of the terms of trade. The two commodities do not have to be consumed simultaneously by one or the other or both countries. It will be sufficient for our purposes if one country consumes only X and the other consumes only Y. The only requirement is that the total world consumption of every commodity is always positive. This does not appear to be an unreasonable assumption.

Figure 2.2 shows that, unless the international price ratio lies in the closed region $\{\frac{1}{2}, 2\}$,[5] both countries will end up specializing in the production of the same commodity. Thus, for values of p higher than 2, both countries will tend to specialize in the production of X, whereas for values of p lower than $\frac{1}{2}$, both countries will tend to specialize in the production of Y. Neither of these situations is viable in the long run if both commodities are to be consumed. Therefore, long-run international equilibrium cannot exist for values of the terms of trade that lie outside the closed region $\{\frac{1}{2}, 2\}$. The only possible

5. The *closed region* $\{\frac{1}{2}, 2\}$ includes all those numbers which lie between $\frac{1}{2}$ and 2, including the numbers $\frac{1}{2}$ and 2 themselves. The *open region* $(\frac{1}{2}, 2)$ differs from the closed region $\{\frac{1}{2}, 2\}$ in that the former does not include the numbers $\frac{1}{2}$ and 2 whereas the latter does.

values of the terms of trade that are consistent—from the point of view of long-run equilibrium—with the assumption that both commodities are always consumed are those that lie in the closed region $\{\frac{1}{2}, 2\}$, which is, of course, determined by the pretrade price ratios in the two countries. But for any value of the terms of trade in the open region $(\frac{1}{2}, 2)$ country A specializes in Y and B in X; that is, *each country specializes in that commodity in whose production it has a comparative advantage*. In this more general case, both countries benefit from trade. But in the specific case where the equilibrium terms of trade coincide with either country's pretrade price ratio, one of the two countries—the one whose pretrade price ratio is equal to the terms of trade—gains nothing while the other becomes the sole beneficiary of the gains from trade. This could very well happen if the two countries are not of equal size, because then it is possible that the total world consumption of the commodity in which the smaller country has a comparative advantage may be larger than the latter's maximum output of the said commodity, thus causing the larger country to produce both commodities. Under these circumstances, the terms of trade will necessarily coincide with the larger country's pretrade price ratio, with all gains from trade accruing to the smaller country. The larger country will merely be forced to change its internal allocation of labor between the two commodities to satisfy the needs of the smaller country.

The division of the gains of trade between the two countries depends on the equilibrium terms of trade. Thus, if the terms of trade coincide with A's (B's) pretrade price ratio, A (B) gains nothing. Further, the closer to A's (B's) pretrade price ratio the terms of trade lie, the larger will be B's (A's) share of the gains. Thus, if the terms of trade are initially equal to $\frac{1}{2}$ (i.e., B's pretrade price ratio) and, as a result of a continuous change in tastes in favor of commodity X, they increase continuously until they reach the value 2 (i.e., A's pretrade terms of trade), the division of the gains from trade will be affected as follows. Initially all the gains will accrue to A, but as the terms of trade increase, the division of gains will shift continuously in favor of country B until the moment when the terms of trade become equal to 2, and then all gains will accrue to country B. This conclusion, of course, makes sense because tastes are assumed to shift continuously in favor of X, which is the commodity in which B has a comparative advantage. The truth of this conclusion can be demonstrated as follows. Let p stand for the terms of trade. As we have seen, p must satisfy the condition

$$\frac{1}{2} \leq p \leq 2. \tag{2.6}$$

Further, on the basis of the analysis of the present section, it should be clear that the labor coefficients for the production or acquisition through trade of commodities X and Y in countries A and B are those given in table 2.4. Two of the four coefficients are constant; the other two, however, are variable depending on the value of p. Observe that as p increases, the amount of

TABLE 2.4

	Country A	Country B
Commodity X	$2p$	6
Commodity Y	2	$6/p$

labor required in A for the acquisition of 1 unit of X (i.e., $2p$) tends to *increase*, whereas the amount of labor required in B for the acquisition of 1 unit of Y (i.e., $6/p$) tends to *decrease*. Therefore, as p increases, country A will find out that it can consume less X for any given consumption of Y because the acquisition of X becomes more costly. Country B, however, will be delighted to find out that the acquisition of Y becomes cheaper, and thus for any level of consumption of X it can consume a higher amount of Y. Consequently, as p increases, the division of the gains from trade shifts in favor of country B and against country A.

The data given in table 2.4 can also help answer the question of the real wage in the two countries. The real wage rate—as opposed to the money wage rate—can be expressed in terms of either commodity. Actually, it is equal to the amount of the commodity in terms of which it is being measured that can be directly produced, or acquired through trade, with the expenditure of 1 unit of labor.

Strictly speaking, the real wage rate expressed in terms of the ith commodity is given by the marginal physical productivity of labor in the production of the ith commodity. Since the preceding definition refers to the average, as opposed to the marginal, physical productivity of labor, it is quite possible that some confusion might arise. However, in the context of our model, the marginal and the average physical productivity of labor are identical.

TABLE 2.5

	Country A	Country B
Real wage rate expressed in terms of:		
Commodity X	$1/2p$	$\frac{1}{6}$
Commodity Y	$\frac{1}{2}$	$p/6$

The real wage rate expressed in either commodity in each of the two countries is given in table 2.5. Note that the entries in table 2.5 correspond to the entries in table 2.4. This should be obvious from the fact that when z units of labor are required for the production of 1 unit of the ith commodity (z being the entry in table 2.4), $1/z$ units of the ith commodity can be produced with 1 unit of labor ($1/z$ being the entry in table 2.5).

The most important observation that can be made about the information given in table 2.5 is this: whether the real wage rate is expressed in terms of

X or *Y* (in both countries), the two rates will be proportional to each other, with *A*'s real wage rate always $3/p \times$ *B*'s wage rate. (That is, $(1/2p)/(\frac{1}{6}) = (\frac{1}{2})/(p/6) = 3/p$.)

Inequality (2.6) can be used to show that the factor of proportionality $(3/p)$ must, in the long run, satisfy the following inequality:

$$1 < \tfrac{3}{2} \le 3/p \le 6. \tag{2.7}$$

Thus, the factor of proportionality will always be greater than unity. This implies, of course, that *A's wage rate will definitely be higher than B's*. This is what we should have been expecting, because, after all, *country A was assumed to be more productive than country B in every line of production.*

The above conclusion can also be established in terms of money wage rates—even though, within the context of our model, money wage rates cannot be uniquely determined. Consider the following problem. Suppose that *B*'s money wage rate is arbitrarily fixed at $1. Then, from inequality (2.7), it follows that *A*'s money wage rate (w_A), also expressed in dollars for convenience, must necessarily satisfy the inequality $1.5 \le w_A \le 6$. It can be shown that if $w_A > 6$, the average cost of production of every commodity in country *A* will be higher than the corresponding cost in *B*. Thus, *B* will undersell *A* in every line of production. But this is not a viable situation in the long run, because *A* will not be able to finance its purchases from *B* indefinitely. On the other hand, if $w_A < 1.5$, *A* will undersell *B* in every line of production. But again, this is not a viable situation in the long run.

In the context of the present model, the argument that country *A* cannot compete with country *B* because the latter's wage rate is lower is absolutely fallacious. When inequality (2.7) is satisfied, inequality (2.6) is also satisfied, and each country specializes in the production of that commodity in which it has a comparative advantage. In general, both countries benefit from trade. The other argument for protection in *B* (i.e., because of *A*'s superiority in every line of production) is equally fallacious: every country necessarily has a comparative advantage by definition.

7. *Production-Possibilities Frontiers*

Even if comparative advantage explains why trade takes place, it certainly cannot explain on what terms. (Ricardo is widely regarded as having maintained that the terms of trade would settle "halfway between" the comparative cost ratios.) For this purpose, as John Stuart Mill emphasized, it is required that demand be introduced into the picture. The concept of the *production-possibilities frontier* now becomes pertinent. This will make it possible to restate the preceding analysis graphically, which will be helpful in two different ways: (1) in assimilating the conclusions established so far, particularly that the major classical conclusions remain valid even if the labor theory of value is discarded, and (2) in understanding the neoclassical theory of international trade, which is the subject matter of the next two chapters.

In general, the production-possibilities frontier of a country producing two commodities, X and Y, shows, on the basis of given factor endowments and technology, the maximum amounts of Y that the economy can produce for any given value of X. Thus, assuming that country A is endowed with L_A units of (homogeneous) labor and that the production of X and Y requires, respectively, a_x and a_y units of labor per unit of output, its production-possibilities frontier will be given by the following equation:

$$L_A = a_x X + a_y Y. \tag{2.8}$$

Equation (2.8) is linear and is represented graphically by a straight line, as shown in figure 2.3. Since the production-possibilities frontier is in this case linear, it can be easily determined by first finding its intercepts with the two axes and then connecting them with a straight line. The x-axis intercept shows the maximum quantity of commodity X that the economy can produce—under the constraints of given factor endowments and technology —when the output of Y is zero; it is given by the ratio L_A/a_x, as shown in figure 2.3. A similar interpretation holds for the y-axis intercept, which is given by L_A/a_y. Any point inside the production-possibilities frontier, such as point M, implies that the economy is not making full use of its resources. Since the pure theory of trade is a full-employment, general-equilibrium theory, in what follows it will be assumed that each economy is always producing somewhere on its production-possibilities frontier.

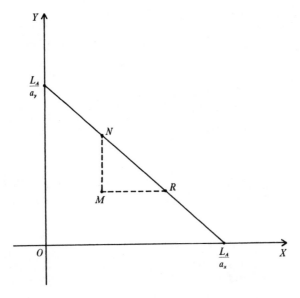

FIGURE 2.3

The absolute slope of A's production-possibilities frontier is given by the ratio

$$\frac{(L_A/a_y)}{(L_A/a_x)} = \frac{a_x}{a_y}. \tag{2.9}$$

Suppose that country A is producing at point N (fig. 2.3) and that, as a result of a change in tastes in favor of X, it moves to point R. In other words, it transfers sufficient amounts of resources from the production of Y to the production of X so that the production of X increases by MR units while the production of Y falls by NM units. How many units of Y did A have to give up per extra unit of X? The answer is MN/MR, which actually is the absolute slope of A's production-possibilities frontier. Therefore, the absolute slope of A's production-possibilities frontier, or, as is usually called, the *marginal-rate of transformation*, has an important meaning: it shows the opportunity cost of X in terms of Y. Further, combining equations (2.2) and (2.9), it follows that the absolute slope of A's production-possibilities frontier is identical to the ratio of commodity prices, that is, p_x/p_y. This important conclusion can be expressed as follows:

$$-\Delta Y/\Delta X = a_x/a_y = p_x/p_y. \tag{2.10}$$

Actually, it is more accurate to say that the slope of A's production-possibilities frontier (PPF) shows the ratio of marginal costs of X and Y, i.e.,

$$\text{absolute slope of } A\text{'s } PPF = \frac{\text{marginal cost of } X}{\text{marginal cost of } Y}.$$

This observation becomes important shortly when international trade is introduced, where the terms of trade (equivalent to the relative prices prevailing in each country) are different from the absolute slope of each country's *PPF*.

Country B's production-possibilities frontier can be derived in a similar way, so there is no need to repeat the preceding discussion. However, it is useful to introduce some additional symbols. Assume that B is endowed with L_B units of labor; its labor requirements per unit of output are b_x and b_y for commodities X and Y, respectively. Therefore, B's production-possibilities frontier is given by the equation

$$L_B = b_x X + b_y Y. \tag{2.11}$$

Its absolute slope (or the opportunity cost of X in terms of Y) is, of course, given by the ratio b_x/b_y.

Notice that A will have a comparative advantage in X and B in Y if the following inequality holds:

$$a_x/a_y < b_x/b_y. \tag{2.12}$$

On the other hand, A will have a comparative advantage in Y and B in X if the opposite inequality holds, that is,

$$a_x/a_y > b_x/b_y. \qquad (2.13)$$

This should become obvious if inequalities (2.12) and (2.13) are rewritten as follows:

$$a_x/b_x < a_y/b_y, \qquad (2.12)'$$

$$a_x/b_x > a_y/b_y. \qquad (2.13)'$$

These are actually the inequalities used in section 4 for the definition of comparative advantage. The importance of inequalities (2.12) and (2.13)—which from a strictly mathematical point of view are equivalent to the inequalities (2.12)' and (2.13)', respectively—follows from the fact that they define comparative advantage directly in terms of opportunity costs.

8. The World Production-Possibilities Frontier

The quite useful concept of the world production-possibilities frontier is illustrated in figure 2.4, which shows the maximum amount of Y that both countries together can produce for any given amount of X, under the assumption that labor is completely immobile between countries. Its construction is rather simple. The triangle TUR represents the production-possibilities frontier of country A, with T as its point of origin. The triangle

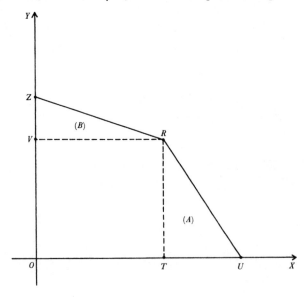

FIGURE 2.4

VRZ represents *B*'s production-possibilities frontier, with *V* as its point of origin. The intercept *Z* of the world production-possibilities frontier is determined by the sum of the maximum quantities of *Y* that both countries could produce if they were to channel all of their resources in the production of *Y*, that is, $OZ = TR + VZ$. Similarly, the intercept *U* is determined by the sum of the maximum quantities of *X* that both countries could produce if they were to channel all of their resources in the production of *X*, that is, $OU = VR + TU$.

The world frontier can now be derived. Note that *B*'s production-possibilities frontier has been assumed flatter than *A*'s; that is, the opportunity cost of *X* in terms of *Y* was assumed to be lower in *B*. Suppose that we are at point *Z*—with both countries producing *Y* only—and assume that we would like to produce an extra unit of *X*. Which country should undertake the production of the extra unit of *X*? Obviously, country *B*, because its opportunity cost of *X* in terms of *Y* is lower. This will continue for the second, third, etc., units of *X* until *B* specializes completely in *X*, that is, until we reach point *R*. From then on, that is, from *R* to *U*, any additional amounts of *X* can only be extracted from *A*. Thus, in the region *ZR*, *A* specializes in *Y* while *B* produces both commodities. On the other hand, in the region *RU*, country *A* produces both commodities while *B* completely specializes in *X*. In particular, at the specific point *R*, country *A* specializes in the production of *Y* and *B* in *X*. Thus, point *R* can be recognized as the *Ricardian point* of complete specialization in each country according to the comparative advantage of each.

The world production-possibilities frontier, as illustrated in figure 2.4, is not a straight line—except in the special case of equal opportunity costs (i.e., when the production-possibilities frontiers of *A* and *B* have the same slope). In general, it consists of two straight-line segments, such as *ZR* and *RU*. Along each of these straight-line segments, opportunity costs are constant. However, the absolute slope of *ZR* is different from, and significantly smaller than, that of *RU*. However, at the Ricardian point *R*, the slope of the world production-possibilities frontier ($\equiv$ opportunity cost of *X* in terms of *Y*) is indeterminate. This indeterminacy of the slope of point *R* accounts for the failure of the Ricardo–Torrens theory of comparative advantage to explain the equilibrium value of the terms of trade. From figure 2.4, it should be obvious that the slope at point *R* can range from the slope of *B*'s production-possibilities frontier to the slope of *A*'s. This coincides with our previous conclusion that the equilibrium terms of trade must necessarily lie between the pretrade price ratios of the two countries or coincide with one or the other of them.

The world production-possibilities frontier can be used in several ways. In the following chapter, it will be used to demonstrate the international equilibrium of the two-country model. In this section, it can be used to illustrate the important idea of the gains from trade.

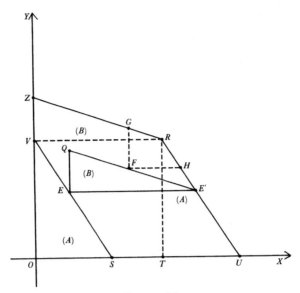

FIGURE 2.5

Consider now figure 2.5. It is similar to figure 2.4 but includes some additional information. Country *A*'s production-possibilities frontier has been drawn with respect to the origin of the diagram, as shown by the line *VS*. Thus, the triangles *OSV* and *TUR* are similar in all respects. Assume that country *A* is producing at point *E*; place *B*'s production-possibilities frontier in such a way as to have its origin at point *E*, as shown by the triangle *EE'Q*. Note that *B*'s production-possibilities frontier, *EE'Q*, must necessarily lie inside the world production-possibilities frontier—except at the singular point *E'*—because *A*'s production-possibilities frontier is steeper than *B*'s. Finally, assume that *B* produces at any point on its frontier—other than *E'*—such as point *F*. It can be shown that the coordinates of point *F* with respect to the origin *O* give the total world output of the two commodities. But point *F* lies inside the world production-possibilities frontier, which means that, with a different pattern of specialization, the world as a whole could move to the boundaries of the world production-possibilities frontier. The workers do not have to move internationally, nor do they have to work harder. If *A* specializes in *X* and *B* in *Y*, the world can reach point *R*, which implies higher output of all commodities.

It should be obvious, however, that whether or not the world moves from point *F* to point *R* depends on demand. Thus, it is conceivable that, with free commodity trade, the world might move from point *F* to some point on the world production-possibilities frontier in the region *ZG*, where the world output of *X* is smaller after trade, or in the region *HU*, where the posttrade world output of *Y* is smaller than before trade started. In both of these cases, it should not be concluded that the world does not necessarily gain from trade. The fact that the consumption of one commodity is reduced while the consumption of the other is increased is not sufficient to support the conclusion that trade may not be profitable. The world can always move to point R—where the output of every commodity increases with trade—so at least potentially everybody could be made better off with trade. If the world chooses a different point than R, it must be assumed that it does so because that other point is preferred to point R. However, the concept of the gains from grade is much more subtle than what this paragraph suggests. This problem is discussed in chapter 16.

Finally, it should be noted that what is called in this section the "world production-possibilities frontier" is not what the world can actually achieve, because this frontier has been derived under the assumption that labor is internationally immobile. Therefore, in cases where one country is superior to another country in every line of production, the world could reach a frontier that includes inside it the frontier of figure 2.4 merely by allowing labor to move to the most productive nation. The same is also true in the case of absolute advantage.

SELECTED BIBLIOGRAPHY

Balassa, B. 1963. An empirical demonstration of comparative cost. *Review of Economics and Statistics* 45: 231–38.
Chipman, John S. 1965. A survey of the theory of international trade, part 1: the classical theory. *Econometrica* 33: 477–519.
Haberler, G. 1936. *The Theory of International Trade*. London: W. Hodge & Co. Chap. 9–11.
MacDougall, G. D. A. 1951. British and American exports: a study suggested by the theory of comparative costs, part I. *Economic Journal* 61: 697–724; reprinted in A.E.A. *Readings in International Economics*. Homewood, Ill.: R. D. Irwin, Inc., 1968.
———. 1952. British and American exports: a study suggested by the theory of comparative costs, part II. *Economic Journal* 62: 487–521.
Meade, J. E. 1955. *The Theory of International Economic Policy*. Vol. 2: *Trade and Welfare*. Oxford: Oxford University Press. Chap. 9.
Mill, J. S. 1902. *Principles of Political Economy*. New York: Appleton. Chap. 17, 18, 25.
Ricardo, David. 1821. *The Principles of Political Economy and Taxation*. London: J. Murray. Chap. 7.
Smith, Adam. 1937. *The Wealth of Nations*. New York: Modern Library.
Stern, R. 1962. British and American productivity and comparative costs in international trade. *Oxford Economic Papers* 14: 275–96.
Williams, J. H. 1929. The theory of international trade reconsidered. *Economic Journal* 39: 195–209; reprinted in A.E.A. *Readings in the Theory of International Trade*. Homewood, Ill.: R. D. Irwin, Inc.

3

Demand and International Equilibrium

1. Indifference Curves[1]

Economists following Pareto, Slutsky, and Hicks, usually depict the tastes of the consumer via the concept of indifference curves. As is well known, an indifference curve is the geometric locus of all alternative combinations of, say, commodities X and Y which enable the consumer to attain a given level of satisfaction, or utility. Thus, each indifference curve corresponds to a certain level of satisfaction. The collection of all indifference curves forms the indifference map. This is shown in figure 3.1, where only three indifference curves have been drawn. Some general properties of indifference curves are noted briefly: (1) they slope downward; (2) they are convex to the origin, as illustrated in figure 3.1; (3) they never intersect each other; and (4) a movement from a lower to a higher indifference curve (such as from I_1 to I_2 in fig. 3.1) implies an increase in the satisfaction or utility enjoyed by the consumer. Finally, note that the object of the consumer is to reach the highest possible indifference curve, that is, attain the highest level of satisfaction, under the assumptions of a fixed money income and fixed commodity prices. The first-order condition for this maximization is that the *marginal rate of substitution* of X for Y (i.e., the maximum number of units of Y that the consumer could give up for an extra unit of X and still continue to enjoy the same level of satisfaction or utility)—which is simply the absolute slope of the indifference curve passing through the equilibrium point—be equal to the price ratio p_x/p_y.

The neoclassical theory makes the simplifying assumptions that the tastes of a society—as opposed to the tastes of the individual consumer—can be conveniently summarized by a *social indifference map* qualitatively similar to the indifference map of an individual consumer, and that the society behaves

1. In the following analysis, mastery of the concept of indifference curves is assumed. Those who wish to refresh their memory should consult any price-theory textbook.

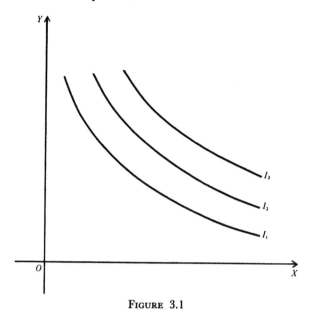

FIGURE 3.1

as if it were trying to attain the highest possible social indifference curve. The validity of this assumption will be examined in chapter 5. For the moment, assume that a meaningful social indifference map exists. Once this is done, the general equilibrium of each country separately, but also the general equilibrium of the world as a whole, can be shown graphically.

Figure 3.2 shows the general equilibrium of a closed economy. The straight line RS is the production-possibilities frontier and the curves I_1, I_2, and I_3 are three social indifference curves. Equilibrium is seen to occur at point E, where the production-possibilities frontier is tangent to the social indifference curve I_2. The analogy between the general equilibrium of the whole economy, on the one hand, and the equilibrium of the individual consumer, on the other, should be noted. In the case of the consumer, the straight line RS represents his budget constraint; in the case of general equilibrium, the line RS represents the production-possibilities frontier. In both cases, the line RS serves as a constraint. In the former case, it is the familiar budget constraint, while in the latter case it is the society's technological constraint: the society cannot produce beyond the boundaries of its production-possibilities frontier. Further, in both cases, the indifference map represents tastes, and the assumption is that both the consumer and the society will move to the highest possible indifference curve. At the equilibrium point (i.e., point E) the slope of the straight line RS is equal to the slope of the indifference curve I_2. In the case of the consumer, the slope of RS is equal to the price ratio p_x/p_y. In the case of the society, the slope of RS gives the opportunity cost of X in terms of Y, which under competitive conditions

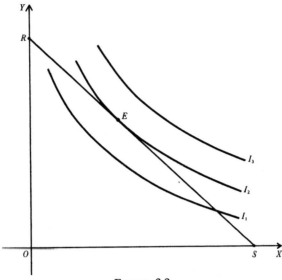

FIGURE 3.2

is equal to the price ratio p_x/p_y. Finally, the slope of the indifference curve I_2 at point E is, in the case of the consumer, the individual consumer's marginal rate of substitution of X for Y; in the case of the society, it is the *social* marginal rate of substitution of X for Y.

Figure 3.3 extends the preceding analysis to international equilibrium. To simplify the analysis, it is assumed that the tastes of the world as a whole can be represented by a single social indifference map. In other words, the world is assumed to behave like a single rational individual whose budget constraint is the line ZRU, which is similar in all respects to the world production-possibilities frontier depicted in figure 2.4. Observe that this assumption is even more restrictive than the assumption that a separate social indifference map exists for each country. It is used here merely because the analysis of international equilibrium is greatly simplified. Incidentally, it should be noted that John Stuart Mill in his theory of international value made such assumptions about demand conditions as to guarantee the existence of a world indifference map. On this point, see Chipman (1965, sec. 1.2).

International equilibrium occurs at the Ricardian point R. It should be obvious that international equilibrium need not take place at point R. Depending upon tastes, it can occur anywhere on the world production-possibilities frontier. Point R is selected because the classical economists considered this to be the usual case; in addition, we want to show how the equilibrium terms of trade can be rigorously determined at this point, where the slope of the production-possibilities frontier ZRU is indeterminate, and

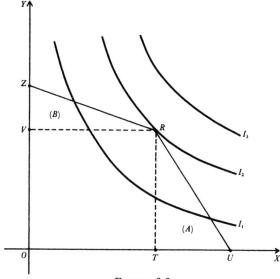

FIGURE 3.3

thus the equilibrium value of relative prices cannot be determined from the characteristics of the world production-possibilities frontier alone: only the limits of the relative prices can be so determined. However, with the introduction of demand, this indeterminacy disappears. Thus, in equilibrium, relative prices must necessarily be equal to the marginal rate of substitution which is perfectly determinate at point R. Therefore, the equilibrium terms of trade (i.e., p_x/p_y) are given by the slope of the indifference curve I_2 at point R.

Figure 3.3 can also be used to verify our earlier conclusion that the terms of trade must lie between the pretrade price ratios of the two countries. This should be obvious, because, if point R is to be the equilibrium point, the marginal rate of substitution of X for Y (i.e., the absolute slope of the indifference curve I_2 at R) must necessarily lie between the absolute slopes of the straight-line segments ZR and RU, which show, respectively, B's and A's pretrade price ratios. If the indifference curve I_2 were steeper (flatter) at point R than the slope of the straight-line segment RU (ZR), the indifference curve would simply intersect the world production-possibilities frontier at point R and equilibrium would occur somewhere on the RU (ZR) straight-line segment, with the equilibrium terms of trade given by A's (B's) pretrade price ratio (i.e., the pretrade price ratio of the country which is producing both commodities at the final international equilibrium position).

The preceding general-equilibrium solution shows: (*a*) the equilibrium terms of trade; (*b*) the pattern of specialization; (*c*) the total world output and consumption of each commodity; and (d) the potential role of free commodity trade in improving the welfare of the world as a whole. However, it conceals much important information, such as the consumption levels of X and Y in the two countries, the quantities of X and Y exported or imported by the two countries, and the manner in which the gains from trade are divided between the two countries. In the following section, it will be shown how this information can be recovered.

2. *International Equilibrium in Terms of Price-Consumption Curves*

To demonstrate international equilibrium in a more disaggregated form than is given in the preceding section, it is necessary to make use of another known tool, namely, the price consumption curve.

Suppose that, instead of having a single social indifference map for the world as a whole, there are two: one for each country. How then can international equilibrium be demonstrated? This can be done geometrically in two ways. First, international equilibrium will be established in terms of price consumption curves. This is done in the present section, and it is a useful way of demonstrating international equilibrium when the production-possibilities frontiers are linear. However, this method cannot be used in general; therefore, the following section extends the analysis of the present section to show international equilibrium in terms of *offer curves*. This second method is much more general than the first, and it can be easily grasped, at least in the context of the classical theory, once international equilibrium in terms of price consumption curves has been understood. The latter will appear quite obvious to readers who have mastered the theory of consumer equilibrium.

It is necessary to explain how a single economy which can buy and sell unlimited quantities of commodities X and Y at given prices attains general equilibrium. This problem can be divided into two subproblems: (1) What should the economy produce to maximize its income (i.e., the value of its output)? (2) Subject to the answer given to question (1), what should the economy consume to maximize social welfare (i.e., reach the highest possible social indifference curve)? Let us consider both of these questions in the order in which they have been presented.

Since our interest lies mainly in relative prices, as opposed to absolute prices, the value of output produced (Q), is expressed in terms of commodity Y. As before, let p stand for the international terms of trade (i.e., $p \equiv p_x/p_y$). Accordingly, the value of total output is given by

$$Q = pX_p + Y_p, \qquad (3.1)$$

where X_p and Y_p are the production levels of commodities X and Y, respectively. The object is to maximize Q, as given by equation (3.1), subject to the production-possibilities frontier of the economy, such as equation (2.8) above. The solution is given graphically in figure 3.4. The straight line KM is the economy's production-possibilities frontier. Its slope (i.e., the opportunity cost of X in terms of Y) is given by the ratio of labor requirements, that is, a_x/a_y. In figure 3.4, it is assumed that the given terms of trade (p_1) are lower than a_x/a_y, that is, $p_1 < a_x/a_y$; which is to say, the opportunity cost of X in the economy was assumed to be higher than the relative price of X in the world economy. It should be obvious that the economy has to produce somewhere on the production-possibilities frontier. On the one hand, it cannot produce outside of the frontier, and on the other, from any point within the frontier it can always move to some region of the frontier where the outputs of both commodities are higher than the corresponding outputs implied by the original point, and thus increase the total value of the economy's output. Now consider any point on the production-possi-bilities frontier, such as point E, and assume that the economy is for the moment producing there. Then draw the *income line* of the economy, as defined by equation (3.1). This income line (whose absolute slope is given by p_1) is a kind of consumption line for the economy; that is, on the assumption that the economy produces at E and the relative price of X in terms of Y (as given by the international market) is p_1, the income line shows the maximum combinations of X and Y that the economy can consume. Observe that this particular income line, as illustrated in figure 3.4 by the broken line through E, must necessarily pass through point E: if the economy

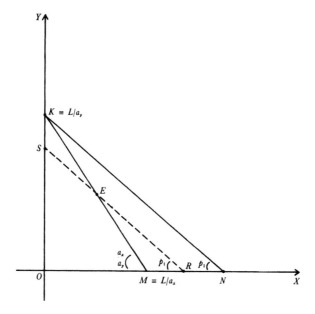

FIGURE 3.4

produces at E it can also consume at E, irrespective of prices. In addition, it must be flatter than the production-possibilities frontier because of our original assumption that $p_1 < a_x/a_y$. Thus, through any arbitrarily chosen production point, such as E, an income line can be drawn with slope equal to the given terms of trade p_1. However, the problem is to determine the optimum production point, that is, the point which will maximize the economy's value of output produced. What this means in terms of figure 3.4 is that a point on the production-possibilities frontier should be determined on the basis of which the income line will lie as far from the origin as possible. The optimum production point is K. As the production point slides downward on the production-possibilities frontier (i.e., from E to M), the income line shifts inward. On the other hand, as the production point slides upward on the frontier (i.e., from E to K), the income line shifts outward, reaching its optimum position when the production point coincides with K. This should come as no surprise, because at point K the economy specializes completely in the production of commodity Y, whose opportunity cost is smaller at home than abroad. The income line KN, which corresponds to the highest possible value of output, is given a special name: the *consumption-possibilities frontier*. The determination of the consumption-possibilities frontier answers the first of the two questions raised earlier.

Note that the consumption-possibilities frontier lies totally outside the production-possibilities frontier, except at the singular point K. This is important, because it follows that while an economy is necessarily constrained by its production-possibilities frontier as far as production is concerned, it is by no means so constrained with respect to consumption. That is, *free trade makes it possible to consume beyond the boundaries of the production-possibilities frontier*. Free trade expands the consumption-possibilities set beyond the boundaries of the production-possibilities frontier; herein lies the whole essence of the gains from trade.

Note also the relationship between the (domestic) opportunity cost of X in terms of Y and the international price ratio. In figure 3.4, it is assumed that $p_1 < a_x/a_y$. To complete the analysis, however, it must be shown what happens when $p \geq a_x/a_y$. The answer is simple. If $p > a_x/a_y$, the family of income lines[2] will be steeper than the production-possibilities frontier, so for income maximization, the economy will have to specialize completely in the production of X (X being relatively cheaper domestically); that is, the consumption-possibilities frontier will pass through M and be steeper than the production-possibilities frontier. What is important is that the consumption-possibilities frontier will lie beyond the economy's production-possibilities frontier, except at the singular (production) point M. On the other hand, if $p = a_x/a_y$, the consumption-possibilities frontier will coincide with the production-possibilities frontier. In this particular case, the economy

2. We speak of a "family of income lines" because an income line passes through every point on the production-possibilities frontier.

will obviously gain nothing from international trade. In addition, its structure of production is indeterminate: it can produce anywhere on the production-possibilities frontier and end up with the same consumption-possibilities frontier.

Let us turn now to the second question: What should the economy consume? The answer is given graphically in figure 3.5, which contains the pertinent information given in figure 3.4 together with the economy's social indifference map. Actually, to avoid confusion, only two social indifference curves have been drawn in figure 3.5. Equilibrium before trade obviously

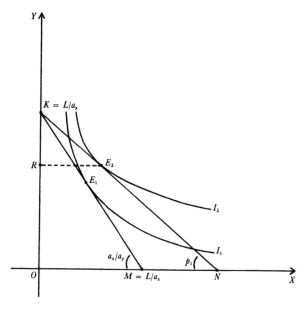

FIGURE 3.5

occurs at point E_1, where the production-possibilities frontier is tangent to the highest possible social indifference curve (i.e., I_1). In other words, before trade, the economy produces *and* consumes at point E_1. However, a distinction between consumption and production equilibria must necessarily be made when the country has access to international trade. As was already shown, production in this particular case (i.e., when $p < a_x/a_y$) takes place at point K, with KN being the consumption-possibilities frontier. Consumption, however, will have to take place at point E_2, where the consumption-possibilities frontier is tangent to the highest possible social indifference curve (i.e., I_2).

Once the posttrade production and consumption equilibria are determined, the exports and imports of the economy can be easily determined by completing the right-angle triangle RKE_2. Thus, since the economy produces

OK units of Y and consumes only OR units, it must necessarily be exporting RK units of Y to the rest of the world. Further, since the economy consumes RE_2 units of X and produces none, it must necessarily be importing RE_2 units of X from the rest of the world. Further, note that

$$p_1 \equiv OK/ON = RK/RE_2,$$

or

$$p_1 \times RE_2 = RK;$$

that is, the value of exports is equal to the value of imports, both being expressed in terms of commodity Y. This is no accident; it follows, rather, from the assumption that our economy spends on X and Y exactly as much as it receives in the form of income from the production of Y. In other words, our economy does indeed consume on the consumption-possibilities frontier, which means that the value of production equals the value of consumption.

What has been done for a single value of p can be repeated for every other value. The general conclusion can be summarized as follows. For all values of p satisfying the inequality $p < a_x/a_y$, the consumption-possibilities frontier will always start from point K (figure 3.5) and be flatter than the production-possibilities frontier. Further, as p falls from a_x/a_y toward zero, the consumption-possibilities frontier rotates through the production equilibrium point K, becoming continuously flatter. But while the production equilibrium point remains unique, the consumption equilibrium point varies with p. The locus of all consumption equilibrium points is the price consumption curve. This is illustrated in figure 3.6(a), where the social indifference map has been omitted to keep the diagram simple. The straight line KM is the economy's production-possibilities frontier, and the curve labeled PCC is the price consumption curve.

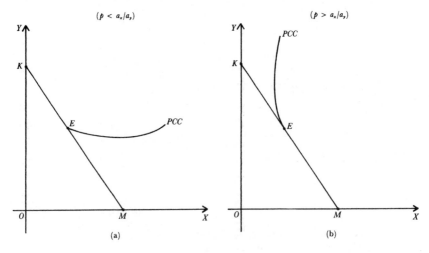

FIGURE 3.6

For all values of p satisfying the inequality $p > a_x/a_y$, the economy produces at M and consumes along the price consumption curve (PCC) as shown in figure 3.6(b). In this case, the consumption-possibilities frontier is always steeper than the production-possibilities frontier. Further, as p increases, the consumption-possibilities frontier rotates through point M, becoming continuously steeper.

Let us now return to the problem of international equilibrium. Assume that A has a comparative advantage in the production of Y and B in X; that is, A's production-possibilities frontier is steeper than B's. International equilibrium is shown in figure 3.7. The triangle $O_B KN$ represents B's

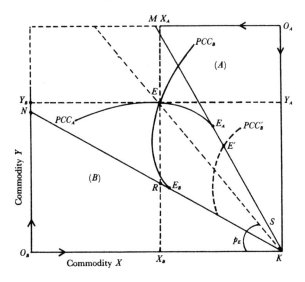

FIGURE 3.7

production-possibilities frontier, with O_B being its origin. The curve PCC_B is B's price consumption curve derived under the assumption that $b_x/b_y < p$, that is, that B's opportunity cost of X in terms of Y is always smaller than the international terms of trade p. On the other hand, the triangle $O_A MK$ is A's production-possibilities frontier, having been rotated through its origin O_A by 180°. The curve PCC_A is A's price consumption curve derived under the assumption that $a_x/a_y > p$, that is, that A's opportunity cost of X in terms of Y is higher than the international terms of trade p. Therefore, country B is seen to specialize completely in the production of X, whereas country A specializes in the production of Y. Accordingly, the total world output of X is given by the horizontal distance $O_B K$ (i.e., B's maximum output of commodity X), and that of Y is given by the vertical distance $O_A K$ (i.e., A's maximum output of Y). Since we have assumed thus far that each country behaves as a single rational individual, it is obvious that the problem is essentially reduced to that of two individuals, A and B, with one (i.e., A) endowed with a fixed quantity of Y and the other (i.e., B) with a fixed quantity of X. From price theory, we know that general equilibrium occurs at the point of intersection between the price-consumption curves of the two consumers.[3] This is shown by point E of figure 3.7. Thus, at point E, A consumes X_A and Y_A (measured from O_A) while B consumes X_B and Y_B (measured from O_B) units of commodities X and Y, respectively. Supply is equal to demand in both markets, and therefore general equilibrium prevails. Country B (A) is exporting (importing) $X_B K$ units of X while it is importing (exporting) $X_B E$ units of Y. The equilibrium terms of trade (p_E) are given by the absolute slope of the vector KE. Observe that $b_x/b_y <$ $p_E < a_x/a_y$—and that KE is steeper than NK but flatter than MK.

Figure 3.7 shows the gains from trade and their division between the two countries. Without trade, each country will necessarily have to consume on its production-possibilities frontier. With trade, as figure 3.7 shows, both countries consume beyond their respective production-possibilities frontiers, because they both specialize completely. In fact, the gains from trade correspond to the area NKM of figure 3.7. The larger this area, the larger the gains from trade. In addition, observe that the area NKM is divided into two parts by the terms-of-trade line KE—the area EKM going to A and the area EKN going to B, so to speak. Therefore, the closer the terms-of-trade line KE lies to B's production-possibilities frontier (i.e., the smaller the difference between b_x/b_y and p_E), the smaller will be B's share of the gains. Similarly, the closer KE lies to A's production-possibilities frontier (i.e., the smaller the difference between a_x/a_y and p_E), the smaller will be A's share of the gains.

As pointed out earlier, the concept of the gains from trade is much subtler than it appears. In general, the introduction of free international trade will make (within each country) some people better off and others worse off compared with the pretrade equilibrium position. But it is not clear whether the society actually becomes better off or worse off when some of its members gain and some lose. Within the context of the classical theory, however, this difficulty does not arise. Labor is the only factor of production, and if any worker becomes better off, all of them do. In fact, the production-possibilities frontier of each country can be scaled down to the relative size of the representative citizen and the analysis carried out on the basis of the data on the production-possibilities frontiers and indifference maps of all individuals. Such analysis would, of course, be more complicated without any distinct advantage, except that it would probably enable us to see better

3. The analysis of the text assumes that both A and B behave as price takers. It is well known that this assumption may be violated in the case of two consumers and that our problem may end up being a problem of bilateral monopoly. However, this assumption is quite legitimate for our purposes because we are not actually dealing with two individuals; rather, we are dealing with two countries, each composed of many individuals.

the relationship between the equilibrium value of p and the division of the gains from trade. However, the latter should be obvious when it is realized that, in this particular case, the production-possibilities frontier of the country as a whole is merely the sum of all individual frontiers with no interaction whatsoever between them.

There is no general rule according to which one can decide which distribution of the gains from trade between countries is the best. International competition will, of course, give rise to a certain distribution, but we cannot be sure that this distribution is the best. Further, it is not unusual for any or all countries of the world to interfere with the free workings of the competitive system through tariffs and other barriers to trade, in an effort to turn the terms of trade in their favor and thus end up with a bigger share of the gains from trade.

Frank B. Graham believed that the equilibrium terms of trade were, as a rule, equal to the pretrade equilibrium price ratio of one of the trading countries; intermediate or "limbo" price ratios were, he thought, the exception. If "limbo" price ratios were the rule, Graham argued, one would observe violent fluctuations in prices because of the (assumed) highly volatile nature of demand. (It should be noted that later econometric studies did not support Graham's belief about the volatile nature of demand. In fact, demand stability rather than instability was borne out by such studies.) Since the terms of trade were empirically stable, "limbo" price ratios must be ruled out.

Graham believed that relative prices are determined by opportunity costs rather than reciprocal demand, as illustrated in the following section by the Marshallian offer curves. The theory of reciprocal demand (he said) relies on changes in the terms of trade as the fundamental means of international adjustment, which is useless and misleading given the observed stability of relative prices. ("Stability" in this context should be interpreted as "constancy" or "rigidity.") Graham believed that international adjustment was more likely to take place through the possibility of transferring resources from one commodity to another under conditions of constant opportunity costs. It should be noted that of greater interest was Graham's effort to liberate the pure theory of trade from the assumption of two commodities and two countries—an effort that had already been begun by Mill and continued by Mangoldt, Edgeworth, and Viner. This topic is treated briefly in the appendix to this chapter.

In the context of the classical model discussed so far, Graham's conclusion is possible in the following cases: (1) when the two trading countries are of unequal size and (2) when the two commodities are consumed in fixed proportions—an assumption that Graham used in one of his numerical examples. The first case is illustrated in figure 3.7. If B were a small country with a production-possibilities frontier given by the triangle $X_B KR$ (instead of $O_B KN$) and if its price consumption curve were the broken curve labeled

PCC'_B, equilibrium would occur on A's production-possibilities frontier, with the terms of trade being equal to A's pretrade price ratio. Country B would specialize completely in the production of X, but A would produce both X and Y. Note that at A's pretrade price ratio, B will consume at point E', and A at E_A (as before trade). However, since the consumption points E' and E_A do not coincide, supply cannot equal demand in any market if A specializes in Y and B in X (i.e., if the supplies of X and Y, respectively, are given by the sides of the original parallelogram of fig. 3.7), for then there would be an excess demand for X and an excess supply of Y. The problem is solved if country A produces at point S on its production-possibilities frontier, which is determined in such a way as to satisfy the equation $E'E_A = KS$.

Note that essentially the same result could have been reached if B were not a small country but its tastes were heavily biased in favor of commodity X and, as a result, the PCC'_B were its original price consumption curve. Therefore, the "size" of a country is not an absolute magnitude which can be measured objectively. Demand considerations are indeed important in this respect. Nevertheless, there is one objectively measurable magnitude which can serve as a sufficient condition for the emergence of the preceding phenomenon. Suppose that B is so small that the maximum amount of X it can produce falls short of the amount of X that A consumes before trade. Then, provided that X is not a Giffen commodity[4] in country A, international equilibrium will always imply that A produces both commodities, with the terms of trade being equal to A's pretrade price ratio and all the gains from trade accruing to the small country B. This is the importance of being unimportant!

The implications of the assumption that commodities are consumed in fixed proportions are illustrated in figure 3.8, which is similar to figure 3.7 except that now it is assumed that A consumes the commodities X and Y in the proportion shown by the slope of the vector $O_A E_A$ and B in the proportion shown by the slope of the vector $O_B E_B$. Equilibrium does indeed occur at point E, but it is unstable. That is, if the terms of trade happen to be equal to the slope of the vector KE, say p_E, all markets will be cleared and general equilibrium would prevail. However, any displacement of the terms of trade from their equilibrium value (p_E) will generate forces which will push them further from equilibrium. For instance, if p were to rise above p_E, an excess demand for X and an excess supply of Y would emerge—as can be verified from figure 3.8. The price ratio p_x/p_y will thus tend to rise on both counts, instead of falling back to p_E. On the other hand, should p ever fall below p_E, it will go on falling because when the terms of trade are lower than p_E, an excess supply of X and an excess demand for Y emerge. Therefore, point E is unstable. But there are another two possible equilibrium points

4. For the concept of "Giffen commodity," see any textbook on price theory.

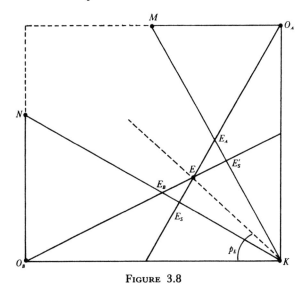

FIGURE 3.8

which are indeed stable. These are E_S and E'_S. But at each of these points, one country produces both commodities, with the equilibrium terms of trade given by its pretrade price ratio and all gains from trade going to the other country. Thus, at E'_S, country A produces both commodities, while at E_S country B does.

Finally, note that the assumption that commodities are consumed in fixed proportions is not sufficient to guarantee that the intersection between the two consumption paths (i.e., point E of fig. 3.8) is an unstable equilibrium. To see this, draw a straight line connecting the origins (O_A, O_B) of the two production-possibilities frontiers. If the intersection of the two consumption paths takes place in the cone NKM but to the northwest of the line connecting O_A and O_B, that intersection will give rise to a stable equilibrium.

The analysis of the present section has relaxed the assumption made in the preceding section, namely, that there exists a world social indifference map. But although the analysis has given further insights into the problems of international equilibrium and the gains from trade, it suffers from two disadvantages. In the first place, figures 3.7 and 3.8 were drawn on the assumption that the terms of trade must lie between the pretrade price ratios of the two countries, which actually was the conclusion derived earlier. However, it appears desirable to have a geometrical solution which does not depend on conclusions derived otherwise. In the second place, figures 3.7 and 3.8 can hardly be used to find the general-equilibrium solutions to the neoclassical and modern theories of trade, notwithstanding the fact that they contain all the necessary ingredients. The purpose of the following section is mainly to remedy these two deficiencies.

3. Offer Curves

International equilibrium requires that for every commodity, the world supply must be equal to the world demand. In particular, within the context of our two-country, two-commodity model, the following equations must be satisfied:

$$X_A^P + X_B^P = X_A^C + X_B^C, \tag{3.2}$$

$$Y_A^P + Y_B^P = Y_A^C + Y_B^C, \tag{3.3}$$

where the superscripts P and C indicate production and consumption, respectively, and the subscripts A and B indicate the countries. Figures 3.7 and 3.8 have been interpreted as showing general equilibrium in precisely this manner, that is, by showing that world supply is equal to world demand in every market. However, general equilibrium can be shown in another way, namely, in terms of the excess demand for each commodity by each country. Figures 3.7 and 3.8 could also be interpreted in this fashion.

The equilibrium conditions (3.2) and (3.3) can be rewritten as follows:

$$(X_A^C - X_A^P) + (X_B^C - X_B^P) = 0, \tag{3.2\ensuremath{'}}$$

$$(Y_A^C - Y_A^P) + (Y_B^C - Y_B^P) = 0. \tag{3.3\ensuremath{'}}$$

The four pairs of parentheses in these equations enclose the excess demands of the two countries for each of the two commodities. For instance, the expression $(X_A^C - X_A^P)$ is A's excess demand for X, which may be either positive or negative. A similar interpretation holds for every other difference in these equations. Actually, these equations can be simplified by introducing the symbol E_i^j to indicate the excess demand of the jth country for the ith commodity. Thus, equations (3.2)$'$ and (3.3)$'$ can be simplified as follows:

$$E_X^A + E_X^B = 0, \tag{3.2\ensuremath{''}}$$

$$E_Y^A + E_Y^B = 0. \tag{3.3\ensuremath{''}}$$

In other words, for general equilibrium it is required that A's excess demand for X plus B's excess demand for X be zero, and that A's excess demand for Y plus B's excess demand for Y be zero. From equations (3.2)$''$ and (3.3)$''$ it is quite obvious that E_X^A and E_X^B cannot be of the same sign—unless they are both zero. The same is true of E_Y^A and E_Y^B. That is, in equilibrium, when one country's excess demand for X (or Y) is positive, that is, when one country is actually importing X (or Y), the other country's excess demand for X (or Y) must be negative, that is, the other country must be exporting it. What is more, the former country's imports must necessarily match the latter country's exports. To verify this, note that in figure 3.7 the coordinates of the equilibrium point E with respect to K as origin give the exports and imports of X and Y for both countries and that equations $(3.2)''$ and $(3.3)''$ are indeed satisfied.

It follows that the excess demands E_X^A, E_Y^A, E_X^B, and E_Y^B depend on the terms of trade. These excess demands can be rigorously derived. It suffices to show how this can be done for only one of the two countries, country A.

Figure 3.6 has shown how A's price consumption curve can be derived. Figure 3.9 shows how to derive A's excess demand for X and Y on the basis of the information given in figure 3.6. Panel (a) reproduces in the lower part

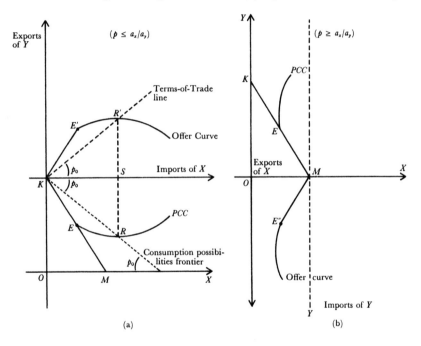

FIGURE 3.9

the information contained in panel (a) of figure 3.6. The only additional information in figure $3.9(a)$ is the introduction of the consumption-possibilities frontier for the specific value of the terms of trade p_0. As has been pointed out, the price consumption curve (PCC) is the locus of consumption equilibrium points. For instance, for $p = p_0$, the economy will produce at K and consume at R. But this implies that A will be willing to offer to the rest of the world the quantity SR of Y in exchange for the quantity KS of X. Now draw a horizontal line at the level of K (as in fig. 3.9) and measure from K, in the positive direction, A's imports of X (i.e., A's positive excess demand for X). Then extend the vertical axis beyond K and measure vertically A's supply of exports of Y (i.e., A's negative excess demand for Y). Finally, notice that the coordinates of point R' with respect to K as origin show A's exports of Y and imports of X, where point R' is the mirror image of point R on the PCC curve. In addition, the vector KR' is the mirror image of the consumption-possibilities frontier KR. The vector KR' is called the terms-of-trade line; its slope is equal to the given terms of trade (p_0).

Point R' is a point on A's *offer curve*, which shows the quantities of X and Y that A is willing to export to, or import from, the rest of the world, as the case may be, at alternative values of the terms of trade. Repeating the same experiment for all values of p satisfying the inequality $p \le a_x/a_y$, we determine one part of A's offer curve as the mirror image of the price-consumption curve. This is shown by the curve $E'R'$ in figure 3.9(a).

For the specific value $p = a_x/a_y$, the country will consume at E, but as noted earlier, its production point is indeterminate. For the moment, assume that production takes place somewhere in the region KE. (Fig. 3.9(b) explains what happens when production takes place in the region EM.) If production takes place at E, both the demand for imports and the supply of exports of country A will be zero. This will give rise to point K of the offer curve. On the other hand, if production takes place at K, the relevant point on the offer curve is E'. Finally, as the production point slides from K to E, the point on the offer curve slides from E' to K. Note again that the linear part KE' of the offer curve is the mirror image of KE of A's production-possibilities frontier.

Figure 3.9(b) shows how the second and final part of A's offer curve can be derived. Country A's offers for all values of p greater than a_x/a_y are considered. In the upper half of the diagram is reproduced the information given in figure 3.6(b). The reader who has mastered the analysis of figure 3.9(a) will have no trouble proving that the second part of A's offer curve is again the mirror image of the price-consumption curve (PCC), with M as its point of origin and the horizontal axis the axis of symmetry. The linear part ME'' corresponds to the case where $p = a_x/a_y$, and production takes place in the region EM of A's production-possibilities frontier.

The two branches of A's offer curve are brought together in figure 3.10. In the first quadrant is the part of the offer curve derived in figure 3.9(a), and in the third quadrant is the part derived in figure 3.9(b). Thus, figure 3.10 gives A's full offer curve. Notice that it necessarily lies in the first and third quadrants only. This follows from the fact that any point on the offer curve necessarily satisfies the equation (value of exports) = (value of imports). Therefore, a country cannot export or import both commodities simultaneously by assumption. Any point of the offer curve in the first quadrant shows how much Y country A is willing to export for a given quantity of imports of X. On the other hand, any point in the third quadrant shows how much X the country is willing to export for a given quantity of imports of Y. To determine the precise offer of the economy at any particular value of the terms of trade, simply draw through the origin a straight line with slope equal to the given value of the terms of trade—called the terms-

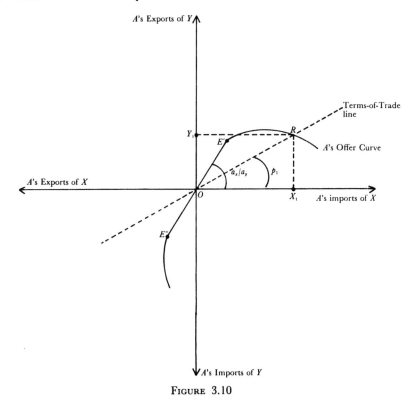

FIGURE 3.10

of-trade line—and determine the point of intersection between it and the offer curve. The coordinates of the point of intersection show A's exports and imports. Thus, for $p = p_1 < a_x/a_y$, A's offer is given by the coordinates of point R; that is, A is willing to export OY_1 units of Y for OX_1 units of imports of X. Note that $p_1 = OY_1/OX_1$. Finally, notice that the straight-line portion $E''OE'$ of the offer curve corresponds precisely to the mirror image of A's production-possibilities frontier, with the origin of the offer curve corresponding to the pretrade equilibrium point on the production-possibilities frontier.

Remember that the offer curve does not depend on demand alone. It also depends on supply. Both the production-possibilities frontier (supply) and the social indifference map (demand) were used for its derivation. This point is made here because Graham believed that the offer curve depended only on demand. It appears that Graham fell into this trap because Edgeworth had derived the offer curve only in the case of fixed supplies of commodities.

The offer curve of any other country can be similarly derived. Figure 3.11 shows B's offer curve. It is similar to figure 3.10 except that now it is B's

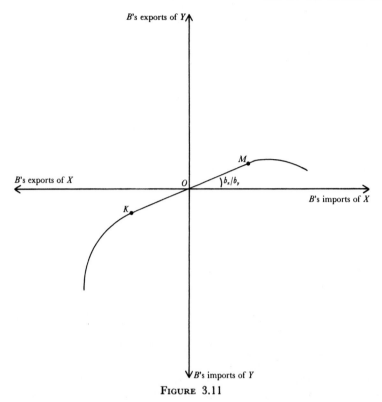

FIGURE 3.11

exports and imports that are being measured along the corresponding axes. Again, the straight-line segment KOM is the mirror image of B's production-possibilities frontier, and its slope is equal to b_x/b_y, that is, the absolute slope of B's production-possibilities frontier.

As noted earlier,[5] general equilibrium occurs when A's excess demand plus B's excess demand for each and every commodity is zero. The offer curves given in figures 3.10 and 3.11 give each country's excess demand ($\pm$) for each commodity for all values of the terms of trade. This information can be used to demonstrate international equilibrium in terms of these offer curves. It is important to note that the corresponding axes of figures 3.10 and 3.11 do not measure the same variables that are relevant for the analysis of general equilibrium. For instance, along the positive direction of the horizontal axis are measured, in figure 3.10, the quantity of A's imports of X and, in figure 3.11, the quantity of B's imports of X. Along the negative direction of the horizontal axis are measured, in figure 3.10, the quantity of A's exports of X and, in figure 3.11, the quantity of B's exports of X. But what we are actually interested in comparing is not A's demand for imports of X and B's

5. See eqs. (3.2)″ and (3.3)″.

demand for imports of X but, rather, A's demand for imports of X and B's supply of exports of X, or A's supply of exports of X and B's demand for imports of X. Similar observations hold for commodity Y. To remedy the situation simply rotate either one of the two diagrams by 180°, so that all axes will correspond to what we would like to compare. In the following analysis, B's diagram has been rotated.

Figure 3.12 brings together the two offer curves, with B's offer curve rotated by 180°. International equilibrium occurs at the intersection of the

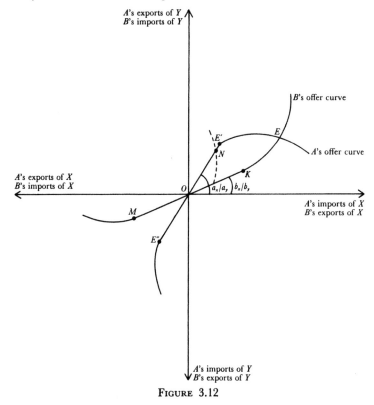

FIGURE 3.12

two offer curves in the first quadrant (i.e., point E). Country A exports Y and imports X, and B exports X and imports Y. The precise quantities of X and Y imported and exported by the two countries are given by the co-ordinates of the equilibrium point E. Further, the equilibrium terms of trade are given by the slope of the vector OE (not drawn). Obviously, the equilibrium terms of trade lie between the pretrade price ratios of the two countries; that is, the vector OE lies between the vectors OE' and OK. In addition, the two offer curves intersect each other in the first quadrant only.

It might seem at this point that the conclusion that the vector OE (showing the equilibrium terms of trade) lies between the vectors OE' and OK is an artificial one because the offer curves might be drawn in a different way and give rise to international equilibrium that might violate our conclusion. However, in the first quadrant, A's offer curve does not exist for $p > a_x/a_y$ and B's offer curve does not exist for $p < b_x/b_y$, because these are the assumptions under which they have been drawn. The parts of these offer curves which correspond to $p > a_x/a_y$ and $p < b_x/b_y$ lie in the third quadrant. Thus, as long as $a_x/a_y > b_x/b_y$, international equilibrium will occur in the first quadrant, with the equilibrium terms of trade (p_E) satisfying the condition $b_x/b_y \leq p_E \leq a_x/a_y$. The analysis can be extended to the case where equilibrium occurs in the third quadrant, i.e., when $a_x/a_y < b_x/b_y$.

On the basis of the above observations, it should be clear that it is impossible to have intersections of the two offer curves in the first and third quadrants simultaneously. However, this does not necessarily imply that international equilibrium is unique, because it is quite possible to have several intersections of the two offer curves in the same quadrant. What is implied is that when $a_x/a_y > b_x/b_y$, and thus $E''E'$ is steeper than MK, international equilibrium will necessarily occur in the first quadrant; i.e., country A will definitely export Y and import X while B will export X and import Y, which is in perfect agreement with the law of comparative advantage. If $a_x/a_y < b_x/b_y$, international equilibrium will necessarily occur in the third quadrant: A (B) will export X (Y) and import Y (X), which again is in agreement with the law of comparative advantage.

The equilibrium terms of trade will coincide with one country's pretrade price ratio if, and only if, the intersection of the two offer curves takes place on the linear part of either offer curve. The broken offer curve in figure 3.12 illustrates the case where equilibrium occurs at point N on the straight-line segment of A's offer curve, with the equilibrium terms of trade coinciding with A's pretrade price ratio and all gains from trade going to B.

Is international equilibrium stable? To aid in answering this question, the first quadrant of figure 3.12 is reproduced in figure 3.13. Again, international equilibrium occurs at point E, with the equilibrium terms of trade given by the slope of the vector OE (not drawn). What happens when the system is out of equilibrium? Will the system return to point E (i.e., is the system stable?) or not (i.e., is the system unstable?). To answer this question, let us use the Walrasian stability condition that the price of a commodity tends to rise (fall) when its excess demand is positive (negative). On the basis of this condition, it can easily be shown that the international equilibrium in figure 3.13 is indeed stable. Thus, consider any value of the terms of trade which is lower than the equilibrium terms of trade. This can be presented graphically by a terms-of-trade line flatter than the vector OE, such as the broken line TOT_1. For the specific value of the terms of trade implied by TOT_1, A's offer is given by the coordinates of point S (i.e., the intersection between TOT_1 and A's offer curve) and B's offer by the co-

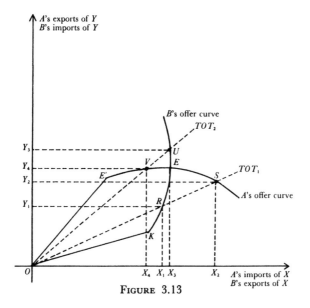

FIGURE 3.13

ordinates of point R (i.e., the intersection between TOT_1 and B's offer curve). That is, A is offering OY_2 units of Y in exchange for OX_2 units of X, and B is offering OX_1 units of X in exchange for OY_1 units of Y. Since $OX_2 > OX_1$ and $OY_2 > OY_1$ (i.e., since the world excess demand for X is positive while that for Y is negative), the price of X will tend to rise and the price of Y will tend to fall. On both counts, the price ratio p_x/p_y will tend to rise and the terms-of-trade line TOT_1 will rotate through the origin and move closer to the vector OE; that is, the system will tend to move back to the equilibrium point E. On the other hand, for any value of the terms of trade higher than the equilibrium value (such as that implied by TOT_2), the world excess demand for X will be negative and that for Y positive. This is also illustrated in figure 3.13. Thus, for the terms of trade implied by TOT_2, country A will be offering OY_4 units of Y in exchange for OX_4 units of X and B will be offering OX_3 units of X in exchange for OY_3 units of Y. Since $OY_3 > OY_4$ and $OX_3 > OX_4$, the price of X will tend to fall and the price of Y will tend to rise; the price ratio p_x/p_y will tend to fall and the terms-of-trade line TOT_2 will rotate through the origin and move closer to the vector OE. Therefore, when the system is not in equilibrium, forces are generated which will push it back to equilibrium. Accordingly, E is a stable equilibrium point.

Not all equilibrium points are stable. Some are indeed unstable. (A case of an unstable equilibrium has already been given in fig. 3.8.) One of the problems that will have to be investigated later relates to the necessary and sufficient conditions for stability.

4. Walras's Law and International Equilibrium

The preceding section shows how the problem of international equilibrium can be handled in terms of offer curves. But however useful the geometrical apparatus of offer curves may be, it is important to notice that they give (directly) more information than is actually necessary for the determination of international equilibrium. The purpose of the present section is to show the redundancy of the information given by the offer curves and to provide a simpler way of dealing with the problem of international equilibrium.

International equilibrium requires that equations (3.2)″ and (3.3)″ be satisfied. In other words, supply must equal demand in every market. However, equations (3.2)″ and (3.3)″ are not independent. When one of them is satisfied, the other is necessarily satisfied as well. This is actually what has come to be known as *Walras's law*: in a system of n markets, when $(n - 1)$ markets are in equilibrium, then by necessity the last market is also in equilibrium. This conclusion should give some assurance to those who have already noticed that each of equations (3.2)″ and (3.3)″ contains only one unknown, p, and that each could be solved for p; hence, there arises the possibility of inconsistent solutions. Walras's law is seen to eliminate the problem of inconsistency by declaring that equations (3.2)″ and (3.3)″ are not independent.

As has been repeatedly pointed out, the value of output produced is equal to the value of output consumed in each of the two countries. Accordingly, the following equations must be satisfied:

$$pX_A^P + Y_A^P = pX_A^C + Y_A^C, \tag{3.4}$$

$$pX_B^P + Y_B^P = pX_B^C + Y_B^C. \tag{3.5}$$

These equations can be rewritten thus:

$$pE_X^A + E_Y^A = 0, \tag{3.4}'$$

$$pE_X^B + E_Y^B = 0. \tag{3.5}'$$

Combining equations (3.4)′ and (3.5)′ gives

$$p(E_X^A + E_X^B) + (E_Y^A + E_Y^B) = 0. \tag{3.6}$$

Equation (3.6) shows that equations (3.2)″ and (3.3)″ are indeed dependent; any solution of (3.2)″ is also a solution of (3.3)″ and vice versa. This should be obvious from equation (3.6), because whenever the expression $(E_A^X + E_B^X)$ is zero, the expression $(E_A^Y + E_B^Y)$ is also zero, and vice versa. The conclusion that should be derived from this analysis is that both equations (3.2)″ and (3.3)″, do not have to be solved to determine the equilibrium value of p. It is sufficient to solve only one of them, for its solution will necessarily satisfy the other equation. The following discussion concentrates on equation (3.2)″.

Figure 3.14 illustrates A's excess demand for commodity X (i.e., E_X^A). The horizontal segment ME_1K corresponds to the horizontal base of A's production-possibilities frontier. At the pretrade equilibrium price ratio, OE_1, A's excess demand for X is indeterminate because its structure of production is indeterminate. If A specializes in the production of Y, it will have to import whatever amount of X will be domestically consumed, given by the distance E_1K. As A continuously reshuffles its resources in favor of X, the output of X increases and the output of Y decreases continuously (i.e., the production point slides along A's production-possibilities frontier,

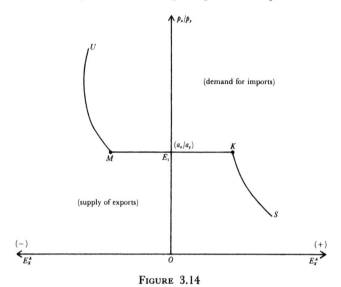

FIGURE 3.14

as given by fig. 3.6, from K to M). Since A's consumption of X remains the same, its excess demand for X falls continuously, as indicated by the movement from K to M. When A specializes in the production of X, its excess demand for X is negative (i.e., A is willing to export X), its precise value being determined by the difference between domestic production and consumption.

So much for the particular value $OE_1 = a_x/a_y$ of p_x/p_y. As p_x/p_y falls below a_x/a_y, country A will specialize in the production of Y and consume along the PCC curve as shown in figure 3.6(a). The domestic consumption of X is, in this case, A's excess demand for X, as shown by the portion KS of the curve in figure 3.14. On the other hand, as p_x/p_y increases above a_x/a_y, country A specializes in the production of X and consumes along the price-consumption curve as shown in figure 3.6(b). The difference between domestic production and consumption constitutes A's supply of exports of X, as shown in figure 3.14 by the curve MU.

Country B's excess demand curve for commodity X (i.e., E_X^B) can be determined in a similar fashion. Qualitatively, it will be similar to A's excess demand for X as shown in figure 3.14. However, for equilibrium in the market for commodity X, it is required that A's demand for imports be equal to B's supply of exports, or that A's supply of exports be equal to B's demand for imports. For this reason, B's excess demand curve for X ideally should be drawn on a diagram where, in the positive direction of the horizontal axis, B's supply of exports of X can be measured and, in the negative direction, B's demand for imports of X can be measured. In other words, the mirror image of B's excess demand curve is used. Finally, B's excess demand curve is superimposed on A's excess demand curve for X, as shown in figure 3.15.

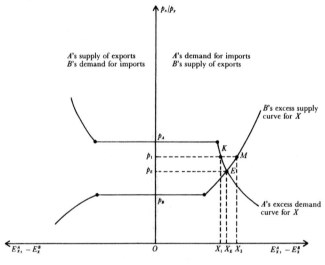

FIGURE 3.15

Equilibrium occurs at the intersection of the two curves, point E. The equilibrium terms of trade are given by Op_E, and the quantity of X traded internationally (i.e., exported from B to A) is given by the distance OX_E. Again, notice that Op_E lies between the pretrade price ratios of A and B, that is, Op_A and Op_B, respectively. Observe that for values of the terms of trade outside the region $p_B p_A$ (i.e., the region defined by the pretrade price ratios of the two countries), the supply curve for exports of one country and the demand curve for imports of the other lie in opposite quadrants. Thus, equilibrium is impossible outside the region $p_B p_A$, assuming, of course, that both commodities are always being consumed. The importance of the last qualification will be discussed in chapter 5.5.

Figure 3.15 appears to be a much simpler geometrical device than that of the offer curves. It may seem that the price of this simplicity is a lack of information for the market of Y, but this is actually not so. Whatever information is needed for the market of commodity Y can be easily recovered from figure 3.15. This can be illustrated by rewriting equations (3.4)' and (3.5)' as follows:

$$E_Y^A = -pE_X^A, \tag{3.4}''$$

$$E_Y^B = -pE_X^B. \tag{3.5}''$$

Thus, the excess demand for Y by either country is equal to the negative of the value of the same country's excess demand for X expressed in terms of commodity Y. For example, in figure 3.15, B is exporting OX_E units of X to country A at the equilibrium terms of trade Op_E. But from equations (3.4)'' and (3.5)'', it can also be deduced that country A is exporting to B an amount of commodity Y equal to the area of the rectangle $OX_E E p_E$.

Figure 3.15 is also useful to the discussion of stability. For any value of p (such as p_1) higher than the equilibrium value, p_E, B's supply of exports of X is larger than A's demand for imports of X. In addition, B's demand for imports of Y (as given by the area of the rectangle $OX_2 M p_1$) is greater than A's supply for exports of Y (as given by the area of the rectangle $OX_1 K p_1$). Thus, the terms of trade will tend to fall. The opposite will, of course, happen when p takes a value lower than p_E.

5. Limitations of the Classical Theory

The classical theory explains that profitable international trade takes place because of the existence of comparative cost differences. But then, why do comparative cost differences exist? Within the context of the labor theory of value, it appears that a necessary condition for the existence of comparative cost differences is the existence of different production functions between countries. If production functions were the same between countries, the labor requirements for the production of any commodity would, by necessity, be the same in all countries; that is, every country would be equally productive in every line of production. This state of affairs, however, leaves no room for international trade. Therefore, it appears that the *sine qua non* for the existence of international trade is the nonidentity of production functions between countries. But if this is so, why do production functions differ between countries? Unfortunately, the classical theory does not offer any answers—although implicitly, in Ricardo's classic example, the reason was climatic differences. But without a satisfactory answer to this important question, the classical theory loses most of its explanatory usefulness. As we shall see later, the modern theory of trade starts with the assumption that production functions are indeed identical among countries and explains the existence of comparative advantage with differences in factor proportions.

The classical theory offers a clear explanation of the gains from trade and as such has made an important contribution to welfare as opposed to positive economics. In addition, it demonstrates convincingly that trade barriers are harmful to the world economy and that free trade is potentially the best policy.

Appendix 3A:
Many Commodities and Many Countries

Trade in Many Commodities and Two Countries

The analysis of chapters 2 and 3 can be easily extended to the case where not two but any number of commodities are produced in two countries.

Let there be n commodities, $X_1, X_2, \ldots, X_n$, and let the labor requirements for the production of 1 unit of the ith commodity in country A be denoted by a_i and in country B by b_i $(i = 1, 2, \ldots, n)$. In addition, let us adopt the following notation:

C_i^A = A's consumption of commodity X_i,

Q_i^A = A's production of commodity X_i,

D_A^A = A's indirect demand (i.e., through the consumption of commodities produced in A) for its own labor,

D_B^A = A's indirect demand for B's labor,
Similar notation with superscript B will be used with the first four terms for country B.

D_A = total demand (by both A and B) for A's labor,

D_B = total demand for B's labor,

L_A = total supply of labor in A, and

L_B = total supply of labor in B.

Arrangement of Commodities in Order of Comparative Advantage

Following the analysis of chapter 2, we can say that A has a comparative advantage in the production of X_i and B in X_j when

$$a_i/b_i < a_j/b_j \qquad (i, j = 1, 2, \ldots, n). \tag{3A.1}$$

On the basis of this definition, the n commodities can be arranged in the order of comparative advantage of country A over country B. Thus, assuming that the following inequalities hold:

$$a_1/b_1 < a_2/b_2 < a_3/b_3 < \cdots < a_{n-1}/b_{n-1} < a_n/b_n, \qquad (3A.2)$$

it should be obvious that country A is relatively more efficient in the production of X_1 as compared with X_2; X_2 as compared with X_3; $\ldots$; X_{n-1} as compared with X_n. From inequalities (3A.2) it is also evident that these relationships are transitive. That is, since A is relatively more efficient in the production of X_1 compared with X_2, and in the production of X_2 compared with X_3, A must also be relatively more efficient in the production of X_1 compared with X_3.

Wages and Prices

Denote the money wage rate in A by w_A and in B by w_B. Before trade starts, the absolute money prices in countries A and B are given, respectively, by equations (3A.3) and (3A.4):

$$P_i^A = w_A a_i \qquad\qquad\qquad\qquad\qquad (3A.3)$$
$$\qquad\qquad (i = 1, 2, \ldots, n).$$
$$P_i^B = w_B b_i \qquad\qquad\qquad\qquad\qquad (3A.4)$$

While absolute prices depend upon the absolute money wage rates in the two countries, relative prices are given by relative labor requirements as explained in chapter 2. Since this discussion concerns mainly relative prices and wages, let us assume, without any loss of generality, that w_A is arbitrarily set equal to unity with only w_B allowed to vary. Actually, w_B, which for convenience will be denoted from this point on simply by w, can vary only within certain limits, which will presently be determined.[1] As the analysis of chapter 2 showed, international equilibrium requires that each country export at least one commodity to secure enough revenue to pay for its imports. Thus, if w increases beyond a certain limit, B's unit costs of production will be higher than the corresponding costs in A, and B will be unable to export anything. On the other hand, if w falls below a certain limit, everything will cost less in B, and A will be unable to export anything.

Theorem: The upper limit for w is given by the ratio a_n/b_n and the lower limit by a_1/b_1; that is:

$$a_1/b_1 \leq w \leq a_n/b_n. \qquad (3A.5)$$

Proof: The upper limit for w is determined in such a way as to make B's unit cost of production of X_n (i.e., the commodity in whose production B has

---

1. The ratio of wage rates, w_B/w_A, is usually called the "factoral terms of trade." It shows the number of units of A's labor that can be exchanged for 1 unit of B's labor.

a comparative advantage compared with any other commodity) equal to A's. That is, the upper limit for w is given by the solution to the equation $a_n = wb_n$. To see why this is so, observe that for any commodity X_i $(i \neq n)$ the following inequality holds:

$$a_i/b_i < a_n/b_n. \tag{3A.6}$$

Thus, if $w = a_n/b_n$, it follows from inequality (3A.6) that

$$a_i < wb_i \qquad (i \neq n). \tag{3A.7}$$

In other words, A's unit costs of production of every commodity except X_n are lower than B's. Since B can conceivably export X_n, the value $w = a_n/b_n$ cannot be ruled out as a possible equilibrium value. However, should w rise slightly above a_n/b_n, A's costs will be everywhere lower than B's, and long-run equilibrium is ruled out. Therefore, the value a_n/b_n is indeed the upper limit for w.

The lower limit for w, on the other hand, is determined in such a way as to make B's unit cost of production of X_1 (i.e., the commodity in whose production A has a comparative advantage compared with any other commodity) equal to A's. That is, the lower limit for w is given by the solution to the equation $a_1 = wb_1$. This follows from the fact that for any commodity X_i $(i \neq 1)$ the following inequality holds:

$$a_1/b_1 < a_i/b_i. \tag{3A.8}$$

Therefore, if $w = a_1/b_1$, we must have

$$wb_i < a_i \qquad (i \neq 1). \tag{3A.9}$$

That is, B will undersell A in every commodity except X_1. Since A can conceivably export X_1, the value $w = a_1/b_1$ cannot be ruled out as a possible equilibrium value. However, should w fall slightly below a_1/b_1, B's costs will be everywhere lower than A's, and long-run equilibrium cannot exist. Therefore, the value a_1/b_1 is indeed the lower limit for w.

Direction of Trade

Theorem: In any general-equilibrium configuration, each country enjoys a comparative advantage (over the other country) in all its export commodities relative to all its import commodities.

Proof: Consider the problem from the point of view of country A. Assume that A exports commodity X_t and imports commodity X_s. Then the following inequalities must hold:

$$a_t < wb_t, \tag{3A.10}$$

$$a_s > wb_s. \tag{3A.11}$$

These inequalities can be rearranged as follows:

$$a_t/b_t < w < a_s/b_s. \tag{3A.12}$$

This proves the theorem.

It is conceivable that one of the inequalities (3A.10) and (3A.11) may be an equality. However, as long as inequalities (3A.2) hold, at least one of the two will be a strict inequality, and this is sufficient for our proof. If inequalities (3A.2) are not strict inequalities, however, and if in particular we have $a_t/b_t = a_s/b_s$, commodities X_t and X_s are identical from the point of view of comparative advantage. In fact, if the equilibrium value of w is such that $a_t = wb_t$ and $a_s = wb_s$, it will be impossible to determine whether X_s or X_t or both will be exported from A to B, or vice versa. This can be seen as follows. As in the two-commodity case, the consumption levels of all commodities are perfectly determined in both countries once the value of w is given. Further, given w, each country will certainly be producing all those commodities (and at levels equal to the world consumption of each) which it can produce more cheaply than the other. But the production and direction of trade as far as commodities X_t and X_s are concerned are not so certain. Thus, since the production levels in each of all other commodities (except X_t and X_s) are known, it is easy to determine the quantity of labor required for their production. Hence, it is easy to determine the residual amount of labor left in each country for the production of X_s and X_t. Denote these residual amounts of labor in A and B by L_A^0 and L_B^0, respectively, and form the following two equations:

$$L_A^0 = a_s Q_s^A + a_t Q_t^A, \tag{3A.13}$$

$$L_B^0 = b_s Q_s^B + b_t Q_t^B. \tag{3A.14}$$

These equations can be considered as the production-possibilities frontiers of two countries, A and B, producing two commodities, X_s and X_t. If $a_s/b_s = a_t/b_t$, the opportunity costs will be the same in the two countries, i.e., the production-possibilities frontiers will have the same slope. As the analysis of chapter 3 shows, despite the fact that the consumption equilibria of the two countries are unique, the production equilibria are indeterminate and so is the pattern of trade as far as these two commodities are concerned.

Inequality (3A.12) is useful in another way. Given any value of w, say w^*, the export and import commodities of country A (and country B, for that matter) can easily be determined as follows. All those commodities for which the inequality $w^* > a_i/b_i$ holds are exported from A to B, and all those commodities for which the inequality $w^* < a_i/b_i$ holds are exported from B to A. (If for a particular commodity, say X_t, we have $w^* = a_t/b_t$, this commodity will in general be produced in both countries. Without further information about demand, it is impossible to say which country will be exporting it.) Thus, given w^*, we can draw a line and break the chain of commodities $X_1, X_2, \ldots, X_n$ into two groups: those at the beginning of the chain which satisfy the inequality $w^* > a_i/b_i$ and thus are exported from A to B, and those at the end of the chain which satisfy the inequality $w^* < a_i/b_i$ and are exported from B to A. A corollary of this is that, if we know that at the existing international equilibrium commodity X_m is exported from A to B, we can then conclude without any further information that all commodities in the chain before X_m, that is, $X_1, X_2, \ldots, X_{m-1}$, are also exported from A to B. Or, if commodity X_t is known to be exported from B to A, then without any further information we can conclude that commodities X_{t+1}, $X_{t+2}, \ldots, X_n$ must also be exported from B to A.

Finally, it should be noted that when $a_1/b_1 < w < a_n/b_n$, both countries gain from trade; when $w = a_1/b_1$, all gains accrue to A; and when $w = a_n/b_n$, all gains accrue to B.

Commodity Prices

The relative prices in the international market depend on w and nothing else. Thus, for any specific value of w, say w^*, A's export and import commodities can be determined as in the preceding section. Assume provisionally that when $w = w^*$, the first m commodities (i.e., $X_1, X_2, \ldots, X_m$) are exported from A to B while the rest (i.e., $X_{m+1}, X_{m+2}, \ldots, X_n$) are exported from B to A. Then the n equilibrium prices will be given by the following equations:

$$P_i = a_i \qquad (i = 1, 2, \ldots, m), \qquad (3A.15)$$

$$P_j = w^* b_j \qquad (j = m + 1, \ldots, n). \qquad (3A.16)$$

Any commodity could be used as numeraire, and these prices could be converted into price ratios, but that is not necessary for our purposes. As they now stand, equations (3A.15) and (3A.16) give the n commodity prices in terms of A's labor units, and this is sufficient for the ensuing analysis.

From equations (3A.15) and (3A.16), it becomes apparent that, as w increases, only the prices of the commodities exported by B are increased. However, this process does not continue forever. In particular, the price P_{m+1} will continue to increase until $wb_{m+1} = a_{m+1}$. When that happens, X_{m+1} will be produced in A and any further increases in w will not affect P_{m+1}. As noted earlier, for the particular value of w which satisfies the equation $wb_{m+1} = a_{m+1}$, commodity X_{m+1} can be imported or exported by A. However, as w rises above this value, X_{m+1} definitely shifts into the category of A's export commodities. As w continues to increase, the same will successively happen to commodities X_{m+2}, X_{m+3}, and so on. Therefore, we conclude that as w increases, A's export commodities tend to become cheaper relative to A's import commodities.

International Equilibrium

As in the case of two commodities, the determination of the equilibrium prices requires the introduction of demand data. It might appear that, since there are n commodity markets, we might have to solve simultaneously n equations, which, of course, cannot be done graphically. However, things are not as bad as they look. As the discussion in the preceding section showed, all prices depend on w only. Therefore, if we could somehow determine the equilibrium value of w, we would be able to determine indirectly all equilibrium prices and also break the chain of commodities $X_1, X_2, \ldots, X_n$ into export and import commodities from the point of view of either country. The following remarkable theorem shows that this can be done.

Theorem: International equilibrium occurs when the following condition is satisfied:

$$D_B^A = L_B - D_B^B. \tag{3A.17}$$

Proof: Consider any value of w satisfying condition (3A.5) and assume that the first m commodities (i.e., $X_1, X_2, \ldots, X_m$) are exported from A to B and the last $(n - m)$ commodities (i.e., $X_{m+1}, \ldots, X_n$) are exported from B to A. Then form the following equations, which follow directly from the definitions given at the beginning of this appendix:

$$D_A^A = \sum_{i=1}^{m} a_i C_i^A, \tag{3A.18}$$

$$D_A^B = \sum_{i=1}^{m} a_i C_i^B, \tag{3A.19}$$

$$D_B^A = \sum_{j=m+1}^{n} b_j C_j^A, \tag{3A.20}$$

$$D_B^B = \sum_{j=m+1}^{n} b_j C_j^B, \tag{3A.21}$$

$$D_A = D_A^A + D_A^B, \tag{3A.22}$$

$$D_B = D_B^A + D_B^B. \tag{3A.23}$$

General equilibrium occurs when each country can actually produce all commodities that it finds profitable to produce at the given value of w and at the precise amounts that are being demanded by both countries together. Now given that country A produces $X_1, \ldots, X_m$ and B produces $X_{m+1}, \ldots,$

X_n, we can determine all alternative combinations of commodities that can be produced in each country as follows:

$$L_A = \sum_{i=1}^{m} a_i Q_i^A, \tag{3A.24}$$

$$L_B = \sum_{j=m+1}^{n} b_j Q_j^B. \tag{3A.25}$$

For general equilibrium, it is required that the following conditions be satisfied:

$$Q_i^A = C_i^A + C_i^B \qquad (i = 1, \ldots, m), \tag{3A.26}$$

$$Q_j^B = C_j^A + C_j^B \qquad (j = m + 1, \ldots, n). \tag{3A.27}$$

Substituting equations (3A.26) and (3A.27) into equations (3A.24) and (3A.25), respectively, we get

$$L_A = \sum_{i=1}^{m} a_i(C_i^A + C_i^B) = D_A \qquad (i = 1, \ldots, m), \tag{3A.28}$$

$$L_B = \sum_{j=m+1}^{n} b_j(C_j^A + C_j^B) = D_B \qquad (j = m + 1, \ldots, n). \tag{3A.29}$$

Therefore, general equilibrium occurs when equations (3A.28) and (3A.29) are satisfied. But these equations are not independent; one of them is redundant. To see why, let us start with the following community budget equations:

$$L_A = \sum_{i=1}^{m} a_i C_i^A + w \sum_{j=m+1}^{n} b_j C_j^A = D_A^A + w D_B^A, \tag{3A.30}$$

$$w L_B = \sum_{i=1}^{m} a_i C_i^B + w \sum_{j=m+1}^{n} b_j C_j^B = D_A^B + w D_B^B. \tag{3A.31}$$

Adding equations (3A.30) and (3A.31) and manipulating them slightly, we get

$$(L_A - D_A) + w(L_B - D_B) = 0. \tag{3A.32}$$

Now equation (3A.32) must always be satisfied, whether or not international equilibrium exists. But if this is so, then it should be obvious that, if $(L_A - D_A) = 0$ (i.e., if eq. [3A.28] is satisfied), then $(L_B - D_B) = 0$ (i.e., eq. [3A.29] is also satisfied), and vice versa. In the following analysis, let us eliminate equation (3A.28) and work with equation (3A.29). The latter is simply a variant of equation (3A.17). This completes the proof of the theorem.

Figure 3A.1 shows how, on the basis of the preceding theorem, international equilibrium can be determined in terms of two curves: A's demand

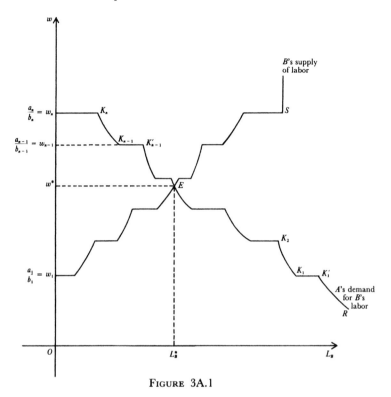

FIGURE 3A.1

for B's labor (D_B^A) and B's supply of labor to A $(L_B - D_B^B)$. Start with A's demand curve for B's labor. For $w > a_n/b_n$, D_B^A must be zero, because, as shown above, A's costs of production will be lower than B's in every line of production and A will demand no commodities and hence no labor from B. Thus, for $w > a_n/b_n$, A's demand curve for B's labor coincides with the vertical axis. For the specific value $w = a_n/b_n$, however, B produces X_n at the same cost as A, while everything else is still produced cheaper in A. The relative commodity prices are still the same in A (compared with the case where $w > a_n/b_n$), and therefore A will continue to consume the same quantities of $X_1, \ldots, X_n$ as before. Nevertheless—and this is the difference now—A does not have to produce commodity X_n at the level of domestic consumption of X_n, although it has to continue producing the rest of the commodities, that is, $X_1, \ldots, X_{n-1}$. Now, if $\overline{C}_n^A$ is the equilibrium consumption of X_n in A when $w = a_n/b_n$, A may be importing all or nothing or any fraction of this amount of X_n from B. This gives rise to the horizontal segment $w_n K_n$ on A's demand curve for B's labor. In particular, the distance $w_n K_n$ is given by the product $b_n \overline{C}_n^A$. Now as w falls below a_n/b_n but remains above a_{n-1}/b_{n-1}, that is, when $a_{n-1}/b_{n-1} < w < a_n/b_n$, commodity X_n will be cheaper in B and it will have to be imported from B. On the other hand, all other commodities will continue to be cheaper in A, and therefore none will have to be imported from B. But as w falls below a_n/b_n, commodity X_n becomes cheaper relative to all other commodities, and A's consumers will tend to substitute X_n for other, more expensive commodities.[2] This will tend to increase the amount of B's labor demanded by A, as shown by the negatively sloped segment K_nK_{n-1}. When $w = a_{n-1}/b_{n-1}$, then B's costs of production of X_{n-1} are equal to A's. Therefore, A can import, in addition to X_n, all or any part of X_{n-1} that it consumes domestically. This gives rise to the straight-line segment $K_{n-1}K'_{n-1}$. This process continues until $w = a_1/b_1$, when B's costs of production of X_1 are equal to A's while A's costs are higher than B's in every other line of production. The straight-line segment $K_1K'_1$ corresponds to the amount of labor that B will have to use for the production of that amount of X_1 consumed by A at $w = a_1/b_1$. For values of w below a_1/b_1, A's demand for B's labor is part of the rectangular hyperbola given by the equation $L_A = wD_B^A$. This follows from the fact that A's income is L_A (measured in terms of A's labor units); A would like to spend this income totally on commodities produced by B, because B's costs are everywhere lower than A's. Hence, A's budget equation becomes:

$$L_A = w(b_1C_1^A + b_2C_2^A + \cdots + b_nC_n^A) = wD_B^A.$$

Country B's supply curve of labor to A is derived in a similar fashion. It coincides with the vertical axis for $w < a_1/b_1$, because in this region B's costs are lower than A's and B consumes everything it produces. In the region $(a_1/b_1) \le w \le (a_n/b_n)$, we have again a step function, as shown in figure 3A.1. The various steps in its derivation have been omitted because the analysis is similar to that provided for the derivation of A's demand curve for B's labor. For $w > a_n/b_n$, A's costs are lower in every line of production and therefore B would be willing to consume nothing that is produced domestically, which means that B would be willing to supply all of its labor to A. Thus, B's supply curve becomes vertical in the region $w > a_n/b_n$. It should be noted that the number of horizontal segments of both curves depicted in figure 3A.1 is equal to the number of commodities, or more precisely, it is equal to the number of distinct ratios a_i/b_i.

Equilibrium is seen to occur at point E, where country B exports indirectly L_B^* units of labor to A in exchange for L_A^* units of A's labor, where $L_A^* =$ area of rectangle $OL_B^*Ew^*$.

Once w^* is determined, all other prices in the system can be determined as explained earlier. In addition, the chain of commodities $X_1, X_2, \ldots, X_n$ can be split into A's export and import commodities. However, what cannot be determined without additional information are the precise amounts of these commodities traded internationally, despite the fact that the aggregate value of A's exports and imports expressed in terms of either A's or B's

2. For simplicity, it is assumed that as the relative price of a commodity falls, more of it is being demanded.

labor units is in general perfectly determined.[3] From this observation follows the important conclusion that shifts in demand within each group of commodities (i.e., A's export commodities and A's import commodities) do not affect the equilibrium value of w and, therefore, relative commodity prices—as long as the aggregate expenditure on each group of commodities remains constant. The important condition, in other words, for international equilibrium is the equality between A's demand for B's labor and B's supply of labor to A, irrespective of the allocation of D_A^A among the commodities produced by A; the allocation of D_B^A among the commodities produced by B; the allocation of D_A^B among the commodities produced by A; and the allocation of D_B^B among the commodities produced by B. However, shifts in demand which involve a redistribution of expenditure from A's export to A's import commodities, or vice versa, will in general affect the equilibrium value of w. In this latter case, the shift in demand will not have a substantial effect on w, or will have none at all, if w^* is equal to one of the ratios a_i/b_i. The importance of this qualification, though, shrinks as the number of commodities increases. This can be seen as follows. The average length of the horizontal segments of the curves depicted in figure 3A.1 decreases as the number of commodities increases, for the average length of the horizontal segments of B's supply curve is given by the ratio L_B/n and the average length of the horizontal segments of A's demand curve is given by $[L_A(a_1/b_1)]/n$. Thus, as n increases, they both decrease. In fact, as $n \to \infty$, both curves become smoothly continuous in the region $a_1/b_1 < w < a_n/b_n$, and a shift of either curve will definitely affect the equilibrium value of w. However, if the number of commodities is small and if the two curves of figure 3A.1 coincide along a horizontal segment—whose length will be relatively large because of the small number of commodities—a shift in demand which causes either curve to shift totally to the left or right will, within limits, fail to produce any change in w^*. If a change in w^* does take place, it will most certainly be smaller than what it would have been had the number of commodities been larger.

Two Commodities and Many Countries

The model of chapter 2 can be generalized easily from another point of view. The number of commodities can be kept to two while the number of countries can be allowed to increase to m $(m > 2)$. This case can be handled quite easily in terms of the concept of the world production-possibilities frontier.

3. This is true except in the limiting case where w^* is equal to one of the ratios a_i/b_i, say a_s/b_s, and commodity X_s is being produced in both countries. Then, as a result of the indeterminacy of the amounts of X_s produced by the two countries (though the total production of X_s is given by the sum of the equilibrium consumption levels of X_s in the two countries), the aggregate value of exports and imports cannot be uniquely determined, although an upper and a lower limit can be established.

Figure 3A.2 shows how the world production-possibilities frontier can be derived when there are five countries, A, B, C, D, and E, producing two commodities, X and Y. The x-axis intercept X_0 shows the maximum amount of X that all countries together can produce when the output of Y is zero. Thus, $OX_0 = K'K + L'L + M'M + N'N + SX_0$, where $K'K$, $L'L$, $M'M$, $N'N$, and SX_0 are the maximum quantities of X that countries A, B, C, D, and E, respectively, can produce. Similarly, the y-axis intercept Y_0 shows the maximum amount of Y that all countries together can produce

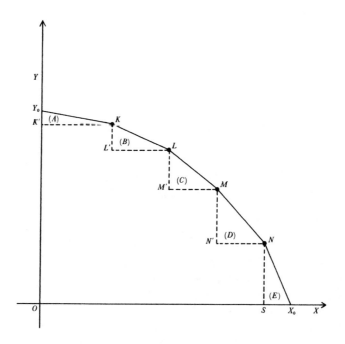

FIGURE 3A.2

when the output of X is zero. Thus, $OY_0 = K'Y_0 + L'K + M'L + N'M + SN$, where $K'Y_0$, $L'K$, $M'L$, $N'M$, and SN are the maximum quantities of Y that countries A, B, C, D, and E, respectively, can produce. The reader should be able to verify that the triangles $K'KY_0$, $L'LK$, $M'ML$, $N'NM$, and SX_0N are the production-possibilities frontiers of countries A, B, C, D, and E, respectively. Further, on the basis of the analysis of chapter 2, the reader should be able to show why the five production-possibilities frontiers have been arranged in the order in which they appear in figure 3A.2.

Given the world production-possibilities frontier, international equilibrium can be determined by the introduction of demand. If demand could be introduced in the form of a world indifference map, the analysis would closely approximate that of chapter 3, section 1. The only difference is that now the world production-possibilities frontier does not consist of only two straight-line segments but many. In fact, the number of straight-line segments of the world production-possibilities frontier is given by the number of countries whose opportunity costs are different from those of all other countries.

Demand could very well be introduced in terms of separate social indifference maps, one for each country. Then general equilibrium could be shown by adding horizontally the excess demand curves for X of all countries as shown in chapter 3. Thus, the analysis is essentially the same as that of the simple two-country, two-commodity model.

Finally, it should be pointed out that the introduction of many countries with different opportunity costs increases the probability that the equilibrium terms of trade will coincide with some country's, say country C's, pretrade price ratio. In that case, country C will gain nothing from international trade; and what is more, any changes in demand (within limits) will merely affect C's internal allocation of resources without having any effect on the terms of trade. It is, of course, conceivable that wider shifts in world demand might shift the equilibrium point from the linear segment LM to another linear segment, say MN. Then country D will assume the role of country C, with the terms of trade shifting from C's to D's pretrade price ratio.

Many Countries and Many Commodities

The analysis can be extended to the general case of m countries and n commodities. However, the rigorous treatment of this case seems to require the application of mathematical tools that go beyond the scope of this book. Therefore, no attempt will be made now to provide a general-equilibrium solution. The discussion will be limited to some general conclusions which follow easily from the preceding analysis.

In this general case, as well as in simpler ones, international equilibrium requires that each country export at least one commodity. In addition, the problem of international equilibrium can be formulated in either one of the following two ways: (a) in terms of a system of n equilibrium conditions, one for each of the n commodity markets, which by Walras's law can be reduced to a system of $(n - 1)$ equations in $(n - 1)$ price ratios, or (b) in terms of a system of m equilibrium conditions, one for each country's labor market, which can be reduced (by Walras's law) to a system of $(m - 1)$ equations in $(m - 1)$ wage ratios. Both approaches will necessarily give rise to identical results.

If $n = m$, either approach will give rise to the same number of equations. Each country will specialize in the production of at least one commodity, and once the equilibrium wage ratios are determined, the price ratios can be determined, and vice versa.

If $n \neq m$, it might appear that the two approaches would give rise to inconsistent results. However, this is not so. For instance, if $n > m$, the first approach would give rise to $(n - 1)$ equations in $(n - 1)$ unknowns while the second approach would give rise to $(m - 1)$ equations in $(m - 1)$ unknowns. But as has been shown earlier in this appendix in the case of two countries and many commodities, the $(n - 1)$ price ratios are necessarily functions of the $(m - 1)$ wage ratios. Thus, in the final analysis, the $(n - 1)$ equations are actually functions of only $(m - 1)$ unknowns, and the question naturally arises as to whether the set of $(n - 1)$ equations is consistent. That this is so follows from the fact that $(n - m)$ commodities will have to be produced in one country or another along with other commodities, and therefore their relative prices will be determined by relative labor requirements. Actually, the system can be thought of as consisting of m composite commodities each of which is being produced by a single country—although these composite commodities cannot be decided a priori. The actual proportions of the various commodities making up each composite good are immaterial from the point of view of international equilibrium. Thus, any shifts in the composition of each and every composite good as a result of a shift in demand will necessarily leave relative prices undisturbed.

If $n < m$, at least $(m - n)$ commodities will have to be produced in more than one country. The $(m - 1)$ wage ratios can be seen to be uniquely determined by the $(n - 1)$ price ratios. The reader is referred to the discussion of the simple case of two commodities and m countries.

Selected Bibliography

Balassa, B. 1963. An empirical demonstration of comparative cost. *Review of Economics and Statistics* 45: 231–38.

Chipman, John S. 1965. A survey of the theory of international trade, part 1: the classical theory. *Econometrica* 33: 477–519.

Graham, F. D. 1923. The theory of international values re-examined. *Quarterly Journal of Economics* 28: 54–86; reprinted in A.E.A. *Readings in the Theory of International Trade*. Homewood, Ill.: R. D. Irwin, Inc., 1949.

Haberler, G. 1936. *The Theory of International Trade*. London: W. Hodge & Co. Chap. 9–11.

Heller, H. R. 1968. *International Trade*. Englewood Cliffs, N.J.: Prentice-Hall, Inc. Chap. 2.

MacDougal, G. D. A. 1951. British and American exports: a study suggested by the theory of comparative costs, part I. *Economic Journal* 61: 697–724; reprinted in A.E.A. *Readings in International Economics*. Homewood, Ill.: R. D. Irwin, Inc., 1968.

———. 1952. British and American exports: a study suggested by the theory of comparative costs, part II. *Economic Journal* 62: 487–521.

Meade, J. E. 1955. *The Theory of International Economic Policy*. Vol. 2: *trade and welfare*. Oxford: Oxford University Press. Chap. 9.

Melvin, J. R. 1969. On a demand assumption made by Graham. *Southern Economic Journal* 36: 36–43.

Metzler, L. A. 1950. Graham's theory of international values. *American Economic Review* 50: 67–110.

Mill, J. S. 1902. *Principles of Political Economy.* New York: Appleton, Century & Crofts, Inc. Chap. 17, 18, 25.

Ricardo, David. 1821. *The Principles of Political Economy and Taxation.* London: J. Murray. Chap. 7.

Smith, Adam. 1937. *The Wealth of Nations.* New York: Modern Library.

Stern, R. 1962. British and American productivity and comparative costs in international trade. *Oxford Economic Papers* 14: 275–96.

Williams, J. H. 1929. The theory of international trade reconsidered. *Economic Journal* 39: 195–209; reprinted in A.E.A. *Readings in the Theory of International Trade.* Homewood, Ill.: R. D. Irwin, Inc. 1949.

III

The Neoclassical Theory

4

Opportunity Cost

The neoclassical theory of international values is based on the fundamental concepts of opportunity cost and social indifference. It is an improvement over the classical theory because it frees the classical conclusions from the restrictive assumption of the labor theory of value. The main architects of the neoclassical theory are Edgeworth, Haberler, Leontief, Lerner, Marshall, and Meade.

The neoclassical theory is discussed in this and the following three chapters. In particular, the present chapter discusses at some length the concept of opportunity cost; chapter 5, the concept of social indifference and comparative advantage; chapter 6, the problem of general equilibrium; and chapter 7, the problem of increasing returns.

As discussed in chapter 2, Haberler insisted that the sole purpose of the labor theory of value was to determine the pretrade price ratios in the two countries. By means of the concept of the production-possibilities frontier (or substitution curve, as he called it), he demonstrated that the restrictive assumption of the labor theory of value can be dispensed with "without having to discard the results obtained from it: these will remain, just as a building remains after the scaffolding, having served its purpose, is removed."[1]

Chapter 2 introduced the concept of the production-possibilities frontier but within the context of the labor theory of value. The latter is now being dropped to make room for a more general theory of production. This discussion therefore begins with a brief survey of the theory of production.

1. Production Functions

Consider a firm using two factors of production, labor, L, and land, T, and producing a single output, q. Its *production function* is merely a statement of

1. Haberler (1936, p. 126).

the maximum quantity of output that it can produce with any specified quantities of labor and land. This can be expressed algebraically as

$$q = f(L, T). \tag{4.1}$$

The production function is a purely physical concept; that is, it is a relationship between the physical quantities of output and input—not their values. The symbol f in equation (4.1) could be thought of as an engineer who could tell us the maximum amount of q that he can possibly produce with given amounts of L and T, irrespective of price.

The production function is usually illustrated graphically by means of the *isoquant map*, as shown in figure 4.1. Each curve, or *isoquant*, is the locus of alternative combinations of labor and land, all of which are capable of producing the same amount of output. Once the production function (4.1) is given, an isoquant can be derived by assigning a particular value to q. Equation (4.1) then becomes an equation in two variables (L and T) and is graphically depicted by means of an isoquant. Thus, isoquant q_2 is simply the graphical representation of the function $f(L, T) = q_2$. The totality of all isoquants, which can be derived by assigning different values to q in equation (4.1), is the isoquant map. Therefore, an isoquant map gives, in principle, all the information included in equation (4.1), no more and no less.

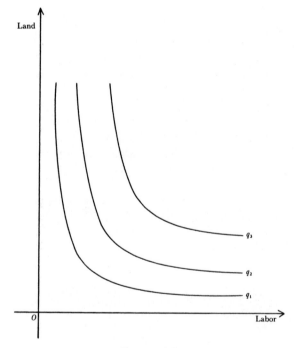

FIGURE 4.1

Qualitatively, an isoquant map looks like an indifference map. However, in the case of an isoquant map, the quantity produced is objectively measurable, whereas in the case of an indifference map, the utility attached to each indifference curve is not objectively measurable.

Isoquants have normally a negative slope—at least within a certain range. Within this range, factors of production are substitutable for one another. The absolute value of the slope of an isoquant is known as the *marginal rate of substitution* of labor for land (MRS_{LT}). It shows the maximum number of units of land that can be given up for an extra unit of labor if the firm is to continue producing the same amount of output. This is illustrated in figure 4.2. Assume that the firm is at point M and that RM (or ΔT) units of land are given up for the additional amount of RN (or ΔL) units of labor. The firm moves from point M to point N; since it remains on the same isoquant, its output does not change. For each additional unit of labor acquired, it gave up, on the average, RM/RN units of land. Now the ratio $RM/RN = -(\Delta T/\Delta L)$ is the absolute slope of the straight line passing through points M and N. Now imagine that point N travels along the isoquant toward M; the slope of the line MN will move closer and closer to the slope of the tangent at M. Actually, the limit of the sequence of numbers given by the

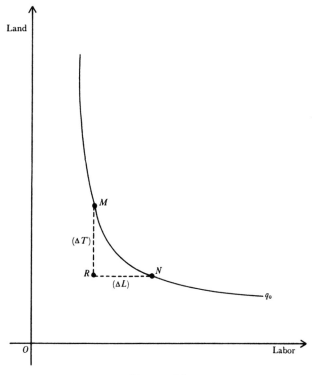

FIGURE 4.2

various values of the slope of MN as N tends to M is simply the slope of the tangent at M. Thus,

$$MRS_{LT} = -dT/dL, \tag{4.2}$$

where dT/dL stands for the slope of the isoquant.[2]

There is a close relationship between the *marginal physical products* of the two factors of production and the marginal rate of substitution of labor for land. (The marginal physical product of a factor, say labor, is the extra amount of output that can be secured by increasing labor by 1 unit while leaving all other factors unchanged.) To see this, let us go back to figure 4.2 and assume again that we are moving from M to N. It is useful, however, to divide this movement into two parts (*a*) a movement from M to R and (*b*) a movement from R to N. In the first step, ΔT units of land are given up, and output necessarily falls. In particular, output will fall by $\Delta T(MPP_T)$ (where $MPP_T \equiv$ marginal physical product of land). On the other hand, moving from R to N implies that the employment of labor is increased by ΔL units. Output necessarily increases this time by the amount $\Delta L(MPP_L)$ (where $MPP_L \equiv$ marginal physical product of labor). Now, since we end up on the same isoquant (i.e., points M and N lie on the same curve), it follows that the reduction of output, $\Delta T(MPP_T)$, is equal to the increase in output, $\Delta L(MPP_L)$. In other words, the following equation necessarily holds:

$$\Delta T(MPP_T) + \Delta L(MPP_L) = 0. \tag{4.3}$$

Making use of equation 4.2, we can rearrange equation (4.3) as follows:

$$MRS_{LT} = -(\Delta T/\Delta L) = MPP_L/MPP_T. \tag{4.4}$$

Consequently, the marginal rate of substitution of labor for land is equal to the ratio of the marginal physical product of labor over the marginal physical product of land.

Each point on an isoquant corresponds to a different technological method of producing the specified output. Given these technological methods, a real choice remains to be made among the alternative methods. This choice is an economic one, because it is not determined by wholly technical or engineering considerations. It depends, in addition, on factor prices and the behavioral assumption that firms try to minimize cost, which is part and parcel of the profit-maximization assumption. Accordingly, given any factor prices, the firm will choose that production technique which minimizes cost. This problem is illustrated in figure 4.3. No further explanation is needed for the two isoquants appearing in this figure. The straight lines T_1L_1, T_2L_2, and T_3L_3 are three illustrative *isocost lines*. Each isocost line shows the alternative combinations of labor and land which can be purchased with a

---

2. The term dT/dL is the first derivative of T with respect to L. Since the isoquant is negatively sloped, dT/dL is negative. However, we are interested in the absolute value of $!T/dL$ and, hence, eq. (4.2).

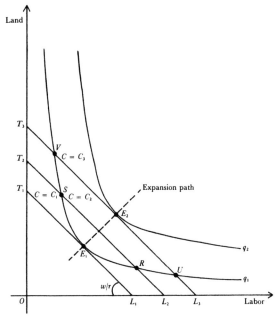

FIGURE 4.3

fixed sum of money. Algebraically, these isocost lines are given by the simple equation

$$C = wL + rT, \tag{4.5}$$

where C = total amount of expenditure, w = wage rate, and r = rent for land services. (The factor prices, w and r, are assumed constant because each firm is assumed to be a price taker in the factor markets.) For any given value of C, equation (4.5) can be represented graphically in the (L, T) plane by a straight line whose absolute slope is equal to the ratio of factor prices. Thus, as shown in figure 4.3, when $C = C_1$, we get the isocost line $T_1 L_1$; when C increases to C_2, we get the line $T_2 L_2$; and when C increases further to C_3, we get the line $T_3 L_3$. Observe that in each case, the L-axis intercept is given by the ratio C/w, while the T-axis intercept is given by the ratio C/r. Thus, as C increases, the isocost line shifts outward (i.e., away from the origin). Similarly, as q increases, we move to isoquants which lie farther from the origin.

It should be obvious from figure 4.3 that if the firm wants to produce q_1 units of output (and, therefore, a combination of labor and land must be selected in such a way as to coincide with the coordinates of some point on the q_1 isoquant), to minimize costs it will have to produce at point E_1; anywhere else, its costs are higher. (Compare points U, R, S, and V with point E_1.) Also, if the firm wants to produce q_2, it will produce at point E_2. Observe that at points E_1 and E_2 the isocost lines are tangent to the respective isoquants. The locus of all such tangencies, as illustrated by points E_1 and E_2, is called the *expansion path*. This is illustrated in figure 4.3 by the broken curve through points E_1 and E_2.

It should be noted that the expansion path gives all the information necessary for the derivation of the firm's *long-run total cost curve*, for an isoquant and isocost line pass through any point along the expansion path. The former gives the amount of output produced, and the latter gives the (minimum) total cost of production. Further, when the total cost curve is determined, the average cost is determined as the ratio C/q and the marginal cost will be given by the slope of the total cost curve, or the derivative dC/dq.

From the preceding analysis, it follows that a necessary condition for cost minimization is that the slope of the isocost line be equal to the slope of the isoquant, that is,

$$w/r = MPP_L/MPP_T. \tag{4.6}$$

This condition can also be written in the form

$$w/MPP_L = r/MPP_T = MC. \tag{4.7}$$

The ratio w/MPP_L is the marginal cost of production if labor were to increase sufficiently and raise output by 1 unit. The ratio r/MPP_T is the marginal cost of production if land were to increase and raise output by 1 unit. That is, increasing total cost by w, we increase the employment of labor by 1 unit, which in turn increases output by MPP_L units. Thus, the per unit cost on the margin (i.e., for the last unit of labor employed) is given by the ratio w/MPP_L. A similar reasoning holds for land as well. In the long run, as equation (4.7) shows, the two ratios must be equal to the unique long-run marginal cost. If that is not the case, total costs can be reduced (while keeping output constant) by transferring expenditure from the factor whose "marginal cost" is higher to the other. It can be shown that at S (fig. 4.3) we have $w/MPP_L < r/MPP_T$ and at R we have $w/MPP_L > r/MPP_T$. Thus, in both cases, a movement toward point E_1 reduces costs.

Equation (4.7) can also be arranged as follows:

$$MPP_L/w = MPP_T/r = 1/MC, \tag{4.7'}$$

where the ratio MPP_L/w (MPP_T/r) shows the extra output which can be produced by spending an extra dollar on L (T).

2. Linear Homogeneous Production Functions

An important production function playing a prominent role in economics in general and international economics in particular is the so-called *linear homogeneous production function*, or the class of production functions characterized by *constant returns to scale*.

The term *returns* refers in general to what happens to output (measured either in physical units or in value) when an input or some combination of inputs are increased. In particular, the term *returns to scale* refers to the relationship between changes in the physical quantity of output and a proportionate change in the physical quantity of all inputs. If the physical quantity of output changes in the same proportion as all physical inputs, we say that the production function is characterized by *constant returns to scale* for the range of input combinations under consideration. That is, if output doubles when all inputs are doubled, returns to scale are constant. On the other hand, if the physical quantity of output changes faster (slower) than all physical inputs, we say that the production function is characterized by *increasing (decreasing) returns to scale*. That is, if output more than doubles when all inputs are doubled, returns to scale are increasing, and if output increases but falls short of being doubled when all inputs are doubled, returns to scale are decreasing.

A linear homogeneous (production) function is the name that mathematicians use to describe (production) functions subject to constant returns to scale. A production function is linear homogeneous if, and only if, it satisfies the equation

$$mq = f(mL, mT), \tag{4.8}$$

where m is any positive real number.

A linear homogeneous production function has the following properties.

1. The *average physical product* of either factor depends only on the proportion in which the factors L and T are used; it does not depend on their absolute amounts. Thus, putting $m = 1/L$, equation (4.8) becomes

$$APP_L \equiv q/L = f(1, T/L) = g(T/L). \tag{4.9}$$

Or, putting $m = 1/T$, we get

$$APP_T \equiv q/T = f(L/T, 1) = h(T/L). \tag{4.10}$$

The symbol APP means "average physical product"; the subscripts L and T indicate the factors of production.

2. The marginal physical products, MPP_L and MPP_T, can likewise be expressed as functions of the ratio T/L alone. This proposition can be proved as follows:

$$MPP_L = \partial q/\partial L = \partial[Lg(T/L)]/\partial L = g(T/L) - (T/L)g'(T/L) = \phi(T/L),$$

$$MPP_T = \partial q/\partial T = \partial[Lg(T/L)]/\partial T = g'(T/L),$$

where primes indicate partial differentiation. Note that in these calculations use was made of equation (4.9); i.e., $q = L(APP_L)$.

3. Total output equals the MPP_L multiplied by the quantity of L used plus the MPP_T multiplied by T. That is,

$$q = L(MPP_L) + T(MPP_T). \tag{4.11}$$

This is *Euler's theorem*. From the economic point of view, this property means that under conditions of constant returns to scale, if each factor is paid the amount of its marginal physical product, the total product will be exhausted exactly by the distributive shares of all factors. For this reason, this property is sometimes referred to as the *adding-up theorem*.

The proof of Euler's theorem is not difficult to establish. Thus, substituting the results obtained in the preceding footnote into the right-hand side of equation (4.11), we get:

$$L(MPP_L) + T(MPP_T) = L[g - (T/L)g'] + T(g')$$

$$= L(g) - T(g') + T(g') = L(g) = q.$$

The independent variable T/L has been omitted for simplicity.

4. As a result of property 2 (i.e., that the MPP of every factor depends only on the ratio T/L) and equation (4.4) (i.e., that the MRS_{LT} is given by the ratio MPP_L/MPP_T), it follows that any straight line through the origin (implying a fixed ratio T/L) will cut all isoquants at points which have the same slope (i.e., the same MRS_{LT}).

5. If any one isoquant is given, the whole isoquant map can be constructed without any further information. This is illustrated in figure 4.4,

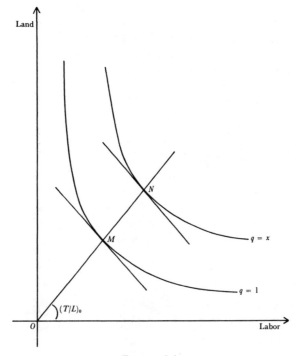

FIGURE 4.4

where for simplicity it is assumed that the unit isoquant is given. To determine a point (such as N) on the (unknown) isoquant which is the locus of alternative combinations of L and T which are capable of producing x units of output, simply draw a straight line through the origin (such as OMN). It will cut the unit isoquant at a certain point (such as point M). Then measure the distance OM and determine point N on the ray through the origin in such a way that the distance ON is equal to x times the distance OM (i.e., $ON = xOM$). Point N will lie on the isoquant $q = x$. That this should be so follows from the definition of constant returns to scale, because the movement from point M to point N implies that all factors are multiplied by the factor x, and therefore output at point N must be x times the output at point M. (Note that the tangents at points M and N in fig. 4.4 are parallel.) In the same way, we can determine all other points on the isoquant $q = x$. Since x stands for any particular value of q, it should be obvious that the whole isoquant map can be so constructed.

6. For any given factor prices (w and r), the expansion path is always a straight line through the origin. This follows from the fact that for cost minimization, it is required that the MRS_{LT} be equal to the factor-price ratio w/r. According to property 4, the MRS_{LT} will remain constant (and equal to the ratio w/r) along a certain ray through the origin.

7. As a result of property 6, the average cost of production (AC) remains constant at all levels of output. This can be seen as follows. By definition,

$$AC = \frac{wL + rT}{q}. \qquad (4.12)$$

Given w and r, factors L and T are always used in the same proportion. When L and T increase by a certain percentage, q also increases by the same percentage (because of the assumption of constant returns to scale). Therefore, both the numerator and the denominator on the right-hand side of equation (4.12) change by the same percentage, and thus, their ratio (i.e., AC) remains constant.

If both w and r increase by a certain percentage, their ratio, w/r, will of course remain the same and so will the expansion path. The average cost curve, however, will shift upward by the percentage by which w and r have gone up. This can be seen more rigorously as follows. Starting with equation (4.12) and making use of equations (4.11), (4.6), and (4.7), we obtain

$$AC = \frac{wL + rT}{q} = \frac{wL + rT}{L(MPP_L) + T(MPP_T)}$$

$$= \frac{r}{MPP_T} \left[\frac{(w/r)L + T}{(MPP_L/MPP_T)L + T} \right] = \frac{r}{MPP_T} = \frac{w}{MPP_L} = MC.$$

Thus, for given w and r, AC is equal to MC. In addition, if the ratio w/r is kept constant, the ratio L/T and the marginal physical productivities of

L and T also remain constant. Accordingly, AC is proportional to w and r.

On the other hand, if w falls while r remains constant, more labor will be used per unit of land (i.e., the ratio $[L/T]$ will rise); the marginal physical product of labor will fall and the marginal physical product of land will rise; and, finally, the marginal and average cost of production will fall. This can be proved as follows. At the original factor prices, say (w^0, r^0), the following equality is, for cost-minimization purposes, satisfied:

$$w^0/r^0 = MPP_L^0/MPP_T^0,$$

or

$$w^0/MPP_L^0 = r^0/MPP_T^0 = MC^0 = AC^0, \qquad (4.13)$$

where MPP_L^0 and MPP_T^0 stand, respectively, for the marginal physical product of labor and land at the initial equilibrium state. When w falls to, say, w^1, equality (4.13) is immediately converted into the inequality

$$w^1/MPP_L^0 < r^0/MPP_T^0. \qquad (4.14)$$

As explained in the section on production functions, costs can be reduced if labor is substituted for land, i.e., if the ratio L/T rises. As this happens, and because of diminishing returns to a variable factor, the MPP_L will tend to fall and the MPP_T will tend to rise. Thus, the left-hand side of inequality (4.14) will tend to increase while the right-hand side will tend to fall. Accordingly, if this substitution proceeds sufficiently, inequality (4.14) will again be converted into an equality as follows:

$$w^1/MPP_L^1 = r^0/MPP_T^1 = MC^1 = AC^1, \qquad (4.15)$$

where the superscript 1 indicates the values at the new equilibrium state. Now recall that $MPP_T^1 > MPP_T^0$. Hence,

$$AC^0 = MC^0 = r^0/MPP_T^0 > r^0/MPP_T^1 = MC^1 = AC^1. \qquad (4.16)$$

This completes the proof.

3. The Production Function of the Industry

The preceding discussion refers to the production function of the firm as opposed to the production function of a whole industry. However, section 2 is silent on this point, for the very good reason that, typically, the production function of a firm is not characterized by constant returns to scale throughout. Instead, increasing returns at the beginning (i.e., the familiar fact of "economies of large-scale production") are followed by constant and decreasing returns successively, presumably because of increasing difficulties of supervision. Accordingly, we observe the usual U-shaped average cost curve for the firm instead of the horizontal average cost curve implied by the linear homogeneous production function. But if the typical production function of a firm is not characterized by constant returns to scale, why study the linear homogeneous production function? The answer follows from the fact that neoclassical and modern writers usually postulate the existence of an industry production function, and for the whole industry, constant returns to scale is not an unrealistic assumption.

Before proceeding any further, we have to question whether it is meaningful or legitimate to bypass the firm and postulate a production function for the industry. In other words, the question is whether it is possible to predict the amount of output produced by an industry when only the *total* amounts of labor and land employed by all firms in the industry are known. For obviously, the actual output produced depends not only on the totals L and T used but also on their allocation among the various firms. Whether this can be done in general seems to be an open question. The rest of this section shows that this can be done if the following simplifying assumptions are made:

1. Each firm produces a single commodity.
2. Whatever the number of *active* firms in an industry at a given time, there is an indefinitely large number of *potential* producers.
3. Entrepreneurship is not a distinct factor of production. That is, the organizing and operating of a firm call for only routine ability and effort, exactly comparable to what is demanded of a hired worker— and hence require the same remuneration.[3]
4. All firms in an industry are alike in the sense that they have access to the same production function. Assume that the common production function will give rise to the usual U-shaped average cost curve for each individual firm at every possible combination of factor prices. Therefore, the present formulation is consistent with the phenomenon of "economies of large-scale production." However, it will be assumed that the output where each firm is able to attain minimum average cost is sufficiently low relative to the total industry output that many firms will be able to operate for the industry to remain purely competitive.
5. The common production function of firms is of the type illustrated by equation (4.1). In other words, output (q) depends only on the amounts of L and T used by the firm and nothing else. Therefore, the phenomenon of technological external effects[4] is assumed away.

3. In equilibrium, the entrepreneur will receive wages for his labor and rent for his land that are neither more nor less than other suppliers of labor and land. However, it should be clear that the function of the entrepreneur is quite distinct in that, in disequilibrium, he may enjoy a temporary profit or suffer a temporary loss. Nevertheless, assume that the entrepreneurs receive no compensation for their risk-bearing function. This can be justified on the grounds that profits and losses do cancel out over time and that all entrepreneurs have a neutral attitude toward these balanced chances of profit and risks of loss.

4. When technological external effects are present, the output of a typical firm does not depend only on the amounts of L and T used by the firm itself, but also on the amounts of L and T used by all other firms in the industry as well as the aggregate industry output. This phenomenon is discussed briefly in chap. 7.

Under these assumptions, the equilibrium price of the commodity produced by the industry must necessarily be equal to the minimum average cost of production. In other words, given any combination of w and r, the expansion path for a typical firm can be determined and the average cost curve derived therefrom. Since, by assumption, there is an infinite number of potential producers with the same average cost curve, the equilibrium price must necessarily be equal to the common minimum average cost. For, if the price were lower than the minimum average cost, no firm would be willing to produce, and if the price were higher than the minimum average cost of production, all active producers would be enjoying positive profits which would attract additional firms into the industry and cause the price to fall. In summary, the long-run industry supply curve is horizontal at the level of the minimum average cost of production, and the long-run equilibrium price is necessarily equal to this minimum average cost.

The preceding analysis shows that all active firms in the industry will use, in the long-run, the same production technique and that their scale of operations will always be determined at the point where the average cost of production is at a minimum. In other words, given any combination of factor prices (w, r), the optimum combination of labor and land that each and every firm will be using can be determined under conditions of long-run equilibrium. The scale of operations of each firm is perfectly determined, and the only unknown that remains to be determined is the number of active firms. The latter obviously depends upon demand. If, at the minimum average cost, the consumers would like to consume an output Q_0 and if each firm is producing q_0, then the number of active firms must be equal to Q_0/q_0. If the quantity demanded increases, the number of firms will increase —with each individual firm doing exactly what each and every other firm was doing before the change in demand. In particular, if the quantity demanded doubles, the number of firms (and, therefore, the employment of L and T) doubles as well. In general, if the quantity demanded is multiplied by the positive number m, the number of firms (and, therefore, the employment of L and T) will be multiplied by the number m. This sounds like constant returns to scale, for both output and inputs always seem to change by the same percentage. Does this mean that we have proved that, under assumptions 1–5 above, there exists an industry production function that is linear homogeneous? Not quite. We are very close to providing such a proof, but we are not there yet. The reason for this becomes obvious as we compare the preceding sequence with the definition of a linear homogeneous production function. Thus, what has just been shown (i.e., that as output doubles, inputs double as well) seems to be the reverse of the order followed in the definition of the (linear homogeneous) production function. In the latter case, output was the dependent variable while inputs were the independent variables. In the former case, though, output appears to be the independent variable while inputs are the dependent variables. In addition, the conclusion that inputs double as output demanded doubles was derived under the assumption that factor prices (w, r) were given. This is closely related to the first observation.

The real question is whether, under assumptions 1–5, industry output (Q) can be expressed as a function of the total quantities of L and T employed by all firms in the industry. This depends upon whether the allocation of the totals L and T among the firms in the industry will be such as to give rise to a unique industry output.

From the preceding analysis, it follows that, in the long run, all active firms always use the factors L and T in exactly the same proportion, because of the assumed identity of production functions. This being the case, when the total quantities of labor and land, say L_0 and T_0 respectively, are given, only one thing is certain: every active firm will be using the two factors in the proportion T_0/L_0. However, this alone is not sufficient for the determination of the industry output. To do so, we would have to know, in addition to the proportion in which the two factors are being used, the optimum scale of operations of each firm. But, as we saw earlier, the optimum scale of operations depends on factor prices. If we were to conclude that the industry output depends not only on the total quantities of L and T employed by the industry but also on factor prices, we would also conclude that an industry production function does not exist.

It soon becomes clear that prior knowledge of factor prices for the determination of industry output is unnecessary when a one-to-one correspondence exists between the factor-price ratio (w/r) and the optimum ratio T/L in which each firm uses L and T in the long run. Under these circumstances, the totals L_0 and T_0 fix the proportion T_0/L_0, which in turn can be optimum if, and only if, a single factor-price ratio exists. Therefore, the ratio T_0/L_0 does, in this case, imply a unique scale of operations for each firm, and when that scale is known, the industry output can easily be determined as the product nq^*, where q^* is the optimum output for each firm and n is the number of firms which can be accommodated by the totals L_0 and T_0.

Figure 4.5 illustrates the point. The solid curves OM, ON, and OR are three illustrative expansion paths corresponding to the factor-price ratios $(w/r)_1$, $(w/r)_2$, and $(w/r)_3$, respectively, with $(w/r)_3 < (w/r)_2 < (w/r)_1$. The points M, N, and R are assumed to be the optimum production points in the three cases. The broken curve through points M, N, and R is assumed to be the locus of all optimum production points as w/r varies from zero to infinity. The one-to-one correspondence between w/r and the optimum ratio T/L implies that any ray through the origin will intersect the MNR curve only once. Thus, assuming that (given T_0 and L_0) the ratio T_0/L_0 is given by the slope of the vector ON (not drawn), N would be the optimum production point for each and every firm and the implied factor-price ratio would be $(w/r)_2$. Further, the ratio L_0/OS gives the number of active firms in the industry.

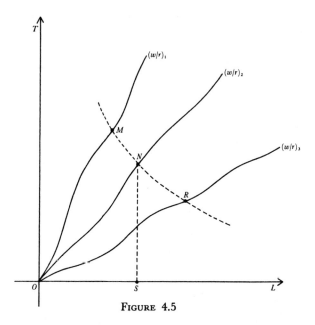

FIGURE 4.5

The real question now is this: Does a one-to-one correspondence exist between factor prices and factor proportions at the level of the firm? Yes. The rigorous proof of this proposition is relegated to appendix 4A.

In summary, on the basis of assumptions 1–5, an industry production function exists which expresses the industry output as a function of the specific aggregate quantities of L and T. Under these assumptions, this industry production function is linear homogeneous, that is, it is characterized by constant returns to scale.

An important property of the industry production function is that any given totals of labor and land, such as L_0 and T_0, are allocated among the active firms of the industry in such a way as to maximize the industry output. This follows from the following two equilibrium conditions:

a) The marginal physical product of every factor is the same in all active firms. This follows directly from the assumed identity of production functions among firms and the fact that each firm is using the same combination of labor and land.

b) Consider the composite factor of production Z that consists of 1 unit of land and (L_0/T_0) units of labor. (Remember that L_0 and T_0 are the given totals of labor and land available to the industry.) Then the average physical product of Z (APP_Z) in every firm is necessarily at a maximum. The easiest way to see this is to note that the average cost of production (AC) is given by

$$AC = \frac{\text{total cost in terms of } T}{\text{total output}} = \frac{p_Z Z}{Z(APP_Z)} = \frac{p_Z}{APP_Z} = \frac{1 + (w/r)(L_0/T_0)}{APP_Z}.$$

Thus, for the given ratio L_0/T_0, the (implied) equilibrium factor-price ratio (w/r) is perfectly determined and so is the rental of the composite factor Z (i.e., $p_Z = 1 + [w/r][L_0/T_0]$). Therefore, minimization of AC necessarily implies maximization of APP_Z.

How do conditions (a) and (b) guarantee that the allocation of L_0 and T_0 among firms is such as to maximize the industry output? Condition (a) implies that, given the number of firms in the industry, the industry output cannot be increased by transferring either labor or land from one firm to another—the marginal physical products of both factors being equal and diminishing everywhere. On the other hand, condition (b) implies that the industry output cannot be increased by increasing or decreasing the number of active firms—through a decrease or increase of the scale of operations of each firm, with condition (a) always being satisfied.

4. The Box Diagram

Let us consider an economy endowed with fixed quantities of labor and land, L_0 and T_0, respectively, and producing two commodities, X and Y. It is assumed that each industry's technology is summarized by a linear homogeneous production function as described in the preceding section. All this information can be conveniently summarized by means of the so-called Edgeworth–Bowley box diagram. This has been done in figure 4.6.

The sides of the parallelogram $O_X M O_Y N$ are determined by the given amounts of labor and land. Thus, the distance $O_X M$ equals L_0 while the distance $O_X N$ equals T_0. Along the lower horizontal axis $O_X M$, we measure, moving from O_X toward M, the amount of labor used in the production of X. Along the left-hand vertical axis, we measure, moving from O_X toward N, the amount of land used in the production of X. Because the amount of each

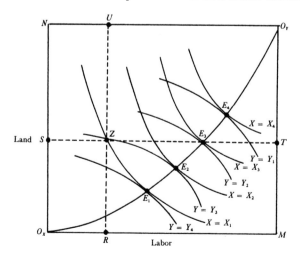

FIGURE 4.6

factor not used in the production of X must be employed in the production of Y by assumption, the upper horizontal axis indicates, moving from O_Y toward N, the amount of labor used in the production of Y. Similarly, along the right-hand vertical axis, we measure, moving from O_Y toward M, the amount of land used in the production of Y. Any point in the box represents four quantities: the amounts of labor and land used in the production of X and Y. For instance, the coordinates of point Z with respect to O_X, that is, $(O_X R, O_X S)$, give us the amounts of labor and land, respectively, that are used in the production of X, while the coordinates of the same point, Z, with respect to O_Y, that is, $(O_Y U, O_Y T)$, give us the amounts of labor and land, respectively, that are used in the production of Y. Finally, note that

$$O_X R + O_Y U = L_0 \quad \text{and} \quad O_X S + O_Y T = T_0.$$

Let us now introduce the isoquant maps of X and Y into the box. Thus, the isoquant map of industry X has been drawn with respect to the origin O_X, and the isoquant map of industry Y has been drawn with respect to the origin O_Y. In order to keep the diagram as clear as possible, there are only four isoquants for each commodity. Now, any point in the box taken at random corresponds to a definite allocation of L and T between the two industries, giving rise to definite production levels of both commodities. Thus, at point Z, in addition to knowing how much L and T are used in the production of both X and Y, we can also read, from the isoquants passing through Z, the amounts of X and Y produced, that is, X_1 and Y_3, respectively. Therefore, this diagram is indeed remarkable because it enables us to represent the relations among six variables in only two dimensions.

As was seen earlier, the MRS_{LT} in each industry must necessarily be equal to the factor-price ratio w/r, in long-run equilibrium. Since factor prices are assumed uniform throughout the economy, it follows that in the long-run, the economy must be allocating L and T in a way that equalizes the MRS_{LT} in the two industries. Therefore, long-run equilibrium will necessarily occur at a point within the box diagram where the isoquants of X and Y happen to be tangential to one another. The locus of all such tangencies between the two sets of isoquants corresponds to Edgeworth's *contract curve*. In figure 4.6, the contract curve is illustrated by the curve $O_X E_1 E_2 E_3 E_4 O_Y$.

Edgeworth actually uses the term "contract curve" to describe the case of a pure exchange economy. Thus, consider the case of two consumers endowed with fixed quantities of two consumer goods. In this case, the dimensions of the box (fig. 4.6) will represent the total available quantities of the two consumer goods, and the two sets of contour lines will represent the indifference maps of the two consumers. The contract curve will be given by the locus of tangencies between the two sets of indifference curves. Observe that any point on the contract curve is Pareto-optimal in the sense that each consumer's utility is at a maximum given the utility level of the other consumer.

The term "optimum efficiency locus" might describe the present case of production better than the term "contract curve." However, the less accurate term "contract curve" is used here because it is used by the majority of economists writing in the area of international economics.

An important property of all points on the contract curve is that, if the economy is on the contract curve, it is impossible to increase the outputs of both X and Y by a mere reallocation of resources. Thus, an increase in the production of X necessarily implies a decrease in the production of Y, and vice versa. Conversely, if the economy is not on the contract curve, the outputs of both X and Y can be increased by a mere reallocation of resources which moves the economy to the contract curve. For instance, if the economy were at point Z of figure 4.6, the output of both commodities could be increased by reallocating resources in such a way as to move from Z to some point on the contract curve in the region E_1E_2. However, this is not possible if the economy is already on the contract curve. Accordingly, the existence of perfect competition, which implies that the economy (in the long run) is producing somewhere along the contract curve, achieves economic efficiency in the sense that resources are optimally used.

Under the assumption of linear homogeneous production functions, the contract curve must lie on one side of the diagonal of the box diagram; that is, it can never cross it, although it may happen to coincide with it. To see why, consider the following two cases.

1) When a point of the contract curve lies on the diagonal, the diagonal itself becomes the contract curve. This follows from the fact that along the diagonal the marginal rates of substitution of labor for land in both industries remain the same, and if they are equal at one point they must be equal everywhere.

2) Consider a typical pair of isoquants intersecting each other on the diagonal as shown in figure 4.7. In panel (a), the two isoquants intersect each other at point K. (A single pair of isoquants is sufficient for our purposes because the same relationship between the MRS_{LT} in X and the MRS_{LT} in Y will necessarily hold at any other point along the diagonal, as a result of the assumed homogeneity.) The straight lines KZ and RKS are the tangents to the isoquants of X and Y, respectively. Thus, at point K, the MRS_{LT} in the production of X (MRS_{LT}^X) is given by the slope c, while the MRS_{LT} in the production of Y (MRS_{LT}^Y) is given by slope a, which is equal to slope b. It is obvious that $MRS_{LT}^X < MRS_{LT}^Y$. Since in every industry the MRS_{LT} diminishes as the ratio L/T increases, it should be clear that all tangencies between the two sets of isoquants must occur in the northwest triangle, above and to the left of the diagonal. As we move above and to the left of the diagonal, the proportion L/T falls in the X industry but rises in the Y industry—compared with the overall proportion, L_0/T_0, along the diagonal. Thus, the MRS_{LT}^X is higher and the MRS_{LT}^Y is lower at points above and to the left of the diagonal, compared with their respective values (i.e., slopes

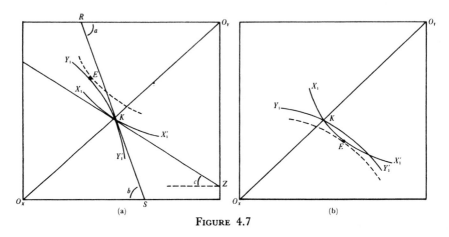

FIGURE 4.7

c and b) along the diagonal. On the other hand, below and to the right of the diagonal, the MRS_{LT}^X is lower and the MRS_{LT}^Y is higher compared with their respective values along the diagonal. Since along the diagonal $MRS_{LT}^X < MRS_{LT}^Y$, below and to the left of the diagonal the inequality between marginal rates of substitution is accentuated. Thus, no tangency can ever occur in this region. As we move to points above and to the left of the diagonal, however, the divergence between marginal rates of substitution tends to disappear on two counts: (1) the MRS_{LT}^X increases and (2) the MRS_{LT}^Y decreases. All tangencies (and, therefore, the contract curve) necessarily lie above and to the left of the diagonal, as illustrated by point E in figure 4.7(a), where a broken isoquant of industry X touches the isoquant of industry Y.

In figure 4.7(b) the inequality $MRS_{LT}^X > MRS_{LT}^Y$ lies along the diagonal. All tangencies (and, therefore, the contract curve) lie below and to the right of the diagonal, as illustrated by point E.

5. The Production–Possibilities Frontier

The main objective of the preceding analysis is to prepare the ground for the derivation of the production-possibilities frontier (also known as the transformation curve). This is precisely the purpose of this section.

The production-possibilities frontier shows the maximum obtainable amount of one commodity for each amount of the other. Also, as noted earlier, it depends on two fundamental data: factor endowments and production functions.

The discussion of the box-diagram technique of the preceding section enables us to derive the important conclusion that perfect competition will lead the economy to allocate its resources somewhere along the contract curve; and since the economy is on the contract curve, it is impossible to increase the output of one commodity without decreasing the output of the other commodity. In other words, perfect competition leads to an optimum allocation of resources. As a result of this important conclusion, it follows that each point on the contract curve corresponds to a point on the production-possibilities frontier (and vice versa), and that perfect competition implies that the economy will actually be producing on the production-possibilities frontier, the precise equilibrium point being determined by demand.

The one-to-one correspondence between points on the contract curve and the production-possibilities frontier can be illustrated graphically by a slightly modified box diagram. Measure again labor and land horizontally and vertically, respectively, but place the origins O_X and O_Y in the northwest and southeast corners, respectively, as shown in figure 4.8. Further, measure the outputs of X and Y with respect to the southwest corner (O), with X being measured horizontally and Y vertically. Now consider a point along the diagonal $O_X O_Y$, such as point M. Observe that the coordinates of point M with respect to the southwest corner (O) show (horizontally) the quantity of labor allocated to X (L_X) and (vertically) the quantity of land allocated to Y (T_Y). Since the units of measurement of both X and Y (and L and T, for that matter) are arbitrary, let us adopt the convention and measure X and Y in the following units. If the economy were to allocate its resources according to some point on the diagonal $O_X O_Y$, the amount of X produced will be equal to the number of units of L used for its production,

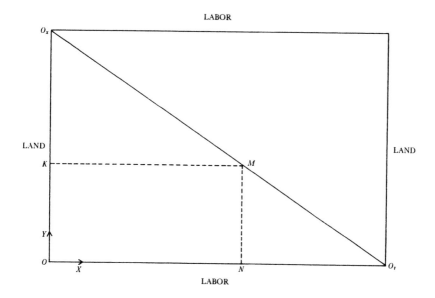

FIGURE 4.8

and similarly, the amount of Y produced will be equal to the number of units of T used for its production. Note that this is possible because of the assumption of constant returns to scale. Thus, at point M on figure 4.8 the economy must be producing KM (or ON) units of commodity X and NM (or OK) units of Y. Therefore, we now have a way to measure the amounts of X and Y implied by the isoquants for X and Y, respectively, passing through point M, Since all isoquants necessarily cross the diagonal of the box only once, this appears to be a unique way of assigning values to X and Y at any given point in the box. All we have to do is draw the isoquants through the specified point and determine their intersections with the diagonal. We then follow the same procedure as with point M to determine the amounts of X and Y produced.

Figure 4.9 shows how to determine a point on the production-possibilities frontier when a point on the contract curve is given. Consider point E, where the two isoquants, X_1X_1 and Y_1Y_1, are tangent to each other. Point E is a point on the contract curve. The isoquant X_1X_1 intersects the diagonal at point M, and therefore the quantity of X produced is given by the distance OR. On the other hand, the Y_1Y_1 isoquant intersects the diagonal at point N, and therefore the quantity of Y produced is given by the distance OS. It should now be clear that the coordinates of point E' show the quantities of X and Y produced (when the economy is allocating its resources according to point E on the contract curve), with X measured horizontally along the lower horizontal side of the box and Y measured vertically along the left-hand side of the box, and with O being, of course, the point of origin. Notice

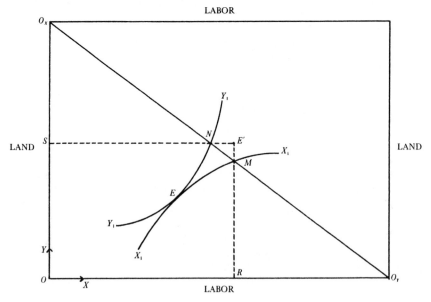

FIGURE 4.9

that point E' always lies above and to the right of the diagonal. In fact point E' lies above and to the right of the diagonal even if point E lies above and to the right of the diagonal.

Once we know how to determine a point on the production-possibilities frontier, given a point on the contract curve, we can derive the whole production-possibilities frontier by repeating the same process for each and every point on the contract curve.

If the contract curve coincides with the diagonal of the box, it should be obvious that the production-possibilities frontier is necessarily a straight line. In particular, with the procedure of figure 4.9, the production-possibilities frontier would coincide with the diagonal, with O being its point of origin. It should be pointed out that the numerical value of the slope of the linear frontier is arbitrary, depending upon the units of measurement of L and T. Further, this is the case which Taussig had in mind in his effort to show that the classical theory is logically correct even though other factors besides labor are used in the production of commodities.

If the contract curve does not coincide with the diagonal, then the production-possibilities frontier will be concave to the origin, as shown in figure 4.10A. To see why, first note that the economy can always reach the broken straight line MK by allocating its resources arbitrarily along the

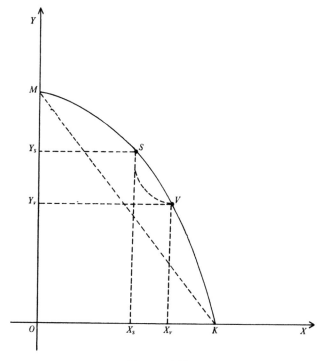

FIGURE 4.10A

diagonal. However, by assumption, the contract curve does not coincide
with the diagonal, and therefore, the production-possibilities frontier will
definitely lie beyond the straight line *MK*—except for the intercepts *M* and
K. But does this necessarily mean that the production-possibilities frontier is
concave to the origin? This will be the case if it can be shown that no part of
the frontier *MSVK* can be convex to the origin. For this purpose, consider any
two points on the frontier, such as points *S* and *V*. At *S* the economy produces
X_S units of *X* and Y_S of *Y*. Similarly, at *V* the economy produces X_V of *X* and
Y_V of *Y*. What can easily be shown is that the economy can always reach all
points that lie on the straight-line segment *SV* (not drawn). Therefore, the
convex broken curve *SV* can be ruled out.

Consider figure 4.10B. It represents the box diagram from which the
production-possibilities frontier of figure 4.10A has been derived. The curve
$O_X S' V' O_Y$ is the contract curve. Points *S'* and *V'* on the contract curve
correspond to points *S* and *V*, respectively, on the production-possibilities
frontier. Point *S'* corresponds to a certain production technique for producing
X and another technique for producing *Y*. Similarly, point *V'* corresponds to
two more production techniques—one for each commodity. In what follows,
assume that no other techniques are used.

Consider now the straight-line segment *S'V'* (fig. 4.10B). As shown in the
appendix 4B, the line *S'V'* is nothing but the set of all points (*P'*) of the form

$$P' = (1 - \lambda)S' + \lambda V',$$

where $0 \leq \lambda \leq 1$. This is true whether we measure the coordinates of *S'*,
V', and *P'* with respect to O_X or O_Y. What are the output levels of *X* and *Y*
at *P'*? Because of constant returns to scale, we have

$$X = (1 - \lambda)X_S + \lambda X_V,$$

$$Y = (1 - \lambda)Y_S + \lambda Y_V.$$

Consider now the point $P = (X, Y)$ in figure 4.10A. We obviously have

$$P = (X, Y) = [(1 - \lambda)X_S + \lambda X_V, (1 - \lambda)Y_S + \lambda Y_V]$$

$$= (1 - \lambda)(X_S, Y_S) + \lambda(X_V, Y_V) = (1 - \lambda)S + \lambda V.$$

Thus, point *P* (fig. 4.10A) must lie somewhere along the straight-line segment
SV. As λ increases from 0 to 1, and thus point *P'* (figure 4.10B) moves from
S' to *V'* along the straight line *S'V'*, point *P* (fig. 4.10A) moves along the
straight line *SV* from *S* to *V*. Accordingly, the broken curve *SV* (fig. 4.10A)
is ruled out. (An alternative proof of the concavity of the production-
possibilities frontier will be given in chaps. 9–11.) In general, the economy
will be able to do better than the straight line *SV*, as illustrated in figure
4.10A. This follows from the fact that the straight-line segment *S'V'* (figure
4.10B) does not coincide with the contract curve.

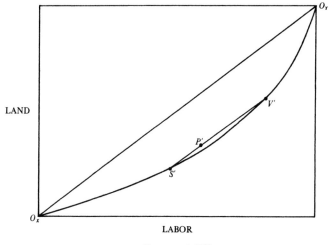

LAND

LABOR

FIGURE 4.10B

The absolute slope of the production-possibilities frontier (known as the marginal rate of transformation), as shown in figure 4.10A, shows the opportunity cost of X in terms of Y, that is, the minimum amount of Y that the economy can possibly give up to obtain an extra unit of X, or, the maximum amount of Y that the economy can obtain by giving up 1 unit of X. Because of the concavity of the production-possibilities frontier, the opportunity cost of X in terms of Y increases as more X is produced. Thus, as we move from point S to point V (see fig. 4.10A), the tangent to the production-possibilities frontier becomes steeper, indicating increasing opportunity cost. It can be verified that in figure 4.10A, increasing opportunity costs exist for every commodity. (Hint: the opportunity cost of X in terms of Y is the reciprocal of the opportunity cost of Y in terms of X.)

It should also be emphasized that a movement along the production-possibilities frontier is much more complicated than what it appears to be from figure 4.10A. Thus, a movement from S to V implies that labor and land are transferred from industry Y to industry X. Since the two industries do not use the two factors in the same proportion (the latter occurring, by the way, only when the production-possibilities frontier is linear), new production techniques will necessarily become optimum in both industries. Therefore a whole reorganization of production takes place. This is an important phenomenon.

The marginal rate of transformation (or the opportunity cost of X in terms of Y) can be shown to be equal to the ratio of the marginal cost of X (MC_X) to the marginal cost of Y (MC_Y). Before rigorous proof of this proposition is provided, it is useful to consider the following heuristic argument. Consider point S on the production-possibilities frontier of figure 4.10A as corresponding to point S' (Fig. 4.10B) on the contract curve. Now consider a slight movement along the contract curve in the neighborhood of S', implying an infinitesimal transfer of resources from industry Y to industry X. The production of X increases infinitesimally by dX and the production of Y decreases infinitesimally by dY. For this infinitesimal transfer of resources, the increase in the total cost of production of X (i.e., dC_X) must be equal to the reduction of the total cost of production of Y (i.e., dC_Y). That is,

$$dC_X + dC_Y = 0. \tag{4.17}$$

But, by definition, we have

$$MC_X \equiv dC_X/dX \qquad \text{and} \qquad MC_Y \equiv dC_Y/dY. \tag{4.18}$$

Introducing equations (4.18) into (4.17) and reorganizing, we obtain

$$-(dY/dX) = MC_X/MC_Y. \tag{4.19}$$

That is to say, the absolute slope of the production-possibilities frontier is equal to the ratio of the marginal cost of X to Y.

Since, under perfectly competitive conditions, marginal costs are also equal to prices, equation (4.19) can be extended as follows:

$$-\frac{dY}{dX} = \frac{MC_X}{MC_Y} = \frac{\text{price of } X}{\text{price of } Y}. \tag{4.20}$$

Thus, under competitive conditions, the marginal rate of transformation (or absolute slope of the production-possibilities frontier) shows relative commodity prices. When perfect competition in the product markets (only) breaks down, the absolute slope of the frontier will continue to show the ratio of marginal costs, but it will, in general, fail to show relative prices.

The rigorous proof of equation (4.20) follows. Consider figure 4.11. As before, measure labor horizontally and land vertically, and place the origins O_X and O_Y in the northwest and southeast corners, respectively, of the box diagram. Consider now point E_0, which, by assumption, lies on the contract curve. The corresponding point on the production-possibilities frontier (following our earlier convention) is, of course, P_0. What is the slope of the production-possibilities frontier at P_0? Consider another point on the contract curve, such as E_1. Obviously, point P_1 on the production-possibilities frontier corresponds to E_1. Consider the slope of the straight line P_0P_1 and imagine that point E_1 moves closer to E_0, causing point P_1 to move closer to point P_0. The limit of the slope of the straight line P_0P_1, as P_1 moves closer to P_0, is simply the slope of the production-possibilities frontier at P_0. But how is this limit determined?

Consider the percentage changes in the outputs of X and Y as we move from E_0 to E_1. Because of the assumed linear homogeneity, we have

$$\frac{\Delta X}{X_0} = \frac{E_0 D}{O_X E_0} \qquad \text{and} \qquad -\frac{\Delta Y}{Y_0} = \frac{E_0 C}{O_Y E_0},$$

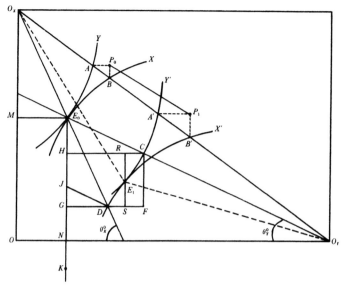

FIGURE 4.11

where X_0 and Y_0 are the outputs of commodities X and Y, respectively, at point P_0 (or E_0). Now observe that the triangles $O_X M E_0$ and $E_0 G D$ are similar. Hence,

$$\frac{\Delta X}{X_0} = \frac{E_0 D}{O_X E_0} = \frac{GD}{ME_0}. \tag{4.21}$$

In addition, the triangles $O_Y E_0 N$ and $C E_0 H$ are similar. Hence,

$$-\frac{\Delta Y}{Y_0} = \frac{E_0 C}{O_Y E_0} = \frac{HC}{O_Y N}. \tag{4.22}$$

Taking now the ratio of the percentage change in Y to X, we obtain

$$-\frac{\Delta Y}{\Delta X} \frac{X_0}{Y_0} = \frac{HC}{O_Y N} \frac{ME_0}{GD}. \tag{4.23}$$

Observe that the distance ME_0 shows the amount of labor allocated to the production of X at P_0 (i.e., L_X^0) and that the distance $O_Y N$ shows the amount of labor allocated to the production of Y at P_0 (i.e., L_Y^0). Introducing these new symbols (L_X^0 and L_Y^0) into equation (4.23) and multiplying both sides by Y_0/X_0, we obtain

$$-\frac{\Delta Y}{\Delta X} = \frac{HC}{GD} \frac{L_X^0}{L_Y^0} \frac{Y_0}{X_0}. \tag{4.24}$$

Now determine the limit of the expression on the right-hand side of equation (4.24) as $\Delta X \to 0$. Since the quantities L_X^0, L_Y^0, Y_0, and X_0 remain constant, let us concentrate on the limit of the ratio HC/GD.

Draw a straight line through D and parallel to $O_Y CE_0$. Let it intersect the perpendicular line $E_0 N$ at J. In addition, imagine a straight line through points C and D and let it intersect $E_0 N$ at K. Given all this, the ratio HC/GD can be rewritten as follows:

$$\frac{HC}{GD} = \frac{HC}{GD}\frac{KE_0}{KE_0} = \frac{HC}{GD}\frac{GE_0 + KG}{HE_0 + KH}$$

$$= \frac{(GE_0/GD) + (KG/GD)}{(HE_0/HC) + (KH/HC)} = \frac{\theta_X^0 + (KG/GD)}{\theta_Y^0 + (KH/HC)} = \frac{\theta_X^0 + (KG/GD)}{\theta_Y^0 + (KG/GD)},$$

$$(4.25)$$

where θ_X^0 and θ_Y^0 are the optimum land/labor ratios in industries X and Y, respectively, at point E_0. Again, θ_X^0 and θ_Y^0 remain constant. The only thing that will change continuously as we move from E_1 to E_0 is the ratio KG/GD. What is the limit of this ratio? Observe that

$$\frac{KG}{GD} = \frac{CF}{DF} = \frac{RE_1 + E_1S}{DS + RC} = \frac{RE_1[1 + (E_1S/RE_1)]}{RC[1 + (DS/RC)]}. \qquad (4.26)$$

In the limit, the slope of $E_1 C$ and the slope of DE_1 will tend to the common slope of the isoquants of X and Y at E_0, that is, $(w/r)_0$. In other words, in the limit the following will be true:

$$\frac{RE_1}{RC} = \frac{E_1S}{DS} = \left(\frac{w}{r}\right)_0. \qquad (4.27)$$

Hence,

$$\frac{E_1S}{RE_1} = \frac{DS}{RC}. \qquad (4.28)$$

Substituting (4.27) and (4.28) into (4.26), we get (in the limit)

$$\frac{KG}{GD} = \frac{RE_1}{RC} = \left(\frac{w}{r}\right)_0. \qquad (4.29)$$

Therefore, the value of the ratio HC/GD as given by equation (4.25) can now be rewritten (in the limit) as follows:

$$\frac{HC}{GD} = \frac{\theta_X^0 + (w/r)_0}{\theta_Y^0 + (w/r)_0}. \qquad (4.30)$$

Finally, introducing the preceding result into equation (4.24), we obtain

$$-\frac{dY}{dX} = \frac{\theta_X^0 + (w/r)_0}{\theta_Y^0 + (w/r)_0}\frac{L_X^0}{L_Y^0}\frac{Y_0}{X_0}. \qquad (4.31)$$

Observe that the symbol $\Delta Y/\Delta X$ has now been replaced by dY/dX.

What is the meaning of the right-hand side of equation (4.31)? For completeness, the equation can be rewritten as follows:

$$\frac{\theta_X^0 + (w/r)_0\, L_X^0}{\theta_Y^0 + (w/r)_0\, L_Y^0}\frac{Y_0}{X_0} = \frac{(T_X^0/L_X^0) + (w_0/r_0)\, L_X^0}{(T_Y^0/L_Y^0) + (w_0/r_0)\, L_Y^0}\frac{Y_0}{X_0}$$

$$= \frac{(r_0 T_X^0 + w_0 L_X^0)/X_0}{(r_0 T_Y^0 + w_0 L_Y^0)/Y_0} = \frac{AC_X^0}{AC_Y^0} = \frac{MC_X^0}{MC_Y^0} = \frac{p_x^0}{p_y^0}.$$

Accordingly, our general conclusion can be stated thus:

$$-\frac{dY}{dX} = \frac{AC_X}{AC_Y} = \frac{MC_X}{MC_Y} = \frac{p_x}{p_y}. \tag{4.32}$$

This completes our proof.

When, as in the classical theory, the production-possibilities frontier is a straight line, relative pretrade prices are uniquely given by the slope of the production-possibilities frontier. However, in the presence of increasing opportunity costs, this is not so. The pretrade prices will be determined by the slope of the production-possibilities frontier at the pretrade equilibrium point, which can only be determined if demand is introduced into the picture. This particular problem will be taken up in the next chapter.

6. *Some Difficulties with the Production-Possibilities Frontier*

The preceding analysis assumes implicitly that factors of production are perfectly mobile and indifferent as between different employments. Problems, however, arise when the assumption of perfect mobility is dropped.

If all factors are perfectly immobile between industries (assuming that factor-price flexibility prevails), the production-possibilities frontier becomes a rectangle and the economy (whether "closed" or "open") will always be producing a fixed combination of X and Y. However, in the intermediate case of imperfect mobility, whether or not a production-possibilities frontier, can be derived, with its slope at any point showing relative prices, is still an open question.

Finally, it should be noted that several attempts have been made to derive the production-possibilities frontier when the factor supplies are variable. Unfortunately, the production-possibilities frontiers so derived lack the important property referred to earlier, namely, that the slope of the frontier at any point shows relative prices. In general, the production-possibilities frontier derived under the assumption that factor supplies are variable can be regarded as a locus of points which lie on a family of production-possibilities frontiers derived with fixed-factor supplies.

Appendix 4A

This appendix attempts to prove rigorously that there exists a one-to-one correspondence between factor prices and factor proportions at the level of the firm.

Given the factor-price ratio, w/r, we can determine uniquely the optimum scale of operations of the firm; that is, we can determine the optimum amounts of labor and land, L^* and T^* respectively, that a typical firm will employ in order to minimize its average cost of production. This can be expressed formally as follows:

$$L^* = L(w/r), \qquad\qquad (4A.1)$$

$$T^* = T(w/r). \qquad\qquad (4A.2)$$

Equations (4A.1) and (4A.2) express the absolute quantities L^* and T^* as functions of the factor-price ratio w/r. However, what we are interested in at the moment is not the relationship between the absolute quantities L^* and T^* and w/r but, rather, the relationship between the optimum factor ratio $\mu = T^*/L^*$ and the factor-price ratio w/r. Let us therefore concentrate on

$$\mu = \frac{T^*}{L^*} = \frac{T(w/r)}{L(w/r)}. \qquad\qquad (4A.3)$$

Is there a one-to-one correspondence between μ and w/r? This will be the case if, and only if, the function (4A.3) is monotonic, that is, if μ is a strictly increasing, or a strictly decreasing, function of w/r. In turn, this condition will be satisfied if the derivative of μ with respect to w/r is either strictly positive, or strictly negative, for all values of w/r. In other words, the function (4A.3) will be monotonic; therefore a one-to-one correspondence will exist between the factor ratio, μ, and the factor-price ratio, w/r, if, and only if, the derivative $d\mu/d(w/r)$ is nonzero and retains the same sign for all values of w/r. Is this condition met?

Differentiating μ as given by equation (4A.3) with respect to w/z, we get

$$\frac{d\mu}{d(w/r)} = \frac{T'L - L'T}{L^2}, \qquad\qquad (4A.4)$$

where L and T are the functions (4A.1) and (4A.2), respectively, and primes indicate differentiation. From equation (4A.4) it is obvious that

$$\text{sign of } \frac{d\mu}{d(w/r)} = \text{sign of } (T'L - L'T).$$

Is the sign of $(T'L - L'T)$ unique? If it is, then a one-to-one correspondence exists between μ and w/r. To answer this question, a way to determine the derivatives L' and T' must be found. First formalize the cost-minimization problem.

Express the average cost of production (AC) as follows, using T as the numeraire:

$$AC = \frac{(w/r)L + T}{f(L, T)},\qquad (4A.5)$$

where $f(L, T)$ is the production function of a typical firm. For minimization of AC, it is required that the partial derivatives of AC with respect to L and T be equal to zero. Thus,

$$\frac{\partial(AC)}{\partial L} = \frac{(w/r)f(L, T) - [(w/r)L + T]f_L(L, T)}{[f(L, T)]^2} = 0,\qquad (4A.6)$$

$$\frac{\partial(AC)}{\partial T} = \frac{f(L, T) - [(w/r)L + T]f_T(L, T)}{[f(L, T)]^2} = 0,\qquad (4A.7)$$

where the subscripts L and T indicate partial differentiation with respect to labor and land, respectively.

Equations (4A.6) and (4A.7) can be reduced to

$$(w/r)f = [(w/r)L + T]f_L,\qquad (4A.6)'$$

$$f = [(w/r)L + T]f_T\qquad (4A.7)'$$

where the arguments of the functions f, f_L, and f_T have been omitted for simplicity.

Note that the ratio of equations (4A.6)′ and (4.A.7)′ gives the familiar condition

$$w/r = f_L/f_T.\qquad (4A.8)$$

That is, for cost minimization it is required that the marginal rate of substitution of labor for land be equal to the factor-price ratio w/r. This condition will necessarily be satisfied at the point where AC is at a minimum. In addition, substituting (4A.8) into (4A.7)′, we get

$$f = [(f_L/f_T)L + T]f_T = Lf_L + Tf_T.\qquad (4A.9)$$

In other words, at the point where AC is at a minimum, Euler's equation must be satisfied. Put differently, AC is minimized at a point where returns to scale are momentarily constant.

Equations (4A.6) and (4A.7) are known as the first-order conditions for minimization of AC. Unfortunately, however, for the problem at hand we shall have to go beyond the first-order conditions and determine the second-order conditions as well.

Consider the following Hessian matrix:

$$H \equiv \begin{bmatrix} \dfrac{\partial^2(AC)}{\partial L^2} & \dfrac{\partial^2(AC)}{\partial L\,\partial T} \\[2ex] \dfrac{\partial^2(AC)}{\partial T\,\partial L} & \dfrac{\partial^2(AC)}{\partial T^2} \end{bmatrix}.\qquad (4A.10)$$

It is well known that the second-order condition for AC minimization is that the Hessian matrix H be positive definite (on this point, see Samuelson [1947], mathematical appendix A). The Hessian matrix H will be positive definite if, and only if,

$$\frac{\partial^2(AC)}{\partial L^2} > 0, \quad \frac{\partial^2(AC)}{\partial T^2} > 0 \quad \text{and} \quad |H| > 0,$$

where $|H|$ is the determinant of H, that is, the Hessian determinant. These second-order partial derivatives must be evaluated to see whether the above conditions are satisfied, or rather, to determine the restrictions (that must be placed on these second-order partial derivatives) for minimization of AC. We have:

$$\frac{\partial^2(AC)}{\partial L^2} = \left\{ \left[\frac{w}{r} f_L - f_{LL}\left(\frac{w}{r}L + T\right) - \frac{w}{r}f_L \right] f^2 \right.$$
$$\left. - 2ff_L\left[\frac{w}{r}f - f_L\left(\frac{w}{r}L + T\right)\right] \right\} \Big/ f^4,$$

$$\frac{\partial^2(AC)}{\partial L\,\partial T} = \left\{ \left[\frac{w}{r} f_T - f_{LT}\left(\frac{w}{r}L + T\right) - f_L \right] f^2 \right.$$
$$\left. - 2ff_T\left[\frac{w}{r}f - f_L\left(\frac{w}{r}L + T\right)\right] \right\} \Big/ f^4,$$

$$\frac{\partial^2(AC)}{\partial T^2} = \left\{ \left[f_T - f_{TT}\left(\frac{w}{r}L + T\right) - f_T \right] f^2 \right.$$
$$\left. - 2ff_T\left[f - f_T\left(\frac{w}{r}L + T\right)\right] \right\} \Big/ f^4,$$

$$\frac{\partial^2(AC)}{\partial T\,\partial L} = \left\{ \left[f_L - f_{TL}\left(\frac{w}{r}L + T\right) - f_T \frac{w}{r} \right] f^2 \right.$$
$$\left. - 2ff_L\left[f - f_T\left(\frac{w}{r}L + T\right)\right] \right\} \Big/ f^4.$$

These second-order partial derivatives have to be evaluated at the point where AC is at a minimum. This means that equations (4A.6)′ and (4A.7)′ as well as equations (4A.8) and (4A.9) must necessarily hold. Making use of these equations, we can easily simplify the above second-order partial derivatives to

$$\frac{\partial^2(AC)}{\partial L^2} = -\left[f_{LL}\left(\frac{w}{r}L + T\right)\right] \Big/ f^2, \qquad (4A.11)$$

$$\frac{\partial^2(AC)}{\partial L\,\partial T} = -\left[f_{LT}\left(\frac{w}{r}L + T\right)\right] \Big/ f^2, \qquad (4A.12)$$

$$\frac{\partial^2(AC)}{\partial T^2} = -\left[f_{TT}\left(\frac{w}{r}L + T\right)\right]\Big/ f^2, \qquad (4A.13)$$

$$\frac{\partial^2(AC)}{\partial T \, \partial L} = -\left[f_{TL}\left(\frac{w}{r}L + T\right)\right]\Big/ f^2. \qquad (4A.14)$$

Note that the ratio $[(w/r)L + T]/f^2$ is a factor common to all expressions on the right-hand side of equations (4A.11)–(4A.14). Therefore, equations (4A.11)–(4A.14) can be simplified as follows:

$$\frac{\partial^2(AC)}{\partial L^2} = -cf_{LL} \qquad (4A.11)'$$

$$\frac{\partial^2(AC)}{\partial L \, \partial T} = -cf_{LT}, \qquad (4A.12)'$$

$$\frac{\partial^2(AC)}{\partial T^2} = -cf_{TT}, \qquad (4A.13)'$$

$$\frac{\partial^2(AC)}{\partial T \, \partial L} = -cf_{TL}, \qquad (4A.14)'$$

where $c \equiv [(w/r)L + T]/f^2 > 0$.

The Hessian matrix H (see eq. [4A.10]) will thus be positive definite if, and only if, the following conditions are satisfied:

$$-cf_{LL} > 0,$$

$$-cf_{TT} > 0,$$

$$|H| = \begin{vmatrix} -cf_{LL} & -cf_{LT} \\ -cf_{TL} & -cf_{TT} \end{vmatrix} = c^2 \begin{vmatrix} f_{LL} & f_{LT} \\ f_{TL} & f_{TT} \end{vmatrix} > 0.$$

Since $c > 0$, these conditions can be simplified to

$$f_{LL} < 0, f_{TT} < 0, \begin{vmatrix} f_{LL} & f_{LT} \\ f_{TL} & f_{TT} \end{vmatrix} > 0. \qquad (4A.15)$$

These conditions imply that the Hessian matrix of the production function is negative definite. (This implies that the production function must be strictly concave in the neighborhood of the point where AC is at a minimum.) In what follows assume that these conditions are indeed satisfied. Note that the conditions $f_{LL} < 0$ and $f_{TT} < 0$ are simply the mathematical expression of the familiar law of diminishing returns to a variable factor.

Having derived the first-order and second-order conditions for minimization of the average cost of production, we return to the problem of whether or not there exists a one-to-one correspondence between the factor-price ratio, w/r, and the optimum factor ratio, μ. As we saw earlier (see eq. [4A.4]), the problem reduces to whether or not the sign of $(T'L - L'T)$ is unique. For this purpose, let us evaluate the derivatives T' and L'.

Given the factor-price ratio, w/r, equations (4A.6)$'$ and (4A.7)$'$ can be solved simultaneously for the optimum values of labor and land employed by the firm, that is, L^* and T^*. But we are not interested in these absolute quantities at the moment. Our first step is the determination of the partial derivatives L' and T'; that is, we want to find out how the optimum quantities L^* and T^* vary as the factor-price ratio varies. For this purpose, differentiate equations (4A.6)$'$ and (4A.7)$'$ totally with respect to w/r, to get

$$\left[\frac{w}{r}f_L + \left(\frac{w}{r}L + T\right)f_{LL} - \frac{w}{r}f_L\right]\frac{dL}{d(w/r)}$$

$$+ \left[f_L + \left(\frac{w}{r}L + T\right)f_{TL} - \frac{w}{r}f_T\right]\frac{dT}{d(w/r)} = f - Lf_L,$$

$$\left[\frac{w}{r}f_T + \left(\frac{w}{r}L + T\right)f_{LT} - f_L\right]\frac{dL}{d(w/r)}$$

$$+ \left[f_T + \left(\frac{w}{r}L + T\right)f_{TT} - f_T\right]\frac{dT}{d(w/r)} = -Lf_T.$$

Making use of equations (4A.8) and (4A.9), we can simplify the above equations to

$$f_{LL}\frac{dL}{d(w/r)} + f_{TL}\frac{dT}{d(w/r)} = \left(f - Lf_L\right)\bigg/\left(\frac{w}{r}L + T\right), \quad (4A.16)$$

$$f_{LT}\frac{dL}{d(w/r)} + f_{TT}\frac{dT}{d(w/r)} = -Lf_T\bigg/\left(\frac{w}{r}L + T\right), \quad (4A.17)$$

or in matrix notation,

$$\begin{bmatrix} f_{LL} & f_{TL} \\ f_{LT} & f_{TT} \end{bmatrix}\begin{bmatrix} L' \\ T' \end{bmatrix} = \begin{bmatrix} \dfrac{Tf_T}{(w/r)L + T} \\ -\dfrac{Lf_T}{(w/r)L + T} \end{bmatrix}. \quad (4A.18)$$

Note that the matrix of this system is simply the Hessian matrix of the production function. Hence, it must be negative definite. The determinant

$$\Delta \equiv \begin{vmatrix} f_{LL} & f_{TL} \\ f_{LT} & f_{TT} \end{vmatrix}$$

must be positive (see [4A.15]).

Solving system (4A.18) by means of Cramer's rule, we get

$$L' = \frac{1}{\Delta}\begin{vmatrix} \dfrac{Tf_T}{(w/r)L + T} & f_{TL} \\ -\dfrac{Lf_T}{(w/r)L + T} & f_{TT} \end{vmatrix} = \frac{f_T}{\Delta[(w/r)L + T]}(Tf_{TT} + Lf_{TL}),$$

$$(4A.19)$$

$$T' = \frac{1}{\Delta} \begin{vmatrix} f_{LL} & \dfrac{Tf_T}{(w/r)L + T} \\ f_{LT} & -\dfrac{Lf_T}{(w/r)L + T} \end{vmatrix} = \frac{-f_T}{\Delta[(w/r)L + T]} (Lf_{LL} + Tf_{LT}).$$

$$(4A.20)$$

Now substitute these results into the expression $T''L - L'T$ to get

$$T''L - L'T = -\left\{ f_T \Big/ \left[\Delta \left(\frac{w}{r} L + T \right) \right] \right\}$$

$$\times [L(Lf_{LL} + Tf_{LT}) + T(Tf_{TT} + Lf_{TL})].$$

$$(4A.21)$$

Since

$$-f_T \Big/ \left[\Delta \left(\frac{w}{r} L + T \right) \right] < 0,$$

the sign of $(T''L - L'T)$ is necessarily the opposite of the sign of $[L(Lf_{LL} + Tf_{LT}) + T(Tf_{TT} + Lf_{TL})]$. What is the sign of this latter expression? Observe that

$$L(Lf_{LL} + Tf_{LT}) + T(Tf_{TT} + Lf_{TL}) = (L, T) \begin{bmatrix} f_{LL} & f_{TL} \\ f_{LT} & f_{TT} \end{bmatrix} \begin{pmatrix} L \\ T \end{pmatrix}.$$

Therefore, what we are actually looking for is the sign of a quadratic form, the matrix of which is the Hessian matrix of the production function of the firm. This Hessian matrix is negative definite at the point where the average cost of production is at a minimum. Hence, the expression in brackets at the far right-hand side of equation (4A.21) must be negative. Accordingly,

$$T''L - L'T > 0, \qquad (4A.22)$$

$$d\mu/d(w/r) > 0. \qquad (4A.23)$$

This means that $\mu \equiv T/L$ is a strictly increasing function of w/r. That is, as labor becomes relatively cheaper (i.e., as w/r falls), each firm will be using relatively more labor per unit of land (i.e., each firm will be using a smaller $\mu \equiv T/L$), at the new minimum average cost point as compared with the old. This being the case, it must be obvious that, given μ, there is only one factor-price ratio, w/r, consistent with perfectly competitive conditions. That is, given μ, only one expansion path will give rise to a minimum average cost point at that value of μ. Hence, any ray through the origin will intersect the "optimality locus" of figure 4.5 only once. This completes the proof of the proposition that there exists a one-to-one correspondence between μ and w/r.

Appendix 4B: Points and Vectors

This appendix discusses briefly the concepts of points and vectors and some of their properties. Comments are restricted to points and vectors in the plane (i.e., the two-dimensional space).

A point in the plane, such as point P_0 in figure 4B.1, can be denoted either by the letter P_0 or in the coordinate form $P_0 = (x_0, y_0)$. Since a point in the plane is associated with an ordered pair (x, y) of real numbers, the geometric term plane can be interpreted as the set of all ordered pairs (x, y) of real numbers.

The operation of addition of real numbers can be generalized to provide a way to add points. If

$$P_0 = (x_0, y_0),$$
$$P_1 = (x_1, y_1),$$

we define their sum to be the point

$$P_2 = P_0 + P_1 = (x_0 + x_1, y_0 + y_1) = (x_2, y_2),$$

where, of course, $x_2 = x_0 + x_1, y_2 = y_0 + y_1$, as shown in figure 4B.1. Further, the product of a point $P = (x, y)$ by a real number λ is given by the new point $\lambda P = (\lambda x, \lambda y)$.

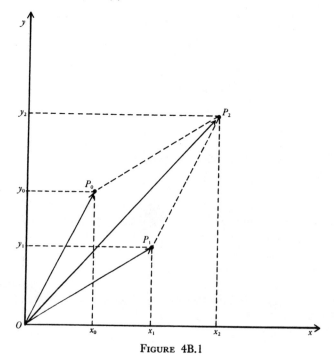

FIGURE 4B.1

At the most elementary level in physics, a vector is defined as a quantity which has both magnitude and direction. Vectors are often represented geometrically by a line with an arrowhead on the end of it. The length of the line indicates the magnitude of the vector, and the arrow denotes its direction. Some vectors lying in a plane are shown in figure 4B.1. In general, a vector may originate at any point in space and terminate at any point. However, it is convenient to have a vector start at the origin of the coordinate system rather than at some other point in space. Once this convention is adopted, a vector becomes perfectly determined when the terminal point of the vector is specified. Thus, there is a one-to-one correspondence between all points in the plane and all vectors which emanate from the origin. This is illustrated in figure 4B.1, points P_0, P_1, and P_2 correspond to the synonymous vectors, and vice versa.

The algebraic operations of addition of points and multiplication of points by real numbers have simple geometric interpretations in the plane (and in space). Here, we speak of addition of vectors and multiplication of vectors by "scalars." The addition of points defined earlier corresponds exactly to the parallelogram rule for adding geometric vectors as illustrated in figure 4B.1. Similarly, multiplication of points by real numbers corresponds to expansion or contraction of the associated vector by the appropriate factor, with negative numbers effecting reversal.

An important geometric concept is the straight line determined by two distinct points, such as points P_1 and P_2 in figure 4B.1. As we saw earlier, $P_0 + P_1 = P_2$, or $P_0 = P_2 - P_1$. Looking at figure 4B.1, we see that every point (P) on the straight-line segment $P_1 P_2$ can be obtained by adding to the point P_1 some positive fraction of the vector (point) $P_0 = P_2 - P_1$. Thus,

$$P = P_1 + \lambda P_0 = P_1 + \lambda(P_2 - P_1) = (1 - \lambda)P_1 + \lambda P_2, \qquad (4B.1)$$

where $0 \le \lambda \le 1$. When $\lambda = 0$, P coincides with P_1; and when $\lambda = 1$, P coincides with P_2. Further, as λ increases continuously from 0 to 1, P slides along the straight-line segment $P_1 P_2$, moving from P_1 to P_2. In particular, when $\lambda = \frac{1}{2}$, P lies halfway between P_1 and P_2. More generally, the distance from P_1 to P is given by λ times the distance from P_1 to P_2. This follows directly from equation (4B.1), which can be rewritten as $P - P_1 = \lambda(P_2 - P_1)$.

Consider figure 4B.2. It is a box diagram similar to that of figure 4.6. (No isoquants have been drawn, because they are not needed for our purposes.) The sides of the box are given by the total amounts of labor and land (L_0, T_0) available to an economy. The coordinates of any point P in the box with respect to O_x show the quantities of labor and land allocated to the production of X (i.e., L_x, T_x). The coordinates of the same point P with respect to O_y show the quantities of labor and land allocated to the production of Y (i.e., L_y, T_y). Since there are two origins, O_x and O_y, and

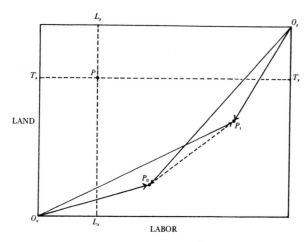

FIGURE 4B.2

there might be confusion as to which origin is the relevant one, write P with a superscript x or y to distinguish between the two. Thus, P^x refers to point P with its coordinates measured with respect to O_x, while P^y refers to point P with its coordinates measured with respect to O_y. Accordingly, $P^x = (L_x, T_x)$, and $P^y = (L_y, T_y)$. Note that the sum of the points P^x and P^y is given by

$$P^x + P^y = (L_x + L_y, \ T_x + T_y) = (L_0, T_0). \qquad (4B.2)$$

Consider now points P_0 and P_1. Looking at them from the point of view of O_x, we can express every point (P^x) along the broken straight-line segment P_0P_1 as

$$P^x = (1 - \lambda)P_0^x + \lambda P_1^x, \qquad (4B.3)$$

where $0 \le \lambda \le 1$.

On the other hand, looking at P_0, P_1 from the point of view of O_y, we can express every point (P^y) along the broken straight-line segment P_0P_1 as

$$P^y = (1 - \lambda)P_0^y + \lambda P_1^y, \qquad (4B.4)$$

where $0 \le \lambda \le 1$.

Theorem: For any given value of λ in the interval $[0, 1]$, the points P^x and P^y in equations (4B.3) and (4B.4) are identical.

Proof: Because of equation (4B.2), it is only necessary to show that the sum $P^x + P^y$ equals (L_0, T_0). Thus, substituting directly from equations (4B.3) and (4B.4) and making use of equation (4B.2), we get

$$P^x + P^y = (1 - \lambda)P_0^x + \lambda P_1^x + (1 - \lambda)P_0^y + \lambda P_1^y$$
$$= (1 - \lambda)(P_0^x + P_0^y) + \lambda(P_1^x + P_1^y) = (L_0, T_0).$$

This completes the proof.

SELECTED BIBLIOGRAPHY

Haberler, G. 1936. *The Theory of International Trade*. London: W. Hodge & Co. Chap. 12.

Lerner, A. P. 1932. The diagrammatical representation of cost conditions in international trade. *Economica* 12: 346–56; reprinted in A. P. Lerner. 1953. *Essays in Economic Analysis*. London: Macmillan & Co.

Samuelson, P. A. 1947. *Foundations of Economic Analysis*. Cambridge, Mass.: Harvard University Press.

Savosnik, K. M. 1958. The box diagram and the production possibility curve. *Ekonomisk Tidskrift* 60: 183–97.

Viner, J. 1937. *Studies in the Theory of International Trade*. New York: Harper & Bros. Chaps. 7, 9.

(Additional references may be found at the end of Chapter 5, p. 140.)

5

Community Indifference and
Comparative Advantage

This chapter is divided into two parts. The first part discusses the fundamental concept of social indifference. The second part discusses the problems
of how to portray general equilibrium (1) in a closed economy, and (2) in a
simple open economy which is a price taker in the international market; in
addition, it provides a neoclassical demonstration of comparative advantage.

A. Community Indifference

The second simplifying assumption made by the neoclassical theory of
international trade is the existence of a logically acceptable social indifference
map, that is, an indifference map qualitatively similar to the well-known
indifference map of an individual consumer that portrays the tastes of the
society at large. Several questions arise. First, what meaning should be
attached to a social indifference curve? Further, do social indifference maps
having the same properties as the indifference map of an individual consumer exist? If they do, how can they be derived? This section is concerned
mainly with these questions. It should be noted that the main justification
for the continued use of social indifference curves is, besides their simplicity,
the fact that they give rise to results which are qualitatively similar to those
derived more laboriously by the use of a totally disaggregated model.

1. Definition and Difficulties

An individual consumer's indifference curve shows all the alternative
combinations of two commodities (X and Y) which are capable of providing
the consumer with the same amount of utility. The consumer is thus indifferent to the alternatives. One might be inclined to apply this definition

to a social indifference curve. But in what sense does social welfare remain constant along a social indifference curve? Since interpersonal comparisons of consumer welfare levels are impossible, this seems to be a rather difficult question.

Tibor Scitovsky[1] defines an indifference curve as the locus of all those minimal combinations of X and Y that are capable of putting each and every consumer in the society on arbitrarily prescribed levels of well-being. That is, given the indifference maps of all consumers, an indifference curve is arbitrarily selected from every map. What minimal combinations of X and Y are needed to put every consumer on his arbitrarily selected indifference curve? Note that, since every consumer remains by assumption on the same indifference curve, the society may be said to be indifferent between one or another combination on the social indifference curve.

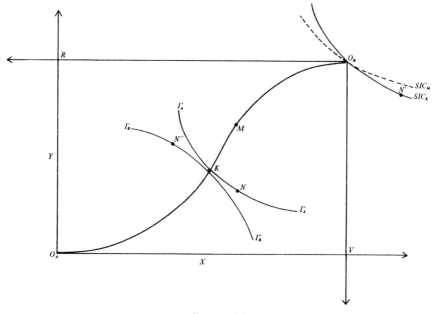

FIGURE 5.1

Scitovsky's definition is illustrated in figure 5.1. Assume two consumers, A and B. Given their indifference maps, select arbitrarily an indifference curve from each map, as shown in figure 5.1 by the indifference curves $I'_A I''_A$ and $I'_B I''_B$, where the subscripts indicate the individuals. Note that A's indifference map is drawn with respect to the O_A origin and B's with respect to O_B. That is, B's indifference map has actually been rotated by $180°$ and placed in such a way that the two arbitrarily selected indifference curves, $I'_A I''_A$ and $I'_B I''_B$, are tangential to each other at point K.

1. See Scitovsky (1942).

What are the minimal combinations of X and Y (measuring them with respect to the origin O_A) which are capable of putting consumer A on indifference curve $I'_A I''_A$ and B on $I'_B I''_B$? One such combination is already known: the origin O_B itself. To determine all such combinations, and thus the social indifference curve, simply slide B's indifference curve, $I'_B I''_B$, along A's indifference curve so that they are always tangential to each other, and let the origin O_B trace out the curve SIC_K. The latter is the social indifference curve we have been looking for. The slope of the SIC_K curve at a particular point is necessarily equal to the slope of the corresponding point of the indifference curves $I'_A I''_A$ and $I'_B I''_B$ at which they are tangent to each other. (For a proof of this statement, i.e., that the slope of a Scitovsky social indifference curve at a certain point is equal to the corresponding slope of the corresponding indifference curves of A and B, see appendix 5A.) For instance, the slope of SIC_K at O_B is equal to the common slope of $I'_A I''_A$ and $I'_B I''_B$ at K. The slope at N', determined by the origin of B's indifference map when the $I'_B I''_B$ curve is tangent to $I'_A I''_A$ at point N, is equal to the slope of N (or N'').

The social indifference curve SIC_K has been derived on the basis of the arbitrarily selected indifference curves $I'_A I''_A$ and $I'_B I''_B$. In order to bring out clearly the consequences of this construction, suppose for the moment that the rectangle $O_A V O_B R$ is a box diagram. Our two-man economy is endowed with the fixed quantities $O_A V$ and $O_A R$ of X and Y, respectively. The indifference maps of A and B have been drawn as before, with the solid curve $O_A K O_B$ being the contract curve, that is, the locus of tangencies between the two sets of indifference curves. It should be noted again that all points on the contract curve are Pareto-optimum points. In other words, starting from a point on the contract curve, it is impossible to improve the well-being of one consumer without making the other consumer worse off. No other points in the box have this important property. Now arbitrarily select some other point (besides K) on the contract curve, such as M. Obviously, the two indifference curves passing through point M are by construction tangential to each other at M. Suppose now that another social indifference curve is defined in relation to the indifference curves passing through M. How would this new social indifference curve compare with SIC_K? Obviously, it will necessarily pass through point O_B, but, in general, it will intersect SIC_K at O_B instead of coinciding with it throughout. This is illustrated by the broken curve SIC_M, which intersects the curve SIC_K at O_B. That the two curves will, in general, intersect each other at point O_B follows from the fact that the common slope of the indifference curves at K is different from the slope at M.

In general, there will be an infinite number of social indifference curves passing through point O_B, each curve being associated with a certain distribution of welfare between the two individuals (in other words, a point on the contract curve). Thus, in general, nonintersecting social indifference curves cannot be drawn. Accordingly, an infinite number of social indifference curves (usually intersecting one another) pass through any point of the positive quadrant. This makes it impossible to assign a single social utility index to any given combination of X and Y available to the society. In addition, we cannot predict the social marginal rate of substitution of X for Y by knowing the aggregate of the two commodities available to the society. We have no way of knowing which social indifference curve (out of the infinite number of social indifference curves passing through the chosen point in the commodity space) will eventually be the relevant one.

Social welfare does not depend only on the total quantities of X and Y available to the society. It also depends on their distribution among the various members of the society (to put it differently, it depends on the distribution of income). Figure 5.2 shows the so-called (unique) utility frontier of the society, which is derived on the basis of the information given in figure 5.1. Consumer A's total utility (U_A) is measured along the horizontal axis and B's (U_B) is measured along the vertical axis. Each point on the utility frontier (figure 5.2) corresponds to a point on the contract curve (fig. 5.1). The utility frontier necessarily slopes downward because, as we move along the contract curve, one consumer becomes better off and the other worse off. In other words, when the economy is on the contract curve (and thus on the utility frontier), it is impossible to make one consumer

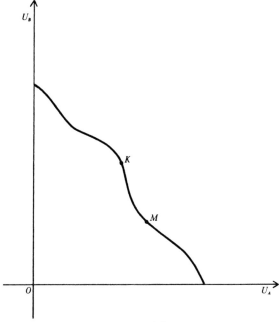

FIGURE 5.2

better off without making the other consumer worse off. Thus, every point on the contract curve or the utility frontier is Pareto optimal. Points K and M on the utility frontier (fig. 5.2) correspond to the synonymous points on the contract curve (fig. 5.1). Every point on the utility frontier necessarily corresponds to a certain level of social welfare, although we have no way of knowing what that level is at the moment. But a point on the utility frontier corresponds not to a single combination of X and Y available to the society but to an infinite number of combinations of X and Y that lie on a social indifference curve as previously derived. Each combination of X and Y (i.e., each point in the commodity space, such as point O_B in fig. 5.1) corresponds to an infinite number of points in the utility space, that is, the whole utility frontier. Thus, the points K and M (and all other points on the utility frontier) of figure 5.2 correspond to the single point O_B in figure 5.1. A different combination of X and Y in the commodity space gives rise to a new utility frontier which might or might not intersect the utility frontier derived on the basis of the assumption that the society is endowed with X_0 and Y_0 units of X and Y, respectively.

2. Justification of Social Indifference Curves in Some Special Cases

The analysis of the preceding section shows convincingly that, in general, social indifference curves with the desired properties do not exist. However, there are several cases in the literature where the use of social indifference curves can be justified. Before proceeding with the discussion of these cases, let us distinguish between two concepts of social indifference curves. Social indifference curves can be drawn (a) to describe *positive behavior* irrespective of the level of social welfare attached to each social indifference curve, or (b) to represent *social welfare*. In addition, welfare statements can be made if either (1) we have an optimizing income-redistribution policy, or (2) we talk about potential welfare as opposed to actual welfare.

Note that, when an optimizing income-redistribution policy is pursued, the social indifference map can be used to describe both the consumption behavior of the economy and changes in social welfare. But in the absence of an optimizing income-redistribution policy, the social indifference map need not indicate changes in social welfare. Thus, a movement from a lower to a higher social indifference curve need not imply an increase in social welfare; it may very well imply a decrease if the income distribution becomes worse. Under these circumstances, we can only talk about potential welfare. For instance, as is shown in chapter 16, although we cannot be sure that free trade improves actual welfare, we can prove that free trade could potentially make everybody better off; that is, free trade improves potential welfare.

The few cases where the use of social indifference curves can be justified are briefly discussed as follows:

1. The simplest and at the same time most trivial case is where the economy is composed of a single individual (i.e., a Robinson Crusoe economy). Here the problem of aggregation of indifference maps does not arise because there exists only one indifference map, which is also the social indifference map. Nevertheless, this case cannot be taken seriously.

2. In a totalitarian state (or even when a planning bureau exists), the indifference map of a dictator (or of the planning bureau) becomes the social indifference map. Here, as in the preceding case, the problem of aggregation does not arise.

3. An apparently more realistic case is a country inhabited with individuals having identical tastes and factor endowments. Thus, these individuals must be equally endowed capitalists (or land owners) and also equally productive workers. The identity of tastes is not unrealistic, particularly within one nation and culture. However, the identity of factor endowments is most certainly violated in the real world.

The box-diagram technique used in the preceding section can be used in the present case to yield a single nonintersecting social indifference map. Thus, considering again two individuals, A and B, endowed with X_0 and Y_0 units of commodities X and Y, respectively, study the box diagram in figure 5.3. The contract curve must necessarily pass through point K on the diagonal, with K lying halfway between points O_A and O_B. This must be so because of the assumed identity of tastes. Thus, at K both consumers consume the same bundle of commodities, and therefore their marginal rates of substitution must be identical. Now, since both consumers have the same

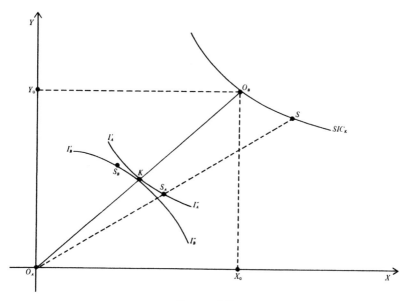

FIGURE 5.3

income, the consumption of quantities X_0 and Y_0 necessarily implies that K is the equilibrium point on the contract curve. The social indifference curve SIC_K has been derived as before on the basis of the indifference curves passing through K. On the assumption of the identity of incomes, this is a unique curve. Observe that any point on SIC_K, such as S, implies that both consumers are consuming exactly the same bundles of commodities, as shown by points S_A and S_B. Point S_A is the midpoint of the straight-line segment joining points O_A and S; point S_B is the point whose distance from O_B is equal to $O_A S_A$. That this is so follows from the fact that the slopes at S_A and S_B must be equal; because tastes are assumed identical, this occurs only when both consumers consume exactly the same bundles of commodities.

What this analysis shows is that, in the present case of identical tastes and endowments (or incomes), a social indifference curve can be constructed as follows. Draw a ray through the origin intersecting a common (to all consumers) indifference curve at a point, such as K. Then, in the case of two consumers, determine the point on the ray whose distance from the origin is twice as long as that of K. For instance, $O_A O_B = 2(O_A K)$ and $O_A S = 2(O_A S_A)$. When the number of consumers is not two but n, then the point on the social indifference curve is that point on the ray which lies n times the distance $O_A K$ from the origin. Repeating the same experiment for all points on the chosen indifference curve, we can construct the whole social indifference curve that corresponds to it.

Note that in this case we have been able to select only one Scitovsky social indifference curve passing through a point in the commodity space, because of the assumed identity of incomes and tastes. If these assumptions are dropped, then according to the analysis of the preceding section, there does not exist a nonintersecting social indifference map.[2]

It should be obvious that a social indifference curve corresponds to a single curve of the common indifference map of all consumers. Repeating, therefore, the same experiment for all such common indifference curves, we can construct the whole social indifference map.

A fundamental property of this social indifference map, is that a movement from a lower to a higher indifference curve implies that the economy as a whole becomes better off because the welfare of each and every consumer goes up; that is, every consumer necessarily moves from a lower to a higher indifference curve. Thus, the present social indifference map can be used for predicting both the consumption behavior of the economy and changes in social welfare.

4. Another case in which the use of a social indifference map is justified is when all individuals have identical tastes which are, in addition, *homo-*

---

2. Eisenberg (1961) has shown that a nonintersecting social indifference map also exists in the case where all individuals have the same proportionate share in total resources and homogeneous (*but not necessarily identical*) tastes.

thetic in the sense that all income-consumption curves are straight lines through the origin. In this case, the contract curve in the box diagram coincides with the diagonal which intersects all indifference curves at points with the same slope. This case also yields a single nonintersecting social indifference map which is actually identical with any of the individual indifference maps. Thus, the technique of the preceding section can be used to show that, whatever point on the contract curve is chosen, the same social indifference curve will be derived.

However, although this social indifference map is capable of describing the *consumption behavior* of the economy, it cannot be used to discuss changes in social welfare. This follows from the fact that the present social indifference map is independent of the distribution of income, on which it gives absolutely no information. Put differently, through any point in commodity space there pass an infinite number of social indifference curves which happen to be identical. Each social indifference curve, however, corresponds to a different distribution of income and thus social welfare. Even though this social indifference map can be used to predict the marginal rate of substitution in consumption when only the aggregates of X and Y are given, there is no way of knowing what the distribution of income is and how it changes as we move from a lower to a higher social indifference curve. As a result, there is no way of knowing (by looking at the aggregates of X and Y) whether social welfare improves as the society moves from a lower to a higher indifference curve.

5. Finally, as Samuelson (1956) has shown, if a social welfare function exists and if income is always reallocated among individuals in such a way as to maximize social welfare, it is possible to derive a social indifference map with all the usual properties of an individual consumer's indifference map. No proof of Samuelson's theorem will be given here. Interested readers are referred to Samuelson's classic paper.

A social welfare function is a function of the form $W = f(U_1, U_2, \ldots, U_n)$, where $W \equiv$ social welfare and $U_i \equiv$ utility enjoyed by the ith individual. For the case of a society consisting of two individuals, the social welfare function can be represented graphically by a family of contour lines in the utility space (U_A, U_B). Welfare maximization can be determined by superimposing these contour lines on the utility frontier (fig. 5.2) and finding the point where the utility frontier touches the highest welfare contour line.

It should be noted that the derivation of the utility frontier of an economy is a much more complicated process than what was suggested earlier with respect to figure 5.2. There, the utility frontier was derived under the assumption that the totals X_0 and Y_0 were given. But in general, an economy can move along its production-possibilities frontier, which means that there are an infinite number of (Pareto-optimum) combinations of X and Y available to the society. However, what has been done for a single combination of X and Y can be repeated for any other. For each such combination there is, therefore, a utility frontier in figure 5.2. The outer envelope of these utility frontiers, which in fact are infinite in number, is the true utility frontier of the economy, and it is with respect to this true utility frontier that the welfare function has to be maximized.

Samuelson (1956) suggests that the problem of aggregation can be bypassed by treating each individual within a country as a separate country. If factor endowments are the same among individuals, or proportional to aggregate endowments, the production-possibilities frontier of each country can be scaled down in proportion to the relative factor endowments of each individual. In this case, we can follow Samuelson's suggestion and treat each individual as a separate country. In the case of the classical theory where there is a single factor of production, this suggestion can indeed be carried through because the condition of proportionality in factor endowments is indeed satisfied. However, with dissimilar factor endowments, the income distribution changes continuously as the economy moves along the production-possibilities frontier, and the simple idea of scaling down the production-possibilities frontier becomes exceedingly complex—though not impossible.

The cases considered so far refer to total aggregation of individual indifference maps. Harry G. Johnson (1959) offers what appears to be a more fruitful approach to this problem, which is actually a compromise between total disaggregation, on the one hand, and total aggregation, on the other. In particular, Johnson considers the two factors of production (which he calls *labor* and *capital*) as separate consuming groups, with each group behaving as a single rational individual. Since the income distribution is perfectly fixed at any point on the production-possibilities frontier (although it usually varies when we move from one point to another), the aggregate quantities consumed are thus perfectly determined for any given commodity-price ratio.

B. General Equilibrium and Comparative Advantage

Assuming that the concept of a social indifference map can be made logically acceptable, the problems arise of how to portray general equilibrium (1) in a closed economy, (2) in a simple open economy which is a price taker in the international market, and (3) in a two-country, two-commodity model. The first two problems will be considered rigorously and the third problem only tentatively. Chapter 6 considers the question of international equilibrium in detail.

1. General Equilibrium in a Closed Economy

Despite all the limitations and shortcomings of the social indifference map, let us nevertheless employ it as a tool of analysis. The only justification for its

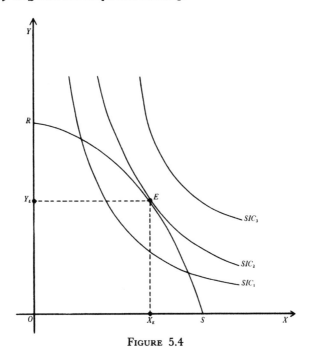

FIGURE 5.4

use, as mentioned earlier, is the great simplification that it makes possible with regard to the problem of general equilibrium; in addition, the conclusions so derived are similar to those derived by more rigorous and laborious ways.

Figure 5.4 portrays the general equilibrium of a closed economy. Curve *RS* is the production-possibilities frontier of the economy. It is a curve concave[3] to the origin and exhibits increasing opportunity costs. As explained in the previous chapter, such a production-possibilities frontier is derived under the assumptions of fixed endowments of labor and land and constant returns to scale. In addition, superimposed on the same diagram are three illustrative social indifference curves. General equilibrium occurs at point *E*, where the production-possibilities frontier is tangent to the highest possible social indifference curve (i.e., SIC_2). Therefore, the economy will produce and consume X_E units of commodity X and Y_E units of Y. The common absolute slope of the production-possibilities frontier and the SIC_2 at point *E* gives the equilibrium price ratio p_X/p_Y, for p for short. *Therefore, in general equilibrium, p is equal both to the marginal rate of transformation,*

---

3. The description of the curve *RS* of fig. 5.4 as a concave curve may give rise to some confusion. Some would like to say that the set of points lying within the production-possibilities block *OSER* is convex in the sense that any straight line joining two points of the set lies totally within the set. There is nothing wrong with either characterization, but confusion can occur.

or the opportunity cost of X in terms of Y (i.e., the absolute slope of the production-possibilities frontier at the equilibrium point), *and to the marginal rate of substitution in consumption of X for Y.*

It is usually said that the economy maximizes social welfare at point E. As the analysis of part A of the present chapter reveals, this may be legitimate under certain conditions. However, this statement is not generally true. For this reason, let us refrain from passing a judgment on social welfare by means of the tenuous concept of the social indifference map. Let us, rather, use the social indifference map for predicting the demand behavior of the economy alone. Otherwise, the impression might be created that the social indifference map is all that is needed in a discussion of the effects of trade on welfare. The question of the effects of trade on welfare will be taken up in chapters 15 and 16, so there is no reason for trying to simplify a rather complex phenomenon at this stage.

In the classical theory, the production-possibilities frontier is a straight line and the (pretrade) equilibrium price ratio can be predicted from the production data (i.e., the labor coefficients) alone without any knowledge about demand—assuming, of course, that both commodities are produced and consumed in equilibrium. Under the more general assumptions of the neoclassical theory, however, increasing opportunity costs are the rule (and constant costs the exception). Therefore, we can no longer predict the (pretrade) equilibrium price ratio without full information about demand, which now becomes as important as supply. In the presence of increasing opportunity costs, the most that can be accomplished without full information about demand (assuming only that both commodities are consumed in equilibrium) is finding the limits within which the pretrade equilibrium price ratio must lie. These limits are, of course, given by the slope of the production-possibilities frontier at the intercepts (i.e., points R and S in fig. 5.4).

2. Equilibrium in a Simple Open Economy

The preceding analysis can easily be extended to a simple open economy which is too small relative to the rest of the world to have any appreciable influence on the formation of international prices. In other words, the assumption now is that our economy can buy and sell unlimited quantities of X and Y at given international prices, p_X^* and p_Y^*. Actually, we are only interested in relative prices. Let us therefore, denote the given international price ratio, p_X^*/p_Y^*, by the symbol p^*. The problem is to show how equilibrium is reached when trade with the rest of the world is possible.

As in the case of the classical theory, our economy will reach general equilibrium in the following two steps:

a) Given p^*, the economy will choose to produce at that particular point on the production-possibilities frontier where national income (expressed in either X or Y) is at a maximum. Mathematically, this problem can be stated as follows: maximize $Q = p^*X + Y$ subject to the constraint $F(X, Y) = 0$, where Q is national income expressed in Y and the function $F(X, Y) = 0$ is the algebraic expression for the production-possibilities frontier.

b) Having chosen the production point, the economy will then have to decide what to consume.

The determination of the optimum production point is illustrated in figure 5.5. The curve RS is the familiar production-possibilities frontier of the economy. The family of parallel straight lines with slope equal to p^* is the geometric representation of the function

$$Q = p^*X + Y. \qquad (5.1)$$

It is a family of contour lines, with each line being the locus of all those combinations of X and Y which have the same value in the international market. The object of the economy is to maximize national income (Q). In this effort, it is constrained by the production-possibilities frontier. (Remember that the economy can produce at any point that lies inside or on the production-possibilities frontier, but not beyond it.) From figure 5.5, it should be obvious that national income is being maximized when the economy produces at point E, that is, at the point where the production-possibilities frontier becomes tangent to the highest income contour line, I_3. Production at a point other than E either is impossible (such as Z) or gives

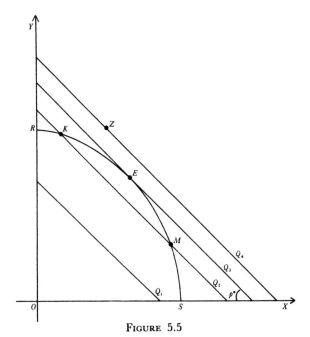

FIGURE 5.5

rise to a national income smaller than Q_3 (such as K). Accordingly, the economy cannot reach a higher income contour line than Q_3 because of the constraint imposed by the production-possibilities frontier. With technological progress, labor growth, and capital accumulation, the production possibilities frontier will, of course, shift outward and enable the economy to reach a higher income contour line. However, with given technology and factor endowments, giving rise to the production-possibilities frontier RS (fig. 5.5), the maximum income that the economy can possibly reach is Q_3.

Following the terminology introduced in chapter 3, let us call the highest income contour line, Q_3, the *consumption-possibilities frontier*. In other words, the economy, by producing at point E, can consume at any point on the consumption-possibilities frontier, that is, the income contour line Q_3, because of the possibility of international trade. Therefore, as the classical theory demonstrates, international trade makes it possible for an economy to consume beyond its production-possibilities frontier despite the fact that it can never produce beyond the boundaries of the production-possibilities frontier. To use Haberler's metaphor, the building (i.e., the possibility of consuming beyond the production-possibilities frontier) remains after the scaffolding (i.e., the labor theory of value) is removed.

Observe that the income contour line Q_3 lies totally outside the production-possibilities frontier, RS, except at the singular point E. Therefore, neglecting the singular point E, we can say immediately that free trade increases potential welfare, for it is possible, with an appropriate distribution of income after trade, to make everybody better off relative to the pretrade position. This question is discussed in detail in chapter 16.

The preceding discussion shows that national income is maximized if the economy produces at point E. But how do we know that the economy will actually produce at E? This is a legitimate question, because in a perfectly competitive economy there is no "planning board" to make this important decision. Nevertheless, this important function is performed by the forces of competition. Since our economy is a price taker in the world market and transportation costs are assumed zero, domestic prices will necessarily coincide with international prices. Point E is the only point on the production-possibilities frontier where domestic and international prices are equal. In addition, observe that at any other point on the production-possibilities frontier, the value of output produced at world prices could increase by merely changing the production pattern. Therefore, Adam Smith's invisible hand will sooner or later guide the economy to produce at point E.

In summary, the economy will produce at that point on the production-possibilities frontier whose absolute slope is equal to the international price ratio, p^*. The tangent to the production-possibilities frontier at the production point so selected becomes the consumption-possibilities frontier of the economy.

Once the consumption-possibilities frontier is determined, the next step is to find out where the economy should consume. Figure 5.6 shows how this part of the problem can be handled. The curves *RPS* and *KPV* are the production-possibilities and consumption-possibilities frontiers, respectively. In addition, on the same diagram are three illustrative social indifference curves. Consumption equilibrium occurs at point *C*, where the consumption-possibilities frontier touches the highest possible social indifference curve. Therefore, the economy produces at *P* and consumes at *C*; that is, it produces X_P and Y_P units of *X* and *Y*, respectively, and consumes X_C and Y_C units of *X* and *Y*, respectively. Accordingly, the economy must be exporting *DP* units of *Y* while importing *DC* units of *X*.

Finally, note that the value of *DC* units of *X* is equal to the value of *DP* units of *Y*. Geometrically, this follows from the fact that the ratio *DP/DC* gives the absolute slope of the consumption-possibilities frontier that is equal to the international price ratio, p^*. Thus, $DP/DC = p^*$, or $DP = p^*(DC)$. That is, the value of exports is equal to the value of imports. From an economic point of view, this equality follows from the fact that the value of output produced is equal to the value of output consumed; that is, both the production and consumption points lie on the same income contour line. Thus,

$$p^*X_P + Y_P = p^*X_C + Y_C,$$

or

$$Y_P - Y_C = p^*(X_C - X_P). \tag{5.2}$$

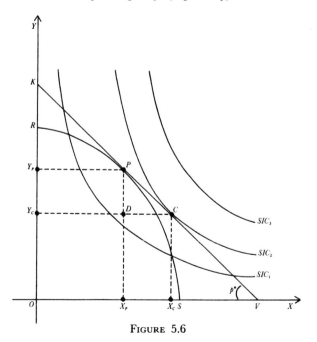

FIGURE 5.6

But $Y_P - Y_C = DP$ and $X_C - X_P = DC$. Therefore, equation (5.2) reduces to the equation $DP = p*(DC)$.

The preceding analysis shows how to determine the quantities of X and Y that the economy would be willing to export or import, as the case may be, for a given value of the international price ratio, p. But this is precisely the information that is required for the determination of a point on the offer curve of the economy involved. Therefore, repeating the same process for all possible values of p, we can determine all points on the country's offer curve; that is, we can determine the country's offer curve.

Compared with the classical theory, the determination of the offer curve in the present case becomes much more complicated because of the existence of increasing opportunity costs. Recall that, in the classical theory where the production-possibilities frontier is linear, the production point coincides with the vertical-axis intercept of the production-possibilities frontier for all values of p lower than the pretrade price ratio. Similarly, for all values of p higher than the pretrade price ratio, the production point coincides with the horizontal-axis intercept of the production-possibilities frontier. As a result of this simplification, the derivation of the offer curve did not seem to be an impossible task. In the presence of increasing opportunity costs, the production point necessarily changes as p changes. This makes the derivation of the offer curve much more difficult. However, thanks to J. E. Meade's ingenious technique (explained in the following chapter), the offer curve can still be derived with little effort.

Note that the preceding analysis can be used to improve our understanding of the gains from trade. For this purpose, assume that the social indifference map describes not only consumption behavior but also changes in social welfare. As noted in part A of the present chapter, this assumption is legitimate only under certain conditions. In particular, it is legitimate in all the special cases discussed in part A with only one exception—the case of identical and homothetic tastes.

Given a social indifference map describing social welfare in addition to consumption behavior, it is obvious (see fig. 5.6) that free international trade enables the economy to move from a lower to a higher social indifference curve, that is, to increase social welfare.

The total gain from trade is usually divided into the following two components:

a) The *gain from international exchange*, or the *consumption gain*, which accrues to the economy when the same bundle of commodities that was produced under autarky is also produced under free trade.

b) The *gain from specialization*, or the *production gain*, which accrues to the economy over and above the consumption gain as a result of the shift of the production point due to the difference between the pretrade and posttrade commodity prices.

Figure 5.7 illustrates the reduction of the total gain into a consumption and a production gain. The curve MP_1P_0N is the economy's production-

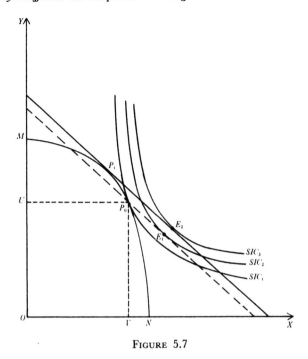

FIGURE 5.7

possibilities frontier. Before trade, equilibrium occurs at point P_0, where the production-possibilities frontier touches the highest possible social indifference curve (SIC_1). When trade opens up, the economy produces at P_1 and consumes at E_2, with the straight line passing through P_1E_2 being the economy's consumption-possibilities frontier. Social welfare improves because the economy moves from a lower social indifference curve (SIC_1) to a higher one (SIC_3). To isolate the consumption gain, assume for the moment that with the opening up of trade, the production point is frozen at P_0. This could be identified as the case of perfect factor immobility between industries and factor-price flexibility, where the economy's production-possibilities frontier becomes the rectangle OVP_0U. Even though production is frozen at P_0, the economy will still benefit from trade. Its consumption point would move from P_0 to E_1. That is, the economy would move from a lower social indifference curve (SIC_1) to a higher one (SIC_2). The movement from SIC_1 to SIC_2 is the consumption gain. The production gain is represented by the movement from E_1 to E_2 as a result of the change in the production pattern (from P_0 to P_1).

3. Neoclassical Demonstration of Comparative Advantage

Assume two countries, A and B, endowed with fixed quantities of two factors of production, labor (L) and land (T), and producing two commodities, X and Y, under constant returns to scale. Denote the pretrade equilibrium

price ratios (p_X/p_Y) in countries A and B by p_A^0 and p_B^0, respectively. Figure
5.8 summarizes the pretrade equilibrium positions of the two countries.
Panel (a) illustrates A's pretrade general equilibrium and panel (b) illustrates B's. The curve ME_AN (KE_BR) is A's $(B$'s) production-possibilities
frontier, while the curve SIC_A (SIC_B) is the highest social indifference curve
that A's $(B$'s) production-possibilities frontier can reach. Thus, before trade,
A (B) produces and consumes at E_A (E_B). Country A's $(B$'s) pretrade price
ratio is given by the slope of the tangent E_AV (E_BU). It has been assumed
that $p_A^0 < p_B^0$, that is, that X is relatively cheaper in A and Y in B before trade.

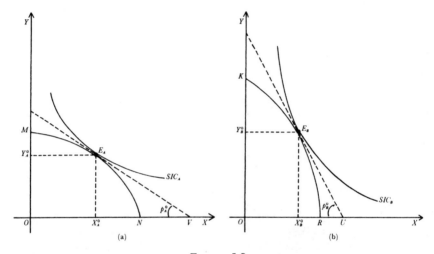

FIGURE 5.8

Under the preceding assumptions, it can be said that country A has a
comparative advantage in the production of X and B in Y. Thus, when
trade is opened up, A will export commodity X and import Y (or B will
export Y and import X). Finally, it can be shown that the equilibrium terms
of trade (p_E) will definitely lie between the pretrade price ratios of the two
countries; that is,

$$p_A^0 < p_E < p_B^0. \tag{5.3}$$

The preceding statements can be proved as follows. First show that
international equilibrium is impossible when the international terms of trade
take a value lower than p_A^0, that is, a value lower than both pretrade price
ratios. Figure 5.9 shows why. It illustrates the behavior of a typical country
whose pretrade price ratio is higher than the international price ratio. Thus,
before trade, the country produces and consumes at E. However, for any
international price ratio lower than the pretrade price ratio, the production
point will move in the region KE of the production-possibilities frontier, as
illustrated by point P. Under these circumstances, the consumption-
possibilities frontier (as illustrated by the straight line $PFCD$) will necessarily

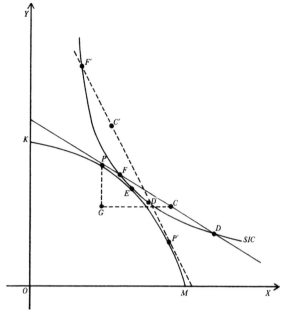

FIGURE 5.9

intersect the social indifference curve *SIC* at two points, such as F and D. Consumption equilibrium should occur somewhere in the region FD of the consumption-possibilities frontier, as shown by point C. Therefore, the typical country of figure 5.9 will want to export commodity Y and import X. When the international price ratio is smaller than both p_A^0 and p_B^0, both countries (A and B) will want to export Y and import X. As the analysis of chapter 3 shows, international equilibrium is impossible under these circumstances.

International equilibrium is also impossible when the international price ratio is higher than p_B^0, that is, when it is higher than both pretrade price ratios. Under these circumstances, both countries will want to export X and import Y, as illustrated by the broken consumption-possibilities frontier $F'C'D'P'$ of figure 5.9, with production occurring at P' and consumption at C'.

Having eliminated all values of the international price ratio that lie outside the open region (p_A^0, p_B^0), we can now show that international equilibrium will necessarily take place for some value of the terms of trade between p_A^0 and p_B^0. In order to prove this assertion as briefly as possible, let us concentrate on the market for commodity X only. The reader is reminded that, in a two-commodity model, when the market for one commodity is in equilibrium the market for the other is necessarily in equilibrium (Walras's law). Therefore, general equilibrium can be discussed in terms of either market alone. This has already been explained in detail in chapter 3.

Adopt the symbol p as a shorthand expression for the international terms of trade and consider the following extreme values: $p = p_A^0$ and $p = p_B^0$. When $p = p_A^0$, A's excess demand for commodity X from the rest of the world is necessarily zero. However, as the preceding analysis shows, at $p = p_A^0$ country B has a positive excess demand for commodity X. Therefore, when $p = p_A^0$, the combined excess demand for X by both countries is necessarily positive. On the other hand, when $p = p_B^0$, B's excess demand for X is necessarily zero while A's becomes negative. Therefore, when $p = p_B^0$, the combined excess demand for X by both countries is necessarily negative. It should be obvious that, because of the (assumed) continuity of the combined excess demand curve for X, there must exist a value of p satisfying the inequality $p_A^0 < p < p_B^0$ at which the combined excess demand for X becomes zero, that is, the market for X is in equilibrium. Finally, it should be noted that when inequality (5.3) is satisfied, country A will export commodity X and import Y.

The preceding conclusions are in full agreement with the conclusions of the classical theory. However, these conclusions depend crucially on the assumption that the tastes of each country can be logically portrayed by a nonintersecting social indifference map. What is the implication of the assumption that a nonintersecting social indifference map exists? It eliminates the possibility of multiple pretrade equilibria which might violate some (but not necessarily all) classical conclusions. Thus, in the presence of multiple pretrade equilibria, we cannot be sure that a country will export the commodity which, in the pretrade equilibrium position, it produces relatively more cheaply than the other country. In addition, the equilibrium terms of trade need not satisfy inequality (5.3).

Figure 5.10 illustrates the preceding statements. Panels (a), (b), and (c) show A's, B's, and the combined excess demand for X, respectively. The solid curves illustrate the case where the pretrade equilibrium prices, p_A^0 and p_B^0, are unique. The relationship among these curves is illustrated for the two values of p, p_A^0, and p_B^0. Note that $UV = U'V'$ and $MN = M'N'$. Thus, the equilibrium terms of trade are p_E, where $p_A^0 < p_E < p_B^0$. Now distort A's excess demand curve as shown by the broken curve in panel (a) and assume that the equilibrium price ratio in A before trade is still p_A^0. This distortion of A's excess demand curve distorts the combined excess demand curve as shown in panel (c) by the broken curve. Note that $NS = N'S'$. The equilibrium terms of trade are now p_E', where the broken combined curve intersects the vertical axis. But $p_E' > p_B^0 > p_A^0$. Therefore, when trade is introduced, both countries tend to specialize in the production of X; that is, they both increase the production of X and decrease the production of Y. Further, when $p = p_E'$, country A exports commodity Y and B commodity X—quite contrary to the classical expectations. It should be pointed out that, had A's pretrade price ratio been p_A^2 instead of p_A^0, the classical conclusions would have been entirely correct.

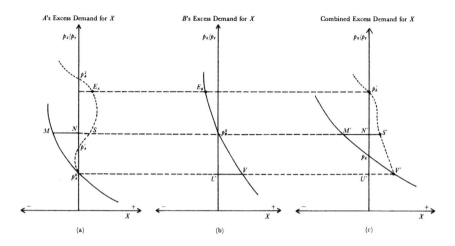

FIGURE 5.10

The existence of multiple pretrade equilibria does not affect the classical conclusions in the following special case. In the presence of increasing opportunity costs, the equilibrium pretrade price ratio of a country cannot be determined without full information about demand. However, the limits within which the pretrade equilibrium price ratio will necessarily lie can be determined under the reasonable assumption that both commodities are consumed by the economy. Denote the lower limit of the pretrade price ratio of the ith country by the symbol p_i^L and the upper limit by p_i^M. Thus, any pretrade equilibrium price ratio in country A (p_A) must satisfy the condition

$$p_A^L < p_A < p_A^M. \tag{5.4}$$

Similarly, the following condition must be satisfied by country B's pretrade price ratio (p_B):

$$p_B^L < p_B < p_B^M. \tag{5.5}$$

It can be shown that if the two regions (p_A^L, p_A^M) and (p_B^L, p_B^M) do not overlap, all classical conclusions remain valid. For instance, if $p_A^M < p_B^L$, country A will be producing X relatively more cheaply than B before trade, and it will definitely (i.e., whether or not multiple pretrade equilibria exist) specialize in the production of X and export it to B, while B will specialize in the production of Y and export it to A. A similar statement can be made when $p_B^M < p_A^L$, with B specializing in the production of X and exporting it to A, and A in Y.

Finally, whether or not multiple pretrade equilibria invalidate the classical conclusions regarding the direction of trade and the limits of the equilibrium terms of trade, the marginal rates of transformation of the participating countries will always be equalized with trade (except in the case of complete specialization). This automatically ensures that the world as a whole will be operating on the world production-possibilities frontier (and not inside it), with the result that all countries can be made potentially better off with trade. Thus, this important classical contribution indeed remains unassailable.

Appendix 5A:
Scitovsky's Social Indifference Curves

This appendix considers (*a*) how the Scitovsky's social indifference curves can be derived and (*b*) what their slope is equal to.

Let X_i and Y_i ($i \equiv A, B$) stand for the quantities of X and Y, respectively, allocated to the ith individual, and let $\bar{U}_A = U_A(X_A, Y_A)$ and $\bar{U}_B = U_B(X_B, Y_B)$ be the equations for two arbitrarily selected indifference curves of A and B, respectively, such as $I_A' I_A''$ and $I_B' I_B''$ of figure 5.1. The problem can be formalized as follows. Given a fixed amount of X, say X_0, to be allocated (in a way which will be determined below) between A and B, what is the minimum amount of Y needed so that its allocation between A and B, along with the allocation of X_0, will put A on indifference curve $I_A' I_A''$ and B on $I_B' I_B''$? In other words, we would like to minimize

$$Y = Y_A + Y_B$$

subject to

$$X_A + X_B - X_0 = 0,$$
$$U_A(X_A, Y_A) - \bar{U}_A = 0,$$
$$U_B(X_B, Y_B) - \bar{U}_B = 0.$$

Form the Lagrangian function

$$Z = Y_A + Y_B + \lambda_1[U_A(X_A, Y_A) - \bar{U}_A]$$
$$+ \lambda_2[U_B(X_B, Y_B) - \bar{U}_B] + \lambda_3(X_A + X_B - X_0), \quad (a)$$

where $\lambda_i(i = 1, 2, 3)$ are the Lagrangian multipliers. For minimization of Y, it is required that the following partial derivatives be zero:

$$\frac{\partial Z}{\partial X_A} = \lambda_1 \frac{\partial U_A}{\partial X_A} + \lambda_3 = 0, \quad (b)$$

$$\frac{\partial Z}{\partial X_B} = \lambda_2 \frac{\partial U_B}{\partial X_B} + \lambda_3 = 0, \quad (c)$$

$$\frac{\partial Z}{\partial Y_A} = 1 + \lambda_1 \frac{\partial U_A}{\partial Y_A} = 0, \quad (d)$$

$$\frac{\partial Z}{\partial Y_B} = 1 + \lambda_2 \frac{\partial U_B}{\partial Y_B} = 0, \quad (e)$$

$$\frac{\partial Z}{\partial \lambda_1} = U_A(X_A, Y_A) - \bar{U}_A = 0, \tag{f}$$

$$\frac{\partial Z}{\partial \lambda_2} = U_B(X_B, Y_B) - \bar{U}_B = 0, \tag{g}$$

$$\frac{\partial Z}{\partial \lambda_3} = X_A + X_B - X_0 = 0. \tag{h}$$

Equations (f), (g), and (h) imply that the three constraints of the problem are indeed satisfied. Combining equations (b) and (c), we get

$$\left(\frac{\partial U_A}{\partial X_A}\right)\bigg/\left(\frac{\partial U_B}{\partial X_B}\right) = \frac{\lambda_2}{\lambda_1}. \tag{i}$$

Further, combining equations (d) and (e), we get

$$\left(\frac{\partial U_A}{\partial Y_A}\right)\bigg/\left(\frac{\partial U_B}{\partial Y_B}\right) = \frac{\lambda_2}{\lambda_1}. \tag{j}$$

Finally, substituting equation (j) into equation (i), we get

$$\left(\frac{\partial U_A}{\partial X_A}\right)\bigg/\left(\frac{\partial U_B}{\partial X_B}\right) = \left(\frac{\partial U_A}{\partial Y_A}\right)\bigg/\left(\frac{\partial U_B}{\partial Y_B}\right),$$

or

$$\left(\frac{\partial U_A}{\partial X_A}\right)\bigg/\left(\frac{\partial U_A}{\partial Y_A}\right) = \left(\frac{\partial U_B}{\partial X_B}\right)\bigg/\left(\frac{\partial U_B}{\partial Y_B}\right). \tag{k}$$

That is, a necessary condition for minimization of Y is that the two commodities be allocated between A and B in such a way that the marginal rates of substitution of the two consumers are equal. This is illustrated in figure 5.1, where the two indifference curves, $I_A' I_A''$ and $I_B' I_B''$, are held in a position tangent to each other.

What is the slope of a Scitovsky social indifference curve at a certain point, say (X_0, Y_0)? To answer this question, rewrite equation (k) in the following form:

$$\frac{dY_A}{dX_A} = \frac{dY_B}{dX_B}, \tag{l}$$

or

$$dY_A = \left(\frac{dY_B}{dX_B}\right) dX_A. \tag{l}'$$

Consider now the differentials

$$dX_0 = dX_A + dX_B, \tag{m}$$

$$dY_0 = dY_A + dY_B. \tag{n}$$

Substitute (l)' into (n) and get

$$dY_0 = \left(\frac{dY_B}{dX_B}\right) dX_A + dY_B. \tag{o}$$

Now consider the ratio

$$\frac{dY_0}{dX_0} = \frac{(dY_B/dX_B)\,dX_A + dY_B}{dX_A + dX_B} = \frac{(dY_B/dX_B)\,dX_A + (dY_B/dX_B)\,dX_B}{dX_A + dX_B} = \frac{dY_B}{dX_B}.$$

(p)

Combining (l) and (p), we finally get

$$\frac{dY_0}{dX_0} = \frac{dY_B}{dX_B} = \frac{dY_A}{dX_A}.$$

(q)

Therefore, the slope of a Scitovsky social indifference curve at a certain point is equal to the corresponding slope of the corresponding indifference curves of A and B (at which the latter are tangent to each other).

SELECTED BIBLIOGRAPHY

Chacholiades, M. 1972. Pre-trade multiple equilibria and the theory of comparative advantage. *Metroeconomica*, Fasc. II.

Eisenberg, E. 1961. Aggregation of utility functions. *Management Science* 7: 337–350.

Haberler, G. 1936. *The Theory of International Trade*. London: W. Hodge & Co. Chap. 12.

Johnson, H. G. 1959. International trade, income distribution, and the offer curve. *Manchester School of Economic and Social Studies* 27: 241–60; reprinted in A.E.A. *Readings in International Economics*. Homewood, Ill.: R. D. Irwin, Inc., 1968.

———. 1960. Income distribution, the offer curve, and the effects of tariffs. *Manchester School of Economic and Social Studies* 28: 215–42.

Leontief, W. W. 1933. The use of indifference curves in the analysis of foreign trade. *Quarterly Journal of Economics* 47: 493–503.

Lerner, A. P. 1932. The diagrammatical representation of cost conditions in international trade. *Economica* 12: 346–56; reprinted in A. P. Lerner. 1953. *Essays in Economic Analysis*. London: Macmillan & Co., 1953.

———. 1934. The diagrammatical representation of demand conditions in international trade. *Economica* N.S. 1: 319–34; reprinted in A. P. Lerner. *Essays in Economic Analysis*.

Marshall, A. 1924. *Money, Credit and Commerce*. New York: Macmillan & Co., Appendix J.

Samuelson, P. A. 1956. Social indifference curves. *Quarterly Journal of Economics* 70: 1–22.

Savosnik, K. M. 1958. The box diagram and the production possibility curve. *Ekonomisk Tidskrift* 60: 183–97.

Scitovsky, T. 1942. A reconsideration of the theory of tariffs. *Review of Economic Studies* 9: 89–110; reprinted in A.E.A. *Readings in the Theory of International Trade*. Homewood, Ill.: R. D. Irwin, Inc., 1949.

Vanek, J. 1959. An afterthought on the real cost-opportunity cost dispute and some aspects of general equilibrium under conditions of variable factor supplies. *Review of Economic Studies* 26: 198–208.

Viner, J. 1937. *Studies in the Theory of International Trade*. New York: Harper & Bros. Chaps. 7, 9.

6

International Equilibrium

As we saw in chapter 3, international equilibrium is usually portrayed in terms of offer curves. Our first problem is to derive the offer curve of a single country. This can be repeated for a second country, and then the analysis of international equilibrium can proceed along the familiar lines of chapter 3.

The derivation of the offer curve in the absence of constant opportunity costs is not an easy task. Edgeworth (1905) summarized the difficulties in the following well-known statement: "There is more than meets the eye in Professor Marshall's foreign trade curves. As it has been said by one who used this sort of curve, a movement along a supply-and-demand curve of international trade should be considered as attended with rearrangements of internal trade; as the movement of the hand of a clock corresponds to considerable unseen movements of the machinery." Edgeworth was actually quoting himself (Edgeworth 1894).

In the early 1930s, Leontief (1933) and Lerner (1934) provided a geometric technique for obtaining a country's offer curve from its social indifference curves and production-possibilities frontier. Twenty years later, the technique introduced by these two writers was finally perfected by James E. Meade in his *Geometry of International Trade* (1952). Meade's ingenious geometric technique is the subject of part A of this chapter, part B deals with the problem of stability of international equilibrium.

A. Meade's Geometric Technique

1. Introduction

The previous chapter shows how, for a given value of the terms of trade, a point on a country's offer curve can be derived from its social indifference curves and production-possibilities frontier. In particular, given the terms of trade, production occurs at the point on the production-possibilities frontier where national income is being maximized, that is, at the point on the production-possibilities frontier at which the latter is tangent to the highest income contour line, known as the consumption-possibilities frontier. Further, consumption occurs at the point on the consumption-possibilities frontier at which the latter is tangent to the highest social indifference curve. Finally, the quantities traded (i.e., the coordinates of a point on the offer curve) are shown by the differences between the quantities consumed and the quantities produced. This procedure can be repeated for all possible values of the terms of trade, until the whole offer curve is derived. Obviously, the same procedure can be repeated for a second country; and then the analysis of international equilibrium can proceed along the familiar lines of chapter 3.

This procedure, though formally correct, nevertheless is abandoned for three reasons. First, it is cumbersome: too much time and effort are required for the job. Second, this procedure is inadequate for the analysis of the effects of, say, tariffs on the welfare of the tariff-imposing country, assuming that the social indifference map does indeed portray welfare. The imposition of a tariff will cause the offer curve of the tariff-imposing country to shift, and it will be extremely difficult to determine whether the country moves to a higher social indifference curve after the imposition of the tariff. Third, there exists an alternative approach distinctly superior to the cumbersome procedure above. This alternative approach is Meade's technique, to which we now turn.

2. *The Need for a Trade Indifference Map*

As we saw in chapter 3, international equilibrium requires that the value of exports be equal to the value of imports. Consider now a simple open economy which can buy or sell unlimited amounts of X and Y in the international market at the fixed prices p_x^0 and p_y^0, respectively. Denote the given international terms of trade (i.e., the price ratio p_x^0/p_y^0) by the symbol p_0. This information can be summarized by the equation

$$p_0 E_X + E_Y = 0, \tag{6.1}$$

where E_X and E_Y denote our country's excess demand for X and Y, respectively. (Since p_0 is positive, it should be obvious that E_X and E_Y must necessarily have opposite signs, unless they are both zero.)

Figure 6.1 illustrates graphically the information summarized by equation (6.1). The straight line *ROK*, which is usually called the *terms-of-trade line*, is the locus of points which satisfy equation (6.1).

Observe that when $E_X > 0$, commodity X is imported, and when $E_X < 0$, commodity X is exported. A similar interpretation holds for E_Y.

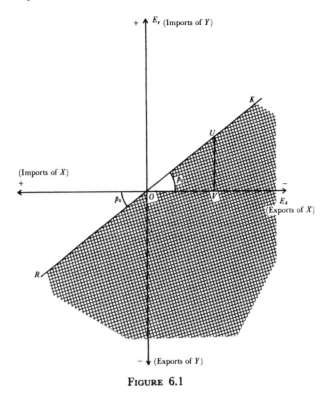

FIGURE 6.1

The first quadrant of figure 6.1 shows exports of X (i.e., negative E_X) and imports of Y (i.e., positive E_Y), and the third quadrant shows imports of X (i.e., positive E_X) and exports of Y (i.e., negative E_Y).

The terms-of-trade line ROK is another form of the budget constraint for our economy. It shows all combinations of exports and imports of X and Y which satisfy the requirement that the value of exports be equal to the value of imports. Thus, for a given amount of exports, such as OV units of X, our economy will be able to get only VU units of Y. Although it could get less than VU units of Y (by destroying, for instance, part of VU), it can never get more. This suggests that our economy can never reach any point which lies above and to the left of the terms-of-trade line. It can, however, reach points in the shaded area, that is, below and to the right of the terms-of-trade line. Nevertheless, our economy will not be able to reach the highest social indifference curve unless it actually operates on the terms-of-trade line. Accordingly, in what follows, let us concentrate on the points which lie on the terms-of-trade line and ignore the rest.

Once it is understood that the terms-of-trade line is a budget constraint, it must be clear that, given p_0, the corresponding point on our country's offer curve, that is, the optimum *trade point*, could easily be determined if somehow indifference curves for trade, not indifference curves for consumption, could be plotted in figure 6.1. Then the optimum trade point would be determined by the tangency of the terms-of-trade line to the highest indifference curve for trade. Hence, the real question is, Do indifference curves for trade, or, as Meade called them, *trade indifference curves*, exist? If they do exist, how can they be derived?

3. Derivation of Trade Indifference Curves

The main tool of Meade's analysis is the concept of the trade indifference map. Figure 6.2 illustrates this concept in the simplest possible case. We measure vertically, moving upward from the origin O, the total amount of Y consumed by the economy, and we measure horizontally, moving leftward from O, the total amount of X consumed by the economy. Accordingly, the social indifference curves have been drawn in the second quadrant with 180° rotation. Each social indifference curve shows (with respect to the origin O) the alternative combinations of consumption levels of X and Y which yield the same level of social welfare.

Assume now that the economy under consideration is an Edgeworth exchange economy endowed with OO' units of commodity X only. Consider point O' as a new origin. Measure vertically, moving upward from O', the imports of Y; horizontally, moving leftward from O', the imports of X;

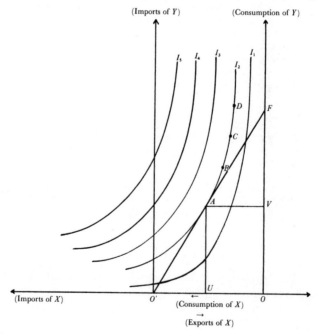

FIGURE 6.2

and rightward from O', the exports of X. The indifference curves $I_1, I_2, I_3, \ldots$, viewed with respect to O' as origin, automatically become *trade indifference curves*. That is, each indifference curve shows, with respect to the origin O', all export-import combinations which, given the initial endowment of OO' of X, will allow the economy to reach the consumption levels indicated by the same curve with respect to the origin O (i.e., to reach a certain level of welfare). For instance, the coordinates of point A with respect to the origin O (i.e., OU and OV) show one combination of consumption levels of X and Y which enables the economy to reach the level of social welfare indicated by the social indifference curve I_2. At the same time, the coordinates of point A with respect to the origin O' (i.e., $O'U$ and UA) show one combination of exports of X and imports of Y which enables the economy to reach the same social indifference curve I_2. Notice that, at point A, we have

$$\text{imports of } Y = UA = OV = \text{consumption of } Y,$$

$$\text{exports of } X = O'U = OO' - OU = OO' - \text{consumption of } X.$$

Similarly, we can say that the coordinates of points A, B, C, and D (which lie on the social indifference curve I_2) give us, with respect to the origin O, four alternative combinations of consumption levels of X and Y which enable the economy to reach the level of social welfare indicated by the social indifference curve I_2. The coordinates of the same points A, B, C, and D give us, with respect to the origin O', four alternative export-import combinations which (given the initial endowment of X) enable the economy to reach the same level of social welfare. In general, then, the indifference curves in figure 6.2, when viewed with respect to the origin O, are the familiar social indifference curves (which, following Meade, we might call consumption indifference curves). (To avoid confusion, the term "consumption indifference curve" will be used instead of the term "social indifference curve," which we have been using so far.) The same indifference curves become trade indifference curves, however, when viewed with respect to the origin O'.

Assume now that the international terms of trade are given by $p_x/p_y = p_0$. Draw a straight line through O' (fig. 6.2) with slope equal to p_0 as shown by $O'AF$. The straight line $O'AF$ is simply our economy's consumption-possibilities frontier viewed with respect to the origin O. Consumption equilibrium necessarily occurs at point A, where the consumption-possibilities frontier is tangent to the highest consumption indifference curve. What is the interpretation of the straight line $O'AF$ when viewed with respect to the origin O'? It is simply our economy's terms-of-trade line. Hence, the tangency at point A can also be viewed as the point where the terms-of-trade line becomes tangent to the highest trade indifference curve.

If we assume that the concept of the trade indifference map can be made acceptable in the general case where the economy's production-possibilities frontier is a concave curve (and not merely a point, as in the present case), this latter interpretation becomes quite useful, for the optimum trade point, as illustrated in figure 6.2 by point A, when viewed with respect to O', can be identified as the tangency between the terms-of-trade line and the highest trade indifference curve. In addition, the economy becomes better off when it moves from a lower to a higher trade indifference curve. The concept of the trade indifference map becomes a powerful tool.

So far, the concept of the trade indifference map has been illustrated by means of a simple exchange economy endowed with a fixed amount of commodity X only. But how is the trade indifference map derived in the general case where the economy's domestic availability of commodities is given by a production-possibilities frontier exhibiting increasing opportunity costs? The information needed for the construction of such a trade indifference map is contained in the consumption indifference map *and* the production-possibilities frontier. But how can we condense all this information into a trade indifference map?

Consider figure 6.3. Measure vertically along the axis OY (i.e., moving north from the origin O) positive quantities of Y, and along the axis OY' (i.e., moving south) negative quantities of Y. Similarly, measure horizontally along the axis OX' (i.e., moving west) positive quantities of X, and along the axis OX (i.e., moving east) negative quantities of X. A set of consumption indifference curves, I_i^c ($i = 1, 2, 3, 4$), has been drawn in the second quadrant as in figure 6.2. The block $OMPN$ is the economy's production-possibilities frontier. It is tangent to the highest consumption indifference curve at point P. Hence, before trade, the economy produces and consumes at point P, enjoying the level of social welfare implied by the consumption indifference curve I_1^c. What are the alternative export-import combinations which enable the economy to reach the consumption indifference curve I_1^c? These export-import combinations are given by a trade indifference curve which can be derived as follows. Imagine that the block $OMPN$ (i.e., the production-possibilities frontier) is moved up the consumption indifference curve I_1^c in such a way that the curve MPN remains tangential to I_1^c and the line MO remains in a horizontal position. The corner of the block $OMPN$ will trace out the required trade indifference curve I_1^t.

In interpreting figure 6.3, recall that imports are shown as positive quantities and exports as negative quantities.

How do we know that the trade indifference curve I_1^t gives us the information we are looking for? Concentrate on a single point on I_1^t, because what is true for one point is true for all. Consider, therefore, point V. At V the country will be exporting OC ($= DV$) units of X in exchange for OD ($= CV$) units (of imports) of Y. Does this export-import combination enable our economy to consume somewhere on the social indifference curve I_1^c?

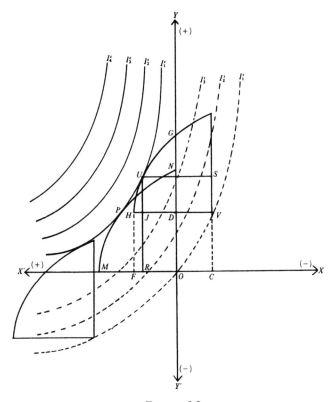

FIGURE 6.3

Further, is it not possible that with this particular combination, our economy might be able to reach a higher social indifference curve than I_1^c? The answers become obvious when it is seen that, after our economy makes the exchange of OC units of X for OD units of Y, the best it can do is to consume along the curve $FHUG$, where the straight line FH is perpendicular. Thus, it will actually consume at point U (where the production block is tangent to I_1^c). It will produce VJ units of X out of which it will export DV units and consume only JD. Similarly, it will produce VS ($= JU$) units of Y which along with the imports of Y given by CV (or RJ) make up the total domestic consumption of Y (i.e., RU). Similar reasoning applies to all other points lying on I_1^t. Therefore, the trade indifference curve I_1^t shows the alternative export–import combinations which enable the economy to reach the consumption indifference curve I_1^c.

In general, a trade indifference curve can be derived for each consumption indifference curve. Imagine the block $OMPN$ (i.e., the production-possibilities frontier) placed tangentially against a consumption indifference curve, such as I_2^c, and then moved along this I_2^c curve. A new trade indifference curve will be traced by the corner of the block $OMPN$, as illustrated by the I_2^t curve. Observe that I_2^t lies consistently above and to the left of I_1^t, since I_2^c lies consistently above and to the left of I_1^c. Consequently, there exists, in general, a trade indifference curve corresponding to every consumption indifference curve; the higher the consumption indifference curve, the higher the corresponding trade indifference curve. Thus, suppose that the trade indifference curve I_i^t corresponds to the consumption indifference curve I_i^c (for $i = 1, 2, \ldots$). Then, if I_5^c is higher than I_3^c, I_5^t must lie totally to the left and above I_3^t, and so on.

4. Properties of the Trade Indifference Map

Some of the most important properties of the trade indifference map are described as follows.

1. There exists a trade indifference curve corresponding to every consumption indifference curve; the higher the consumption indifference curve, the higher the corresponding trade indifference curve.

2. The slope of a trade indifference curve at any point is equal to the slope of the corresponding consumption indifference curve and the slope of the production-possibilities frontier at the corresponding point. Thus, in terms of figure 6.4, the slope of the trade indifference curve I_1^t through T_1 is necessarily equal to the slope of the consumption indifference curve I_1^c and the slope of the production-possibilities frontier at point C_1. This can be

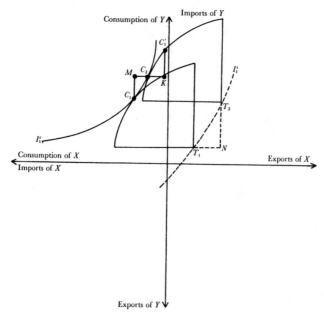

FIGURE 6.4

proved as follows. Let the production block slide along I_1^c from C_1 to C_2, with its corner moving from T_1 to T_2. The movement from T_1 to T_2 implies that the exports of X increase by $T_1 N$ and the imports of Y by NT_2. Further, the increase in exports of X (i.e., $T_1 N$) can be decomposed into: (a) a decrease in the consumption of X by MC_2 (since on I_1^c we move from C_1 to C_2) and (b) an increase in the production of X by $C_2 K$ (since on the production block $T_2 C_2$ we move from C_1' to C_2). Therefore, $T_1 N = MC_2 + C_2 K$. Similarly, the increase in imports of Y (i.e., NT_2) can be decomposed into: (a) an increase in the consumption of Y by $C_1 M$ and (b) a decrease in the production of Y by KC_1'. Thus, $NT_2 = C_1 M + KC_1'$. (Note that point C_1' on the production block $T_2 C_2$ corresponds to point C_1 on the production block $T_1 C_1$.)

The slope of the straight-line segment joining points T_1 and T_2 on I_2^t equals $NT_2 / T_1 N = (C_1 M + KC_1')/(MC_2 + C_2 K)$. Let the production block $T_2 C_2$ slide along the consumption indifference curve I_1^c until it coincides with the production block $T_1 C_1$. The ratio $C_1 M/MC_2$ will approach the slope of the I_1^c curve at point C_1, and the ratio $KC_1'/C_2 K$ will approach the slope of the production block at point C_1 (or C_1'). Since at point C_1 the production block is tangent to the I_1^c curve, we must have (in the limit)

$$\frac{C_1 M}{MC_2} = \frac{KC_1'}{C_2 K} \quad \text{or} \quad \frac{C_2 K}{MC_2} = \frac{KC_1'}{C_1 M}.$$

Therefore,

$$\frac{NT_2}{T_1 N} = \frac{C_1 M + KC_1'}{MC_2 + C_2 K} = \frac{C_1 M[1 + (KC_1'/C_1 M)]}{MC_2[1 + (C_2 K/MC_2)]} = \frac{C_1 M}{MC_2} = \frac{KC_1'}{C_2 K}.$$

In words, the slope of the I_1^t curve at T_1 is equal to the slope of the I_1^c curve and the slope of the production block at the point C_1.

3. As a result of property 2, it follows that if the I_i^c curve is negatively sloped, the I_i^t curve will also be negatively sloped.

4. Likewise, if the I_i^c curve is always convex, the I_i^t curve will also be convex under conditions of increasing opportunity costs.[1]

These properties are also discussed (more rigorously) in appendix 6A.

5. The Offer Curve

The trade indifference map can be used for the purpose of deriving the offer curve. As the preceding section demonstrates, there is a trade indifference curve corresponding to every consumption indifference curve; the higher the consumption indifference curve, the higher the trade indifference curve. Further, for any given international price ratio, the economy will consume

---

1. For the derivation of trade indifference curves under conditions of decreasing opportunity costs as well as for some other important properties of the trade indifference map, see Meade, 1952).

on the consumption-possibilities frontier at the point where the latter is tangent to the highest consumption indifference curve. But as should be clear by now, the optimum trade point can be determined by the tangency of the terms-of-trade line, which is parallel to the consumption-possibilities frontier, to the highest possible trade indifference curve. As the international price ratio changes, the terms-of-trade line rotates through the origin so that its slope is again equal to the (new) international price ratio. A new tangency is determined between the (new) terms-of-trade line and the highest possible trade indifference curve, giving us another point on the offer curve. By allowing the international terms of trade to vary from zero to infinity, we can thus trace out all tangencies between the successive terms-of-trade lines and the trade indifference curves, that is, all optimum trade points. The locus of all these tangencies, or optimum trade points, is the economy's offer curve.

Figure 6.5 illustrates the derivation of the offer curve. Consider the terms-of-trade line TOT_1, which is tangent to the trade indifference curve I_1^t at the origin. For the terms of trade implied by TOT_1, say p_1, our economy does not wish to participate in international trade. (Put differently, p_1 corresponds to our economy's pretrade equilibrium price ratio.) Imagine that commodity X becomes progressively more expensive in the international market. The terms-of-trade line will rotate through the origin, becoming steeper and steeper, as illustrated by the terms-of- trade lines TOT_2 and TOT_3. As this happens, the optimum trade point (i.e., the tangency between

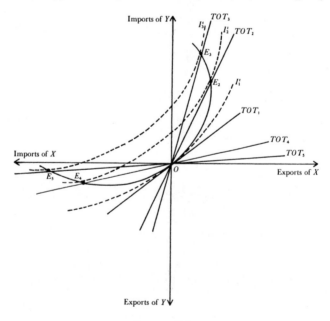

FIGURE 6.5

the rotating terms-of-trade line and the trade indifference curves) will move from the origin into the first quadrant, as illustrated by points E_2 and E_3. The locus of all optimum trade points in the first quadrant is given by the continuous curve OE_2E_3. In particular, this is the part of the offer curve which corresponds to terms of trade higher than p_1. The remaining part of the offer curve is derived by allowing the international terms of trade to fall continuously from p_1 to zero. As this happens, the terms-of-trade line will rotate through the origin, becoming flatter and flatter than TOT_1, as illustrated by the terms-of-trade lines TOT_4 and TOT_5. The optimum trade point will move from the origin into the third quadrant, as illustrated by points E_4 and E_5. The locus of all optimum trade points in the third quadrant (i.e., OE_4E_5) is the other part of the offer curve. Accordingly, the offer curve is given by the solid curve $E_5E_4OE_2E_3$.

It should be clearly understood why figure 6.5 has *three* trade indifference curves but *five* terms-of-trade lines. First, note that the I_1^t curve passes through the origin. It follows that the I_1^t curve corresponds to the consumption indifference curve (say I_1^c) that the country's production-possibilities frontier touches tangentially in the absence of international trade. Further, the slope of I_1^t at the origin, as shown by the slope of the terms-of-trade line TOT_1, necessarily corresponds to the pretrade price ratio, that is, the slope of the I_1^c curve at the pretrade equilibrium point. From the analysis so far, it must be clear that our economy will consume on the I_1^c curve—and that, therefore, the optimum trade point will be on the I_1^t curve—if, and only if, the international price ratio is equal to the pretrade price ratio, as shown by the slope of TOT_1. For any other international price ratio, the economy will be able to consume on a higher consumption indifference curve than the I_1^c curve and, therefore, trade on a higher trade indifference curve than the I_1^t curve. Accordingly, the only point of the I_1^t curve that belongs to the offer curve is the origin O.

For any international price ratio other than the one that coincides with the pretrade price ratio (i.e., the slope of TOT_1), our economy will be consuming on a higher consumption indifference curve than the I_1^c curve and, therefore, trade on a higher trade indifference curve than the I_1^t curve. For this reason, all trade indifference curves lower than the I_1^t curve have been omitted from figure 6.5 as irrelevant to our problem. However, given any other trade indifference curve higher than the I_1^t curve,[2] the terms-of-trade line will necessarily become tangent to it at two different points for two different values of the international price ratio. For instance, points E_2 and E_4 lie on the same trade indifference curve I_2^t and points E_3 and E_5 lie

---

2. We are now interested in trade indifference curves which lie partially in the first and third quadrants, for any trade indifference curves higher than the I_1^t curve but lying totally in the second quadrant will be out of reach for our economy. The possibility of a trade indifference curve lying in the first and second, or the second and third, quadrants has been ignored for convenience.

on I_3^c. This is demonstrated in figure 6.6 in terms of more familiar tools. The curve $ORP_3E_1P_2S$ is the economy's production-possibilities frontier, while I_1^c and I_2^c are two consumption indifference curves. In the absence of international trade, the economy produces and consumes at point E_1 (which corresponds to the origin of fig. 6.5). For the international price ratio given by the slope of the consumption-possibilities frontier P_2E_2 and which is higher than the pretrade price ratio (i.e., the slope of I_1^c at E_1), the economy will produce at P_2 and consume at E_2 on the consumption indifference curve I_2^c. This situation corresponds to point E_2 of figure 6.5. In addition our economy can consume on the consumption indifference curve I_2^c if the international price ratio becomes equal to the slope of the consumption-possibilities frontier P_3E_3. This situation corresponds to point E_4 of figure 6.5. Thus, the economy can reach the same consumption indifference curve I_2 for two distinct values of the international price ratio—one higher and one lower than the pretrade price ratio. At the higher terms of trade, the economy exports X and imports Y (i.e., the optimum trade point lies in the first quadrant of fig. 6.5), and at the lower terms of trade, the economy imports X and exports Y (i.e., the optimum trade point lies in the third quadrant of fig. 6.5).

The offer curve illustrated in figure 6.5 has two important properties: (*a*) it passes through the origin and lies totally above and to the left of the

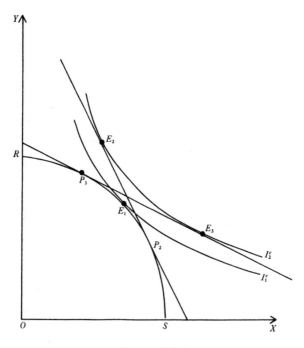

FIGURE 6.6

terms-of-trade line TOT_1, whose slope is equal to the pretrade price ratio, and (*b*) the terms-of-trade line TOT_1 is tangent to the offer curve at the origin, that is, the slope of the offer curve at the origin shows the pretrade price ratio. The first property follows directly from the fact that all trade indifference curves higher than I_1' (i.e., the trade indifference curve passing through the origin) lie above and to the left of I_1'. The second property follows from the assumed continuity of the offer curve and the fact that the terms-of-trade line TOT_1 is tangent to I_1' at the origin.

A more rigorous proof of the second property—the first should be obvious from figure 6.5—is as follows. We know that for any point on the offer curve, equation (6.1), reproduced below for convenience, must be satisfied:

$$pE_X + E_Y = 0. \tag{6.1}$$

Taking the total differential, we have $E_X \, dp + p \, dE_X + dE_Y = 0$, or $dE_Y/dE_X = -p - E_X(dp/dE_X)$. This last equation reduces to $dE_Y/dE_X = -p$, where $E_X = 0$. This proves our proposition.

Having derived the offer curve, we can determine the optimum trade, consumption, and production points for any given value of the terms of trade. Assume that in figure 6.7 the terms of trade are given by the slope of TOT_2, which intersects the offer curve at point O'. Place the production block in position with its corner at O'. By the nature of the construction of the trade indifference curve (I_2') passing through O', the production block

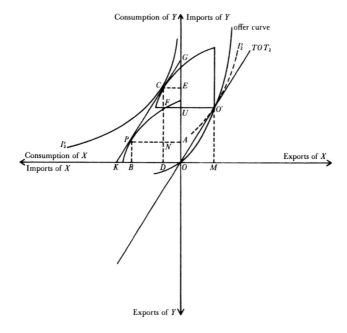

FIGURE 6.7

will be tangential to the corresponding consumption indifference curve (I_2^c) at the corresponding point (C). The common slope of the production block and the consumption indifference curve at point C is equal to the slope of the trade indifference curve at O'; that is, the slope of the terms-of-trade line TOT_2 is equal to the slope of the consumption-possibilities frontier *KPCG*. The coordinates of point O' (in the first quadrant) with respect to the origin O show the quantities of X and Y that our economy is willing to export and import, respectively, at the given terms of trade. The quantities of X and Y consumed are shown by the coordinates of point C (in the second quadrant) with respect to the origin O. Finally, the quantities produced are shown by the coordinates of point C with respect to the corner of the production block O'. The value of output consumed in terms of commodity X is given by the horizontal distance OK. If commodity Y is used as the numeraire, however, the value of output consumed is given by the vertical distance OG. In addition, the same measurements show the value of output produced. This is easily verified if we imagine the production block sliding downward along the consumption-possibilities frontier and the terms-of-trade line until its corner O' coincides with the origin of the diagram (O). Since the production block continues to be tangential to the consumption-possibilities frontier (say at point P), the value of output produced must be equal to the value of output consumed.

It might be useful to consider the following relationships in figure 6.7:

$$AP = OB = O'F = MD, \qquad OA = BP = FC = UE,$$
$$EC = UF = OD, \qquad DC = OE,$$
$$OB - OD = DB = NP = UO' = OM = \text{exports of } X,$$
$$OE - OA = AE = NC = DC - FC = DF = OU = MO' = \text{imports of } Y.$$

6. International Equilibrium

The same procedure can be repeated to derive the offer curve of a second country. International equilibrium can then be shown in terms of the two offer curves by superimposing one diagram on the other, after one country's diagram has been rotated 180° to match the axes of the other.

Figure 6.8 illustrates how international equilibrium can be determined. Assume that B's diagram has been rotated 180°. In the first quadrant of figure 6.8, measure along the horizontal axis A's exports of X and B's imports of X, and along the vertical axis measure A's imports of Y and B's exports of Y. Similarly, in the third quadrant, measure along the horizontal axis A's imports of X and B's exports of X, and along the vertical axis A's exports of Y and B's imports of Y. In the second quadrant, measure along the horizontal axis A's consumption of X, and along the vertical axis A's consumption of Y. In the fourth quadrant, measure along the horizontal axis B's consumption of X, and along the vertical axis B's consumption of Y.

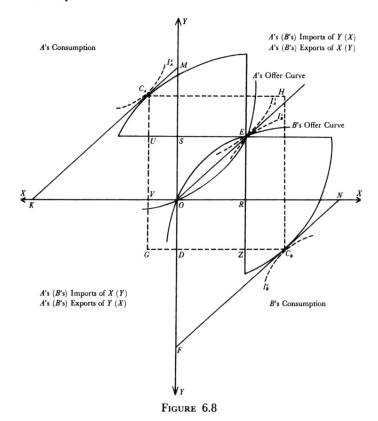

FIGURE 6.8

International equilibrium occurs at point E in the first quadrant where the two offer curves intersect each other. Country A exports OR units of X to B, and B exports OS units of Y to A. The equilibrium terms of trade are given by the slope of the vector OE, which is equal to the ratio OS/OR. Country A is consuming at point C_A in the second quadrant (i.e., OV units of X and VC_A units of Y), and country B at point C_B in the fourth quadrant (i.e., OD units of Y and DC_B units of X). Country A is producing EU units of X and UC_A units of Y, while B is producing EZ units of Y and ZC_B units of X. Thus, the total production of X by both countries is given by $EU + ZC_B = GZ + ZC_B = GC_B$, and the total production of Y is given by $EZ + UC_A = GU + UC_A = GC_A$. The sides of the rectangle GC_BHC_A show the total production of X and Y. But the sides of the same rectangle also show the total consumption of X and Y, because $SU + DC_B = GD + DG_B = GC_B$ and $VC_A + RZ = GV + VC_A = GC_A$. In other words, the rectangle GC_BHC_A can be considered a *production box*. The coordinates of point E with respect to the corner C_A show A's production (or endowments) of X and Y, while the coordinates of E with respect to C_B show B's production of X and Y. Similarly, the coordinates of point O with respect to $C_A(C_B)$ show A's (B's) consumption of X and Y, and the coordinates of O with respect to E (or vice versa) show A's exports of X and imports of Y. Note that the terms-of-trade line OE is tangent to A's trade indifference curve I_A^t and B's curve I_B^t at point E. Note, too, that A's consumption-possibilities frontier KC_AM is tangent to A's consumption indifference curve I_A^c and that B's consumption-possibilities frontier is tangent to B's consumption indifference curve I_B^c. Therefore, all equilibrium conditions are indeed satisfied.

Figure 6.8 brings together production, consumption, and trade in an ingenious way. A multitude of relationships are brought to light in figure 6.8. This diagram, which we owe to J. E. Meade, is the culmination of the neoclassical model.

Figure 6.8 can also be used to show that the equilibrium terms of trade have to lie between the pretrade price ratios of the two countries. This is shown in Figure 6.9, where only the tangents to the two offer curves of figure 6.8 at the origin have been drawn. Thus, the line TOT_A has a slope equal to A's pretrade price ratio (p_A) and TOT_B has a slope equal to B's pretrade price ratio (p_B). Country A's offer curve must lie above and to the left of TOT_A, and B's below and to the right of TOT_B. Therefore, the only area where the two offer curves can intersect is the shaded cone in the first quadrant. This means that the equilibrium terms of trade will definitely lie between p_A and p_B.

What the preceding analysis and figure 6.9 show is that, if international equilibrium exists, it will necessarily occur in the region (p_A, p_B). But how do we know that international equilibrium necessarily exists?

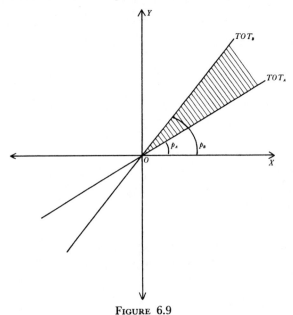

FIGURE 6.9

Country A's offer curve necessarily lies above TOT_A (fig. 6.9). Assume, therefore, that the international price ratio is initially equal to p_A and let it rise continuously. Country A's offer curve will start from the origin and lie above TOT_A. How would A's offer curve behave as the international price ratio tends to infinity, that is, as commodity X tends to become infinitely more expensive relative to Y? Obviously, as $p \to \infty$, country A can acquire unlimited amounts of Y by offering only an infinitesimal amount of X. But this means that, as $p \to \infty$, A's offer curve will tend to approach asymptotically the vertical axis. Thus, A's offer curve will not remain in the shaded area of figure 6.9 but will eventually go beyond it.

Applying the same argument to country B, we observe that, as $p \to 0$, B's offer curve will start from the origin with slope equal to p_B, lie below TOT_B, and approach the horizontal axis asymptotically. Therefore, on the assumption that the two offer curves are indeed continuous they will necessarily intersect each other at least once in the shaded area of figure 6.9.

It should be noted that if $p_A > p_B$, then TOT_A will become steeper than TOT_B and the shaded cone will move the third quadrant. This conclusion depends upon the assumption that the pretrade equilibrium price ratios are unique. As was shown earlier, the existence of multiple pretrade equilibria might violate this conclusion.

B. Elasticities, Stability, and Multiple Equilibria

This section is devoted to the properties of international equilibrium, in particular, whether or not it is stable and unique. Also, the necessary and sufficient conditions for stability will be discussed.

1. Three Important Elasticities

Consider the offer curve in figure 6.10. Define three elasticities in relation to this offer curve at any selected point, such as K, as follows.

a) The *elasticity of the offer curve*, denoted by ε, is defined as

$$\varepsilon \equiv \frac{\% \text{ change in imports}}{\% \text{ change in exports}} = \frac{dY/Y}{dX/X} = \frac{dY}{dX}\frac{X}{Y}. \tag{6.2}$$

Given equation (6.2), the elasticity of the offer curve at point K can be determined as follows. First draw the tangent to the offer curve at K and let it intersect the horizontal axis at point D. Then draw a vertical line through K and let it intersect the horizontal axis at point C. Now the slope of the tangent to the offer curve at K coincides with the derivative dY/dX at K. Therefore,

$$\varepsilon = \frac{CK}{DC} \times \frac{OC}{CK} = \frac{OC}{DC}. \tag{6.3}$$

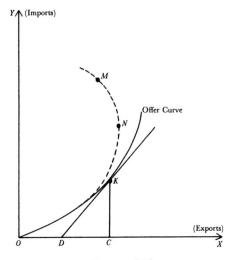

FIGURE 6.10

As long as point D lies between the origin and point C (as in fig. 6.10), the elasticity of the offer curve will be positive and greater than unity. If the offer curve were a straight line through the origin, point D would coincide with the origin and ε would be equal to unity at all points of the offer curve. If the offer curve were backward bending, as shown by the broken curve in figure 6.10, and if we were to estimate ε at a point (such as M) on the backward-bending portion of the curve, then point D would lie to the right of point C; the distance DC would be negative and so would ε. (This is also seen from the fact that the derivative dY/dX at the backward-bending portion of the offer curve is negative.) At the point where the offer curve stops sloping upward and begins bending backward, that is, the point (such as N) where the tangent becomes perpendicular, ε becomes infinite, because OC is strictly positive, while DC becomes zero.

  b) The *elasticity of demand for imports*, denoted by e, is defined as

$$e \equiv \frac{\% \text{ change in imports}}{\% \text{ change in the relative price of imports}}.$$

Since, along the offer curve, the value of exports equals the value of imports, that is, $p_x X = p_y Y$, the relative price of imports (i.e., p_y/p_x) is given by the ratio X/Y. Thus, the above formula becomes

$$e = \frac{(dY/Y)}{[d(X/Y)]/(X/Y)} = \frac{dY}{d(X/Y)} \frac{X}{Y^2} = \frac{dY}{(Y\,dX - X\,dY)/Y^2} \frac{X}{Y^2}$$

$$= \frac{(dY/dX)(X/Y)}{1 - [(dY/dX)(X/Y)]} = \frac{\varepsilon}{1 - \varepsilon}. \tag{6.4}$$

Using equation (6.3), we can measure the elasticity of demand for imports, e, as follows:

$$e = \frac{\varepsilon}{1 - \varepsilon} = \frac{OC/DC}{1 - (OC/DC)} = \frac{OC}{DC - OC}. \tag{6.5}$$

From equations (6.4) and (6.5), it follows that when the elasticity of the offer curve, ε, is positive and greater than unity, the elasticity of demand for imports, e, is negative and greater than unity (in absolute terms), that is, the demand for imports is elastic. When ε is infinite, $e = -1$. As was noted earlier, ε becomes infinite when the tangent to the offer curve becomes vertical and $DC = 0$. Thus, from equation (6.5), when $DC = 0$, $e = -1$. The same conclusion can be derived from equation (6.4) after it is rearranged as follows:

$$e = \frac{1}{(1/\varepsilon) - 1}. \tag{6.4}'$$

Thus, as $\varepsilon \to \infty$, $(1/\varepsilon) \to 0$ and $e \to (-1)$.

Furthermore, when ε tends to unity from above (i.e., when ε assumes a sequence of values such as $2, 1.9, 1.8, 1.7, \ldots, 1$), then e tends to $-\infty$, that is, the demand for imports becomes infinitely elastic. Also note that when $0 < \varepsilon < 1$, the elasticity of demand for imports necessarily becomes positive, which means that imports are necessarily a Giffen good.[3] Finally, notice that when ε is negative (i.e., when the offer curve is backward bending), the elasticity of demand is necessarily negative but less than unity in absolute terms.

It seems more interesting to consider ε as a function of e instead of considering e as a function of ε, as we have been doing so far. Thus, solving equation (6.4) for ε, we get

$$\varepsilon = \frac{e}{1 + e}. \tag{6.6}$$

In general, the elasticity of demand for imports is expected to be negative.[4] If it is also greater than unity in absolute terms (i.e., $e < -1$), then $\varepsilon > 0$ and the offer curve will be upward sloping, that is, it will look like the solid curve of figure 6.10. On the other hand, if the demand for imports is inelastic (i.e., $-1 < e < 0$), then $\varepsilon < 0$, which implies that the offer curve will be backward bending (in the region where $\varepsilon < 0$). Conversely, if the

---

3. A Giffen good is a commodity whose consumption falls as its price falls. Notice that while it is necessary that the imported commodity be a Giffen good for the imports demand elasticity to be positive, this is not a sufficient condition (see n. 4 below).

4. Even if the imported commodity were a Giffen good, the elasticity of demand for imports might still be negative because imports ≡ domestic consumption − domestic production. Thus, even if domestic consumption falls as imports become cheaper, it does not necessarily follow that imports also fall because domestic production falls too. Imports will fall if, and only if, domestic consumption falls faster than domestic production. This is ruled out as unrealistic.

offer curve is backward bending, the demand for imports is necessarily inelastic in that region, and vice versa.

c) The *elasticity of supply of exports*, denoted by η, is defined as

$$\eta \equiv \frac{\% \text{ change in exports}}{\% \text{ change in relative price of exports}}.$$

The relative price of exports is simply the ratio p_x/p_y, which along the offer curve is given by the ratio Y/X. Substituting the ratio Y/X for the relative price of exports in the above formula, we get

$$\eta \equiv \frac{dX/X}{[d(Y/X)]/(Y/X)} = \frac{dX}{d(Y/X)} \frac{Y}{X^2}$$

$$= \frac{dX}{(X\,dY - Y\,dX)/X^2} \frac{Y}{X^2} = \frac{1}{[(dY/dX)(X/Y)] - 1} = \frac{1}{\varepsilon - 1}. \qquad (6.7)$$

In addition, using equation (6.3), we can measure the elasticity of supply of exports, η, as

$$\eta = \frac{1}{\varepsilon - 1} = \frac{1}{(OC/DC) - 1} = \frac{DC}{OC - DC}. \qquad (6.8)$$

Finally, adding the elasticity of demand for imports as given by equation (6.4) to the elasticity of supply of exports as given by equation (6.7), we get

$$e + \eta = -1, \qquad (6.9)$$

or

$$\eta = -(1 + e). \qquad (6.9)'$$

That is to say, the sum of the elasticities of the demand for imports (e) and supply of exports (η) is always equal to -1. Therefore, when the demand for imports is elastic (i.e., $e < -1$), the elasticity of supply of exports must be positive, that is, the supply of exports must be upward sloping. However, when the demand for imports becomes inelastic (i.e., $-1 < e < 0$), the elasticity of supply of exports is necessarily negative and the supply curve for exports becomes backward bending.

As noted earlier, when $e < -1$, the offer curve is positively sloped, and when $-1 < e < 0$, it is backward bending. Therefore, when the supply of exports becomes backward bending, so does the offer curve, and when the supply for exports is upward sloping, the offer curve is also upward sloping. These relationships can be easily verified. Let Z and M stand for exports and imports, respectively, and denote their prices by p_z and p_m. Along the offer curve, we necessarily have $(p_m/p_z)M = Z$; that is, the value of imports equals the value of exports. If the demand for imports (M) is elastic, then as p_m/p_z falls, the product $(p_m/p_z)M$ rises. But $(p_m/p_z)M = Z$; hence Z rises, too. Thus, when the demand for imports (M) is elastic, Z ($\equiv$ supply of exports) rises as p_m/p_z falls, or as p_z/p_m rises. Now the supply of exports is the relationship between Z and p_z/p_m. Thus, when the demand for imports is elastic, Z is an increasing function of p_z/p_m and the supply curve for exports is upward sloping. In addition, M is a decreasing function of p_m/p_z, or an increasing function of p_z/p_m. It follows that, when the demand for imports is elastic, both Z and M change in the same direction as p_m/p_z changes, and thus the offer curve is upward sloping.

When the demand for imports is inelastic, as p_m/p_z falls (or as p_z/p_m rises), the product $(p_m/p_z)M$, and therefore Z, falls. Hence, as p_z/p_m rises, Z falls, which shows that the supply of exports is backward bending. In addition, M is an increasing function of p_z/p_m. Hence, as p_m/p_z changes, Z and M necessarily move in opposite directions, and the offer curve becomes backward bending.

The relationships among the three elasticities (e, η, and ε) and the shape of the offer curve are summarized in table 6.1, where it is assumed that the elasticity of demand for imports is strictly negative.

TABLE 6.1

	e (Elasticity of Demand for Imports)	$\eta = -(1+e)$ (Elasticity of Supply of Exports)	$\varepsilon = e/(1+e)$ (Elasticity of the Offer Curve)	Shape of the Offer Curve
Case 1. . . .	$e = -\infty$	$\eta = \infty$	$\varepsilon = 1$	Elasticity of offer curve is, in general, unity at origin. When offer curve is a straight line through origin, $\varepsilon = 1$ throughout its length.
Case 2. . . .	$e < -1$	$\eta > 0$	$\varepsilon > 1$	Offer curve is upward sloping. Its tangent (at any point in this region) intersects the horizontal axis at latter's positive part, as shown in fig. 6.10.
Case 3. . . .	$e = -1$	$\eta = 0$	$\varepsilon = \infty$	Offer curve is perpendicular. This is illustrated in fig. 6.10 by point N.
Case 4. . . .	$-1 < e < 0$	$\eta < 0$	$\varepsilon < 0$	Offer curve is backward bending.

2. Stability

As indicated in chapter 3, the general equilibrium of a two-commodity model can be demonstrated in terms of a single market because of Walras's Law. Thus, if the market for X is in equilibrium, the market for Y must also be in equilibrium, and vice versa. This is seen from the fact that equation (6.1) holds for both countries. Using the superscripts A and B to indicate the countries and adding these two equations together, we get

$$p(E_X^A + E_X^B) + (E_Y^A + E_Y^B) = 0. \qquad (6.10)$$

Thus, when $E_X^A + E_X^B = 0$, it follows that $E_Y^A + E_Y^B = 0$, and vice versa. Therefore, general equilibrium in a two-commodity model can be determined by concentrating on a single market. Is it also possible to study the stability of a two-commodity model by concentrating on a single market? In other words, is it true that, when an equilibrium point in the market for commodity X is stable, the corresponding equilibrium in the market for commodity Y is also stable? This is indeed the case. Thus, when the market for X is stable, the market for Y is also stable, and vice versa.

Suppose that $p = p_0$ is an equilibrium price; that is, at $p = p_0$ both the market for X and the market for Y are cleared. Suppose, further, that the equilibrium reached in the market for X is stable. That is, for relative prices higher than p_0, the supply of X is greater than the demand for X, and for relative prices lower than p_0, the demand for X is larger than the supply of X. Does it necessarily follow that the corresponding equilibrium in the market for Y is also stable? That is, does it follow that for relative prices higher than $1/p_0$ the supply of Y is larger than the demand for Y, and for relative prices lower than $1/p_0$ the demand for Y is larger than the supply of Y? The answer is yes. As we have seen, whether or not the system is in equilibrium, the following equation holds:

$$p(E_X^A + E_X^B) + (E_Y^A + E_Y^B) = 0. \qquad (6.10)$$

Given that $p > 0$, it follows that, when the sum $(E_X^A + E_X^B)$ is positive, the sum $(E_Y^A + E_Y^B)$ is necessarily negative, and when $(E_X^A + E_X^B)$ is negative, the sum $(E_Y^A + E_Y^B)$ is positive. Thus, the statement "for $p > p_0$, we have $(E_X^A + E_X^B) < 0$" is equivalent to "for $1/p < 1/p_0$, we have $(E_Y^A + E_Y^B) > 0$," and the statement "for $p < p_0$, we have $(E_X^A + E_X^B) > 0$" is equivalent to "for $1/p > 1/p_0$, we have $(E_Y^A + E_Y^B) < 0$," and vice versa. Therefore, when the equilibrium in the market for X is stable, the corresponding equilibrium in the market for Y is also stable; and when the equilibrium in the market for Y is stable, the corresponding equilibrium in the market for X is also stable. Similarly, when the equilibrium in one market is unstable, the corresponding equilibrium in the other market is also unstable. Let us discuss the stability of the system by concentrating on a single market. (Refer back to the analysis of chap. 3, sec. 4.)

Whether a particular position of equilibrium is stable or not depends on the process of adjustment that is specified. Unfortunately, there is not a unique process of adjustment that one can specify. The main drawback of the process we are using is the implicit assumption that the value of exports equals the value of imports at all times, that is, that both countries

are always on their respective offer curves. This is in the spirit of the
Walrasian *tâtonnement* process, in which no trade takes place except at the
final equilibrium. Alfred Marshall, on the other hand, analyzed stability in
terms of points which were off the offer curves. (The mathematical formulation of Marshall's analysis is given in Samuelson [1947].) The stability
condition derived below depends crucially on the assumed specific dynamical
generalization of the static model. For other dynamic assumptions, it should
not be surprising if a different stability condition or conditions are found.

Let us discard the market for Y and concentrate on the market for X.
Suppose that at the equilibrium point, commodity X is being exported from
B to A. (It should be noted that this is not a restrictive assumption.) What
are the necessary and sufficient conditions for the equilibrium to be stable?

On the basis of the notation adopted earlier in this chapter, the equilibrium
condition for the market of commodity X is given by

$$E_X^A + E_X^B = 0. \tag{6.11}$$

In other words, the sum of A's and B's excess demand for commodity X
must be zero. Observe that both E_X^A and E_X^B are functions of the price
ratio p_x/p_y, which we shall simply denote by the letter p. For stability, it is
required that the aggregate demand curve for X at the equilibrium point
be downward sloping, as shown in figure 6.11 by the solid curve DD. Thus,
for any p higher than p_0, the aggregate excess demand for X is negative,
causing p to fall. For instance, at $p = p_2$, there is negative excess demand

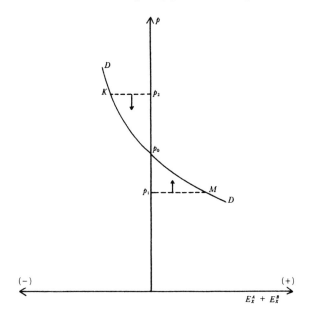

FIGURE 6.11

(or positive excess supply) for X equal to the horizontal distance Kp_2, and the price ratio will tend to fall toward p_0, as shown by the arrow on the diagram. Similarly, for any p lower than p_0, the aggregate demand for X is positive, causing p to rise. Thus, for $p = p_1$ there is a positive excess demand (or negative excess supply) for X equal to the horizontal distance p_1M, and p will tend to rise toward p_0.

The slope of the demand curve DD of figure 6.11 is given by the first derivative of the function $(E_X^A + E_X^B)$ with respect to p. For stability, it is required that the slope of DD at the equilibrium point be negative, that is,

$$\frac{dE_X^A}{dp} + \frac{dE_X^B}{dp} < 0. \tag{6.12}$$

for the value of p satisfying equation (6.11).

Inequality (6.12) can be rewritten as

$$\left(\frac{dE_X^A}{dp} \frac{p}{E_X^A}\right) \frac{E_X^A}{p} + \left(\frac{dE_X^B}{dp} \frac{p}{E_X^B}\right) \frac{E_X^B}{p} < 0. \tag{6.13}$$

The term in the first pair of parentheses is the elasticity of A's demand for imports (which we shall denote by the symbol e_A). The term in the second pair of parentheses is the elasticity of B's supply of exports (which we shall denote by η_B).[5] Inequality (6.13) can now be simplified to

$$\frac{1}{p} (e_A E_X^A + \eta_B E_X^B) < 0. \tag{6.13'}$$

Since p is necessarily positive and, further, at the equilibrium point we necessarily have (see eq. [6.11])

$$E_X^A = -E_X^B > 0,$$

inequality (6.13)' reduces to

$$e_A - \eta_B < 0. \tag{6.14}$$

(Remember that we have been assuming that X is exported from B to A. Thus, $E_X^A > 0$ and $E_X^B < 0$.)

Inequality (6.14) is a necessary and sufficient condition for the stability of international equilibrium. It is expressed in terms of A's demand elasticity for imports and B's supply elasticity of exports. By making use of equation (6.9)', condition (6.14) can be expressed in terms of the demand elasticities for imports of the two countries. Thus, substituting from (6.9)',

$$e_A + e_B < -1. \tag{6.15}$$

Inequality (6.15) is known as the *Marshall–Lerner condition*. However, it seems more accurate to say that this is the Marshallian condition, because only Marshall was interested in the stability of a pure trade model such as

---

5. Let us use the symbols adopted in the preceding section for the three elasticities. The subscripts A and B indicate the country whose elasticity is being considered.

the one discussed in this chapter.[6] Lerner's interest was with the foreign-exchange market.

Since both demand elasticities for imports are generally negative, the Marshallian condition (which is both necessary and sufficient for the stability of the present model) requires that the sum of the elasticities of demand for imports in absolute terms be greater than unity. It follows that a sufficient (but not necessary) condition for stability is that the demand for imports of one of the two countries be elastic at the equilibrium point. In terms of offer curves, therefore, a sufficient (but not necessary) condition for stability is that the offer curve of one of the two countries be upward sloping (i.e., not backward bending) around the equilibrium point. To put it differently, a necessary (but not sufficient) condition for instability is that both demand curves for imports (i.e., A's demand for imports of X and B's demand for imports of Y) be inelastic at the equilibrium point, which in terms of the offer curves means that both offer curves must necessarily be backward bending around the equilibrium point for the occurrence of instability. It should be emphasized that this is only a necessary condition. That is, it is quite possible for both offer curves to be backward bending at the equilibrium point and yet equilibrium be stable—because condition (6.15) is satisfied. An example of this case is given in the following section.

3. Multiple Equilibria

The preceding analysis deals with the problem of *local stability*. An equilibrium point is said to be *locally stable* if, for any small displacements around it, the system returns to the original equilibrium. On the other hand, if the system returns to the equilibrium point irrespective of how large the displacement is, the system is called *globally stable*. A globally stable equilibrium is necessarily unique, for if a second equilibrium exists, a displacement from the first equilibrium point which puts the economy on the second cannot possibly generate forces that will bring the system back to the original equilibrium; otherwise, the second point would not be an equilibrium point.

The history of the pure theory of trade is replete with cases of (posttrade) multiple equilibria. Marshall provided a geometric argument to the effect that offer curves have an odd number of intersections, with each unstable point bounded by two stable ones.[7] Several modern economists, most notably Bhagwati and Johnson,[8] Scarf, and Gale, have provided examples where Marshall's proposition is not generally true. From the point of view of pure theory, many strange possibilities cannot be ruled out by a priori reasoning.

6. In fact, as noted earlier, Marshall had postulated a different dynamic system than the one discussed in the text (see Samuelson 1947).
7. See Marshall (1879, pp. 24–25; 1923, pp. 352–54).
8. Johnson (private correspondence) has changed his mind on this particular point.

The real problem is that of multiple (posttrade) equilibria. Figure 6.12 illustrates the point. We have three equilibria, E_1, E_2, and E_3. Point E_2 is unstable while points E_1 and E_3 are stable. This is in agreement with the Marshallian proposition that the number of equilibria is odd, with each unstable equilibrium bounded by two stable ones. For any terms of trade (p_x/p_y) smaller than the slope of the vector OE_2 (not drawn), the system will tend to move to point E_1. On the other hand, for any terms of trade higher than the slope of the vector OE_2, the system will converge to E_3.

The multiplicity of equilibria illustrated in figure 6.12 is necessarily due to the inelasticity of demand for imports of both countries which gives rise to backward-bending offer curves. If at least one of the offer curves were upward sloping (and not backward bending) throughout, there would be only one stable intersection. This can be seen geometrically from figure 6.12. It also follows from the fact that the demand for imports of the country whose offer curve is upward sloping is necessarily greater than unity. Thus, condition (6.15) is satisfied, and equilibrium must be stable. However, we cannot have more than one equilibria, for if we did, all of them would be stable, which is impossible.

The existence of multiple equilibria raises the question of whether equilibrium is determinate. Given sufficiently large disturbances, the system would move from one (stable) equilibrium to another, thus leading to very volatile price fluctuations. In fact, as the number of equilibrium points tends to infinity, we approach the state of "neutral equilibrium." An extreme case would be when the two offer curves coincide over a certain region.

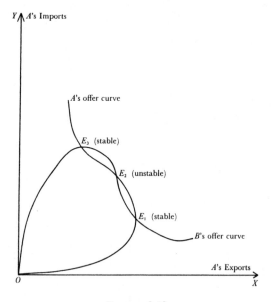

FIGURE 6.12

The existence of multiple equilibria has important policy implications. An equilibrium point which is considered "optimum" from the point of view of one country is not, in general, "optimum" from the point of view of the other country. For instance, in the presence of two stable equilibria, with the first being more favorable to A and the second more favorable to B, it seems natural to assume that A and B will be pursuing inconsistent policies. Thus, the real question is whether there exists a stable equilibrium point corresponding to a division of the gains from trade which can be considered as "fair" by all participating countries.

Appendix 6A: Trade-Indifference Curves

This appendix gives an alternative proof (in terms of differential calculus) of the fundamental property of trade indifference curves, namely, that the slope of a trade indifference curve at any point is equal to the slope of the corresponding consumption indifference curve and the slope of the production-possibilities frontier at the corresponding point. The curvature of trade indifference curves is briefly discussed.

Let

$$Y_c = U(X_c) \qquad (a)$$

be the equation of the I_1^c curve, and let

$$Y_p = F(X_p) \qquad (b)$$

denote the production-possibilities frontier. When the production block is tangent to the consumption indifference curve, the following condition is necessarily satisfied:

$$\frac{dY_c}{dX_c} = \frac{dY_p}{dX_p}, \qquad (c)$$

or

$$U' = F', \qquad (c)'$$

where primes indicate differentiation.

Now define E_X and E_Y as

$$E_X \equiv X_c - X_p, \qquad (d)$$

$$E_Y \equiv Y_c - Y_p = U(X_c) - F(X_p). \qquad (e)$$

Thus, E_X and E_Y show the excess demand for X and Y, respectively.

Solving (d) for X_c and substituting into (e), we get

$$E_Y = U(E_X + X_p) - F(X_p). \qquad (e)'$$

Differentiating E_Y totally with respect to E_X, we get

$$\frac{dE_Y}{dE_X} = [U'(E_X + X_p)]\left(1 + \frac{dX_p}{dE_X}\right) - F'(X_p)\frac{dX_p}{dE_X}$$

$$= U'(E_X + X_p) + [U'(E_X + X_p) - F'(X_p)]\frac{dX_p}{dE_X}. \qquad (f)$$

Equation (f) reduces to

$$\frac{dE_Y}{dE_X} = U' = F' \qquad (f)'$$

as a result of equation (c)'.

What is the meaning of equation (f)'? It is simply that *the slope of the trade indifference curve is equal to the slope of the corresponding social indifference curve and the slope of the production possibilities frontier at the corresponding point.*

Consider now the second derivative of E_Y with respect to E_X. Differentiating dE_Y/dE_X as given by equation (f)', we get

$$\frac{d^2E_Y}{dE_X{}^2} = \frac{d[U'(E_X + X_p)]}{dX_E} = [U''(E_X + X_p)]\left(1 + \frac{dX_p}{dE_X}\right). \qquad (g)$$

To make any progress, we need to evaluate the derivative dX_p/dE_X. For this purpose, take the total differential of equation (c)'. We have $U'' dX_c = F'' dX_p$, or

$$\frac{dX_c}{dX_p} = \frac{F''}{U''}. \qquad (h)$$

From equation (d) it follows that

$$dE_X = dX_c - dX_p, \qquad (i)$$

or

$$\frac{dE_X}{dX_p} = \frac{dX_c}{dX_p} - 1 = \frac{F''}{U''} - 1 = \frac{F'' - U''}{U''}$$

(where use has been made of equation [h]). Therefore,

$$\frac{dX_p}{dE_X} = \frac{U''}{F'' - U''}. \qquad (j)$$

Finally, introducing this result into equation (g), we get

$$\frac{d^2E_Y}{dE_X^2} = U''\left(1 + \frac{U''}{F'' - U''}\right) = \frac{U''F''}{F'' - U''}, \qquad (k)$$

where the arguments of the functions U and F have been omitted for simplicity.

What is the significance of equation (k)? It gives information about the curvature of the trade indifference curve. If the right-hand side of equation (k) is positive, then the trade indifference curve will be convex: it will have the same curvature as the social indifference curves. If it is negative, the trade indifference curve will be concave.

By assumption, the social indifference curves are convex to the origin. This means that $U'' > 0$. If the production-possibilities frontier is concave to the origin, we must have $F'' < 0$. In this case, the trade indifference curve will be convex, that is, it will have the same curvature as the social indifference curve.

What if the production-possibilities frontier is convex to the origin? Then $F'' > 0$, and we can distinguish between the following two cases:

a) When $F'' > U'' > 0$, $d^2 E_Y/dE_X^2 > 0$ and the trade indifference curve will be convex, just like the social indifference curve. That is, when the production-possibilities frontier is convex like the social indifference curves, but its slope (in absolute terms) decreases faster than the slope of the social indifference curve, then the trade indifference curve will be convex.

b) When $0 < F'' < U''$, $d^2 E_Y/dE_X^2 < 0$ and the trade indifference curve will be concave.

SELECTED BIBLIOGRAPHY

Chipman, J. S. 1965. A survey of the theory of international trade: part 2, the neoclassical theory. *Econometrica* 33: 685–760.

Edgeworth, F. Y. 1894. The theory of international values. *Economic Journal* 4: 35–56; reprinted in F. Y. Edgeworth. *Papers Relating to Political Economy*. London: Macmillan & Co., 1925.

———. 1905. Review of Henry Cunynghame's *A geometrical political economy*. *Economic Journal* 15: 62–71; reprinted in F. Y. Edgeworth. *Papers Relating to Political Economy*. London: Macmillan & Co., 1925.

Heller, H. R. 1968. *International Trade*. Englewood Cliffs, N.J.: Prentice-Hall, Inc., Chaps. 3, 4, 5.

Leontief, W. W. 1933. The use of indifference curves in the analysis of foreign trade. *Quarterly Journal of Economics* 47: 493–503.

Lerner, A. P. 1934. The diagrammatical representation of demand conditions in international trade. *Economica* N.S. 1: 319–34; reprinted in A. P. Lerner. *Essays in Economic Analysis*. London: Macmillan & Co., 1953.

Marshall, A. 1879. *The Pure Theory of Foreign Trade*. (Printed for private circulation in 1879; reprinted in 1930.) London: London School of Economics and Political Science.

———. 1923. *Money, Credit, and Commerce*. London: Macmillan & Co., Ltd.

Meade, J. E. 1952. *A Geometry of International Trade*. London: George Allen & Unwin, Ltd. Chaps. 1–4.

Samuelson, P. A. 1947. *Foundations of Economic Analysis*. Cambridge, Mass.: Harvard University Press.

7

Increasing Returns

The analysis so far has been based on the assumption of constant returns to scale. When this assumption is dropped, several difficulties arise, in particular, the problems created by the phenomenon of increasing returns to scale.[1]

Increasing returns to scale are an indisputable fact of life. However, the treatment of increasing returns in the field of international trade theory has been scanty and unsatisfactory, because of the enormous difficulties encountered in incorporating the phenomenon of increasing returns in a general-equilibrium model. The problem is essentially the resultant divergence between private and social costs—but stability also.

Increasing returns are usually attributed to certain "economies"— economies which are reflected in cost reductions. But here we have to distinguish between economies which are *internal* and those which are *external* to the *firm*. In fact, our discussion of constant returns to scale is not inconsistent with the existence of economies which are internal to the firm. Thus, despite the fact that the production function of the industry is characterized by constant returns to scale, the production function of the firm is permitted to exhibit successively increasing, constant, and decreasing returns to scale, giving rise to the usual U-shaped average cost curve. The first phase of increasing returns in the firm's production function is due to *internal economies*, such as division of labor within the firm. Sooner or later, these internal economies come to an end. They are succeeded by constant and decreasing returns to scale largely because of the increasing difficulties of supervision. If the internal economies to the firm were to continue indefinitely, perfect competition would break down because eventually one firm

1. This chapter is slightly more technical than the rest of the book. It can be skipped, for the analysis of the rest of the book does not depend on it.

would become so large that it would be able to supply the whole industry output. Recall that the supply curve of a purely competitive firm does not exist in the region of decreasing average cost. When the internal economies of a firm continue indefinitely to give rise to a continuously falling average cost curve, the firm will find it profitable to increase output beyond all bounds, provided that its average cost curve dips below the average revenue curve after a certain point and continues to fall indefinitely. Thus, the firm will eventually become so large that it will be able to affect the price of its product, i.e., it will stop being a perfect competitor. Accordingly, unlimited increasing returns due to internal economies are incompatible with perfect competition.

The compatibility of increasing returns with perfectly competitive conditions is saved by the concept of *external economies*—a concept introduced into the literature by Marshall in 1890 and later refined by Edgeworth, Haberler, Knight, Viner, Kemp, Meade, and others. The basic idea behind this concept is that the cost curves of individual firms shift downward as the industry's output expands. The lower costs can be attributed to either (*a*) lower factor prices or (*b*) increased efficiency of each firm. The first type of external economies, that is, those which are due to lower factor prices, are called *pecuniary*; the second, that is, those which are due to increased efficiency, are called *technological*. The pecuniary external economies present no new difficulties, whereas the technological external economies do. Actually, *pecuniary external economies* cannot be observed in the case of primary factors. They can only be observed in the case of intermediate goods when the supplying industry is either a monopoly or a decreasing-cost industry subject to *technological external economies*. In the former case, perfect competition is ruled out; in the latter, the pecuniary economies arise because of the existence of the second species of external economies, i.e., those of the technological variety.

The introduction of *technological external economies* gives rise to two major difficulties. First, the economy may not produce on the production-possibilities frontier under perfectly competitive conditions. Second, even if it does, the slope of the production-possibilities frontier will no longer give the ratio of commodity prices, except under certain specific circumstances. Both of these complications have been ignored in the pure theory of trade by means of several simplifying assumptions. It is usually assumed that the technological external economies are such that they do not prevent the economy from producing on its production-possibilities frontier, and that the slope of the frontier is equal to the ratio of commodity prices. The latter assumption is justified in several ways. Meade (1952, p. 33) assumes "either that the economies of scale are external to the individual firms and that there is a system of taxes and subsidies which equates price to marginal social cost in each competitive industry, or that the economies of scale are internal to large monopolistic firms and that the State controls each industry in such a way that it produces up to the point at which the price is equal to the marginal social cost of production." On the other hand, Kemp (1964, p. 111) assumes "that all external economies to the firm are . . . of equal severity in both industries, in the sense that the ratio of marginal private cost to marginal social cost is the same in both industries." Essentially the same assumption is also made by Matthews (1950).

When the preceding complications are assumed away, increasing returns to scale present new problems only to the extent that the production-possibilities frontier is convex to the origin—and not concave, as in the case of constant returns to scale. In other words, when the production-possibilities frontier maintains the concave-to-the-origin shape, the formal analysis of increasing returns to scale does not differ at all from the analysis of constant returns to scale. However, *this is the result of the specific assumption that relative prices are given by the marginal rate of transformation and is totally unrelated to the shape of the production-possibilities frontier.* In general, the price ratio will be different from the slope of the production-possibilities frontier, and the geometrical analysis of constant returns to scale has to be amended. Appendix 7A gives an example where, in the presence of external economies, a perfectly competitive economy may not be able to produce on its production-possibilities frontier.

The rest of the analysis of this chapter will incorporate increasing returns rigorously within the context of an admittedly simple model. The assumption that the marginal rate of transformation reflects relative prices will be dropped. As a result, the analysis of increasing returns will have to be different from that of constant returns whether the production-possibilities frontier is convex or concave to the origin.

1. A Simple Model of a Closed Economy

Let us look at a closed economy consisting of two industries which use a single homogeneous primary factor of production, called labor, existing at a fixed quantity (L) inelastically supplied, and which produce commodities Y and X, respectively. The two industries are subject to, respectively, constant returns and increasing returns due to technological external economies, a necessary assumption for the existence of pure competition. Finally, assume that the production of 1 unit of Y requires exactly 1 unit of labor.

Figure 7.1 summarizes these assumptions. The first quadrant shows the production function of the first industry, a straight line through the origin with a 45° slope. Along the horizontal axis measure labor, and along the vertical axis measure Y and labor. For example, when L_1 units of labor are used to produce OA units of Y, then $OA = OL_1$. Since the labor supply is fixed at OL, the vertical distance BA shows the quantity of labor used in the production of X.

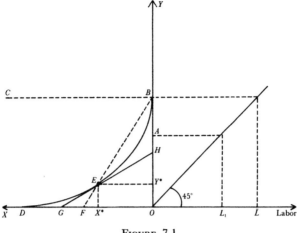

FIGURE 7.1

The second quadrant shows the production function of X as well as the production-possibilities frontier for the economy. Consider point B as the origin for the production function of X and measure along the vertical axis, moving from B to A, the amount of labor used in the production of X and along the horizontal line BC the output of X. Then, the curve BD is the production function of X, characterized by increasing returns. This same curve, considered from the viewpoint of the origin O, is the production-possibilities frontier.

Let us consider now some formal relationships. Note that the real wage rate expressed in terms of Y is equal to unity. Further, assuming that q units of X are equivalent to 1 unit of Y in the market place when the quantities X^* and Y^* are produced (i.e., $1/q = p_x/p_y = p$), we have:

labor used in the production of $Y^* = Y^*$,

labor used in the production of $X^* = L - Y^*$,

wage bill expressed in terms of $Y = L$,

wage bill expressed in terms of $X = qL$,

value of output expressed in terms of $Y = pX^* + Y^*$,

value of output expressed in terms of $X = X^* + qY^*$.

Since prices will be equal to their respective average costs of production, the value of output must equal the wage bill, that is,

$$L = pX^* + Y^*. \tag{7.1}$$

Geometrically, equation (7.1) is shown by the straight line passing through points B and E of figure 7.1, which represents the community budget line. Therefore, if the economy happens to be in equilibrium at point E, it necessarily follows that $p \neq MRT$, as illustrated in figure 7.1, where $MRT =$ marginal rate of transformation, or the opportunity cost of X in terms of Y. We could easily conclude that the commodity whose production function is subject to increasing returns to scale (X in our case) will be relatively more expensive than the MRT would indicate.

Actually, the equality $p = MRT$ implies losses to the producers of X. Thus, assuming that the money wage rate is unity, we have

total cost of production $= \$L$, $\quad p_y = \$1$, $\quad$ and $\quad p_y Y^* = \$Y^*$.

If $p = MRT$, then $p_x = p = MRT$. Therefore, the market value of X^* would be equal to $(MRT)X^*$, which geometrically is equal to the distance Y^*H. Since the total cost of production of X^* is equal to Y^*B, such pricing would necessarily involve losses to the producers of X equal to the distance HB. This state of affairs cannot be viable in the long run.

Let us now introduce demand by means of the neoclassical device of the social indifference map. Figure 7.2 reproduces the production-possibilities frontier of figure 7.1 but with the direction of the horizontal axis reversed and with some additional information about demand. The community budget line must necessarily start at the vertical-axis intercept of the production-possibilities frontier, point A. In addition to the production-possibilities frontier, figure 7.2 shows the Hicksian price consumption curve (PCC), starting at point A. This is all that is needed for our purposes.

Production takes place on the production-possibilities frontier (AB) by assumption. Consumption takes place on the PCC. Therefore, general equilibrium occurs at the intersection of the two curves, point E.

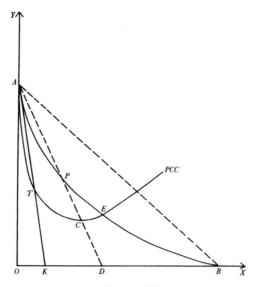

FIGURE 7.2

At the equilibrium point E, the marginal rate of substitution in consumption $(MRS = p)$, that is, the slope of the line AE (not drawn), is higher than the MRT, that is, the slope of the production-possibilities frontier at E. Therefore, one of the Pareto-optimality conditions is not satisfied and the economy is unable to maximize its welfare. This can be achieved only through appropriate economic policy measures.

It is usually said that, under conditions of increasing returns, competitive equilibrium will exist if the indifference curves are "more convex" than the production-possibilities frontier.[2] This condition is also considered necessary for stability.[3] However, these conclusions are based on the incorrect assumption that $p = MRT$. In the general case examined here, this condition is irrelevant.

2. The Offer Curve

Let us derive a country's offer curve. Since the "offers" are given by the differences between domestic consumption and production, our analysis has to start with a discussion of consumption and production equilibria.

Consumption occurs at the point where the budget line touches the highest social indifference curve. The price consumption curve (PCC) of figure 7.2 summarizes the situation when the budget line passes through point A. Note that when trade opens up, the budget line will not necessarily pass through A. The problem is much more difficult for the production equilibria, where the possibility of multiple equilibria arises.[4]

It is convenient to break down the range of values of p into three regions. Consider the budget lines AK (i.e., the tangent to the production-possibilities frontier at point A) and AB (i.e., the straight line joining the two axis intercepts of the production-possibilities frontier). Region a corresponds to that range of values of p which implies steeper budget lines than AK, region b corresponds to values of p which lie between those implied by the budget lines AK and AB; and region c corresponds to that range of values of p which implies flatter budget lines than AB.

In region a, the relative price of X is higher than the limit of the ratio of average costs of production at point A, as shown by the slope of AK. Therefore, in region a, the production of X will be profitable, and it will be even more so as the output of X increases. Consequently, the economy will produce at B.

If p is equal to the slope of AB, production can take place at either A or B. However, the production equilibrium will be stable at A and unstable at B, because at A the average cost of production of X is higher than its price. Despite the fact that it falls as X expands, it will continue to remain higher

2. See Chipman (1965), Matthews (1950), and Young (1958).
3. See Meade (1952, pp. 33–34).
4. For an excellent discussion along the same lines, see Kemp (1964).

than its price. However, at point B, the producers of X will be able to cover their costs; hence, point B can be considered as a production equilibrium point. It is unstable, though, in the sense that any movement away from B will generate forces which will put the economy back to point A.

If p is equal to the slope of AK, equilibrium can again take place at either A or B. However, point B is now stable and A unstable.

If the price ratio lies in region c, the economy, in the absence of permanent subsidization, will specialize in the production of Y.

The most interesting possibility is when the price ratio lies in region b. Here there are three possible production equilibria. To illustrate, consider a price ratio equal to the slope of the budget line $APCD$. The three possible production equilibria are A, P, and B. Points A and B are stable while the middle point P is unstable, as can easily be verified.

For price ratios in regions a and c, unique production equilibria exist at points B and A, respectively. For the limiting price ratios shown by the slopes of AK and AB, there are two production equilibria at points A and B, with point B stable in the former case and A in the latter. For price ratios in region b, there are three production equilibria at points A and B and at the intersection between the budget line through A and the production-possibilities frontier.

The offer curve is derived in figure 7.3. The production-possibilities frontier and the price consumption curve (PCC) as well as the two limiting budget lines have been drawn in the fourth quadrant. Point A of figure 7.2 coincides now with the origin of the diagram, through which are drawn the two limiting price ratios.

For terms of trade in region c, our economy will specialize in the production of Y and consume along the PCC to the right of point C. Therefore, the economy will export Y and import X. In particular, the offer curve for this range of relative prices will lie in the first quadrant (actually, it will be the mirror image of that part of the PCC to the right of C). This is shown in figure 7.3 by the curve $C'D$.

If the terms of trade coincide with the slope of AB, there will be two production equilibria and a single consumption equilibrium. Therefore, two offers arise as shown by points C' (in the first quadrant) and C'' (in the third quadrant).

For terms of trade in region a, our economy will specialize in the production of X and consume along the PCC'. The portion of the offer curve which corresponds to this range is given by the curve FG in the third quadrant. Since this part coincides with the offer curve under Ricardian assumptions (with AB being the Ricardian production-possibilities frontier), the various steps in its derivation have been omitted.

When the terms of trade coincide with the slope of AK, there are two production equilibria (points A and B) and two offers. One is shown by point F in the third quadrant (implying production at point B) and the

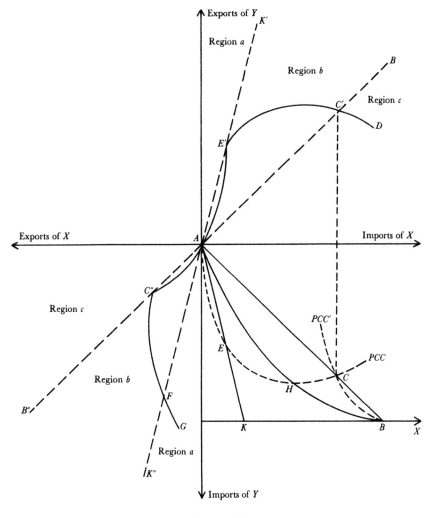

FIGURE 7.3

other shown by point E' in the first quadrant (corresponding to consumption at E, in the fourth quadrant, and implying production at A).

When the terms of trade lie in region b, there are three possible production equilibria which necessarily give rise to three offers. If production takes place at point A, consumption will take place along the PCC between points E and C. The offers that arise in this case are shown by the curve $E'C'$ in the first quadrant, which is the mirror image of the part EC of the PCC in the fourth quadrant. If production takes place at B, consumption will take place on the PCC' from point C upward. This gives rise to the part of the offer curve $C''F$, which appears in the third quadrant. It is derived in precisely the same way as the part *FG* was derived. If production takes place at the intersection of a budget line drawn from point *A* and the production-possibilities frontier, then we can distinguish among the following cases:

i) If the terms of trade are equal to the slope of the budget line *AH* (not drawn), then consumption coincides with production and the corresponding point on the offer coincides with the origin of the diagram (i.e., point *A*).

ii) If the terms of trade lie between the slopes of *AK* and *AH*, *X* will be imported and *Y* will be exported. Curve *AE'* in the first quadrant is the part of the offer curve which describes the present case.

iii) If the terms of trade lie between the slopes of *AH* and *AB*, then *X* will be exported and *Y* imported. The part of the offer curve which corresponds to this particular case is the part *AC"* in the third quadrant.

In summary, the offer curve is shown by the curve *GFC"AE'C'D*. The portion *E'C'D* implies specialization in the production of *Y*, whereas the portion *C"FG* implies specialization in *X*. The middle portion, *C"AE'*, corresponds to incomplete specialization.[5]

3. International Equilibrium

Consider first a simple open economy, that is, an economy which is a price taker in the international market. The behavior of our economy can be summarized in figure 7.4, which reproduces the offer curve of figure 7.3. Note that the tangent (*PP'*) has been drawn to the offer curve at the origin; its slope shows the pretrade price ratio in our economy. (The proof given earlier in relation to constant returns to scale to the effect that the slope of the offer curve at the origin shows pretrade relative prices is valid for the present case as well. That proof did not depend upon the characteristics of production functions.) If the international price ratio lies in region *c*, our economy will definitely specialize in the production of *Y* and import *X*. The terms-of-trade line will necessarily intersect the offer curve in the first quadrant and in the region *CD* only. Similarly, if the international price ratio lies in region *a*, the terms-of-trade line will necessarily intersect the offer curve in the third quadrant in the region *E'G* only. Thus, our economy, specializing completely in the production of *X*, will export *X* and import *Y*. Finally, for any price ratio in region *b*, the direction of trade of our economy as well as its specialization in production remain indeterminate. In this region there are always three offers. For instance, if the international price ratio is equal to the domestic pretrade price ratio, our economy can do one of three things. (i) It can continue to produce and consume exactly as before trade, with the origin on the diagram being the equilibrium trade point. However, this offer is unstable and, in addition, is less preferable, in general,

5. For a brief discussion of the problems involved for the generalization of the preceding analysis when the number of factors is increased to two, see Chacholiades (1970).

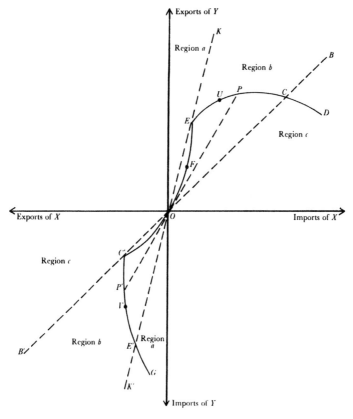

FIGURE 7.4

to the third alternative. (ii) It can specialize in the production of Y, with the equilibrium offer given by point P in the first quadrant. (iii) It can specialize in the production of X, with the equilibrium offer given by point P' in the third quadrant. Both offers P and P' are stable. However, the last offer (P') is preferred because the implied income of the economy expressed in terms of any commodity is higher in this case than the other two, as can be seen from the fact that the consumption-possibilities frontiers implied by the first two alternatives are identical and lie inside the consumption-possibilities frontier implied by the last alternative. In general, it will be to the advantage of a country to specialize in the production of the commodity whose production function is characterized by increasing returns to scale.

For any international price ratio giving rise to a terms-of-trade line steeper than PP' but flatter than KK', there will again be three offers as illustrated by points U, F, and V (the line UFV has been omitted for simplicity). Points U and F lie in the first quadrant, while V lies in the third. This same pattern will necessarily be observed for all terms-of-trade lines lying between KK' and PP'. The offers U and V, implying complete specialization in Y and X, respectively, are stable, while the offer F, implying incomplete specialization, is unstable.

For terms-of-trade lines lying between PP' and CC', there will again be three offers: one in the first quadrant along the region PC of the offer curve and two in the third quadrant lying, respectively, along the regions OC' and $C'P'$ of the offer curve. The middle offer along the region OC' is again unstable, while the other two are stable.

A major difference between the present case of increasing returns and the case of constant returns to scale is that in the latter case, when the international terms of trade coincide with the pretrade price ratio, our economy cannot participate (profitably) in international trade. This is not so under increasing returns to scale. Whether or not the international price ratio coincides with the pretrade price ratio, our economy will always participate in international trade. Another major difference between constant and increasing returns to scale is the existence of multiple offers in the latter but not in the former case, with the resulting instability of the offer implying incomplete specialization.

Once the preceding analysis is well understood, the introduction of a second country (or the rest of the world) with a similarly shaped offer curve presents no additional problems. In general, there will be multiple equilibria and, what is more, the direction of trade cannot be decided a priori, except in a special case. Figure 7.5 illustrates the general case of three equilibria: E_1, E_2, and E_3. At point E_1, country A is completely specializing in the production of Y, and B in X; thus, A exports Y and B exports X. At E_3, the pattern of production specialization is opposite that at E_1. However, at E_2, both countries produce both commodities, with A exporting Y and B exporting X. From the preceding analysis, points E_1 and E_3 are stable while E_2 is unstable. In general, an equilibrium point implying incomplete specialization in both countries (such as E_2) is unstable.

No attempt will be made here to provide an explicit dynamic adjustment mechanism according to which the world economy will behave when it happens to be out of equilibrium. It seems sufficient to point out that the Walrasian stability conditions are satisfied at points E_1 and E_3. However, it should be emphasized that this characterization of stable equilibria is not sufficient to explain where the world economy would move if it happened to be at E_2 and a minor shock threw it out of equilibrium. Would it move toward E_1 or E_3? Whether the terms-of-trade line becomes steeper or flatter than OE_2 after the shock, both E_1 and E_2 pass the Walrasian stability test. Without the introduction of more specific assumptions about the dynamic adjustment mechanism at work, it is impossible to say whether the world economy will settle at E_1 or E_3. The outcome would seem to depend on chance. To illustrate the possibility alluded to earlier, namely, that, in the presence of increasing returns, profitable trade can take place even if the

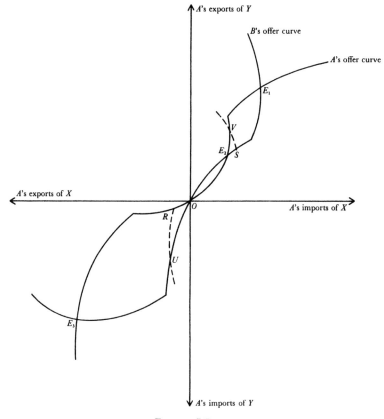

FIGURE 7.5

pretrade prices of the two countries are identical, imagine B's (or A's) offer curve in figure 7.5 rotating through the origin until it becomes tangent to A's (B's) offer curve at the origin. Then, point E_2 will coincide with the origin while points E_1 and E_3 will continue to exhibit the same properties as in figure 7.5.

Figure 7.5 illustrates the case where the stable equilibria E_1 and E_3 imply complete specialization in both countries. However, this is not necessary, as illustrated by the broken curves RU and SV, implying stable equilibria at U and V, respectively. At U, country A specializes completely in X while B produces both commodities. At V, country B specializes in X while A produces both X and Y.

As noted earlier, the direction of trade is indeterminate except in a special case. Thus, in terms of the terminology of figures 7.2–7.4, the direction of trade can be predicted only if A's region b does not coincide with B's region b. In particular, if B's region b lies above and to the left of A's in the first quadrant, equilibrium will necessarily occur in the third quadrant, with

A exporting X and importing Y. On the other hand, if B's region b lies below and to the right of A's in the first quadrant, equilibrium will necessarily occur in the first quadrant, with A exporting Y and importing X.

There is no requirement, as in the case of constant returns to scale (barring multiple pretrade equilibria), for the equilibrium terms of trade to lie between the pretrade price ratios. This can be seen in the case where the pretrade prices are identical in the two countries and yet trade takes place at prices that are in general different from the common pretrade price ratio.

Note that there is no necessity for the terms of trade to be different at the three equilibrium points E_1, E_2, and E_3. In other words, it is quite possible for all three points (E_1, E_2, and E_3) to lie on a straight line through the origin. This is illustrated in figure 7.6, which is similar to figure 7.2 except that now the production-possibilities frontier, shown here by the curve KPM, is common to both countries A and B. At the international terms of trade, $p = p_0$, given by the absolute slope of either KC_BPC_AR or $DC'_BC'_AM$, either country can produce at any of the three points K, P, or M. When production

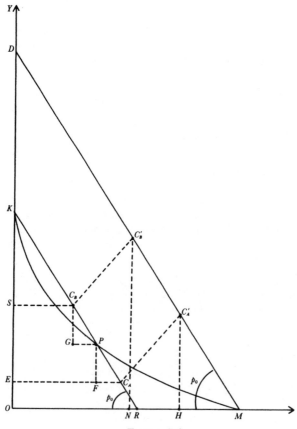

FIGURE 7.6

occurs at M, the consumption-possibilities frontier is given by $DC'_BC'_AM$, and when production occurs either at K or P, the consumption-possibilities frontier is given by KC_BPC_AR. Further, when A's consumption-possibilities frontier is given by KC_BPC_AR, country A consumes at C_A, and when it is given by $DC'_BC'_AM$, then A consumes at C'_A. The corresponding consumption points for country B are, respectively, C_B and C'_B. The triangle C_BGP is identical to PFC_A, the triangle KSC_B is identical to C'_AHM, and the triangle KEC_A is identical to C'_BNM. Therefore, there are three equilibrium points as follows:

a) Both countries produce at P, with A consuming at C_A and B at C_B. Thus, B will be exporting $GP = FC_A$ units of X to country A in exchange for $FP = GC_B$ units of Y. Note that, in this particular case, country A consumes inside its production-possibilities frontier. Hence, country A becomes worse off (in this particular case) after the introduction of trade. But country B benefits, mostly at the expense of country A.

b) Country B produces at K (i.e., B specializes completely in Y) and consumes at C_B, while A produces at M (i.e., A specializes completely in X) and consumes at C'_A. Thus, A exports $HM = SC_B$ units of X to B in exchange for $KS = HC'_A$ units of Y. In this case, while B continues to consume at C_B, as in the first case, country A's consumption of both commodities increases: A moves from C_A to C'_A. Compared with the pretrade position, both countries clearly gain after the introduction of trade, although A gets the lion's share.

c) Country A produces at K and consumes at C_A, and B produces at M and consumes at C'_B. Thus, A specializes in Y and B in X. In particular, A exports $KE = NC'_B$ units of Y to country B in exchange for $NM = EC_A$ units of X. As in case (a), A becomes worse off with trade. Country B's gains are much higher in this case than in the previous two.

It is apparent that a country gains most when it specializes in the production of that commodity (X) whose production function is characterized by increasing returns to scale. Therefore, it will be to the interest of a country to pursue a trade policy that will eventually enable the country to specialize in the production of X. But what happens when both countries pursue such a policy? (a) One of the two countries may be satisfied with the meager gains of specialization in the "wrong" commodity, until finally stable equilibrium is reached. (b) Both countries might interfere with the free flow of goods to the point where the latter is actually shrunk to zero. (c) The governments of the two countries may get together and agree upon an equitable distribution of the gains between them. Thus, the country which eventually specializes completely in the production of X (i.e., the commodity whose production function is characterized by increasing returns to scale) might agree to make an income transfer (annually) to the other country, which agrees to specialize completely in Y (i.e., the commodity whose production function is characterized by constant returns to scale).

Appendix 7A: An Example of External Economies

This appendix gives an example of external economies which may prevent a perfectly competitive economy from producing on its production-possibilities frontier.

Let the output of commodity X depend on labor (L_x) and land (T_x) used in industry X and on the amount of labor (L_y) used in the production of commodity Y. Further, assume that the output of commodity Y depends on the amounts of labor (L_y) and land (T_y) used directly in the production of Y. The production functions take the form

$$X = X(L_x, T_x, L_0 - L_x), \tag{i}$$

$$Y = Y(L_y, T_y), \tag{ii}$$

since $L_y = L_0 - L_x$, where $L_0 \equiv$ total amount of labor available to the economy. The marginal rate of substitution of labor for land in industry X is given by

$$MRS_{LT}^X = -\frac{dT}{dL} = \frac{dX/dL}{dX/dT} = \frac{(\partial X/\partial L_x) - (\partial X/\partial L_y)}{\partial X/\partial T_x}. \tag{iii}$$

Similarly, the marginal rate of substitution of L for T in industry Y is given by

$$MRS_{LT}^Y = -\frac{dT}{dL} = \frac{\partial Y/\partial L_y}{\partial Y/\partial T_y}. \tag{iv}$$

The economy will be allocating its resources along the contract curve of the box diagram if the following condition is satisfied:

$$MRS_{LT}^X = MRS_{LT}^Y. \tag{v}$$

However, perfect competition will bring about the following equality:

$$\frac{\partial X/\partial L_x}{\partial X/\partial T_x} = MRS_{LT}^Y = \frac{w}{r}, \tag{vi}$$

where w/r is the factor-price ratio. Therefore, unless the partial derivative $\partial X/\partial L_y$ is zero, equation (v) cannot be satisfied and the economy will end up producing inside its production-possibilities frontier. In the present case, where by assumption $\partial X/\partial L_y > 0$, equation (v) is indeed not satisfied and the economy will indeed be producing inside its frontier.

This illustration is based on an interaction between the output of one industry and the factors employed by the other. In the absence of such interaction, it appears that condition (vi) will imply condition (v) and the economy will produce on its production-possibilities frontier.

Even if the economy does produce on its production-possibilities frontier, the equilibrium price ratio, measuring the marginal rate of substitution in consumption, will in general be different from the slope of the production-possibilities frontier, because the latter measures the ratio of marginal social costs whereas the former measures the ratio of marginal private costs—and social costs are lower than private costs when technological external economies exist. This difficulty has been circumvented in the literature quite expeditiously by means of several simplifying assumptions.

SELECTED BIBLIOGRAPHY

Chacholiades, M. 1970. Increasing returns and the theory of comparative advantage. *Southern Economic Journal* 37: 157–62.

Chipman, J. S. 1965. A survey of the theory of international trade: part 2, the neoclassical theory. *Econometrica* 33: 685–760.

Kemp, M. C. 1964. *The Pure Theory of International Trade.* Englewood Cliffs, N.J.: Prentice-Hall, Inc. Chap. 8.

Lerner, A. P. 1932. The diagrammatical representation of cost conditions in international trade. *Economica* 12: 346–56; reprinted in A. P. Lerner. 1953. *Essays in Economic Analysis.* London: Macmillan & Co., 1953.

Matthews, R. C. O. 1950. Reciprocal demand and increasing returns. *Review of Economic Studies* 17: 149–58.

Meade, J. E. 1952. *A Geometry of International Trade.* London: George Allen & Unwin, Ltd. Chaps. 1–4.

Young, A. A. 1928. Increasing returns and economic progress. *Economic Journal* 38: 527–42; reprinted in A.E.A. *Readings in Economic Analysis.* Vol. 1, Edited by R. V. Clemence. Cambridge, Mass.: Addison-Wesley Press, 1950.

IV

The Modern Theory

8

Factor Intensity and Factor Abundance

1. Introduction

The preceding chapters show that the direction of trade is determined by the pretrade equilibrium price ratios, ignoring, of course, the cases of pretrade multiple equilibria and increasing returns to scale. Further, these pretrade price ratios depend upon the production-possibilities frontiers of the trading countries, as well as their respective demand conditions.[1] Therefore, the factors which determine the structure of trade can be traced back to differences in (a) the production-possibilities frontiers of the countries involved and (b) their demand conditions.

The neoclassical theory, contrary to the classical theory, does not attempt to go beyond these generalizations and, thus, offers no hypothesis as to why the pretrade price ratios differ between countries. (These comments should not be misconstrued to mean that the neoclassical theory is useless. Its value springs from the fact that, in addition to being a great pedagogical tool, it serves as an introduction to the modern theory.) The modern theory, on the other hand, makes a heroic attempt to predict the pattern of trade on the basis of the observable characteristics of the pretrade autarkic equilibria. In a sense, the modern theory begins where the neoclassical theory leaves off.

The modern theory may be broken down into the following two propositions:

a) The *cause* of international trade is to be found largely in differences between the factor endowments of different countries. In particular, a

1. The Ricardian doctrine of comparative advantage seems to have been developed on the basis of labor coefficients alone. However, the doctrine, for its logical validity, requires some demand restrictions. This creeps into the analysis through the implicit assumption that both commodities are produced and consumed in both countries in their respective pretrade equilibrium positions. In other words, any corner solutions in the pretrade situation are ruled out. In the absence of such restrictions on demand, the opening up of trade need not necessarily result in any change in consumption or production in either country. For further details, see chaps. 2 and 3.

country will have a comparative advantage in the production of that commodity which uses more intensively the country's more abundant factor. This proposition is known as the *Heckscher–Ohlin theorem.*

b) The *effect* of international trade is to tend to equalize factor prices as between countries, thus serving to some extent as a substitute for factor mobility. This proposition is known as the *factor-price equalization theorem.*

As it turns out, neither proposition is generally true. Their validity depends on certain factual assumptions to be analyzed.[2]

This chapter deals with the concepts of factor intensity and factor abundance. This is imperative before we discuss the Heckscher–Ohlin theorem in the following chapter.

2. *The Determinants of the Shape of the Production–Possibilities Frontier*

The modern theory makes the assumption that tastes are largely similar between countries. To simplify, let us initially assume that demand conditions in all countries are identical and homothetic. In particular, assume that there exists a single, homothetic social indifference map which summarizes the tastes of all countries. (The importance of homotheticity will become evident in chap. 9, sec. 1.) Under these circumstances, any differences in the pretrade equilibrium price ratios must be attributed to differences in the production-possibilities frontiers of the countries involved. What factors are, then, responsible for any differences in the shapes of the production-possibilities frontiers between countries?

As we saw in chapter 4, the production-possibilities frontier of a country depends on: (*a*) its factor endowments and (*b*) the production functions of the various commodities. Consequently, any differences in the shape of the production-possibilities frontiers of, say, two countries must necessarily be attributed either to differences in their production functions or to differences in their factor endowments, or both.

The phrase "differences in their production functions" requires careful interpretation. Consider two countries (*A* and *B*) each endowed with two factors of production (labor and land) and each producing two commodities (*X* and *Y*). When we say that "any differences in the shape of the production-

2. The founders of the modern theory are Heckscher (1919) and Ohlin (1933). Ohlin's writings were greatly influenced by Heckscher. The latter, whose work was not made available in English until 1949, acknowledged Wicksell's influence on his thought. In fact, Heckscher stated forthrightly that trade equalizes factor rewards completely. Ohlin, on the other hand, asserted that there was only a *tendency* toward factor-price equalization as a result of free trade. The partial-equalization argument was later made rigorous by Stolper and Samuelson (1941). A few years later, Samuelson (1948, 1953) extended the argument to establish the case for complete equalization. It should be noted that Samuelson's work prompted Robbins to rediscover a seminar paper which Lerner (1953) wrote in 1933 as a student in which he demonstrated in a rigorous fashion the conditions for complete specialization.

possibilities frontiers of the two countries must necessarily be attributed to . . . *differences in their production functions,*" we do not mean differences in the production function of commodity X versus the production function of commodity Y. Rather, we mean differences in the production function of each commodity separately between countries. In other words, we mean differences in the production function of X between countries A and B and, similarly, differences in the production function of Y between A and B. It should be noted, however, that should the production function of X be identical with that of Y, then from a purely economic point of view, we essentially have a *single* commodity (despite the difference in appearance and even use of X and Y), since, with an appropriate choice of units of measurement, 1 unit of X will consist of exactly the same factors (or inputs) as 1 unit of Y. The implications of this, first noted by Robinson (see Lerner [1953], pp. 73, 76), will become apparent later in this and the following three chapters.

The modern theory, in contrast to the classical theory, postulates the existence of linear homogeneous production functions which are also identical between countries. Thus, following the illustration given in the preceding paragraph, we can say that the modern theory postulates that the production function of commodity X is the same in both countries (A and B). The same, of course, holds for commodity Y as well. On the other hand, the production function of commodity X must necessarily be different from that of Y. On the basis of these assumptions, the modern theory concludes that any differences in the shapes of the production-possibilities frontiers of two countries must be found in differences in factor endowments.

On the basis of the preceding analysis, the modern theory advances the hypothesis that the cause of trade lies with differences in factor endowments, in particular, that a country will tend to have a comparative advantage in those commodities which use more intensively the country's more abundant factors.

3. *The Meaning of "Factor Intensity"*

Before the cause and effect of international trade are analyzed in detail, it is important to understand the meaning of *labor-intensive* or *land-intensive commodities*, as well as the meaning of *labor-abundant* or *land-abundant countries*. The purpose of this section is to clarify the concept of *factor intensity*. The following section will clarify the concept of *factor abundance*.

Throughout this chapter, let us assume constant returns to scale. Under these circumstances, the whole isoquant map is a blown-up version of the unit isoquant. Thus, once the unit isoquant is given, the whole production function (or isoquant map) is simultaneously determined. Further, the expansion paths (or scale lines) are straight lines passing through the origin (for further details, see chap. 4). As a result, this discussion will be conveniently restricted to the unit isoquants.

Figure 8.1 illustrates the concept of *factor intensity* under the simplifying assumption of fixed coefficients of production. The two *L*-shaped isoquants, *XX'* and *YY'*, are assumed to be the unit isoquants for commodities *X* and *Y*, respectively. The two broken lines, *OR* and *OS*, represent the expansion paths for *X* and *Y*, respectively. The slopes of the expansion paths *OR* and *OS* show the proportions in which the factors labor and land are used in the production of *X* and *Y*, respectively. More precisely, the slope of the vector *OR* shows the number of units of labor per unit of land that are required in the production of commodity *X*; and the slope of the vector *OS* shows the number of units of labor per unit of land that are required in the production of *Y*. Since the vector *OS* is steeper than the vector *OR*, it is obvious that commodity *Y* requires more labor per unit of land than commodity *X*. Thus figure 8.1 shows that, per unit of land, commodity *X* requires *OK* units of labor, whereas commodity *Y* requires *OL* units of labor, with *OL* > *OK*. This is expressed by saying that *commodity Y is labor intensive relative to commodity X.*

When the problem is considered from the point of view of the number of units of land per unit of labor, it is obvious that commodity *X* requires more units of land per unit of labor than commodity *Y*. Thus, figure 8.1 shows that, per unit of labor, commodity *X* requires *ON*, and commodity *Y* requires

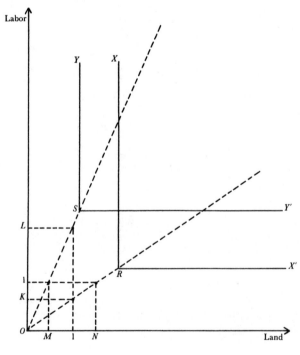

FIGURE 8.1

OM, units of land, with $ON > OM$. Again, this can be expressed by saying that *commodity X is land intensive relative to commodity Y*. This does not contradict the previous statement, namely, that commodity Y is labor intensive relative to commodity X. In fact, the two statements represent two different ways of expressing the same thing. In other words, when we say that commodity X is land intensive relative to commodity Y, we necessarily imply that commodity Y is labor intensive relative to commodity X, and vice versa.

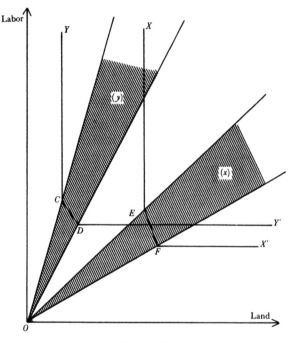

FIGURE 8.2A

With a single technique for producing X and a single technique for producing Y, it is obvious that the two commodities can always be classified unambiguously into labor intensive and land intensive. The only exception to this general conclusion is the case where the two expansion paths coincide, a case which, as indicated previously, degenerates into the single-commodity case (from our point of view), and we exclude it by assumption, at least for the time being. (The generalization of this conclusion to the case of more than two commodities is straightforward.) Usually, however, more than one production technique for producing each commodity is known. Can we also classify unambiguously the two commodities in terms of factor intensity in this general case? Not always. There are some cases where this is true, of course. Figures 8.2 illustrate a simple case where it is still possible to rank commodities in terms of factor ratios. Figure 8.2A illustrates the case where

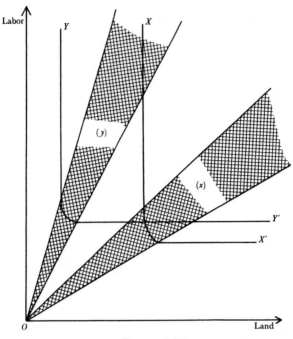

FIGURE 8.2B

only two techniques are known for each commodity (fig. 8.2B illustrates the same point when the isoquants are smoothly continuous). Thus, the two techniques for producing 1 unit of X are given by the coordinates of points E and F, and the two techniques for producing 1 unit of Y are given by the coordinates of points C and D. On the assumption that the techniques E and F can be combined (without any interaction between them) to produce 1 unit of X and the techniques C and D can be combined to produce 1 unit of Y, it must be clear that 1 unit of commodity X can be produced by any one combination of labor and land that lies on the straight-line segment EF and that 1 unit of commodity Y can be produced by any one combination of labor and land that lies on the straight-line segment CD. Thus, the expansion path for X must necessarily lie in the shaded cone x, and the expansion path for Y must necessarily lie in the shaded cone y. This must also be true for the case of smoothly continuous isoquants illustrated in figure 8.2B. Figures 8.2 show that commodity Y is labor intensive relative to commodity X or, what is the same thing, that commodity X is land intensive relative to commodity Y. This follows from the fact that the shaded cones x and y, that is, the regions of efficient input ratios, do not overlap.

Figure 8.3 illustrates a more difficult case. The expansion path for industry X can lie in either cone a or cone c, and the expansion path for industry Y can lie in either cone b or cone c. Since cone c is common to both

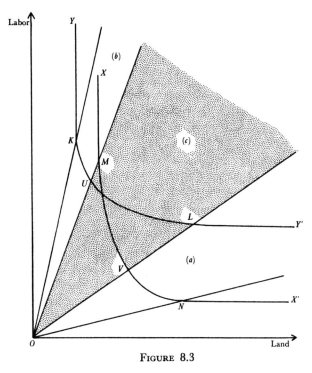

FIGURE 8.3

industries, it seems impossible to rank the two commodities unambiguously in terms of factor intensities. But this need not be so. The problem hinges on the way the optimum expansion paths of X and Y are selected. How is this selection performed under perfectly competitive conditions?

As we have already seen in chapter 4, the selection of the optimum expansion path for an industry depends upon factor prices. In particular, given the factor-price ratio (w/r), the optimum expansion path will be determined by the condition that the marginal rate of substitution of labor for land be equal to the given factor-price ratio. Assuming both industries pay identical factor prices, it follows that the optimum expansion paths of the two industries—to be used for purposes of ranking the commodities in terms of factor intensities—must necessarily correspond to identical marginal rates of substitution of labor for land. But since factor prices are not given to begin with, how can we decide which commodity is labor intensive and which land intensive? Put differently, how can we exclude the possibility that one commodity is considered labor intensive for some factor-price ratios but land intensive for other factor-price ratios? It follows that commodities can be unambiguously ranked in terms of factor intensities if, and only if, prior knowledge of factor prices is unnecessary. Hence, commodity Y is defined to be labor intensive relative to another commodity X if commodity Y uses more units of labor per unit of land than commodity X for all factor-price ratios. This definition is illustrated in figure 8.3, where, for any factor-price ratio, the optimum expansion path for industry Y is steeper than the corresponding optimum expansion path for industry X. Observe that the slope of the isoquant XX' at V is steeper than the slope of YY' at U. Therefore, for any factor-price ratio for which the optimum expansion path for industry Y falls in the shaded cone c, the optimum expansion path for industry X will necessarily lie in cone a, and for any factor-price ratio for which the optimum expansion path for industry X falls in the shaded cone c, the optimum expansion path for industry Y will necessarily lie in cone b.

The condition that the slope of XX' at V be steeper than the slope of YY' at U is sufficient but not necessary for the ranking of commodities X and Y. It should be clear that *a necessary condition for Y to be labor intensive is that any ray through the origin should cut the two unit isoquants at points such that Y's isoquant is flatter than X's.* For instance, the tangent to XX' at M should by necessity be steeper than the tangent to YY' at U. Thus, for the factor-price ratio for which X's expansion path coincides with the vector OM, Y's expansion path will by necessity be steeper than OM. The point on YY' where the slope is equal to the slope of XX' at M necessarily lies in the region KU. Conversely, for the factor-price ratio for which Y's expansion path coincides with the vector OU, X's expansion will by necessity be flatter than OU.

Unfortunately, there exist particular pairs of isoquants for which commodities X and Y cannot be unambiguously ranked in terms of factor intensity and the Heckscher–Ohlin requirements cannot be met. Figures 8.4 illustrate this case, which has come to be known in the literature as the case of factor-intensity reversals. Figure 8.4A illustrates the case where Y's unit isoquant is L shaped whereas X's unit isoquant is smoothly continuous. Commodity Y's isoquant has been so constructed that it touches X's isoquant at point S only. (Since units of measurement for X and Y can be arbitrarily selected, this construction does not depend on any particular assumptions other than the assumption that Y's isoquant is L shaped and X's smoothly continuous.) Commodity Y's expansion path is uniquely given by the vector OS. However, X's expansion path is not uniquely given; it depends upon the factor-price ratio. When the factor-price ratio is given by the absolute value of the slope α of X's isoquant at point S, X's expansion path coincides with Y's. However, for any factor-price ratio lower than α (such as that given by the absolute value of the slope of XX' at point N), X's expansion path becomes flatter than Y's. This implies that Y is labor intensive relative to X. On the other hand, for any factor-price ratio higher than α (such as that given by the absolute value of the slope of XX' at point U), X's expansion path becomes steeper than Y's. This implies that X is labor intensive relative to Y. Therefore, in this particular case, an unequivocal classification of commodities by factor intensity is impossible.

Figure 8.4B is similar to figure 8.4A except that now Y's isoquant also has been drawn as a smoothly continuous curve. The basic assumption that

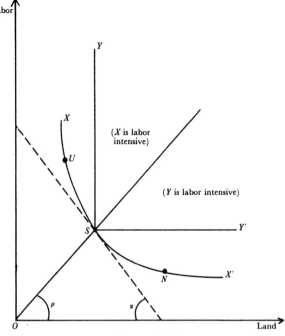

FIGURE 8.4A

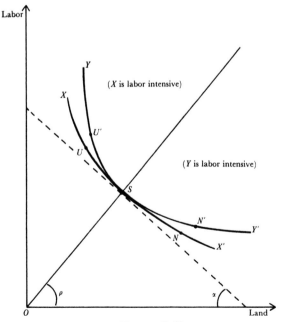

FIGURE 8.4B

characterizes the construction of this diagram is this: any ray through the origin and flatter than OS will intersect the two-unit isoquants at points where the marginal rate of substitution of land for labor is higher in industry X than in Y; and any ray steeper than OS will cut the two unit isoquants at points where the marginal rate of substitution of land for labor is higher in Y than in X. This is a necessary and sufficient condition for the existence of a single factor-intensity reversal. In general, when more than one reversal is admitted, the preceding condition will not be met.

The conclusion reached earlier with regard to figure 8.4A applies equally to figure 8.4B. Consider a factor-price ratio lower than α (where α is the absolute value of the slope of either isoquant at point S), such as the slope of XX' at point N. Commodity X's expansion path would then be given by the vector ON (not drawn). To see whether Y's expansion path is steeper or flatter than X's at this factor-price ratio, simply consider the marginal rate of substitution of land for labor in industry Y along the expansion path ON. By assumption, it must be lower than that of industry X along ON. Therefore, for the specific value of the factor-price ratio we have chosen, Y's expansion path must necessarily be steeper than ON and, in particular, it will be given by a vector lying between OS and ON. Thus, for values of the factor-price ratio lower than α, Y is labor intensive relative to X. In the same way, it can be shown that for values of the factor-price ratio higher than α, Y's expansion path will necessarily be flatter than X's and, therefore, X will be labor intensive relative to Y. It is impossible to classify commodities unequivocally by factor intensity.

What meaning could possibly be attached to the Heckscher–Ohlin theorem in the presence of factor-intensity reversals? When commodities cannot be unambiguously classified into labor and land intensive, the Heckscher–Ohlin theorem becomes very difficult to follow, since it is based on the implicit assumption that commodities can indeed be classified a priori in terms of factor intensity. When this implicit assumption is not met, the structure of trade need not coincide with the Heckscher–Ohlin theorem. But does this imply that factor-intensity reversals will necessarily render the Heckscher–Ohlin theorem invalid? Not at all. It all depends upon the overall factor proportions (i.e., the ratios of labor to land) in the two countries.

As we saw in chapter 4, under constant returns to scale, the contract curve in the Edgeworth–Bowley box diagram must necessarily lie on one side of the diagonal: it can never cross it. This necessarily implies that no matter what type of isoquants we are dealing with, the two commodities can unequivocally be classified by factor intensity once the overall factor proportions are given. This is illustrated in figure 8.5. The sides of the box diagram (i.e., O_xN, and O_xM) show the aggregate endowments of labor and land for the economy in question. The slope of the diagonal (ρ) shows the overall factor proportions. When resources are allocated with reference to the coordinates of a point below and to the right of the diagonal, such as U,

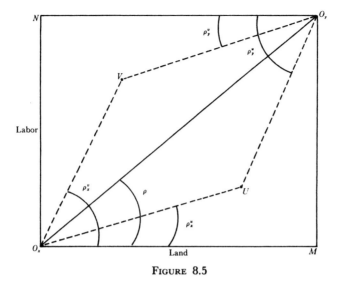

FIGURE 8.5

commodity X is necessarily land intensive relative to Y $(\rho_x^u < \rho_y^u)$. On the other hand, when resources are allocated in accordance with the coordinates of any point above and to the left of the diagonal, such as V, commodity X is necessarily labor intensive relative to Y $(\rho_x^v > \rho_y^v)$. Accordingly, when the contract curve lies on one side of the diagonal, one commodity will always be labor intensive relative to the other for all admissible efficient resource allocations.

Does the preceding argument mean that the phenomenon of factor-intensity reversals cannot be damaging to the Heckscher–Ohlin theorem? Not at all. All we know is that, given the overall factor endowments of, say, country A, we can rank commodities X and Y in terms of factor intensity, but from the point of view of country A. The same experiment can be repeated for a second country, B, of course, but there is no guarantee that the two rankings will not be contradictory. For instance, while we are absolutely sure that commodity X will always be labor intensive relative to Y from the point of view of country A, we cannot possibly be absolutely sure that commodity X will also be labor intensive in country B as well. It may very well be land intensive in B. In other words, in the presence of factor-intensity reversals, it is possible (but not necessary) that commodity X may be labor intensive relative to Y in one country, but land intensive relative to Y in the other country. Under what circumstances would A's ranking of X and Y be consistent with, or contradictory to, B's?

Consider again figures 8.4. If the overall ratio of labor to land in a particular country were given by the slope of the vector OS, the contract curve in the box diagram would necessarily coincide with the diagonal. The production-possibilities frontier would be a straight line, and X and Y

would have identical factor intensities. On the other hand, if the overall labor land ratio were given by a vector flatter than OS, such as ON, then commodity Y would be labor intensive relative to X. Finally, if the overall labor land ratio were given by a vector steeper than OS, such as OU, then commodity X would be labor intensive relative to Y. Accordingly, if the overall labor/land ratios of both countries were given by vectors lying on the same side of OS, the commodity rankings in terms of factor ratios of the two countries would be consistent; otherwise, they would be contradictory. How were these conclusions established?

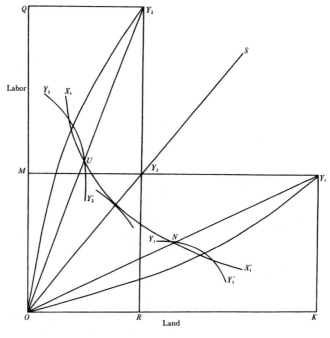

FIGURE 8.6

Consider figure 8.6. It is a combination of three box diagrams. The vectors OS, OY_1, and OY_2 (which are simply the diagonals of the three box diagrams) correspond to the vectors OS, ON, and OU, respectively, of figure 8.4. Thus, when the overall labor/land ratio is given by the slope of OS (as shown by the box diagram ORY_3M), the marginal rate of substitution of land for labor in X and Y will necessarily be equal along the diagonal of the box diagram; the unit isoquants are by assumption tangent to each other at S (fig. 8.4). Hence, the contract curve will coincide with the diagonal and the labor land ratios used in the two industries will be equal to each other and also to the overall labor/land ratio of the economy in general. On the other hand, when the labor/land ratio is lower than the slope of OS

(as shown by the box diagram OKY_1M), the contract curve must lie below the diagonal if Y is to be labor intensive relative to X. Is there any reason why the contract curve should lie below and to the right of the diagonal of the box diagram OKY_1M? The answer lies in the assumption that any ray through the origin and flatter than OS (fig. 8.4B) will intersect the two unit isoquants at points where the marginal rate of substitution of land for labor is higher in industry X than in Y. What this means is that for any pair of isoquants passing through a point lying on the diagonal OY_1 (fig. 8.6), such as X_1X_1' and Y_1Y_1' passing through N, Y's isoquant will be flatter than X's at N. But as explained in chapter 4, this necessarily implies that the contract curve lies below and to the right of the diagonal OY_1.

When the overall labor land ratio is higher than the slope of OS (as shown by the box diagram ORY_2Q), the contract curve lies above the diagonal and X becomes labor intensive relative to Y, for X's isoquants along the diagonal OY_2 are flatter than Y's. This is illustrated in figure 8.6 by the typical pair X_1X_1' and Y_2Y_2'—the former being flatter than the latter at U. Again, this relationship, which follows from the assumption that any ray steeper than OS (fig. 8.4) will cut the two one-unit isoquants at points where the marginal rate of substitution of land for labor is higher in Y than X, implies that the contract curve necessarily lies above and to the left of the diagonal OY_2 and, therefore, that X is labor intensive relative to Y.

It is interesting to note that, should the overall labor/land ratios in both countries be equal to the slope of the vector OS (figs. 8.4 and 8.6), then (*a*) the production-possibilities frontiers will become straight lines with equal slope (whose numerical value is quite arbitrary, depending on the units of measurement for X and Y), and (*b*) assuming that both commodities are being consumed in both countries in the autarkic state, the pretrade relative prices will be equal and thus no trade will take place.

The same conclusions would follow if the production functions of X and Y are identical. Thus, by an appropriate choice of units of measurement for X and Y, the two one-unit isoquants can be made to coincide. Accordingly, the commodity-price ratio will necessarily be equal to unity irrespective of factor prices. Thus, we end up again with the classical equal-costs case.

To summarize, the vector OS (figs. 8.4 and 8.6) divides the diagram into two nonoverlapping cones. If the overall factor proportions of both countries fall in the same cone, then a unique classification of commodities in terms of factor intensity will hold for both countries. On the other hand, if the overall factor proportions of the two countries lie in different cones, the ranking of commodities will be contradictory between countries.

When the ranking of commodities is contradictory between countries, the logic of the Heckscher-Ohlin theorem breaks down because it is impossible for both countries to export the commodity which uses more intensively their abundant factor. For instance, suppose that the factor proportions of country A are lower, and those of country B higher, than the slope of the vector OS (fig. 8.6). Country B will classify X as labor intensive relative to Y, while country A will classify X as land intensive relative to Y. If country A is considered labor abundant and country B land abundant, while X is labor intensive relative to Y in A but land intensive in B, the Heckscher–Ohlin theorem would predict that both countries will export commodity X, which, as we saw in chapters 2–7, is impossible. The situation does not improve if A were considered land abundant relative to B. (Indeed, as the following section shows, A should be classified as land abundant relative to B under all acceptable definitions.)

4. Definitions of Relative Factor Abundance

The preceding section discusses the concept of "factor intensity" rather thoroughly. Before a rigorous statement of the Heckscher–Ohlin theorem is made, however, let us consider the concept of factor abundance. This is necessary because there are various (often contradictory) criteria which can be used for this purpose.

Consider a model of two countries, A and B, with each country endowed with two homogeneous factors of production called labor and land. In particular, assume that A is endowed with L_A units of labor and T_A units of land, and B with L_B units of labor and T_B units of land. Under what circumstances would it be reasonable to say that country A is labor abundant relative to country B? The first definition of relative factor abundance that could be used in the present case is as follows.

Definition 1 (physical definition): Country A is said to be labor abundant relative to country B if country A is endowed with more units of labor per unit of land relative to B, that is, if the following inequality holds:

$$\frac{L_A}{T_A} > \frac{L_B}{T_B}. \qquad (8.1)$$

Observe that "factor abundance" is a relative concept. When we conclude that A is labor abundant relative to B, we necessarily imply that B is land abundant relative to A. This follows directly from equality (8.1), which can be rearranged as

$$\frac{T_B}{L_B} > \frac{T_A}{L_A}. \qquad (8.2)$$

Inequality (8.2) tells us that B has more units of land per unit of labor relative to A, that is, B is land abundant relative to A.

This definition of relative factor abundance is called the *physical definition*, because factor abundance is decided on the basis of the physical quantities of factor endowments. It has been used in the literature by Samuelson, Leontief, and others. But despite its great simplicity in a simplified model, serious conceptual difficulties arise in empirical investigations because of the implied *homogeneity* of factors of production. The traditional trichotomy of factors into capital, labor, and land is useful for some purposes. However, one should never forget that each of these three major classes of factors of production consists of rather heterogeneous as opposed to homogeneous objects. The factor "capital" should be understood to include all kinds of *produced means of production*, such as buildings, machinery of all sorts, buses, airplanes, and so on. In the same way, labor cannot be considered a homogeneous factor, in view of differences in the educational background, motivation, health, nutrition, and other qualities of workers. Similarly, two different parcels of land cannot be expected to be identical in all respects. In view of these (and many other) differences between the Heckscher–Ohlin model and the real world, great care should be exercised in applying the theory to any real world situation. These comments point to the necessity of a many-factor, many-commodity model, but then no simple hypothesis about the structure of trade can be made.

The physical definition of factor abundance is based on the relative physical abundance of the two factors of production. However, Ohlin himself was concerned not with physical but with *economic* abundance as it is reflected by relative factor prices in the autarkic state. In particular, he defined factor abundance as follows.

Definition 2 (price definition) : Country A is said to be labor abundant relative to country B if, at the pretrade autarkic equilibrium state, labor is relatively cheaper in A than in B. More precisely, A is said to be labor abundant relative to B if, at the pretrade autarkic equilibrium state, the following inequality holds:

$$\frac{w_A}{r_A} < \frac{w_B}{r_B}, \tag{8.3}$$

where w and r stand for the money wage rate and rent, respectively, with the subscripts indicating the country.

Are the two definitions of factor abundance, namely, the physical and price definitions, equivalent? In other words, is it necessarily true that, in the autarkic pretrade equilibrium state, labor is relatively cheaper in that country which is endowed with relatively more units of labor? More precisely, does the inequality $L_A/T_A > L_B/T_B$ necessarily imply the inequality $(w/r)_A < (w/r)_B$, where $(w/r)_A$ and $(w/r)_B$ are the pretrade equilibrium factor-price ratios in countries A and B, respectively? Unfortunately, the answer turns out to be negative.

As already mentioned, the price definition reflects relative *economic* abundance while the physical definition reflects merely relative *physical* abundance. What is the difference between physical versus economic abundance? The former is based on the absolute quantities of factors that exist in each country. The latter is based on the same factor quantities but relative to demand. Factor prices—on the basis of which factor abundance is decided when the price definition is used—are, like commodity prices, determined by both supply and demand. But while the price definition is based on both supply and demand influences, the physical definition is based solely on supply, ignoring completely the influence of demand. Hence, we cannot rule out the possibility that demand conditions might outweigh supply conditions with the result that the two definitions of factor abundance might give rise to contradictory classifications of the countries involved. For instance, assume that A is labor abundant relative to B on the basis of the physical definition. Further, assume that A's consumers have a stronger bias toward consuming labor-intensive commodities than B's consumers. Under these circumstances, it is not impossible for labor to be relatively more expensive in A before trade. Then A would be classified as labor abundant according to the physical definition but land abundant according to the price definition. This point becomes clearer as we proceed.

For completeness, it should be mentioned that a third definition of factor abundance has been proposed by Lancaster (1957) as follows.

Definition 3 (Lancaster's definition): A country is said to be abundant in that factor which is used intensively by the country's exported commodity.

Is Lancaster's definition of factor abundance appropriate for the Heckscher–Ohlin theorem? Not at all. On the basis of this definition, the Heckscher–Ohlin theorem is by necessity tautologically true. The Heckscher–Ohlin theorem asserts that a country exports that commodity which uses relatively more intensively its abundant factor, while Lancaster's definition calls abundant that factor which is being used more intensively by the exported commodity. On the basis of Lancaster's definition, the Heckscher–Ohlin theorem is by definition true—and it can never be refuted. But tautologies cannot help us explain the observed structure of trade. In this connection, one is reminded of Samuelson's observation that "the tropics grow tropical fruits because of the relative abundance there of tropical conditions."[3]

It is interesting to note that, on the basis of Lancaster's definition and when the ranking of commodities in terms of factor intensity is contradictory between countries, both countries will be considered abundant in the same factor, which is a nonsensical conclusion, because factor abundance, like comparative advantage, is a relative concept.

SELECTED BIBLIOGRAPHY

Heckscher, E. 1919. The effect of foreign trade on the distribution of income. *Ekonomisk Tidskrift* 21: 1–32.
Lancaster, K. 1957. The Heckscher–Ohlin trade model: a geometric treatment. *Economica* 24: 19–39.

3. See Samuelson (1948, p. 182).

Lerner, A. P. 1953. *Essays in Economics Analysis*, pp. 67–100.

Ohlin, B. 1933. *Interregional and International Trade*. Cambridge, Mass.: Harvard University Press. Chaps. 1–5, App. III.

Samuelson, P. A. 1948. International trade and the equalization of factor prices. *Economic Journal* 68: 165–184.

———. 1953. Prices of factors and goods in general equilibrium. *Review of Economic Studies* 21: 1–20.

Stolper, W. F., and P. A. Samuelson. 1941. Protection and real wages. *Review of Economic Studies* 9: 58–73.

(Additional references may be found at the end of Chapter 9, p. 227.)

9

The Heckscher-Ohlin Theorem

This chapter discusses the proofs of the Heckscher-Ohlin theorem in the two-commodity case. In addition, it extends the analysis to many countries and many commodities, and finally it points out some differences between the Classical and the Heckscher–Ohlin theories.

1. The Heckscher-Ohlin Theorem: When the Physical Definition of Factor Abundance is Adopted

Consider two countries, A and B, endowed with fixed quantities of two factors of production, labor (L) and land (T), inelastically supplied and producing two commodities, X and Y, under conditions of constant returns to scale. Assume that both countries have the same production functions, that pure competition rules throughout, and that A is relatively labor abundant (and thus B is land abundant) on the basis of the physical definition of factor abundance. Finally, assume that commodity X is labor intensive relative to Y for all factor-price ratios. Under these assumptions, the following proposition is necessarily true.

If the two countries produced the two commodities in the same proportion, that is, if in the autarkic equilibrium state the following equation held:

$$\frac{\text{output of } X \text{ in } A}{\text{output of } Y \text{ in } A} = \frac{\text{output of } X \text{ in } B}{\text{output of } Y \text{ in } B},$$

then commodity X would be relatively cheaper in A than in B, that is, the following inequality would hold:

$$\frac{\text{price of } X \text{ in } A}{\text{price of } Y \text{ in } A} < \frac{\text{price of } X \text{ in } B}{\text{price of } Y \text{ in } B}.$$

Alternatively, at the same relative commodity prices, A would be producing relatively more X than Y compared with B. That is, the following inequality would hold:

$$\frac{\text{output of } X \text{ in } A}{\text{output of } Y \text{ in } A} > \frac{\text{output of } X \text{ in } B}{\text{output of } Y \text{ in } B}.$$

This proposition can be easily established as follows. Given any factor-price ratio (i.e., w/r), the optimum coefficients of production can be determined. This can be done by determining the points on the unit isoquants of X and Y where the absolute value of the slope of each isoquant is equal to the given ratio w/r. The coordinates of these points are the optimum coefficients of production. Assume that these coefficients are a_{Lx}, a_{Ly}, a_{Tx}, and a_{Ty}, where the first subscript indicates the factor and the second the commodity. These coefficients are common to both countries (because of the assumption of identical production functions). Since it has been assumed that X is labor intensive relative to Y, the following inequality must also be satisfied:

$$\frac{a_{Lx}}{a_{Tx}} > \frac{a_{Ly}}{a_{Ty}}. \tag{9.1}$$

The commodity-price ratio is given by

$$\frac{p_x}{p_y} = \frac{(w/r)a_{Lx} + a_{Tx}}{(w/r)a_{Ly} + a_{Ty}}. \tag{9.2}$$

Finally, for full employment it is required that the following two equations be satisfied:

$$a_{Lx}X + a_{Ly}Y = L, \tag{9.3}$$

$$a_{Tx}X + a_{Ty}Y = T, \tag{9.4}$$

where L and T indicate overall factor endowments. Solving equations (9.3) and (9.4) for X and Y, we get

$$X = \frac{1}{\Delta}(La_{Ty} - Ta_{Ly}), \tag{9.5}$$

$$Y = \frac{1}{\Delta}(Ta_{Lx} - La_{Tx}), \tag{9.6}$$

where

$$\Delta \equiv a_{Lx}a_{Ty} - a_{Ly}a_{Tx}. \tag{9.7}$$

Consider the following ratio:

$$\frac{X}{Y} = \frac{La_{Ty} - Ta_{Ly}}{Ta_{Lx} - La_{Tx}} = \frac{(L/T)a_{Ty} - a_{Ly}}{a_{Lx} - (L/T)a_{Tx}}, \tag{9.8}$$

Equation (9.8) can be simplified to

$$\frac{X}{Y} = C\,\frac{\rho - \rho_y}{\rho_x - \rho} > 0, \tag{9.8}'$$

where

$$C \equiv \frac{a_{Ty}}{a_{Tx}}, \qquad \rho \equiv \frac{L}{T}, \qquad \rho_x \equiv \frac{a_{Lx}}{a_{Tx}}, \qquad \rho_y \equiv \frac{a_{Ly}}{a_{Ty}}.$$

The right-hand side of equation $(9.8)'$ is necessarily positive because ρ is a weighted average of ρ_x and ρ_y. This can be proved as follows. By definition,

$$\rho \equiv \frac{L}{T} = \frac{L_x}{T} + \frac{L_y}{T} = \frac{L_x}{T_x}\frac{T_x}{T} + \frac{L_y}{T_y}\frac{T_y}{T} = \lambda_x\rho_x + \lambda_y\rho_y, \tag{9.9}$$

where L_x and L_y = total amount of labor used for the production of X and Y, respectively, T_x and T_y = total amount of land used for the production of X and Y, respectively, $\rho \equiv L/T$, $\rho_x \equiv L_x/T_x$, $\rho_y \equiv L_y/T_y$, $\lambda_x \equiv T_x/T$, $\lambda_y \equiv T_y/T$, and $\lambda_x + \lambda_y = 1$. Accordingly, ρ must necessarily lie between ρ_x and ρ_y, a fundamental property of weighted averages. Hence, the numerator and the denominator of the right-hand side of $(9.8)'$ are either both positive or both negative, as the case may be. In the present case, where, by assumption, $\rho_y < \rho < \rho_x$, they are both positive.

Differentiating the ratio X/Y with respect to ρ, we get

$$\frac{d(X/Y)}{d\rho} = C\,\frac{\rho_x - \rho_y}{(\rho_x - \rho)^2}. \tag{9.10}$$

The sign of this derivative coincides with the sign of the difference $\rho_x - \rho_y$. Since, by assumption, $0 < \rho_y < \rho_x$ in the present case, the derivative of X/Y with respect to ρ must be positive. This means that the higher the value of ρ, the higher the value of the ratio X/Y. Since ρ is assumed to be higher in A than in B (i.e., $\rho_B < \rho_A$), at the same relative factor and commodity prices, A is producing more X per unit of Y than B. This proves the second part of the proposition. The first part, however, follows directly from the second (and vice versa). Starting from a position where relative commodity prices are identical and A is producing more X per unit of Y than B, we can freeze A's production and allow B to move along its production-possibilities frontier (in the direction of the axis for commodity X) until it produces the same ratio X/Y as country A. Because of the underlying increasing opportunity costs (see the discussion in chap. 4), X becomes relatively more expensive in B than in A. This completes the proof of the proposition.

Figure 9.1 illustrates the preceding proposition. Any vector through the origin (such as OM) will intersect the two production-possibilities frontiers at points (such as S and T) such that A's slope is flatter than B's. This means that when both countries produce the two commodities in the same proportion, X is relatively cheaper in A. On the other hand, given point T on

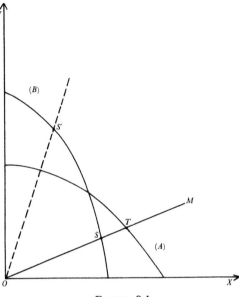

FIGURE 9.1

A's production-possibilities frontier, a point on B's production-possibilities frontier (such as S') can be determined such that the slope of B's production-possibilities frontier is equal to the slope of A's production-possibilities frontier at T. Figure 9.1 illustrates that, at the same relative prices, A produces more X than B per unit of Y (i.e., the vector OS' is necessarily steeper than the vector OM).

Let us now show that, under the additional assumption that demand conditions are identical in the two countries and, in particular, that they are given by a homothetic social indifference map, country A will necessarily have a comparative advantage in the production of X (i.e., the commodity which uses more intensively A's abundant factor), and B in Y. It is emphasized (and it will become evident from the following analysis) that the existence of a single social indifference map summarizing the demand conditions of both countries is not sufficient for the Heckscher-Ohlin theorem. It has to be coupled with the assumption of homotheticity. This is, no doubt, a much stronger assumption than similarity of tastes. In other words, what is actually required is not only similarity of tastes between A and B but similarity of tastes between income levels as well (i.e., the income consumption curves must be straight lines through the origin).

Figure 9.2 illustrates the problem for the simple case where in the autarkic state both countries reach the same social indifference curve II'. Before trade, country A is in equilibrium at point E_A and country B at E_B. Because of the law of diminishing marginal rate of substitution, the slope of the

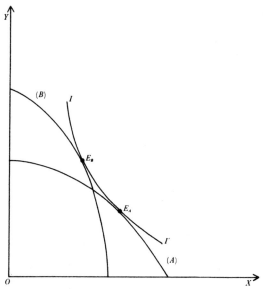

FIGURE 9.2

indifference curve II' at E_A is flatter than its slope at E_B. Therefore, in autarkic equilibrium, X is relatively cheaper in A than in B. Consequently, A has a comparative advantage in X (i.e., the commodity which uses more intensively A's abundant factor), and B in Y (i.e., the commodity which uses more intensively B's abundant factor). It should be noted that in this special case, the assumption of homotheticity of tastes is not necessary for the Heckscher-Ohlin theorem, similarity of tastes seems to be sufficient.

So far so good. But what if the two countries reach *different* social indifference curves at their respective pretrade equilibrium positions? Can we still prove that A will have a comparative advantage in X and B in Y? If we assume that the social indifference map is homothetic, the answer is yes. This more difficult case is illustrated in figures 9.3. Figure 9.3A illustrates the case where country B is small and country A is large, and figure 9.3B illustrates the opposite case, where country A is small and B is large.

First consider figure 9.3A. Before trade is opened up, country A is in equilibrium at point E_A. The common slope of A's production-possibilities frontier and social indifference curve I_3 at point E_A (in absolute terms) shows A's pretrade equilibrium price ratio. Let us call this price ratio p_A. As was previously shown, B's production-possibilities frontier at point N must be steeper than A's at point E_A. However, because of the assumption of homotheticity of tastes, the social indifference curve I_1 passing through point N must have the same slope at N as the slope of the social indifference curve I_3 at point E_A. Therefore, the social indifference curve passing through

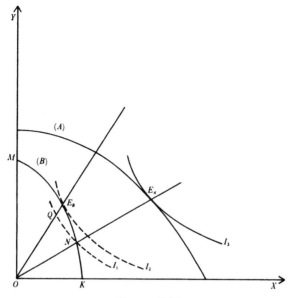

FIGURE 9.3A

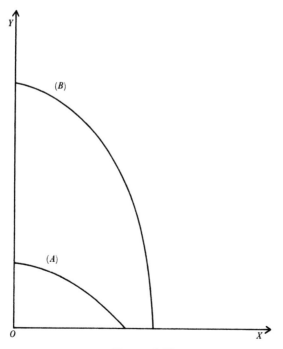

FIGURE 9.3B

N must necessarily intersect B's production-possibilities frontier from left to right, indicating that pretrade equilibrium in B must necessarily occur somewhere in the region MN of B's production-possibilities frontier, say at point E_B. Let p_B stand for B's pretrade equilibrium price ratio (as given by the common slope of B's production-possibilities frontier and the broken social indifference curve I_2 at point E_B). What remains to be shown is that $p_B > p_A$, implying that A has a comparative advantage in X and B in Y. This can be easily established as follows. Because of the assumed homotheticity of tastes, the slope of the broken indifference curve I_2 at E_B is equal to the slope of the broken indifference curve I_1 at Q. Therefore, the pretrade equilibrium price ratios of both countries can be read from the social indifference curve I_1. Thus, p_B is given by the absolute value of the slope of I_1 at point Q, and p_A is given by the absolute value of the slope of I_1 at point N. Because of the law of diminishing marginal rate of substitution, we must conclude that $p_A < p_B$, which is exactly what we set out to prove.

It is redundant to repeat the analysis for figure 9.3B. Under the assumption of identical and homothetic tastes, it can be shown that A has a comparative advantage in X and B in Y.

It is important to emphasize once more the role of the homotheticity assumption and show where it crucially enters into the proof of the Heckscher-Ohlin theorem. Remember that the homotheticity assumption was used twice: first, to show that the indifference curves I_3 and I_1 have the same slope at points E_A and N, respectively, and second, to show that the indifference curves I_2 and I_1 have the same slope at points E_B and Q, respectively. The first step seems to eliminate the region NK of B's production-possibilities frontier as a possible candidate for pretrade equilibrium in B. However, this is not crucial to the argument. In fact, if pretrade equilibrium in B occurs in the region NK, the Heckscher-Ohlin conclusion follows immediately, since all points in this region have an absolute slope steeper than the slope of A's production-possibilities frontier at point E_A. The importance of the first step is that it eliminates the possibility of the slope of I_1 at N being smaller than the slope of I_3 at E_A. In the same way, it can be shown that the importance of the second step in the use of the homotheticity assumption is that it eliminates the possibility of the slope of I_2 at E_B being smaller than the slope of I_1 at Q. More precisely, our proof establishes that $p_A = $ slope of I_3 at $E_A = $ slope of I_1 at $N < $ slope of I_1 at $Q = $ slope of I_2 at $E_B = p_B$. The homotheticity assumption is used twice: first, to eliminate the possibility of having slope of I_3 at $E_A > $ slope of I_1 at N, and second, to eliminate the possibility of having slope of I_1 at $E_B < $ slope of I_1 at Q.

Similarity of tastes and homotheticity are sufficient for the Heckscher-Ohlin theorem. It should be emphasized, though, that they are not necessary. In other words, the Heckscher-Ohlin theorem could be true even in the absence of these assumptions on demand conditions. What *is* necessary is that the slope of A's production-possibilities frontier at E_A be smaller (in absolute terms) than the slope of B's production-possibilities frontier at point E_B.

It should also be pointed out that, without any restrictions on demand, the direction of trade might be opposite to what the Heckscher-Ohlin theorem would predict, even though all other assumptions regarding production functions and so on are actually met.

As chapter 5 shows, the existence of pretrade multiple equilibria in one or both countries makes it virtually impossible to predict the direction of trade by simply comparing the pretrade equilibrium price ratios. Thus, even if we were told that $p_A < p_B$ in the pretrade position, we could not possibly conclude that A has a comparative advantage in X and B in Y.

Finally, it should be remembered that the preceding analysis is based on the assumption that commodity X is labor intensive relative to Y for all factor-price ratios. In other words, the phenomenon of factor-intensity reversals has been excluded by assumption. How should the preceding conclusions be amended in the presence of factor-intensity reversals? Without going into any detail, we can easily reach the following conclusions for the simple case where only one factor-intensity reversal exists.

a) If the overall factor proportions of the two countries (i.e., ρ_A and ρ_B) are such that a unique classification of X and Y in terms of factor intensity holds in both countries (see chap. 8, sec. 3), then the preceding analysis can be applied step by step to show that, under the rest of the assumptions outlined at the beginning of this section, the labor-abundant country will have a comparative advantage in the production of the labor-intensive commodity, and the land-abundant country in the land-intensive commodity. The proof of this statement can be undertaken along the same lines of analysis used for the case where the phenomenon of factor-intensity reversals had been assumed away.

b) If the overall factor proportions of the two countries are such that a contradictory classification of X and Y in terms of factor intensity is adopted in the two countries, the Heckscher-Ohlin theorem cannot possibly be correct for both countries simultaneously. However, it will always be correct for one of the two countries. But does this mean that the Heckscher-Ohlin theorem does not entirely lose its validity in the present case? Not at all, for we cannot predict a priori the country for which the theorem will remain valid.

2. The Heckscher-Ohlin Theorem: When the Price Definition of Factor Abundance is Adopted

Let us investigate the validity of the Heckscher-Ohlin theorem on the basis of the price definition of factor abundance.

Assume again that commodity X is labor intensive relative to Y for all factor-price ratios. To show that the Heckscher-Ohlin theorem is true, it must be demonstrated that the country which produces X relatively more cheaply in the pretrade equilibrium state is necessarily the labor-abundant country, with factor abundance decided on the basis of the price definition. In other words, it must be shown that the country with the lowest pretrade commodity-price ratio p_x/p_y is also the country with the lowest pretrade factor-price ratio w/r. This can be done by showing that the commodity-price ratio p_x/p_y is a strictly increasing function of the factor-price ratio w/r. Hence, a low p_x/p_y implies a low w/r, and a high p_x/p_y a high w/r.

The proposition that the price ratio p_x/p_y is a strictly increasing function of the factor-price ratio w/r (assuming, of course, that X is the labor-intensive commodity) can be proved as follows. Consider the case of fixed coefficients of production. As shown in the preceding section (see eq. [9.2]), the commodity-price ratio is a function of the factor-price ratio as follows:

$$\frac{p_x}{p_y} = \frac{(w/r)a_{Lx} + a_{Tx}}{(w/r)a_{Ly} + a_{Ty}}. \tag{9.11}$$

Equation (9.11) can be rewritten as

$$\frac{p_x}{p_y} = c\,\frac{(w/r)\rho_{x+1}}{(w/r)\rho_{y+1}}, \tag{9.12}$$

where c is a constant defined by the ratio a_{Tx}/a_{Ty}. Remember that equation (9.12) is valid in both countries because of the assumed identity of production functions between countries.

Differentiating p_x/p_y as given by equation (9.12) with respect to w/r, we get

$$\frac{d(p_x/p_y)}{d(w/r)} = c\,\frac{\rho_x - \rho_y}{[(w/r)\rho_y + 1]^2} > 0, \tag{9.13}$$

which is positive, since, by assumption, $\rho_x > \rho_y$. This shows that the commodity-price ratio p_x/p_y is a strictly increasing function of the factor-price ratio w/r.

For completeness, it should be pointed out that, should commodity Y be the labor-intensive commodity (i.e., $\rho_y > \rho_x$), the ratio p_x/p_y will be a strictly decreasing function of w/r, which is again sufficient for the validity of the Heckscher–Ohlin theorem.

The case of variable coefficients is slightly more complicated. The coefficients a_{Lx}, a_{Tx}, a_{Ly}, and a_{Ty} are themselves functions of the factor-price ratio w/r. This is important in the following differentiations. For simplicity, the convention of using primes is adopted in differentiating the coefficients a_{Lx}, a_{Tx}, a_{Ly}, and a_{Ty} with respect to the ratio w/r.

Differentiating p_x/p_y as given by equation (9.11) with respect to w/r, we get

$$\frac{d(p_x/p_y)}{d(w/r)} = \frac{\begin{aligned}[a_{Lx} + a'_{Tx} + (w/r)a'_{Lx}][(w/r)a_{Ly} + a_{Ty}] \\ - [a_{Ly} + (w/r)a'_{Ly} + a'_{Ty}][(w/r)a_{Lx} + a_{Tx}]\end{aligned}}{[a_{Lx}(w/r) + a_{Ty}]^2}. \tag{9.14}$$

Equation (9.14) can be greatly simplified by making use of the marginal conditions which have to be satisfied for cost minimization. Thus, the marginal rate of substitution of labor for land should be equal to the factor-price ratio w/r in each industry; that is,

$$MRS^X_{LT} = -\frac{da_{Tx}}{da_{Lx}} = -\frac{a'_{Tx}}{a'_{Lx}} = w/r, \tag{9.15}$$

$$MRS^Y_{LT} = -\frac{da_{Ty}}{da_{Ly}} = -\frac{a'_{Ty}}{a'_{Ly}} = w/r, \tag{9.16}$$

where MRS^i_{LT} stands for the marginal rate of substitution of labor for land in the ith industry.

From equations (9.15) and (9.16) it follows that

$$a'_{Tx} + \frac{w}{r} a'_{Lx} = 0, \tag{9.15'}$$

$$a'_{Ty} + \frac{w}{r} a'_{Ly} = 0. \tag{9.16'}$$

Using equation (9.15)' and (9.16)', we can simplify equation (9.14) as follows:

$$\frac{d(p_x/p_y)}{d(w/r)} = \frac{a_{Lx}a_{Ty} - a_{Ly}a_{Tx}}{[a_{Ly}(w/r) + a_{Ty}]^2} = c\frac{\rho_x - \rho_y}{[(w/r)\rho_y + 1]^2}. \tag{9.17}$$

Now equation (9.17) is identical to equation (9.13), and therefore, the conclusion must be the same as the conclusion reached under the simplified assumption of fixed coefficients of production; that is, the commodity-price ratio p_x/p_y is a strictly increasing function of w/r.

From the preceding analysis it follows that, in the absence of factor-intensity reversals, the Heckscher-Ohlin theorem is necessarily true on the basis of the price definition, for the country with the lower commodity-price ratio p_x/p_y (in the pretrade equilibrium state) will necessarily be the country with the lower factor-price ratio w/r, given that X is labor intensive relative to Y for all factor-price ratios. It should be emphasized that our analysis is based on the implicit assumption that, before trade, both commodities are produced and consumed in both countries, which is not unreasonable. In cases where only one commodity is produced in at least one country before trade, the Heckscher-Ohlin conclusion may be reversed. This point will be taken up in chapter 11.

Nowhere in the preceding proof were we required to assume the identity of consumption patterns between countries. Consequently, in the absence of factor-intensity reversals and when the price definition of factor abundance is used, the Heckscher-Ohlin theorem will necessarily be true irrespective of any differences in tastes in the two countries.

Does the Heckscher-Ohlin theorem remain valid when factor-intensity reversals are allowed? Not in general. This follows from the fact that the price ratio p_x/p_y is no longer a monotonic function of the factor-price ratio w/r. For the simple case of a single factor-intensity reversal, the following conclusions pertain.

a) If the overall factor proportions of the two countries are such that a unique classification of X and Y in terms of factor intensity holds in both countries, the preceding analysis can be applied step by step to show that, before trade, the labor-intensive commodity will be relatively cheaper in the labor-abundant country (i.e., the country with the lower w/r, ratio before trade).

b) If the overall factor proportions of the two countries are such that a contradictory classification of X and Y in terms of factor intensity is adopted by the two countries, the Heckscher-Ohlin theorem cannot possibly be correct for both countries simultaneously, although it will always be true for one of the two countries.

If the number of factor-intensity reversals is greater than one, conclusion (*b*) will continue to be correct but conclusion (*a*) can no longer be maintained. The analysis of the factor-price equalization theorem in chapter 11 will facilitate a better understanding of these cases.

3. The Heckscher-Ohlin Theorem: Summary

a) In the absence of factor-intensity reversals, the Heckscher-Ohlin theorem is necessarily true on the basis of the price definition of factor abundance. The identity of tastes between countries is unnecessary to assume in the present case. But incomplete specialization before trade is in general required.

b) In the absence of factor-intensity reversals, the Heckscher-Ohlin theorem will be true on the basis of the physical definition of factor abundance if tastes are homothetic and similar between countries. The latter assumption is sufficient but not necessary for the validity of the theorem.

c) In the presence of factor-intensity reversals, the Heckscher-Ohlin theorem is not true in general.

4. Many Countries and Many Commodities

The preceding conclusions can be easily generalized to the case of many countries. Assume that there are $n > 2$ countries which can be classified in the order of factor abundance on the basis of either the price or the physical definition. In particular, assume that

$$\frac{L_1}{T_1} < \frac{L_2}{T_2} < \cdots < \frac{L_n}{T_n}, \qquad (9.18)$$

where L_i = total labor endowment of the ith country and T_i = total land endowment of the ith country. On the basis of the physical definition of factor abundance, the first country is land abundant relative to the second, the second country is land abundant relative to the third, and so on down the line to the nth country.

Without any loss of generality, also assume that tastes are similar and homothetic between countries and that commodity X is land intensive relative to Y for all factor-price ratios. Therefore, the preceding classification of countries in the order of factor abundance will not be affected if we were to use the price definition.

On the basis of the analysis of sections 1–3 of the present chapter, the following inequalities would necessarily hold before trade opens up:

$$p_1 < p_2 < \cdots < p_n,$$

where p_i = the pretrade equilibrium price ratio (i.e., [price of X]/ [price of Y]) of the ith country. That is, considering any pair of countries, we can definitely say that the land-abundant country will be producing X relatively more cheaply than the labor-abundant country before trade. But does this conclusion enable us to determine a priori the direction of trade for all n countries? Not at all. All we can be sure of is that the first country will be exporting commodity X in exchange for Y and that the nth country will be exporting commodity Y in exchange for X. But the direction of trade of the countries in between (countries $2, 3, \ldots, n - 1$) cannot be predicted without introducing demand into the picture. However, this much can be said. Demand conditions can be introduced to "break the chain" into exporters of X and exporters of Y. If, for instance, the third country exports commodity X and imports Y, then the preceding countries (the first and second) must also export X and import Y. This is very similar to appendix 3A in relation to the classical theory. Therefore, no further discussion is necessary.

Let us turn now to the case of two countries (A and B) but many ($m > 2$) commodities. Some economists have contended that introducing more commodities into the analysis does not destroy the conclusions reached in sections 1–3.[1] In particular, assuming away the possibility of factor-intensity reversals, these economists contend that it is still possible to rank the commodities (from technological data and factor supply data) in terms of factor ratios and *thereby uniquely rank them in terms of comparative advantage as in the*

---

1. See Jones (1956) and Bhagwati (1964).

classical system. Demand conditions will then "break the chain" into exports and imports. Unfortunately, this proposition is false. There is no need to give rigorous proof; a counterexample should be sufficient.

Assume that there are three commodities, X, Y, and Z, and that X is labor intensive relative to Y and Y is labor intensive relative to Z (and therefore X is also labor intensive relative to Z) for all factor-price ratios. Assume also that country A is endowed with 350 units of labor and 600 units of land, and B with 300 units of labor and 600 units of land. Assume further that international commodity trade equalizes factor prices between countries.

Consider now a general-equilibrium situation. In particular, assume that the optimum coefficients of production (in both countries) at the observed equilibrium point are as follows: 1 unit of X requires 1 unit of labor and 1 unit of land; 1 unit of Y requires 1 unit of labor and 2 units of land; and 1 unit of Z requires 1 unit of labor and 3 units of land. On the basis of these assumptions and the factor endowments of A and B, we can formulate the following full-employment equations:

$$X_A^P + Y_A^P + Z_A^P = 350, \tag{9.19}$$

$$X_A^P + 2Y_A^P \quad 3Z_A^P = 600, \tag{9.20}$$

$$X_B^P + Y_B^P + Z_B^P = 300, \tag{9.21}$$

$$X_B^P + 2Y_B^P + 3Z_B^P = 600. \tag{9.22}$$

The term $X_A^P \equiv$ amount of X produced in country A, and so on.

We have four equations in six unknowns; therefore, we cannot, without further information, determine the equilibrium values for all variables. Note that *this situation is created by the fact that there are more commodities than factors of production*. For the moment, treat the output of the third commodity as a parameter and solve equations (9.19) and (9.20) for X_A^P and Y_A^P and equations (9.21) and (9.22) for X_B^P and Y_B^P. The solutions are

$$X_A^P = 100 + Z_A^P, \tag{9.23}$$

$$Y_A^P = 250 - 2Z_A^P, \tag{9.24}$$

$$X_B^P = Z_B^P, \tag{9.25}$$

$$Y_B^P = 300 - 2Z_B^P. \tag{9.26}$$

Since only nonnegative solutions are acceptable, equation (9.24) restricts the value of Z_A to less than 125; that is,

$$0 \leq Z_A^P \leq 125. \tag{9.27}$$

Similarly, equation (9.26) restricts the value of Z_B^P to

$$0 \leq Z_B^P \leq 150. \tag{9.28}$$

Let us introduce another piece of exogenous information about the general-equilibrium situation we are assuming exists. In particular, suppose that the total production and consumption of Z in both countries is 100 units. Can we also determine the aggregate production of X and Y? The answer is yes. Thus,

$$X_W^P \equiv X_A^P + X_B^P = 100 + Z_A^P + Z_B^P = 100 + Z_W^P, \qquad (9.29)$$

$$Y_W^P \equiv Y_A^P + Y_B^P = 250 - 2Z_A^P + 300 - 2Z_B^P = 550 - 2Z_W^P, \qquad (9.30)$$

where the subscript W indicates the total "world output." Since, by assumption, $Z_W^P = 100$, it must also be true that $X_W^P = 200$ and $Y_W^P = 350$.

What is the direction of trade? Can we determine it uniquely? If so, does it correspond to what the Heckscher-Ohlin theorem would predict? Unfortunately, the answers are all negative, mainly because, although we know the combined outputs of countries A and B for each one of the three commodities—and thus we know a point on the world production-possibilities frontier—we cannot determine *uniquely* the individual outputs of A and B. That is, the structure of production is indeterminate as in the classical equal-costs case.

To illustrate the implications of the indeterminacy of the structure of production, let us first introduce demand into the picture. We can follow the Heckscher-Ohlin tradition and suppose that tastes are homothetic and similar between countries. Therefore, irrespective of prices, both countries will be consuming the three commodities in the same proportion. Since we already know the aggregate production of X, Y, and Z (200, 350, and 100, respectively), we can infer that the three commodities must be consumed in the proportion $4X:7Y:2Z$ in both countries.

What are the precise amounts of X, Y, and Z consumed in A and B? That depends on the division of income between A and B, which in turn depends upon the equilibrium factor prices. Even without knowing the equilibrium factor prices, we can still determine upper and lower limits for the ratio Q_A/Q_B, where $Q_i \equiv$ income of the ith country. Thus,

$$\frac{Q_A}{Q_B} = \frac{(w/r)350 + 600}{(w/r)300 + 600}, \qquad (9.31)$$

or, dividing both numerator and denominator by w/r,

$$\frac{Q_A}{Q_B} = \frac{350 + (r/w)600}{300 + (r/w)600}. \qquad (9.31)'$$

The factor-price ratio w/r can vary from 0 to ∞. When $w/r = 0$, it follows from equation (9.31) that $Q_A/Q_B = 1$, and when $w/r = \infty$, or $r/w = 0$, it follows from (9.31)' that $Q_A/Q_B = \frac{7}{6}$. That is, the income ratio can only vary between 1 and $\frac{7}{6}$, or

$$1 < \frac{Q_A}{Q_B} < \frac{7}{6}. \qquad (9.32)$$

Assume that, at the particular equilibrium we are interested in, the income ratio is $Q_A/Q_B = \frac{13}{12}$. Therefore, the outputs of X, Y, and Z must be absorbed by countries A and B in the proportion 13:12. The equilibrium consumption levels are:

$$X_A^c = 104 \qquad Y_A^c = 182 \qquad Z_A^c = 52$$
$$X_B^c = 96 \qquad Y_B^c = 168 \qquad Z_B^c = 48,$$

where the superscript c indicates consumption.

As long as A produces only 3 units of Z or less, it will definitely export Y and import X and Z. For instance, suppose that A produces only 2 units of Z. The pattern of production of both countries will then be

$$X_A^p = 102 \qquad Y_A^p = 246 \qquad Z_A^p = 2$$
$$X_B^p = 98 \qquad Y_B^p = 104 \qquad Z_B^p = 98$$
$$X_W^p = 200 \qquad Y_W^p = 350 \qquad Z_W^p = 100.$$

Therefore, A must be exporting to B 64 units of Y in exchange for 2 units of X and 50 units of Z. But this pattern of trade is precisely what some economists thought could never occur, for Y is labor intensive relative to Z but land intensive relative to X. This clearly shows that commodities cannot be uniquely ranked in terms of comparative advantage as in the classical system—whether the price or the quantity definition of factor abundance is used.

If (as the preceding analysis shows) commodities cannot be uniquely ranked in terms of comparative advantage, is there any way in which the Heckscher-Ohlin theorem can be reformulated and be logically consistent in the presence of more than two commodities? Probably, because in a deeper sense the Heckscher-Ohlin (or the factor-proportions) theory points to an indirect exchange of factors between countries—an exchange which tends to equalize the proportion in which the two factors are indirectly (through commodities) absorbed despite the fact that the labor/land ratios differ between countries. It is this fundamental property of the Heckscher-Ohlin model which is not lost even when the number of commodities is allowed to increase.

Assume that countries A and B have identical and homothetic tastes. On the basis of this assumption alone, the consumption levels of all commodities in country A will necessarily be proportional to the corresponding consumption levels in country B. In other words,

$$C_i^A = \lambda C_i^B, \tag{9.33}$$

where $C_i^A = A$'s consumption level of the ith good, $C_i^B = B$'s consumption level of the ith good, and $\lambda = $ factor of proportionality. The factor of proportionality (λ) depends on the precise equilibrium value of the factor-price ratio. In what follows, λ will be treated as a constant because it will be assumed that the world economy is already in equilibrium. Our job is to study the properties of this equilibrium.

Let us now follow the Heckscher-Ohlin theorem and assume that the techniques of production at the observed international equilibrium are identical between countries. Let the symbols a_{Li} and a_{Ti} denote the amounts of labor and land, respectively, required for the production of 1 unit of the ith commodity in either country. The total amounts of labor and land absorbed by countries A and B are calculated as follows:

$$L_A^D \equiv \sum_{i=1}^{n} a_{Li} C_i^A \tag{9.34}$$

$$T_A^D \equiv \sum_{i=1}^{n} a_{Ti} C_i^A, \tag{9.35}$$

$$L_B^D \equiv \sum_{i=1}^{n} a_{Li} C_i^B, \tag{9.36}$$

$$T_B^D \equiv \sum_{i=1}^{n} a_{Ti} C_i^B. \tag{9.37}$$

The new symbols are self-evident. For instance, L_A^D denotes the total amount of labor absorbed (or demanded) by country A, and so on.

Applying equation (9.33) to equations (9.34)–(9.37) gives

$$L_A^D \equiv \sum_{i=1}^{n} a_{Li} C_i^A = \lambda \sum_{i=1}^{n} a_{Li} C_i^B = \lambda L_B^D, \tag{9.38}$$

$$T_A^D \equiv \sum_{i=1}^{n} a_{Ti} C_i^A = \lambda \sum_{i=1}^{n} a_{Ti} C_i^B = \lambda T_B^D. \tag{9.39}$$

That is, the amounts of labor and land absorbed by A are proportional to the respective amounts absorbed by B, with λ being the factor of proportionality.

Denote L_A and $\bar{T}_A$ as A's endowments of labor and land, respectively. Similarly, let L_B and $\bar{T}_B$ denote the corresponding endowments for B. It is further convenient to define the following:

$$L \equiv L_A + L_B, \tag{9.40}$$

$$\bar{T} \equiv \bar{T}_A + \bar{T}_B. \tag{9.41}$$

That is, L and $\bar{T}$ show the aggregate amounts of labor and land, respectively, which exist in both countries together.

Full employment in both countries requires that the following equations be satisfied:

$$L = L_A^D + L_B^D = \lambda L_B^D + L_B^D = (1 + \lambda) L_B^D, \tag{9.42}$$

$$\bar{T} = T_A^D + T_B^D = \lambda T_B^D + T_B^D = (1 + \lambda) T_B^D. \tag{9.43}$$

It is clear from equations (9.38)–(9.39) and (9.42)–(9.43) that

$$\frac{L_A^D}{T_A^D} = \frac{L_B^D}{T_B^D} = \frac{L}{\bar{T}}. \tag{9.44}$$

Consider now the budget equations of countries A and B:

$$wL_A + r\bar{T}_A = wL_A^D + rT_A^D, \tag{9.45}$$

$$wL_B + r\bar{T}_B = wL_B^D + rT_B^D, \tag{9.46}$$

or

$$w(L_A^D - L_A) + r(T_A^D - \bar{T}_A) = 0, \tag{9.45}'$$

$$w(L_B^D - L_B) + r(T_B^D - \bar{T}_B) = 0. \tag{9.46}'$$

Also, from equations (9.42)–(9.43) it follows that

$$(L_A^D - L_A) + (L_B^D - L_B) = 0, \tag{9.42}'$$

$$(T_A^D - \bar{T}_A) + (T_B^D - \bar{T}_B) = 0. \tag{9.43}'$$

Hence, when $(L_A^D - L_A)$ is positive, $(T_A^D - \bar{T}_A)$ must be negative, $(L_B^D - L_B)$ must be negative, and $(T_B^D - \bar{T}_B)$ must be positive. In other words, when country A is importing labor indirectly, it must be exporting land, and country B must be exporting labor and importing land.

The above conclusions are illustrated in figure 9.4. The sides of the box show the aggregate amounts of labor and land (L and $\bar{T}$). The coordinates of point Z show, with respect to the O_A origin, A's factor endowments, and with respect to the O_B origin, B's factor endowments. Equilibrium will occur somewhere along the diagonal $O_A O_B$ (eq. [9.44]). In particular, equilibrium will occur somewhere in the region UV because the equilibrium factor prices (w and r) are positive. This is illustrated by point E. Therefore, A must be exporting GZ units of land to B in exchange for ZH units of labor.

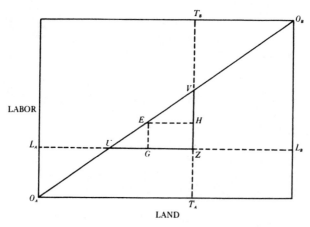

FIGURE 9.4

It is important to note that the quantities GZ and ZH are the net (not the gross) exports and imports of labor and land. Finally, note that the precise position of the equilibrium point E depends on the equilibrium value of the factor-price ratio: we must have $(w/r)ZH = GZ$.

Consider now the case illustrated in figure 9.4 where A will necessarily be exporting land to B in exchange for labor. We can classify the n commodities into two categories: A's exportables (those commodities exported by A to B) and A's importables (those imported by A from B). (We know that we cannot uniquely classify commodities in this fashion, but we are only interested in the general properties of any feasible classification, i.e., a classification which is consistent with general equilibrium.) Let us adopt the following symbols: X_i = amount of ith commodity exported from A to B $(i = 1, 2, \ldots, s)$ and M_j = amount of jth commodity exported from B to A $(j = s + 1, s + 2, \ldots, n)$. Then the quantities $(L_A^D - L_A)$, $(T_A^D - \bar{T}_A)$, $(L_B^D - L_B)$, and $(\bar{T}_B^D - \bar{T}_B)$ can be defined directly in terms of the quantities of A's exportables and importables. Thus,

$$L_A^D - L_A = \sum_{j=s+1}^{n} a_{Lj}M_j - \sum_{i=1}^{s} a_{Li}X_i > 0, \tag{9.47}$$

$$T_A^D - \bar{T}_A = \sum_{j=s+1}^{n} a_{Tj}M_j - \sum_{i=1}^{s} a_{Ti}X_i < 0. \tag{9.48}$$

Since $L_B^D - L_B = -(L_A^D - L_A)$ and $(T_B^D - \bar{T}_B) = -(T_A^D - \bar{T}_A)$, these are the only equations we need.

Inequalities (9.47) and (9.48) can be simplified by introducing the optimum labor/land ratios $\rho_i \equiv a_{Li}/a_{Ti}$ for $i = 1, 2, \ldots, n$, which gives us

$$\sum_{j=s+1}^{n} \rho_j(a_{Tj}M_j) > \sum_{i=1}^{s} \rho_i(a_{Ti}X_i), \tag{9.47'}$$

$$\sum_{j=s+1}^{n} a_{Tj}M_j < \sum_{i=1}^{s} a_{Ti}X_i. \tag{9.48'}$$

Dividing the left-hand side of (9.47)' by the left-hand side of (9.48)' and the right-hand side of (9.47)' by the right-hand side of (9.48)', we get the fundamental inequality

$$\frac{\sum_{j=s+1}^{n} \rho_j(a_{Tj}M_j)}{\sum_{j=s+1}^{n} a_{Tj}M_j} > \frac{\sum_{i=1}^{s} \rho_i(a_{Ti}X_i)}{\sum_{i=1}^{s} a_{Ti}X_i}, \tag{9.49}$$

or, defining

$$z_i \equiv \frac{a_{Ti}X_i}{\sum_{i=1}^{s} a_{Ti}X_i}, \qquad z_j \equiv \frac{a_{Tj}M_j}{\sum_{j=s+1}^{n} a_{Tj}M_j}$$

$$\left(\text{thus } \sum_{i=1}^{s} z_i = 1 \quad \text{and} \quad \sum_{j=s+1}^{n} z_j = 1\right)$$

and substituting into (9.49), we finally get

$$\sum_{j=s+1}^{n} \rho_j z_j > \sum_{i=1}^{s} \rho_i z_i. \tag{9.49}'$$

That is, *the weighted average of the labor/land ratios of A's imported commodities must be higher than the weighted average of the labor/land ratios of A's exported commodities, with the weights being given by the relative amounts of land absorbed by each commodity within each group.*

Therefore, although it cannot be said that every commodity exported by A (i.e., the land-abundant country) must be land intensive relative to every commodity imported by A, it can be said that *A's exportables as a group are necessarily land intensive relative to A's importables as a group*, with "factor intensity" defined in terms of the weighted averages as shown by inequality (9.49)'.

In conclusion, note that the familiar case of two commodities is a special case of this more general formulation. Then the land-abundant country can export land in exchange for labor only by exporting the land-intensive commodity in exchange for the labor-intensive commodity.

5. *The Identity of Production Functions between Countries*

One of the crucial assumptions of the Heckscher-Ohlin theorem is that production functions are identical between countries. In fact, Ohlin appears to have taken it for granted that production functions are the same everywhere. He based his conclusion on the observation that, at any time, the same causes everywhere produce the same results. In his words, "the physical conditions of production . . . are everywhere the same."[2] This assumption seems necessary for the Heckscher-Ohlin theorem. Otherwise, any empirical evidence contrary to that indicated by factor proportions could always be explained by arbitrary differences in production functions. But such an explanation would contribute nothing to our understanding of the causes of trade.

The assumption that production functions are identical between countries raises the fundamental question of the proper definition of two concepts, namely, production functions and factors of production. As Samuelson noted, the concept "factor of production" can be used in at least three different senses: (*a*) as a concrete input item (such as raw materials) purchasable in the market place; (*b*) as a nonappropriable factor (such as weather conditions) that is free (in the sense that its price is zero) though not available in unlimited quantities; and (*c*) as a condition bearing on production (such as technological knowledge). By including all three categories

2. See Ohlin (1933, p. 14).

under "factors of production," we can no doubt make the production functions identical between countries.

Ricardo's production functions illustrate the point. He specifically assumed the following relationships between labor input (L) and cloth output (C):

$$\text{Portugal:} \quad C = L/90,$$
$$\text{England:} \quad C = L/100.$$

If labor, of course, were considered the only "factor of production," it would be obvious that England and Portugal would indeed have different production functions. However, the two countries may be regarded as sharing a common production function, $C = f(L, W_1, W_2, \ldots, W_n)$, where W_i signifies one aspect of "the peculiar powers bestowed by nature" (Ricardo's phrase), such as temperature, humidity, and so on, that are considered relevant for the production of cloth. It could be said that England and Portugal share the same production function but that they operate in different regions of the production function. In other words, considering the factors W_i as parameters, we can rewrite the common production function as follows:

$$C = f(L, W_1, W_2, \ldots, W_n) = g(L).$$

Since the parameters $W_1, \ldots, W_n$ will take different values in the two countries, the function $g(L)$ will necessarily be different despite the fact that the function $f(L, W_1, \ldots, W_n)$ is common to both countries.

By considering every conceivable circumstance affecting output as a separate factor, we can no doubt make the production functions identical between countries. But this seems to be a useless tautology. It would be more appropriate to include in the concept "factor of production" only the concrete input items purchasable in the marketplace. But then, we can no longer pretend on the basis of a priori reasoning alone that the production functions are identical between countries. Under these circumstances, the Heckscher-Ohlin theorem cannot be a sufficient explanation of the pattern of trade. With different production functions, trade can take place between any two countries with similar factor endowments and similar consumption patterns. But serious problems arise after the assumption is dropped that production functions are identical between countries. It would then be required to explain when and how production functions come to differ—a necessary prerequisite for the use of the theory of comparative advantage to predict (ex ante) the pattern of trade.

6. Some Differences Between the Classical and the Heckscher-Ohlin Theories

The classical and the Heckscher-Ohlin theories constitute two different hypotheses in relation to the structure of trade. First, the classical doctrine is based on the labor theory of value, while the Heckscher-Ohlin theorem is necessarily based on a more general theory of production, postulating at least two factors of production. (It should be noted that when the number of factors is greater than two, the concept of "factor intensity" is very difficult to interpret.)

Second, the classical theory emphasizes the gains from trade. That is, the classical theory is a contribution to welfare economics. On the other hand, the modern theory is a contribution to positive economics.

Third, if we restrict our comments to the two-commodity case, the classical theory requires only that demand conditions in the two countries be such that both commodities are being produced and consumed in both countries in the autarkic equilibrium state. On the other hand, the Heckscher-Ohlin theorem assumes that tastes are largely similar between countries, which appears to be a stronger assumption.

Fourth, in the classical theory, the distribution of income necessarily remains the same after as before trade, because of the existence of a single factor of production. As a result, the derivation of the offer curves can proceed directly from the indifference maps of individuals (as explained in chaps. 2–6) instead of having to postulate the existence of social indifference maps, as we were practically forced to do with the neoclassical and modern theories. To be sure, the Heckscher-Ohlin theorem could proceed from the indifference maps of individuals, but this approach has the disadvantage that it cannot be easily handled with simple analytical tools. Another consequence of income distribution remaining constant in the classical theory as opposed to the Heckscher-Ohlin theorem is that, in the classical theory, the welfare of every individual unequivocally improves with trade; or, in the limiting case where a large country trades with a small one and the equilibrium terms of trade coincide with the large country's pretrade equilibrium price ratio, the welfare of each individual citizen of the large country necessarily remains at the same level as it were before trade. Thus, in the classical theory the introduction of trade does not make anybody worse off. The same unqualified statement cannot be made about the Heckscher-Ohlin theorem.

Fifth, multiple pretrade equilibria can be easily ruled out in the case of the classical theory. The only requirement is that both commodities be produced and consumed in both countries in the autarkic equilibrium state. (Note that the latter condition does not require that every individual consume both commodities.) But again, the same statement cannot be made about the Heckscher-Ohlin theorem. Thus, comparative advantage can be decided on the basis of pretrade price ratios with certainty only in the classical theory.

Finally, and perhaps most important, the classical theory attributes comparative advantage to arbitrary differences in production functions. On the other hand, the Heckscher-Ohlin theorem postulates the identity of production functions between countries and attributes comparative advantage to differences in factor proportions.

SELECTED BIBLIOGRAPHY

Bhagwati, J. 1964. The pure theory of international trade. *Economic Journal* 74: 1–78.
Heckscher, E. 1919. The effect of foreign trade on the distribution of income. *Ekonomisk Tidskrift* 21: 1–32.
Jones, R. W. 1956. Factor proportions in the Heckscher-Ohlin theorems. *Review of Economic Studies* 24: 1–10.
Lancaster, K. 1957. The Heckscher-Ohlin trade model: a geometric treatment. *Economica* 24: 19–39.
Lerner, A. P. 1953. *Essays in Economics Analysis*, pp. 67–100.
Ohlin, B. 1933. *Interregional and International Trade*. Cambridge, Mass.: Harvard University Press. Chaps. 1–6, App. 3.
Samuelson, P. A. 1948. International trade and the equalization of factor prices. *Economic Journal* 68: 165–184.
———. 1949. International factor price equalization once again. *Economic Journal* 59: 181–97.

(Additional references may be found at the end of Chapter 11, p. 266.)

10

Factor Proportions, Factor Prices, and Commodity Prices

1. Introduction

The preceding chapter analyzes the first proposition of the modern theory, namely, the hypothesis that the *cause* of trade is to be found largely in differences between the factor endowments of different countries, in particular, the hypothesis that a country has a comparative advantage in the production of that commodity which uses more intensively the country's relatively abundant factor. This proposition has come to be known as the *Heckscher-Ohlin theorem*.

We shall now analyze the second proposition of the modern theory, namely, the hypothesis that the *effect* of trade is to tend to equalize factor prices as between countries, thus serving to some extent as a substitute for factor mobility. This proposition, which has come to be known as the *factor-price equalization theorem*, has attracted the attention of many distinguished trade theorists in the last two and a half decades. In 1919 Heckscher stated that trade would equalize factor rewards completely. Ohlin (1933), on the other hand, cited several reasons why full factor-price equalization would not occur in practice. He asserted, however, that there was a tendency (but only a tendency) toward factor-price equalization. Samuelson (1948) initiated the investigation of the conditions under which complete factor-price equalization would follow.

It appears that, as far as the two-country, two-factor, two-commodity case is concerned, Samuelson stated everything that has ever been said subsequently. Since this book is mainly confined to the restrictive case of two factors and two commodities, Samuelson's analysis will be followed rather closely. The present chapter deals with the relationship between factor proportions, factor prices, and commodity prices. The proof of the factor-price equalization theorem will be taken up in chapter 11.

2. The Basic Model

Consider two countries (A and B), each endowed with two homogeneous factors of production called labor (L) and land (T) and producing two commodities (X and Y). In addition, assume the following:

i) pure competition in both product and factor markets.
ii) nonreversible and different factor intensities of the two commodities at all factor prices;
iii) identical production functions for each commodity between countries;
iv) linear homogeneous production functions in each commodity (i.e., constant returns to scale);
v) the outputs of commodities dependent only on inputs of factors which enter into their respective production processes and factors indifferent between uses and of the same quality in both countries;
vi) incomplete specialization in production in each country; and
vii) absence of trade impediments (such as tariffs, and quotas) and transportation costs.

The argument is usually simplified further by assuming initially that the two homogeneous factors (labor and land) are inelastically supplied in both countries. In other words, the available quantities of labor and land are independent of their prices.

It should be noted at the outset that the purpose of assumption (vii) is to ensure that, under free trade, commodity prices are equalized between countries. All other assumptions ensure a one-to-one correspondence between commodity prices and factor prices. The heart of the factor-price equilization theorem is to show that, as a result of assumptions (i)–(vi), there exists a one-to-one correspondence between commodity prices and factor prices. Once this is established, it can be easily seen that factor prices will indeed be equalized through free commodity movements, because commodity prices will be the same everywhere.

It should be emphasized that "factor prices" in this context does not mean prices of the factors of production themselves (i.e., the price of a piece of land, and so on). It means, rather, the *rentals* for the *services* of these factors, such as the wage rate for the services of labor and the rent for the services of land, per unit of time. The equalization of factor rentals is neither a necessary nor a sufficient condition for the equalization of the prices of the factors of production. This follows directly from the fact that the relation between a factor's rental and its price is determined, among other things, by the rate of interest, and the rate of interest is equalized between countries only in special circumstances. Thus, it is entirely possible for, say, one acre of homogeneous land to earn the same real rental in both countries and yet command substantially different market prices in the two countries. The confusing use of the term "factor prices" instead of "factor rentals" in the literature is unfortunate.

3. Factor Prices and Factor Intensities

The given technical possibilities of production, as summarized by the production functions, imply a definite relationship between relative factor prices (i.e., w/r), optimum factor proportions in the two industries, and relative costs of production of commodities—which under the assumption of pure competition are equal to the relative commodity prices (i.e., p_x/p_y). This section analyzes the relationship between w/r and factor proportions only. The following section considers the relationship between factor proportions, factor prices, and commodity prices.

For any given factor-price ratio (i.e., w/r) the optimum coefficients of production of both commodities can be determined by determining the points on the unit isoquants of commodities X and Y where the marginal rate of substitution of labor for land is equal to the given factor-price ratio w/r.[1] The coordinates of these points are the optimum coefficients of production. The ratio of the optimum coefficients of each commodity shows, of course, the proportion in which the factors labor and land are being used in the production of these commodities.

Figure 10.1 illustrates the case for commodity X. The isoquant XX' is the unit isoquant. The factor-price ratio w/r is assumed to be given by the ratio OM/ON. Given the factor-price ratio, point E was determined on the unit isoquant where the slope is equal to the given w/r. The coordinates of point E (i.e., a_{Lx}^0, a_{Tx}^0) are the optimum coefficients of production for the given factor-price ratio. The slope of the vector OE with respect to the vertical axis shows the labor/land ratio in the production of X (i.e., ρ_x) for the originally given factor-price ratio.

What happens to the labor/land ratios of both industries when the factor-price ratio varies? As w/r falls, both factor ratios, ρ_x and ρ_y, tend to rise. Geometrically, as w/r falls, we move southeast on each unit isoquant as illustrated by the movement from E to E' in figure 10.1. This implies that the labor coefficient increases (from a_{Lx}^0 to a_{Lx}') while the land coefficient decreases (from a_{Tx}^0 to a_{Tx}'), and therefore the ratio $\rho_x = a_{Lx}/a_{Tx}$ necessarily rises. What is the basic economic reason for this? As w/r falls, costs can be reduced by substituting the relatively cheaper factor, labor, for the more expensive factor, land. Therefore, as w/r falls, both industries will tend to become more labor intensive (i.e., both ρ_x and ρ_y will rise) in an attempt to

---

1. It should be clear that the equality between the marginal rate of substitution of labor for land and the factor-price ratio w/r, i.e.,

$$MRS_{LT} = w/r, \qquad (10.1)$$

is required for cost minimization.

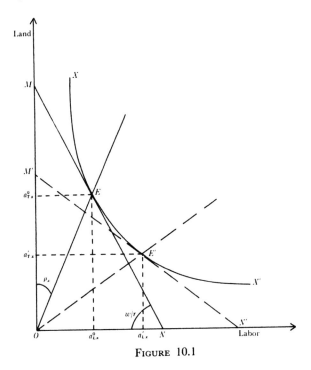

FIGURE 10.1

continue minimizing costs. On the other hand, as w/r rises, both industries will tend to become more land intensive.

Figure 10.2 illustrates the relationship between factor prices and factor proportions, on the assumption that commodity X is labor intensive relative to Y for all factor-price ratios. The curve XX' represents the relationship between w/r and ρ_x, while the curve YY' represents the relationship between w/r and ρ_y. Both curves have been drawn downward sloping, which implies that, as the factor-price ratio w/r falls, both industries become more labor intensive (i.e., both ρ_x and ρ_y increase). Further, the curve XX' lies totally to the right of the curve YY', implying that commodity X is labor intensive relative to Y for all factor-price ratios. Figure 10.2 summarizes the relationship between w/r and ρ_x and ρ_y. Thus, for any given factor-price ratio, we can quickly determine the optimum factor proportions in the two industries without having to refer back to figure 10.1. For instance, assuming that the factor-price ratio is given by the distance OM, the optimum factor proportions for industries X and Y are ρ_x^0 and ρ_y^0, respectively.

It follows, from the general principles of production, that both industries tend to become more labor intensive as labor becomes relatively cheaper (i.e., as the factor-price ratio w/r falls). But is the increase in both ρ_x and ρ_y consistent with the assumption of *fixed overall factor supplies*? And if so, how can the two statements be reconciled?

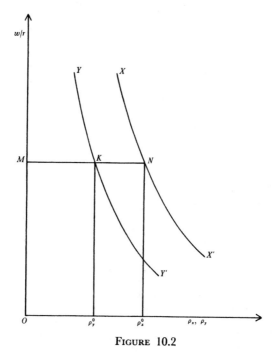

FIGURE 10.2

As shown in chapter 9, section 1, the overall factor-endowment ratio (ρ) in a country is a weighted average of the factor proportions of the two industries. More precisely,

$$\rho = \frac{T_x}{T} \rho_x + \frac{T_y}{T} \rho_y. \qquad (10.2)$$

Since we have been assuming that X is labor intensive relative to Y, we must necessarily have

$$\rho_y < \rho < \rho_x. \qquad (10.3)$$

Now start from a position where equation (10.2) is satisfied and assume that the factor-price ratio w/r falls. Both ρ_x and ρ_y will tend to increase, and equation (10.2) will not be satisfied if we keep the original allocation of land between X and Y (i.e., eq. [10.2] will not be satisfied if ρ_x and ρ_y increase while T_x and T_y remain constant). However, if a heavier weight is given to ρ_y than to ρ_x (i.e., if T_y increases and T_x falls sufficiently), then equation (10.2) will be reestablished. This can best be illustrated by means of the box diagram. However, let us first discuss the following lemma.

Lemma: Given the optimum factor proportions in the two industries and assuming that the outputs of X and Y are always selected in such a way as to keep land fully employed, an increase in the output of the labor-intensive commodity at the expense of the land-intensive commodity necessarily increases the aggregate demand for labor; and an increase in the output of the land-intensive commodity at the expense of the labor-intensive commodity necessarily decreases the aggregate demand for labor.

That this is true follows from the fact that, per unit of land, the labor-intensive industry employs more labor than the land-intensive industry. Thus, if X changes by ΔX and Y by ΔY subject to the condition that

$$a_{Tx}\,\Delta X + a_{Ty}\,\Delta Y = 0 \tag{10.4}$$

(that is, subject to the condition that the aggregate employment of land remains constant), the total demand for labor will change by

$$\Delta L = a_{Lx}\,\Delta X + a_{Ly}\,\Delta Y = a_{Tx}\rho_x\,\Delta X + a_{Ty}\rho_y\,\Delta Y. \tag{10.5}$$

Solving (10.4) for ΔY and substituting into (10.5), we get

$$\Delta L = a_{Tx}\rho_x\,\Delta X + a_{Ty}\rho_y(-a_{Tx}/a_{Ty})\,\Delta X = a_{Tx}(\rho_x - \rho_y)\,\Delta X. \tag{10.6}$$

Hence, if $\rho_x > \rho_y$, the sign of ΔL will be the same as the sign of ΔX. That is, an increase in the output of the labor-intensive commodity (and therefore a fall in Y) will cause the aggregate demand for labor to increase; and a decrease in the output of the labor-intensive commodity X will cause the aggregate demand for labor to fall—assuming, of course, that land remains fully employed and the same techniques of production remain in use.

Interchanging the roles of labor and land, it becomes obvious that as the output of the labor-intensive commodity increases at the expense of the land-intensive commodity in such a way that labor remains fully employed, the aggregate demand for land decreases; and when the output of the land-intensive commodity increases at the expense of the labor-intensive commodity, the aggregate demand for land increases.

Consider now figure 10.3. The sides of the box diagram show the overall factor endowments. The amounts of L and T used in industry X (L_x and T_x, respectively) are measured from the origin O_x. Similarly, the amounts of L and T used in industry Y (L_y and T_y) are measured from the origin O_y. Assume that commodity X is labor intensive relative to Y and suppose that the factor-price ratio is such that the economy happens to be initially at point E_1 on the contract curve. Thus, O_xC units of labor and O_xM units of land are used in the production of X. The slope of the vector O_xE_1 with respect to the T_x-axis shows the labor/land ratio used in industry X (ρ_x^1). Similarly, O_yH units of labor and O_yF units of land are used in the production of Y. The slope of the vector O_yE_1 with respect to the T_y-axis shows the labor/land ratio used in industry Y (ρ_y^1).

Assume now that the factor-price ratio w/r falls An explanation for this is given in the following section. As w/r falls, both industries become more labor intensive. In particular, assume that ρ_x increases from ρ_x^1 to ρ_x^2 and ρ_y increases from ρ_y^1 to ρ_y^2. How can both industries become more labor in-

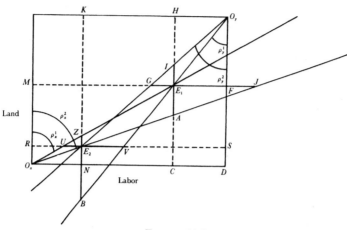

FIGURE 10.3

tensive given that the same totals of labor and land continue to be employed by the economy as a whole? Figure 10.3 shows that this is possible because the output of the labor-intensive industry (X) contracts while the output of the land-intensive industry (Y) expands. Thus, the maintenance of full employment at the higher labor/land ratios requires that the economy move from E_1 to E_2. The necessity for this movement can be justified in several ways.

a) Consider the initial position at E_1. What would the total labor requirements be if, as both ρ_x and ρ_y increase, both industries were to continue employing the same amounts of land they were employing before the increase in the labor/land ratios? The total labor requirements in X would be MJ and in Y they would be FG. The aggregate demand for labor by both industries would be $MJ + FG = MG + FG + GJ$. Since the total supply of labor is only $MG + GF$, an excess demand for labor would emerge given by the horizontal distance GJ. How could this excess demand for labor be eliminated if both industries continue to maintain the factor ratios ρ_x^2 and ρ_y^2? According to the lemma, this can be accomplished by allowing the labor-intensive industry to contract and the land-intensive industry to expand. Imagine that the horizontal line $MGFJ$ shifts downward continuously (in a parallel fashion). It will intersect the two expansion paths O_xJ and O_yG at points such as J and G, respectively. The horizontal distance JG will always give the excess demand for labor under the assumption that all the available land is always employed. As the line $MGFJ$ shifts downward, that is, as land is transferred from X to Y and therefore X contracts while Y expands, the excess demand for labor decreases. The latter shrinks to zero when the horizontal line $MGFJ$ coincides with $RUVS$. Thus, when RM units of land are transferred from X to Y, the aggregate demand for labor equals the aggregate supply.

b) Consider again the initial position at E_1. What would the total land requirements be if, as both ρ_x and ρ_y increase, both industries were to continue employing the same amounts of labor they were employing before the increase in the labor/land ratios? The aggregate demand for land would obviously be $CA + HI$, which falls short of the aggregate supply of land by AI. What can be done to eliminate this excess supply of land, assuming that X and Y will maintain the ratios ρ_x^2 and ρ_y^2, respectively? Again, according to the lemma, the output of the land-intensive industry (Y) should expand and the output of the labor-intensive industry should contract. As the vertical line $HIAC$ moves leftward in a parallel fashion, that is, as labor is transferred from X to Y, the excess supply of land (given by the vertical distances between the vectors E_2A and E_2I) necessarily shrinks. In particular, the excess supply of land shrinks to zero when NC units of labor are transferred from X to Y.

c) Assume that the optimum factor ratios in X and Y are ρ_x^1 and ρ_y^1, respectively, and the economy happens to be at E_1. What would happen to the aggregate demand for labor if we let X contract and Y expand while keeping land fully employed? Again, on the basis of the lemma, there will emerge an excess supply of labor. In particular, if RM units of land are transferred from X to Y, the aggregate demand for labor would be $RU + VS$. Thus, an excess supply of labor would emerge given by the distance UV. It is precisely this excess supply of labor which enables both industries to become more labor intensive as the factor-price ratio w/r falls. Thus, at the higher factor ratios, ρ_x^2 and ρ_y^2, industry X would be able to employ an additional amount of labor given by the distance UE_2; and industry Y would be able to employ E_2V extra units of labor.

d) Assume again that the optimum factor ratios in X and Y are ρ_x^1 and ρ_y^1, respectively, and allow X to contract and Y to expand from their respective levels at E_1. What would happen to the aggregate demand for land assuming that labor is always fully employed? It will definitely increase, because the expanding industry is the land-intensive industry. In particular, when NC units of labor are transferred from X to Y, the aggregate demand for labor would be given by the sum $KB + NZ$, which is larger than the aggregate supply (KN) by the amount ZB. This excess demand for land is eliminated, of course, when both industries become more labor intensive, which is another way of saying that they become less land intensive.

The preceding analysis—in particular, the conclusion that as w/r falls both ρ_x and ρ_y increase—is valid whether factor-intensity reversals are absent or not. The complications of factor-intensity reversals will be studied in chapter 11, section 2.

4. Factor Prices and Commodity Prices

It has already been said that the production functions imply a definite relationship between the optimum labor/land ratios in the two industries, the relative factor prices, and the relative costs of production of commodities. Section 3 analyzes the relationship between factor prices and the optimum labor/land ratios. This section analyzes the relationship between factor prices and commodity prices.

The basic proposition is that, as the factor-price ratio w/r falls, that is, as labor becomes relatively cheaper, the labor-intensive commodity becomes cheaper relative to the land-intensive commodity. In our example where X is the labor-intensive commodity, as w/r falls, the commodity-price ratio p_x/p_y also falls.

A heuristic proof of this proposition follows. Its correct equivalent has already been given in chapter 9, section 2.

If the factor proportions, ρ_x and ρ_y, in industries X and Y, respectively, remain constant as the factor-price ratio w/r falls (as, for instance, in the case of fixed coefficients of production), the relative cost of the labor-intensive commodity would also fall, that is, p_x/p_y would fall. A difficulty arises in the case of variable proportions where, as w/r falls, labor is being substituted for land in both industries. Could this substitution of labor for land reverse the direction of change of the relative commodity-price ratio? In other words, is it possible that p_x/p_y might increase as w/r falls? The answer is definitely no. Let us see why.

In figure 10.4, the production-possibilities frontier corresponds to the box diagram of figure 10.3. As shown in chapter 4, the production-possibilities frontier (under the present assumptions of constant returns to scale and differing factor intensities between commodities X and Y) is necessarily concave to the origin. Points E_1 and E_2 on the frontier correspond to the synonymous points on the contract curve of figure 10.3. Under these

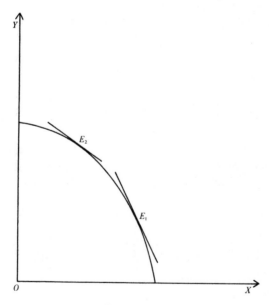

FIGURE 10.4

circumstances, as the factor-price ratio w/r falls and the economy moves from point E_1 to point E_2, commodity X becomes cheaper relative to Y, as indicated by the fact that the production-possibilities frontier is flatter at point E_2 compared with point E_1.

This can be summarized as follows. As the factor-price ratio w/r falls, both industries tend to become more labor intensive (or less land intensive) in order to minimize costs. That is, both industries tend to substitute the cheaper factor (labor) for the more expensive factor (land). In the context of general equilibrium, this substitution of labor for land in both industries is possible if, and only if, the output of the land-intensive industry expands at the expense of the output of the labor-intensive industry. As a result, the labor-intensive commodity tends to become cheaper relative to the land-intensive commodity because of the underlying increasing opportunity costs.

Perhaps it seems unusual to consider the factor-price ratio as the independent variable and the commodity-price ratio as the dependent variable. In static analysis this is immaterial. But what would a probable dynamic sequence of events be? A dynamic sequence of events would probably proceed along opposite lines, with the commodity-price ratio playing the role of the independent variable and the factor-price ratio being the dependent variable. This can be illustrated as follows (see figs. 10.3 and 10.4). Assume that the economy is originally in equilibrium at point E_1 but it moves to E_2 as a result of a change in tastes. The first impact of the change in tastes would be reflected immediately in a lower price of commodity X (whose demand has fallen) relative to Y. What would this change in commodity prices imply for the active producers of X and Y? Obviously, the producers of Y will enjoy positive profits and the producers of X will suffer losses. The ensuing profits in industry Y and losses in industry X will attract resources from industry X to industry Y. But since, by assumption, industry X is labor intensive relative to Y, the proportion in which labor and land will be released by industry X will not be the same as the proportion in which industry Y would be willing to absorb the two factors. In particular, there will emerge an excess demand for land and/or an excess supply of labor; and both of these forces will cause the factor-price ratio w/r to fall. As w/r falls, of course, both industries will substitute labor for land (i.e., both industries will become more labor intensive or less land intensive), and this process will continue until a new equilibrium is established.

This sequence of events is no doubt more appealing than the original exposition. However, for our purposes, whatever reasons are given for the relationship between factor prices and commodity prices are immaterial, although it must be admitted that the second version approximates the actual sequence of events better than the first. Our main purpose is to establish a one-to-one correspondence between factor prices and commodity prices. Put differently, our analysis is basically static.

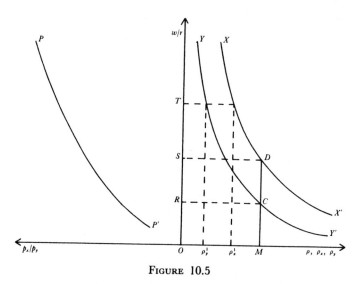

5. The Range of Factor Prices and Commodity Prices in a Closed Economy

Sections 3 and 4 are conveniently summarized in figure 10.5. The first quadrant contains the information in figure 10.2. The fact that both curves (i.e., XX' and YY') are drawn downward sloping indicates that, as the factor-price ratio w/r falls (rises), both commodities tend to become more (less) labor intensive. Further, the curve XX' lies totally to the right of curve YY', indicating our assumption that commodity X is labor intensive relative to Y for all factor-price ratios.

In the second quadrant, the commodity-price ratio p_x/p_y is measured along the horizontal axis and in the negative direction. The curve PP' shows the relationship between the factor-price ratio w/r and the commodity-price ratio p_x/p_y. As can be easily verified, the curve PP' implies that, as the factor-price ratio (w/r) falls (rises), the commodity-price ratio also falls (rises), and vice versa. The reason why this relationship should hold between the factor-price ratio w/r and the commodity-price ratio p_x/p_y has already been explained in the preceding section.

The analysis so far, as summarized in figure 10.5, has been concerned with the relationships between optimum factor proportions, factor prices, and commodity prices implicit in the given technological possibilities of production. In a particular economy, however, with a given factor endowment, only a limited range of the techniques available can actually be used efficiently. How do we know this? Remember that the contract curve lies on one side of the diagonal. Therefore, the techniques implied by the opposite side (i.e., the area in which the contract curve does not lie) are never used. What is the possible range of factor prices, commodity prices, and optimum factor proportions after the introduction of the overall factor-endowment ratio?

Consider a country whose factor endowment of labor relative to land (i.e., L/T) is given by the distance OM of figure 10.5. We can be sure that, when both commodities are being produced, a labor/land ratio greater than OM will be used in industry X and a labor/land ratio smaller than OM will be used in industry Y. This follows directly from the assumption that, at uniform factor prices, industry X will be using a higher labor/land ratio than industry Y (i.e., $\rho_x > \rho_y$) and the observation that the overall factor-endowment ratio (total labor/total land $= OM$) is a weighted average of the proportions used in the two industries, the exact weights being the relative proportions of total land applied to each use.[2] In the limiting case where only X is being produced, industry X necessarily uses the two factors in the same proportion as the overall factor proportion OM; and when only Y is being produced, industry Y necessarily uses the two factors in the existing overall proportion OM.

What is the possible range of the factor-price ratio? Clearly, if something of both goods is to be produced, the factor-price ratio can only range between points S and R (i.e., $OR < w/r < OS$). This can best be seen by noting that, for any factor-price ratio higher than the distance OS, such as OT, both industries will be using the factors labor and land in proportions smaller than the overall labor/land ratio, OM. In particular, for $w/r = OT$, we have $\rho_x = \rho_x^1 < OM$ and $\rho_y = \rho_y^1 < OM$. Under these circumstances, the full-employment assumption cannot be fulfilled. No matter what the outputs of X and Y are, there will always be a surplus of labor (i.e., positive excess supply of labor) and/or a deficit of land (i.e., positive excess demand for land). The former will cause the wage rate to fall, while the latter will cause the rent for the services of land to rise, and both of these forces will cause the factor-price ratio w/r to fall.

Similarly, if the factor-price ratio is smaller than OR, both industries will be using the factors labor and land in proportions higher than the overall labor/land ratio (i.e., OM). Under these circumstances, there will always be a deficit of labor (i.e., positive excess demand for labor) and/or a surplus of land (i.e., positive excess supply of land). Again, the former will cause the wage rate to rise, while the latter will cause the rent to fall, and both of these forces will cause the factor-price ratio w/r to rise.

When the factor-price ratio equals OR, industry Y will be using labor and land in the same proportion as that in which these factors exist in the economy (i.e., OM), while industry X will be using a labor/land ratio higher than OM. Under these circumstances, only Y will be produced. The output

2. See equation (10.2).

of X has to be zero; otherwise the full-employment assumption will again be violated.

Similarly, when the factor-price ratio equals OS, industry X will be using a labor/land ratio equal to OM while industry Y will be using a ratio smaller than OM. Again, the economy will completely specialize in the production of X, with the output of Y being set equal to zero. Any positive production of Y necessarily violates the full-employment assumption.

For any factor-price ratio in the range $OR < w/r < OS$, both commodities will necessarily have to be produced if full employment is to be preserved. In this range, neither commodity is using a labor/land ratio equal to OM. Therefore, specialization in the production of only one commodity will necessarily violate the full-employment assumption. However, since in this range $\rho_y < OM < \rho_x$, a proper combination of outputs of X and Y can be found to satisfy the full-employment assumption. Further, as the factor-price ratio falls continuously from the value OS to the value OR, the output of commodity X falls while the output of commodity of Y increases. This proposition has already been established in section 3, and no additional discussion is necessary.

Can we determine the precise amounts of X and Y produced for factor-price ratios in the range $OR < w/r < OS$? Unfortunately, this cannot be done on the basis of the information given in figure 10.5. For this, we have to know the land coefficients, a_{Tx} and a_{Ty}, as well as the total amount of land available. Thus, the full-employment equations are

$$a_{Lx}X + a_{Ly}Y = L, \tag{10.7}$$

$$a_{Tx}X + a_{Ty}Y = T. \tag{10.8}$$

Since by definition

$$a_{Lx} = \rho_x a_{Tx}; \qquad a_{Ly} = \rho_y a_{Ty}; \qquad L = \rho T,$$

equation (10.7) can be rewritten as follows:

$$\rho_x a_{Tx}X + \rho_y a_{Ty}Y = \rho T. \tag{10.7}'$$

If, in addition to ρ_x, ρ_y, and ρ, we also know the coefficients a_{Tx} and a_{Ty} as well as the total quantity of land (T), we can solve equations $(10.7)'$ and (10.8) for X and Y to get

$$X = \frac{Ta_{Ty}}{\Delta}(\rho - \rho_y), \tag{10.9}$$

$$Y = \frac{Ta_{Tx}}{\Delta}(\rho_x - \rho), \tag{10.10}$$

where $\Delta = a_{Tx}a_{Ty}(\rho_x - \rho_y)$.

However, despite the fact that we cannot determine the outputs of X and Y unless we know a_{Tx}, a_{Ty}, and T, in addition to ρ, ρ_x, and ρ_y, we can nevertheless determine the proportion in which L and T will be allocated in the production of X and Y for full employment. Thus, taking the ratio of X and Y as given, respectively, by equations (10.9) and (10.10), we get

$$\frac{X}{Y} = \frac{a_{Ty}}{a_{Tx}} \frac{\rho - \rho_y}{\rho_x - \rho}. \tag{10.11}$$

Equation (10.11) can also be rearranged as follows:

$$\frac{\rho - \rho_y}{\rho_x - \rho} = \frac{a_{Tx}X}{a_{Ty}Y} = \frac{T_x}{T_y}, \tag{10.12}$$

where T_x is the total amount of T used in the production of X and T_y is the total amount of T used in the production of Y. Equation (10.12) shows that the ratio T_x/T_y depends only on the ratios ρ, ρ_y, and ρ_x.

It should be noted that, as long as ρ lies between ρ_x and ρ_y, the ratio T_x/T_y is necessarily positive. On the other hand, should ρ become smaller (or higher) than ρ_x and ρ_y, the ratio T_x/T_y would become negative. Since negative production is not possible, such an arrangement has to be ruled out, which explains once more why the only possible range for the factor-price ratio is $OR \le w/r \le OS$ (see fig. 10.5). Finally, if $\rho = \rho_y$, then $T_x/T_y = 0$, that is, $T_x = 0$ and $T_y = T$; and if $\rho = \rho_x$, $T_x/T_y \to \infty$, that is, $T_x = T$ and $T_y = 0$.

The allocation of labor, of course, is given by $L_x = \rho_x T_x$ and $L_y = \rho_y T_y$, or

$$\frac{L_x}{L_y} = \frac{\rho_x(\rho - \rho_y)}{\rho_y(\rho_x - \rho)}. \tag{10.13}$$

Observe that in the extreme case of fixed coefficients of production, the two curves XX' and YY' would become vertical, with the range of variation of the factor-price ratio becoming infinite. On the other hand, if the production functions of X and Y were identical, except for a scale factor, the curves XX' and YY' would coincide and the range of variation of w/r would necessarily shrink to a single point. In this special case, the equilibrium factor-price ratio would depend only on the overall factor-endowment ratio: it is independent of demand conditions.

How does technological change affect the range of variation of w/r? In particular, suppose that, as a result of a technological innovation, *the labor-intensive industry* (X) *becomes more labor intensive* at every value of w/r. How would this change affect the range of variation of w/r? Figure 10.5 shows that the range of variation of w/r necessarily increases in this case because the curve XX' shifts totally to the right. Essentially the same conclusion follows when, as a result of a technological innovation, *the land-intensive industry becomes more land intensive* at every value of w/r. Here, the curve YY' shifts totally to the left and the vertical distances between XX' and YY' increase.

We have just seen that the permissible range of variation of both the factor-price ratio and the labor/land ratios in the two industries are rather limited once the overall labor/land ratio is given. But what about the commodity-price ratio? It is reasonable to expect that the commodity-price ratio will necessarily vary within narrow limits, too? Not at all. After the introduction of the overall factor-endowment ratio, the curve PP' of figure 10.5 is necessarily distorted. This is illustrated in figure 10.6, which reproduces only the second quadrant of figure 10.5. The solid curve PP' of figure 10.6 corresponds to the curve PP' of figure 10.5. However, the curve showing the relationship between the commodity-price ratio and the factor-price ratio is $KS'R'R$. For factor prices in the admissible range (OR and OS), the relationship between factor prices and commodity prices corresponds to that originally given by the curve PP'. Now consider points S and R. At $w/r = OS$, the economy is specializing entirely in the production of commodity X. The distance SS' (or OP_2) shows the ratio

$$\frac{\text{marginal cost of commodity } X}{\text{marginal cost of commodity } Y} = \frac{MC_x}{MC_y}.$$

But the ratio of marginal costs may or may not be equal to the ratio of commodity prices, since the economy is completely specializing in the production of X. As shown in chapter 4, the slope of the production-possibilities frontier shows the ratio of marginal costs rather than the ratio of commodity prices. But with pure competition prevailing in the commodity markets, marginal costs are equal to prices, provided that both commodities are being produced. If, however, a commodity is not produced, we must

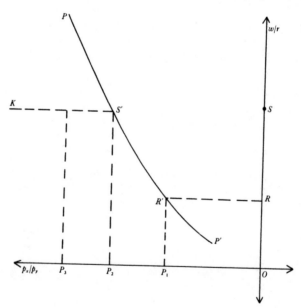

FIGURE 10.6

allow for the possibility that its price is lower than its marginal cost, i.e., price < marginal cost. Thus, when commodity Y is not being produced, we must have $MC_y \geq p_y$. Since commodity X is produced, and thus $MC_x = p_x$, we must also have $(MC_x/MC_y) \leq (p_x/p_y)$. This is exactly what is being allowed for by the horizontal broken line KS' of figure 10.6. Similar arguments can be provided for the justification of the broken line $R'R$ of figure 10.6, where we allow for the possibility that $p_x \leq MC_x$.

To understand better what is involved, assume that our economy is a small open economy which takes international prices as given. Assume initially that the international price ratio is given by OP_2 and thus our country specializes in the production of commodity X. The factor-price ratio is given by OS, which is simply the marginal rate of substitution of labor for land in the production of commodity X when all available land and labor are used in the production of X. In this case, the ratio of marginal costs equals the ratio of commodity prices. Now suppose that the demand for commodity X increases in the international market, causing the international price ratio to rise to OP_3. Since by assumption our economy is small and cannot affect international prices, the commodity-price ratio OP_3 must necessarily prevail in our economy as well. However, since our economy was already specializing in the production of X, its allocation of resources will not be affected: the factor ratio used in industry X (i.e., ρ_x) and the factor-price ratio (w/r) will remain at their original levels (i.e., $\rho_x = OM$ and $w/r = OS$, as shown in figure 10.5). Thus, while the commodity-price ratio is free to rise above OP_2, the factor-price ratio will continue to be given by OS. This explains the horizontal part KS' of figure 10.6. A similar argument can be provided for the horizontal part $R'R$.

While the possible range of variation of the commodity-price ratio is in general infinite, the permissible range when both commodities are produced is drastically limited. For instance, in figure 10.6 the range of variation of p_x/p_y when both commodities are produced is limited to $OP_1 < p_x/p_y < OP_2$. Two factors determine this limited range of the commodity-price ratio: the permissible range of variation of the factor-price ratio and the gentleness of the slope of the curve PP'. Thus, for any given range of w/r, the flatter the curve PP', the larger the range of variation of p_x/p_y. What actually determines the slope of the curve PP'? Broadly speaking, and subject to the qualification made below, the larger the divergence between the labor/land ratios of the two industries, the flatter the curve PP' and, therefore, the larger the variation of the commodity-price ratio (when, of course, both commodities are being produced).

As we saw before (see eq. [9.17]),

$$z = \frac{d(p_x/p_y)}{d(w/r)} = c \frac{\rho_x - \rho_y}{[(w/r)\rho_y + 1]^2} > 0 \quad (\rho_x > \rho_y).$$

It can easily be shown that

$$\frac{\partial z}{\partial \rho_x} > 0 \quad \text{and} \quad \frac{\partial z}{\partial \rho_y} < 0.$$

Thus, given ρ_y, the higher ρ_x is (and thus the higher the difference $\rho_x - \rho_y$ is), the higher z will be and the flatter the curve PP' of figures 10.5 and 10.6 will be. On the other hand, given ρ_x, the smaller ρ_y is (and thus the higher the difference $\rho_x - \rho_y$ is), the higher will be z and the flatter the curve PP' will be.

However, this does not mean that, as the difference $\rho_x - \rho_y$ becomes larger in general, the curve PP' becomes flatter irrespective of the individual values of ρ_x and ρ_y. To show that this more general statement cannot be correct, imagine that both ρ_x and ρ_y increase by the same amount so that the difference $\rho_x - \rho_y$ remains the same. Then z (i.e., the slope of the curve PP') must fall because the denominator of the ratio

$$\frac{\rho_x - \rho_y}{[(w/r)\rho_y + 1]^2}$$

increases while the numerator remains the same. If we were to freeze ρ_y at the higher value and allow ρ_x to increase (and thus allow the difference $\rho_x - \rho_y$ to rise), it would take some time before the original value of z could be restored. In the meantime, we shall have a situation where the difference $\rho_x - \rho_y$ is larger than what it was originally although z is smaller. This shows that the general statement that z increases as the difference $\rho_x - \rho_y$ becomes larger is not generally true.

6. Equilibrium in a Closed Economy

Within the range of variation permitted by technology and factor endowment, the equilibrium factor-price ratio and the equilibrium commodity-price ratio will be determined by the forces of demand. In particular, the equilibrium w/r and p_x/p_y will be determined by the condition that the marginal rate of transformation of X for Y (given by the absolute value of the slope of the production-possibilities frontier, which in turn is equal to the ratio of the marginal cost of X to the marginal cost of Y) be just equal to the marginal rate of substitution of X for Y in consumption (which is given by the ratio of the marginal utility of X to the marginal utility of Y).

Assuming, for simplicity, that demand conditions are given by a social indifference map, the complete general-equilibrium solution can be summarized as follows. In figure 10.7, the production-possibilities frontier (Y_0EX_0) is superimposed on the social indifference map. Equilibrium occurs at point E. The quantities OX_1 and OY_1 of commodities X and Y, respectively, are being produced and consumed. From figure 10.7 we can

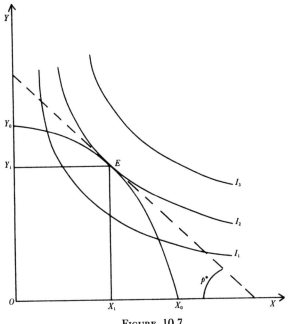

FIGURE 10.7

read off the commodity-price ratio p_x/p_y as the absolute value of the common slope of the production-possibilities frontier and the social indifference curve I_2 at point E, as shown by the broken line through E. Call this equilibrium commodity-price ratio p^*. With this information, we can read directly from figure 10.8 (which is a combination of figs. 10.5 and 10.6) the equilibrium factor-price ratio (w^*) and the equilibrium factor ratios in the

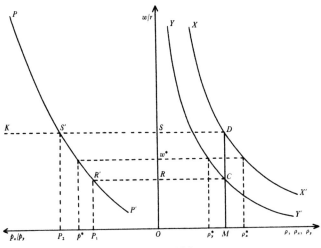

FIGURE 10.8

two industries, namely ρ_x^* and ρ_y^*. The absolute equilibrium values of labor and land used in the two industries can be easily recovered from the box diagram (not reproduced here) by simply drawing the expansion paths of the two industries with slopes (with respect to the land axis) equal to ρ_x^* and ρ_y^*, respectively. These expansion paths will necessarily intersect each other somewhere on the contract curve. The coordinates of the point of their intersection with respect to the origin O_x show the total quantities of labor and land used in the production of commodity X; the coordinates of the same point with respect to the origin O_y show the total quantities of labor and land used in the production of commodity Y.

As a result of the assumption that demand conditions are given by a social indifference map, the possibility of multiple equilibria is necessarily ruled out.

SELECTED BIBLIOGRAPHY

Heckscher, E. 1919. The effect of foreign trade on the distribution of income. *Ekonomisk Tidskrift* 21: 1–32.

Lerner, A. P. 1953. *Essays in Economics Analysis*, pp. 67–100.

Ohlin, B. 1933. *Interregional and International Trade*. Cambridge, Mass.: Harvard University Press. Chaps. 1–6, App. 31.

Samuelson, P. A. 1948. International trade and the equalization of factor prices. *Economic Journal* 68: 165–184.

———. 1949. International factor price equalization once again. *Economic Journal* 59: 181–97.

(Additional Bibliography may be found at the end of Chapter 11.)

The Factor-Price Equalization Theorem

This chapter deals with the proof of the factor-price equalization theorem and with the empirical relevance of its assumptions. In particular, the analysis of this chapter shows that, under the assumptions enumerated in chapter 10, section 2, free commodity trade (equalizing relative commodity prices between countries) necessarily completely equalizes factor prices between countries. Under these conditions, commodity trade is a perfect substitute for factor mobility between countries.

1. The Factor-Price Equalization Theorem

Given the assumption that production functions are identical between countries, the basic relationship between relative factor prices (i.e., w/r), factor proportions in the two industries, and relative commodity prices (i.e., p_x/p_y), as is illustrated in figure 10.5, is necessarily the same in both countries. This is a tremendous simplification in our diagrammatic apparatus. But if this is so, what is the difference between the two countries? The answer is simple: factor endowments. Different factor endowments necessarily imply different regions for autarkic equilibrium factor-price ratios and factor proportions in the two industries. In addition, the relationship between relative factor prices and relative commodity prices (the curve $KS'R'P'$ of fig. 10.8) will necessarily be different between the two countries. Therefore, different factor endowments will force the two countries to operate in different regions of the same curves, with due allowance for the horizontal segments of the curves showing the relationship between relative factor prices and relative commodity prices.

We already know that profitable trade will take place if, and only if, the (unique) pretrade equilibrium commodity-price ratios are different between the two countries. In addition, the effect of free trade (with zero transportation costs) will be to equalize the relative commodity prices in the two countries at a level somewhere between the two pretrade equilibrium price ratios, with the posttrade equilibrium terms of trade determined by the supply and demand conditions in the two countries taken together. We are assuming here that social indifference maps (with regular convexity) exist; hence the complications of pretrade multiple equilibria are ignored. With these general statements in mind, let us use the diagrammatic apparatus developed earlier in chapter 10 to demonstrate that, under the (rather restrictive) assumptions enumerated in chapter 10, section 2, factor prices will be completely equalized through trade in commodities. In addition, we can show the importance of some of these assumptions for the rigorous proof of the factor-price equalization theorem.

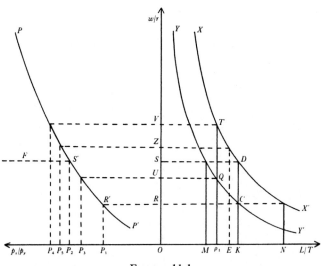

FIGURE 11.1

Consider figure 11.1. Assume that A's overall factor proportions are given by the distance OK. Therefore, country A's relative factor-price region, permitted by the factor-endowment ratio OK, is given by RS, and its relative commodity-price region with incomplete specialization is given by P_1P_2. We can distinguish between these two cases: (*a*) country B's overall factor-endowment ratio lies in the region MN; and (*b*) country B's overall factor-endowment ratio lies outside the region MN. We shall consider both of these cases in turn. It is obvious, however, that complete factor-price equalization will never occur in the second case, because the range of variation of w/r in country A does not overlap the range of variation of w/r in country B. These two regions overlap only in case (*a*), and this is the only case where factor-price equalization is possible.

Case a: This case can be decomposed into three subcases:
  i) B's overall factor-endowment ratio equal A's (i.e., it is also given by the distance OK);
  ii) B's overall factor-endowment ratio lying in the region MK; and
  iii) B's overall factor-endowment ratio lying in the region KN.

In case a(i), where the overall factor-endowment ratios of the two countries coincide, both the relative factor-price region and the relative commodity-price region are given, respectively, by RS and P_1P_2 (assuming incomplete specialization) for both countries. Is factor-price equalization possible? Not only is it possible, but it is a necessity, for, given any commodity-price ratio, we can uniquely determine the factor-price ratio for *both* countries, since the distorted PP' curves of A and B in the second quandrant of figure 11.1 coincide completely. The equalization of commodity prices through commodity trade will necessarily bring about (in the present case) complete equalization of factor prices. Or will it? Observe that the relationships illustrated in figure 11.1 are all in terms of relative, not absolute, factor prices. Given the equilibrium commodity-price ratio, the only thing that can be determined from figure 11.1 is the factor-price ratio—and not the *individual factor rentals* expressed in terms of either commodity. Does this mean that commodity trade will equalize only the factor-price ratio between countries? Not at all. As we saw in chapter 4, from the relative factor prices, we can move to the absolute marginal productivities of labor and land in the two industries because of the assumption of constant returns to scale. This is possible because all marginal physical productivities are functions of the relevant labor/land ratios—and not the absolute quantities of labor and land used. The labor/land ratios are perfectly determined when w/r is given. Therefore, commodity trade will equalize factor prices both relatively and absolutely.

If we could be assured unequivocally that tastes are indeed identical in the two countries and, in particular, that they are being given by the same social indifference map, would it be reasonable to conclude that profitable trade will not take place between the two countries? Not at all, for while we know that the overall factor-endowment ratio of the two countries is the same, we know nothing about the relative sizes of the two countries. Put differently, the identity of factor proportions does not imply that the production-possibilities frontiers of the two countries coincide. It simply means that any ray through the origin will cut the two frontiers at points of equal slope. Under these conditions, similarity of tastes[1] between countries is sufficient to eliminate profitable trade only in the special case where the two countries happen to be of equal size and their production-possibilities

---

1. Recall that "similarity of tastes between countries" means that the *same* social indifference map portrays tastes in each and every country. The common social indifference map need not be homothetic. Homotheticity is always stated separately because it is an additional condition.

frontiers coincide. In general, however, when the two countries are of unequal size, similarity of tastes has to be supplemented by homotheticity of tastes if all profitable trade is to be ruled out. However, as explained in chapter 9, while these two assumptions are sufficient to eliminate all profitable trade, neither assumption is by itself necessary.

In the present case, the Heckscher-Ohlin theorem is correct (i.e., the labor-abundant country will export the labor-intensive commodity, and the land-abundant country will export the land-intensive commodity) only when the price definition of factor abundance is used. On the basis of the physical definition, the Heckscher-Ohlin theorem would predict no trade, but the outcome would obviously depend on tastes.

Consider now case $a(\text{ii})$. Country B's overall factor-endowment ratio lies somewhere in the region MK. Assume that it is actually equal to the distance $O\rho_1$. Note that, on the basis of the physical definition of factor abundance, country B is T-abundant relative to A (or A is L-abundant relative to B). Country B's relevant region of relative commodity prices (when both commodities are produced) is given by P_3P_4. Is factor-price equalization possible now? Yes, because, while the relevant regions of relative factor and commodity prices of the two countries do not completely coincide, they do overlap. In particular, the two regions of relative factor prices overlap in the area US, while the two regions of relative commodity prices overlap in the area P_3P_2. If demand conditions in the two countries are such as to cause the pretrade equilibrium relative commodity prices in the two countries to lie in the region P_3P_2, then the posttrade equilibrium relative commodity prices will also lie in the same region (i.e., P_3P_2). Again, factor-price equalization is seen to be complete. But this is not the only possibility. The posttrade equilibrium commodity-price ratio may very well lie in the region P_2P_4, or in the region P_1P_3 (as can be verified). In both of the cases, factor-price equalization cannot possibly be complete.

If the posttrade equilibrium commodity-price ratio lies in the region P_2P_4, country A will definitely specialize completely in the production of X. Accordingly, factor prices cannot be equalized (either relatively or absolutely), except in the limiting case where the posttrade equilibrium commodity-price ratio happens to be equal to OP_2. This is illustrated by the commodity-price ratio OP_5, which causes the factor-price ratio (w/r) to be equal to OS in country A (because A necessarily specializes in the production of X) and OZ in country B, with $OZ > OS$.

The failure of complete factor-price equalization in this case is due to the fact that one of the two countries (country A) specializes completely in the production of only one of the two commodities (commodity X). But this implies that assumption (vi) of chapter 10, section 2, above is being violated. Since all other assumptions are not violated, only a limited migration of labor from A (the country with low wages) to B (the country with high wages) is necessary to bring about complete factor-price equalization. In particular, sufficient amounts of labor should migrate from A to B to reduce A's factor-endowment ratio from OK to OE.

If factor prices are not equalized completely in the present case, is there any tendency toward factor-price equalization? Yes. Assuming that the posttrade equilibrium commodity-price ratio is given by OP_5, we must necessarily infer, on the assumption that both countries produce both commodities before trade, that A's pretrade commodity-price ratio must be higher, and B's lower, than OP_5. Hence, A's pretrade equilibrium factor-price ratio must be higher than OZ, and B's lower than OS. Free commodity trade, therefore, causes factor prices in the two countries to move closer together.

If the posttrade equilibrium price ratio lies in the region P_1P_3, country B will specialize completely in the production of Y and factor-price equalization cannot be complete, although there will be a tendency toward equalization. The posttrade equilibrium factor-price ratio (w/r) will necessarily be higher in country B relative to country A. Again, only limited labor migration from A to B will completely eliminate any gap between factor prices in the two countries.

The failure of complete factor-price equalization witnessed thus far has been attributed to the fact that one of the two countries is completely specializing in the production of only one commodity. In *all* cases, we have seen that complete factor-price equalization could be brought about if a sufficient amount of labor migrated from A to B. The fundamental reason for the failure of complete factor-price equalization is the great disparity between factor proportions in the two countries. This disparity in factor proportions is evident in the complete specialization in production of at least one of the two countries. Thus, if sufficient labor were to migrate from A to B (thus causing ρ_A to fall and ρ_B to rise and, therefore, causing the difference $\rho_A - \rho_B$ to shrink), the great dissimilarity in overall factor proportions would be eliminated and factor prices would be completely equalized, with neither country specializing completely in production. Finally, note that in all of the preceding cases there is always a tendency toward factor-price equalization.

Is the Heckscher-Ohlin theorem correct in case a(ii)? Chapter 9 proves that the Heckscher-Ohlin theorem is always true on the basis of the price definition of factor abundance *and* in the absence of factor-intensity reversals. Since factor-intensity reversals are absent in the present case, the Heckscher-Ohlin theorem must necessarily be true on the basis of the price definition. Difficulties arise only when the physical definition of factor abundance is being used. When does the Heckscher-Ohlin theorem become incorrect on the basis of the physical definition?

In case a(ii), country A is labor abundant relative to country B and commodity X is labor intensive relative to commodity Y. According to the Heckscher-Ohlin theorem, country A must be exporting to B commodity X

and it must be importing from *B* commodity *Y*. Accordingly, the Heckscher-Ohlin theorem will be valid if, and only if, the pretrade commodity-price ratio (p_x/p_y) is lower in *A* than in *B*. Is the latter condition necessarily satisfied in the present case? No. If *A*'s pretrade commodity-price ratio lies in the region P_1P_3, or if *B*'s pretrade commodity-price ratio lies in the region P_2P_4, then the Heckscher-Ohlin theorem will be correct. But when both pretrade commodity-price ratios lie in the region P_2P_3, the Heckscher-Ohlin theorem is not necessarily correct. In the latter case, demand conditions may be such as to render commodity *X* relatively cheaper in *B* than in *A* before trade. In this case, the factor-price equalization theorem will necessarily be correct.

Case a(iii) is similar to case a(ii), except that the roles of the two countries are now interchanged, and will not be discussed here.

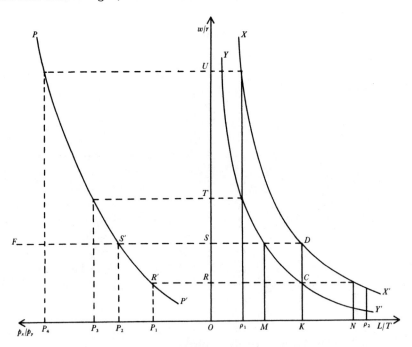

FIGURE 11.2

Case b: Country *B*'s overall factor-endowment ratio (ρ_B) lies outside the region *MN*. This means that the permissible ranges of variation of relative factor prices in the two countries do not overlap at all, and thus complete factor-price equalization is definitely out of the question. This is illustrated in figure 11.2, which reproduces the basic relationships among factor proportions, relative factor prices, and relative commodity prices as shown in figure 11.1. Again, *A*'s factor-endowment ratio is given by the distance

OK, A's permitted range of variation of relative factor prices is given by RS, and A's permitted range of variation of relative commodity prices with incomplete specialization is given by P_1P_2.

The following two possibilities exist:

i) Country B's factor-endowment ratio lies in the region OM (i.e., country B is land abundant relative to country A, or A is labor abundant relative to B, on the basis of the physical definition). In particular, assume that B's factor-endowment ratio is given by ρ_1. The permitted range of variation of B's relative factor prices is then given by TU, while the permitted range of variation of its relative commodity prices is given by P_3P_4. Under these circumstances, the following conclusions can be derived. In the first place, both the pretrade factor-price ratio (w/r) and the pretrade commodity-price ratio (p_x/p_y) of country B will necessarily be higher than the corresponding pretrade equilibrium relative prices in country A. As a result, country A is labor abundant relative to country B on the basis of the price definition of factor abundance. In this case, both the physical definition and the price definition of factor abundance give rise to the same conclusions irrespective of tastes. In addition, country A will export commodity X and country B will export commodity Y, which is in line with the Heckscher-Ohlin theorem (on the basis of both the price definition and the physical definition of factor abundance). The equilibrium terms of trade will lie somewhere in the region P_1P_4. If they lie in the region P_1P_2, country A will produce both commodities while country B will specialize completely in the production of commodity Y; if they lie in the region P_3P_4, country B will produce both commodities while country A will specialize completely in the production of commodity X; and if they lie in the region P_2P_3, country A will specialize completely in the production of commodity X and country B will specialize completely in the production of commodity Y. In all cases, at least one country specializes completely in the production of only one commodity. This violates one of the assumptions of the factor-price equalization theorem. After trade, the factor-price ratio (w/r) will necessarily continue to be higher in country B than in A. However, the pretrade divergence between factor prices in the two countries will tend to become smaller. In other words, despite the fact that complete factor-price equalization is impossible (because the regions RS and TU do not overlap), there will nevertheless be a tendency toward factor-price equalization.

ii) Country B's factor-endowment ratio is higher than ON; for example, $\rho_B = \rho_2$. This is similar to possibility (i), with the roles of the two countries reversed, and therefore will not be elaborated here.

It should again be stressed that the failure of complete factor-price equalization in the present case (b) is due to the fact that one of the fundamental assumptions of the factor-price equalization theorem, namely, incomplete specialization in both countries, is being violated. But again, the violation of the assumption of incomplete specialization is due to the fact that the factor-endowment ratios of the two countries are very dissimilar. Only a limited migration of labor from the labor-abundant country to the land-abundant country (with factor abundance decided on the basis of the physical definition) is all that is necessary to eliminate the possibility of complete specialization and thus to permit commodity trade to establish complete factor-price equalization.

A problem exists in the possible divergence between the price definition and the physical definition of factor abundance. What are the necessary and sufficient conditions under which the two definitions will give rise to contradictory classifications? In the absence of factor-intensity reversals, the two definitions give rise to identical results when the possible ranges of variation of factor prices do not overlap. The first condition necessary for a possible divergence between the two definitions is that the ranges of variation of factor prices in the two countries overlap. In terms of figures 11.1 and 11.2, B's factor-endowment ratio must lie in the region MN. The second condition is that the pretrade relative commodity prices must lie in the region where the possible ranges of variation of relative commodity prices with incomplete specialization overlap. This is illustrated in figure 11.1 by the region P_3P_2, assuming that $\rho_B = \rho_1$. Third, each country must have a very strong preference for the commodity which uses intensively its abundant factor, with factor abundance decided on the basis of the physical definition. Refer back to figure 11.1 and assume that $\rho_B = \rho_1$; a divergence between the two definitions will arise if the pretrade relative commodity prices lie in the region P_3P_2 and if, in addition, commodity X is relatively more expensive in A than in B. For commodity X to be relatively more expensive in A than in B, it is necessary that A (the L-abundant country) have a strong preference for commodity X (i.e., the L-intensive commodity), and B (the T-abundant country) for commodity Y (i.e., the T-intensive commodity).

While these three conditions are necessary they are not sufficient. The sufficient condition, of course, is that, before trade, the L-intensive commodity must be relatively cheaper in the T-abundant country.

Let us consider briefly the case of variable factor supplies. Could the preceding analysis of the factor-price equalization theorem be applied equally to the case where the factor supplies are not perfectly inelastic? Yes. The only difference now is that the overall factor-endowment ratio is not rigidly fixed; it is, rather, a function of the factor-price ratio (w/r). Thus, in determining the possible range of variation of the factor-price ratio, we have to draw, in the first quadrant of figure 11.2, a curve showing the behavior of the overall factor-endowment ratio as a function of the factor-price ratio, instead of a vertical line at the given overall factor-endowment ratio. The intersection of this factor-endowment curve with the curves XX' and YY' will determine the range of variation of w/r. Once this is done, the analysis can proceed along lines similar to the analysis of the case of perfectly inelastic factor supplies.

Is the above conclusion also true for the Heckscher-Ohlin theorem? Unfortunately, variable factor supplies can conceivably give rise to additional difficulties for the Heckscher-Ohlin theorem, for it may not be possible to uniquely classify countries into labor abundant and land abundant on the basis of the physical definition *for all factor-price ratios*. In other words, the factor-endowment curves of the two countries in the first quadrant of figures 11.1 and 11.2 may intersect each other any number of times. Then, one country will be classified as labor abundant for some factor-price ratios but land abundant for some others. Would the difficulties disappear if we were to base our classification of countries into labor and land abundant on the pretrade equilibrium factor-endowment ratios? Certainly not, for we still cannot exclude the possibility that the so-defined labor-abundant country may export the land-intensive commodity.

2. Factor-Intensity Reversals

Thus far, the phenomenon of factor-intensity reversals has been completely ignored. In the absence of factor-intensity reversals, we have been able to derive the following conclusions:

1. A *tendency* toward factor-price equalization exists.

2. Factor prices will be equalized between countries provided that the divergence between the factor proportions of the two countries is not too large. Put differently, the failure of complete factor-price equalization is necessarily due to a large disparity between the factor proportions of the two countries.

3. The Heckscher-Ohlin theorem is necessarily true on the basis of the price definition of factor abundance.

4. The Heckscher-Ohlin theorem is *not* necessarily true on the basis of the physical definition of factor abundance.

How does the phenomenon of factor-intensity reversals affect the preceding conclusions? Figure 11.3 illustrates the case of a single factor-intensity reversal. In particular, commodity X is assumed to be labor intensive for relative factor prices smaller than W_N; land intensive for relative factor prices higher than W_N; and, for the specific factor-price ratio W_N, as labor-intensive as commodity Y. These assumptions are reflected in the properties of the curves XX' and YY' (in the first quadrant). The curve XX' lies to the right of YY' for $w/r < W_N$; it lies to the left of YY' for $w/r > W_N$; and it intersects YY' at $w/r = W_N$, that is, at point N.

How is the PP' curve in the second quadrant affected by the factor-intensity reversal at N? According to equation (9.17), the commodity-price ratio, p_x/p_y, is an increasing function of the factor-price ratio, w/r, only when commodity X is labor intensive relative to Y. If X is land intensive relative to Y, the ratio p_x/p_y becomes a decreasing function of w/r. If X is as labor intensive as Y, the ratio p_x/p_y becomes a constant,—its precise value de-

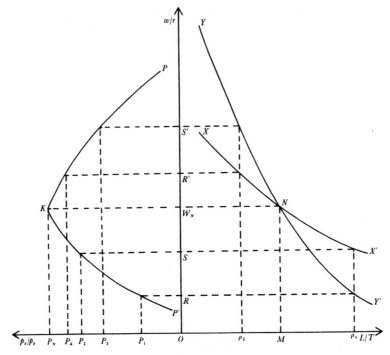

FIGURE 11.3

pending on the arbitrarily chosen units of measurement of X and Y. Accordingly, the PP' curve (in the second quadrant) is drawn upward sloping in the region $0 < w/r < W_N$, where X is labor intensive, backward bending in the region $w/r > W_N$, where X is land intensive; and vertical at the specific value $w/r = W_N$, where both X and Y have identical labor/land ratios.

What are the implications of the nonmonotonicity of the PP' curve[2] of figure 11.3? The immediate consequence is that the one-to-one correspondence between relative commodity prices and relative factor prices is lost. To be sure, given a factor-price ratio, we can uniquely determine a commodity-price ratio, as can be verified by the fact that *any* horizontal line will cut the PP' curve only once. However, the converse is no longer true. In other words, given a commodity-price ratio, we have two factor-price ratios consistent with the originally given commodity-price ratio, as can be verified by the fact that any vertical line that cuts the PP' curve (with the exception of $P_N K$) will cut it twice.

Why is it important that, after the introduction of factor-intensity reversals, the one-to-one correspondence between relative commodity prices and relative factor prices is lost? Because even with incomplete specialization

2. By which we mean that the PP' curve is neither upward sloping throughout nor downward sloping, throughout.

in both countries, the equality of commodity prices between countries (through free commodity trade) need not necessarily imply equality of factor prices between countries as well. The outcome depends upon additional information regarding factor proportions in the two countries.

The new problems created by factor-intensity reversals will be discussed in terms of the following three cases:

Case 1: The factor-endowment ratios of both countries are either larger or smaller than OM (see fig. 11.3), where OM is the optimum labor/land ratio for both X and Y when the factor-price ratio is equal to W_N. This case presents no new problems besides those already discussed in the preceding section. Although commodities X and Y cannot be uniquely classified into labor intensive and land intensive on the basis of their respective production functions alone (as illustrated by the fact that the curves XX' and YY' in the first quadrant of fig. 11.3 intersect each other at point N), the additional condition on factor endowments, namely, that both ρ_A and ρ_B be either smaller or larger than OM, restricts the area of substitutability in a way that prevents the factor-intensity reversal from being actually observed. In other words, factor proportions are such that the contract curves of both countries lie on the same side of the diagonal of their respective box diagrams. Therefore, in the absence of complete specialization, factor prices will be completely equalized between countries. The Heckscher–Ohlin theorem will also be true on the basis of the price definition of factor abundance. However, on the basis of the physical definition, the Heckscher–Ohlin theorem will be true only if tastes are largely similar (and homothetic) between countries.

Case 2: The factor-endowment ratio of one of the two countries is equal to OM. Assume that it is A's factor-endowment ratio that is equal to OM (i.e., $\rho_A = OM$). This case can be conveniently subdivided into the following three subcases:

a) $\rho_A = \rho_B = OM$. This corresponds to the classical case of equal comparative costs. In other words, the production-possibilities frontiers of both countries are parallel straight lines with their common slope equal to P_N (see fig. 11.3). As we have seen in chapter 3, no trade takes place in this case. However, factor prices are equal in both countries in the autarkic state, and they will continue to remain equal after the possibility of trade is allowed.

The assumption that the two commodities have different factor intensities is an important one. As noted earlier, if the factor intensities of the two commodities were actually the same, the curves XX' and YY' would coincide and the range of variation of factor prices in each country would shrink to a single point. Under these circumstances, differing factor-endowment ratios between countries would necessarily imply different factor prices between countries—both before and after trade. Factor prices can only be equal if, and only if, the factor-endowment ratios of the two countries are equal. However, this leads to the equal comparative-costs case with no trade —and factor prices are equal between countries in the autarkic equilibrium state to begin with. In the present case where the curves XX' and YY' do not coincide but intersect each other at N, the conclusion must be the same, because, when $\rho_A = \rho_B = OM$, the only observable production techniques are those implied by point N. The rest of the curves become irrelevant.

b) $\rho_A = OM$ but $\rho_B > OM$, and in particular, $\rho_B = \rho_1$. In this case, A's production-possibilities frontier will again be a straight line. Its absolute slope will be equal to P_N, as in case (a) above. The only factor-price ratio consistent with full employment in A is still W_N. However, the possible range of variation of the factor-price ratio in B is now given by RS, while the range of variation of the commodity-price ratio (with incomplete specialization) is given by P_1P_2. Thus, before trade, X will be relatively cheaper in B than in A, and the posttrade equilibrium commodity-price ratio will definitely lie in the region P_1P_N. Thus, country A will always specialize in the production of commodity Y. However, country B will either specialize in the production of commodity X (when the commodity-price ratio lies in the region P_2P_N) or produce both commodities (when the commodity-price ratio lies in the region P_1P_2). Factor-price equalization cannot possibly take place, since A's equilibrium factor-price ratio (W_N) does not lie in the region RS (i.e., B's permissible range of variation of relative factor prices). However, there will be a tendency toward factor-price equalization. In this case, the Heckscher–Ohlin theorem seems to be correct from the point of view of country B, which is exporting that commodity (X) which uses intensively its abundant factor (L). This is true on the basis of both the price and the physical definitions of factor abundance: they both give rise to the same classification of countries. However, from the point of view of country A, the Heckscher–Ohlin theorem cannot be applied, because in this country the two commodities have equal factor intensities. But if we were to use the classification of country B, the Heckscher–Ohlin theorem would also hold from the point of view of country A as well.

c) $\rho'_A = OM$ but $\rho_B < OM$, and in particular, $\rho_B = \rho_2$. As in the preceding case, in the autarkic equilibrium state X will be relatively cheaper in B than in A. Country B, which is the land-abundant country now on the basis of both the price and the quantity definitions, will export commodity X. But X is also the land-intensive commodity now. Hence, the Heckscher–Ohlin theorem is again correct, subject to the qualification made in the preceding case in relation to country A. Complete factor-price equalization is again impossible, because W_N (i.e., A's equilibrium factor-price ratio) does not lie in the region $R'S'$ (i.e., B's permissible range of variation of relative factor prices). However, there will definitely be a tendency toward factor-price equalization.

It should be pointed out that in case (*b*) a limited migration of labor from *B* to *A*, and in case (*c*) a limited migration of labor from *A* to *B*, would bring about complete factor-price equalization between the two countries.

Case 3: The factor-endowment ratio of one country is higher than *OM*, while the factor-endowment ratio of the other country is lower than *OM*. Assume that $\rho_A > OM$ and $\rho_B < OM$. This is the case of factor-intensity reversals proper. This important case is illustrated in figure 11.4, which reproduces the basic relationships exhibited in figure 11.3. To facilitate the exposition, assume that *A*'s factor-endowment ratio remains fixed at ρ_1 and allow *B*'s factor-endowment ratio to vary in the region *OM*. This enables us to cover all the important subcases of this important case.

Is factor-price equalization possible? Is there a tendency toward equalization? Is the Heckscher–Ohlin theorem correct? These are the important questions, but the answers are rather disappointing.

Given that $\rho_A = \rho_1$, the range of variation of *A*'s relative factor prices is given by *RS* while its range of variation of relative commodity prices (with incomplete specialization) is given by $P_1 P_2$. As long as $\rho_B < OM$, the range of variation of *B*'s relative factor prices will necessarily lie above *A*'s range (i.e., *RS*). Therefore, complete factor-price equalization is ruled out. What is even

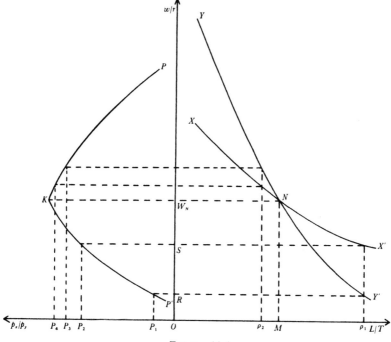

FIGURE 11.4

more disappointing in this case is that even a tendency toward factor-price equalization need not exist. More precisely, in this case free trade in commodities will necessarily cause factor prices to move in the same direction in both countries, and the difference between them may either narrow or widen according to circumstances. How has this conclusion been derived? Observe that commodity X is labor intensive in A but land intensive in B. Therefore, if A exports X and B exports Y, the factor-price ratio w/r will tend to rise in both countries because both countries export their labor-intensive commodity. On the other hand, if A exports Y and B exports X, the factor-price ratio w/r will fall in both countries because both countries export their land-intensive commodity. Under these circumstances, the disparity between factor prices may expand or contract, depending on which factor-price ratio changes faster.

In the present case, country A is classified as labor abundant relative to B, from the point of view of both the price and the quantity definitions of factor abundance. Notice also that this conclusion holds *irrespective of any differences in tastes between countries.* However, because of the fact that commodity X is labor intensive relative to Y in country A but land intensive relative to Y in country B, the Heckscher-Ohlin theorem cannot possibly be correct from the point of view of both countries. (The Heckscher-Ohlin theorem requires that both countries export commodity X!)

Is it possible to predict, in the present case, the pattern of trade—even though the Heckscher-Ohlin theorem cannot be correct for both countries— from the knowledge that $\rho_A > OM$ and $\rho_B < OM$? Definitely not. Remember that the direction of trade depends on the pretrade equilibrium relative commodity prices. Keeping $\rho_A = \rho_1$ and letting ρ_B fall from OM toward zero, we can see that, even without any information on tastes in the two countries, the pattern of trade will necessarily be reversed. Thus, if $\rho_B = \rho_2$, the range of variation of B's commodity-price ratio (with incomplete specialization) will be given by P_3P_4. Therefore, X will be relatively cheaper in A, so that A will export X and B will export Y.

On the other hand, if ρ_B is reduced sufficiently from its original value, ρ_2, the range of variation of B's commodity-price ratio can be made to lie totally to the right of P_1P_2. In this case, X will be relatively cheaper in B than in A, and therefore, B will be exporting commodity X and A will be exporting Y.

The preceding analysis is based on the assumption that only one reversal separates the factor-endowment ratios of the two countries. However, the analysis can be easily generalized to the case where n $(n > 1)$ reversals separate ρ_A from ρ_B. In particular, if n is *odd*, none of the preceding conclusions will be affected. Thus, countries can be uniquely classified into labor abundant and land abundant on the basis of either the price or the physical definition. However, A's classification of commodities will be contradictory to B's, so that the Heckscher–Ohlin theorem cannot be correct.

Complete factor-price equalization is ruled out because the permissible factor-price ranges of the two countries do not overlap. As a result of the contradictory classification of commodities, even a tendency toward equalization may not exist.

On the other hand, if *n* is *even*, a commodity is unequivocally classified into labor intensive, or land intensive, in both countries. But the direction of trade is indeterminate. Thus, the labor-abundant country may export either the labor-intensive or the land-intensive commodity. If the labor-abundant country exports the labor-intensive commodity (and thus the land-abundant country exports the land-intensive commodity), factor prices in the two countries will move toward each other, despite the fact that complete factor-price equalization is impossible. But if the pattern of trade is the opposite, that is, if the labor-abundant country exports the land-intensive commodity and the land-abundant country exports the labor-intensive commodity, there will be a tendency for factor prices in the two countries *to move away from each other*.

Figure 11.5 illustrates this analysis of multiple reversals. It is similar to figure 11.4, except that now there are four reversals as the curves *XX'* and

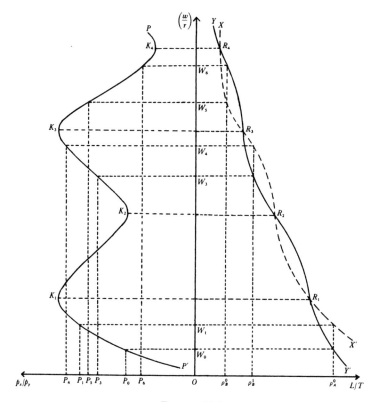

FIGURE 11.5

YY' (in the first quadrant) intersect each other four times at points R_1, R_2, R_3, and R_4. As a result, the PP' curve assumes the twisted shape shown in the second quadrant. Assume now that ρ_A is equal to ρ_A^0, as shown in figure 11.5. Then A's range of variation of the factor-price ratio will be given by $W_0 W_1$, and its range of variation of the commodity-price ratio will be given by $P_0 P_1$. If ρ_B were equal to ρ_B^0, then ρ_A would be separated from ρ_B by three (i.e., an *odd* number of) reversals. Country B's range of variation of w/r would be given by $W_5 W_6$, and its range of variation of p_x/p_y would be given by $P_5 P_6$. Several things are obvious. (*a*) Since $\rho_A^0 > \rho_B^0$ and the factor-price ratio w/r assumes higher values in the range $W_5 W_6$ than in the range $W_0 W_1$, that is, $(w/r)_A < (w/r)_B$, A will be classified as labor abundant relative to B on the basis of either the price or the physical definition of factor abundance. (*b*) Since it is always (i.e., before and after trade) true that $(w/r)_A < (w/r)_B$ (because the region $W_0 W_1$ is uniformly lower than the region $W_5 W_6$), complete factor-price equalization is ruled out. (*c*) Commodity X is labor intensive relative to Y in country A but land intensive relative to Y in country B. Hence, the Heckscher–Ohlin theorem cannot be correct. (*d*) Any pattern of trade is possible. If A exports X and B exports Y, then both A's and B's posttrade factor-price ratios will be higher than their respective pretrade levels. On the other hand, if A exports Y and B exports X, then both A's and B's posttrade factor-price ratios will be lower than their respective pretrade levels. Hence, in neither case is there reason to believe that there exists a tendency toward factor-price equalization.

Suppose now that ρ_B is equal to ρ_B^1, as shown in figure 11.5, with ρ_A separated from ρ_B by only two (i.e., an *even* number of) reversals. What difference does this make to conclusions (*a*)–(*d*)? It is obvious that A is still labor abundant relative to B on the basis of both the price and the quantity definitions of factor abundance, and that complete factor-price equalization is ruled out because it is always true that $(w/r)_A < (w/r)_B$. However, commodity X is labor intensive relative to Y in both countries. But the direction of trade need not be that predicted by the Heckscher-Ohlin theorem (i.e., A exporting X and B exporting Y). This conclusion does not necessarily depend on differences in tastes between A and B. Imagine that the curves and factor-endowment ratios have been drawn in such a way as to make the region $P_3 P_4$ (i.e., B's range of variation of the commodity-price ratio) lie uniformly to the right of $P_0 P_1$. Under these circumstances, B will necessarily be exporting X and A will be exporting Y *irrespective of tastes*. Note that if A exports X and B exports Y, factor prices in the two countries will be moving toward each other, that is, there will be a tendency toward factor-price equalization. On the other hand, if A exports Y and B exports X, factor prices in the two countries will be moving away from each other.

This section can be summarized thus:

i) The Heckscher-Ohlin theorem is not generally true whether the price definition or the quantity definition of factor abundance is used. However, in the absence of factor-intensity reversals between the factor-endowment ratios of the two countries, the Heckscher-Ohlin theorem is true only on the basis of the price definition; on the basis of the physical definition, the outcome depends on tastes.

ii) Commodity trade will equalize factor prices completely only in the absence of factor-intensity reversals between the factor-endowment ratios of the two countries and provided that neither country specializes completely in the production of one commodity. In the presence of factor-intensity reversals between ρ_A and ρ_B, commodity trade may have any effect whatsoever on factor prices. Incomplete specialization in both countries *is* consistent with widely differing factor prices between countries.

3. The Empirical Relevance of the Assumptions of the Factor-Price Equalization Theorem

No logical objections can be raised against the factor-price equalization theorem. If the assumptions enumerated in chapter 10, section 2, are correct, factor prices will be completely equalized between countries via free trade in commodities. But how far are these assumptions correct in the real world, and what conclusions can be reached in analyzing any actual situation?

It goes without saying that the assumption of perfect competition cannot be relaxed. The introduction of oligopolistic market structures, wage and price rigidities, and so on, necessarily impede the equalization of factor prices via commodity movements, because under these circumstances, commodity prices are not equal to the costs of production. Therefore, knowing factor prices (and thus costs of production), we cannot uniquely determine commodity prices, let alone the reverse proposition of going from commodity prices to factor prices.

Whether factor-intensity reversals may or may not impede factor-price equalization depends on the factor endowments of the two countries, as explained in the preceding section. Minhas (1962) first noted that, if the production functions of the two commodities are characterized by a constant elasticity of substitution[3] and if the elasticity coefficient is different between the two industries, then factor-intensity reversals will necessarily occur. This is an important objection to the factor-price equalization theorem from an empirical point of view if, in addition, the factor-endowment ratios of the two countries are actually separated by factor-intensity reversals. Otherwise, the existence of factor-intensity reversals as such need not impede factor-price equalization.

The assumption of identical production functions for each commodity between countries has already been discussed in chapter 9. For the present, if production functions are different as between countries, factor prices cannot be equalized. However, if the differences are of the sort attributed to

---

3. Minhas calls this form of production function "homohypallagic."

neutral technological progress, *relative* factor prices will still be equalized, although no equality of *absolute* factor prices can take place. This topic is discussed in chapters 12–13.

The assumption of constant returns to scale cannot be relaxed either. With variable returns to scale, whether increasing or decreasing, and even with the assumption that the production functions are homogeneous (of a degree different from unity), absolute factor prices do not depend only on the labor/land ratios used in the two industries; they depend, in addition, on the scales of output. Under these circumstances, the most that can be expected is relative factor-price equalization. Finally, with increasing returns due to economies internal to the firm, perfect competition breaks down, which, as we have seen, necessarily impedes factor-price equalization.

Differences in the quality of factors have been particularly emphasized by Harrod and Viner.[4] Differences in the educational background, motivation, health and nutrition, and other sociological characteristics of workers should prevent us from describing labor as a homogeneous factor. The wide heterogeneity of capital goods (specialized production and transportation equipment) and the well-known difficulties connected with this heterogeneity should also prevent us from regarding "capital" as a single homogeneous factor of production. The same can also be said for the factor "land." The fact is, in the real world, it is not two homogeneous factors of production (in the two countries) we must contend with, but many. However, new problems are created for the factor-price equalization theorem when the number of factors of production is increased $(n > 2)$. Unfortunately, this more general case is beyond the scope of this book.

The consequences of complete specialization—and the impact of differences in factor endowments between the two countries as well as the impact of differences in factor intensities of the two commodities on specialization in production—are examined in sections 1 and 2 of this chapter.

It is obvious that trade restrictions and transportation costs exist in the real world, which means that commodity trade does not really equalize relative commodity prices in the real world. Even if there were a one-to-one correspondence between factor prices and commodity prices, complete factor-price equalization would still not occur in the real world, because of the absence of complete commodity-price equalization. The most we can hope for is a *tendency* toward equalization.

The general conclusion that one can derive from these comments is that the conditions for factor-price equalization through commodity trade are so restrictive that they are unlikely to be fulfilled, even approximately, in the real world. Haberler (1961) expressed the opinion that "we must thus conclude that the Lerner–Samuelson theory, though formally correct, rests on such restrictive and unrealistic assumptions that it can hardly be regarded

4. See Viner (1952, pp. 29, 131).

as a valuable contribution to economic theory." Harrod (1959, p. 37) described the factor-price equalization theorem as a *curiosum* in economics. John S. Chipman (1965, p. 479), on the other hand, expressed the opinion that the modern theory "represents probably the most complex and impressive theoretical structure that has yet been developed in economic thought." Both of these positions are extremes. The truth probably lies somewhere in between. It can be argued that, although the assumptions of the factor-price equalization theorem are violated in the real world, the importance of the theorem itself springs mainly from the fact that it directs our attention toward the examination of the relevant variables that determine the impact on factor prices of free trade in commodities. The factor-price equalization theorem can tell us how far we can hope to go toward world efficiency, while maintaining barriers to factor movements, through free commodity trade plus technical assistance plus, possibly, capital movements (the latter two being "foreign aid").

SELECTED BIBLIOGRAPHY

American Economic Association. 1968. *Readings in International Economics*. Edited by Caves and Johnson. Homewood, Ill.: R. D. Irwin, Inc. Chaps. 1–6, 30.
———. 1950. *Readings in the Theory of International Trade*. Edited by Ellis and Metzler. Homewood, Ill.: R. D. Irwin, Inc. Chap. 13.
Balassa, B. 1961. The factor-price equalization controversy. *Weltwirtschaftliches Archiv* 87: 111–123.
Bhagwati, J. 1964. The pure theory of international trade. *Economic Journal* 74: 1–78.
Brown, A. J. 1957. Professor Leontief and the pattern of world trade. *Yorkshire Bulletin of Economic and Social Research* 9: 63–75.
Chacholiades, M. 1972. Multiple pre-trade equilibria and the theory of comparative advantage. *Metroeconomica* Fasc. II.
Chipman, J. S. 1965. A survey of the theory of international trade: part 1, the classical theory. *Econometrica* 33: 477–519.
———. 1965. A survey of the theory of international trade: part 2, the neo-classical theory. *Econometrica* 33: 685–760.
———. 1966. A survey of the theory of international trade: part 3, the modern theory. *Econometrica* 34: 18–76.
Clement, M. O., R. L. Pfister, and K. J. Rothwell. 1967. *Theoretical Issues in International Economics*. Boston: Houghton-Mifflin Co. Chaps. 1, 2.
Corden, W. M. 1965. *Recent Developments in the Theory of International Trade*. Princeton University Special Papers in International Economics No. 7.
Haberler, G. 1961. *A Survey of International Trade Theory*. Princeton University Special Papers in International Economics, No. 1, 2nd Ed.
Harrod, R. F. 1959. *International Economics*, 4th ed. Cambridge: Cambridge University Press.
Heckscher, E. 1919. The effect of foreign trade on the distribution of income. *Ekonomisk Tidskrift* 21: 1–32.
Jones, R. W. 1956. Factor proportions and the Heckscher-Ohlin theorem. *Review of Economic Studies* 24: 1–10.

Kemp, M. C. 1969. *The Pure Theory of International Trade and Investment*. Englewood Cliffs, N.J.: Prentice-Hall, Inc. Part I.

Lancaster, K. 1957. The Heckscher-Ohlin trade model: a geometric treatment. *Economica* 24: 19–39.

Leontief, W. W. 1956. Factor proportions and the structure of American trade. *Review of Economics and Statistics* 38: 386–407.

Lerner, A. P. 1953. *Essays in Economics Analysis*. London: Macmillan & Co., pp. 67–100.

Meade, J. E. 1955. *The Theory of International Economic Policy. Vol. 2: Trade and Welfare*. Oxford: Oxford University Press. Chaps. 19–23.

Melvin, J. R. 1968. Production and trade with two factors and three goods. *American Economic Review* 58: 1249–68.

Metzler, L. A. 1948. The theory of international trade. In H. S. Ellis, (Ed.). *Survey of Contemporary Economics*. Philadelphia: The Blakiston Co., 1948.

Michaely, M. 1964. Factor proportions in international trade: current state of the theory. *Kyklos* 17, Fasc. 4.

Minhas, B. 1962. The homohypallagic production function, factor intensity reversals, and the Heckscher–Ohlin theorem. *Journal of Political Economy* 70: 138–56.

Mundell, R. A. 1960. The pure theory of international trade. *American Economic Review* 40: 301–22.

Ohlin, B. 1933. *Interregional and International Trade*. Cambridge, Mass.: Harvard University Press. Chaps. 1–4, App. 3.

Samuelson, P. A. 1948. International trade and the equalization of factor prices. *Economic Journal* 68: 165–184.

———. 1953. Prices of factors and goods in general equilibrium. *Review of Economic Studies* 21: 1–20.

———. 1967. Summary on factor price equalization. *International Economic Review* 8: 286–95.

Stolper, W. F., and P. A. Samuelson. 1941. Protection and real wages. *Review of Economic Studies* 9: 58–73.

Vanek, J. 1960. An alternative proof of the factor price equalization theorem. *Quarterly Journal of Economics* 74: 633–40.

Viner, J. 1953. *International Trade and Economic Development*. New York: Free Press.

V

Economic Growth
and Trade

The Effects of Economic Growth
on Trade

The preceding chapters are limited by the assumption that the two fundamental data which delimit the production-possibilities frontier, namely, factor
endowments and technology, are given. But in the real world, neither
factor endowments nor technology remain static. With the passage of time,
factor endowments grow and new and more efficient methods of production
replace old and inefficient ones. Factor-endowment growth and technical
progress give rise to some interesting economic problems the study of which
forms the *theory of the effects of economic growth on trade.*

We shall now be concerned with the *comparative static analysis* of the effects
of labor growth and capital accumulation, on the one hand, and technical
progress, on the other, on the growing country's consumption, production,
demand for imports, supply of exports, terms of trade, factor prices, and social
welfare. The major architect of this analysis is Harry G. Johnson (1958),
though the idea of export and import bias originated with John R. Hicks'
article on the long-run dollar problem (1953). In addition, contributions
have been made by Bhagwati (1958), Corden (1956), Findlay and Grubert
(1959), and Rybczynski (1955).

This chapter deals with the effects of economic growth. The discussion
is rather general in the sense that it does not distinguish among the three
main sources of economic growth.

A. The Effects of Growth on the Small Country

Let us begin our analysis with a discussion of the effects of economic growth
on a small country that is a price taker in the international market. To
simplify, assume that the units of measurement of commodities X and Y are

such that the given international price ratio, p_x/p_y, is unity. Needless to say, this is not a crucial assumption: it is merely convenient.

1. Definitions

The main sources of economic growth are labor growth, capital accumulation, and technical progress. Their common characteristic is that they cause the production-possibilities frontier of the growing economy to shift outward through time. In the next chapter, we shall have to distinguish among these three sources of economic growth. For present purposes, it will suffice to concentrate on the resultant outward shift of the production-possibilities frontier and study its effects on the consumption and production patterns of the growing economy, as well as its volume of trade, at the initial terms of trade.

Assume that our simple economy is in long-run equilibrium. In particular, assume that at this initial equilibrium our economy produces X_p units of X (exportables) and Y_p units of Y (importables), consumes X_c units of X and Y_c units of Y, and exports $Z \equiv X_p - X_c$ units of X in exchange for $M \equiv Y_c - Y_p$ units of Y. Therefore, the real national income, Q, of our economy (expressed in terms of either commodity) is given by

$$Q = X_p + Y_p = X_c + Y_c \tag{12.1}$$

and the volume of trade, V, by

$$V = M = Y_c - Y_p = Z = X_p - X_c \tag{12.2}$$

Let us now introduce the following definitions:

$$\text{average propensity to produce exportables} \equiv \frac{X_p}{Q} \equiv \theta_x^p,$$

$$\text{average propensity to produce importables} \equiv \frac{Y_p}{Q} \equiv \theta_y^p,$$

$$\text{average propensity to consume exportables} \equiv \frac{X_c}{Q} \equiv \theta_x^c,$$

$$\text{average propensity to consume importables} \equiv \frac{Y_c}{Q} \equiv \theta_y^c,$$

$$\text{average propensity to import importables} \equiv \frac{M}{Q} \equiv \theta_m,$$

$$\text{average propensity to export exportables} \equiv \frac{Z}{Q} \equiv \theta_z,$$

$$\text{average propensity to trade} \equiv \frac{V}{Q} \equiv \theta_v.$$

Note that θ = average propensity, p = production, c = consumption, x = exportables, y = importables, m = imports, z = exports, and v = volume of trade.

Given the above definitions and equations (12.1) and (12.2), we can easily formulate the following relationships:

$$\theta_x^p + \theta_y^p \equiv \theta_x^c + \theta_y^c \equiv 1 \tag{12.3}$$

(by dividing all terms in eqs. [12.1] by Q) and

$$\theta_v \equiv \theta_m \equiv \theta_y^c - \theta_y^p \equiv \theta_z \equiv \theta_x^p - \theta_x^c \tag{12.4}$$

(by dividing all terms in eqs. [12.2] by Q).

Suppose now that our economy's production-possibilities frontier shifts outward. Given sufficient time, our economy will reach a new equilibrium. In general, our economy will produce, consume, export, and import amounts at the new equilibrium different from the corresponding amounts at the initial equilibrium. What follows concerns the differences between the new and the old quantities. Using the operator Δ to indicate the difference between the value of a certain variable at the new equilibrium and its value at the initial equilibrium, we can write ΔX_p for the "difference in X_p"; ΔX_c for the "difference in X_c"; and so on. (Assume that at the new equilibrium our economy continues to export X and import Y.) Thus, using the superscripts 0 and 1 to indicate the values at the initial equilibrium and the new one, respectively, we have

$$\Delta Q = Q^1 - Q^0, \quad \Delta X_p = X_p^1 - X_p^0,$$
$$\Delta Y_p = Y_p^1 - Y_p^0, \quad \Delta X_c = X_c^1 - X_c^0,$$
$$\Delta Y_c = Y_c^1 - Y_c^0, \quad \Delta V = V^1 - V^0,$$
$$\Delta M = M^1 - M^0, \quad \Delta Z = Z^1 - Z^0.$$

Since equations (12.1) and (12.2) must hold at both equilibria, the following equations must be true:

$$\Delta Q = \Delta X_p + \Delta Y_p = \Delta X_c + \Delta Y_c, \tag{12.5}$$
$$\Delta V = \Delta M = \Delta Y_c - \Delta Y_p = \Delta Z = \Delta X_p - \Delta X_c. \tag{12.6}$$

Let us now introduce the following definitions:

marginal propensity to produce exportables $\equiv \dfrac{\Delta X_p}{\Delta Q} \equiv \xi_x^p,$

marginal propensity to produce importables $\equiv \dfrac{\Delta Y_p}{\Delta Q} \equiv \xi_y^p,$

marginal propensity to consume exportables $\equiv \dfrac{\Delta X_c}{\Delta Q} \equiv \xi_x^c,$

marginal propensity to consume importables $\equiv \dfrac{\Delta Y_c}{\Delta Q} \equiv \xi_y^c,$

$$\text{marginal propensity to import importables} \quad \equiv \frac{\Delta M}{\Delta Q} \equiv \xi_m,$$

$$\text{marginal propensity to export exportables} \quad \equiv \frac{\Delta Z}{\Delta Q} \equiv \xi_z,$$

$$\text{marginal propensity to trade} \quad \equiv \frac{\Delta V}{\Delta Q} \equiv \xi_v.$$

The Greek letter ξ stands for marginal propensity.

Dividing all terms of equations (12.5) by ΔQ and applying the preceding definitions, we get

$$\xi_x^p + \xi_y^p = \xi_x^c + \xi_y^c = 1. \tag{12.7}$$

Dividing all terms of equations (12.6) by ΔQ and applying the preceding definitions, we get

$$\xi_v = \xi_m = \xi_y^c - \xi_y^p = \xi_z = \xi_x^p - \xi_x^c. \tag{12.8}$$

The literature on growth makes use of some additional concepts, namely, "rates of growth" and "output elasticities." The various rates of growth are defined as follows:

$$\text{rate of growth of output} \quad \equiv \frac{\Delta Q}{Q^0} \equiv \lambda_q,$$

$$\text{rate of growth of production of exportables} \quad \equiv \frac{\Delta X_p}{X_p^0} \equiv \lambda_x^p,$$

$$\text{rate of growth of production of importables} \quad \equiv \frac{\Delta Y_p}{Y_p^0} \equiv \lambda_y^p,$$

$$\text{rate of growth of consumption of exportables} \quad \equiv \frac{\Delta X_c}{X_c^0} \equiv \lambda_x^c,$$

$$\text{rate of growth of consumption of importables} \quad \equiv \frac{\Delta Y_c}{Y_c^0} \equiv \lambda_y^c,$$

$$\text{rate of growth of imports (of importables)} \quad \equiv \frac{\Delta M}{M^0} \equiv \lambda_m,$$

$$\text{rate of growth of exports (of exportables)} \quad \equiv \frac{\Delta Z}{Z^0} \equiv \lambda_z,$$

$$\text{rate of growth of (the volume of) trade} \quad \equiv \frac{\Delta V}{V^0} \equiv \lambda_v.$$

The Greek letter λ stands for rate of growth.

Given equations (12.2) and (12.6) and applying the preceding definitions, we get

$$\lambda_v \equiv \lambda_m \equiv \lambda_z. \tag{12.9}$$

The definitions of output elasticities are as follows:

output elasticity of supply of exportables $\equiv \dfrac{\Delta X_p}{\Delta Q} \dfrac{Q^0}{X_p^0} \equiv \eta_x^p,$

output elasticity of supply of importables $\equiv \dfrac{\Delta Y_p}{\Delta Q} \dfrac{Q^0}{Y_p^0} \equiv \eta_y^p,$

output elasticity of demand for exportables $\equiv \dfrac{\Delta X_c}{\Delta Q} \dfrac{Q^0}{X_c^0} \equiv \eta_x^c,$

output elasticity of demand for importables $\equiv \dfrac{\Delta Y_c}{\Delta Q} \dfrac{Q^0}{Y_c^0} \equiv \eta_y^c,$

output elasticity of demand for imports $\equiv \dfrac{\Delta M}{\Delta Q} \dfrac{Q^0}{M^0} \equiv \eta_m,$

output elasticity of supply of exports $\equiv \dfrac{\Delta Z}{\Delta Q} \dfrac{Q^0}{Z^0} \equiv \eta_z,$

output elasticity of (the volume of) trade $\equiv \dfrac{\Delta V}{\Delta Q} \dfrac{Q^0}{V^0} \equiv \eta_v.$

The Greek letter η stands for output elasticity.

We now have

$$\eta_v = \eta_m = \eta_z, \tag{12.10}$$

which corresponds to equation (12.9).

The relationships among marginal propensities, average propensities, rates of growth, and output elasticities are simple and can be summarized as follows.

$$\frac{\text{marginal propensity}}{\text{average propensity}} = \frac{\text{rate of growth}}{\text{rate of growth of output}} = \text{output elasticity}$$

This equation follows directly from the definitions. Thus,

$$\lambda_x^p \equiv \frac{\Delta X_p}{X_p^0} = \frac{\Delta X_p}{\Delta Q} \frac{Q^0}{X_p^0} \frac{\Delta Q}{Q^0} = \frac{\xi_x^p}{\theta_x^p} \lambda_q = \eta_x^p \lambda_q, \tag{12.11}$$

$$\lambda_x^c \equiv \frac{\Delta X_c}{X_c^0} = \frac{\Delta X_c}{\Delta Q} \frac{Q^0}{X_c^0} \frac{\Delta Q}{Q^0} = \frac{\xi_x^c}{\theta_x^c} \lambda_q = \eta_x^c \lambda_q, \tag{12.12}$$

$$\lambda_y^p \equiv \frac{\Delta Y_p}{Y_p^0} = \frac{\Delta Y_p}{\Delta Q} \frac{Q^0}{Y_p^0} \frac{\Delta Q}{Q^0} = \frac{\xi_y^p}{\theta_y^p} \lambda_q = \eta_y^p \lambda_q, \tag{12.13}$$

$$\lambda_y^c \equiv \frac{\Delta Y_c}{Y_c^0} = \frac{\Delta Y_c}{\Delta Q} \frac{Q^0}{Y_c^0} \frac{\Delta Q}{Q^0} = \frac{\xi_y^c}{\theta_y^c} \lambda_q = \eta_y^c \lambda_q, \qquad (12.14)$$

$$\lambda_m \equiv \frac{\Delta M}{M^0} = \frac{\Delta M}{\Delta Q} \frac{Q^0}{M^0} \frac{\Delta Q}{Q^0} = \frac{\xi_m}{\theta_m} \lambda_q = \eta_m \lambda_q, \qquad (12.15)$$

$$\lambda_z \equiv \frac{\Delta Z}{Z^0} = \frac{\Delta Z}{\Delta Q} \frac{Q^0}{Z^0} \frac{\Delta Q}{Q^0} = \frac{\xi_z}{\theta_z} \lambda_q = \eta_z \lambda_q, \qquad (12.16)$$

$$\lambda_v \equiv \frac{\Delta V}{V^0} = \frac{\Delta V}{\Delta Q} \frac{Q^0}{V^0} \frac{\Delta Q}{Q^0} = \frac{\xi_v}{\theta_v} \lambda_q = \eta_v \lambda_q. \qquad (12.17)$$

The rate of growth of output (λ_q) is a weighted average of the rate of growth of production of exportables (λ_x^p) and the rate of growth of production of importables (λ_y^p). In addition, λ_q is a weighted average of the rate of growth of consumption of exportables (λ_x^c) and the rate of growth of consumption of importables (λ_y^c). These statements can be proved as follows:

$$\lambda_q \equiv \frac{\Delta Q}{Q^0} = \frac{\Delta X_p + \Delta Y_p}{Q^0} = \frac{X_p^0}{Q^0} \frac{\Delta X_p}{X_p^0} + \frac{Y_p^0}{Q^0} \frac{\Delta Y_p}{Y_p^0} = \theta_x^p \lambda_x^p + \theta_y^p \lambda_y^p, \qquad (12.18)$$

$$\lambda_q \equiv \frac{\Delta Q}{Q^0} = \frac{\Delta X_c + \Delta Y_c}{Q^0} = \frac{X_c^0}{Q^0} \frac{\Delta X_c}{X_c^0} + \frac{Y_c^0}{Q^0} \frac{\Delta Y_c}{Y_c^0} = \theta_x^c \lambda_x^c + \theta_y^c \lambda_y^c. \qquad (12.19)$$

Since all average propensities are positive and less than unity, it follows from equations (12.3) and (12.18) that λ_q is a weighted average of λ_x^p and λ_y^p, and from equations (12.3) and (12.19) that λ_q is a weighted average of λ_x^c and λ_y^c. Hence, λ_q must always lie between λ_x^p and λ_y^p, and between λ_x^c and λ_y^c.

The rate of growth of production of exportables (λ_x^p) is a weighted average of the rate of growth of the volume of trade (λ_v) and the rate of growth of consumption of exportables (λ_x^c). This is proved as follows:

$$\lambda_v = \lambda_z = \frac{\Delta Z}{Z^0} = \frac{\Delta X_p - \Delta X_c}{X_p^0 - X_c^0} = \frac{(\Delta X_p / X_p^0) - [(\Delta X_c / X_c^0)(X_c^0 / X_p^0)]}{1 - (X_c^0 / X_p^0)}$$

$$= \frac{\lambda_x^p - \lambda_x^c (X_c^0 / X_p^0)}{1 - (X_c^0 / X_p^0)},$$

or

$$\lambda_x^p = [1 - (X_c^0 / X_p^0)]\lambda_v + (X_c^0 / X_p^0)\lambda_x^c. \qquad (12.20)$$

Since $0 < X_c^0 / X_p^0 < 1$, λ_x^p is a weighted average of λ_v and λ_x^c, and its value must always lie between λ_v and λ_x^c.

The rate of growth of consumption of importables (λ_y^c) is a weighted average of the rate of growth of the volume of trade (λ_v) and the rate of growth of production of importables (λ_y^p). Therefore, λ_y^c must always lie between λ_v and λ_y^p. This can be proved as follows:

$$\lambda_v = \lambda_m = \frac{\Delta M}{M^0} = \frac{\Delta Y_c - \Delta Y_p}{Y_c^0 - Y_p^0} = \frac{(\Delta Y_c / Y_c^0) - [(\Delta Y_p / Y_p^0)(Y_p^0 / Y_c^0)]}{1 - (Y_p^0 / Y_c^0)}$$

$$= \frac{\lambda_y^c - \lambda_y^p (Y_p^0 / Y_c^0)}{1 - (Y_p^0 / Y_c^0)},$$

or

$$\lambda_y^c = [1 - (Y_p^0 / Y_c^0)]\lambda_v + (Y_p^0 / Y_c^0)\lambda_y^p. \tag{12.21}$$

Our statement follows when we observe that $0 < Y_p^0 / Y_c^0 < 1$.

2. Growth Under Classical Assumptions (Complete Specialization)

Let us now analyze the effects of economic growth on the growing country's consumption, production, demand for imports, and supply of exports. Recall that our growing economy is a simple open economy, that is, it can trade unlimited amounts of X and Y at given international prices. Again, we assume for convenience that the given international price ratio is unity. Even in this simple case, it is useful to distinguish between the classical theory, where the production-possibilities frontier is linear and our economy specializes completely in the production of exportables, and the neoclassical and modern theories, where the production-possibilities frontier is concave to the origin (implying increasing opportunity costs) and our economy produces both commodities before and after growth. In this section, we consider the classical case (or the case of complete specialization), and in the following section, we consider the neoclassical-modern case (or the case of incomplete specialization).

Figure 12.1 illustrates the general nature of the effects of growth on production, consumption, demand for imports, and supply of exports in the classical case. The 45° straight line $P_1 K_1$ is the original consumption-possibilities frontier, with production taking place at point P_1 and consumption at C_1. Therefore, our economy is assumed to be specializing in the production of X, exporting $X_1 P_1$ units of X in exchange for $X_1 C_1$ units of Y. The absolute slope of the consumption-possibilities frontier $K_1 P_1$ is unity, which is consistent with our assumption that the given international price ratio is unity.

At the initial, pregrowth equilibrium, the average propensity to produce exportables, and so on, can be measured as follows:

$$\theta_x^p = \frac{OP_1}{OP_1} = 1; \qquad \theta_x^c = \frac{OX_1}{OP_1} < 1; \qquad \theta_y^p = \frac{\text{zero}}{OP_1} = 0;$$

$$\theta_y^c = \frac{OY_1}{OK_1} = \frac{X_1 P_1}{OP_1} < 1; \qquad \theta_m = \theta_z = \theta_v = \frac{X_1 P_1}{OP_1} = \frac{OY_1}{OK_1}.$$

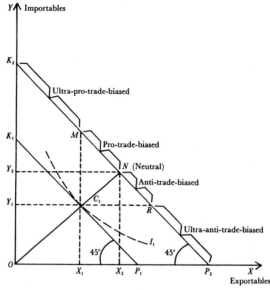

FIGURE 12.1

In addition, we can verify equations (12.3) and (12.4) thus:

$$\theta_x^p + \theta_y^p = 1 + 0 = 1;$$

$$\theta_x^c + \theta_y^c = \frac{OX_1}{OP_1} + \frac{X_1P_1}{OP_1} = \frac{OP_1}{OP_1} = 1;$$

$$\theta_y^c - \theta_y^p = \frac{X_1P_1}{OP_1} - 0 = \frac{X_1P_1}{OP_1} = \theta_v;$$

$$\theta_x^p - \theta_x^c = 1 - \frac{OX_1}{OP_1} = \frac{OP_1 - OX_1}{OP_1} = \frac{X_1P_1}{OP_1} = \theta_v.$$

With economic growth the production-possibilities frontier (not drawn) shifts outward. What happens to the optimum production point depends on exactly how the production-possibilities frontier shifts outward. Figure 12.1 is based on the implicit assumption that, after the production-possibilities frontier shifts outward, the country continues to enjoy a comparative advantage in the production of commodity X. In the classical theory, this will always be the case when economic growth is due to labor growth. However, if growth is due to technical progress, this need not be so. Thus, if technical progress is heavily biased in favor of commodity Y (i.e., if Y's labor coefficient, a_y, falls faster than X's labor coefficient, a_x, through time), the comparative advantage of the country may very well shift from X to Y. To simplify, assume the latter possibility away.

Since, by assumption, the country continues to enjoy a comparative advantage in the production of X after the production-possibilities frontier shifts outward, it will continue to specialize completely in the production of X. Accordingly, the optimum production point will shift to the right along the horizontal axis. This is illustrated in figure 12.1 by the shift of the production point from P_1 to P_2. As a result, the new consumption-possibilities frontier is given by the straight line K_2P_2, which is parallel to K_1P_1 because of the assumed constancy of the international price ratio. With no further information about demand, the only statement that can be made about the new consumption point is that it will lie somewhere on the post-growth consumption-possibilities frontier, K_2P_2. However, the region K_2M implies "inferiority" in X, and the region RP_2 "inferiority" in Y. If we wish to exclude inferiority by assumption, we can restrict the consumption point to the region MNR. We shall return to this point shortly.

With no further information about the postgrowth position of the optimum consumption point, several propensities and rates of growth can be determined merely with the information that the production point shifts from P_1 to P_2. Thus, we can determine the marginal propensity to produce exportables (ξ_x^p), the marginal propensity to produce importables (ξ_y^p), the rate of growth of output (λ_q), the output elasticity of supply of exportables (η_x^p), and the rate of growth of production of exportables (λ_x^p) as follows:

$$\xi_x^p \equiv \frac{\Delta X_p}{\Delta Q} = \frac{P_1P_2}{P_1P_2} = 1, \qquad \xi_y^p \equiv \frac{\Delta Y_p}{\Delta Q} = \frac{\text{zero}}{P_1P_2} = 0,$$

$$\lambda_q \equiv \frac{\Delta Q}{Q^0} = \frac{P_1P_2}{OP_1} = \frac{K_1K_2}{OK_1} = \frac{C_1N}{OC_1},$$

$$\eta_x^p \equiv \frac{\Delta X_p}{\Delta X}\frac{Q^0}{X_p^0} = \frac{P_1P_2}{P_1P_2}\frac{OP_1}{OP_1} = 1,$$

$$\lambda_x^p \equiv \frac{\Delta X_p}{X_p^0} = \frac{P_1P_2}{OP_1}.$$

We can verify equation (12.11) as follows:

$$\eta_x^p\lambda_q = 1\frac{P_1P_2}{OP_1} = \lambda_x^p.$$

What is the effect of economic growth on the growing country's relative dependency on trade as revealed by the average propensity to trade? In other words, does growth tend to increase or decrease the average propensity to trade (θ_v)?

When growth does not affect the average propensity to trade (i.e., when the average propensity to trade remains constant), the growth is *neutral*. When the average propensity to trade tends to increase with growth, the growth is *protrade biased*. When the average propensity to trade tends to fall, the growth is *antitrade biased.* We can predict whether the average propensity to trade increases, decreases, or remains constant with growth by comparing the pregrowth *average* propensity to trade (θ_v) with the *marginal* propensity to trade (ξ_v). Thus, if $\xi_v > \theta_v$, then θ_v must be increasing; if $\xi_v < \theta_v$, then θ_v must be decreasing; and if $\xi_v = \theta_v$, then θ_v must remain constant. Accordingly, neutral growth occurs when $\xi_v = \theta_v$; protrade-biased growth occurs when $\xi_v > \theta_v$; and antitrade biased growth occurs when $\xi_v < \theta_v$.

Two extreme cases of growth can be distinguished: *ultra-protrade-biased growth,* in which $\xi_v > 1$ (implying that the absolute increase in the volume of trade, ΔV, is larger than the absolute increase in national income, ΔQ, so that the growing country becomes absolutely less self-sufficient); and *ultra-antitrade-biased growth,* in which $\xi_v < 0$ (implying that the absolute volume of trade actually falls, i.e., $\Delta V < 0$, so that the growing country becomes absolutely more self-sufficient).

Figures 12.2A and 12.2B illustrate the five types of growth. Figure 12.2A measures horizontally the value of output produced (Q), and vertically the value of the volume of trade (V). At any equilibrium state, the equilibrium values of Q and V will be represented by the coordinates of a point below and to the right of the 45° line (OR). At the pregrowth equilibrium state, our economy's position is at point E. The average propensity to trade is shown by the slope of the vector OE. Assume now that the economy grows and its national income increases from Q^0 to Q^1. If point E moves along the vector ON, then growth is neutral (N); if E moves to the region GD (where the line ED is parallel to OR), then growth is protrade biased (P); if E moves

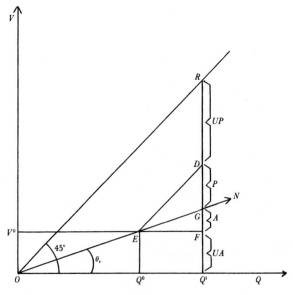

FIGURE 12.2A

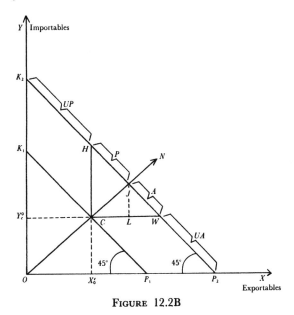

FIGURE 12.2B

to the region DR, then growth is ultra protrade biased (UP); if E moves to the region FG, then growth is antitrade biased (A); and if E moves to the region Q^1F, growth is ultra antitrade biased (UA).

Figure 12.2B, similar to figure 12.1, illustrates the five types of growth in terms of the familiar diagram of the consumption-possibilities frontier. Before growth, the economy produces at P_1 and consumes at C; after growth, the economy produces at P_2 and the consumption point can lie, in general, anywhere on the new consumption-possibilities frontier, K_2P_2. If C moves along the vector ON, growth is neutral; if C moves to the region HJ, growth is protrade biased; if C moves to the region K_2H, growth is ultra protrade biased; if C moves to the region JW, growth is antitrade biased; and if C moves to the region WP_2, growth is ultra antitrade biased. These conclusions follow when we note that $\Delta X_p = \Delta Q = P_1P_2 = CW = CH$, $V^0 = OY_c^0 = X_c^0C$, and ΔV is given by the vertical distance from the post-growth consumption point to the horizontal line Y_c^0CW. Thus, in the region K_2H, $\Delta V > \Delta Q$ (or $\xi_v > 1$); and in the region WP_2, $\Delta V < 0$ (or $\xi_v < 0$). Further, if C moves to J, we have

$$\xi_v \equiv \frac{\Delta V}{\Delta Q} = \frac{LJ}{CW} = \frac{X_c^0C}{OP_1} = \frac{V_0}{Q^0} = \theta_v.$$

From this, it follows that if C moves to the region HJ, we have $1 > \xi_v > \theta_v$ (because $LJ < \Delta V < \Delta Q = CH$); and if C moves to the region JW, we have $0 < \xi_v < \theta_v$ (because $LJ > \Delta V > 0$). The preceding conclusions are conveniently summarized in table 12.1.

TABLE 12.1

Type of Growth	Range of the Marginal Propensity to Trade (ξ_v) (1)	Range of the Rate of Growth of the Volume of Trade (λ_v) $\lambda_v = (\xi_v/\theta_v)\lambda_q$ (2)	Range of the Output Elasticity of the Volume of Trade (η_v) $\eta_v = \xi_v/\theta_v$ (3)
Neutral	$\xi_v = \theta_v$	$\lambda_v = \lambda_q$	$\eta_v = 1$
Protrade biased	$\theta_v < \xi_v < 1$	$\lambda_q < \lambda_v < (1/\theta_v)\lambda_q$	$1 < \eta_v < 1/\theta_v$
Ultra protrade biased . . .	$\xi_v > 1 > \theta_v$	$\lambda_v > (1/\theta_v)\lambda_q$	$1/\theta_v < \eta_v$
Antitrade biased	$0 < \xi_v < \theta_v$	$0 < \lambda_v < \lambda_q$	$0 < \eta_v < 1$
Ultra antitrade biased . . .	$\xi_v < 0 < \theta_v$	$\lambda_v < 0 < \lambda_q$	$\eta_v < 0$

Because of the strict relationship which exists between the marginal and average propensities to trade and the rates of growth of the volume of trade and output, the classification of growth into five types can be accomplished in terms of the rate of growth of the volume of trade. Accordingly, column (2) of table 12.1 gives the appropriate range of the rate of growth of the volume of trade for each type of growth. This follows from the entries in column (1) and from equation (12.17), which is partially reproduced in the heading of column (2) for convenience. Similarly, column (3) gives the range of the output elasticity of the volume of trade (η_v) for each type of growth. Again, the results follow from either column (1) or column (2) and the equation $\eta_v = \xi_v/\theta_v$. The three alternate ways of classifying growth into its five types, as given in table 12.1, can be used in any particular situation.

It is interesting to note that, in the classical case of complete specialization in exportables before and after trade, where $\theta_y^p = \xi_y^p = 0$, we necessarily have $\xi_v = \xi_y^c - \xi_y^p = \xi_y^c$ and $\theta_v = \theta_y^c - \theta_y^p = \theta_y^c$, where equations (12.8) and (12.4), respectively, are used. Accordingly, growth can be classified, in this case, in terms of the marginal propensity and the average propensity to consume importables. The same classification can be made in terms of the output elasticity of demand for importables (η_y^c), since $\eta_y^c = \xi_y^c/\theta_y^c = \eta_v$, and in terms of the rate of growth of consumption of importables (λ_y^c), since $\lambda_y^c = \eta_y^c\lambda_q = \eta_v\lambda_q = \lambda_v$.

3. Neoclassical and Modern Theories (Incomplete Specialization)

Within the context of the classical theory, the growing country necessarily specializes completely in the production of exportables before and after trade. In other words, economic growth causes the optimum production point to slide along the axis of exportables. As we have seen, this implies that $\theta_y^p = \xi_y^p = 0$, $\xi_v = \xi_y^c - \xi_y^p = \xi_y^c$, and $\theta_v = \theta_y^c - \theta_y^p = \theta_y^c$. As a result, growth can be classified (within the context of complete specialization) in terms of the marginal propensity to consume importables (ξ_y^c) and the average propensity to consume importables (θ_y^c), that is, in terms only of the consumption behavior of the growing country.

However, when the assumption of constant opportunity costs is replaced by the assumption of increasing costs, the classification of growth becomes more difficult, due mainly to the fact that, in general, increasing opportunity costs imply incomplete specialization—and the classification of growth necessarily depends on the behavior of both the optimum consumption point and the optimum production point. Put differently, the marginal propensity to trade (ξ_v) is given by the difference $(\xi_y^c - \xi_y^p)$. Unlike the classical case of complete specialization, where $\xi_y^p = 0$, in the present case, $\xi_y^p \neq 0$ in general. Therefore, the value of ξ_v (and thus the type of growth) cannot be predicted from the knowledge of the marginal propensity to consume importables (ξ_y^c) alone. We need to know, in addition to ξ_y^c, the value of the marginal propensity to produce importables (ξ_y^p). We therefore conclude that, in the case of incomplete specialization, the effect of growth on the volume of trade (and thus the classification of growth) depends on the combined behavior of consumption and production. For analytical purposes, however, it is convenient to consider separately the effects on the country's volume of trade of the consumption and production shifts associated with growth, before considering their combined effect.

As explained earlier, economic growth results in an outward shift of the production-possibilities frontier. This causes the consumption-possibilities frontier to shift outward in a parallel fashion. Since consumption necessarily takes place on the consumption-possibilities frontier and the latter is also tangent to the production-possibilities frontier at the equilibrium production point, the pregrowth and postgrowth consumption-possibilities frontiers are all that are needed for the classification of the consumption and production effects.

The consumption effect is *neutral* when growth leaves the average propensity to consume importables (θ_y^c) constant; when the average propensity to consume importables (θ_y^c) tends to increase with growth, the consumption effect is *protrade biased*; and when θ_y^c tends to fall with growth, the consumption effect is *antitrade biased*. Accordingly, when $\xi_y^c = \theta_y^c$, the consumption effect is neutral; when $\xi_y^c > \theta_y^c$, it is protrade biased; and when $\xi_y^c < \theta_y^c$, it is antitrade biased. In addition, there are the two extreme cases of *ultra protrade biased* (consumption effect), in which $\xi_y^c > 1$ (implying that the absolute increase in the consumption of importables, ΔY_c, is larger than the absolute increase in national income, ΔQ), and *ultra antitrade biased* (consumption effect), in which $\xi_y^c < 0$ (implying that the domestic consumption of importables falls absolutely, i.e., $\Delta Y_c < 0$).

Note that the above classification of the consumption effect coincides with the classification of growth (or, what is the same thing, the classification of the combined effect of the production and consumption shifts) in the case of complete specialization, for in the latter case, $\xi_v = \xi_y^c$ and $\theta_v = \theta_y^c$.

Hence, figure 12.2B can be used to illustrate the classification of the consumption effect in general.

Because of equations (12.3) and (12.7), the consumption effect can also be classified in terms of the behavior of the domestic consumption of exportables. Table 12.2 summarizes the classification.

TABLE 12.2   *Classification of the consumption effect*

Type of Consumption Effect	Range of the Marginal Propensity to Consume Importables (ξ_y^c) (1)	Range of the Marginal Propensity to Consume Exportables (ξ_x^c) $\xi_x^c \equiv 1 - \xi_y^c$ $\theta_x^c \equiv 1 - \theta_y^c$ (2)
Neutral	$\xi_y^c = \theta_y^c$	$\xi_x^c = \theta_x^c$
Protrade biased.	$\theta_y^c < \xi_y^c < 1$	$0 < \xi_x^c < \theta_x^c$
Ultra protrade biased	$+\infty > \xi_y^c > 1$	$-\infty < \xi_x^c < 0$
Antitrade biased	$0 < \xi_y^c < \theta_y^c$	$\theta_x^c < \xi_x^c < 1$
Ultra antitrade biased	$-\infty < \xi_y^c < 0$	$+\infty > \xi_x^c > 1$

The production effect can be similarly classified. Thus, when growth leaves unchanged the average propensity to produce exportables (θ_x^p), that is, $\xi_x^p = \theta_x^p$, the production effect is *neutral*; when the average propensity to produce exportables (θ_x^p) tends to increase with growth, that is, $\xi_x^p > \theta_x^p$, the production effect is *protrade biased*; and when θ_x^p tends to fall with growth, that is, $\xi_x^p < \theta_x^p$, the production effect is *antitrade biased*. Again, there are the two extreme cases of *ultra protrade biased* (production effect), in which $\xi_x^p > 1$ (implying that the absolute increase in the production of exportables, ΔX_p, is larger than the absolute increase in national income, ΔQ), and *ultra antitrade biased* (production effect), in which case $\xi_x^p < 0$ (implying that the domestic production of exportables falls absolutely). As before, because of equations (12.3) and (12.7), the production effect can be classified, alternatively, in terms of the behavior of the production of importables. The classification is summarized in table 12.3.

TABLE 12.3   *Classification of the production effect*

Type of Production Effect	Range of the Marginal Propensity to Produce Exportables (ξ_x^p) (1)	Range of the Marginal Propensity to Produce Importables (ξ_y^p) $\xi_y^p = 1 - \xi_x^p$ $\theta_y^p = 1 - \theta_x^p$ (2)
Neutral	$\xi_x^p = \theta_x^p$	$\xi_y^p = \theta_y^p$
Protrade biased.	$\theta_x^p < \xi_x^p < 1$	$0 < \xi_y^p < \theta_y^p$
Ultra protrade biased	$+\infty > \xi_x^p > 1$	$-\infty < \xi_y^p < 0$
Antitrade biased	$0 < \xi_x^p < \theta_x^p$	$\theta_y^p < \xi_y^p < 1$
Ultra antitrade biased	$-\infty < \xi_x^p < 0$	$+\infty > \xi_y^p > 1$

A comparison of tables 12.2 and 12.3 reveals that largely similar inequalities were used to classify both the production effect and the consumption effect, except for one major difference: the consumption effect emphasizes (initially) the behavior of the domestic consumption of importables, whereas the production effect emphasizes the behavior of the domestic production of exportables. The roles of the two commodities are reversed as we move from the classification of the consumption effect to the classification of the production effect because, other things equal, increased consumption of importables tends to increase the volume of trade while increased consumption of exportables tends to decrease the volume of trade. On the other hand, increased production of exportables, like increased consumption of importables, tends to increase the volume of trade.

Figure 12.3 illustrates the five types of production effect. Production before growth occurs at P, with the straight line MPF being the economy's pregrowth consumption-possibilities frontier, which shifts (in a parallel fashion) to $NRSUV$ after growth. If the postgrowth optimum production point coincides with point S, the production effect will be neutral; if it shifts to the region SU, it will be protrade biased; if it shifts to the region UV, it will be ultra protrade biased; if it shifts to the region RS, it will be antitrade biased; and if it shifts to the region NR, it will be ultra-antitrade biased.

The preceding classification of the consumption and production effects was performed in order to study the overall effect of growth on the average propensity to trade, which in turn depends on the sum of the consumption and production effects. These two effects can be added simply by determining in each case the range of variation of the marginal propensity to trade (ξ_v).

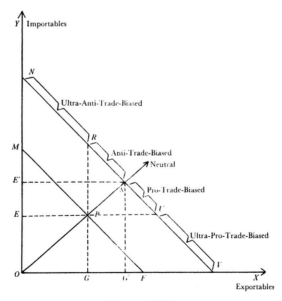

FIGURE 12.3

That is, we need only determine the upper and the lower limits of ξ_v. We can do this by using equations (12.4) and (12.8) and the inequalities given in tables 12.2 and 12.3. For example, if the consumption effect is neutral (i.e., $\xi_x^c = \theta_x^c$) while the production effect is protrade biased (i.e., $\theta_x^p < \xi_x^p < 1$), the upper limit of ξ_v is given by

$$(\xi_v)^U = (\xi_x^p)^U - (\xi_x^c)^L = 1 - \theta_x^c$$

and the lower limit by

$$(\xi_v)^L = (\xi_x^p)^L - (\xi_x^c)^U = \theta_x^p - \theta_x^c = \theta_v,$$

where the superscripts U and L stand for the upper limit and the lower limit, respectively. Hence, $\theta_v < \xi_v < 1 - \theta_x^c < 1$. The limits of ξ_v in all other cases have been similarly calculated, and the results are summarized in table 12.4. Note that when both effects are biased in the same direction, the total effect is similarly biased, and when one effect is neutral, the bias of the total effect is in the same direction as the bias of the other effect. If, however, the two effects are biased in opposite directions, the total effect cannot be easily predicted. When the production effect is ultra antitrade biased, the total effect is also ultra antitrade biased, except when the consumption effect is ultra protrade biased, and then the total effect can be anything. Similarly, when the consumption effect is ultra antitrade biased, the total effect is also ultra antitrade biased, except when the production effect is ultra protrade biased, and then the total effect can be anything.

Figure 12.4 illustrates the various types of growth in terms of shifts of the offer curve of the growing country. The given international terms of trade are shown by the slope of the terms-of-trade line TOT. Our country's original offer curve is the solid curve OE_0K; equilibrium, before growth, occurs at E_0. The broken curves UP, P, N, A, and UA show how the growing country's offer curve will tend to shift with growth that is ultra protrade biased, protrade biased, neutral, antitrade biased, and ultra antitrade biased, respectively. The analysis of the present section enables us to identify the points E_{UP}, E_P, E_N, E_A, and E_{UA} only—not the whole new offer curves. The implicit assumption made in figure 12.4 is that the type of growth is independent of the specific value of the terms of trade, but this is not correct in general. As concerns the case of the small country which is a price taker in the international market, the only relevant points on the new offer curves are E_{UP}, E_P, E_N, E_A, and E_{UN}; therefore, the behavior of the offer curves elsewhere is irrelevant. However, when the assumption of the small country is dropped, this is no longer true. How, then, can the analysis of the present section be applied to the case of a large country whose purchases and sales of commodities X and Y in the international market affect the terms of trade?

TABLE 12.4

Production Effect $\xi_v = \xi_x^P - \xi_x^c$ $\theta_v = \theta_x^P - \theta_x^c$	Consumption Effect				
	Neutral $\xi_x^c = \theta_x^c$	Protrade biased $0 < \xi_x^c < \theta_x^c$	Ultra protrade biased $-\infty < \xi_x^c < 0$	Antitrade biased $\theta_x^c < \xi_x^c < 1$	Ultra antitrade biased $1 < \xi_x^c < +\infty$
Neutral $\xi_x^P = \theta_x^P$	$\xi_v = \xi_x^P - \xi_x^c$ $= \theta_x^P - \theta_x^c = \theta_v$ (N)	$\theta_v = \theta_x^P - \theta_x^c$ $= (\xi_v)^L < \xi_v < (\xi_v)^U$ $= \theta_x^P < 1$ (P)	$\theta_v < \theta_x^P - \theta_x^c$ $< \xi_v < (\xi_v)^U$ $= +\infty$ $(P \text{ or } UP)$	$0 > \theta_x^P - 1 = (\xi_v)^L$ $< \xi_v < (\xi_v)^U$ $= \theta_x^P - \theta_x^c = \theta_v$ $(A \text{ or } UA)$	$-\infty = (\xi_v)^L$ $< \xi_v < (\xi_v)^U$ $= \theta_x^P - 1 < 0$ (UA)
Protrade biased $\theta_x^P < \xi_x^P < 1$	$\theta_v = \theta_x^P - \theta_x^c = (\xi_v)^L$ $< \xi_v < (\xi_v)^U$ $= 1 - \theta_x^c < 1$ (P)	$\theta_v = \theta_x^P - \theta_x^c = (\xi_v)^L$ $< \xi_v < (\xi_v)^U = 1$ (P)	$\theta_v < \theta_x^P = (\xi_v)^L < \xi_v$ $< (\xi_v)^U = +\infty$ $(P \text{ or } UP)$	$0 > \theta_x^P - 1 = (\xi_v)^L$ $< \xi_v < (\xi_v)^U$ $= 1 - \theta_x^c$ with $\theta_v < 1 - \theta_x^c < 1$ $(\text{Not } UP)$	$-\infty = (\xi_v)^L < \xi_v$ $< (\xi_v)^U = 0$ (UA)
Ultra protrade biased $1 < \xi_x^P < +\infty$	$\theta_v < 1 - \theta_x^c = (\xi_v)^L$ $< \xi_v < (\xi_v)^U$ $= +\infty$ $(P \text{ or } UP)$	$\theta_v < 1 - \theta_x^c = (\xi_v)^L$ $< \xi_v < (\xi_v)^U$ $= +\infty$ $(P \text{ or } UP)$	$1 = (\xi_v)^L < \xi_v$ $< (\xi_v)^U = +\infty$ (UP)	$0 = (\xi_v)^L < \xi_v$ $< (\xi_v)^U = +\infty$ $(\text{Not } UA)$	$-\infty = (\xi_v)^L < \xi_v$ $< (\xi_v)^U = +\infty$ $(\text{All types possible})$
Antitrade biased $0 < \xi_x^P < \theta_x^P$	$-\theta_x^c = (\xi_v)^L < \xi_v$ $< (\xi_v)^U$ $= \theta_x^P - \theta_x^c = \theta_v$ $(A \text{ or } UA)$	$-\theta_x^c = (\xi_v)^L < \xi_v$ $< (\xi_v)^U = \theta_x^P < 1$ $(\text{Not } UP)$	$0 = (\xi_v)^L < \xi_v$ $< (\xi_v)^U = +\infty$ $(\text{Not } UA)$	$-1 = (\xi_v)^L < \xi_v$ $< (\xi_v)^U$ $= \theta_x^P - \theta_x^c = \theta_v$ $(A \text{ or } UA)$	$-\infty = (\xi_v)^L < \xi_v$ $< (\xi_v)^U$ $= \theta_x^P - 1 < 0$ (UA)
Ultra antitrade biased $-\infty < \xi_x^P < 0$	$-\infty = (\xi_v)^L < \xi_v$ $< (\xi_v)^U$ $= -\theta_x^c < 0$ (UA)	$-\infty = (\xi_v)^L < \xi_v$ $< (\xi_v)^U = 0$ (UA)	$-\infty = (\xi_v)^L < \xi_v$ $< (\xi_v)^U = +\infty$ $(\text{All types possible})$	$-\infty = (\xi_v)^L < \xi_v$ $< (\xi_v)^U$ $= -\theta_x^c < 0$ (UA)	$-\infty = (\xi_v)^L < \xi_v$ $< (\xi_v)^U = -1$ (UA)

NOTE: Parenthetical material beneath equations refers to type of growth (N = neutral, P = protrade biased, UP = ultra protrade biased, A = antitrade biased, UA = ultra antitrade biased). $(\xi_v)^U$ = upper limit of ξ_v; $(\xi_v)^L$ = lower limit of ξ_v.

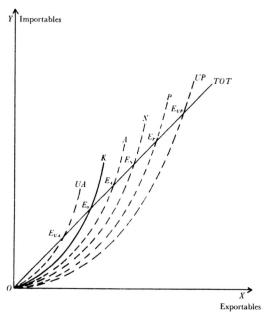

FIGURE 12.4

B. The Effects of Growth on the Large Country: Complete Specialization

Assume that there are two countries, A and B, producing two commodities, X and Y. At the original equilibrium position, assume that A is exporting commodity X and B is exporting commodity Y. Their general-equilibrium positions can be shown in terms of the familiar offer curves. Assume that only country A grows. Thus, only A's offer curve shifts through time while B's remains the same, although the equilibrium point on B's offer curve will shift because A's offer curve shifts. How does A's growth affect the terms of trade?

Using the analysis of section A, we can predict how A's offer curve at the *initial* equilibrium terms of trade will shift. But in the present case, by assumption, the terms of trade will not remain constant. Nevertheless, the preceding analysis becomes sufficient for the determination of the effect of A's growth on the terms of trade when we make the additional assumption that international equilibrium is unique and stable before and after growth. Let us now proceed with the simple case of the classical theory where the production-possibilities frontier is linear and at least one country specializes completely in the production of only one commodity.

Consider figure 12.5. The production block $B_0K_1B_1$ is B's (linear) production-possibilities frontier, which is assumed to remain constant throughout. The production block $A_0A_1K_1$ is A's pregrowth production-possibilities frontier. Accordingly, the pregrowth world production-possibilities frontier is given by $A_1K_1B_1$. Tastes are assumed given by a world social indifference map, illustrated in figure 12.5 by the indifference curves I_1I_1' and I_2I_2'. Equilibrium occurs initially at point K_1, with the equilibrium price ratio, p_x/p_y, given by the absolute slope of the indifference curve I_1I_1' at K_1.

Assume now that A's production-possibilities frontier shifts outward in a parallel fashion, as illustrated by the production block $A_0A_2K_2$ (fig. 12.5). This shift of A's production-possibilities frontier may be due to either *labor growth* (labor being the only factor of production) or *neutral technical progress*, causing both labor coefficients, a_x and a_y, to fall by the same percentage. How does the shift of A's production-possibilities frontier affect (*a*) the world production-possibilities frontier and (*b*) A's terms of trade? The world production-possibilities frontier shifts to $A_2K_2B_3$. Postgrowth equilibrium will occur somewhere along $A_2K_2B_3$, the precise equilibrium point being determined by tastes. In the example given in figure 12.5, equilibrium occurs at E, with the postgrowth equilibrium price ratio given by A's domestic price ratio. Thus, in figure 12.5, A's terms of trade deteriorate with growth, that is, the price ratio p_x/p_y falls. But this need not be the case, for, depending

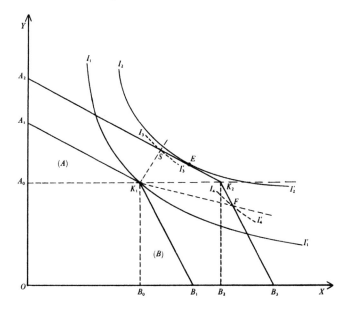

FIGURE 12.5

on tastes, postgrowth equilibrium may occur at K_2 or even in the region $K_2 B_3$. In the latter case, A's terms of trade definitely improve. Under what conditions do A's terms of trade deteriorate with growth? Under what conditions do they improve?

Concentrating for the moment on the geometry of figure 12.5, we can prove that, if commodity Y is neutral (i.e., if the consumption of Y remains constant as income changes), the relative price of X remains constant; if Y is superior or normal (i.e., if the consumption of Y tends to increase as income increases), p_x/p_y falls; and if Y is inferior (i.e., if the consumption of Y tends to decrease as income increases), p_x/p_y increases with growth. To prove this, note that, when Y is neutral, the income consumption curve will be horizontal, as illustrated by the broken line $A_0 K_1 K_2$. Hence, at K_2 all curves maintain the same slopes they originally had at K_1, equilibrium shifts from K_1 to K_2, and the marginal rate of substitution of X for Y (and thus the relative price of X) remains constant.

On the other hand, when commodity Y is a superior good, the income consumption curve through K_1 will be upward sloping, as illustrated by the broken curve $K_1 S$. Therefore, the indifference curve $I_3 I_3'$ passing through S will intersect the world production-possibilities frontier at S from above, with equilibrium occurring somewhere in the region SK_2, implying a lower relative price for X. When commodity Y is inferior, the income consumption curve through K_1 will be negatively sloped, as illustrated by the broken curve $K_1 F$. Accordingly, the indifference curve $I_4 I_4'$ passing through F will intersect the world production-possibilities frontier at F from left to right, with equilibrium occurring somewhere in the region FK_2 and implying a higher relative price for X.

The conclusion that A's terms of trade can change in either direction with A's growth is reached also when each country's tastes are represented separately by a social indifference map. Thus, we can easily identify the effect of A's growth on A's terms of trade by determining the type of growth experienced by A, which in the present, classical, complete-specialization case coincides with the type of A's consumption effect. If A's consumption effect (and therefore A's growth) is anything but ultra antitrade biased, A's demand for imports (or supply of exports) becomes absolutely larger with growth at the pregrowth terms of trade. If it is assumed that international equilibrium is unique and stable before and after growth, A's terms of trade, p_x/p_y, will deteriorate with growth. However, if A's consumption effect is ultra antitrade biased, A's growth will definitely be ultra antitrade biased and its terms of trade, p_x/p_y, will improve with growth, that is, the ratio p_x/p_y will increase.

That A's growth can affect A's terms of trade either favorably or unfavorably appears inescapable. But is it not possible to eliminate certain types of consumption behavior and, thus, narrow down the range of possible outcomes? In particular, can we not eliminate the possibility that A's consumption effect may be ultra antitrade biased? If A's growth is the result of technical progress, the ultra antitrade-biased consumption effect cannot be excluded on the basis of a priori reasoning, but when A's growth is the result of sheer labor growth, the exclusion of the ultra-antitrade-biased consumption effect is inevitable.

Suppose that A's citizens have identical tastes and factor endowments. Then A's demand for Y at the pregrowth terms of trade will increase *pari passu* with A's labor and output. That is, A's consumption effect will be *neutral*: every resident of country A will be doing after growth exactly the same thing they were doing before growth. The consumption effect will also be neutral if A's residents are assumed to have identical and homothetic tastes. But what if we drop these assumptions? Here again, we can exlude the possibility of an ultra-antitrade-biased consumption effect, for as A's workers, and therefore consumers, increase, it is impossible for A's demand for any commodity to fall at the pregrowth terms of trade. Country A's old consumers will continue to consume the same quantities after growth as before, and A's new consumers cannot have a negative demand for any commodity. Accordingly, in the absence of any shift in tastes, and with the growth of labor, A's consumption effect cannot possibly be ultra antitrade biased; therefore, *A's terms of trade will definitely deteriorate.*

How does A's labor growth affect the level of social welfare in A and in B? To simplify, assume that A's citizens have identical tastes and factor endowments, and the same for B's citizens. Therefore, we can determine the effect of A's labor growth on the level of social welfare in A by determining its effect on the welfare of A's "Representative Citizen." Similarly, we can determine the effect of A's labor growth on the level of social welfare in B by determining its effect on the welfare of B's "Representative Citizen."

Consider country B first. How does A's labor growth affect the welfare of B's Representative Citizen? Remember that B's production-possibilities frontier can be scaled down in proportion to its Representative Citizen. Under these circumstances, it should be clear that *the welfare of B's Representative Citizen necessarily improves with A's labor growth.* Because, on the one hand, B's Representative Citizen specializes completely in the production of Y and, on the other hand, A's increased (net) supply of X and demand for Y cause the commodity-price ratio p_x/p_y to fall, and, therefore, the budget line of B's Representative Citizen rotates outward through the Y-axis intercept of his (scaled-down) production-possibilities frontier.

Observe that when A's growth is the result of technical progress, B's Representative Citizen may become either better off (when A's growth is not ultra antitrade biased and the price ratio p_x/p_y falls) or worse off (when A's growth is ultra antitrade biased and the price ratio p_x/p_y rises).

When A's growth is the result of sheer labor growth, A's Representative Citizen necessarily becomes worse off, for, given his uniquely determined (scaled-down) production-possibilities frontier, his budget line rotates inward through the X-axis intercept of his (scaled-down) production-possibilities frontier, thus reaching equilibrium at a lower indifference curve. When we say that A's growth makes A's Representative Citizen worse off, we do not mean that free trade is not beneficial to A but, rather, that *its citizens are forced to give up part of the gains they used to enjoy from trade before growth.* Eventually, as A's growth proceeds, A's citizens may be forced back to the level of welfare they enjoyed under autarky.

What happens to the welfare of A's Representative Citizen when A's growth is the result of technical progress? We have to distinguish between the *terms-of-trade effect,* which is due to the favorable or unfavorable change in the commodity-price ratio p_x/p_y, and the *wealth effect,* which is due to the outward shift of A's production-possibilities frontier, implying a corresponding outward shift of the production-possibilities frontier of A's Representative Citizen. The wealth effect if always favorable to the welfare of A's Representative Citizen, but the terms-of-trade effect can go either way. Accordingly, when the terms-of-trade effect is also favorable (when A's growth is ultra antitrade biased), A's Representative Citizen definitely becomes better off with growth. When the terms-of-trade effect is unfavorable, the outcome obviously depends on whether the unfavorable terms-of-trade effect outweighs the favorable wealth effect, and vice versa.

The case of technical progress is illustrated in figure 12.6. The curve SK is A's production-possibilities frontier before growth. Since A is specializing completely in the production of X, consider K as a new origin and draw A's offer curve through K, as shown by KGE (in the manner of chap. 6, part A).

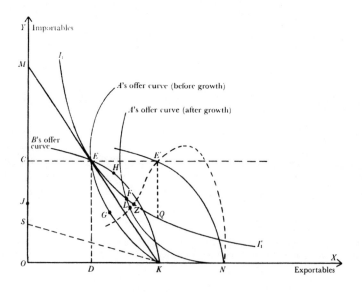

FIGURE 12.6

In addition, superimpose *B*'s offer curve, *KHE*. The two offer curves intersect each other at *E*. Hence, before growth, *A* exports *DK* units of *X* to *B* in exchange for *DE* units of *Y*, with the equilibrium terms of trade given by the ratio *DE/DK* or the absolute slope of *MEK*. Line is *A*'s pregrowth consumption-possibilities frontier. Observe that, before growth, *A* reaches the social indifference curve I_1I_1'.

Suppose now that, as a result of neutral technical progress, *A*'s production-possibilities frontier shifts outward in a parallel fashion, as illustrated by the broken curve *JN* (not drawn). How does this shift affect *A*'s social welfare? (Note that the social indifference map in the present case describes social welfare; that is, a movement from a lower to a higher social indifference curve necessarily implies that *A*'s social welfare increases. Figure 12.6 could be scaled down in proportion to *A*'s Representative Citizen, thus directly showing the effect of growth on the economic welfare of *A*'s Representative Citizen.) If *A*'s production-possibilities frontier is allowed to shift outward sufficiently, it can be made tangent to the social indifference curve I_1I_1' or a higher one; then *A*'s social welfare cannot possibly deteriorate with growth. The paradoxical reduction in *A*'s level of social welfare arises only when *A*'s postgrowth production-possibilities frontier (*JN*) cannot reach the social indifference curve I_1I_1'. Further, if *A*'s terms of trade (p_x/p_y) do not deteriorate with growth, *A*'s social welfare will definitely increase with growth, for then *A*'s consumption-possibilities frontier would start at *N* and be at least as steep as its pregrowth consumption-possibilities frontier *MEK*. But if *A*'s postgrowth production-possibilities frontier does not reach the indifference curve I_1I_1' and if *A*'s terms of trade deteriorate (i.e., p_x/p_y falls), the possibility that *A*'s social welfare may deteriorate with growth cannot be ruled out. This possibility is illustrated in figure 12.6.

Consider *A*'s postgrowth production point *N* and draw *B*'s offer curve through *N*. The horizontal distances between *B*'s offer curve through *K* and the new one through *N* must always be equal to *KN*; in particular, *EE'* = *KN*. To complete the picture, draw *A*'s new offer curve through *N*. If *A*'s offer curve should intersect *B*'s in the region *E'N* (as is the case when *A*'s growth is ultra antitrade biased), *A*'s terms of trade and social welfare will improve. Thus, a necessary condition for *A* to become worse off with growth is that its offer curve intersect *B*'s at a point which lies beyond point *E'*. In addition, the new equilibrium point should lie below the indifference curve I_1I_1'. How can this happen? Observe that *A*'s postgrowth offer curve will necessarily intersect the indifference curve I_1I_1' to the right and below the initial equilibrium point *E*. Another condition necessary for the paradoxical reduction in *A*'s level of social welfare is that the latter intersection occur somewhere in the region *EQ* (point *F*, in fig. 12.6). Equilibrium should occur on *A*'s post-growth offer curve somewhere in the region *FN* (point *L* in fig. 12.6). This requires that *B*'s offer curve be backward bending, as illustrated by the broken curve *NE'ZL*. A final necessary (but not sufficient) condition for *A*'s social welfare to decrease with technical progress is that *B*'s demand for imports be inelastic.

There are some important differences between the present case of technical progress and the previous case of labor growth. In the latter case *A*'s social welfare always deteriorates, but in the former case the outcome can go either way. In fact, in the presence of large technical progress, the growing country always benefits from growth. In the case of technical progress, the growing country can pursue an optimum tariff policy (to be discussed in chap. 20) and always gain from growth; that is, the growing country, *A*, can force the other country, *B*, with a tariff, to trade anywhere on its (i.e., *B*'s) offer curve. Since *B*'s offer curve through *N* (fig. 12.6) lies beyond *B*'s offer curve through *K*, *A*'s social welfare will always improve with technical progress when an optimum tariff policy is being pursued. However, even an optimum tariff policy cannot prevent the deterioration of *A*'s social welfare when *A*'s growth is the result of sheer labor growth, in which case, the production-possibilities frontier of *A*'s Representative Citizen remains the same after growth as before but the offer curve of *B* *scaled down in proportion to A's Representative Citizen* shifts unfavorably (it shrinks), because, by assumption, the number of *A*'s citizens increases.

The paradox that a growing country can become worse off with growth was first noted by Edgeworth (1894, pp. 40–42). More recently, Bhagwati (1958) has dealt with this phenomenon, which he calls "immiserizing growth."

C. The Effects of Growth on the Large Country: Incomplete Specialization

The analysis of section A can be used to predict the effect of growth on the terms of trade of the growing country when it is assumed that international equilibrium is unique and stable. Therefore, only ultra-antitrade-biased growth improves the growing country's terms of trade: all other types of growth tend to deteriorate them. At the original equilibrium terms of trade, all types of growth, except ultra antitrade biased, tend to increase the growing country's absolute demand for imports and supply of exports. Since the other country's (i.e., the rest of the world's) demand for imports and supply of exports remain the same, it follows that, at the pregrowth equilibrium terms of trade, there will emerge a positive excess demand for *A*'s importables (Y) and a positive excess supply of *A*'s exportables (X), causing the relative price of *A*'s exportables (i.e., p_x/p_y) to fall. On the other hand, if the growth is ultra antitrade biased, the growing country's demand for imports and supply of exports, at the pregrowth equilibrium terms of trade, will fall absolutely with growth. Consequently, there will emerge a positive excess demand for *A*'s exportables (X) and a positive excess supply of *A*'s importables, causing

A's terms of trade to improve with growth (i.e., causing the commodity-price ratio p_x/p_y to rise).

When A's growth is not ultra antitrade biased and B's demand for imports is elastic (i.e., B's offer curve is upward sloping), the physical quantity of both A's exports of X and its imports of Y will increase with growth. But when A's growth is ultra antitrade biased and B's demand for imports is elastic, both A's imports of Y and its exports of X will fall. On the other hand, when B's demand for imports is inelastic, the physical quantity of A's imports of Y will fall and the quantity of its exports of X will rise for all types of growth except ultra antitrade biased. When A's growth is ultra antitrade biased, A's imports will rise while its exports will fall. These conclusions are illustrated in figure 12.7. Before growth, equilibrium occurs at E. With A's ultra-anti-

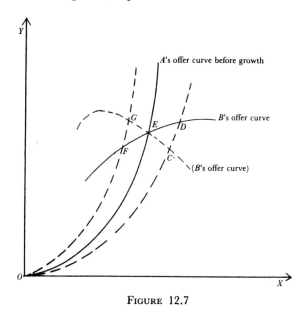

FIGURE 12.7

trade-biased growth, A's offer curve shifts to OFG, with equilibrium occurring either at F (when B's demand for imports is elastic) or at G (when B's demand for imports is inelastic). With any other type of growth besides ultra anti-trade biased, A's offer curve will shift to the right, as illustrated by the broken curve OCD. Equilibrium will occur either at D (when B's demand for imports is elastic) or at C (when B's demand for imports is inelastic).

SELECTED BIBLIOGRAPHY

Bhagwati, J. 1958. Immiserizing growth: a geometrical note. *Review of Economic Studies* 25: 201–5; reprinted in the A.E.A. *Readings in International Economics*. Homewood, Ill.: R. D. Irwin, 1968.

Corden, W. M. 1956. Economic expansion and international trade: a geometric approach. *Oxford Economic Papers* 8: 223–8.

Edgeworth, F. Y. 1894. The theory of international values. *Economic Journal* 4: 35–50.

Findlay, R., and H. Grubert. 1959. Factor intensities, technological progress and the terms of trade. *Oxford Economic Papers* 11: 111–21.

Hicks, J. R. 1953. An inaugural lecture. *Oxford Economic Papers* 5: 117–35.

Johnson, H. G. 1958. *International Trade and Economic Growth*. London: George Allen & Unwin, Ltd. Chap. 3.

Rybczynski, T. M. 1955. Factor endowment and relative commodity prices. *Economica* 22: 336–41.

The Sources of Economic Growth and International Trade

When we know A's type of growth, we can predict whether A's terms of trade will tend to improve or deteriorate with growth. But can we predict what type of growth A will experience if we know the factors responsible for the outward shift of A's production-possibilities frontier? In particular, can we predict the type of A's growth if we know, for instance, that it is the result of sheer labor growth, or sheer capital accumulation, or a combination of labor growth and capital accumulation, or technical progress? Further, how does A's growth affect the level of social welfare in A? Let us take a closer look at the factors that work behind the scenes, so to speak, and cause the growing country's production-possibilities frontier to shift outward.

1. Factor Increases

Assume again that there are two countries, A and B, endowed with two factors of production, labor, L, and capital, K, and producing two commodities, X and Y. Both commodities are produced under constant returns to scale, and commodity X is labor intensive relative to commodity Y. Assume, further, that B's factor endowments and technology, as well as tastes, remain constant throughout. Thus, B's behavior can be represented conveniently by its offer curve, which remains constant throughout. The system is in long-run equilibrium to begin with, but we need not restrict ourselves, at this stage, to the case where A necessarily exports commodity X (i.e., the labor-intensive commodity).

How does an increase in A's factor endowments affect A's demand for imports and supply of exports at the pregrowth terms of trade? We must first determine the type of production effect which A will experience (at the pregrowth terms of trade) and then draw on the analysis of chapter 12 to determine A's type of growth.

Consider the familiar box diagram of country A, as illustrated in figure 13.1, and assume that at the pregrowth international equilibrium position, country A is producing at point E on the contract curve, O_xEO_y. Note that, because of constant returns to scale, the absolute quantities of X and Y produced by A can be made equal to the distances O_xE and O_yE, respectively, by an appropriate choice of units of measurement. Accordingly, $X_p^0 = O_xE$, $Y_p^0 = O_yE$, where X_p^0, Y_p^0 stand for A's pregrowth production levels of X and Y, respectively.

When A's factor endowments grow, A's box diagram expands. In particular, an increase in A's factor endowments can be represented in figure 13.1 either by a shift of the origin for commodity Y into the region MO_yN, while X's origin remains constant at O_x, or by a shift of the origin for commodity X into the region CO_xD, while Y's origin remains constant at O_y. For present purposes, let us shift Y's origin. The type of A's production effect depends crucially on the exact location of the new origin for commodity Y.

We already know that, as A's factor endowments grow, the type of A's production effect depends on what happens to the outputs of commodities X and Y. In order to determine the type of production effect which country A will experience after an increase in its factor endowments, we must first determine the differences ΔX_p and ΔY_p *under the assumption that the commodity*

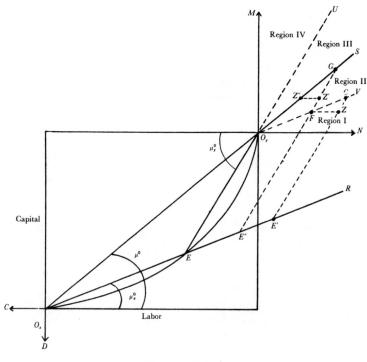

FIGURE 13.1

prices remain constant at their pregrowth level. Because of the one-to-one correspondence which exists between commodity prices and factor prices, on the one hand, and between factor prices and the optimum capital/labor ratio, on the other, we can determine the differences ΔX_p and ΔY_p by assuming that the pregrowth optimum capital/labor ratios μ_x^0 and μ_y^0 in industries X and Y, respectively, continue to be optimum after growth. The ratios μ_x^0 and μ_y^0 are illustrated in figure 13.1 by the slopes of the pregrowth expansion paths of industries X and Y, respectively. After growth, industry X will be producing somewhere along its pregrowth expansion path, $O_x ER$, and industry Y along an expansion path which will start at Y's new origin (i.e., a point in the region $MO_y N$) and be parallel to Y's pregrowth expansion path, $O_y E$. The postgrowth equilibrium point will occur at the intersection of Y's postgrowth expansion path with X's.

In figure 13.1, draw through the pregrowth origin for commodity Y, O_y, three straight lines: $O_y S$, $O_y V$, and $O_y U$, with $O_y S$ being merely an extension of the diagonal $O_x O_y$; $O_y V$ being parallel to X's expansion path $O_x ER$; and $O_y U$ being an extension of Y's expansion path, $O_y E$. These three lines divide the quadrant $MO_y N$ into four regions (or cones). Now consider the *incremental capital/labor ratio*, $\Delta K/\Delta L$. When $\Delta K/\Delta L$ is equal to the pregrowth overall capital/labor ratio μ^0, that is, the slope of the diagonal $O_x O_y$, Y's origin will shift to a point on the line $O_y S$; when $\Delta K/\Delta L = \mu_x^0$, Y's origin will shift to a point on the line $O_y V$; when $\Delta K/\Delta L = \mu_y^0$, Y's origin will shift to a point on the line $O_y U$; when $\Delta K/\Delta L < \mu_x^0$, Y's origin will shift to a point in region I; when $\mu_x^0 < \Delta K/\Delta L < \mu^0$, Y's origin will shift to a point in region II; when $\mu^0 < \Delta K/\Delta L < \mu_y^0$, Y's origin will shift to a point in region III; and finally, when $\Delta K/\Delta L > \mu_y^0$, Y's origin will shift to a point in region IV.

Theorem: Assume that $\mu_x^0 < \mu_y^0$ and that prices remain constant at their pregrowth levels. As A's capital and labor increase by ΔK and ΔL, respectively, X_p and Y_p will change as follows:

a) When $\Delta K/\Delta L = \mu^0$, X_p and Y_p will grow at the same rate, that is, $\lambda_x^p = \lambda_y^p$. Further, $\zeta_x^p = \theta_y^p$ and $\zeta_x^p = \theta_x^p$. Hence, A's production effect is neutral.

b) When $\Delta K/\Delta L < \mu_x^0$, we necessarily have $\Delta X_p > 0$ and $\Delta Y_p < 0$. Hence, $\zeta_y^p < 0$ and $\zeta_x^p > 1$.

c) When $\mu_x^0 < \Delta K/\Delta L < \mu^0$, we necessarily have $\Delta X_p > 0$ and $\Delta Y_p > 0$. In addition, we have $\lambda_x^p > \lambda_y^p$; $1 > \zeta_x^p > \theta_x^p$; and $0 < \zeta_y^p < \theta_y^p$.

d) When $\mu^0 < \Delta K/\Delta L < \mu_y^0$, we necessarily have $\Delta X_p > 0$ and $\Delta Y_p > 0$. In addition, we have $\lambda_y^p > \lambda_x^p$; $1 > \zeta_y^p > \theta_y^p$; and $0 < \zeta_x^p < \theta_x^p$.

e) Finally, when $\Delta K/\Delta L > \mu_y^0$, we necessarily have $\Delta X_p < 0$ and $\Delta Y_p > 0$. Hence, $\zeta_x^p < 0$ and $\zeta_y^p > 1$.

Proof: The truth of part (a) follows directly from the analysis of chapter 9. For a given factor-price ratio, the ratio X_p/Y_p depends only on the overall factor-endowment ratio, μ. When $\Delta K/\Delta L = \mu^0$, μ remains constant and so does the ratio X_p/Y_p. Accordingly, X_p and Y_p must be growing at the same rate (i.e., $\lambda_x = \lambda_y$). Since the rate of growth of output (λ_q) is a weighted average of the rate of growth of $X_p(\lambda_x^p)$ and the rate of growth of $Y_p(\lambda_y^p)$, it follows that $\lambda_q = \lambda_x^p = \lambda_y^p$, implying that the production effect is neutral.

This argument can be verified geometrically. Assume that Y's origin shifts to point G (fig. 13.1). Postgrowth equilibrium must occur at E'', where the broken line GE'' is parallel to O_yE. Since we measure X_p and Y_p by the distances from the equilibrium point on the contract curve to the origins for X and Y, respectively, we have $\Delta X_p = EE''$ and $\Delta Y_p = FG$. Note that the triangles O_xEO_y and O_yFG are similar. Consequently,

$$\lambda_x^p \equiv \frac{\Delta X_p}{X_p^0} = \frac{EE''}{O_xE} = \frac{FG}{O_yE} = \frac{\Delta Y_p}{Y_p^0} \equiv \lambda_y^p. \tag{13.1}$$

Thus, the outputs of X and Y increase at the same rate. Recalling equation (12.18), we have

$$\lambda_x^p = \lambda_y^p = \lambda_q. \tag{13.2}$$

Substituting from (13.2) into equations (12.11) and (12.13), we get

$$\xi_x^p = \theta_x^p \quad \text{and} \quad \xi_y^p = \theta_y^p.$$

In words, the marginal propensity to produce X (ξ_x^p) is equal to the average propensity to produce X (θ_x^p), and the marginal propensity to produce Y (ξ_y^p) is equal to the average propensity to produce Y (θ_y^p).

To prove part (b), note that, for any point along the vector O_yV (implying $\Delta K/\Delta L = \rho_x^0$), such as points F and C, the change in Y_p is zero (i.e., $\Delta Y_p = 0$). Consider point Z in region I and the line CZE', which is parallel to O_yE. Obviously, $ZE' < CE'$; hence $\Delta Y_p < 0$. However, $\Delta X_p = EE' > 0$. This can be verified as follows. When $\Delta K/\Delta L = \mu_x^0$, then X_p can increase and absorb all ΔK and ΔL, with Y_p remaining constant. But when $\Delta K/\Delta L < \mu_x^0$, this is not possible, for all ΔK will be used up before all ΔL is employed (see fig. 13.1). Suppose that ΔL and ΔK are given by the coordinates of point Z with respect to O_y. The total amounts of L and K will then be given by the coordinates of Z with respect to O_x. If we keep Y_p constant at $Y_p^0 = O_yE$ and allow X_p to expand to O_xE'', the total amounts of L and K employed in both industries will be given by the coordinates of point F with respect to O_x. Under the circumstances, K will be fully employed, but there will still be a certain amount of unemployment of L, as shown by the horizontal distance FZ. This unemployment of labor can be removed, as we saw in chapter 10, by allowing the output of the labor-intensive commodity (X) to expand and the output of the land-intensive commodity (Y) to contract. Accordingly, X_p will have to expand beyond O_xE'' and Y_p will have to fall below O_yE. In particular, X_p will have to expand to $O_x E'$ and Y_p to ZE'. Hence, $\Delta X_p > 0$ and $\Delta Y_p < 0$, and therefore, $\xi_x^p > 1$ and $\xi_y^p < 0$.

Given the preceding analysis, an increase in factor endowments that causes Y's origin to shift to some point in region I, such as the shift from O_y to Z, can be decomposed into the following two shifts: α a shift from O_y to F (on the vector $O_y V$), implying that $\Delta X_p^\alpha > 0$ and $\Delta Y_p^\alpha = 0$, and β a shift from F to Z (corresponding to a sheer labor increase), implying that $\Delta X_p^\beta > 0$ and $\Delta Y_p^\beta < 0$, where the superscripts α and β indicate the changes which correspond to the shifts α and β, respectively. The total change in X_p is given by $\Delta X_p = \Delta X_p^\alpha + \Delta X_p^\beta > 0$, and the total change in Y_p is given by $\Delta Y_p = \Delta Y_p^\alpha + \Delta Y_p^\beta < 0$.

A corollary to this conclusion is what is known in the literature as the *Rybczynski theorem*: when only labor grows, the output of the labor-intensive commodity expands and the output of the land-intensive commodity contracts (at the pregrowth prices). The same is true for sheer capital accumulation. Thus, as K grows with L remaining constant, the output of the K-intensive commodity expands and the output of the L-intensive commodity contracts.

Part (c) is proved as follows. Assume that ΔL and ΔK are given by the coordinates of point Z' with respect to O_y. Shifting Y's origin to Z' implies that both X_p and Y_p necessarily increase, because $O_x E'' > O_x E$ and $Z'E'' > FE'' = O_y E$. In addition, as we saw earlier (eq. [13.1]), $EE''/O_x E = FG/O_y E$. Since $FG > FZ'$, we necessarily have $\lambda_x^p = EE''/O_x E = FG/O_y E > FZ'/O_y E = \lambda_y^p$. Since λ_q is a weighted average of λ_x^p and λ_y^p (see eq. [12.18]), we necessarily have $\lambda_x^p > \lambda_q > \lambda_y^p$. Combining the inequality $\lambda_x^p > \lambda_q$ with equation (12.11), we get $\xi_x^p > \theta_x^p$. Similarly, combining the inequality $\lambda_q > \lambda_y^p$ with equation (12.13), we get $\xi_y^p < \theta_y^p$. Recalling that $\Delta Y_p > 0$, we conclude that $0 < \xi_y^p < \theta_y^p$ and $1 > \xi_x^p > \theta_x^p$.

Again, the shift of Y's origin from O_y to Z' can be decomposed into a shift from O_y to Z'', implying an equiproportional increase in factors and outputs, and a shift from Z'' to Z', implying an increase in labor only, causing X_p to increase further and Y_p to fall. Since Z' lies above and to the left of the vector $O_y V$, the overall change in Y_p is positive. Hence, both X_p and Y_p increase, with X_p increasing faster than Y_p.

Part (d) is similar to part (c), and part (e) is similar to part (b), except that the roles of the two commodities are reversed.

What type of production effect does A experience in each of cases (a)–(e)? With the exception of case (a), where the production effect is always neutral, we cannot predict the type of A's production effect in the last four cases on the basis of the information we have thus far. We need to know, in addition, which commodity is being exported by A (see table 13.1).

Note that the four regions of figure 13.1, which are used as the basis for classifying A's production effect (as shown in table 13.1), depend on the pregrowth prices. If we start with a different set of pregrowth prices (and

TABLE 13.1   *Classification of A's production effect*

Incremental Capital Labor Ratio, $\Delta K/\Delta L$	Marginal Propensity to Produce X (ξ_x^p) (1)	Marginal Propensity to Produce Y (ξ_y^p) (2)	Type of Production Effect when A Exports the labor-intensive commodity (X) (3)	when A exports the capital-intensive commodity (Y) (4)
(a) $\mu_x^0 < \Delta K/\Delta L = \mu^0 < \mu_y^0$	$\xi_x^p = \theta_x^p$	$\xi_y^p = \theta_y^p$	N	N
(b) $\Delta K/\Delta L < \mu_x^0 < \mu_y^0$	$\xi_x^p > 1$	$\xi_y^p < 0$	UP	UA
(c) $\mu_x^0 < \Delta K/\Delta L < \mu^0 < \mu_y^0$	$\theta_x^p < \xi_x^p < 1$	$0 < \xi_y^p < \theta_y^p$	P	A
(d) $\mu_x^0 < \mu^0 < \Delta K/\Delta L < \mu_y^0$	$0 < \xi_x^p < \theta_x^p$	$\theta_y^p < \xi_y^p < 1$	A	P
(e) $\Delta K/\Delta L > \mu_y^0 > \mu_x^0$	$\xi_x^p < 0$	$\xi_y^p > 1$	UA	UP

NOTE: N = neutral, P = protrade biased, UP = ultra protrade biased, A = antitrade biased, UA = ultra antitrade biased.

thus a point on the contract curve different from E), the same factor increases may give rise to different results. This is illustrated in figures 13.2. Figure 13.2A partially reproduces figure 13.1 (in particular, the area MO_yN). Capital is measured vertically and labor horizontally. The slope of the vector O_yS shows the pregrowth overall capital/labor ratio which exists in A. Figure 13.2B is similar to figure 10.5. The capital/labor ratios μ, μ_x, and μ_y are measured horizontally, the factor-price ratio r/w is measured vertically.

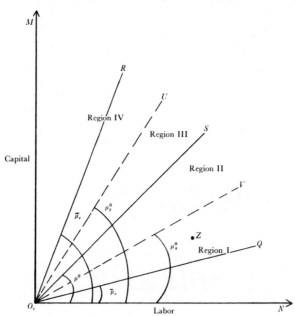

FIGURE 13.2A

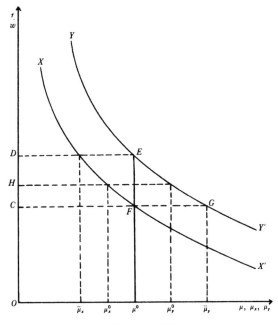

FIGURE 13.2B

The curves XX' and YY' give the optimum values of μ_x and μ_y, respectively, for given values of r/w. Given the overall capital/labor ratio μ^0, the ratio r/w can vary between OC and OD only. Hence, $\bar{\mu}_x < \mu_x \leq \mu^0$ and $\mu^0 \leq \mu_y < \bar{\mu}_y$. Given $\bar{\mu}_x$ and $\bar{\mu}_y$, we can draw two vectors in figure 13.2A, O_yQ and O_yR, with slopes equal to $\bar{\mu}_x$ and $\bar{\mu}_y$, respectively. For any value of r/w between the limits OC and OD, such as OH, we can determine the optimum values of μ_x and μ_y, as illustrated by the values μ_x^0 and μ_y^0, respectively. Assume that the pregrowth factor-price ratio was actually given by OH. Then the four regions of figure 13.1 will be given by the synonymous regions in figure 13.2A. Consider a point, such as Z, lying in region I. If ΔL and ΔK were given by the coordinates of Z with respect to O_y, then X_p would expand and Y_p would contract with growth. But this necessarily depends on the particular pregrowth prices we have chosen. If the factor-price ratio were sufficiently higher than OH, the vector O_yV could have been flatter than the vector O_yZ (not drawn); then both X_p and Y_p would increase with growth, with X_p increasing faster than Y_p. *When the factor increases, ΔL and ΔK, determine a point in the cone RO_yQ, the type of A's production effect cannot be predicted without further information about the pregrowth factor-price ratio. On the other hand, if the factor increases, ΔL and ΔK, determine a point in the cone QO_yN, then X_p will increase and Y_p will fall with growth, irrespective of the pregrowth value of the factor-price ratio. Similarly, if the factor increases, ΔL and ΔK, determine a point in the cone MO_yR, then X_p will fall and Y_p will increase with growth, irrespective again of* *the pregrowth factor-price ratio*. Note, finally, that the cones MO_yR and QO_yN depend on the pregrowth capital/labor ratio, μ^0.

What type of growth would country A experience in each of the preceding five cases of factor increases we have studied? That depends, in addition to the production effect, on the consumption effect. (Note that when only one factor increases, the extra income goes to the augmented factor and the consumption effect is a pure income effect of demand. On the other hand, if both factors increase, the incomes of both factors increase and the consumption effect becomes a weighted sum of income effects on demand.) The classification of A's production effect (summarized in table 13.1) can be used to determine the resultant type of overall growth, under the various types of consumption behavior, directly from table 12.4. Further, given the type of overall growth, the effect of factor-endowment growth on A's terms of trade can be predicted and, making use of the one-to-one correspondence between the commodity-price ratio and the factor-price ratio, the effect of growth on factor prices can be inferred.

Let us consider the effect of overall growth on the level of social welfare in the growing country, A. Assume that country A consists of identical individuals with respect to tastes and factor endowments both before and after growth. What is the effect of A's growth on the welfare of its Representative Citizen? Let us first distinguish between the *terms-of-trade effect*, which is due to the change in the commodity-price ratio, and the *wealth effect*, which is due to the shift of the production-possibilities frontier of A's Representative Citizen. Other things equal, A's Representative Citizen will tend to become better off when A's terms of trade improve (this occurs only with ultra-antitrade-biased growth); he will tend to become worse off when A's terms of trade deteriorate; and he will be indifferent when A's terms of trade remain constant. Other things equal, A's Representative Citizen will tend to become better off with an outward shift of his (scaled-down) production-possibilities frontier, which occurs when he has more capital to work with, that is, when the overall capital/labor ratio, μ, increases; he will tend to become worse off when his production-possibilities frontier shifts inward, which occurs when μ falls; and he will be indifferent when his production-possibilities frontier remains constant, which occurs when μ remains constant. The total effect on the welfare of A's Representative Citizen depends on the combined effect of both the wealth effect and the terms-of-trade effect. When neither effect is unfavorable, A's Representative Citizen will definitely become better off with growth, and when neither effect is favorable, he will definitely become worse off. But when one effect is favorable while the other is unfavorable, the total effect on the welfare of A's Representative Citizen will be indeterminate, the outcome depending on which of the two effects outweighs the other. Can we go beyond these generalizations and predict the total effect of growth on the welfare of A's Representative Citizen in each of the five cases of factor increases?

Table 13.2 shows the nature of the wealth effect, the terms-of-trade effect, and the overall effect on the welfare of A's Representative Citizen. Column (1) shows the nature of the income effect, which depends on the relationship between μ^0 and $\Delta K/\Delta L$. Thus, when $\Delta K/\Delta L > \mu^0$, the wealth effect is necessarily favorable; when $\mu^0 > \Delta K/\Delta L$, the wealth effect is unfavorable; and when $\mu^0 = \Delta K/\Delta L$, the wealth effect is zero (or neutral). Columns (2) and (3) reproduce columns (3) and (4) of table 13.5. Column (4) shows the nature of the consumption effect, which is neutral, because all citizens are, by assumption, identical with respect to tastes and factor endowments. Columns (5) and (6) show the type of overall growth. The information in columns (2)–(4), along with table 12.4, is used to determine the overall growth (cols. [5] and [6]). Columns (7) and (8) show the terms-of-trade effect, which depends on the nature of the overall growth, given in columns (5) and (6). Columns (9) and (10) show the *total* effect of growth on the welfare of A's Representative Citizen by combining the entries in column (1) with the corresponding entries in columns (7) and (8). It is clear from columns (9) and (10) that, *when country A exports the labor-intensive commodity (X), A's Representative Citizen becomes worse off with growth when the incremental capital/labor ratio, $\Delta K/\Delta L$, is either equal to or less than the pregrowth overall capital/labor ratio, μ^0.* Then, A's Representative Citizen has less capital to work with after growth, on the one hand, and A's terms of trade deteriorate, on the other. Further, when A exports the labor-intensive commodity X, A's Representative Citizen becomes definitely better off only when $\Delta K/\Delta L > \mu_y^0$; when $\mu^0 < \Delta K/\Delta L < \mu_y^0$, the outcome is indeterminate. On the other hand, when A exports the capital-intensive commodity Y, A's Representative Citizen becomes worse off only when $\Delta K/\Delta L = \mu_0$; in all other cases, the outcome is indeterminate.

2. Technical Progress

Technical progress is an important factor of growth. It occurs when increased output can be obtained over time from given resources of capital and labor. It can take a variety of forms. Let us define some of the simpler varieties.

Embodied technical progress occurs when progress is *embodied* in *new* capital goods; it becomes effective after the installation of the new capital goods (usually machines) in which it is embodied. Since, with the passage of time, new and more productive capital goods come into existence, capital can no longer be assumed to be homogeneous. On the contrary, capital becomes essentially a mixed stock of capital goods of different "vintages." Capital goods of one vintage are different from those of another: because of embodied technical progress, capital goods of a more recent vintage are more productive than capital goods of an earlier vintage, other things equal.

Labor can also be treated in a similar fashion. Thus, other things equal, the workers of the most recent "vintage" (i.e., those who have had their

TABLE 13.2 *The effects of factor increases*

Incremental Capital Labor Ratio (ΔK/ΔL) (1)	Income Effect on A's Representative Citizen (1)	Production Effect			Overall Growth		A's Terms-of-Trade Effect		Total Effect on the Welfare of A's Representative Citizen	
		when A exports the L-intensive commodity (X) (2)	when A exports the K-intensive commodity (Y) (3)	Consumption Effect (4)	when A exports the L-intensive commodity (X) (5)	when A exports the K-intensive commodity (Y) (6)	when A exports the L-intensive commodity (X) (A's terms of trade = p_x/p_y) (7)	when A exports the K-intensive commodity (Y) (A's terms of trade = p_y/p_x) (8)	when A exports the L-intensive commodity (X) (9)	when A exports the K-intensive commodity (Y) (10)
(a) $\mu_x^0 < \Delta K/\Delta L = \mu^0 < \mu_y^0$	Neutral (production possibilities frontier remains constant)	N	N	N	N	N	Unfavorable (deteriorate)	Unfavorable (deteriorate)	Unfavorable (worse off)	Unfavorable (worse off)
(b) $\Delta K/\Delta L < \mu_x^0 < \mu_y^0$	Unfavorable (production possibilities frontier shifts inward)	UP	UA	N	P or UP	UA	Unfavorable (deteriorate)	Favorable (improve)	Unfavorable (worse off)	Indeterminate (may become better off, worse off, or remain indifferent)
(c) $\mu_x^0 < \Delta K/\Delta L < \mu^0 < \mu_y^0$	Unfavorable (production-possibilities frontier shifts inward)	P	A	N	P	A or UA	Unfavorable (deteriorate)	Indeterminate (may, improve, deteriorate or remain constant)	Unfavorable (worse off)	Indeterminate (may become better off, worse off, or remain indifferent)

(d) $\mu_x^0 < \mu^0 < \Delta K/\Delta L < \mu_y^0$	Favorable (production-possibilities frontier shifts outward)	A	P	N	A or UA	P	Indeterminate (may improve, deteriorate, or remain constant)	Unfavorable (deteriorate)	Indeterminate (may become better off, worse off, or remain indifferent)	Indeterminate (may become better off, worse off, or remain indifferent)
(e) $\Delta K/\Delta L > \mu_y^0 > \mu_x^0$	Favorable (production-possibilities frontier shifts outward)	UA	UP	N	UA	P or UP	Favorable (improve)	Unfavorable (deteriorate)	Favorable (better off)	Indeterminate (may become better off, worse off, or remain indifferent)

NOTE: N = neutral, P = protrade biased, UP = ultra protrade biased, A = antitrade biased, UA = ultra antitrade biased.

305

training most recently) are more productive than those of earlier vintages.

We shall be concerned primarily with the various types of *disembodied technical progress*, which applies equally to all workers and capital goods. In other words, disembodied technical progress implies that increased output can be obtained over time from given quantities of labor and capital through time irrespective of the "vintage" of workers and capital goods. In fact, labor and capital are assumed to be two homogeneous factors, with no two units of the same factor being in any way different with respect to productivity.

Disembodied technical progress in general can be viewed as an inward shift of all isoquants of an industry undergoing technical progress. In what follows, assume that constant returns to scale prevail before and after the occurrence of technical progress and that technical progress occurs in a once-and-for-all fashion.

CLASSIFICATION OF DISEMBODIED TECHNICAL PROGRESS

Disembodied technical progress is usually classified into neutral, labor saving, and capital saving. But in the literature, there exist several sets of definitions of neutral, labor-saving, and capital-saving technical progress. In general, the different definitions give rise to different classifications of otherwise similar phenomena. Needless to say, each particular set of definitions is adapted to a certain purpose. We shall adopt the Hicksian definitions (Hicks 1964), which are the most appropriate for our purposes.

Neutral Technical Progress occurs in an industry when increased output is obtained from given quantities of labor and capital and, in addition, when the same factor ratio, K/L, is optimal before and after the change for each and every value of the factor-price ratio. In other words, the isoquants of the industry undergoing technical progress shift inward and, in addition, the marginal rate of substitution of labor for capital is the same before and after the technical change for all possible values of the capital/labor ratio in the industry. This type of disembodied technical progress amounts to a mere renumbering of the isoquants of the industry undergoing change.

Mathematically, this type of technical progress can be expressed as follows. Assume that $Q = Q(K, L)$ is a production function characterized by constant returns to scale. Then neutral technical progress implies that $Q^* = \lambda Q(K, L)$, where $\lambda > 1$ and $Q^* =$ the new amount of output produced with K and L. Thus, $Q^* = \lambda Q$, with Q the maximum amount of output which was obtained from the employment of K and L before the technical progress took place. Since $\partial Q^*/\partial L = \lambda(\partial Q/\partial L)$ and $\partial Q^*/\partial K = \lambda(\partial Q/\partial K)$, it follows that $(\partial Q^*/\partial L)/(\partial Q^*/\partial K) = (\partial Q/\partial L)/(\partial Q/\partial K)$. The renumbering of isoquants follows directly from the equation $Q^* = \lambda Q$.

Labor-Saving Technical Progress occurs in an industry when increased output is obtained from given quantities of labor and capital. In addition, at the factor prices which existed before the change, a smaller amount of labor per unit of capital (i.e., a smaller labor/capital ratio) is optimally employed after the change than before. Thus, labor is being saved per unit of capital employed. But this does not mean that only the factor labor is being saved while the other factor, capital, is not. Since each isoquant shifts inward, despite the combination of L and K originally used to produce a specified amount of output there will be at least one new combination of smaller L and K capable of producing that same amount of output after the change.

The case of labor-saving technical progress is illustrated in figure 13.3, where the curve bb is the unit isoquant before the change and the curve aa is the unit isoquant after the change. Note that the new isoquant lies totally inside the old isoquant. For any factor-price ratio, such as that shown by the slope of bb at E_0, the ratio K/L used after the change is higher than that used before the change, as shown by the fact that the vector OE_1 is steeper than the vector OE_0, where the slope of the aa isoquant at point E_1 is equal to the slope of the bb isoquant at E_0. This same relationship must hold for all factor prices.

Labor-saving technical progress in a certain industry tends to make that industry capital intensive relative to what the industry was before the change. When the industry uses labor and capital in the same proportion before and after the change, the marginal rate of substitution of labor for capital is smaller after the change than before. This is illustrated in figure 13.3 where the slope at E_0 is steeper than the slope at M. Accordingly, an industry which experiences labor-saving technical change will employ labor and capital in the same proportion before and after the change if, and only if, labor becomes, after the change, sufficiently cheaper relative to capital.

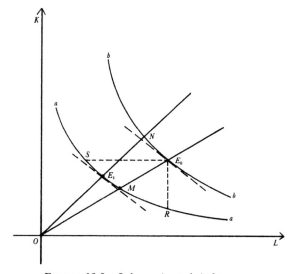

FIGURE 13.3 *Labor-saving technical progress*

Capital-Saving Technical Progress occurs in an industry when increased output is obtained from given quantities of labor and capital. In addition, at the factor prices which existed before the change, a smaller amount of capital per unit of labor (i.e., a smaller capital/labor ratio) is optimally employed after the change than before. Therefore, capital is being saved per unit of labor employed. Again, this does not mean that only the factor capital is being saved.

The case of capital-saving technical progress is illustrated in figure 13.4. Again, the curves bb and aa are the unit isoquants before and after the change, respectively. For any given value of the factor-price ratio, such as that implied by the slopes at points E_0 and E_1, the factor ratio K/L is lower after the change, as illustrated by the fact that the vector OE_1 is flatter than the vector OE_0.

Capital-saving technical progress in a certain industry tends to make that industry labor intensive relative to what the industry was before the change. For the same capital/labor ratio, the marginal rate of substitution of labor for capital is therefore higher after the change than before. This is illustrated in figure 13.4, where the slope at M is steeper than the slope at E_0. Accordingly, an industry which experiences capital-saving technical change will employ labor and capital in the same proportion before and after the change if, and only if, capital becomes, after the change, sufficiently cheaper relative to labor.

The original Hicksian definitions are worded differently. Hicks (1964, pp. 121–22) says that "we can classify inventions according as their initial effects are to increase, leave unchanged, or diminish the ratio of the marginal

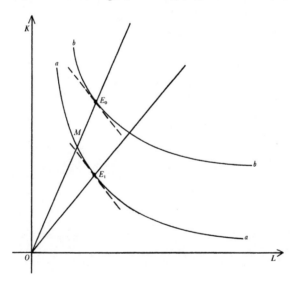

FIGURE 13.4   *Capital-saving technical progress*

product of capital to that of labour. We may call these inventions 'labour-saving,' 'neutral,' and 'capital-saving' respectively. 'Labor-saving' inventions increase the marginal product of capital more than they increase the marginal product of labour, 'capital-saving' inventions increase the marginal product of labour more than that of capital, 'neutral' inventions increase both in the same proportion." In other words, Hicks compares the slopes of the unit isoquants of figures 13.3 and 13.4 at points E_0 and M, that is, the *marginal rates of substitution at the original factor proportions used by the industry.* On the other hand, our definitions center on the comparison between the slopes of the vectors OE_0 and OE_1, under the assumption that the slope of the isoquant bb at E_0 is equal to the slope of the isoquant aa at E_1.

These definitions of neutral, labor-saving, and capital-saving technical progress can be formulated mathematically as follows. Let $F(K, L)$ be the original production function and $G(K, L)$ the production function after the technical progress takes place. In general, the function $G(K, L)$ can be expressed as

$$G(K, L) = F(\alpha K, \beta L), \tag{13.3}$$

where $\alpha > 1$ and $\beta > 1$. (In general, α and β can be considered as functions of the ratio K/L, with the proviso that $\alpha > 0$, $\beta > 0$ and that the ratio α/β is always equal to, greater than, or smaller than unity.) Therefore,

$$MPP_K^a \equiv \frac{\partial G}{\partial K} = \alpha \frac{\partial F}{\partial K} = \alpha MPP_K^b, \tag{13.4}$$

$$MPP_L^a \equiv \frac{\partial G}{\partial L} = \beta \frac{\partial F}{\partial L} = \beta MPP_L^b, \tag{13.5}$$

where $MPP^a \equiv$ marginal physical product after the change and $MPP^b \equiv$ marginal physical product before the change, with the subscripts L and K indicating the factor whose marginal product is being considered. Considering now the marginal rate of substitution of L for K before and after the change, we have

$$MRS_{LK}^a \equiv \frac{MPP_L^a}{MPP_K^a} = \frac{\beta MPP_L^b}{\alpha MPP_K^b} = \frac{\beta}{\alpha} MRS_{LK}^b. \tag{13.6}$$

Accordingly, if $\alpha = \beta$, then $MRS_{LK}^a = MRS_{LK}^b$ and thus technical progress is neutral; if $\beta > \alpha$, then $MRS_{LK}^a > MRS_{LK}^b$ and thus the technical progress is capital saving; and if $\beta < \alpha$, then $MRS_{LK}^a < MRS_{LK}^b$ and thus the technical progress is labor saving. Therefore, the relationship between the coefficients α and β is all that is needed for the classification of technical progress.

This formulation emphasizes another aspect of the classification of disembodied technical progress. From equation (13.3) it follows that disembodied technical progress is factor augmenting. That is, the effective amount of capital increases from K to αK and the effective amount of labor increases from L to βL. But classification into neutral, labor saving, and capital saving depends on whether $\alpha = \beta$, $\alpha > \beta$, or $\alpha < \beta$, respectively. If both factors are augmented at the same rate ($\alpha = \beta$), the technical progress is neutral; if capital is augmented at a higher rate than labor ($\alpha > \beta$), technical progress is labor saving; and if labor is augmented at a higher rate than capital ($\alpha < \beta$), technical progress is capital saving. Labor-saving technical progress ($\alpha > \beta$) can now be decomposed into *neutral* technical progress (where both factors are augmented by β) and purely capital-augmenting technical progress (where capital is further augmented by the factor $\alpha - \beta$). On the other hand, capital-saving technical progress ($\alpha < \beta$) can be decomposed into neutral and purely labor-augmenting technical progress.

TECHNICAL PROGRESS IN THE LABOR-INTENSIVE INDUSTRY (X)

Assume for the moment that A is a small country which can buy and sell unlimited amounts of commodities X and Y in the international market at given prices. Assume further that X and Y are produced with two factors, labor, L, and capital, K, and that X is labor intensive relative to Y. How does technical progress in each of the two industries of country A affect A's demand for imports and supply of exports, that is, A's volume of trade at the pregrowth prices? We must first determine the type of production effect A will experience by analyzing the behavior of X_p (A's output of X) and Y_p (A's output of Y) with the occurrence of one or another type of disembodied technical progress either in industry X or in Y.

A simple but important proposition is that the relative price of the commodity undergoing technical progress is necessarily lower after the change for any given factor prices because, with technical progress, the unit isoquant for the said commodity necessarily shifts inward, closer to the origin. Irrespective of the type of technical progress, a lower isocost line will be tangent to it after the change than before, and hence, the average cost of production, which is equal to the price of the commodity, is necessarily lower after the change for any given factor prices. For any given factor prices, the price of the other commodity whose production function does not shift (by assumption) necessarily remains the same. Accordingly, the relative price of the first commodity (which undergoes technical progress) necessarily falls. For instance, if, by assumption, technical progress occurs in industry X only, the price ratio p_x/p_y will necessarily be lower after technical progress for any given factor prices.

1) Neutral Technical Progress in Industry X. How does neutral technical progress in industry X affect A's box diagram and its production-possibilities frontier? As noted earlier, neutral technical progress in any industry results in a mere renumbering of that industry's isoquants, with each isoquant corresponding to a higher output after the change than before. From a purely geometrical point of view, as industry X experiences neutral technical progress, its isoquants (inside the box diagram), and therefore the contract curve, will be the same after the change as before. Does this mean that the country's production-possibilities frontier will also remain the same? No, for despite the fact that the isoquants and the contract curve do not appear to change with neutral technical progress, the renumbering of X's isoquants necessarily causes the production-possibilities frontier to shift outward. This is illustrated in figure 13.5, where the curve RP_0M is A's production-possibilities frontier. With neutral technical progress in industry X, A's production-possibilities frontier shifts to RP_1P_2N because, for any point on the contract curve (not shown), the output of Y is the same before and after the change while the output of X is necessarily higher after the change. For instance, when OY_1 units of commodity Y are produced (as implied by a certain point on the contract curve), the output of commodity X increases from Y_1P_0 to Y_1P_1. Note that the production-possibilities frontier necessarily has the same Y-axis intercept, R, after the change as before, for the distance OR shows the maximum output of Y which could be obtained if all resources were employed in the production of Y; since industry Y does not undergo any change, A's production-possibilities frontier must necessarily start at the same point, R, after industry X experiences technical progress (neutral or any other type).

Assume now that the international price ratio, p_x/p_y, is given by the absolute slope of A's pregrowth production-possibilities frontier at P_0.

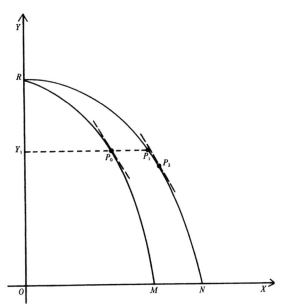

FIGURE 13.5 *Neutral technical progress in industry X*

Hence, P_0 is A's optimum production point before the change. Given that p_x/p_y remains constant, where would A produce after the change? Observe that each and every point on the (constant) contract curve implies the same marginal rate of substitution of labor for capital in both industries after as well as before the change. Hence, each and every point on the contract curve implies the same factor-price ratio after as well as before the change. In addition, each point on the contract curve implies the same output for Y. If the factor-price ratio were kept constant at the pregrowth level, A's production point would therefore shift from P_0 to P_1. But at P_1, the slope of A's production-possibilities frontier is necessarily flatter than the slope at P_0 (for any given factor prices, commodity X becomes relatively cheaper after industry X experiences technical progress). Accordingly, at the pregrowth commodity prices, A will be producing somewhere in the region P_1N, as illustrated by point P_2. To summarize, the slope at P_1 is flatter than the slope at P_0; therefore, the point on RP_1P_2N where the slope is equal to the slope at P_0 must lie in the region P_1N, as shown by the point P_2. After the occurrence of neutral technical progress in industry X, the output of commodity Y will necessarily fall absolutely while the output of X will increase at given commodity prices.

2) Labor-Saving Technical Progress in the Labor-Intensive Industry X. What would happen to the output of X (X_p) and the output of Y (Y_p) at the internationally given commodity prices if industry X's technical progress were not neutral but labor saving? Consider first the effect (of labor-saving technical progress in industry X) on X_p and Y_p at the pregrowth equilibrium factor prices. Recall that industry X will necessarily tend to become less labor intensive (or more capital intensive) relative to its pre-technical-change status. In particular, if we assume that factor prices remain at their pregrowth equilibrium level, X's expansion path after the change will be steeper than its expansion path before the change. This is illustrated in figure 13.6, where X's expansion before the change is given by the vector O_xE_0 and after the change by the steeper vector O_xE_1. Observe that, at the pregrowth factor prices, Y's expansion path remains the same, as illustrated in figure 13.6 by the straight line $O_yE_1E_0$. Accordingly, the equilibrium point in the box diagram will shift from E_0 (before) to E_1 (after) and Y's output will fall from O_yE_0 to O_yE_1. Commodity X's output will increase for two reasons: (i) at E_0, X's output is higher after the change, because with (any type of) technical progress increased output can be obtained from the same amounts of labor and capital; and (ii) the shift from E_0 to E_1 necessarily implies a movement from a lower to a higher isoquant for industry X.

These changes in X_p and Y_p (i.e., $\Delta X_p > 0$ and $\Delta Y_p < 0$) assume that factor prices are kept constant at their pregrowth level. We are actually interested in the changes in X_p and Y_p when commodity prices remain constant at their pregrowth level. Recall that, for the same factor prices

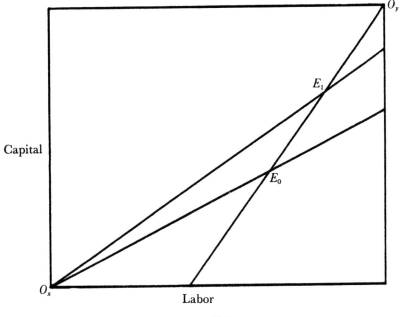

FIGURE 13.6

(before and after the change), the commodity-price ratio p_x/p_y is necessarily lower after the occurrence of technical progress in industry X and that, because of increasing opportunity costs, as p_x/p_y is allowed to increase to the pregrowth level, X_p will tend to increase further and Y_p will tend to fall further, from the levels they had reached at point E_1 in figure 13.6. These changes in X_p and Y_p reinforce the initial changes corresponding to the shift from E_0 to E_1 (fig. 13.6). Accordingly, the total change in X_p and Y_p is a fortiori the same as in the preceding case of neutral technical change.

3) Capital-saving Technical Progress in the Labor-Intensive Industry X. Figure 13.6 can also be used to illustrate the case of capital-saving technical change in industry X. Now the original expansion paths for X and Y are given by the vectors $O_x E_1$ and $O_y E_1 E_0$, respectively. Consider what happens to X_p and Y_p at the pregrowth equilibrium factor prices. With capital-saving technical progress, industry X becomes less capital intensive (or more labor intensive), with its expansion path shifting from $O_x E_1$ to $O_x E_0$. Equilibrium shifts from E_1 to E_0, with Y's output greater at E_0 than at E_1. Nothing, of course, can be said about the change in X_p, because its outcome depends on the strength of the inward shift of X's isoquants. For instance, if the isoquant passing originally through E_1 shifts to the isoquant that now passes through E_0, the output of industry X will be the same at the two points; if the isoquant passing originally through E_1 shifts to a position below point E_0, the output of industry X will be higher at E_0 (after the change) than at E_1 (before the change); and if the isoquant passing originally through E_1 shifts to a position above point E_0, the output of industry X will be smaller at E_0 (after the change) than at E_1 (before the change). In general, therefore, the sign of ΔX_p (at given factor prices) is indeterminate.

We also have to consider the changes that occur in X_p and Y_p as the commodity-price ratio p_x/p_y is allowed to rise to its pregrowth level. Again, because of increasing opportunity costs, Y_p will fall from and X_p will increase to the levels they had reached at point E_0.

It can also be verified that the total change in X_p and Y_p at the pregrowth equilibrium commodity prices is indeterminate. This will not be done here. Also, there is no need to analyze the effects on X_p and Y_p of technical progress in industry Y. To do so, merely reverse the roles of the two factors and proceed as above. The results are summarized in table 13.3, where the last two columns show the nature of the production effect depending on whether A is exporting commodity X or Y.

TABLE 13.3   *The effect of technical progress on X_p and Y_p*

			Production Effect	
Technical Progress	Sign of ΔX_p	Sign of ΔY_p	when A exports the labor-intensive commodity X	when A exports the capital-intensive commodity Y
In industry X:				
Neutral	$\Delta X_p > 0$	$\Delta Y_p < 0$	UP	UA
Labor saving . .	$\Delta X_p > 0$	$\Delta Y_p < 0$	UP	UA
Capital saving .	?	?	All types possible	All types possible
In industry Y:				
Neutral	$\Delta X_p < 0$	$\Delta Y_p > 0$	UA	UP
Labor saving . .	?	?	All types possible	All types possible
Capital saving .	$\Delta X_p < 0$	$\Delta Y_p > 0$	UA	UP

Drop the assumption that the commodity prices are fixed in the international market. What is the effect of the various types of technical progress on A's terms of trade? First determine the type of overall growth that A will experience with technical progress. As we have seen, A's type of overall growth depends, in addition to the production effect, on the consumption effect. Using the information in chapter 12, part A, especially table 12.4, we can determine A's type of overall growth as well as the effect on A's terms of trade (see table 13.4). Note that A's terms of trade are given by the ratio (price of A's exportables)/(price of A's importables). An increase in the latter ratio implies that A's terms of trade improve, and a decrease implies that they deteriorate.

What is the effect of technical progress on the level of social welfare in A? Assume again that A's citizens are identical with respect to tastes and factor

TABLE 18.4 *The effect of technical progress on A's terms of trade*

Technical Progress	A Exports the L-Intensive Commodity X — Production effect	consumption effect N	P	UP	A	UA	A Exports the K-Intensive Commodity Y — Production effect N	consumption effect	P	UP	A	UA
In the labor-intensive industry X:												
Neutral . . . UP	UP	G: P or UP / TOT: deteriorate	G: P or UP / TOT: deteriorate	G: UP / TOT: deteriorate	G: Not UA / TOT: deteriorate	?	UA	G: UA / TOT: improve	G: UA / TOT: improve	?	G: UA / TOT: improve	G: UA / TOT: improve
Labor-saving . . . UP	UP	G: P or UP / TOT: deteriorate	G: P or UP / TOT: deteriorate	G: UP / TOT: deteriorate	G: not UA / TOT: deteriorate	?	UA	G: UA / TOT: improve	G: UA / TOT: improve	?	G: UA / TOT: improve	G: UA / TOT: improve
Capital-saving . . . ?	?	?	?	?	?	?	?	?	?	?	?	?
In the capital-intensive industry Y:												
Neutral . . . UA	UA	G: UA / TOT: improve	G: UA / TOT: improve	?	G: UA / TOT: improve	G: UA / TOT: improve	UP	G: P or UP / TOT: deteriorate	G: P or UP / TOT: deteriorate	G: UP / TOT: deteriorate	G: not UA / TOT: deteriorate	?
Labor-saving . . . ?	?	?	?	?	?	?	?	?	?	?	?	?
Capital-saving . . . UA	UA	G: UA / TOT: improve	G: UA / TOT: improve	?	G: UA / TOT: improve	G: UA / TOT: improve	UP	G: P or UP / TOT: deteriorate	G: P or UP / TOT: deteriorate	G: UP / TOT: deteriorate	G: not UA / TOT: deteriorate	?

NOTE: G = type of overall growth, TOT = terms of trade, N = neutral, P = protrade biased, UP = ultra protrade biased, A = antitrade biased, UA = ultra antitrade biased.

endowments, which implies that the consumption effect is neutral. As before, we can distinguish between two effects on the welfare of A's Representative Citizen: a *terms-of-trade effect*, which has already been determined in table 13.4, and a *wealth effect*, which corresponds to the outward shift of the production-possibilities frontier of A's Representative Citizen as in the classical theory (chap. 12), the wealth effect is always favorable: the production-possibilities frontier of A's Representative Citizen always shifts outward with technical progress. However, as shown in table 13.4, the terms-of-trade effect may go either way. When it is favorable (i.e., when A's terms of trade improve), A's Representative Citizen becomes better off with growth. This occurs with certainty in only two cases: (i) when A exports the labor-intensive commodity and either neutral or capital-saving technical progress occurs in the capital-intensive industry, and (ii) when A exports the capital-intensive commodity and either neutral or labor-saving technical progress occurs in the labor-intensive industry.

When either neutral or capital-saving technical progress occurs in the capital-intensive industry and, in addition, country A exports the capital-intensive commodity, A's terms of trade deteriorate. Similarly, when A exports the labor-intensive commodity and, in addition, either neutral or labor-saving technical progress occurs in the labor-intensive industry, A's terms of trade deteriorate. In these two cases, the total effect on the welfare of A's Representative Citizen depends on which of the two effects outweighs the other—the wealth effect or the terms-of-trade effect.

The effect on A's terms of trade is indeterminate in the following two cases: (i) when capital-saving technical progress occurs in the labor-intensive industry, and (ii) when labor-saving technical progress occurs in the capital-intensive industry. As a result, the total effect on the welfare of A's Representative Citizen is, in general, indeterminate. If A's terms of trade do not deteriorate, A's Representative Citizen becomes better off; if they do deteriorate, A's Representative Citizen may become better off (when the favorable wealth effect outweighs the unfavorable terms-of-trade effect) or worse off (when the unfavorable terms-of-trade effect outweighs the favorable wealth effect).

Two final comments are in order. (i) If technical progress of whatever type and in whichever industry is large enough to cause the production-possibilities frontier of A's Representative Citizen to shift sufficiently outward so that it at least touches the indifference curve where A's Representative Citizen was consuming in the pregrowth equilibrium state, A's Representative Citizen will definitely become better off with growth, irrespective of what happens to A's terms of trade. Thus, the phenomenon of "immiserizing growth" occurs only when technical progress is rather small. (ii) If country A pursues an optimum tariff policy (discussed in chap. 20), technical progress will always make A's Representative Citizen better off.

SELECTED BIBLIOGRAPHY

Bhagwati, J. 1958. Immiserizing growth: a geometrical note. *Review of Economic Studies* 25: 201–5; reprinted in the A.E.A. *Readings in International Economics*. Homewood, Ill.: R. D. Irwin, 1968.

Clement, M. O., R. L. Pfister, and K. J. Rothwell. 1967. *Theoretical Issues in International Economics*. Boston: Houghton Mifflin Co. Chap. 3.

Corden, W. M. 1956. Economic expansion and international trade: a geometric approach. *Oxford Economic Papers* 8: 223–8.

Edgeworth, F. Y. 1894. The theory of international values. *Economic Journal* 4: 35–50.

Findlay, R., and H. Grubert. 1959. Factor intensities, technological progress and the terms of trade. *Oxford Economic Papers* 11: 111–21.

Heller, H. R. 1968. *International Trade*. Englewood Cliffs, N.J.: Prentice-Hall, Inc. Chap. 7.

Hicks, J. R. 1964. *The Theory of Wages*, 2nd Ed. London: Macmillan & Co., Ltd.

———. 1953. An inaugural lecture. *Oxford Economic Papers* 5: 117–35.

Johnson, H. G. 1958. *International Trade and Economic Growth*. London: George Allen & Unwin, Ltd. Chap. 3.

———. 1962. *Money, Trade and Economic Growth*. Cambridge, Mass.: Harvard University Press. Chap. 4; reprinted in the A.E.A. *Readings in International Economics*. Homewood, Ill.: R. D. Irwin, 1968.

Kemp, M. C. 1964. *The Pure Theory of International Trade*. Englewood Cliffs, N.J.: Prentice-Hall, Inc.

Meier, G. M. 1963. *International Trade and Development*. New York: Harper & Row. Chap. 2–3.

Rybczynski, T. M. 1955. Factor endowment and relative commodity prices. *Economica* 22: 336–41.

Samuelson, P. A. 1956. Social indifference curves. *Quarterly Journal of Economics* 70: 1–22.

14

Growth in a Simple Open Economy

The modern theory of international trade is basically a long-run *static* theory. It postulates the existence of two homogeneous factors of production which are usually assumed to remain in fixed supply throughout. Johnson (1962, chap. 4), among others, has developed a useful comparative-statics framework within which the assumptions of given technology and factor endowments can be relaxed. In fact, chapters 12 and 13 are largely based on Johnson's work. But even though a comparative-statics analysis is useful, it leaves much to be desired, for it considers all changes in factor endowments as totally exogenous phenomena. Even though modern economists take, with some justification, the rate of growth of the labor force as given exogenously by demographic factors, the same claim cannot be made for capital, because the factor capital should be understood to mean "produced means of production," for example, machines. How do these capital goods (i.e., machines) get to be produced, and how does their stock change through time? Is it legitimate to assume that the stock of machines as well as its changes through time are given exogenously? To answer these questions, the model of chapters 8 and 9 has to be amended to include explicitly the capital-goods sector.

When the capital-goods sector is introduced into the model explicitly, the current stock of capital (machines) will be the integral of net saving and investment from the beginning of time until the current period. The current change of the stock of capital will be equal to the net saving and investment of the current period. Since the acts of saving and investment form an integral part of the economic process, the stock of capital and its growth cannot be taken as exogenous; they are, rather, endogenous, with their respective equilibrium values determined by the behavior of the economic system itself. Thus, contrary to the modern theory of trade (which takes the overall capital/labor ratio as given), the overall capital/labor ratio will now be a variable. In addition, the overall capital/labor ratio will not be a variable whose value is being determined by factors which lie totally outside the scope of the economic system; that is, it will not be an exogenous variable. It will, rather, be an endogenous variable, at least partially, with its long-run equilibrium value, if it exists, determined by the general-equilibrium solution of the system. For this purpose, a truly dynamic model must be developed. This is the purpose of the present chapter. A dynamic model of a simple open economy will be set up to show how the long-run equilibrium capital/labor ratio, and therefore the pattern of specialization, is determined.

This dynamic model can be considered as an integration of the one-sector and two-sector growth models developed by Solow (1956) and Uzawa (1961), respectively, because, on the one hand, relative prices will be held constant by assumption (and this makes our model akin to Solow's one-sector growth model) and, on the other hand, two sectors (a consumption-goods sector plus a capital-goods sector) will be explicitly considered (and this makes our model akin to Uzawa's two-sector growth model).

1. The Assumptions

Let us start the discussion by enumerating the assumptions on which the analysis is based.

1. There are two factors of production, machines (K) and labor (L).

2. There are two products, newly produced machines (Q_k) and consumption goods (Q_c). (Note that both Q_k and K refer to machines; the former is the current output of machines and the latter is the stock of machines at a point in time.)

3. The production functions of both machines and consumption goods $(Q_k$ and $Q_c)$ are characterized by constant returns to scale. Therefore, these production functions can be written in the following form:

$$Q_k = F_k(K_k, L_k) = L_k F_k[(K_k/L_k), 1] = L_k f_k(\mu_k), \qquad (14.1)$$

$$Q_c = F_c(K_c, L_c) = L_c F_c[(K_c/L_c), 1] = L_c f_c(\mu_c), \qquad (14.2)$$

where $K_k \equiv$ machines used in the production of machines; $L_k \equiv$ labor used in the production of machines; $K_c \equiv$ machines used in the production of consumption goods; $L_c \equiv$ labor used in the production of consumption goods; $\mu_k \equiv K_k/L_k$; $\mu_c \equiv K_c/L_c$; $f_k(\mu_k) \equiv F_k[(K_k/L_k), 1] =$ per capita output in the capital-goods industry; and $f_c(\mu_c) \equiv F_c[(K_c/L_c), 1] =$ per capita output in the consumption-goods industry.

4. Machines do not depreciate.[1]

---

1. Exponential depreciation can be easily substituted for zero depreciation. The latter assumption will be maintained throughout for simplicity.

5. The price of machines (p_k) and the price of the consumption good (p_c) are given in the international market.

6. Saving (S) is proportional to income (Y); that is,

$$S = sY, \qquad (14.3)$$

where $s \equiv$ marginal (and average) propensity to save and

$$Y \equiv Q_c + (p_k/p_c)Q_k. \qquad (14.4)$$

7. All saving is invested in newly produced machines. In other words, the possibility of a Keynesian inconsistency between saving and investment at full employment is ruled out.

8. Labor grows exponentially at the natural rate n. In other words,

$$L = L_0 e^{nt}, \qquad (14.5)$$

where $L =$ labor supply at time t and $L_0 =$ labor supply at time 0.

2. Equilibrium in the Short Run

Given these assumptions, we can draw upon the analyses of chapters 6–11 to determine the short-run equilibrium of the model, that is, the equilibrium of the model during a single time period. Thus, at the beginning of the period, the economy will be endowed with a certain amount of labor (which is historically determined) and a certain stock of machines (which is the result of capital accumulation in the past and, therefore, perfectly determined). On the basis of the historically given supply of labor (L_0) and the stock of machines (K_0), we can determine the production-possibilities frontier of the economy. Further, the equilibrium production points is that point where the production-possibilities frontier becomes tangent to the highest income-contour line, with slope equal to the given international price ratio, as explained in chapter 5. Finally, once the equilibrium production point is determined, the equilibrium absorption point[2] can be determined by the condition that saving (which is assumed to be proportional to income) is being used to purchase newly produced machines.

The preceding description of the short-run equilibrium process is illustrated in figure 14.1. The output of consumption goods (Q_c) and income (Y) are measured along the horizontal axis, while the output of machines (Q_k) is measured along the vertical axis. The curve MPN is the economy's production-possibilities frontier for the time period under consideration. Where should the economy produce? As explained earlier in the book, the economy should produce at that point where income is being maximized.

---

2. The term "absorption point" is substituted for "consumption point" used earlier in the book, because "consumption point" implies that both commodities are consumed, which is not the case now. The term "absorption point" seems to describe the present situation better.

Imagine that the family of income contour lines with common absolute slope equal to the internationally given price ratio p_c/p_k is superimposed on figure 14.1. The economy will then produce at that point where the production-possibilities frontier is tangent to the highest income contour line. This is illustrated by point P, where the production-possibilities frontier is tangent to the straight line ZPT, this being the highest income contour line. Having determined the optimum production point, we can measure the economy's maximum income in terms either of the consumption good or of the capital good. In the former case, the economy's maximum income will be given by the horizontal distance OT, and in the latter case, by the vertical distance OZ.

The equilibrium absorption point must lie on the highest income contour line ZPT. But how can it be determined? For this purpose, we can concentrate on either the demand for Q_c or the demand for Q_k. Let us choose the latter. The demand for Q_k (Z_k) is obviously equal to the value of saving expressed in terms of the capital good. In other words,

$$Z_k = (p_c/p_k)S = s(p_c/p_k)Y. \tag{14.6}$$

Equation (14.6) is represented graphically by the vector OU whose slope is given by $s(p_c/p_k)$. Since Y is given by the distance OT, the economy must be saving and investing in newly produced machines in the amount TD. Thus, the equilibrium absorption point must lie on the income contour line ZPT,

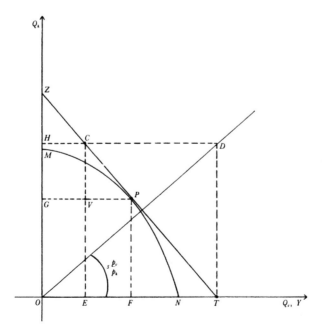

FIGURE 14.1

and the absolute quantity of capital goods demanded must be equal to the
vertical distance TD. Obviously, the equilibrium absorption point occurs
at the intersection of the horizontal line through point C (i.e., DC) and
the income contour line ZPT (i.e., point C). But how do we know that the
horizontal line through D will intersect the income contour line ZPT in the
first quadrant? Put differently, how do we know that the distance TD will
not be larger than the distance OZ? Aggregate expenditure on both Q_c and
Q_k is equal to the value of output produced. Since the value of output
produced expressed in terms of the capital good is given by OZ, the economy
can never demand a larger quantity of capital goods than OZ. In other
words, the average propensity to save can never be larger than unity. In fact,
it is less than unity, since the economy is assumed to spend part of its income
on Q_c. Thus, $0 < s < 1$, and $TD = s\,(OZ)$; that is, $TD < OZ$.

Having determined the equilibrium production and absorption points, we
can determine the quantities of Q_c and Q_k traded by the economy in the
international market as the differences between the levels of production and
consumption of each commodity. Therefore, in the example of figure 14.1,
the economy must be exporting $EF = VP$ units of the consumption good in
exchange for $GH = VC$ units of the capital good.

This graphical solution can be clarified by setting up the problem in the
form of a system of simultaneous equations. This is a necessary step for the
determination of the long-run equilibrium solution. The system of equations
is

$$Q_k = L_k f_k(\mu_k), \tag{14.1}$$

$$Q_c = L_c f_c(\mu_c), \tag{14.2}$$

$$K = K_k + K_c, \tag{14.7}$$

$$L = L_k + L_c, \tag{14.8}$$

$$p_k \frac{\partial Q_k}{\partial K} = p_k f_k' = r,$$

or

$$f_k' = \frac{r}{p_k} \tag{14.9}$$

$$p_c \frac{\partial Q_c}{\partial K} = p_c f_c' = r,$$

or

$$f_c' = \frac{r}{p_c}, \tag{14.10}$$

$$p_k \frac{\partial Q_k}{\partial L} = p_k(f_k - \mu_k f_k') = w,$$

or

$$f_k - \mu_k f'_k = \frac{w}{p_k}, \tag{14.11}$$

$$p_c \frac{\partial Q_c}{\partial L} = p_c(f_c - \mu_c f'_c) = w, $$

or

$$f_c - \mu_c f'_c = \frac{w}{p_c}, \tag{14.12}$$

$$\frac{f_c - \mu_c f'_c}{f'_c} = \frac{f_k - \mu_k f'_k}{f'_k} = \frac{w}{r}, \tag{14.13}$$

$$Y = Q_c + \frac{p_k}{p_c} Q_k = L_c f_c + p L_k f_k, \tag{14.14}$$

$$Z_k = \frac{S}{p} = \frac{sY}{p}, \tag{14.6}$$

$$Z_c = (1 - s)Y, \tag{14.15}$$

where the additional symbols in the above equations are: $p \equiv p_k/p_c$, $r =$ money rental per unit of capital, $w =$ money wage rate, $Z_k =$ absolute quantity of new capital goods demanded (i.e., current investment evaluated in terms of the capital good), and $Z_c =$ absolute quantity of consumption goods demanded (i.e., current consumption evaluated in terms of the consumption good).

What is the interpretation of these equations? Equations (14.1) and (14.2) are the two production functions discussed earlier. Equations (14.7) and (14.8) are the full-employment conditions. Equations (14.9)–(14.12) are the familiar marginal productivity conditions. Equation (14.13), which follows from equations (14.9)–(14.12), is the condition that the marginal rate of substitution of labor for capital in the two industries must be equal. This is the condition which guarantees that the economy will allocate its resources according to the coordinates of some point on the contract curve in the box diagram and produce somewhere along the production-possibilities frontier. In fact, equations (14.1), (14.2), (14.7), (14.8), and (14.13) can be used to derive a relationship between Q_k and Q_c which is simply the mathematical expression for the economy's production-possibilities frontier.[3] Equation (14.14) expresses national income (Y) as the value of output produced, while equations (14.6) and (14.15) show the aggregate demand for capital goods and consumption goods, respectively.

3. Note that we have five equations in six unknowns: Q_k, Q_c, L_k, L_c, K_k, and K_c. Thus, four equations can be used to eliminate the four unknowns L_k, L_c, K_k, and K_c. The last equation, i.e., the production-possibilities frontier equation, will simply be an equation in Q_k and Q_c.

Let us write the equation for the economy's production-possibilities frontier as

$$G(Q_k, Q_c) = 0. \tag{14.16}$$

It is impossible to derive an explicit expression for the production-possibilities frontier. Note, too, that the equilibrium production point (on the production-possibilities frontier) is determined by the condition

$$-\frac{dQ_c}{dQ_k} = \frac{(dG/dQ_k)}{(dG/dQ_c)} = p. \tag{14.17}$$

Thus, starting with equation (14.17), we can determine the optimum production point (Q_k^*, Q_c^*) and work backwards, with the system of five equations we have formulated, to determine the equilibrium values of all other variables in the system, that is, L_k^*, L_c^*, K_k^*, and K_c^*, where the asterisks are used to indicate equilibrium quantities. We can also determine the ratios

$$\mu_k^* = \frac{K_k^*}{L_k^*} \quad \text{and} \quad \mu_c^* = \frac{K_c^*}{L_c^*}.$$

When Q_k^* and Q_c^* are known, equation (14.14) can be used to determine the equilibrium value of output produced, Y^*. Equations (14.6) and (14.15) can be used to determine the equilibrium quantities Z_k^* and Z_c^*. The differences $(Z_k^* - Q_k^*)$ and $(Z_c^* - Q_c^*)$ are the economy's excess demand for capital goods and consumption goods, respectively, and they must satisfy the equation

$$p(Z_k^* - Q_k^*) + (Z_c^* - Q_c^*) = 0.$$

Thus far, we have worked with the aggregate variables Y, Z_k, and Z_c. Consider now the per capita version of these variables, defined as

$$y \equiv \frac{Y}{L} = \frac{L_c}{L} f_c + p \frac{L_k}{L} f_k, \tag{14.18}$$

$$z_k \equiv \frac{Z_k}{L} = \frac{sy}{p}, \tag{14.19}$$

$$z_c \equiv \frac{Z_c}{L} = (1 - s)y. \tag{14.20}$$

The per capita income (y) turns out to be of crucial importance to the analysis of long-run equilibrium. For this reason, let us devote the rest of this section to refining equation (14.18).

Note the following relationship:

$$\mu \equiv \frac{K}{L} = \frac{K_k + K_c}{L} = \frac{K_k}{L_k}\frac{L_k}{L} + \frac{K_c}{L_c}\frac{L_c}{L} = \frac{L_k}{L}\mu_k + \frac{L_c}{L}\mu_c. \tag{14.21}$$

Equation (14.21) can be solved simultaneously with the equation

$$\frac{L_k}{L} + \frac{L_c}{L} = \frac{L}{L} = 1$$

for the ratios L_k/L and L_c/L. Thus,

$$\frac{L_k}{L} = \frac{\mu - \mu_c}{\mu_k - \mu_c}, \qquad (14.22)$$

$$\frac{L_c}{L} = \frac{\mu_k - \mu}{\mu_k - \mu_c}. \qquad (14.23)$$

Substituting equations (14.22) and (14.23) into (14.18) gives us

$$y = \left(\frac{\mu_k - \mu}{\mu_k - \mu_c}\right)f_c + p\left(\frac{\mu - \mu_c}{\mu_k - \mu_c}\right)f_k. \qquad (14.24)$$

Equation (14.24) expresses the per capita income in terms of the ratios μ, μ_k, and μ_c and the price ratio, p. Now p is given in the international market and the ratios μ_c and μ_k are uniquely determined when p and μ are known. Thus, given p, we can determine the corresponding factor-price ratio w/r on the basis of which we can determine the optimum ratios μ_c^* and μ_k^*. The latter ratios will actually be observed if and only if μ falls between these ratios, for μ is always a weighted average of the *observed* ratios μ_c and μ_k. Thus, if $\mu_c^* < \mu_k^*$ and μ lies outside the region (μ_c^*, μ_k^*), the country will be specializing completely in the production of one commodity only, as is shown in chapters 8–9. In particular, if $\mu < \mu_c^* < \mu_k^*$, the economy will be specializing in the production of Q_c, with $\mu_c = \mu$ and $L_k = K_k = 0$. On the other hand, if $\mu_c^* < \mu_k^* < \mu$, the economy will be specializing in Q_k, with $\mu_k = \mu$ and $L_c = K_c = 0$. With this understanding, we can state that y is a function of μ. In particular, when both commodities are produced, y is given by equation (14.24), with $\mu_c = \mu_c^*$ and $\mu_k = \mu_k^*$; when the economy is specializing in Q_c, y is given by equation (14.25); and when the economy is specializing in Q_k, y is given by equation (14.26):

$$y = f_c(\mu) \qquad \text{(specialization in } Q_c\text{)}, \qquad (14.25)$$

$$y = pf_k(\mu) \qquad \text{(specialization in } Q_k\text{)}. \qquad (14.26)$$

In the short run, μ is of course given. With the passage of time, however, μ will in general change as K and L grow until long-run equilibrium is established. It is interesting to see how changes in μ affect y.

If the economy is specializing completely in one or the other commodity, it should be obvious from equations (14.25) and (14.26) that y changes in the same direction as μ, because $f_c' > 0$ and $f_k' > 0$. But what if the economy is producing both commodities? Is it still true that y changes in the same direction as μ? Differentiating y (as given by eq. [14.24]) with respect to μ, and remembering that $\mu_c = \mu_c^*$ and $\mu_k = \mu_k^*$, we get

$$\frac{dy}{d\mu} = \frac{f_c - pf_k}{\mu_c^* - \mu_k^*}. \tag{14.27}$$

What is the sign of the derivative $dy/d\mu$ in this case? Is it still positive? Although it may not be obvious, it is necessarily positive, for an increase in μ implies that the amount of capital allocated to the representative citizen increases. Thus, his production-possibilities frontier shifts outward, resulting in an increase of his income (y), however measured, at the original prices. Even though this intuitive reasoning shows that $dy/d\mu$ must be positive, we have to show that this is so by proving that the right-hand side of equation (14.27) is necessarily positive. How can this be done?

Observe that the value of output produced in the consumption-good industry (expressed in terms of the consumption good) per unit of labor employed in the consumption-good industry is given by f_c and that the value of output produced in the capital-good industry (expressed in terms of the consumption good) per unit of labor employed in the capital-good industry is given by pf_k. Further, the value of output produced in either industry is necessarily equal to the total cost of production of that output. Since factor prices are assumed identical for both industries, when one industry uses absolutely more labor and capital than the other industry, the value of output produced by the first industry must necessarily be higher than the value of output produced by the second. Now f_c and pf_k in equation (14.27) show the value of output produced in the consumption-good industry and the capital-good industry, respectively, per unit of labor employed in each industry. Since labor is only one of two factors, whether $f_c \gtrless pf_k$ depends upon the amount of capital per unit of labor used in each industry, that is, μ_c and μ_k. Thus, if $\mu_c > \mu_k$, f_c must necessarily be higher than pf_k, and if $\mu_c < \mu_k$, f_c must be lower than pf_k. That is,

$$\mu_c \gtrless \mu_k \leftrightarrow f_c \gtrless pf_k,$$

which necessarily implies that the right-hand side of equation (14.27) is positive.

A more direct mathematical proof of the conclusion that the right-hand side of equation (14.27) is positive can be given in several ways. The following is not the easiest, but it is a by-product of a further simplification of equation (14.24) that will be quite useful to our future investigations. Let us rewrite equation (14.24) as

$$y = \left(\frac{1}{\mu_k - \mu_c}\right)[\mu_k f_c - p\mu_c f_k + \mu(pf_k - f_c)]. \tag{14.24}'$$

The expression in brackets can be simplified as follows. However, first observe that from equations (14.11) and (14.12) it follows that

$$p(f_k - \mu_k f_k') = f_c - \mu_c f_c',$$

or

$$pf_k - f_c = p\mu_k f_k' - \mu_c f_c' = f_c'(\mu_k - \mu_c), \tag{14.28}$$

because $p = f_c'/f_k'$. The latter follows from equations (14.9) and (14.10). From equations (14.13) we have

$$\mu_k f_c = (w/r)\mu_k f_c' + \mu_k \mu_c f_c',$$

$$p\mu_c f_k = (w/r)\mu_c f_k' p + \mu_c \mu_k f_k' p = (w/r)\mu_c f_c' + \mu_c \mu_k f_c'.$$

Thus,

$$\mu_k f_c - p\mu_c f_k = (w/r)\mu_k f_c' + \mu_k \mu_c f_c' - (w/r)\mu_c f_c' - \mu_c \mu_k f_c'$$

$$= (w/r)f_c'(\mu_k - \mu_c). \tag{14.29}$$

Substituting equations (14.28) and (14.29) into equation (14.24)' and simplifying, we get

$$y = [(w/r) + \mu]f_c' = [(w/r) + \mu]pf_k'. \tag{14.30}$$

Thus, $dy/d\mu = f_c' > 0$.

For completeness, note that

$$\frac{dz_k}{d\mu} = \frac{s}{p}\frac{dy}{d\mu} > 0, \tag{14.31}$$

$$\frac{dz_c}{d\mu} = (1 - s)\frac{dy}{d\mu} > 0. \tag{14.32}$$

3. Equilibrium in the Long Run

The problem of long-run equilibrium is an interesting one. The short-run equilibrium considered in the preceding section is based on the assumption that the overall capital/labor ratio μ is historically given. The analysis is deliberately limited to the short run, where the system does not have the time to react on the given value of μ. In the long run, however, this assumption has to be dropped, and the system will be allowed to react on the overall capital/labor ratio. As long as μ changes through time, the short-run equilibrium solution will change continuously. Only when the value of μ is stabilized at some level will the short-run equilibrium solution be repeated continuously. This long-run equilibrium state of affairs is called *steady-state growth*. When steady-state growth is achieved, both labor and capital, as well as aggregate income, consumption, investment, exports, and imports, will all grow at the natural rate n. Only the per capita counterparts of these variables will remain constant. The major task in this section is to determine the long-run equilibrium value of μ and show whether or not a system will be driven automatically to that value, that is, whether or not a system will be stable.

Let us first consider a methodological problem. In a real economy, not only does μ change with the passage of time but other short-run parameters change as well. Thus, shifts in international supply and demand relations affect p, which in turn affects μ_c^* and μ_k^*; and technical progress causes the functions f_k and f_c to shift upward through time, and so on. Why then does our long-run analysis consider only the changes in the overall capital/labor ratio? The importance of changes in the various parameters of a system should not be underestimated, and certainly it would be foolish to imply that the changes of μ through time are somehow more important than the changes of any other short-run parameters. However, all other changes except those of the overall capital/labor ratio are *exogenous* in the sense that they cannot be determined by the equations of our model. They represent phenomena which our system takes as given. In other words, we lack the information necessary to predict the behavior of these short-run parameters through time. As a result, we make the easiest assumption, namely, that they remain constant. On the other hand, μ changes through time as a result of labor growth and capital accumulation. But whereas labor growth is also considered exogenous, capital accumulation is not. Therefore, despite the fact that at any point in time μ can be considered as given, its behavior through time as well as its long-run equilibrium value can be *endogenously* determined.

Let us now return to the analysis of the long-run equilibrium of our simple model. From equation (14.5), we have

$$\frac{dL}{dt} \equiv \dot{L} = nL_0 e^{nt} = nL,$$

or

$$\frac{\dot{L}}{L} = n. \tag{14.33}$$

The rate of increase of the capital stock dK/dt, or $\dot{K}$, is given by $\dot{K} = Z_k = (sY)/p$. Thus,

$$\frac{\dot{K}}{L} = z_k = s\frac{y}{p}. \tag{14.34}$$

Differentiating the ratio $\mu \equiv K/L$ with respect to time (t) and substituting from equations (14.33) and (14.34), we get

$$\frac{d\mu}{dt} \equiv \dot{\mu} = \frac{L\dot{K} - K\dot{L}}{L^2} = \frac{\dot{K}}{L} - \frac{K}{L}\frac{\dot{L}}{L} = \frac{sy}{p} - \mu n. \tag{14.35}$$

Steady-state growth occurs when $\dot{\mu} = 0$, that is, when $s(y/p) - \mu n = 0$, or

$$y/p = \mu \frac{n}{s}. \tag{14.36}$$

Equation (14.36), which is the condition for steady-state growth, can also be cast in terms of the natural rate of growth of labor (n), of the marginal propensity to save, and of the capital/output ratio (v). Thus, rewrite equation (14.36) as

$$n = \frac{ys}{p\mu} = \frac{(Y/L)s}{p(K/L)} = \frac{s}{p(K/Y)} = \frac{s}{v}. \tag{14.36'}$$

Note that $v \equiv pK/Y$, that is, capital has to be measured in the same units as income.

Let us introduce the variables

$$\phi \equiv \phi(\mu; p) = y/p, \tag{14.37}$$

$$\psi \equiv \psi(\mu; n, s) = \mu \frac{n}{s}. \tag{14.38}$$

The long-run equilibrium condition (14.36) can now be rewritten as

$$\phi(\mu; p) = \psi(\mu; n, s). \tag{14.36'}$$

Both ϕ and ψ are functions of μ. In addition, changes in p affect only the function ϕ, whereas changes in either n or s affect only the function ψ. Let us attempt the solution of equation (14.36)' graphically.

In figure 14.2, the ratios μ, μ_c, and μ_k are measured along the horizontal axis, moving rightward from the origin; the variables f_c, f_k, ϕ, and ψ are measured along the vertical axis, moving upward from the origin. The functions f_c, f_k, and ψ are given by the synonymous curves in the first quadrant. The function $\psi = \mu(n/s)$ is given by a vector through the origin with slope equal to the ratio n/s. The functions $f_c(\mu_c)$ and $f_k(\mu_k)$ start from the origin, by assumption, and they are both strictly concave in the sense that the tangent to either curve at any point will lie totally above the curve except at the point of tangency itself.[4] The strict concavity of the functions f_c and f_k is the result of diminishing returns to capital. In particular, the slope of the f_c curve (f_c') at any point gives the marginal physical product of capital in the consumption-goods industry. The slope of the f_k curve (f_k') at any point gives the marginal physical product of capital in the capital-goods industry. Since $f_c'' < 0$ and $f_k'' < 0$ (because of the assumption

---

4. A function $f(x)$ is said to be concave in a certain region if, for any two points x_1, and x_2 in the specified region, the following relationship holds

$$f[\lambda x_1 + (1 - \lambda)x_2] \geq \lambda f(x_1) + (1 - \lambda) f(x_2), \qquad o \leq \lambda \leq 1.$$

It is *strictly* concave if the strict inequality holds for all λ such that $o < \lambda < 1$ and $x_1 \neq x_2$.

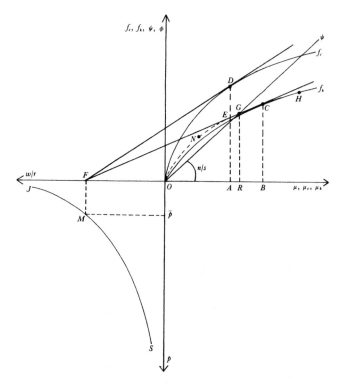

that the marginal physical product of capital is diminishing in both industries), both the f_c curve and the f_k curve are strictly concave.

To determine the long-run equilibrium value of μ, the function $\phi = y/p$ must be represented graphically. As noted earlier, y is a function of μ. In particular, it is given by equations (14.25), (14.26), and (14.30). But how can the variable y/p or ϕ be represented graphically? Consider the third quadrant of figure 14.2. Along the horizontal axis, we measure, moving leftward from the origin, the factor-price ratio w/r, and along the vertical axis, moving downward from the origin, we measure the commodity-price ratio $p = p_k/p_c$. The curve *JMS* in the third quadrant shows the familiar one-directional relation of commodity prices to factor prices. Thus, starting with the commodity-price ratio $\bar{p}$ given in the international market, we determine the corresponding factor-price ratio *OF* which will prevail in the country, in the absence of complete specialization. Given any value of the factor-price ratio, such as *OF*, we can determine the optimum capital/labor ratios of both industries as follows. Draw from point *F* the tangents to the curves f_c and f_k as shown by *FD* and *FEC*, respectively. Then project the tangency points *D* and *C* on the horizontal axis as shown by the broken lines

DA and *CB*. The horizontal distance *OA* is the optimum capital/labor ratio in the consumption-goods industry, and the distance *OB* is the optimum capital/labor ratio in the capital-goods industry. It should be noted that in figure 14.2 it is implicitly assumed that the capital good is capital intensive relative to the consumption good for all factor prices. This is confirmed by the fact that *OB* > *OA*. The real question, however, concerns the logic behind this construction. Why can the optimum capital/labor ratios μ_c^* and μ_k^* be determined in the fashion just described? The answer is implicit in the analysis of short-run equilibrium.

Consider any point on the f_c curve, such as point *D*. At *D*, the average physical product of labor in the Q_c industry is given by the vertical distance *AD*, the capital/labor ratio (μ_c) by the horizontal distance *OA*, and the marginal physical product of capital (f_c') by the slope of the f_c curve at *D*, that is, *AD/FA*. What is the marginal rate of substitution of labor for capital at point *D*? By definition, we must have

$$MRS_{LK}^c = \frac{MPP_L^c}{MPP_K^c} = \frac{f_c - \mu_c f_c'}{f_c'} = \frac{f_c}{f_c'} - \mu_c$$

$$= \frac{AD}{(AD/FA)} - OA = FA - OA = FO. \qquad (14.39)$$

That is, the marginal rate of substitution of labor for capital at *D* is given by the distance *FO*, that is, the intercept of the tangent to the f_c curve at *D* with the (w/r) axis. Repeating the same exercise for the capital-good industry, we can easily establish a similar relationship. We already know that when both commodities are produced, the marginal rate of substitution of labor for capital in either industry has to be equal to the common factor-price ratio w/r. Hence, the technique of figure 14.2.

Let us derive the $\phi = y/p$ curve in the first quadrant of figure 14.2. All we have to do is apply equations (14.25), (14.26), and (14.30), after dividing both sides of these equations by p. Thus, if the overall capital/labor ratio μ is larger than *OB* (i.e., the optimum capital/labor ratio of the capital-intensive industry), $\phi = y/p$ will be given by the f_k curve because the economy will be specializing in the production of the capital good. Further, for $OA \leq \mu \leq OB$, $\phi = y/p$ will be given by the straight-line segment *EC*. Finally, for $\mu < OA$, $\phi = y/p$ will be given by f_c/p, as shown by the broken curve *OE*, because the country will be specializing in the production of the consumption good.

Note that the broken curve *OE* has been drawn to lie totally above the f_k curve in the region $\mu \leq OA$, except at the origin, where the two curves coincide. Is this necessary, or is it because the curve has simply been drawn that way? The broken curve *OE* must necessarily lie totally above the f_k curve. This follows from the fact that, in this region, the economy specializes in the production of the consumption good. This pattern of specialization necessarily implies that the per capita income, however measured, is at a maximum. In other words, the income contour line lies farther from the origin when the economy produces at the intercept of the production-possibilities frontier with the Q_c axis, as compared with any other point, on the frontier, and, in particular, with the intercept of the frontier with the Q_k axis.

Steady-state growth occurs at the intersection of the ϕ curve (i.e., $ONEGCH$) with the ψ curve (i.e., the vector OG). That is, long-run equilibrium occurs at point G, with the overall capital/labor ratio given by the distance OR.

In this illustration, the economy necessarily produces both commodities, since $OA < OR < OB$. But this is not always so. For instance, if the natural rate of growth of labor were a little higher, so that the ψ curve were a little steeper than the vector OE (not drawn), such as the vector ON (not drawn), the economy's long-run equilibrium capital/labor ratio would be smaller than OA and the economy would specialize completely in the production of the consumption good which is the labor-intensive commodity. On the other hand, if n were a little smaller, so that the ψ curve were flatter than the vector OC (not drawn), such as the vector OH (not drawn), the overall long-run equilibrium capital/labor ratio would be higher than OB and the economy would specialize completely in the production of the capital-intensive commodity, that is, Q_k.

The equilibrium point G in figure 14.2 is globally stable. That is, if the economy starts with a capital/labor ratio different from OR, there will be a continuous change through time until $\mu = OR$. Why? For one thing, G is the only intersection of the ϕ curve with the ψ curve. In addition, for values of μ in the region $\mu < OR$, $\phi - \psi > 0$ or $y/p - (\mu n)/s = \dot{\mu}/s > 0$, that is, $\dot{\mu} > 0$. But a *positive* $\dot{\mu}$ means that μ *increases* through time. On the other hand, for values of μ in the region $\mu > OR$, $\phi - \psi < 0$ or $y/p - (\mu n)/s = \dot{\mu}/s < 0$, that is, $\dot{\mu} < 0$, so a *negative* $\dot{\mu}$ means that μ *decreases* through time. Accordingly, irrespective of the initial capital/labor ratio, the economy will sooner or later attain and maintain the equilibrium capital/labor ratio OR; that is, it will attain the steady-state growth path which, as figure 14.2 shows, is uniquely determined.

The long-run equilibrium portrayed in figure 14.2 is unique. But is this an inherent property of our model, or is it something accidental? A closer look at figure 14.2 will show that, if a long-run equilibrium exists at all, it will have to be unique and globally stable. Why? Because the ψ curve is a vector through the origin, while the ϕ curve is concave. In particular, the ϕ curve is concave in the region EC but strictly concave elsewhere. Equilibrium can occur in the concave region EC if, and only if, the ψ curve is steeper than EC, that is, if, and only if, $n/s > f_c'(\mu_c^*) = p f_k'(\mu_k^*)$. Put differently, equilibrium cannot occur in the region EC when the ψ curve is parallel to EC.

Therefore, if equilibrium exists, it has to be unique because the ψ curve cannot intersect the ϕ curve more than once.

Another important question arises in relation to the existence of a steady-state growth path. Does it always exist? Or better, what are the necessary and sufficient conditions for its existence? From figure 14.2, it should be clear that two conditions are necessary and sufficient: (*a*) the tangent to the ϕ curve at the origin must be steeper than the ψ curve, and (*b*) the ϕ curve must become flatter than the ψ curve past a certain point. Each condition is necessary, and together they are sufficient for the existence of a steady-state growth path. Thus, if the ψ curve (or vector) is steeper than the tangent to the ϕ curve at the origin, no intersection will ever occur between the two curves other than the origin. The overall capital/labor ratio will fall continuously through time. This case would arise if the natural rate of growth of labor (n) is exceedingly high and the average propensity to save (s) exceedingly low. Eventually, the economy disappears, and thus this case is uninteresting. On the other hand, if the economy is so productive that the marginal physical product of capital in the capital-goods industry (i.e., the slope of the f_k curve) never falls below the ratio n/s, again no intersection would occur between the two curves (ϕ and ψ), but this time, the overall capital/labor ratio would tend to rise continuously. This would certainly be the case if n were zero and f_k' remained nonnegative throughout. In what follows, assume that a unique, globally stable, long-run equilibrium exists.

The first condition, namely, that the tangent to the ϕ curve at the origin be steeper than the ψ curve, can be stated as $(1/p)f_c'(0) > n/s$. But this condition seems to depend on p. Can we reformulate it so that it is independent of p? We can do so with a slightly stronger condition. Recall that the broken curve OE must necessarily lie above the f_k curve in the region $\mu < OA$. In general, the ϕ curve will not lie below the f_k curve irrespective of p, if we assume, of course, that Q_k is capital intensive relative to Q_c. Therefore, a stronger condition would be for the ψ curve to be flatter than the slope of the f_k curve at the origin, i.e., $f_k'(0) > n/s$. This condition also holds in the case where Q_c is capital intensive relative to Q_k.

Although the pattern of specialization is perfectly determined once the steady-state growth path is attained, nothing can be said about the pattern of specialization during the transitional period when the system is moving toward long-run equilibrium. Any pattern of specialization is possible during this transitional period, as can be verified from figure 14.2. But even when the steady-state growth path is attained, we cannot be sure, from the construction of figure 14.2, which commodity is exported and which imported, unless the economy is completely specialized in the production of a single commodity. This does not mean, of course, that at point G the pattern of specialization is indeterminate. On the contrary, it is perfectly determinate, but it is not obvious from figure 14.2 which is the exported and which the imported commodity. However, all the information is available for the determination of the pattern of specialization at point G. Thus, the per capita demand for newly produced capital goods is given by $z_k = s(RG)$. On the other hand, the per capita output of capital goods, say y_k, is given by

$$y_k = \frac{L_k}{L} f_k(\mu_k^*) = \frac{\mu - \mu_c^*}{\mu_k^* - \mu_c^*} f_k(\mu_k^*) = \frac{OR - OA}{OB - OA} BC = \frac{AR}{AB} BC.$$

In addition, applying equation (14.24) directly gives us

$$RG = \frac{RB}{AB} AE + \frac{AR}{AB} BC,$$

or

$$z_k = s(RG) = s\left(\frac{RB}{AB} AE + \frac{AR}{AB} BC\right).$$

The imports of capital goods will be zero if $z_k = y_k$, that is,

$$s = \frac{(AR)(BC)}{(RB)(AE) + (AR)(BC)} \equiv s_0 < 1. \tag{14.40}$$

On the other hand, if $s > s_0$, the capital good will be imported (i.e., $z_k > y_k$), and if $s < s_0$, the capital good will be exported (i.e., $z_k < y_k$). It should be clear now why the pattern of specialization is not obvious from figure 14.2. We do not know what the value of s is, because an infinite number of values of s is consistent with equilibrium at point G.

The assumption that the capital good is capital intensive relative to the consumption good can be reversed and the long-run equilibrium of the system determined along the lines of the analysis of this section.

4. Comparative Dynamics

So far, the discussion has been limited to the problems of uniqueness, existence, and stability of long-run equilibrium under the assumption that the parameters p, n, and s assume certain specific values. It would be interesting to consider the effects of changes in these parameters on the long-run equilibrium values of the variables in our model. For instance, how would the long-run equilibrium capital/labor ratio (or the rate of growth, or per capita consumption, or per capita income, and so on) be affected by a change in p, or n, or s? All these are questions of *comparative dynamics*. Despite the fact that there are not enough equations to determine the behavior of these parameters through time, changes in these parameters will nevertheless occur. In addition, from the point of view of policy, if the government could somehow affect these parameters, what would be the best policy?

Any changes in n or s affect the ψ curve only, and any changes in p affect the ϕ curve only. Let us start with the effects of a once-and-for-all change in the natural rate of growth of labor, n.

Suppose that n increases from, say, n_0 to n_1. How does the new steady-state growth path compare with the old? In terms of figure 14.2, as n increases, the ψ curve tends to become steeper. This implies that the equilibrium capital/labor ratio and thus per capita income will necessarily fall; and since per capita income falls, per capita consumption and per capita investment also fall. In addition, the per capita output of the consumption-goods industry (i.e., the labor-intensive commodity) will tend to rise and the per capita output of the capital-goods industry will tend to fall. In other words, $y_c \equiv (L_c/L)f_c(\mu_c^*)$ rises and $y_k \equiv (L_k/L)f_k(\mu_k^*)$ falls. This follows from the Rybczynski theorem studied in chapter 13, but we can also see this directly from figure 14.2. If n increases so much that the ψ curve becomes steeper than the vector OE (not drawn), the economy will specialize completely in the production of Q_c. But what if the new equilibrium falls in the region EG, where the country continues to produce both commodities? As we saw earlier, $y_k = (AR)(BC)/AB$; and as equilibrium moves closer to point E, the distance AR shrinks (while BC and AB remain constant), causing y_k to fall. In a similar fashion, it can be shown that

$$y_c = \frac{\mu_k^* - \mu^*}{\mu_k^* - \mu_c^*} f_c(\mu_c^*) = \frac{RB}{AB} AD.$$

Thus, as μ falls, RB rises while AB and AD remain the same; hence, y_c rises. Note that if the new equilibrium occurs in the region EG of the ϕ curve, the economy will continue to produce both commodities and the factor-price ratio will continue to be given by OF. But what if the new equilibrium occurs in the region ONE and the economy specializes in the production of Q_c? Will the factor-price ratio remain constant in this case, too? Obviously not. The economy will be producing somewhere along the region OD of the f_c curve, and the tangent to the f_c curve in this region will necessarily intersect the (w/r)-axis to the right of F. Therefore, the factor-price ratio will necessarily fall. Note too that all aggregates in the system $(K, \dot{K}, Z_c, Y, Q_c, Q_k,$ and imports and exports) will now grow at the faster rate n_1.

Let us turn now to the parameter s. How does a once-and-for-all change in s affect the long-run equilibrium of the system? From figure 14.2, it can be shown that an increase in s will cause the overall capital/labor ratio to rise and a decrease in s will cause it to fall. Therefore, when s falls, the per capita income also falls, and when s rises, the per capita income rises. We know this from the fact that the ϕ curve is upward sloping, implying a higher per capita income in terms of the capital good as μ rises. Does this also mean that the per capita consumption falls when s falls and it rises when s rises? Not necessarily. As s changes, per capita consumption can go either way despite the fact that the per capita income will change in the same direction as s. In particular, per capita consumption is given by equation (14.20), or

$$z_c = (1 - s)y = (1 - s)p\phi. \qquad (14.20)'$$

Steady-state growth requires that equation (14.36) be satisfied. But equation (14.36) can be solved for s. Thus,

$$s = n\mu/\phi. \qquad (8.36)''$$

Substituting equation (14.36)'' into equation (14.20)', we get

$$z_c = (1 - s)p\phi = \left(1 - \frac{n\mu}{\phi}\right)p\phi = (\phi - n\mu)p.$$

Since p is assumed constant, by an appropriate choice of the units of measurement we can make it equal to unity. Thus,

$$z_c = \phi - n\mu. \qquad (14.41)$$

Equation (14.41) is given graphically in figures 14.3. The ϕ curve is the familiar curve derived in figure 14.2. A vector is drawn through the origin with slope equal to n. In figure 14.3A, the straight-line segment RH is flatter than the vector $n\mu$; in figure 14.3B, they are parallel. The per capita consumption is now given by the vertical distances between the ϕ curve and the vector $n\mu$. Draw another curve (z_c) which shows directly the vertical

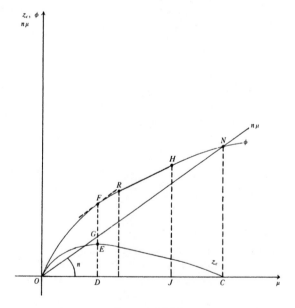

FIGURE 14.3A

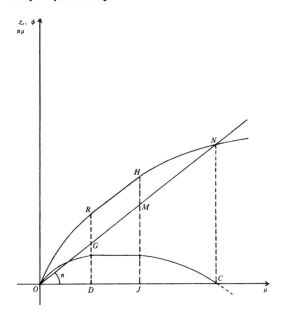

FIGURE 14.3B

differences between the ϕ curve and the vector $n\mu$ (i.e., per capita consumption) for all values of μ. Observe that z_c is initially rising, because for the existence of long-run equilibrium it is required that the slope of the ϕ curve at the origin be greater than n/s. Since $s < 1$, the slope to the ϕ curve at the origin will definitely be greater than n if it is already greater than n/s ($> n$). Beyond a certain point, the z_c curve becomes downward sloping. In fact, beyond a certain point, per capita consumption becomes negative. Nevertheless, this part of the curve is totally irrelevant, because equilibrium will certainly take place in the region where z_c is positive. Graphically, z_c becomes negative for values of μ beyond the intersection of the ϕ curve with the vector $n\mu$. Thus, given the value of s, we can determine the long-run equilibrium of the system by rotating the vector $n\mu$ upward until its slope becomes equal to n/s. This will be the ψ curve of figure 14.2, so equilibrium can be determined as before. As s increases, the ψ curve becomes flatter and the equilibrium capital/labor ratio as well as the per capita income necessarily rise. On the other hand, as s falls, the ψ curve becomes steeper and the equilibrium capital/labor ratio as well as the per capita income necessarily fall. However, per capita consumption does not behave in this fashion. If the initial equilibrium capital/labor ratio is smaller than OD, per capita consumption will tend to move in the same direction as s. But if the initial equilibrium capital/labor ratio is larger than OD, as s increases per capita consumption will either fall immediately (fig. 14.3A) or remain constant for a while and then fall (fig. 14.3B).

From the preceding discussion, it follows that per capita consumption is maximized at a specific value of μ (as shown in fig. 14.3A) or over a certain region of values of μ (as illustrated in fig. 14.3B). Since there is a one-to-one correspondence between μ and s, there will be a certain value (or region of values) of s at which per capita consumption is maximized. How can we determine the value(s) of the average propensity to save for which per capita consumption is maximized? In figure 14.3A, per capita consumption is maximized when $\mu = OD$. At that point, we have $\phi = DF$. Long-run equilibrium will now occur at point F (where $\mu = OD$) if, and only if, the vector ψ coincides with the vector OF (not drawn), that is, if $n/s = DF/OD$ or $s = n(OD)/DF$. But $n = DG/OD$. Therefore

$$ s = \frac{DG}{OD}\frac{OD}{DF} = \frac{DG}{DF} < 1. $$

Figure 14.3B illustrates the case where per capita consumption is maximized over a range of values of μ and s. In this case, per capita consumption is maximized for any value of μ in the region $OD \leq \mu \leq OJ$. The corresponding range of s is, of course, $DG/DR \leq s \leq JM/JH$.

The optimum value of s is uniquely determined only when maximization of per capita consumption implies complete specialization in one or the other commodity. If both commodities are produced, there will be an infinite number of values of s and μ that will be compatible with that maximum level of per capita consumption. In particular, per capita consumption is maximized when $dz_c/d\mu = \phi' - n = 0$, or

$$ \phi' = n. \tag{14.42} $$

That is, per capita consumption is maximized when the slope of the ϕ curve is equal to the rate of growth of labor. If the slope of the straight-line segment (RH) of the ϕ curve, where the economy is actually producing both commodities, is equal to n, as in figure 14.3B, the z_c curve will become horizontal over that region. Thus, maximal per capita consumption occurs over this whole range of values of μ and a corresponding range of values of s.

Why should there be this important difference between the case of complete specialization and the case of complete diversification (i.e., the case where both commodities are produced)? Let us first attempt a common-sense interpretation of equation (14.42). Assume that the economy has been on a steady-state growth path—not necessarily the maximum per capita consumption path. Had μ been higher all along, per capita income would have been higher. How much higher depends on the marginal product of capital expressed in terms of the consumption good (MPP_k), since per capita income is measured in terms of the consumption good. Therefore, when the economy is specializing in the consumption good, we have $MPP_k = f'_c(\mu_c)$; when it is specializing in the capital good, we have $MPP_k = pf'_k(\mu_k)$; and when it is producing both commodities, we have $MPP_k = f'_c(\mu_c) = pf'_k(\mu_k)$. Thus, having a bit more capital per unit of labor, that is, $\Delta\mu$, at this time would yield $MPP_k \, \Delta\mu$ more per capita output. But not all of this is available for consumption. Having a bit more capital per unit of labor now commits the economy (under the steady-state growth rules of the game) to some additional investment now and in the future, to keep the slightly higher μ constant: K and L must grow at the fixed rate n in long-run equilibrium. In particular, an extra bit of capital per unit of labor ($\Delta\mu$) now means that an output of $n \, \Delta\mu$ of capital goods (or $np \, \Delta\mu$ of consumption goods) per unit of labor is required simply to maintain μ at its higher level. Clearly, if $MPP_k \, \Delta\mu > np \, \Delta\mu$ or $MPP_k > np$, a larger μ will yield some extra per capita consumption now and forever. If $MPP_k < np$, a larger μ now will imply a smaller per capita consumption now and forever. Thus, per capita consumption is at a maximum when $MPP_k = np$. Note that $MPP_k = dy/d\mu$; hence, the equation $MPP_k = np$ is equivalent to equation (14.42).

When the economy is specializing completely in the production of one commodity only, as μ increases, MPP_k falls continuously; therefore, there exists one, and only one, value of μ at which equation (14.42) is satisfied. However, when the country is producing both commodities, MPP_k does not necessarily fall as μ increases. This is because μ is a weighted average of μ_c and μ_k; and as μ changes, the weights of μ_c and μ_k change, leaving μ_c and μ_k themselves unchanged. Thus, MPP_k remains constant in this range, as evidenced by the linear segment RH of figures 14.3. If this constant value of MPP_k (along the straight-line segment RH) coincides with the product np (which is constant by assumption), there will be a whole range of values of μ giving rise to the same maximum per capita consumption.

The condition for maximum per capita consumption is described in the literature as the "golden rule" condition (or as the "neo-neoclassical growth theorem"). It should be noted, however, that it is a technical condition and not a normative rule. Thus, if the economy's actual capital/labor ratio were larger than the "golden rule" capital/labor ratio, per capita consumption could be raised both immediately and in the future by reducing the average propensity to save to the "golden rule" level. In this case, the "golden rule" is a normative prescription for increasing welfare, unless the economy derives utility from the mere possession of capital in addition to the utility it derives from consumption. But if the economy's actual capital/labor ratio ($\bar{\mu}$) is smaller than the "golden rule" capital/labor ratio (μ_g), the increase in the average propensity to save required to raise $\bar{\mu}$ to μ_g would entail a sacrifice of immediate consumption for the sake of higher future consumption. This would involve an intertemporal choice between present and future consumption, the basis for which is not provided by the model.

These comments hold not only for the case where per capita consumption is maximized at a specific value of μ (as shown in fig. 14.3A) but also in the case where it is maximized over a certain region of values of μ (as shown in fig. 14.3B). But in the latter case the argument is slightly more complicated. Thus, in figure 14.3B, per capita consumption is maximized for any value of μ in the region $OD \leq \mu \leq OJ$. As noted earlier, the corresponding range of s is $DG/DR \leq s \leq JM/JH$. If the actual value of s is smaller than DG/DR, per capita consumption can increase in the future only if immediate consumption is sacrificed; therefore, in this case the "golden rule" cannot serve as a normative prescription for increasing welfare because the model does not provide for the required intertemporal choice between present and future consumption. Now assume that the actual average propensity to save is higher than JM/JH. Per capita consumption could increase now and in the future if the average propensity to save were allowed to fall to JM/JH. But should s be allowed to fall below JM/JH? Yes, it should be allowed to fall to DG/DR, the smallest value of s which maximizes per capita consumption, for as s falls from JM/JH to DG/DR, current consumption increases without any sacrifice of future consumption. This is clearly a welfare gain, under the proviso given in the preceding paragraph.

To summarize, as s increases, the overall capital/labor ratio (μ) and per capita income (y) increase. Per capita consumption (z_c) may increase, decrease, or remain constant.

Suppose now that, as the average propensity to save, s, increases, the per capita consumption, z_c, increases also. Is it possible for the rate of growth of z_c to be higher than the rate of growth of y? Observe that the rate of growth of y is a weighted average of the rate of growth of z_c and z_k, because

$$y = z_c + pz_k, \tag{14.43}$$

$$\Delta y = \Delta z_c + p\,\Delta z_k, \tag{14.44}$$

$$\frac{\Delta y}{y} = \frac{\Delta z_c}{y} + p\,\frac{\Delta z_k}{y} = \left(\frac{\Delta z_c}{z_c}\right)\left(\frac{z_c}{y}\right) + \left(\frac{\Delta z_k}{z_k}\right)\left(\frac{pz_k}{y}\right). \tag{14.45}$$

From equation (14.19) it is clear that z_k increases faster than y, since both s and y increase. Accordingly, the rate of growth of y must be smaller than the rate of growth of z_k but higher than the rate of growth of z_c. This is sensible, because as s and thus μ increase, a larger amount of saving will be needed to maintain μ at the higher level. This makes the rate of growth of z_c fall short of the rate of growth of y.

How does a change in s affect the long-run equilibrium volume of trade? Contrary to the comparative-static analysis of the preceding chapter, where the long-run equilibrium volume of trade was uniquely determined before and after growth, in the present case the aggregate volume of trade is growing before and after the change in s at the natural rate of growth (n). Accordingly, we must either compare the aggregate volume of trade before with the aggregate volume of trade after the change in s at a single point in time or, better, compare the per capita volume of trade before with the per capita volume of trade after the change in s, because the per capita volume of trade is indeed uniquely determined. How does a change in s then affect the per capita volume of trade? To illustrate, assume that s increases. We distinguish among the following three cases.

a) Assume that our economy is specializing in the production of Q_c before and after the increase in s. Then $\mu_c = \mu$. As s increases, $\mu = \mu_c$ increases, too. Therefore, $y = f_c(\mu_c)$ increases. Since Q_c is exported by assumption, the per capita volume of trade, measured by the difference $(f_c - z_c)$, will definitely increase, because f_c ($= y$) increases faster than z_c. In fact, z_c might even decrease.

In terms of the terminology adopted in chapter 12, in the present case the production effect is neutral while the consumption effect is either protrade biased or ultra protrade biased. Hence, the overall effect of the increase in s on the per capita volume of trade is either protrade biased or ultra protrade biased.

b) Assume that our economy is specializing in the production of Q_k before and after the increase in s. Then $\mu_k = \mu$. As s increases, $\mu = \mu_k$ increases, too. Therefore, f_k ($= y/p$) increases. Now the volume of trade, measured by the amount of Q_c imported, may increase or decrease. But if the volume of trade actually increases, it cannot increase as fast as y.

Here again, in terms of the terminology adopted in chapter 12, the production effect is necessarily neutral while the consumption effect is either antitrade biased or ultra antitrade biased. Accordingly, the overall effect of the increase in s on the per capita volume of trade is either antitrade biased or ultra antitrade biased.

c) Assume that both commodities (i.e., Q_c and Q_k) are being produced before and after the increase in s. Here, an increase in s will cause μ and y to increase. However, the per capita output of the consumption-goods industry $(L_c f_c/L)$ will fall and the per capita output of the capital-goods industry $(L_k f_k/L)$ will rise. But what happens to the per capita volume of trade? It appears that anything is possible, except in the case where Q_c is exported and z_c increases with s. Then the per capita volume of trade will definitely fall. This is so because the per capita volume of trade is given by the difference $(f_c - z_c)$, or, if we apply the terminology of chapter 12, because in this special case the production effect is ultra antitrade biased while the consumption effect is protrade biased. In all other cases, the outcome cannot be determined by a prior analysis.

With regard to the parameter p, how do changes in p affect the ϕ curve only? Consider figure 14.4. When $p = p_0$, the ϕ curve is given by $OE'C'H$. When p increases to $p = p_1$, the corresponding factor-price ratio falls from OF to OF' and points A', B', C', D', and E' shift to A, B, C, D, and E, respectively. The new ϕ curve at $p = p_1$ is given by $OECH$. That is, as p rises, the ϕ curve shifts downward and to the right in the region $\mu < OB'$; it remains stable in the region $\mu \geq OB'$. Reversing the procedure, we can also find out how the ϕ curve shifts when p falls. Thus, if p were initially at

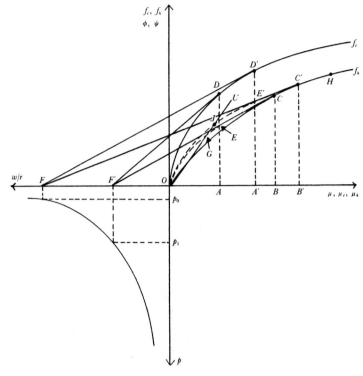

FIGURE 14.4

p_1 and fell to p_0, the ϕ curve would shift from $OECH$ to $OE'C'H$. In other words, as p falls, the ϕ curve shifts upward and to the left in the region $\mu < OB'$; it remains stable in the region $\mu \geq OB'$. Point B' is not fixed; it depends on the lower of the two values of p considered.

The limit of the ϕ curve as p increases beyond bounds is the f_k curve itself. Thus, as p increases, point C will travel along the f_k curve toward the origin; its limiting position is surely the origin. The broken part (OE, or OE') of the ϕ curve will thus disappear completely as p increases beyond a certain point.

Suppose now that the economy has been on a steady-state growth path for some time and then p changes. The system, given sufficient time, will move to another steady-state growth path. How does the new path compare with the old? If the economy was originally specializing in the production of Q_k, an increase in p will leave the intersection between the ϕ curve and the vector ψ totally unaffected. This is so because, in terms of figure 14.4, if $p = p_0$ and the economy is specializing in Q_k, equilibrium would occur, on the ϕ curve, to the right of point C', such as point H. But as we have seen, when p increases, the ϕ curve remains stable in the region $\mu > OB'$, that is, beyond point C'. Hence, the intersection at H will not be affected. Does this mean that the new steady-state growth path will be identical to the old? Not in every respect. The long-run equilibrium capital/labor ratio and ϕ (i.e., y/p) will, of course, remain the same. But the per capita income expressed in Q_c (i.e., y) and the per capita consumption z_c will rise in proportion to p. This follows from the fact that the ratio y/p remains constant while p rises. The per capita investment, however, given by $z_k = s\phi$, will necessarily remain the same. Therefore, under these circumstances, an increase in p (i.e., an improvement in the terms of trade) will simply raise the per capita consumption and hence the per capita imports of Q_c in proportion to p and y. Note that since μ remains constant, the production-possibilities frontier of the respresentative citizen will necessarily remain the same before and after the increase in p. His consumption-possibilities frontier will change, though, because of the change in p. In particular, the production point will remain the same, but the absorption point will imply higher consumption of Q_c but the same investment in Q_k compared with the initial steady-state growth path. The preceding argument can be reversed for moderate decreases in p—moderate in the sense that the economy continues to specialize completely in Q_k after the reduction in p.

Suppose now that at the initial steady-state growth path the economy is specializing in the production of the consumption good. How does a change in p affect this path in the long run? That is, how does the new path compare with the old? In this case, the initial equilibrium occurs somewhere in the region OE or OE' (fig. 14.4), as the case may be. This part of the ϕ curve shifts when p changes. Therefore, even the equilibrium capital/labor ratio will have to change in this case. Suppose that the vector OU in figure 14.4 is the ψ vector. When $p = p_0$, equilibrium occurs at point J. On the other hand, when $p = p_1$, equilibrium occurs at point G. It follows that, as p rises, μ falls; and as p falls, μ rises. That is, p and the equilibrium capital/labor ratio move, in this case, in opposite directions. What happens to the per capita income (y), per capita consumption (z_c), and per capita investment (z_k) as p changes in this case? Recall that the economy is assumed to specialize completely in the production of Q_c before and after the change in p. Accordingly, y is identical with $f_c(\mu)$. As p falls (i.e., as the terms of trade improve), μ increases and thus f_c increases. Per capita consumption necessarily increases proportionally to per capita income, since $z_c = (1 - s)y$. On the other hand, per capita investment rises more than proportionally to per capita income, because $z_k = sy/p$ and y/p rises faster than y because p falls. Finally, since the economy is specializing in Q_c, it must be importing Q_k. Hence, z_k shows per capita imports of the economy. Per capita imports therefore increase more than proportionally to per capita income. But how can this be so? Since per capita exports are given by $y - z_c = sy$, per capita exports must be increasing proportionally to y. These two conclusions can be reconciled in the presence of balanced trade because z_k is not measured in the same units as y and z_c. Thus, measuring z_k in terms of Q_c gives us $pz_k = sy$, and pz_k does increase proportionally to y. The volume of trade therefore increases proportionally to per capita income. This discussion can be reversed for moderate increases in p, that is, increases in p which do not make it profitable for the economy to produce both commodities.

Let us analyze the effects of a once-and-for-all change in p when the economy is producing both commodities before and after the change. Can we still predict the changes in μ, y, z_c, z_k, and per capita exports and imports? Suppose that $p = p_1$ initially, as shown in figure 14.4. In this case, the ψ vector (not drawn) must intersect the ϕ curve somewhere along the straight-line segment EC. Let p fall to p_0 and assume that at the new steady-state growth path the economy continues to produce both commodities; that is, the ψ vector intersects the new ϕ curve somewhere in the region $E'C'$. Two things are obvious from figure 14.4: (a) the new equilibrium capital/labor ratio must necessarily be larger than the old, and (b) f_c, f_k, and ϕ are necessarily larger at the new steady state. The first conclusion follows directly from the fact that, as p falls, the ϕ curve shifts upward in the region $\mu < OB'$. This also shows that the equilibrium value of ϕ (i.e., y/p) must necessarily be larger at the new equilibrium for two reasons: the ϕ curve shifts upward, and μ increases. Finally, f_c and f_k increase, because, as p falls, both industries tend to become more capital intensive. In particular, μ_c increases from OA to OA', and μ_k increases from OB to OB'. Since z_k is proportional to y/p, it must necessarily increase proportionally to y/p. But it will increase more than proportionally to y because p is lower at the new equilibrium and, therefore, the rate of increase of y/p must be higher than the rate of increase in y. Does y necessarily increase? No. Note that there is a minimum p, say p_m, at which the economy is specializing completely in the production of Q_c but the marginal rate of transformation (i.e., the slope of the production-possibilities frontier at the Q_c-axis intercept) is equal to p_m. Further, there is a maximum p, say p_M, at which the economy is completely specializing in the production of Q_k and with $MRT = p_M$. Assume that $p > p_M$ and let it decrease continuously to p_m. In the region $p \geq p_M$, the economy will continue to maintain the same capital/labor ratio and specialize completely in Q_k. Since $y = pf_k$ in this region, y will fall proportionally to p. The moment p falls below p_M, μ tends to increase and the economy produces both commodities. The reduction in p and the increase in μ affect y in diametrically opposite ways. For a given μ, y falls as p falls, and for a given p, y increases as μ increases. The outcome, of course, depends upon which of these two forces is stronger. While nothing can be said a priori, the following general statement is probably correct. For values of p immediately lower than p_M, the effect of the reduction in p will be stronger than the effect of the increase in μ, and for values of p immediately higher than p_m, the effect of p is weaker than the effect of μ. This follows from the observation that, for $p \geq p_M$, y falls as p falls and, for $p \leq p_m$, y increases as p falls. Because of continuity, therefore, we must expect the order of importance of p and μ to change at least once somewhere in the region $p_m < p < p_M$. In general, the reversal of importance of p and μ might occur an odd number of times. But what is more important than this pathological phenomenon is the fact that, as p falls, y and, therefore, per capita consumption might fall while the country is exporting Q_c and importing Q_k. In other words, it is possible that an improvement of the terms of trade of a small country might cause such a change in the capital/labor ratio as to make the per capita income and per capita consumption of the country actually fall after the terms-of-trade improvement. Alternatively, a deterioration of the terms of trade might cause a change in the capital/labor ratio that will make the per capita income and per capita consumption higher. It should be noted that these conclusions are independent of the classification of commodities according to factor intensities.

The effect on the volume of trade cannot be decided a priori. Thus, concentrating on the difference between z_k and domestic per capita production of Q_k, we observe that, as p falls, z_k increases but the outcome on the per capita output of Q_k (q_K) is indeterminate. For as μ increases, q_K increases at the same p. But p falls as well, and it has an adverse effect on q_K.

SELECTED BIBLIOGRAPHY

Bardhan, P. K. 1970. *Economic Growth, Development, and Foreign Trade.* New York: Wiley-Interscience.

Johnson, H. G. 1962. *Money, Trade and Economic Growth.* Cambridge, Mass.: Harvard University Press. Chap. 4; reprinted in the A.E.A. *Readings in International Economics.* Homewood, Ill.: R. D. Irwin, 1968.

———. 1971. The theory of trade and growth: a diagrammatic analysis. In J. Bhagwati, R. Jones, R. A. Mundell, and J. Vanek (Editors). *Trade, Balance of Payments, and Growth,* Essays in Honor of Charles P. Kindleberger. New York: American Elsevier Publishing Co., 1971.

Kemp, M. C. 1969. *The Pure Theory of International Trade and Investment.* Englewood Cliffs, N.J.: Prentice-Hall, Inc. Chaps. 10–11.

Solow, R. M. 1956. A contribution to the theory of economic growth. *Quarterly Journal of Economics* 70: 65–94; reprinted in J. E. Stiglitz and H. Uzawa (Editors). *Readings in the Modern Theory of Economic Growth.* Cambridge, Mass.: The M.I.T. Press, 1969.

Stiglitz, J. E. 1970. Factor price equalization in a dynamic economy. *Journal of Political Economy* 78: 456–88.

Swan, T. W. 1956. Economic growth and capital accumulation. *Economic Record* 32: 334–61; reprinted in J. E. Stiglitz and H. Uzawa (Editors). *Readings in the Modern Theory of Economic Growth.* Cambridge, Mass.: The M.I.T. Press, 1969.

Uzawa, H. 1961. On a two-sector model of economic growth. *Review of Economic Studies* 29.

———. 1963. On a two-sector model of economic growth II. *Review of Economic Studies* 30: 105–18; reprinted in J. E. Stiglitz and H. Uzawa (Editors). *Readings in the Modern Theory of Economic Growth.* Cambridge, Mass.: The M.I.T. Press, 1969.

VI

Trade and Welfare

15

Trade and the Welfare of Individuals

Do countries benefit from international trade? This issue was intentionally avoided in earlier chapters despite the fact that our starting point, the Ricardo–Torrens theory of comparative advantage, purported to show that free international trade is beneficial to all trading countries—or, in the limiting case, international trade does not hurt any country. It was pointed out then that the concept of social welfare is rather subtle. A more careful examination of the doctrine that trade is better than no trade is now in order.

It is usually taken for granted, especially in public debate over commercial policy, that international trade and specialization is beneficial to all participating countries. This is mainly due to the fact that classical and neo-classical writers have always felt that in some sense perfect competition represents an optimal situation. There are various explanations for this belief, but the following two seem to be the most common and interesting.

a) A market transaction is voluntary; hence, no party can be hurt by a voluntary transaction, because he can always refuse to trade. For example, a worker might choose to work for what might appear to be a relatively low wage only because in the end he can consume more as compared with the extreme case where he himself would have to produce everything. He may resent the fact that his wage is low, but he nevertheless accepts it because he is better off with it than without it. It is thought that a similar argument can show that international trade is beneficial to all participating countries. Thus, it may be argued, participation in international trade is free, if countries participate in international trade, they do so voluntarily; hence, international trade (and specialization) is mutually beneficial—one party does not gain what the other loses—and, therefore, free trade is better than no trade. What is wrong with this argument? It suggests that with the opening up of trade, all members of all countries become better off because their participation is voluntary. But voluntary in what sense? Does a single individual in a certain country have a choice between his pretrade and post-trade equilibrium positions? In other words, can a single individual refuse to participate in international trade and be no worse off than in his pretrade position? Not necessarily. With the opening up of trade, the consumption-possibilities frontier (or the equilibrium budget line) of each consumer will be different from what it used to be in the pretrade equilibrium position. Despite the fact that some consumers will definitely become better off after the introduction of trade, we cannot rule out the possibility that some consumers may become worse off. Actually, an individual consumer can refuse the exchange of the services of the factors of production he owns for the commodities and services he can get in the market—but then he would have to produce, with the factors he owns, everything he consumes. The fact that no individual does that is proof that participation in production and exchange even after the introduction of trade is still beneficial to all. But this does not mean that every individual becomes better off after the introduction of trade; it means, rather, that, even if international trade hurts some individuals, these individuals are still better off than if each were to produce everything he consumed.

b) A second, more sophisticated argument attempts to show, not that each individual is made better off after the introduction of international trade, but that in some sense the sum total of satisfactions is maximized. But this involves the notion of adding the utilities of different individuals; that is, it is assumed that it is possible to compare and weight the utilities of different individuals. To many modern economists, interpersonal comparisons of well-being are both impossible and "unscientific," although the preceding generation of economists used to make interpersonal comparisons of well-being almost without question. Today, the welfare of an economy is clearly considered to be no more than a heterogeneous collection of individual welfares.

How can the effect of international trade on social welfare be evaluated? As mentioned in chapter 1, it can be postulated that social welfare depends on the welfare of the individuals comprising the society, and on nothing else. The mathematical expression of this statement is the Bergson–Samuelson social welfare function in its general form, discussed in the following chapter. This function is usually made a little more specific by attributing to it an ethical property, namely, that social welfare increases when one individual becomes better off with no one else being worse off. Now if the introduction of international trade were to make everybody better off, we could conclude that the introduction of international trade increases social welfare. Unfortunately, however, some individuals become worse off after the introduction of international trade; and ethical neutrality prevents us from passing judgment on cases where some individuals lose. How then can we evaluate the effect of international trade on social welfare when some people lose?

Two possibilities are open to us: (*a*) We can assume that society has a social welfare function and implements it consistently (i.e., society always achieves that distribution of income which maximizes social welfare). In this case, we can aggregate the preferences of all individuals into a single social preference system (as explained in chap. 6) and show that the introduction of international trade improves social welfare: after trade, the economy necessarily moves from a lower to a higher social indifference curve. (*b*) Or we can use the so-called *compensation principle* and talk about what society could potentially do. In other words, even though some individuals do become worse off after the introduction of international trade, we can show that every individual *could* be made better off (or, in the limiting case, no worse off). To be ethically neutral, we have to consider all possible income distributions. This is not difficult to do, because, as we have seen, the consumption-possibilities frontier lies beyond the boundaries of the production-possibilities frontier, except at the optimum production point, where the two frontiers coincide. As a result, the cum-trade utility frontier can be shown to lie, in general, beyond the autarkic utility frontier, except at one or more points where the two utility frontiers may be tangent to each other.

The rest of this chapter deals with the effect of international trade on the welfare of the citizens of the trading countries. The question of whether international trade increases social welfare will be taken up in the following chapter.

1. Some Cases in Which the Introduction of International Trade Improves the Welfare of Everybody

In earlier chapters, several simple cases are discussed in which international trade improves the welfare of all individuals of all trading countries or—in the limiting case where the posttrade equilibrium prices are equal to the pretrade equilibrium prices of an economy—it does not *hurt* anybody. Let us review some of these cases briefly.

First, consider the classical theory where it is assumed that there exists one factor of production, labor, and all commodities are produced under constant returns to scale. The introduction of trade cannot hurt anybody in this case. The worst that could happen is for every individual to enjoy the same level of welfare after as before the introduction of international trade. This occurs in the limiting case where the pretrade domestic price ratio coincides with the posttrade international price ratio. How can this proposition be proved?

Consider again the simple case of two commodities, X and Y, with a_x and a_y being the respective labor coefficients. We know that the domestic price ratio (p_x/p_y) before trade is given by the ratio a_x/a_y. Further, if the international price ratio, p $(\equiv p_x/p_y)$, is larger than a_x/a_y, our economy will specialize in the production of X; if $p < a_x/a_y$, our economy will specialize in the production of Y; and if $p = a_x/a_y$, the production point is indeterminate—any pattern of specialization is possible.

Consider now an individual endowed with L_0 units of labor. His budget equation in the autarkic state is

$$wL_0 = p_x X + p_y Y. \qquad (15.1)$$

However,

$$p_x = wa_x \quad \text{and} \quad p_y = wa_y. \qquad (15.2)$$

Substituting equations (15.2) into equation (15.1) and simplifying, we get

$$L_0 = a_x X + a_y Y. \qquad (15.3)$$

Equation (15.3) is the individual's budget line in the autarkic state. The individual will choose that bundle of X and Y which maximizes his welfare as illustrated by figure 15.1. The straight line MN is the individual's budget line as given by equation (15.3). The individual maximizes his welfare at point E_1, where his budget line touches the highest indifference curve, I_1.

Suppose now that our economy can buy and sell unlimited quantities of X and Y in the international market at the relative price $p_0 > (a_x/a_y)$. What would happen to the welfare of our typical individual with this new development? Refer to equation (15.1). What are the prices p_x and p_y equal

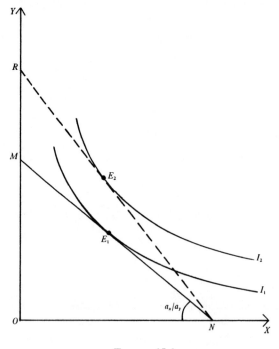

FIGURE 15.1

to now? Since our economy will specialize completely in the production of X (because $p_0 > a_x/a_y$), p_x will continue to be given by the domestic average cost of production, wa_x. But what about p_y? This cannot be determined by the domestic average cost, because Y cannot profitably be produced at home; that is, as we saw in chapter 2, we must necessarily have $p_y <$ domestic average cost of production $= wa_y$. How is p_y determined then? By definition, $p_0 = p_x/p_y$. Thus,

$$p_y = p_x/p_0 = w(a_x/p_0). \tag{15.4}$$

Substituting again p_x and p_y into equation (15.1) and simplifying, we get

$$L_0 = a_x X + (a_x/p_0) Y. \tag{15.5}$$

Equation (15.5) is the new budget equation of our typical consumer. How does this equation compare with equation (15.3)? They are both linear and they both have the same X-axis intercept: L_0/a_x. Which is steeper? The slope of the autarkic budget line, as given by equation (15.3), is given by a_x/a_y; and the slope of the free-trade budget line, as given by equation (15.5), is given by $a_x/(a_x/p_0) = p_0$. Since $p_0 > a_x/a_y$ by assumption, the free-trade budget line must be steeper, as shown in figure 15.1 by the broken line NR. Therefore, after the introduction of international trade, the consumer will reach equilibrium at point E_2 on the higher indifference curve I_2. Accordingly, free trade will make our typical individual—and thus all individuals— better off.

It can be shown, following the same line of reasoning, that when the international price ratio is smaller than a_x/a_y, the free-trade budget line of the typical individual will start at M and be flatter than the autarkic budget line MN. Hence, the free-trade budget line will lie totally outside the autarkic budget line, except at the singular point M, and therefore, the typical individual (and thus all individuals) will again become better off with trade. In the limiting case where $p = a_x/a_y$, the free-trade budget line will coincide with the autarkic budget line, and the typical individual will remain as well off after the introduction of trade as in the autarkic state.

Essentially the same analysis holds in the case in which the economy is endowed not with one but with two primary factors of production, labor (L) and land (T), and the production-possibilities frontier of the economy is a straight line. Note that the production-possibilities frontier becomes a straight line if, and only if, at the given overall labor/land ratio, the marginal rate of substitution of labor for land is the same in both X and Y. But the two industries may have the same marginal rate of substitution of labor for land either for all values of the overall labor/land ratio or for only the specific value of the overall labor/land ratio that our economy happens to be endowed with. However, the reason why the production-possibilities frontier is linear is immaterial. The only requirement is that it be linear; this implies that both industries always use the two factors in the overall proportion in which they exist in the economy at large. We can easily show that trade improves the welfare of all individuals in this case as well.

Consider a typical individual endowed with L_0 units of labor and T_0 units of land. Note that L_0 and T_0 are arbitrarily chosen. It is possible for either L_0 or T_0 to be zero. The budget equation of our typical individual is, in general, given by the equation

$$wL_0 + rT_0 = p_x X + p_y Y. \qquad (15.6)$$

In addition, in the autarkic state, the following marginal productivity conditions necessarily hold:

$$w = p_x MPP_L^X = p_y MPP_L^Y, \qquad (15.7)$$

$$r = p_x MPP_T^X = p_y MPP_T^Y. \qquad (15.8)$$

The term $MPP_L^X \equiv$ the marginal physical product of labor in the production of X, and so on.

Since, by assumption, the labor/land ratios in the two industries are always equal to the overall labor/land ratio, and since MPP_L^X and MPP_T^X are functions of the labor/land ratio used in the X industry while MPP_L^Y and MPP_T^Y are functions of the labor/land ratio used in the Y industry, the marginal physical products of both factors in both industries must be uniquely determined and they must necessarily remain constant throughout at the uniquely determined level.

Now rewrite equation (15.6) as

$$\frac{w}{r} L_0 + T_0 = \frac{p_x}{r} X + \frac{p_y}{r} Y. \qquad (15.6)'$$

The factor-price ratio, w/r, is by assumption uniquely determined. Therefore, we can introduce a new symbol, I_0, to represent the income of the typical individual in terms of units of land; that is,

$$I_0 \equiv \frac{w}{r} L_0 + T_0. \qquad (15.9)$$

Observe that I_0 is a constant. It is independent of the equilibrium production point, and therefore, it will remain constant even after the introduction of international trade.

Solving equation (15.8) for p_x/r and p_y/r, we get

$$\frac{p_x}{r} = \frac{1}{MPP_T^X}, \qquad (15.10)$$

$$\frac{p_y}{r} = \frac{1}{MPP_T^Y}. \qquad (15.11)$$

Substituting equations (15.9)–(15.11) into equation (15.6)', we get

$$I_0 = \left(\frac{1}{MPP_T^X}\right) X + \left(\frac{1}{MPP_T^Y}\right) Y. \qquad (15.12)$$

Equation (15.12) is the typical individual's budget equation in the autarkic state. It is a linear equation and is represented graphically by a straight line whose absolute slope is equal to the ratio MPP_T^Y/MPP_T^X. By a simple division of equations (15.10) and (15.11), it becomes clear that the ratio MPP_T^Y/MPP_T^X is simply the domestic price ratio p_x/p_y prevailing in the autarkic state. Qualitatively, this budget equation looks like the straight line MN of figure 15.1.

Let us now introduce international trade by assuming that our economy can buy and sell unlimited quantities of X and Y in the international market at the relative price $p_0 > MPP_T^Y/MPP_T^X$. Thus, X is assumed to be relatively more expensive in the international market, and therefore, our economy will specialize completely in the production of X. Such being the case, equation (15.10) will continue to hold after the introduction of international trade. But what about equation (15.11)? Will it continue to hold, too? No. By assumption, the international price of Y (p_y^*) will be lower than the domestic average cost of production of Y (r/MPP_T^Y). In other words, after the introduction of trade, we must have

$$p_y^* < r/MPP_T^Y.$$

How is p_y^* to be determined? Again, we have $p_0 \equiv p_x/p_y^*$, or

$$p_y^* = \frac{p_x}{p_0} = \frac{r}{p_0 MPP_T^X}.$$

Thus,

$$\frac{p_y^*}{r} = \frac{1}{p_0 MPP_T^X}. \qquad (15.13)$$

Substituting equations (15.10) and (15.13) into equation (15.6)', we get

$$I_0 = \left(\frac{1}{MPP_T^X}\right) X + \left(\frac{1}{p_0 MPP_T^X}\right) Y. \qquad (15.14)$$

Equation (15.14) is simply the budget equation of our typical individual after the introduction of international trade. How does this budget equation compare with the budget equation of the autarkic state, that is, equation (15.12)? Again, they are both linear and have the same X-axis intercept. Which is steeper? Again, the free-trade budget equation, because the slope of the budget equation in the autarkic state is given by the ratio MPP_T^Y/MPP_T^X while the slope of the budget equation after the introduction of free trade is given by $(1/MPP_T^X)/(1/p_0 MPP_T^X) = p_0$, which by assumption is larger than the ratio MPP_T^Y/MPP_T^X. Therefore, the situation is again similar to that illustrated in figure 15.1.

Similar reasoning will show that, when the international price ratio is smaller than the ratio MPP_T^Y/MPP_T^X, the free-trade budget line of the typical individual will have the same Y-axis intercept as the budget line under autarky, with the latter being steeper than the former. Hence, the free-trade budget line will lie totally outside the budget line under autarky, except at their common Y-axis intercept, and therefore, the typical individual (and thus all individuals) will again become better off with trade. In the limiting case where the international price ratio is equal to the domestic price ratio under autarky, the free-trade budget line will coincide with the autarkic budget line and the typical individual will continue to enjoy, after the introduction of trade, the same level of welfare he used to enjoy in the autarkic state.

A third and last case to be considered is when all members of our economy are identical in every respect. That is, they have the same tastes and factor ownership. As before, all production functions are characterized by constant returns to scale. A great simplification is possible in the present case: the economy's production-possibilities frontier can be scaled down in proportion to each individual (i.e., the representative citizen), and then the scaled-down production-possibilities frontier can be used to show the equilibrium production and consumption positions of each individual.

In figure 15.2, the curve $MP_3E_1P_2N$ is the scaled-down production-possibilities frontier of the typical individual. Before trade, the typical

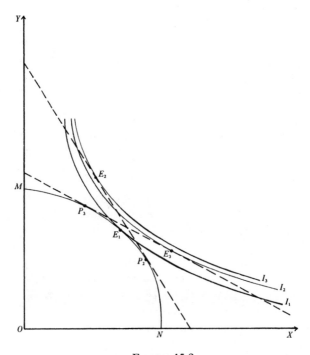

FIGURE 15.2

individual is in equilibrium at point E_1. Now assume that our economy can buy and sell unlimited quantities of X and Y at given international prices. Whether the international price ratio p_x/p_y is higher, as shown by the broken line E_2P_2, or smaller, as shown by the broken line E_3P_3, than the domestic price ratio under autarky, the introduction of international trade will definitely improve the welfare of the typical individual, except in the limiting case where the international price ratio is equal to the domestic price under autarky, in which case the introduction of trade will neither hurt nor benefit the typical individual.

2. International Trade May Hurt Some Individuals

International trade takes place because the relative pretrade equilibrium commodity prices differ between countries. With the opening up of trade, these relative commodity prices tend, in the absence of transportation costs, toward complete equality. What effect, if any, does this change in relative commodity prices have on the income distribution of the trading countries? And what is the effect on the welfare of each individual? The answers to these questions necessarily depend on factor ownership and tastes.

When factor ownership is uniform, the distribution of income is independent of factor prices. For instance, suppose that, in an economy composed of n individuals,

$$L_i/T_i = L/\bar{T} \quad (i = 1, 2, \ldots, n),$$

where $L_i \equiv$ labor owned by the ith individual, $T_i \equiv$ land owned by the ith individual,

$$L \equiv \sum_{i=1}^{n} Li,$$

$$\bar{T} \equiv \sum_{i=1}^{n} T_i.$$

The proportion of the ith individual's income (I_i) to total income (I) is given by

$$\frac{I_i}{I} = \frac{wL_i + rT_i}{wL + r\bar{T}} = \frac{T_i[w(L_i/T_i) + r]}{\bar{T}[w(L/\bar{T}) + r]} = \frac{T_i}{\bar{T}} = \frac{L_i}{L}, \qquad (15.15)$$

which is constant and independent of factor prices. Therefore, the introduction of international trade will not affect the distribution of income in the present case. But what about the welfare of each individual? Can we reasonably expect that the introduction of international trade will make everybody better off? Or would trade make some people better off without making others worse off? In other words, can we eliminate the possibility that the introduction of international trade will hurt some individuals? First, a way must be found to determine the general equilibrium of the economy before and after the introduction of international trade in terms of the excess demand functions of all individuals. Then, we can see whether or not all individuals move to higher indifference curves after the introduction of international trade. How can this be done without getting involved in an unmanageable number of equations?

When factor ownership is uniform (in the sense that each individual owns the two factors of production in the same proportion as the economy's overall factor-endowment ratio), general equilibrium can easily be determined by considering each individual as an island. Then, on the basis of his factor endowments and tastes, we can determine his excess demand curves as in the case of countries. In other words, we have to determine each individual's production-possibilities frontier, superimpose the latter on the individual's indifference map, and so on. Of course, when the excess demand curves are so derived, they will have to be summed laterally for the determination of the general equilibrium of the economy—a procedure that must be quite familiar by now.

Is the assumption of uniformity of factor ownership crucial to the suggested procedure? If so, why? The answer is rather simple. When we proceed from the production-possibilities frontier of the individual citizen (not the economy), we necessarily assume that it is always economical for each individual to organize production and employ fully his own factors at all possible factor-price ratios. In other words, no individual will ever have the need to exchange one factor for another in the factor market in order to be able to organize production and fully employ the factors available to him by adopting those production techniques that happen to be optimum for the economy as a whole. When factor ownership is uniform, this is no doubt true, since, under constant returns to scale, scale is immaterial. But when factor ownership is not uniform, this need not be so. This is, of course, easily illustrated by the case where some individuals (at least) own only one factor, such as labor, and both commodities require both factors, labor and land. Therefore, we conclude that uniformity of factor ownership is both necessary and sufficient for the suggested procedure of solving the general-equilibrium problem.

Let us assume now that we have been able to determine the equilibrium commodity-price ratio (p_x/p_y) of the economy. We can then classify all individuals into the following three categories. (a) Those who produce exactly as much as they need for their personal consumption. These people are self-sufficient. Not only do they not have to exchange factors of production (which is ruled out by the assumption that factor ownership is uniform), but they have no need to exchange commodities. (b) Those who, in the general-equilibrium situation, exchange commodity X for commodity Y. That is, they produce more X and less Y than what they consume. (c) Those who, in the general-equilibrium situation, exchange commodity Y for commodity X. In other words, they produce less X and more Y than what they actually consume.

These categories are illustrated in figure 15.3. Figure 15.3(a) illustrates the case of a typical individual, Mr. A, who belongs to the first category; part (b) illustrates the case of a typical individual, Mr. B, who belongs to the second category; and part (c) illustrates the case of a typical individual, Mr. C, who belongs to the third category. In all panels, the curve MN is the individual's production-possibilities frontier, UV is the individual's consumption-possibilities frontier, II' is the indifference curve that the individual can reach at the autarkic general-equilibrium situation, P_0 is the optimum production point, and C_0 is the optimum consumption point. In part (a), illustrating the case of self-sufficient individuals, the consumption point coincides, of course, with the production point. In the other two cases, the consumption point is different from the production point. How does the introduction of international trade affect the welfare of each individual?

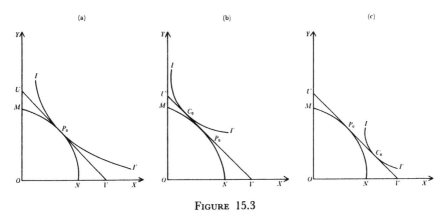

FIGURE 15.3

Consider first the self-sufficient Mr. A. The introduction of international trade cannot possibly hurt him. He is self-sufficient, and he can always reach the pretrade level of satisfaction by continuing to produce and consume at P_0. But is this what he will actually do? No—unless the international price ratio is equal to the economy's pretrade price ratio. When the international price ratio is different from $(p_x/p_y)_0$, Mr. A can definitely improve his welfare by participating in international trade. Thus, any budget line (other than UV) tangent to Mr. A's production-possibilities frontier will necessarily intersect the indifference curve II'. This means that Mr. A can reach a higher indifference curve after the introduction of international trade.

Mr. A's total gain from trade can be decomposed into a consumption gain and a production gain in the manner discussed in chapter 5, part B. Thus, with the same production (point), he can do better through exchange (consumption gain), but he can do still better by shifting his production point (production gain).

Can we infer from this that the introduction of international trade will make Mr. B and Mr. C better off as well? No. In fact, we can show that when the international price ratio is different from $(p_x/p_y)_0$, that is, the pretrade price ratio, one individual will become better off and the other worse off. Suppose that commodity X is relatively cheaper in the international market. Mr. C can reach a higher indifference curve than II', since any budget line tangent to his production-possibilities frontier and flatter than UV will necessarily intersect II'. What about Mr. B? Can he improve his welfare, or at least maintain the same level, after the introduction of international trade? No, because any budget line tangent to Mr. B's production-possibilities frontier and flatter than UV will fail to reach II'.

But why is it not possible for Mr. B to maintain at least the same level of welfare he used to enjoy before trade? Why is he different from Mr. A, who can at least maintain his pretrade level of welfare by refusing to trade? In other words, why is it not possible for Mr. B to refuse to participate in international trade and at the same time maintain his pretrade level of well-being? The crucial difference between Mr. A and Mr. B is that, while the former did not need any cooperation from the rest of the economy to reach the indifference curve II', the latter did. In other words, while Mr. A was self-sufficient, Mr. B had to exchange X for Y in the commodity market. Still better, Mr. A was consuming along his production-possibilities frontier while Mr. B was consuming beyond his production-possibilities frontier. After the introduction of international trade, those individuals (like Mr. C) who want to exchange Y for X at $(p_x/p_y)_0$ will simply refuse transactions with Mr. B at the pretrade terms: they will demand more units of X per unit of Y. What this means is that Mr. B will be unable, after the introduction of international trade, to reach the indifference curve II'.

Another way of looking at this problem is to regard Mr. C as a net supplier of the good whose price goes up; hence, he benefits. On the other hand, Mr. B is a net demander of the good whose price goes up; hence he loses.

Do Mr. B's losses account fully for Mr. C's gains? This is an important question which will be answered satisfactorily later in the next chapter. Briefly, the gainers could compensate the losers for their losses so that in the end some individuals are better off without anybody being worse off.

Let us now discuss another important case where the introduction of international trade hurts some individuals. Drop the assumption that factor ownership is uniform. Once this is done, there are an infinite number of alternative assumptions that could be made with regard to factor ownership. Since our main interest lies in the demonstration that trade may actually hurt some individuals, let us adopt the simplifying assumption that in our economy there are two classes of people: workers and landlords. The landlords own all the land, but they do not offer any labor services. The latter are being offered by the workers, who do not own any land at all. Of course, in any real world situation, workers will own some land and landlords will offer some labor services. However, our assumption will bring out quite sharply the consequences of nonuniformity in factor ownership.

Assume that our economy produces two commodities, X and Y, under constant returns to scale. For the given overall labor/land ratio in our economy, commodity Y is assumed to be land intensive relative to X. Note that the complication of factor-intensity reversals is of no consequence to this classification, because, as demonstrated in chapter 8, the two commodities can *always* be classified uniquely into labor intensive and land intensive when the overall labor/land ratio is given. Assume that our economy can buy and sell unlimited quantities of X and Y in the international market at fixed prices, p_0. In particular, assume that the international price ratio, p_x/p_y, is smaller than the pretrade domestic price ratio. That is, X is cheaper (and Y more expensive) in the international market. What happens when trade opens up?

Since, by assumption, X is relatively cheaper in the international market, our economy will be exporting Y in exchange for X. Thus, the domestic production of Y, that is, the land-intensive commodity, will rise and the domestic production of X will fall. What happens to factor prices? As a result of the shift toward increased production of the land-intensive commodity, both commodities will tend to become more labor intensive and the marginal physical product of labor will fall while the marginal physical product of land will rise in both industries. Thus, the factor-price ratio w/r (see eqs. [15.7] and [15.8]) will definitely fall. What happens to the workers' and landlords' *relative* share in real national income?

National income is the sum of the income of workers (wL) plus the income of landlords $(r\bar{T})$, or $wL + r\bar{T}$. Therefore, the relative income of workers is given by $wL/(wL + r\bar{T})$, and equals (using eqs. [15.7] and [15.8] and simplifying)

$$\frac{MPP_L \cdot L}{MPP_L \cdot L + MPP_T \cdot \bar{T}} = \frac{L}{L + (MPP_T \cdot \bar{T}/MPP_L \cdot)}. \tag{15.16}$$

Note that a superior dot has replaced the superscripts X and Y from the symbols MPP_T and MPP_L, because we can use the marginal productivities of both factors in either of the two industries. Thus, we can use either the pair (MPP_L^X, MPP_T^X) or the pair (MPP_L^Y, MPP_T^Y). An examination of equation (15.16) reveals that, as the production of Y increases at the expense of X and therefore the ratio $MPP_T \cdot /MPP_L \cdot$ increases, the *relative income of workers falls*.

Similar reasoning shows that, as resources are being transferred from industry X to industry Y, the *relative income of landlords rises*. Thus, the relative income of landlords is

$$\frac{MPP_T \cdot \bar{T}}{MPP_L \cdot L + MPP_T \cdot \bar{T}} = \frac{\bar{T}}{(MPP_L \cdot /MPP_T \cdot)L + \bar{T}}. \tag{15.17}$$

Accordingly, when MPP_L'/MPP_T' falls, the relative income of landlords rises.

We cannot conclude from the preceding analysis that the introduction of trade necessarily makes the workers worse off and the landlords better off. All we have proved so far is that the *relative* income of workers falls and the *relative* income of landlords rises. In order to conclude anything about the welfare of each group, we must first determine what happens to the *absolute* income of each group. If international trade actually increases national income, the absolute income of workers might still increase even though their relative income falls: a smaller share from a large pie may very well be bigger than a larger share from a small pie. However, with the introduction of trade, all prices change, which presents a dilemma in terms of absolute income. Do we evaluate income at the pretrade or posttrade prices? We seem to be heading toward an index number problem, which, fortunately, can be avoided.

In principle, it is possible to determine whether an individual's welfare has increased or decreased only if it can be shown that that individual has moved to a higher or a lower indifference curve. This presupposes a detailed knowledge of the indifference map of the individual. But it is possible to predict the effect of international trade on the welfare of each worker and landlord without such information. In particular, we can demonstrate that, with the introduction of international trade, each worker becomes worse off while each landlord becomes better off irrespective of the peculiarities of each individual's indifference map.

Consider the budget line of the ith worker as given by the equation

$$wL_i = p_x X + p_y Y,$$

or

$$L_i = \left(\frac{p_x}{w}\right) X + \left(\frac{p_y}{w}\right) Y. \tag{15.18}$$

As long as both commodities are domestically produced, equations (15.7) and (15.8) will be satisfied. Solving equations (15.7) for (p_x/w) and (p_y/w), we get

$$p_x/w = 1/MPP_L^X, \tag{15.19}$$

$$p_y/w = 1/MPP_L^Y. \tag{15.20}$$

Substituting equations (15.19) and (15.20) into equation (15.18), we get

$$L_i = (1/MPP_L^X)X + (1/MPP_L^Y)Y. \tag{15.21}$$

Equation (15.21) is the budget equation of the ith worker. It depends only on the marginal physical product of labor in the two industries. Assuming that the introduction of international trade does not cause our country to specialize completely in the production of Y (and that something of both commodities is being produced both before and after trade), we can use equation (15.21) to show how the budget line of the ith worker shifts with the opening up of trade. For this purpose, it is only necessary to find out how trade affects the marginal physical product of labor in both industries.

As we saw earlier, with the introduction of trade the production of Y (i.e., the land-intensive commodity) expands while the production of X (i.e., the labor-intensive commodity) contracts, and both commodities tend to become more labor intensive. As a result of diminishing returns to factor proportions, the marginal physical product of labor will fall in both industries after the introduction of international trade, because more units of labor are combined with each unit of land in both industries. In other words, with the introduction of international trade, both MPP_L^X and MPP_L^Y fall.

What happens to the budget equation of the ith worker? First, it becomes flatter because the international price ratio (p_x/p_y) is by assumption lower than the domestic pretrade price ratio. But second, and more important, it shifts totally toward the origin; that is, the posttrade budget line of the ith worker lies completely inside the corresponding pretrade budget line. How can this important proposition be proved?

Observe that all budget lines are straight lines. To find out whether the pretrade budget line of an individual lies beyond his posttrade budget line, we have only to compare the corresponding intercepts of the two budget lines with the two axes. Thus, the X-axis intercept of the ith worker's budget line is given by the product $L_i MPP_L^X$, and the Y-axis intercept is given by the product $L_i MPP_L^Y$.[1] Since both MPP_L^X and MPP_L^Y fall with the opening up of trade, both intercepts will be smaller after trade. Therefore, the posttrade budget line of the ith worker will lie totally inside his pretrade budget line, although their slopes will differ.

What happens, then, to the welfare of the ith worker? Since, with the introduction of trade, the budget line of the ith worker shifts totally toward the origin, he must necessarily be consuming on a lower indifference curve after trade compared with his pretrade position. Hence, the ith worker is definitely hurt by the introduction of international trade. This conclusion does not depend on the details of his indifference map. The effect of international trade on the welfare of the ith worker is a general conclusion; it holds for each and every worker.

Similar reasoning shows that trade makes every landlord better off. Thus, the budget equation of the ith landlord is given by

$$rT_j = p_x X + p_y Y,$$

or

$$T_j = (p_x/r)X + (p_y/r)Y. \tag{15.22}$$

---

1. Given a budget equation $M = aX + bY$, where M, a, and b, are parameters, we can determine the X-axis intercept by putting $Y = 0$ and solving the budget equation for X. Similarly, the Y-axis intercept is determined by putting $X = 0$ into the budget equation and solving for Y. Thus, the X-axis intercept $= M/a$ and the Y-axis intercept $= M/b$.

Substituting (p_x/r) and (p_y/r) as given by equations (15.10) and (15.11), respectively, into equation (15.22), we get

$$T_j = (1/MPP_T^X)X + (1/MPP_T^Y)Y. \qquad (15.23)$$

Equation (15.23) is the budget equation of the *j*th landlord. It depends only on the marginal physical product of land in the two industries. Assuming again that our economy produces something of both commodities before and after the introduction of trade, we can use equation (15.23) to show how the budget line of the *j*th landlord shifts with the opening up of trade. As we saw earlier, with the opening up of trade, both industries tend to become more labor intensive or less land intensive. As a result, both MPP_T^X and MPP_T^Y rise, and both intercepts of the *j*th landlord's budget line (i.e., $T_j MPP_T^X$ and $T_j MPP_T^Y$) increase. The budget line of the *j*th landlord will shift totally outward, and irrespective of the details of his indifference map, the *j*th landlord will definitely become better off after trade. The same conclusion holds, of course, for all landlords.

To summarize, if the introduction of international trade renders the land-intensive commodity more expensive, the production of the land-intensive commodity will expand while the production of the labor-intensive commodity will contract. Both industries will tend to become more labor intensive, thus causing the marginal physical product of labor to fall everywhere (i.e., both MPP_L^X and MPP_L^Y fall) and the marginal physical product of land to rise everywhere (i.e., both MPP_T^X and MPP_T^Y rise). But the *X*-axis and *Y*-axis intercepts of the *i*th worker's budget line are given, respectively, by $L_i MPP_L^X$ and $L_i MPP_L^Y$, and the corresponding intercepts of the *j*th landlord's budget line are given by $T_j MPP_T^X$ and $T_j MPP_T^Y$. Hence, each worker's budget line shifts unequivocally inward and each landlord's budget line shifts unequivocally outward after the introduction of trade.[2] As a result, each worker becomes worse off and each landlord becomes better off with trade.

This conclusion depends only on the direction of change of the commodity-price ratio after the introduction of trade, and nothing else. In particular, it does not depend on the validity of the Heckscher–Ohlin theorem. Whether or not factor prices are completely equalized through commodity trade is also immaterial. Also, factor-intensity reversals will not affect our conclusion that *the factor used intensively in the commodity whose price rises after the introduction of trade benefits positively from trade while the other factor is definitely hurt.*

What is the effect of international trade on our economy's welfare? This is a very difficult question, because some people benefit from trade while others are hurt by it. To judge the effect of trade on welfare, we need either a means of weighing losses versus gains or a policy that compensates for losses. We shall return to this important question later in the next chapter.

---

2. Can it be proved that, when the introduction of international trade renders the land-intensive commodity cheaper, the budget line of each worker will shift outward and the budget line of each capitalist will shift inward?

Now assume that our economy has been exporting Y and importing X from the rest of the world at the given international prices. What would happen to our economy's welfare if, as a result of a shift in international demand from X to Y, the terms of trade of our economy improved (i.e., the international price ratio p_x/p_y fell)? Does the welfare of our economy improve as well? Again, we cannot be sure, because from the preceding analysis, each worker will be hurt while each landlord will benefit from the terms-of-trade improvement. Since interpersonal comparisons of well-being are both impossible and "unscientific," we must reserve judgment on the question of whether welfare improves when the terms of trade improve. It can be similarly shown that a deterioration in the terms of trade will benefit every worker and hurt every landlord. But we cannot tell at this stage whether welfare will improve or deteriorate.

So far, we have been assuming that the introduction of international trade does not bring about complete specialization. In other words, after the introduction of trade, our economy continues to produce both commodities. What happens if this assumption is dropped? Can we still conclude that one factor will definitely be injured by the introduction of trade while the other will definitely benefit from it? No. Consider the case where both commodities are produced and the international price ratio p_x/p_y starts falling continuously. As long as the economy continues to produce both commodities, the preceding analysis will hold; that is, the factor (L) used intensively in the production of the commodity whose price falls (X) will be hurt while the factor (T) used intensively in the production of the commodity whose price rises (Y) will benefit from trade. But beyond a crucial price ratio—corresponding to the slope of the economy's production-possibilities frontier at the Y-axis intercept—the production of X will cease completely, and further reductions in the commodity-price ratio p_x/p_y will alter neither the production point nor the marginal physical productivities of the two factors in the production of Y. The budget equations (15.18) and (15.22), beyond the critical value of p_x/p_y at which the country specializes completely in the production of Y, become

$$L_i = \left(\frac{p_x}{w}\right) X + \left(\frac{p_y}{w}\right) Y = \left(\frac{p_y}{w} \frac{p_x}{p_y}\right) X + \left(\frac{p_y}{w}\right) Y$$

$$= \left(\frac{p_x/p_y}{MPP_L^Y}\right) X + \left(\frac{1}{MPP_L^Y}\right) Y, \tag{15.24}$$

$$T_j = \left(\frac{p_x}{r}\right) X + \left(\frac{p_y}{r}\right) Y = \left(\frac{p_y}{r} \frac{p_x}{p_y}\right) X + \left(\frac{p_y}{r}\right) Y$$

$$= \left(\frac{p_x/p_y}{MPP_T^Y}\right) X + \left(\frac{1}{MPP_T^Y}\right) Y. \tag{15.25}$$

Remember that after p_x/p_y falls below its critical value, the marginal physical products of labor and land in the Y industry, that is, MPP_L^Y and MPP_T^Y, remain constant. Therefore, when p_x/p_y falls below its critical value, the Y-axis intercepts of both budget lines, $L_i MPP_L^Y$ and $T_j MPP_T^Y$, remain constant, while both X-axis intercepts, $L_i MPP_L^Y/(p_x/p_y)$ and $T_j MPP_T^Y/(p_x/p_y)$, tend to increase. Both of these cases are similar to the case of a consumer who is endowed with fixed income and consumes two commodities X and Y, with the price of Y held constant and the price of X allowed to fall continuously. After the commodity-price ratio p_x/p_y falls below its critical value, both workers and landlords will tend to become better off compared with their positions at the critical value of p_x/p_y. Under these circumstances, a terms-of-trade improvement will definitely imply an improvement in the welfare of the country as a whole. But how does the posttrade welfare positions of workers and landlords compare with their pretrade positions? One thing is clear: the welfare of each landlord increases definitely because it increases continuously as p_x/p_y falls. We cannot tell about the welfare of the workers, for as p_x/p_y falls, each worker individually and as a group becomes continuously worse off, until p_x/p_y reaches its critical value. Beyond that point, as p_x/p_y continues to fall, each worker (and the group as a whole) tends to become better off. Thus, the outcome is necessarily indeterminate.

These conclusions are illustrated diagrammatically in figure 15.4(a), which reproduces the information contained in figure 11.1. Thus, the curve PP' in the second quadrant shows the relationship between the commodity-price ratio p_x/p_y and the factor-price ratio w/r; the curve XX' in the first quadrant shows the relationship between the marginal rate of substitution of labor for land in the production of X and the labor/land ratio (ρ_x) used in the production of X; and the curve YY' shows the relationship between the marginal rate of substitution of labor for land in Y and the labor/land ratio (ρ_y) used in Y. The overall labor/land ratio is given by the distance OM. The factor-price ratio can vary from OR to OS depending on the commodity-price ratio; ρ_y can vary from ON to OM; and ρ_x can vary from OM to OG. Note that, after the introduction of the overall labor/land ratio, the relationship between commodity prices and factor prices is given by the solid curve $KS'R'R$.

Figure 15.4(b) shows, in the first quadrant, the curves of the marginal physical product of labor, MPP_L^X and MPP_L^Y, as functions of ρ_x and ρ_y, respectively. Both of these curves are necessarily downward sloping because of diminishing returns. Note that only the solid parts of these curves are relevant to this discussion, because the following inequalities must necessarily be satisfied: $OM \leq \rho_x \leq OG$ (or $OM' \leq \rho_x \leq OG'$) and $ON \leq \rho_y \leq OM$ (or $ON' \leq \rho_y \leq OM'$). Note also that the two marginal productivity curves may intersect each other, but this complication is of no significance to this discussion.

In the first quadrant of figure 15.4(c) are drawn two curves (MPP_T^X and

MPP_T^Y) showing the marginal physical product of land in the production of X and Y as functions of ρ_x and ρ_y, respectively. These two curves are upward sloping, because when the labor/land ratio increases in any industry, the marginal physical product of land necessarily increases. Again, only the solid parts of these two curves are relevant. Let us now derive the budget line of a worker endowed with 1 unit of labor, and the budget line of a landlord endowed with 1 unit of land, for any commodity-price ratio.

Assume that the pretrade price ratio is equal to OP_0. The optimum labor/land ratios in the production of X and Y are ρ_x^0 and ρ_y^0, respectively.

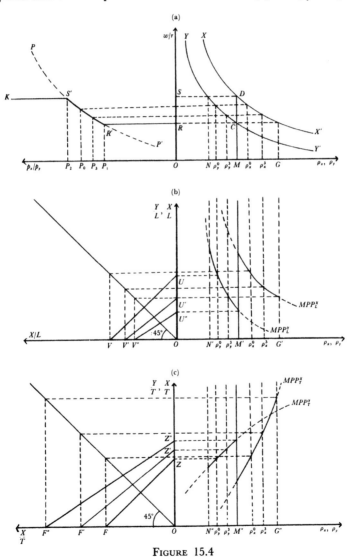

FIGURE 15.4

Hence, the marginal physical product of labor in X is given by OV and in Y by OU, and the budget line of our worker is given by the straight line VU in the second quadrant of figure 15.4(b). Similarly, the marginal physical product of land in X is given by OF and in Y by OZ. Thus, the budget line of our landlord is given by the straight line FZ in the second quadrant of figure 15.4(c). Note that FZ is parallel to VU and their common slope is equal to OP_0.

Now suppose that the country participates in international trade and that the international price ratio p_x/p_y, considered a constant by our economy, is given by OP_3. The domestic price ratio will necessarily fall from OP_0 to OP_3, and both labor/land ratios, ρ_x and ρ_y, will increase from ρ_x^0 and ρ_y^0 to ρ_x^3 and ρ_y^3, respectively. The marginal physical product of labor will fall in Y from OU to OU' and in X from OV to OV', and the budget line of our worker will shift inward from UV to $U'V'$. Similarly, the budget line of our landlord will shift outward from ZF to $Z'F'$. Again, $Z'F'$ is parallel to $U'V'$ and their common slope is equal to OP_3. Thus, $Z'F'$ and $U'V'$ are flatter than ZF and UV. Note that, without any knowledge about the indifference curves of landlords and workers, we can conclude that, with the introduction of trade, landlords become better off and workers become worse off.

Now assume that the international price ratio falls to OP_1. This is the critical value of the price ratio p_x/p_y referred to earlier. At this commodity-price ratio, the budget line of a typical worker will be given by $U''V''$ and the budget line of a typical landlord will be given by $Z''F''$. Our economy will completely specialize in the production of Y. Consider now what happens when the international price ratio falls below its critical value OP_1. How do the two budget lines shift? They will simply rotate through their respective Y-axis intercepts, becoming flatter and flatter. Thus, starting from a position where $p_x/p_y = OP_1$ and allowing p_x/p_y to fall, we can see that both workers and landlords will tend to become better off. Can we compare their pretrade with their posttrade positions? The budget line of a typical landlord lies definitely farther from the origin in the posttrade position, but the posttrade budget line of a typical worker may lie totally inside the corresponding pretrade budget line or it may intersect it. In the former case, the introduction of trade will definitely hurt the workers, while in the latter case the result is in general indeterminate: the indifference map of each worker will necessarily be needed for such evaluation, and the outcome can go either way.

SELECTED BIBLIOGRAPHY

The selected bibliography will be found at the end of chapter 16, p. 391.

16

The Gains from International Trade

1. The Social Welfare Function

The preceding chapter makes clear that the introduction of international trade can be expected to make some people better off and others worse off. In what sense, then, can we claim that international trade increases the welfare of all trading countries? As noted earlier, the difficulty arises essentially because of the impossibility of making interpersonal comparisons of well-being. We saw that the introduction of international trade hurt the workers and benefited the landlords in our model, but we cannot say whether trade increased or decreased social welfare. For this purpose, we need either a policy that compensates for losses or a means of somehow weighing the losses of the workers against the gains of the landlords. The latter method requires a judgment of an essentially ethical nature—and no two observers can be counted on to agree that a country benefits or suffers from international trade.

Ethical judgments have nothing to do with economics. But if we are willing to make them explicit, we can determine definitely whether or not the introduction of international trade improves social welfare.

Ethical judgments can be formalized in the shape of a Bergson–Samuelson social welfare function: $W(U_1, U_2, \ldots, U_n)$, where $U_i \equiv$ utility indicator of the ith individual in the economy. The social welfare function is supposed to characterize some ethical belief: yours, mine, the state's, God's, and so on. It is only required "that the belief be such as to admit of an unequivocal answer as to whether one configuration of the economic system is 'better' or 'worse' than any other or 'indifferent,' and that these relationships are transitive; i.e., A better than B, B better than C, implies A better than C, etc." (Samuelson 1947, p. 221). It is important to remember that the social welfare function is intrinsically ascientific: it either summarizes or implies a detailed set of ethical judgments regarding the way in which one man's welfare is to be "added" to another's.

No two observers can be counted on to make identical judgments. If we had to wait until we were given a specific social welfare function before we could say anything about the effect of trade on social welfare, we would not get very far. What we really want to do is to say as much as can be said that will be true on the basis of ethical propositions of a broad and commonly accepted kind. So we shall confine ourselves to those social welfare functions for which an increase in one person's welfare—the welfare of all other members of the society remaining the same—leads to an increase in social welfare. The totality of such functions is usually referred to as the Paretian class. This class of social welfare functions requires only the very broad ethical judgment that it is a good thing to make one man better off if nobody else is made worse off. No statement made on this basis requires the making of any interpersonal comparisons.

It seems that any statements made about the effect of international trade on social welfare on the basis of the Paretian class of social welfare functions (i.e., statements that are true for *all* social welfare functions which belong to the Paretian class) will meet a negligible amount of objection, because only a very broad ethical judgment ("that it is a good thing . . . ") is required and nothing else. But can we really get very far with the Paretian class of social welfare functions?

Assume that our economy consists only of two individuals, *A* and *B*. In figure 16.1, the utility of *A* (U_A) is measured along the horizontal axis and

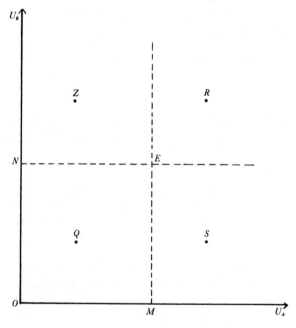

FIGURE 16.1

the utility of B (U_B) is measured along the vertical axis. Consider point E. At E the utility enjoyed by A is given by the horizontal distance OM and the utility of B is given by the vertical distance ON. (The construction of fig. 16.1 does not imply that utility is measurable; U_A and U_B are assumed to be arbitrarily chosen ordinal utility indicators.) If the economy before trade happens to be at E, the introduction of trade actually increases social welfare if the economy moves to a point northeast of E, such as point R. On the other hand, if the economy moves to a point southwest of E, such as Q, social welfare decreases after trade. Both of these conclusions are true for any Paretian social welfare function. It should be noted, however, that both of these cases imply that both individuals become either better off (point R) or worse off (point Q) with the introduction of trade. What about the case where one individual becomes better off while the other becomes worse off, as illustrated by points S and Z? Unless we know precisely the shape of the social welfare contour line passing through E, we cannot possibly say whether social welfare increases with the opening up of trade. Yet this is precisely the problem we want to avoid. If we are forced to con- clude that nothing can be said in these cases unless a social welfare function is completely specified, our results cannot claim generality. Is there a way around this difficulty? This question can be answered after the concept of the utility-possibility frontier, or for short, the utility frontier, is mastered.

2. The Utility-Possibility Frontier

Continue to assume that our economy consists of two individuals, A and B. The utility frontier shows the maximum level of well-being that B can enjoy, given the level of well-being enjoyed by A—or the maximum level of well- being that A can enjoy, given the level of well-being enjoyed by B. In chapter 5, the utility frontier is derived for the simple case where the economy happens to be endowed with fixed quantities of two commodities, X and Y. But how can the utility frontier be derived when the economy is endowed with fixed quantities of two factors of production, L and T, and produces, under constant returns to scale, two commodities, X and Y?

Consider figure 16.2. The curve MSN is the economy's production- possibilities frontier. Choose any point, S, on this frontier. The coordinates of S denote a specific quantity of X and Y. From S, drop lines parallel to the axes and form the Edgeworth–Bowley box $OCSD$. Now draw in the $OCSD$ box the indifference maps of A and B, with O as A's origin and S as B's. Every point in the box fixes six variables: X_A, X_B, Y_A, Y_B, U_A, and U_B, where $X_A \equiv$ amount of X allocated to A; $X_B \equiv$ amount of X allocated to B; $Y_A \equiv$ amount of Y allocated to A; $Y_B \equiv$ amount of Y allocated to B; $U_A \equiv U_A (X_A, Y_A) \equiv$ ordinal level of satisfaction of A; and $U_B \equiv U_B (X_B, Y_B) \equiv$ ordinal level of satisfaction of B. Now determine the locus of tangencies between the two sets of indifference curves as shown by the

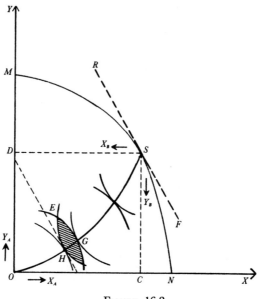

FIGURE 16.2

contract curve *OS*. Note that only points on the contract curve *OS* are Pareto optimal. That is, starting from any point not lying on the contract curve, such as *E*, we can always make at least one consumer better off without making the other worse off. Thus, a movement from *E* to *H* makes *B* better off, with *A* remaining on the same indifference curve; a movement from *E* to *G* makes *A* better off, with *B* remaining on the same indifference curve; and a movement from *E* to any point in the shaded area bounded by the two indifference curves through *E* makes both consumers better off. This is not possible when we start off from a point on the contract curve. Thus, starting at *H*, any movement which makes *A* better off necessarily makes *B* worse off, and any movement which makes *B* better off makes *A* worse off. Hence, all points on the contract curve are Pareto optimal.

From the contract curve *OS*, which is associated with the single production point *S*, we can read off the maximal combinations of U_A and U_B and plot them in the utility space (U_A, U_B) as shown by the downward-sloping curve *S'S'* in figure 16.3. For each point *S* on the production-possibilities frontier, we therefore, determine a utility curve (*S'S'*) in the utility space. Repeating the same experiment for each and every point on the production-possibilities frontier, we shall thus be able to derive an infinite number of such utility curves. But what is the true (or grand) utility-possibility frontier for the economy? The outer envelope of the individual utility curves (such as *S'S'*) were derived with respect to each point on the production-possibilities frontier. But there is a possible shortcut in the derivation of the utility frontier which will enable us to see some important

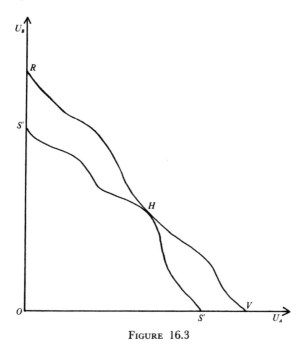

FIGURE 16.3

relationships between the production-possibilities frontier and the true utility frontier.

We can use an efficiency relationship to choose the point or points that belong to the true utility frontier from each contract curve OS associated with every output point S. Pareto-optimality, which exists only along the true utility frontier, requires that it should be impossible by any shift in production cum exchange to make one consumer better off without making the other worse off. But this criterion is met only when the marginal rate of transformation in production (i.e., the slope of the production-possibilities frontier at the specified point) is equal to the marginal rate of substitution in consumption. This is illustrated in figure 16.2 by points S and H. Production takes place at S, and the marginal rate of transformation is indicated by the absolute slope of the tangent to the production-possibilities frontier at S, that is, the slope of the broken line RSF. The marginal rate of substitution (along the contract curve OS) equals the slope at S only at point H. Hence, point H is a point along the contract curve OS which belongs to the true utility-possibilities frontier. In fact, it corresponds to point H in figure 16.3.

What is the rationale behind the optimality rule that the marginal rate of substitution (MRS_{XY}) must be equal to the marginal rate of transformation (MRT_{XY})? Suppose that $MRS_{XY} = 3$ and $MRT_{XY} = 2$. How can we prove that the point on the contract curve, where $MRS_{XY} = 3$, cannot possibly belong to the true utility frontier? The equality $MRT_{XY} = 2$

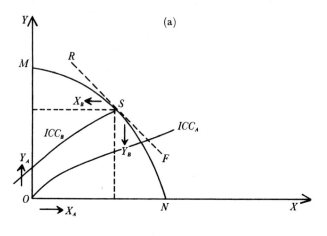

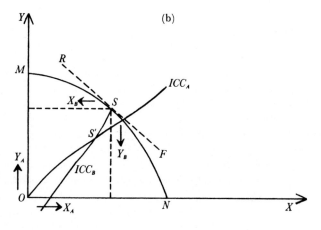

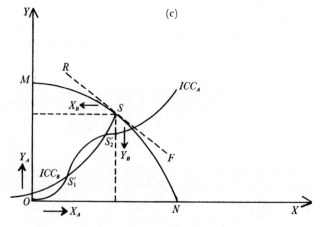

FIGURE 16.4

implies that the economy can increase the output of X by 1 unit by transferring resources from Y to X and reducing the output of Y by 2 units. Assume that we do just that. We have 1 extra unit of X and 2 less units of Y. Leaving A undisturbed, take away 3 units of Y from B and replace them by 1 unit of X. Since $MRS_{XY} = 3$, B is left indifferent. But we have an extra unit of Y left over. Since, by allocating this extra Y arbitrarily between A and B, we can make either A or B or both better off, the initial situation could not have been Pareto-optimal, that is, the original point in the utility space could not have been on the true utility frontier.

Repetition of this process for each point on the production-possibilities frontier will yield the true utility frontier. In figure 16.3, the true utility frontier is illustrated by the curve RHV. Note that the curve $S'HS'$ must be tangent to RHV at point H.

Is there a one-to-one correspondence between points on the production-possibilities frontier and the true utility frontier? Not necessarily. In fact, in general, a point on the production-possibilities frontier can correspond to none, one, two, or any number of points on the true utility frontier. However, a point on the true utility frontier necessarily corresponds to a single point on the production-possibilities frontier. How can we prove these propositions?

We already know that a point on a contract curve will give rise to a point on the true utility frontier if $MRT = MRS$. In turn, the condition $MRT = MRS$ is satisfied at the point(s) where the income consumption curves of A (emanating from 0) and B (emanating from S) for $p_x/p_y = MRT = $ slope of the production-possibilities frontier at S intersect each other. Figure 16.4(a) illustrates the possibility that the condition $MRT = MRS$ is not satisfied along the contract curve OS; figure 16.4(b) illustrates the possibility that the condition $MRT = MRS$ is satisfied only once along the contract curve; and figure 16.4 (c) illustrates the possibility that the condition $MRT = MRS$ is satisfied at two different points (S'_1 and S'_2) on the contract curve. There are other examples where the two income consumption curves intersect each other any number of times. In the limiting case where the indifference maps of A and B are identical and homothetic, there will be a point on the production-possibilities frontier for which the two income consumption curves will coincide throughout (this point is simply the pretrade equilibrium point). In this case, no other point on the production-possibilities frontier will correspond to any point on the true utility frontier, the latter being generated totally by that unique point on the production-possibilities frontier.

How do we know that a point on the true utility frontier corresponds to a unique point on the production-possibilities frontier? This is implicit in the discussion on Scitovsky's social indifference curves in chapter 5. Consider figure 16.5, which is similar to figure 16.4 but with the indifference curves of A and B drawn tangentially through the optimum point S' and the corresponding Scitovsky social indifference curve drawn tangentially to the

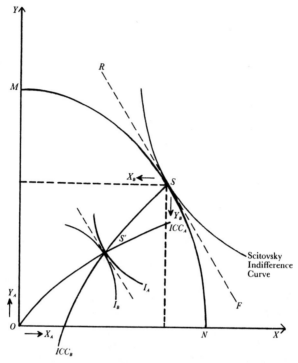

FIGURE 16.5

production-possibilities frontier at S. The slope of the Scitovsky social
indifference curve at a certain point is necessarily equal to the slope of the
corresponding point of either individual's indifference curve. Therefore, it is
obvious from figure 16.5 that the Scitovsky indifference curve must be tangent
to the production-possibility frontier at S and it must lie beyond the production-possibility frontier elsewhere. This implies that, if A remains on his
indifference curve I_A through S', any point on the production-possibilities
frontier MSN other than S will necessarily put B on a lower indifference
curve than I_B. Hence, point S on the production-possibilities frontier is the
only point where B's utility is maximized for a given level of utility for A
implied by the indifference curve I_A. Thus, when A's utility level is held
constant, there is one and only one point on the production-possibilities
frontier where B's utility is maximized, which is another way of saying that a
point on the utility frontier corresponds to a unique point on the production-
possibilities frontier.

The shape, curvature, and position of the utility-possibility frontier
depend on the particular indices selected to represent individual levels of
well-being. But the direction of slope is invariant. Normally, it will slope
downward: A can be made better off if, and only if, B becomes worse off.

However, in the presence of externalities (economies or diseconomies) in consumption, the utility frontier may, in certain regions, slope upward. If we confine ourselves to the Paretian class of social welfare functions, it becomes obvious that all those parts which slope upward can be ruled out as positions of maximum welfare: everybody can be made better off if the economy happens to be at an upward-sloping section of the utility frontier. The following ignores the possibility that the utility frontier may, in certain regions, slope upward.

What is the significance of the true utility frontier? First of all, no point outside the true utility frontier is attainable by our economy. Further, social welfare measured in terms of any Paretian social welfare function can never be maximized at a point lying inside the utility frontier. If we start from any point inside the utility frontier, it will always be possible to reorganize production and exchange and make everybody better off. Social welfare will therefore be at a maximum at some point on the true utility frontier. Does this conclusion imply that a movement from a point inside the utility frontier to a point on the utility frontier always represents an increase in social welfare? Not necessarily. The economy may very well move from a higher to a lower social welfare contour line, and social welfare may thus decrease.

Must the economy always operate on its true utility frontier? No. The economy will necessarily operate on its true utility frontier if it produces on its production-possibilities frontier and, further, if the marginal rate of transformation is equal to the marginal rate of substitution. But both of these conditions can be violated, as we saw in earlier chapters. Under our simplified assumptions of constant returns to scale, perfect competition, and complete absence of external effects, both conditions will be met and the economy will indeed be operating somewhere on the utility frontier. Exactly where on the frontier depends on the distribution of income, which in turn depends on factor ownership. Since factor ownership, at least in the context of our model, is considered exogenous, the final equilibrium point on the true utility frontier will be arbitrarily determined. In fact, by arbitrarily changing the factor ownership, we can make the economy operate on any point on the true utility frontier.

Perfect competition will, under several assumptions, put the economy on its true utility frontier. On the other hand, social welfare is maximized at some point on the true utility frontier. Does the solution attained under perfect competition necessarily maximize social welfare? No. Many great economists have fallen into the trap of believing that perfect competition necessarily maximizes social welfare. But this need not be so. The equilibrium point attained under perfect competition necessarily depends on factor ownership. To say that perfect competition puts the economy on the best or optimum point on the true utility frontier is to assert that the initial factor ownership is somehow optimum, and this need not be true.

The point on the utility frontier where social welfare is maximized—the bliss point—can be determined only with reference to a social welfare function that is completely specified. Without complete specification of the social welfare function, it is absolutely impossible to determine the bliss point. We are sure only that it lies somewhere on the utility frontier. Figure 16.6 illustrates the determination of the bliss point. The curve *REV* is the economy's true utility frontier. The curves W_1, W_2, and W_3 are only three social welfare contour (or indifference) lines. The contour lines are necessarily downward sloping, because our social welfare function is Paretian. A movement from a lower to a higher social welfare contour line causes social welfare to increase. Social welfare is seen to be maximized at point *E*, where the true utility frontier touches the highest contour of the welfare function. Remember that the bliss point, *E*, is the point of maximum welfare only in relation to the family of social welfare contours drawn. For a different set of contours, another point on the utility frontier (*REV*) will become the bliss point.

As noted earlier, perfect competition will put our economy on the utility frontier. But there is no guarantee that perfect competition will put the economy at point *E*, assuming that a social welfare function is completely specified and thus the bliss point, *E*, is perfectly determined. If perfect competition does not put the economy at *E*, how is it possible for social welfare to be maximized? For instance, suppose that perfect competition puts the economy at point *N*. How is it possible to secure a movement *along*

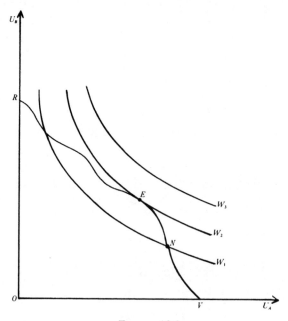

FIGURE 16.6

the utility frontier from N to E? This can be accomplished by a proper redistribution of wealth in the form of lump-sum transfers which destroy none of the conditions necessary for the economy to operate on its true utility frontier.

3. The Gains From International Trade: The Case of the Small Country

The preceding section is intentionally confined to a closed economy. But the tools we have developed can be effectively used to enlighten our discussion of the gains from trade. Let us begin with the simple case of a country that is too small to affect its terms of trade. Section 4 deals with the more general case of a country that is large enough to affect its terms of trade.

Given the international terms of trade $(p \equiv p_x/p_y)$ and the production-possibilities frontier, we can determine a consumption-possibilities frontier which is simply the highest income contour line generated by the equation

$$\text{income} = pX_p + Y_p$$

which the production-possibilities frontier can reach. The consumption-possibilities frontier lies beyond the production-possibilities frontier, except at the optimum production point (X_p, Y_p), where the two frontiers coincide (i.e., they are tangential). Using the technique of the preceding section, we can determine, on the basis of the consumption-possibilities frontier, what may be called society's cum-trade true utility frontier. The relationship between the cum-trade true utility frontier and the true utility frontier under autarky is crucial, because the gains from trade will in the end depend on the relationship between these two frontiers.

Let us derive first the cum-trade utility frontier. Again, assume for simplicity that our economy consists of two individuals A and B. Given their indifference maps and the international price ratio p, we can determine uniquely the income consumption curve for each individual. Now consider figure 16.7. The straight line UV is assumed to be the consumption-possibilities frontier. With respect to the origin of the diagram, draw the income consumption curve of A as shown by ICC_A. Now rotate by $180°$ B's diagram of the income consumption curve and place its corner at U, as shown by ICC_B. Then slide the origin of B's income consumption curve along the consumption-possibilities frontier and determine the region RN on the consumption-possibilities frontier where the two income consumption curves intersect each other at least once in the first quadrant, or, where they are tangential. The region RN on the consumption-possibilities frontier is the only region where the condition $MRS = MRT = p$ is satisfied for some income distribution. The cum-trade utility frontier corresponds to this region (RN) only. The regions UR and NV have no counterpart on the cum-trade utility frontier. Put differently, the region RN is definitely superior

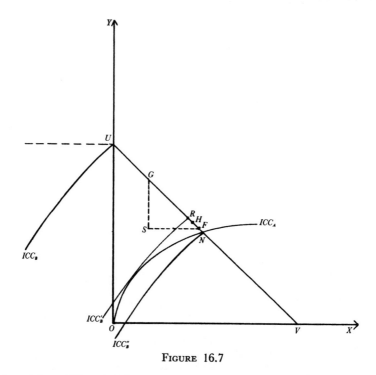

FIGURE 16.7

to the regions *UR* and *NV* in the sense that, for any distribution of utilities (i.e., U_A and U_B) corresponding to a point in either region *UR* or *NV*, there will always be a point or points in the region *RN* which will yield higher utilities for both *A* and *B*. The truth of this proposition follows directly from the analysis of the preceding section and in particular from the construction of figure 16.5.

Figure 16.8 shows the cum-trade utility frontier, *CD*, derived on the basis of the consumption-possibilities frontier of figure 16.7. What is the relationship between this and the autarkic utility frontier? One thing is certain: the autarkic utility frontier cannot lie beyond the cum-trade utility frontier *CD*, because the autarkic production-possibilities frontier cannot lie beyond the consumption-possibilities frontier. Thus, for any point (*S*) on the production-possibilities frontier that lies inside the consumption-possibilities frontier *UV*, there will correspond a utility curve *S'S"* in the utility space (fig. 16.8) that will lie totally inside the cum-trade utility frontier. This is because, for any point *S* that lies inside the consumption-possibilities frontier, there will be points on the frontier (i.e., region *FG*) implying larger quantities of *X* and *Y*; and any of these points will yield a utility curve in figure 16.8 which will lie totally beyond the *S'S"* curve. For instance, point *H* in figure 16.7 will give rise to the utility curve *H'H"* in figure 16.8, which necessarily lies uniformly beyond *S'S"*. Note that the curve *H'H"* is tangent

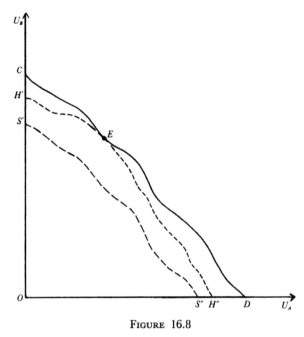

FIGURE 16.8

to the cum-trade utility frontier at point E, because we selected point H to lie in the region RN. Had we picked a point in the region GR of figure 16.7, we would have ended up with a utility curve in figure 16.8 lying between $S'S''$ and CD without touching either of them. Does this argument prove that the autarky utility frontier will lie completely inside the cum-trade utility frontier? No. All we have proved is that all points on the production-possibilities frontier which lie inside the consumption-possibilities frontier will yield utility curves which will lie inside the cum-trade utility frontier. But what about the equilibrium production point, that is, the point where the consumption-possibilities frontier is tangent to the production-possi-bilities frontier? Will not this point at least yield a utility curve in figure 16.8 that will be tangent to the cum-trade utility frontier at one or more points? That depends on the position of the production point. If it lies in the region RN (fig. 16.7), it will necessarily yield a utility curve in figure 16.8 that will be tangent to the cum-trade utility frontier at one or more points. However, if it lies in the regions UR or NV, it will yield a utility curve that will lie totally inside the cum-trade utility frontier. It is therefore appropriate to distinguish clearly between these two cases: (*a*) If the equilibrium production point lies in the regions UR or NV, the cum-trade utility frontier will lie totally beyond the autarkic utility frontier. (*b*) If the equilibrium production point lies in the region RN, the cum-trade utility frontier will normally lie outside the autarkic utility frontier but with the two frontiers tangent to each other at one or more points. Of course, should the region RN shrink to a single point—as in the case of identical and homothetic tastes, where the region *RN* actually coincides with the equilibrium production point before and after trade—the two utility frontiers will completely coincide.

Consider now case (*a*). What can be said about the effect of trade on social welfare? Does the opening up of trade necessarily improve social welfare? Consider figure 16.9, which is similar to figure 16.8. The curve *CD* is the cum-trade utility frontier, while the curve *FG* is the autarkic frontier. By assumption, *FG* lies uniformly inside *CD*. Before trade, the economy is somewhere on *FG*, such as point *M*. With the opening up of trade, the economy moves somewhere on *CD*. Does this movement necessarily imply an increase in social welfare? In other words, does the country become better off with trade?

If we knew that the economy moved from *M* to a point on *CD* in the region *RS* where both *A* and *B* become better off with trade, we could unequivocally claim that trade improved social welfare, because, for *any* Paretian welfare function, the country can reach a higher welfare contour line with trade. This is so because all Paretian welfare functions give rise to welfare contour lines that are strictly negatively sloped; and higher welfare contour lines imply higher social welfare. Thus, the welfare contour line passing through *M* cannot cross *CD* in the region *RS*; and any point in the region *RS* will definitely lie on a higher welfare contour line. This conclusion is true for all Paretian welfare functions. It is also independent of whether or

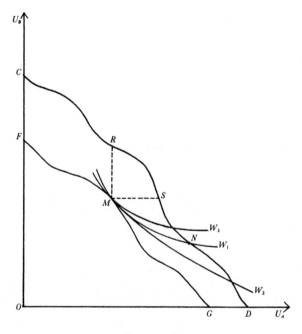

FIGURE 16.9

not social welfare before trade was actually being maximized at M. To put it differently, it is immaterial to our conclusion (that all points in the region RS are superior to M) whether the welfare contour line through M is or is not tangent to the autarkic utility frontier FG at M.

What if one individual becomes worse off with trade, that is, what if the economy moves from M to some point in the region CR or the region SD? Can we still claim that our economy becomes better off with trade? Unfortunately, nothing can be said about this important case. Suppose that the economy moves from M to N. Now A becomes better off (i.e., U_A increases) and B becomes worse off (i.e., U_B decreases) with trade. What happens to social welfare? That depends on the specific social welfare function we happen to be adopting. For instance, the welfare contour line passing through M may pass through N (as illustrated by W_1), or below N (as illustrated by W_2), or above N (as illustrated by W_3). If the actual welfare contour line is W_1, social welfare will remain the same; if it is W_2, social welfare will improve; and if it is W_3, social welfare will deteriorate. Thus, the outcome depends on the specific social welfare function adopted. Some people will pass the ethical judgment that N is superior to M, others will prefer M to N, and still others will be indifferent between the two points. This is a sad conclusion, because if there is nothing we can say in general— that is, for *all* Paretian social welfare functions—we cannot possibly claim that trade is unquestionably superior to no trade. How can this difficulty be resolved?

Consider again figure 16.9. We have already seen that, if the economy moves from M to any point in the region RS (including points R and S), social welfare will definitely improve. But perfect competition cannot be expected to shift the economy from M to a point in the region RS. However, recall that we can make the economy move along its utility frontier through a system of lump-sum transfers. Hence, irrespective of the actual posttrade equilibrium point on the cum-trade utility frontier, say point N, the economy could be made to move to some point in the region RS where everybody becomes better off and thus social welfare unquestionably improves. We can therefore say that trade is *potentially* superior to no trade, because for *any* Paretian welfare function, our country, through a system of lump-sum transfers, can be made to reach a higher welfare contour line after trade. Does this conclusion depend on the initial position of M? Not at all. The same can be said of any point on the autarkic utility frontier, because the cum-trade utility frontier lies uniformly outside the autarkic frontier. Therefore, potentially, everybody can be made better off with trade, because no matter what the original equilibrium point on the autarkic utility frontier is, there will always be a region on the cum-trade utility frontier that will imply that everybody is better off with trade. In other words, compensated free trade is better than no trade *for all income distributions*. As Samuelson (1939, p. 204) put it: "Although it cannot be shown that every individual *is* made better off by the introduction of trade, it can be shown that through trade every individual *could* be made better off (or in the limiting case, no worse off). In other words, if a unanimous decision were required in order for trade to be permitted, it would always be possible for those who desired trade to buy off those opposed to trade, with the result that all could be made better off."

Conversely, it is impossible under autarky to make everyone better off than at the equilibrium free-trade point, because the autarkic utility frontier cannot lie beyond the cum-trade utility frontier. Thus, given any point on the cum-trade utility frontier, it is impossible to find a point on the autarkic utility frontier where *everybody* is better off under autarky.

When the production-possibilities frontier is linear, the equilibrium production point will coincide, in general, with either point U or point V of figure 16.7. Since neither U nor V can be expected to lie in the region RN (both consumers will usually want to consume something of both commodities), trade is in general potentially better than no trade. In the limiting case where the international price ratio happens to coincide with the slope of the linear production-possibilities frontier, the consumption-possibilities frontier will coincide with the production-possibilities frontier and the cum-trade utility frontier will coincide with the autarkic utility frontier. In this case, trade need not take place, but even if it does—because the production point is indeterminate—it need not affect the welfare of anybody. In this limiting case, we can thus safely say that trade is not potentially inferior to no trade.

Case (*b*), where the cum-trade utility frontier is tangent to the autarkic utility frontier at one or more points, occurs in general when the production possibilities frontier is curvilinear rather than linear. As noted earlier, the two utility frontiers will be tangent to each other at one or more points if, and only if, the posttrade equilibrium production point lies in the region RN (fig. 16.7). Assuming that this is actually the case, can we still assert that trade is potentially better than no trade? This cannot possibly be true for *all* Paretian welfare functions and *all* income distributions. In particular, for those welfare functions for which social welfare is maximized at a point of tangency between the autarkic and the cum-trade utility frontiers—and there is an infinite number of such Paretian welfare functions—social welfare will not increase after the introduction of international trade, assuming that the pre-trade income distribution is optimum. But social welfare need not decrease either in the present case. Hence, although it cannot be claimed that with the introduction of trade everybody could become better off for *all* income distributions and *all* Paretian welfare functions, we can definitely say that the introduction of trade need not make anybody worse off (potentially).

Figure 16.10 illustrates the point. The curve CD is the cum-trade utility frontier and the broken curve FG is the autarkic utility frontier. The two utility frontiers are tangent at E, which corresponds to the posttrade

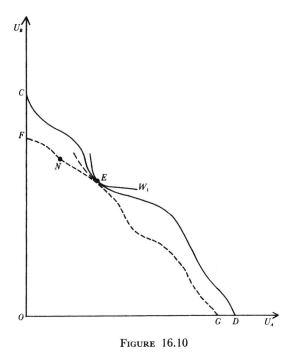

FIGURE 16.10

equilibrium production point on the production-possibilities frontier (point *H*, say of fig. 16.6). If social welfare happens to be maximized at *E*, we cannot claim that free trade makes everybody better off (potentially). For the economy could reach point *E* even without trade. However, and this is important, free trade need not make anybody worse off in a potential sense. This is obvious because the autarkic utility frontier cannot possibly lie beyond the cum-trade utility frontier. Finally, note that even in the present case a slightly modified welfare contour line (as shown by the broken contour line through E_1) could imply increased social welfare after the introduction of trade.

4. The Gains From International Trade: The Case of the Large Country

The preceding analysis depends on the assumption that our country is too small to affect the international price ratio. Do the same conclusions hold for a country that is large enough to affect the international price ratio? To answer this question, we have to find out how free trade affects the utility frontier of the economy. As a first step, we have to determine the economy's consumption-possibilities frontier. But the trading opportunities of the large country cannot be represented by a linear offer curve of the rest of the world; therefore, a way must be found to represent the commodity combinations attainable by trade.

Figure 16.11 shows the offer curve of the rest of the world. The curve *MN* in figure 16.12 is our economy's production-possibilities frontier. For any international price ratio p_x/p_y, we can determine two things: (*a*) the optimum production point on our economy's production-possibilities frontier by the condition $MRT = p_x/p_y$ and (*b*) the equilibrium trade point on the offer curve of the rest of the world by drawing a vector with slope equal to the given international price ratio through the origin of figure 16.11 until it intersects the offer curve—the intersection being the equilibrium trade point. For instance, for the international price ratio given by the slope of TOT_1 (fig. 16.11) or the slope of *UV* (fig. 16.12), the equilibrium trade point for the rest of the world is T_1 (fig. 16.11) and the optimum production point for our economy is P_1 (fig. 16.12). If our economy were small, the straight line UP_1V (fig. 16.12) would have been its con-sumption-possibilities frontier. What happens now that the rest of the world is willing to trade at point T_1 only? Our economy can produce at P_1 and consume at C_1 only where the distance P_1C_1 (fig. 16.12) is equal to the distance OT_1 (fig. 16.11). Point C_1 is a point on our economy's consumption-

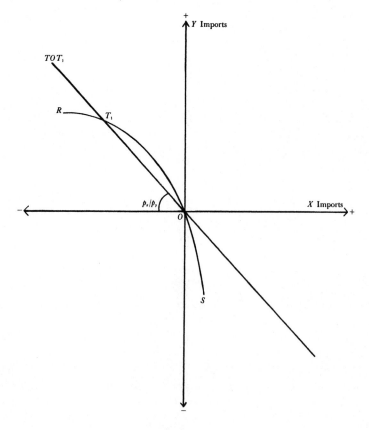

FIGURE 16.11

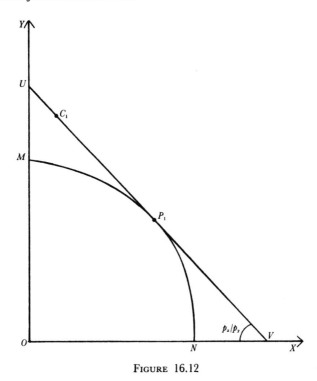

FIGURE 16.12

possibilities frontier. Repetition of this process for all values of p_x/p_y will yield our country's free-trade consumption-possibilities frontier, which will definitely lie beyond our economy's production-possibilities frontier except at one point—the point where the slope of the production-possibilities frontier is equal to the slope of the offer curve of the rest of the world at the origin.

Note that not all points on the production-possibilities frontier are acceptable candidates as production points under free trade. Point C_1 (fig. 16.12) has to lie in the first quadrant; but for some values of p_x/p_y, and hence for some points on the production-possibilities frontier, point C_1 will lie in the second or fourth quadrants. These points, however, are not relevant.

Figure 16.13 shows the consumption-possibilities frontier (CD) and the production-possibilities frontier (MN). The two frontiers are tangential at point R. Elsewhere, the consumption-possibilities frontier (CD) lies beyond the production-possibilities frontier (MN). But what about the corresponding utility-possibilities frontiers? From the preceding analysis, it follows that the autarkic utility frontier cannot lie beyond the cum-trade utility frontier and the cum-trade utility frontier cannot lie inside the autarkic utility frontier—but the two frontiers can be tangent to each other at one or more points depending on the number of intersections between the income

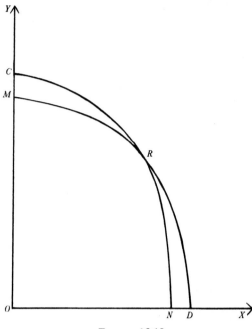

FIGURE 16.13

consumption curve of *A* drawn with respect to *O* and the income consumption curve of *B* drawn with respect to *R* (as in fig. 16.4) for a price ratio equal to the common slope of the two frontiers at *R* (fig. 16.13). If no intersection between the two income consumption curves just described exists, then the cum-trade utility frontier will lie totally outside the autarkic utility frontier, and compensated free trade (i.e., free trade accompanied by optimal transfers) will definitely be better than no trade at all. But what if the two utility frontiers are tangent to each other at one or more points? Can we still assert that compensated free trade is superior to no trade? As is pointed out in section 3, such a statement cannot be made for *all* Paretian welfare functions and all income distributions. Even in this limiting case, however, trade cannot be proved potentially inferior to no trade.

In summary, compensated free trade is superior to no trade; or in the limiting case, compensated free trade is not inferior to no trade. This conclusion remains valid for all countries. Chapter 20 considers the proposition that restricted trade is better than free trade.

5. *The Gains From Trade: The World as a Whole*

So far, we have been dealing with the effect of international trade on a single country's welfare. Let us now demonstrate that international trade improves the potential welfare of all trading countries.

Chapter 2 shows how the world production-possibilities frontier can be constructed when the production-possibilities frontiers of the individual countries are linear; that under autarky the world is in general producing *inside* the world frontier; and that free trade enables the world to produce *on* the world frontier. We can now show that this conclusion holds even in the case where the production-possibilities frontiers of the individual countries are curvilinear and argue that compensated free international trade is superior to no trade, or, in the limiting case, compensated free trade is not inferior to no trade, for the world as a whole.

How can the world production-possibilities frontier be derived in the presence of increasing opportunity costs in individual countries? Assume that we have two countries, *A* and *B*. In figure 16.14, *A*'s production-possibilities frontier is given by the curve *MN*. Country *A*'s production block (*ONEM*) will remain in this position throughout. Now rotate *B*'s production block by 180° and place it tangent to *A*'s production block as shown by *HCED*. Let *B*'s production block slide along *A*'s production block in such a way that the curve *CED* remains tangential to *MEN*, *CH* remains parallel to the horizontal axis, and *HD* remains parallel to the vertical axis. The corner of *B*'s production block will now trace out the broken curve *FHG*, which is simply the world production-possibilities frontier. It shows the

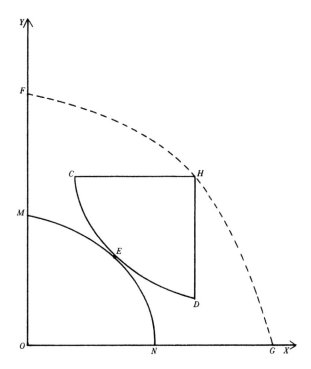

FIGURE 16.14

maximum amount of one commodity that the world as a whole can produce given the amount of production of the other.

What condition must be satisfied if the world is to produce on the world frontier *FHG* and not inside it? From the construction of figure 16.14, the two countries must be producing at points on their individual production-possibilities frontiers where their respective opportunity costs are the same, since the two production frontiers in figure 16.14 are required to be tangential. What is the commonsense meaning of this condition?

Suppose that A's marginal rate of transformation (MRT_{XY}^A) is 3 and B's (MRT_{XY}^B) 2. How can we show that the world is not producing on the world frontier? Assume that A reduces its production of X by 1 unit while B increases its production of X by 1 unit. The total world production of X remains constant. What happens to the world output of Y? Since $MRT_{XY}^A = 3$, A's output of Y will increase by 3 units; and since $MRT_{XY}^B = 2$, B's output of Y will fall by only 2 units. Therefore, the world output of Y will increase by $3 - 2 = 1$ unit. By the suggested reallocation of resources, the world can increase the output of Y without reducing the output of X. Thus, the initial allocation could not have been optimal, that is, the world could not have been producing on the world frontier. Note that when $MRT_{XY}^A = MRT_{XY}^B$ it is impossible to increase the output of one commodity without reducing the output of the other.

As we have seen, international trade takes place when the pretrade price ratios of the two countries differ. But the pretrade price ratios merely reflect the equilibrium marginal rates of transformation under autarky. Hence, international trade takes place when the pretrade marginal rates of transformation differ between countries. In other words, international trade takes place when the world is not producing on the world production-possibilities frontier. But free trade equalizes relative prices (and hence marginal rates of transformation) between countries. Free trade thus makes it possible for the world as a whole to produce on the world frontier and not inside it. Does it necessarily follow that the world as a whole actually becomes better off with free international trade? Free trade will in general make some people better off and others worse off. Under these circumstances, nothing can be said in general about the effect of free international trade on world welfare. However, free international trade is *potentially* better than no trade from the point of view of the world as a whole. Thus, starting from any pretrade equilibrium position implying $MRT_{XY}^A \neq MRT_{XY}^B$, we can increase the world output of both commodities. Let each individual get what he was consuming before trade. By arbitrarily distributing the excess production—over the pretrade levels—to all individuals around the world, we can make every individual better off, or at least we can make some better off without making others worse off. It is in this sense of *potential welfare* that we conclude that free trade is better than no trade, from the point of view of each individual country and of the world as a whole.

For completeness, the limiting case where in the pretrade equilibrium position $MRT_{XY}^A = MRT_{XY}^B$ must be noted. Here, the opening up of international trade will not be followed by any international transactions; hence, every individual will retain his pretrade status.

SELECTED BIBLIOGRAPHY

Baldwin, R. 1952. The new welfare economics and gains in international trade. *Quarterly Journal of Economics* 66: 91–101; reprinted in R. E. Caves and H. G. Johnson (Editors). *Readings in International Economics*. Homewood, Ill.: R. D. Irwin, Inc., 1968.

Kemp, M. C. 1969. *The Pure Theory of International Trade and Investment*. Englewood Cliffs, N.J.: Prentice-Hall, Inc. Chap. 12.

Samuelson, P. A. 1938. Welfare economics and international trade. *American Economic Review* 28: 261–66; reprinted in J. Stiglitz (Editor). *The Collected Scientific Papers of Paul A. Samuelson*. Cambridge, Mass.: The M.I.T. Press, 1966.

———. 1939. The gains from international trade. *Canadian Journal of Economics and Political Science* 5: 195–205; reprinted in H. Ellis and L. Metzler (Editors). *Readings in the Theory of International Trade*. Homewood, Ill.: R. D. Irwin, Inc., 1950.

———. 1962. The gains from international trade once again. *Economic Journal* 72: 820–29; reprinted in J. Stiglitz (Editor). *The Collected Scientific Papers of Paul A. Samuelson*. Cambridge, Mass.: The M.I.T. Press, 1966.

Stolper, W., and P. A. Samuelson. 1941. Protection and real wages. *Review of Economic Studies* 9: 58–73; reprinted in H. Ellis and L. Metzler (Editors). *Readings in the Theory of International Trade*. Homewood, Ill.: R. D. Irwin, 1950.

Samuelson, P. A. 1947. *Foundations of Economic Analysis*. Cambridge, Mass.: Harvard University Press.

VII

International Trade Policy

17

Forms of Trade Control

Chapter 16 demonstrates that free international trade is potentially better than no trade from the point of view both of the world as a whole and of each individual trading country. This thesis has never been successfully refuted, despite the fact that most arguments for protection are asserted with great conviction. Yet in the real world, the free flow of trade has been, as a rule, impeded by several trade-control devices, such as tariffs, quotas, and exchange controls. Chapters 17–20 analyze the effects of these trade-control devices. This chapter deals with the forms of trade controls.

Trade controls can be classified into two major categories: those trade controls that directly influence prices, such as taxes and subsidies, and those that directly influence quantities, such as quotas and exchange controls.[1] Taxes or subsidies, as well as quotas, may be imposed on exports or imports, so there are really four trade controls operating through prices and two trade controls operating through quantities, as shown in table 17.1.

In general, taxes (whether on imports or exports) can be imposed in any one of the following three ways:

a) *The ad valorem basis:* This tax, or "duty," is legally fixed in the form of a percentage on the value of the commodity imported or exported, inclusive or exclusive of transport cost. For instance, if an ad valorem import duty of 10 percent is fixed on the value of imports, exclusive of transport cost, an importer of commodities valued at $100 is required to pay $10 import duty to the government. In general, if t_a is the ad valorem import duty, the importer is

1. Such "monetary controls" as exchange controls and multiple exchange rates will not be discussed. However, quotas and exchange controls can be shown to produce the same economic results, and any system of multiple exchange rates can be shown to be equivalent to a system of import and export taxes and subsidies.

TABLE 17.1

	Controls Operating Through:		
	prices		quantities
	taxes	subsidies	quotas
Exports	Export tax	Export subsidy	Export quota
Imports	Import tax (or tariff)	Import subsidy	Import quota

required to pay $(1 + t_a)p_m$ per unit imported, where p_m is the price accruing to the foreign exporter and $t_a p_m$ is the tax revenue per unit imported.

b) *The specific basis:* This tax is legally fixed in the form of an absolute amount of domestic currency per unit imported or exported. For instance, if a tariff of $1 is imposed on every unit of a particular commodity imported irrespective of its price, an importer must pay $\$(p_m + t_s)$ per unit imported, where p_m is the price accruing to the foreign exporter and t_s is the tax revenue per unit imported.

c) *The combined basis:* This is a combination of an ad valorem tax *plus* a specific tax. For instance, if an importer is required to pay to the government $\$t_s$ (specific duty) plus $t_a \times 100$ percent on the price of the commodity (p_m) per unit imported, the importer will be paying to the government $t_s + t_a p_m$ per unit imported; his per unit cost (inclusive of the tax) will be equal to $t_s + (1 + t_a)p_m$.

Given the price of the commodity exported or imported, as the case may be, there is a one-to-one correspondence between ad valorem rates and specific rates. Consider the case of a commodity imported into the United States whose price in the international market is $\$p_m$. A specific import duty of $\$t_s$ implies that the per unit cost to the U.S. importer is $p_m + t_s$. On the other hand, an ad valorem rate of t_a implies that the per unit cost to the U.S. importer is $(1 + t_a)p_m$. The two import duties will be equivalent if

$$(1 + t_a)p_m = p_m + t_s,$$

or

$$t_a p_m = t_s, \tag{17.1}$$

or

$$t_a = t_s/p_m. \tag{17.1}'$$

On the assumption that p_m is known, given t_a we can determine t_s directly from equation (17.1), and given t_s we can determine t_a directly from equation (17.1)'. In the same way, it can be shown that any tax imposed on the combined basis is equivalent to a uniquely determined ad valorem rate. This demonstration does not imply that it is of no consequence whether one or another of the three methods is used to fix the tax rate legally. This analysis assumes that p_m is known, but p_m may or may not be known. If it is known to begin with, it may not remain constant through time, even though factor supplies, technology, and tastes remain everywhere the same, for p_m is a "money" (or absolute) price depending on monetary conditions. During an inflationary period, where p_m will be rising, the ad valorem rate equivalent to a specific rate will tend to fall. During a deflationary period, where p_m will be falling, the ad valorem rate equivalent to a specific rate will tend to rise. This can be verified with equation $(17.1)'$. Given t_s, as p_m rises t_a falls, and as p_m falls t_a rises. [2]

Since subsidies are merely negative taxes, what has been said in relation to export and import taxes necessarily holds for export and import subsidies as well. Thus, subsidies may be imposed on an ad valorem, specific, or combined basis; the equivalence between ad valorem and specific rates holds for subsidies as well.

What follows concerns ad valorem rates only because we will continue to concentrate on relative prices, for which all taxes or subsidies must be expressed in the form of ad valorem rates. Once the equilibrium relative prices are determined, there will be a one-to-one correspondence between the "absolute price level" and the specific rates equivalent to the originally imposed ad valorem rates. Therefore, the effects of the equivalent specific rates will be identical, in long-run equilibrium, to the effects of the ad valorem rates.

Quotas, as opposed to taxes and subsidies on imports and exports, control the absolute quantities of exports or imports, as the case may be. A government may wish to limit the imports of a particular commodity to a certain maximum quantity (import quota) per unit of time. For this reason, it may issue import licences that it may either sell to importers at a competitive price or just give away as gifts to importers on a first-come, first-served basis. (Alternatively, the government may consider it desirable to limit the *value* of imports by providing the importers with a limited amount of foreign currency for the purchase of a particular commodity.) Observe that, while the government can restrict the quantity of a particular commodity imported into the country, it cannot force importers to import a larger quantity than they would have imported under free-trade conditions.

A government may consider it desirable to restrict the exports of a particular commodity to a certain maximum quantity (export quota) per unit of time. Thus, exporters may be licensed to sell abroad only a certain quota of the product. Again, while the government is capable of directly

2. Another difference between ad valorem and specific rates occurs where various qualities of a certain commodity exist and a flat ad valorem rate is used for all qualities. Then the absolute per unit tax (i.e., the equivalent specific tax) will be lower for cheaper qualities. On the other hand, if a flat specific tax is used, the equivalent ad valorem rate will be lower for the more expensive qualities.

reducing exports below their free-trade level, it is impossible to force the exporters through this kind of quantitative restriction to increase their exports beyond the level where they achieve profit maximization.

SELECTED BIBLIOGRAPHY

The selected bibliography will be found at end of chapter 20, p. 444.

18

Import and Export Taxes: The Case of
the Small Country

Consider the case of a small country whose buying and selling in the international market does not have any appreciable effect on international prices. For this purpose, Meade's geometric technique, explained in chapter 6 and reviewed below, is used.

Assume that our economy is endowed with two factors of production, labor, L, and land, T, and that it produces, under constant returns to scale, two commodities, X and Y, with X being labor intensive relative to Y. Assume that tastes can be summarized by a social indifference map and that our economy can trade commodities X and Y in the international market at the given prices $\bar{p}_x$ and $\bar{p}_y$, respectively. For convenience, the given international price ratio $\bar{p}_x/\bar{p}_y$ will be represented by the symbol $\bar{p}$. (In general, p will indicate the international price ratio and $\bar{p}$ a specific value of p.) The free-trade, long-run equilibrium position is illustrated in figure 18.1, which is similar to figure 6.2 in all essential respects. Thus, the terms-of-trade line is given by TOT, with slope equal to $\bar{p}$, and our economy's offer curve is given by OFR in the first quadrant. The straight line ECD in the second quadrant, parallel to TOT, is the consumption-possibilities frontier, and the economy's production block is given by RC. The production block has been placed tangential to the consumption-possibilities frontier at the equilibrium consumption point C; its corner lies necessarily on the terms-of-trade line TOT, as shown by point R.

1. The Imposition of a Nonprohibitive Tariff

How would the imposition of an ad valorem import duty (i.e., a tariff), t, affect the equilibrium position of figure 18.1? Nothing that our economy does will affect international prices, $\bar{p}_x$ and $\bar{p}_y$. Therefore, the rest of the world

399

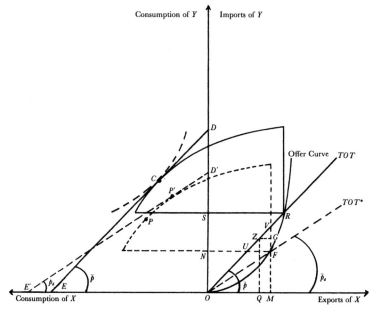

FIGURE 18.1

will continue to trade along the terms-of-trade line TOT. But now the domestic price ratio (p_d) will no longer be equal to the international price ratio; as a result, domestic production, consumption, exports, and imports will all, in general, change after the imposition of the tariff. What is the relationship between the domestic price ratio (p_d) and $\bar{p}$? A full answer is given later in this chapter. For the moment, let us simplify our analysis by assuming that the tariff is *nonprohibitive*. In other words, assume that the ad valorem rate is such that our economy continues, after the imposition of the tariff, to import commodity Y and export commodity X.

The imposition of a nonprohibitive tariff, t, will necessarily make the domestic price of commodity Y (p_y^d) higher than the international price $\bar{p}_y$. In particular,

$$p_y^d = (1 + t)\bar{p}_y. \tag{18.1}$$

The domestic price of commodity X (p_x^d), however, will continue to be equal to the international price $\bar{p}_x$. Accordingly, the domestic price ratio, after the imposition of the tariff, will be given by

$$\bar{p}_d = \frac{p_x^d}{p_y^d} = \frac{\bar{p}_x}{(1 + t)\bar{p}_y} = \left(\frac{1}{1 + t}\right)\bar{p} < \bar{p}. \tag{18.2}$$

The symbol p_d is the domestic price ratio in general and the symbol $\bar{p}_d$ is a specific value of p_d. From equation (18.2), the domestic price ratio, $\bar{p}_d$, will definitely be lower than the corresponding international price ratio, $\bar{p}$. Consider, in figure 18.1, the broken terms-of-trade line TOT^*, whose slope is given by $\bar{p}_d$. What would the equilibrium trade point have been in the absence of tariffs if the international price ratio had been equal to $\bar{p}_d$? Equilibrium would have occurred at F (at the point where the terms-of-trade line TOT^* intersects our economy's offer curve), $E'P'D'$ would have been the consumption-possibilities frontier, P' with respect to the origin O would have been the equilibrium consumption point, and P' with respect to F would have been the equilibrium production point. But now the situation is slightly different. While the domestic price ratio is $\bar{p}_d$ and the economy will definitely be producing on the production block at point P', the international price ratio is $\bar{p}$ and the rest of the world will trade in equilibrium somewhere along the terms-of-trade line TOT. If our economy were to consume at P' and trade at F, international equilibrium would not exist, for point F does not lie on the terms-of-trade line TOT. Yet we know that, when the domestic price ratio is $\bar{p}_d$, our economy will produce at P' on the production block FP', the consumption-possibilities frontier will be given by $E'P'D'$, and consumption will occur at P', thus giving rise to the trade point F. How can these facts be reconciled? There is a difference between the case where the international price ratio is $\bar{p}_d$ and the present case, where it is actually $\bar{p}$, with regard to the tariff revenue which in the present case accrues to the government. Thus, in addition to the income accruing to the domestic factors of production, given by OE' in terms of X or by OD' in terms of Y, we have the tariff revenue that actually enables the country as a whole (i.e., private consumers and government) to consume beyond point P' and trade northwest of point F. In fact, as we shall see, the country will end up trading somewhere along the terms-of-trade line TOT, the precise equilibrium point depending on the way in which the government is actually using the tariff revenue.

What is the tariff revenue equal to? Although it can be measured in either commodity (as we shall see), assume that the government initially collects the tariff revenue in terms of the imported commodity Y. Thus, our economy is exporting OM units of X. The rest of the world exports to our economy, in exchange for OM of X, MV units of Y, the amount MF accruing to the private consumers while the residual FV accrues to the government in the form of tariff revenue—all this from the construction of TOT^*. Thus, $\bar{p}_d = MF/OM$ and $\bar{p} = (MV)/(OM)$. But $\bar{p} = (1 + t)\bar{p}_d$ (see equation [18.2]). Hence, $(1 + t)MF/(OM) = (MV)/(OM)$, or

$$(1 + t)MF = MV,$$

$$tMF = MV - MF = FV.$$

In words, if the private consumers of our economy import MF units of Y, the government will collect tMF units of Y, which is actually given by the vertical distance FV.

What alternative combinations of X and Y are available to the government? Since the private consumers of our economy are importing from the rest of the world MF units of Y, the tariff revenue of the government in terms of abstract purchasing power will be $t\bar{p}_y(MF)$. With this tariff revenue, the government can buy

$$t\bar{p}_y(MF)/\bar{p}_y = tMF = FV$$

units of Y. Observe that the government is not required to pay any tax; hence it can buy Y at the international price $\bar{p}_y$. The maximum amount of X that the government could buy if it were to spend the whole tariff revenue on X is

$$t\bar{p}_y(MF)/\bar{p}_x = tMF/\bar{p} = FV/\bar{p} = UF.$$

It is evident that the government can actually purchase any combination along the straight-line segment UV, all quantities measured with respect to F, of course. The problem is similar to that of a consumer (endowed with a fixed income) facing given market prices. Thus, the straight-line segment UV, with F as origin, is simply the budget line of the government. Depending on the way the government actually spends the tariff revenue, equilibrium will occur somewhere on UV.

The government's equilibrium consumption point on UV, viewed with respect to F as origin, is actually the equilibrium trade point for the economy as a whole. As we have seen, private consumption gives rise to the trade point F. But the coordinates of F (with respect to the origin O) show, respectively, X's excess domestic production over domestic production (i.e., private exports of $X = OM$) and Y's excess domestic consumption over domestic production (i.e., private imports of $Y = MF$). Since all domestic production is actually used up in this fashion, the government can consume X or Y only through imports from abroad. Suppose that the government actually consumes FG of Y and ZG of X. The government's equilibrium consumption point is assumed to be given by Z. What are the total quantities of X and Y exported and imported, respectively? Private imports of Y are MF and government imports of Y are FG, giving rise to a grand total of imports of Y equal to MG or QZ. On the other hand, private exports of X are given by OM while government imports of X are given by ZG or QM. Hence, total exports of X are given by the difference $OM - QM = OQ$. The coordinates of point Z thus actually give us the total quantities of X and Y exported and imported, respectively.

So far we have been assuming that the government spends its tariff revenue to buy X and Y directly for public consumption. But what happens when the government, instead of spending its tariff revenue on X and Y, decides to redistribute it to the consumers in the form of, say, lump-sum transfers or a general income tax reduction? In a study of the effects of a tariff imposed for any purpose, except that of raising revenue, it seems more plausible to assume that the government already has a budget financed by other means and that the government can therefore be expected to return to the consumers, in one way or another, the tariff revenue. In addition, by assuming that the government returns the tariff revenue to the consumers, we do not have to introduce an arbitrary assumption about the use of the tariff revenue: the social indifference map can also be used for this purpose. But having introduced this new assumption, how is international equilibrium to be determined?

Given the international price ratio $\bar{p}$, it follows that (*a*) international equilibrium has to occur somewhere along the terms-of-trade line TOT (fig. 18.1) quite irrespective of any trade taxes (or subsidies) imposed by our economy; and (*b*) the domestic price ratio will be $\bar{p}_d$, as shown by equation (18.2). Point (*b*) follows directly from the logic by which equation (18.2) was derived. Point (*a*) is justified by observing that international prices remain constant, by assumption, irrespective of any taxes or subsidies imposed by our economy, and that the value of exports of the rest of the world to our economy must, in equilibrium, be equal to the value of our exports to the rest of the world, both aggregates being evaluated at international prices. It may be helpful to consider the problem from the point of view of our economy. Assume that, at the domestic price ratio $\bar{p}_d$, our economy produces X_p and Y_p units of commodities X and Y, respectively. The value of output produced (I) at domestic market prices is

$$I = \bar{p}_d X_p + Y_p.$$

In national-income accounting, I is usually called the net national income at factor cost, that is, the income which accrues directly to the factors of production. In the absence of import taxes, I will also be equal to the domestic expenditure on X and Y. However, under the present circumstances, where a tariff is imposed, the domestic aggregate expenditure (E) will be higher than I by the tariff revenue. What is the tariff revenue equal to? Recall that I is expressed in terms of commodity Y at the domestic price ratio $\bar{p}_d$. Hence, the tariff revenue must be so expressed, too. To demonstrate, let us first evaluate the tariff revenue in terms of abstract purchasing power. Thus,

$$\text{tariff revenue} = t\bar{p}_y(Y_c - Y_p),$$

where Y_c = total domestic consumption of Y. To express the tariff revenue in terms of commodity Y at domestic prices, divide the above expression by p_y^d (not $\bar{p}_y$). Thus,

$$\text{tariff revenue in terms of } Y = t\frac{\bar{p}_y}{p_y^d}(Y_c - Y_p) = \frac{t}{1+t}(Y_c - Y_p)$$

using equation (18.1). Therefore, the domestic aggregate expenditure is

$$E = \bar{p}_d X_p + Y_p + \left(\frac{t}{1+t}\right)(Y_c - Y_p).$$

The budget line for our economy is given by

$$E = \bar{p}_d X_c + Y_c,$$

or

$$\bar{p}_d X_p + Y_p + \left(\frac{t}{1 + t}\right)(Y_c - Y_p) = \bar{p}_d X_c + Y_c,$$

or

$$\bar{p}_d(X_p - X_c) = \left(\frac{1}{1 + t}\right)(Y_c - Y_p), \qquad (18.3)$$

or

$$\bar{p}(X_p - X_c) = (Y_c - Y_p). \qquad (18.4)$$

Equation (18.4) states what was concluded earlier: that the value of our exports must be equal to the value of our imports provided both aggregates are evaluated at the international prices. If exports and imports are evaluated at domestic prices, they cannot possibly be equal, as equation (18.3) reveals. In particular, the value of imports, $Y_c - Y_p$, will be higher than the value of exports, $\bar{p}_d(X_p - X_c)$.

Having established that, when $\bar{p}$ is given, the domestic price ratio will be given by equation (18.2), assuming the tariff is nonprohibitive, and that international equilibrium requires that equation (18.4) be satisfied, let us determine international equilibrium. Figure 18.2 reproduces all the essential information from figure 18.1. The straight lines TOT and TOT^* are identical to the corresponding lines in figure 18.1. The curve OFR is again our economy's offer curve. Equilibrium has to occur somewhere along the terms-of-trade line TOT. To determine the precise equilibrium point along TOT, we have to use the conclusion that the domestic price ratio is given by the slope of TOT^*. Thus, equilibrium will occur at a point S on TOT where the slope of our economy's trade indifference curve passing through S is equal to $\bar{p}_d$, that is, the slope of TOT^*. For this purpose, imagine that the terms-of-trade line TOT^* shifts continuously upward in a parallel fashion. Trace out the tangencies between the family of parallel terms-of-trade lines and the trade indifference curves, as shown by the broken curve FS. International equilibrium necessarily occurs at point S.

Point S must lie somewhere along the straight-line segment OR; it cannot lie beyond R. What is the reason for this? The trade indifference curve passing through R is by assumption tangent to the terms-of-trade line TOT. All other trade indifference curves necessarily intersect the line TOT. But any trade indifference curve passing through any point of TOT beyond R must be steeper than TOT at the point of intersection. Hence, equilibrium can occur only in the region OR. This argument also shows that the equilibrium point S must necessarily lie to the left of our country's offer curve. Note, too, that when the broken line FS is negatively sloped, as shown in

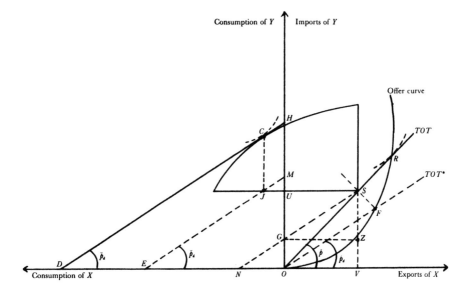

FIGURE 18.2

figure 18.2, the total consumption of both commodities increases as we move from F to S; hence, both commodities are superior or both are normal. On the other hand, if FS is positively sloped, the consumption of one commodity decreases as we move from F to S, that is, one commodity is inferior.

Having determined the equilibrium point S, let us place our economy's production block in position with its corner at S, as shown in figure 18.2. Draw the tangent to the production block at its tangency point with the highest social indifference curve, point C. This is shown by DCH, which by necessity is parallel to TOT^*. Draw lines (EJM and NGS) parallel to TOT^* through points S and J, where J lies on the horizontal base of the production block and directly below C. Thus, SJ = domestic production of X, and JC = domestic production of Y. The value of output domestically produced and evaluated at factor cost is now given by ND in terms of X and by GH in terms of Y. In particular, $EN = JS$ = domestic production of X, and $DE = CJ/\bar{p}_d$ = value of domestic production of Y in terms of X at domestic prices. Further, $HM = CJ$ = domestic production of Y and $GM = \bar{p}_d(EN)$ = value of domestic production of X in terms of Y at domestic prices. But while ND and GH measure the value of the net national income in our economy in terms of commodities X and Y, respectively, the total expenditure on X and Y by our economy is given by DO in terms of X and by

OH in terms of *Y*. Therefore the tariff revenue expressed in terms of *X* (at domestic prices) is given by the horizontal distance *NO*. Expressed in terms of *Y*, the tariff revenue is given by the vertical distance *OG*. What is the ad valorem rate of tariff equal to? We saw earlier that the tariff revenue expressed in terms of *Y* (at the domestic price ratio $\bar{p}_d$) is equal to $(t/1 + t) \times (Y_c - Y_p)$; but $Y_c - Y_p = OU$. Therefore, we can form the equation $[t/(1 + t)]OU = OG$. Solving for *t*, we get

$$t = \frac{OG}{OU - OG} = \frac{OG}{GU}.$$

Observe that the triangles *OGN* and *ZSG* are similar. Since *GU = ZS*, by a well-known property of similar triangles it becomes apparent that

$$t = \frac{OG}{GU} = \frac{NO}{OV} = \frac{NG}{GS}. \tag{18.5}$$

These are three convenient measures of the ad valorem tariff rate.

2. The Effects of the Nonprohibitive Tariff

The major conclusions of the preceding section are summarized below.

1. The imported commodity becomes relatively more expensive in the domestic market, as shown by equation (18.2). Note that the domestic price ratio can no longer be equal to $\bar{p}$. For $t > 0$, we necessarily have $\bar{p} > \bar{p}_d$.

2. As the domestic price ratio falls below $\bar{p}$, the domestic output of the imported commodity, *Y*, expands at the expense of the output of the exported commodity, *X*. This is usually called the *protective effect* of the tariff.

3. Since commodity *Y* is assumed to be land intensive relative to *X*, it follows that the imposition of the (nonprohibitive) tariff raises the real wage of the factor land and lowers the real wage of the factor labor both relatively and absolutely. This follows from the analysis in chapter 15. This is usually called the *redistribution effect* of the tariff.

4. With revenue redistribution the volume of trade, expressed in terms of international prices, falls after the imposition of the tariff. This follows from the fact that point *S* lies between the origin and point *R* (see fig. 18.2). This conclusion remains valid when the government does not redistribute the tariff revenue to all consumers in general if the offer curve is not backward bending. This is made clear in chapter 19.

5. As a result of the protective effect of the tariff, the economy will end up consuming inside the free-trade consumption-possibilities frontier but outside the production-possibilities frontier. This is illustrated in figure 18.3. The curve MP_2P_1N is our economy's production-possibilities frontier. Before the imposition of the tariff, our country produces at P_1 and consumes somewhere along the straight-line segment KP_1, with *Y* the imported

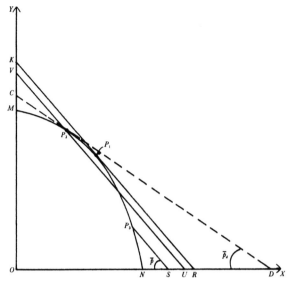

FIGURE 18.3

commodity. The straight line KP_1R is our economy's free-trade consumption-possibilities frontier. After the imposition of the tariff, the domestic price ratio falls to $\bar{p}_d$ and production shifts from P_1 to P_2. The slope of the tangent to the production-possibilities frontier at P_2, that is, the broken line CP_2D, is equal to $\bar{p}_d$. Where will our economy consume? Certainly not on the straight-line segment CP_2, which would neglect the tariff revenue. As we saw earlier, in equilibrium the value of exports equals the value of imports when both aggregates are evaluated at international prices. Hence, our economy will be consuming somewhere along the straight-line segment VP_2, which is parallel to KP_1R. But all points along VP_2 lie inside KP_1R. Hence, the cum-tariff equilibrium consumption point must necessarily lie inside the free-trade consumption-possibilities frontier but outside the production-possibilities frontier.

6. The tariff will also have an effect on the consumption levels of both X and Y (i.e., X_c and Y_c). To determine exactly how X_c and Y_c are affected by the tariff, consider figure 18.4, which reproduces the free-trade consumption-possibilities frontier (KP_1R) of figure 18.3 together with the straight line VP_2U, which is parallel to KP_1R and passes through P_2. Production occurs before the imposition of the tariff at P_1 and after at P_2. Assume that, before the tariff is imposed, consumption occurs at C_1. Consumption will necessarily occur after the imposition of the tariff somewhere along the straight-line segment VP_2. The precise posttariff equilibrium consumption point partially depends on how the government chooses to spend the tariff revenue. Let us therefore make the neutral assumption that the government

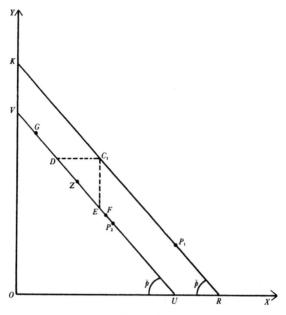

FIGURE 18.4

redistributes the tariff revenue to consumers. The outcome will then depend on consumer tastes. Since we have been assuming that tastes are summarized by a social indifference map, the final outcome will clearly depend on the characteristics of this map. To determine the effect of the tariff on X_c and Y_c, we have to derive the income consumption curve through C_1, on the assumption that the domestic price ratio is $\bar{p}$. If both commodities are superior, this income consumption curve, not drawn, will intersect VP_2 somewhere in the region DE, say at Z. The slope of the social indifference curve passing through Z will be equal to $\bar{p}$ in absolute terms. Consumption equilibrium will occur at a point where the slope of the social indifference curve at this point is equal, in absolute terms, to the domestic price ratio $\bar{p}_d$, which is smaller than $\bar{p}$. This will necessarily occur somewhere in the region ZP_2. But this means that, after the imposition of the tariff and provided that both commodities are superior, Y_c will fall definitely while X_c may either increase or decrease.

If X is inferior, the income consumption curve through C_1 will intersect VP_2 somewhere in the region EP_2, say at F, where the absolute slope of the social indifference curve is $\bar{p}$. Hence, consumption equilibrium, after the imposition of the tariff, will occur somewhere in the region FP_2. Therefore, Y_c will definitely fall after the imposition of the tariff and X_c will definitely rise.

If Y is inferior, the income consumption curve through C_1 will intersect VP_2 somewhere in the region VD, say at point G. Hence, consumption equilibrium after the imposition of the tariff will occur somewhere in the region GP_2. Therefore, X_c may increase or decrease and Y_c may also increase or decrease. If Y_c increases, however, X_c necessarily falls; and if X_c increases, Y_c necessarily falls. Thus, unless the imported commodity is inferior, the imposition of the tariff will necessarily cause the consumption of the imported commodity to fall.

3. The Cum-Tariff Consumption-Possibilities Frontier, Prohibitive Tariffs, and Welfare Loss

To evaluate the effect of a tariff (whether prohibitive or nonprohibitive) on potential welfare, we must first derive the cum-tariff consumption-possibilities frontier. Remember that the tariff is imposed on commodity Y only—the commodity that was imported before the imposition of the tariff. After the imposition of the tariff, the domestic price ratio will fall from $\bar{p}$ to $\bar{p}_d$ only when Y continues to be imported. Under these circumstances, our economy will produce at P_2 (see fig. 18.3), that is, the point where the broken line CD with absolute slope equal to $\bar{p}_d$ becomes tangent to the production-possibilities frontier, and consume somewhere along the straight-line segment VP_2. We can thus see that VP_2 is a part of our economy's cum-tariff consumption-possibilities frontier. But where is the rest of the cum-tariff consumption-possibilities frontier?

First determine the permissible range of variation of the domestic price ratio, p_d. We know that p_d cannot fall below $\bar{p}_d$. That is, commodity Y cannot become relatively more expensive than Y's international price plus the tariff. But there is no reason why it cannot become cheaper, although it cannot fall below the level set by the international market. Therefore, the domestic price ratio will necessarily satisfy the relationship $\bar{p}_d \leq p_d \leq \bar{p}$. When $p_d = \bar{p}_d$, production occurs at P_2; when $p_d = \bar{p}$, production occurs at P_1; and when $\bar{p}_d < p_d < \bar{p}$, production occurs somewhere between P_1 and P_2 at the point where the marginal rate of transformation equals p_d.

Observe that when $\bar{p}_d < p_d < \bar{p}$, consumption will necessarily coincide with domestic production, for commodity Y cannot be exported, because it is still cheaper in the international market ($p_d < \bar{p}$). On the other hand, commodity Y cannot be imported either, because the sum of the international price plus the tariff is certainly higher than the domestic price ($\bar{p}_d < p_d$). By the same token, X cannot be exported, because $\bar{p}_d < p_d$. Therefore, when $\bar{p}_d < p_d < \bar{p}$, the consumption and production points will necessarily coincide and they will lie on the production-possibilities frontier in the region P_1P_2 (see fig. 18.3). Accordingly, the region P_1P_2 is another part of our economy's cum-tariff consumption-possibilities frontier.

Consider the value $p_d = \bar{p}$. Production necessarily occurs at P_1. Consumption can take place anywhere along the straight-line segment P_1R because now X can be imported and Y exported. Since by assumption there is no tariff on X, our economy will behave in this region as if completely free trade existed: the tariff on Y will not interfere because Y is no longer imported.

Therefore, the cum-tariff consumption-possibilities frontier is given by VP_2P_1R, which is not necessarily concave. It lies inside the free-trade consumption-possibilities frontier except in the region P_1R, where the two frontiers coincide. The straight-line segment VP_2 will disappear completely if P_2 coincides with M—or if the absolute slope of the production-possibilities frontier at M is equal to, or higher than, $\bar{p}_d$.

If the tariff is not imposed on Y alone but on all imports, our analysis will have to be modified slightly. When Y is imported, $p_d = \bar{p}_d < \bar{p}$. On the other hand, when X is imported, $p_d = (1 + t)\bar{p} > \bar{p}$. Thus, p_d can now vary within the limits $\bar{p}_d = \bar{p}/(1 + t)$ and $(1 + t)\bar{p}$, that is, $\bar{p}/(1 + t) \leq p_d \leq (1 + t)\bar{p}$. When $\bar{p}/(1 + t) < p_d < (1 + t)\bar{p}$, no trade takes place, as before. The cum-tariff consumption-possibilities frontier in this case will be given by VP_2P_3S, where P_3S is parallel to KP_1R and point P_3 is determined by the requirement that the absolute slope of the production-possibilities frontier be equal to $(1 + t)\bar{p}$. In this case, the cum-tariff consumption-possibilities frontier lies inside the free-trade consumption-possibilities frontier except at the singular point P_1. Note that the regions VP_2 and P_3S can be made to disappear by raising the tariff sufficiently. Then the cum-tariff consumption-possibilities frontier will coincide completely with our economy's production-possibilities frontier.

Both VP_2P_1R and VP_2P_3S do not lie inside the production-possibilities frontier; they lie partially outside it while they coincide with it over the regions P_2P_1 and P_2P_3, respectively. Thus, our economy cannot be forced by a tariff to consume inside its production-possibilities frontier; it can still consume beyond the production-possibilities frontier, although this possibility is rather restricted relative to the free-trade consumption-possibilities frontier.

This analysis can be used to determine the minimum rate at which the tariff becomes prohibitive. Consider figure 18.5. The curve $MEPR$ is our economy's production-possibilities frontier. In the autarkic state, equilibrium occurs at E, where the production-possibilities frontier becomes tangent to the highest possible social indifference curve (SIC). When trade opens up, our country produces at P and consumes at C. An infinitesimal tariff will cause the economy to produce somewhere in the region EP and very close to P. It will continue to import Y and export X. Now suppose that the tariff rate is allowed to rise continuously. The production point will travel along the production-possibilities frontier from P toward E. Trade will continue for a while at a continuously diminishing rate, but it will stop completely when the tariff rate reaches a certain minimum value. What is this minimum tariff rate equal to? First observe that trade ceases completely when the tariff rate is raised sufficiently to make the production point coincide with

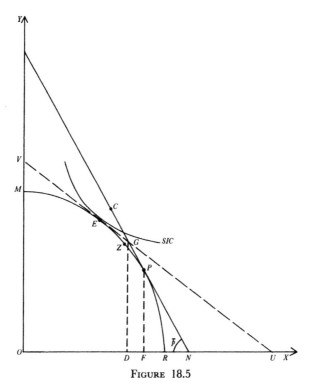

FIGURE 18.5

the pretrade equilibrium point E. Thus, for any production point in the region EP (but excluding point E), such as Z, the economy will continue to import Y, for production will occur at Z if p_d is equal to the slope of the production-possibilities frontier at Z and consumption will occur at Z if p_d is equal to the slope of the social indifference curve passing through Z. Since at Z only the first condition is satisfied, it follows that commodity Y will continue to be imported. At E, however, the marginal rate of substitution in consumption equals the marginal rate of transformation in production. If p_d is made equal to the slope at E, trade will cease completely. Now draw the tangent to the production-possibilities frontier at E and determine the point (G) where it intersects the pretariff consumption-possibilities frontier. The maximum domestic price ratio, p_d^*, consistent with zero trade is now given by the ratio DG/DU. On the other hand, $\bar{p} = DG/DN$. Finally, from equation (18.2), we have $t = (\bar{p} - p_d^*)/p_d^*$. Therefore, the minimum value of t at which the tariff becomes prohibitive, say t^*, is given by

$$t^* = \frac{\bar{p} - p_d^*}{p_d^*} = \frac{(DG/DN) - (DG/DU)}{DG/DU} = \frac{(1/DN) - (1/DU)}{1/DU}$$

$$= \frac{DU - DN}{DN}. \qquad (18.6)$$

The specific value t^* can also be determined in figure 18.2. There, p_d^* will be represented by the slope of the offer curve at the origin and equation (18.6) applied. Therefore, the tariff is prohibitive when $t \geq t^*$.

What is the effect of the tariff on the potential welfare of our small country? We saw in figure 18.3 that the cum-tariff consumption-possibilities frontier (VP_2P_1R) lies mostly inside the free-trade consumption-possibilities frontier, although it coincides with it over the region P_1R. Therefore, if the region P_1R does not give rise to any points on the free-trade utility-possibilities frontier, restricted trade is potentially inferior to free trade (for the small country) because the cum-tariff utility-possibilities frontier will lie uniformly inside the free-trade utility-possibilities frontier. But there is no guarantee that this will be the case. The cum-tariff utility-possibilities frontier can in general be expected to coincide with the free-trade utility-possibilities frontier over a certain region. Then, for some Paretian welfare functions, restricted trade will not be shown to be inferior to free trade. However, free trade will never be shown to be inferior to restricted trade, because the free-trade utility-possibilities frontier cannot lie inside the cum-tariff utility-possibilities frontier. If the tariff is imposed on imports in general and not only imports of commodity Y, the cum-tariff consumption-possibilities frontier $(VP_2P_1P_3S$ in fig. 18.3) will lie totally inside the free-trade consumption-possibilities frontier, except for the singular point P_1, where the two frontiers become tangential. Then, as in the comparison between free trade and autarky and with the same reservations, free trade is potentially superior to restricted trade. It is emphasized that these conclusions apply only to the case of the small country.

4. The Imposition of an Export Tax

What if our country imposes an export tax instead of a tariff? The analysis of the tariff can be applied step by step to the case of the export tax. It does not matter which money price is taxed, because one good is exchanged for another in trade, and hence there is only one relative price. From the point of view of long-run equilibrium analysis, it is immaterial whether a tax is imposed on exports or imports: the outcome will be identical. This symmetry is demonstrated as follows.

When a tax, t, on exports, X, is imposed, the domestic price, p_y^d, of imports, Y, will continue to be identical with the international price, $\bar{p}_y$, while the domestic price of X (i.e., p_x^d)—on the assumption that X continues to be exported after the imposition of the export tax—will satisfy the equation $p_x^d(1 + t) = \bar{p}_x$. Thus,

$$p_x^d = \left(\frac{1}{1+t}\right)\bar{p}_x.$$

Accordingly,

$$p_d = \frac{p_x^d}{p_y^d} = \left(\frac{1}{1 + t}\right)\frac{\bar{p}_x}{\bar{p}_y} = \left(\frac{1}{1 + t}\right)\bar{p} = \bar{p}_d.$$

This is identical to the result obtained with equation (18.2). From this point, the analysis of the export tax follows the analysis of the tariff step by step. For this reason, no further discussion of the problem is given.

That the effects of an export tax are identical to the effects of an import tax (provided the tax revenue is spent in the same way) holds only from the point of view of the long-run static theory. With regard to the effects on the balance of payments and the level of employment (i.e., in the short run), a tariff operates in an expansionary, stimulating fashion whereas an export tax operates in a contractive, depressive manner.

SELECTED BIBLIOGRAPHY

The selected bibliography will be found at the end of chapter 20, p. 444.

19

Import and Export Taxes: The Case of the Large Country

Let us extend the analysis of import and export taxes to a two-country model (A and B) where either country's actions are substantial enough to affect international prices. Again, international equilibrium is usually portrayed in terms of offer curves, which we can derive under free-trade conditions. But how can offer curves be derived when import and export taxes interfere with the free flow of trade? In what follows, assume that only country A imposes trade taxes. The offer curve of country B is thus assumed given and invariant.

1. The Trade-Tax-Distorted Offer Curve

We now have enough information to derive a *trade-tax-distorted offer curve*, that is, the offer curve that shows the willingness of a country to export and import commodities at world (not domestic) prices. What the preceding chapter actually accomplishes is the derivation of a single point on the trade-tax-distorted offer curve by assuming that the international price ratio is given. By repeating the same exercise for all possible values of the international price ratio, we can thus trace out the whole trade-tax-distorted offer curve. Note that, the *trade-tax*-distorted offer curve is discussed here, because it is immaterial to the analysis whether an import or export tax is imposed.

There is no need to repeat the analysis for each and every possible value of the international price ratio. Let us, however, compare the trade-tax-distorted offer curve with the free-trade offer curve in general and then predict the effect of import and export taxes on the international price ratio, that is, the *barter terms of trade* of the trade-tax-imposing country.

414

As we have seen, given the international price ratio $\bar{p}$, the relevant point on the trade-tax-distorted offer curve can be determined only after it has been decided how the government disposes of the tax revenue. In particular, the government may spend the tax revenue on either commodity or on any feasible combination of X and Y, or it may redistribute the tax revenue among the private consumers. Let us distinguish among the following three cases (a) the government spends the tax revenue on the exported commodity, X; (b) the government spends the tax revenue on the imported commodity, Y; and (c) the government redistributes the tax revenue among the private consumers. If the government actually spends the tax revenue on both X and Y (either in some arbitrary fashion or according to some existing government tastes summarized in a government indifference map), the outcome will, of course, lie somewhere between (a) and (b).

Consider figure 19.1. The curve O_A is A's free-trade offer curve. If the international price ratio is equal to the slope of the terms-of-trade line TOT, country A would trade, under free-trade conditions, at point M. If a trade tax (i.e., a tariff or an export tax), t, imposed, at what point would country A trade? Consider the broken terms-of-trade line TOT^*, whose slope is equal to the slope of $TOT \times (1/1 + t)$. If the government does not re-distribute the tax revenue to the private consumers, A's private sector will want to import DN of Y and export OD of X. If the government spends the tariff revenue on the exported commodity X, the relevant point on the

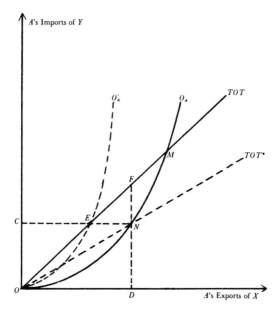

FIGURE 19.1

trade-tax-distorted offer curve would be E. Now point E lies to the left of point N, and this will always be the case for all values of the international price ratio. Therefore, given any point on the free-trade offer curve, such as N, the corresponding point on the trade-tax-distorted offer curve will lie directly to the left of N if the government spends the tax revenue on the exported commodity X. But how can point E be precisely determined when N and t are known? Point E lies at the intersection of the terms-of-trade line TOT with the horizontal line CN. But we already know that

$$\frac{DN}{OD} = \frac{DF}{OD}\left(\frac{1}{1+t}\right) = \frac{OC}{CE}\left(\frac{1}{1+t}\right) = \frac{DN}{CE}\left(\frac{1}{1+t}\right),$$

or

$$\frac{1}{OD} = \left(\frac{1}{1+t}\right)\frac{1}{CE},$$

or

$$CE/CN = 1/(1+t),$$

or

$$1 + t = CN/CE,$$

or

$$t = (CN - CE)/CE = EN/CE = EN/(CN - EN). \qquad (19.1)$$

Equation (19.1) has a very simple interpretation. At the international price ratio $p = DF/OD$, the private sector of country A imports DN of Y from country B in exchange for OD of X. However, not all X given up by A's private sector accrues to B. Country A's government collects EN of X, and thus only $CE = CN - EN$ accrues to B. It is no wonder, then, that the tax rate is equal to the ratio EN/CE. The amount EN is the tax revenue (in terms of X at world prices) that accrues to A's government, while CE is simply A's exports of X, or A's imports of Y expressed in terms of X at world prices

Equation (19.1) can also be solved for EN as follows:

$$EN = \left(\frac{t}{1+t}\right)CN. \qquad (19.2)$$

Therefore, point E can be determined as follows. Draw a horizontal line through N and let it intersect the vertical axis at C. Point E must now be determined in such a way as to satisfy equation (19.2) (or eq. [19.1]). For instance, if t is 25 percent, we must have

$$EN = \frac{0.25}{1.25}CN = \frac{1}{5}CN.$$

In other words, for $t = 0.25$, point E will lie to the left of N one-fifth of the distance CN. Therefore, for $t = 0.25$ and assuming that the government spends the tax revenue on X, the trade-tax-distorted offer curve will lie to the left of the free-trade offer curve. It can easily be derived by reducing the original horizontal distances between the free-trade offer curve and the vertical axis by 20 percent (i.e., $\frac{1}{5}$), as shown by the broken curve O'_A. In general, the trade-tax-distorted offer curve can be derived by shifting the free-trade offer curve to the left in such a way that the horizontal distances between the free-trade offer curve and the trade-tax-distorted offer curve are equal to $[1/(1 + t)] \times 100$ percent of the horizontal distances between the free-trade offer curve and the vertical axis.

What would the trade-tax-distorted offer curve be if the government should spend the tax revenue on the imported commodity? Consider again figure 19.1. For the international price ratio $p = DF/OD$, the private sector of country A wants to trade at N, and the tax revenue in terms of commodity Y at world prices is equal to NF. Therefore, when the government spends the tax revenue on Y, the relevant point on the trade-tax-distorted offer curve will be F. In other words, country B will be exporting DF of Y in exchange for OD of X. However, only DN of Y accrues to A's private sector; the rest (i.e., NF) accrues to A's government. Therefore, the tax rate must be equal to the ratio NF/ND. That this is so follows again from the relationship

$$\frac{DN}{OD} = \left(\frac{1}{1 + t}\right)\frac{DF}{OD},$$

or

$$DN = \left(\frac{1}{1 + t}\right)DF,$$

or

$$1 + t = DF/DN,$$

or

$$t = (DF - DN)/DN = NF/DN. \tag{19.3}$$

Therefore, point F lies directly above N, and the vertical distance NF is equal to $t \times 100$ percent of the vertical distance DN. The same relationship must necessarily hold between any other point on the free-trade offer curve (i.e., the point where A's private sector would like to trade) and the corresponding point on the trade-tax-distorted offer curve. Accordingly, when the government spends the tax revenue on Y, the trade-tax-distorted offer curve can be easily derived by shifting the free-trade offer curve upward in such a way that the vertical differences between the two offer curves are equal to $t \times 100$ percent of the corresponding vertical distances between the free-trade offer curve and the horizontal axis.

There is one fundamental difference between the case where A's government spends the tax revenue on the exported commodity, X, and the case where it spends it on the imported commodity, Y. In the former case, the trade-tax-distorted offer curve lies totally to the left of the free-trade offer curve—the two offer curves can never intersect. In the latter case, however, the trade-tax-distorted offer curve will intersect the free-trade offer curve if the latter becomes backward bending (i.e., if A's demand for imports by the private sector becomes inelastic). This can be illustrated in figure 19.1. Note that point F depends on point N alone. Thus, the behavior of the free-trade offer curve beyond point N is irrelevant as concerns the determination of point F and the rest of the trade-tax-distorted offer curve from the origin to F. Therefore, should the free-trade offer curve become backward bending beyond point N, it will intersect the trade-tax-distorted offer curve. This is shown more clearly in figure 19.2, where O_A is the free-trade offer curve and O_A' the trade-tax-distorted offer curve. The intersection of the trade-tax-distorted offer curve with the free-trade offer curve when the government spends the tax revenue on the imported commodity but not on the exported commodity will have implications for the analysis of the effects of the trade tax.

If the government chooses to spend the tax revenue on both commodities, the trade-tax-distorted offer curve will lie somewhere between the trade-tax-distorted curves just derived under the assumption that the government spends the tax revenue only on X or only on Y, its precise position depending

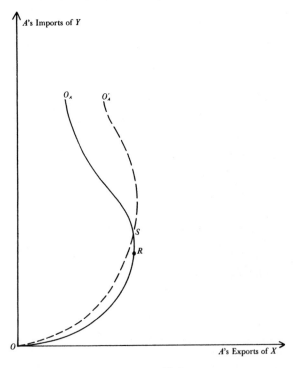

FIGURE 19.2

on the proportion in which the government allocates the tax revenue between X and Y.

Let us consider the case where A's government redistributes the tax revenue among A's consumers. Here it is no longer possible to derive the trade-tax-distorted offer curve in a mechanical fashion, as in the first two cases. The outcome will depend upon the characteristics of the social indifference map. However, on the basis of the analysis of the preceding section, the trade-tax-distorted offer curve will definitely lie totally to the left of the free-trade offer curve, except at the origin, as in the case where the government spends the tax revenue on the exported commodity X. This should be obvious from figure 18.2. Point S, which is the point on the trade-tax-distorted offer curve corresponding to point F on the free-trade offer curve, always lies along the vector OR but never beyond point R. Therefore, any ray through the origin will by necessity cut the trade-tax distorted offer curve before it cuts the free-trade offer curve. Accordingly, the trade-tax-distorted offer curve will lie closer to the origin than the free-trade offer curve. This necessarily implies that the trade-tax-distorted offer curve lies to the left of the free-trade offer curve.

How can the trade-tax-distorted offer curve be derived under the assumption that A's government redistributes the tax revenue among A's consumers? The answer lies in the construction of figure 18.2. For convenience, all necessary information is transferred to figure 19.3. Thus, O_A is A's free-trade

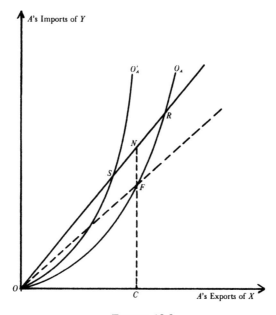

FIGURE 19.3

offer curve. Consider point F on O_A. How can we find the corresponding point on the trade-tax-distorted offer curve? Recall that under free-trade conditions, A's consumers would like to trade at F only when the domestic price ratio is given by the slope of the vector OF (i.e., CF/OC). When a tax is imposed, however, and the domestic price ratio happens to be given by the slope of the vector OF, A's consumers will not actually trade at F because they will be subsidized by the government by means of the tax revenue redistribution, which enables them to spend more on X and Y than they would have spent under free-trade conditions. Where would they trade in the presence of a trade tax whose revenue is redistributed among A's consumers? We must first determine all combinations of exports of X and imports of Y which have the same value at world prices. These combinations will all lie on a straight line through the origin (see TOT in fig. 18.2), with slope equal to the international price ratio corresponding to the domestic price ratio CF/OC.

The desired straight line will be perfectly determined once another point on it (besides the origin) is determined. Simply determine point N directly above F in such a way that the distance FN is $t \times 100$ percent of the distance CF. Therefore, all combinations of exports and imports implying "value of exports = value of imports" estimated at world prices corresponding to the domestic price ratio CF/OC are given by the straight line ON. Country A's consumers will, in equilibrium, trade somewhere along ON. The precise trade point, S, is where the slope of the trade indifference curve at its intersection with the line ON is equal to CF/OC. Repeating the same experiment for all points on the free-trade offer curve, we can determine the trade-tax-distorted offer curve as shown by O'_A in figure 19.3.

2. Trade Taxes and the Barter Terms of Trade

Consider figure 19.4. The curves O_A and O_B are the free-trade offer curves of countries A and B, respectively. Equilibrium under free-trade conditions occurs at E, where A exports CE units of X to B in exchange for OC units of Y. The equilibrium terms of trade are given by the slope of the vector OE, that is, OC/CE. Now suppose that A imposes a trade tax. What will happen to A's barter terms of trade? In other words, after the imposition of the trade tax, will A be able to exchange 1 unit of X (A's exported commodity) for more or fewer units of Y (A's imported commodity) compared with free-trade equilibrium? That will depend on: (a) the nature of B's offer curve; (b) whether A's government spends the tax revenue (or a substantial amount of it) on the imported commodity; and (c) whether A's demand for imports at the free-trade equilibrium position is elastic or inelastic, if A's government spends the tax revenue on the imported commodity.

International equilibrium will always occur somewhere along B's free-trade offer curve, O_B: by assumption, B does not impose any trade taxes,

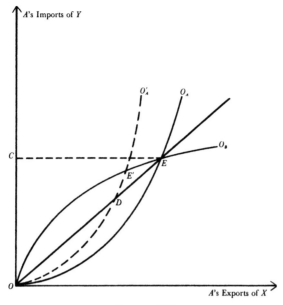

FIGURE 19.4

and *A*'s terms of trade will be given by the slope of the vector passing through the origin and the equilibrium point on *B*'s offer curve. If *B*'s offer curve were a straight line through the origin—as it is in the preceding chapter, where *A* is assumed to be small—*A*'s terms of trade would remain the same after the imposition of the trade tax irrespective of how *A*'s government uses the tax revenue and irrespective of whether or not *A*'s demand for imports is elastic at the free-trade equilibrium point *E*. However, if *B*'s offer curve is not a straight line, the outcome will depend on whether *A*'s demand for imports at free-trade world prices increases or decreases. If it increases, *A*'s terms of trade will tend to deteriorate. If it decreases, they will tend to improve.

According to the analysis of the preceding section, when *A*'s government spends the tax revenue on the exported commodity, or when it redistributes the tax revenue among *A*'s consumers, the trade-tax-distorted offer curve will definitely lie to the left of the free-trade offer curve, as shown by the broken curve O'_A in figure 19.4. In these two cases, *A*'s demand for imports falls at the free-trade world prices after the imposition of the trade tax (compare points *E* and *D*), equilibrium shifts from *E* to *E'*, and *A*'s terms of trade improve (the vector *OE'* is steeper than the vector *OE*). This is the result that one would normally expect, but it is by no means the only possibility.

When *A*'s government spends the tax revenue on the imported commodity *Y*, *A*'s trade-tax-distorted offer curve will lie above and to the right of *A*'s free-trade offer curve over the backward-bending region of *A*'s free-trade offer curve, as can be seen from figure 19.2. (Note that the trade-tax-distorted offer curve remains to the left of the free-trade offer curve immediately after the latter becomes backward bending.) Thus, in figure 19.2, the free-trade offer curve becomes vertical at R and backward bending beyond R, and it is intersected by the trade-tax-distorted offer curve at S, which lies beyond R in the backward-bending region of O_A. Accordingly, for world prices such that A's demand for imports is elastic before the imposition of the trade tax, A's trade-tax-distorted offer curve will lie to the left of the free-trade offer curve. If free-trade equilibrium occurs in this region of the free-trade offer curve (where A's demand for imports is elastic), the imposition of the trade tax will definitely improve A's terms of trade. When point D (fig. 19.4) lies to the left and below point E along the vector OE, equilibrium will occur somewhere in the region OE of B's offer curve, which implies that A's terms of trade will improve.

If A's demand for imports is inelastic at the free-trade equilibrium point and A's government spends the tariff revenue on the imported commodity, the possibility that A's terms of trade will deteriorate after the imposition of the trade tax cannot be ruled out. This is shown graphically by means of figure 19.2. Draw B's offer curve in such a way as to intersect O_A at the latter's backward-bending region beyond S, and then show that A's terms of trade deteriorate after the imposition of the trade tax.

This can also be proved rigorously in such a way that the results can be generalized to the case where the government spends only a fraction, λ, of the tax revenue on the imported commodity while it spends the rest on the exported commodity. Let the function $Y_c(1/\bar{p}_d)$ stand for the demand for imports of Y by A's consumers and Y_g the demand for imports of Y by A's government. The domestic price ratio (p_x/p_y) will be given by $\bar{p}_d$ as before, while the international price ratio will be given by $\bar{p}$. Given the trade tax, t, we must have $\bar{p}_d = \bar{p}/(1 + t)$. What is A's tax revenue in terms of commodity Y equal to? Obviously, it must be given by tY_c. Now if only the fraction λ $(0 \leq \lambda \leq 1)$ of this tax revenue is actually spent on Y, A's government's demand for imports of Y (i.e., Y_g) will be given by λtY_c. Accordingly, A's total demand for imports of Y, say Z, will be given by:

$$Z \equiv Y_c + Y_g = Y_c + \lambda tY_c = (1 + \lambda t)Y_c. \qquad (19.4)$$

To determine how Z changes as t increases from zero to a positive value in the neighborhood of the free-trade equilibrium point (i.e., when $p_d = \bar{p}$), differentiate equation (19.4) with respect to t:

$$dZ/dt = \lambda Y_c + (1 + \lambda t)(dY_c/dt). \qquad (19.5)$$

What is the value of the derivative dY_c/dt? The quantity Y_c is a decreasing function of $1/\bar{p}_d$, and given $\bar{p}$, $\bar{p}_d$ is also a function of t. Therefore,

$$\frac{dY_c}{dt} = \frac{dY_c}{d(1/\bar{p}_d)} \frac{d(1/\bar{p}_d)}{dt}. \qquad (19.6)$$

However,

$$\frac{1}{\bar{p}_d} = \frac{1+t}{\bar{p}} \; ;$$

hence,

$$\frac{d(1/\bar{p}_d)}{dt} = \frac{1}{\bar{p}} . \qquad (19.7)$$

Substituting equation (19.7) into equation (19.6), we get

$$\frac{dY_c}{dt} = \frac{dY_c}{d(1/p_d)} \frac{1}{\bar{p}} . \qquad (19.6)'$$

Recall that, at the free-trade equilibrium $(t = 0)$, $p_d = \bar{p}$ and that the elasticity of demand for imports by A's consumers (e_A) is given by

$$e_A \equiv \frac{dY_c}{d(1/p_d)} \frac{(1/p_d)}{Y_c} . \qquad (19.8)$$

Therefore, equation (19.6) can be simplified to

$$(dY_c/dt)_{t=0} = e_A Y_c. \qquad (19.9)$$

Substituting equation (19.9) into equation (19.5), and remembering that we are interested in the value of dZ/dt when $t = 0$, we get

$$(dZ/dt)_{t=0} = \lambda Y_c + (dY_c/dt)_{t=0} = Y_c(\lambda + e_A). \qquad (19.10)$$

Equation (19.10) gives the rate of change of Z with respect to t when $t = 0$. It is obvious that, as t increases, A's total demand for imports increases (and therefore A's terms of trade deteriorate) when the sum $\lambda + e_A$ is positive. In other words, the necessary and sufficient condition for the deterioration of A's terms of trade, after A's government imposes an infinitesimal trade tax and spends only the fraction λ of the tax revenue on the imported commodity, is $\lambda + e_A > 0$, or

$$\lambda > -e_A. \qquad (19.11)$$

In words, A's terms of trade will deteriorate after the imposition of the trade tax if, and only if, the absolute value of A's elasticity of demand for imports at the free-trade equilibrium position is smaller than the fraction λ of the tax revenue spent by A's government on the imported good. When A's government spends all tax revenue on the exported commodity, then $\lambda = 0$. Since, in general, $e_A < 0$, inequality (19.11) cannot be satisfied. On the other hand, when A's government spends the tax revenue on the imported commodity, $\lambda = 1$, and inequality (19.11) will be satisfied when A's demand for imports at the free-trade equilibrium point is inelastic.

3. *Trade Taxes and Domestic Prices*

For problems of domestic resource allocation and income distribution, what is important is not whether the terms of trade of the tax-imposing country improve or deteriorate after the imposition of the trade tax but, rather, whether the domestic price ratio falls below or rises above the free-trade equilibrium price ratio. Do we have $p_d > \bar{p}$, or $p_d = \bar{p}$, or $p_d < \bar{p}$ after the imposition of the trade tax (where $\bar{p}$ = the free-trade equilibrium price ratio)?

Note that, since in the case of nonprohibitive trade taxes there exists a one-to-one correspondence between the domestic price ratio (p_d) and the terms of trade (p) as shown by equation (18.3), the preceding comparison between p_d and $\bar{p}$ can easily be turned into a comparison between the equilibrium value of p after the imposition of the trade tax, say p_e, and $\bar{p}$. Thus, we shall have to determine which one of the following relations holds:

$$p_d = \frac{1}{1+t} p_e \gtreqless \bar{p}.$$

The issue is not whether A's terms of trade improve, deteriorate, or remain the same after the imposition of the trade tax. Rather, we are comparing $[1/(1 + t)]/p_e$ and $\bar{p}$; or, multiplying both by $(1 + t)$, we can say that the comparison is between p_e and $(1 + t)\bar{p}$. If $p_e > (1 + t)\bar{p}$ after the tax, the domestic price ratio will be higher than $\bar{p}$; if $p_e = (1 + t)\bar{p}$, p_d will be equal to $\bar{p}$ after the tax; and if $p_e < (1 + t)\bar{p}$, p_d will be lower than $\bar{p}$. Therefore, if A's barter terms of trade deteriorate after the imposition of the trade tax, p_d will definitely fall below $\bar{p}$, because, if $p_e < \bar{p}$, we must also have $p_e < (1 + t)\bar{p}$. But problems arise when A's barter terms of trade improve, which is no doubt the most usual case. Will A's barter terms of trade improve so much that $p_e > (1 + t)\bar{p}$, or will they improve only slightly, so that $p_e < (1 + t)\bar{p}$? In the latter case, A's terms of trade improve but the domestic price ratio falls (i.e., p_d and p move in opposite directions), which means that the imported commodity becomes more expensive, after the imposition of the trade tax, in the tax-imposing country while it becomes cheaper in the rest of the world. Thus, the output of Y in A will tend to rise, in this case, after the imposition of the trade tax; this is, no doubt, the normal case. In other words, A will be able to "protect" its import-competing industries via the trade tax. However, it is not inconceivable that the imposition of a trade tax by A may turn the barter terms of trade so much in A's favor that $p_e > (1 + t)\bar{p}$. In this case, the imposition of the trade tax by A will make commodity Y cheaper everywhere. Therefore, A's production of Y will necessarily fall after the imposition of the trade tax. This is indeed a paradoxical outcome, because trade taxes (and especially tariffs) are imposed by politicians who want to *protect* the import-competing industries. Under what conditions will this paradox occur?

Assume for the moment that A's government spends a fraction λ of the tariff proceeds on the imported commodity and a fraction $(1 - \lambda)$ on the exported commodity, with $0 \leq \lambda \leq 1$. As noted earlier, the general equilibrium of the present model can be formulated in terms of the demand and supply relations of either commodity. Let the function $D(1/p_d)$ denote the demand for imports of Y by A's private consumers and let the function $S(1/p)$ denote B's supply of exports of Y. The demand for imports of Y by A's government, as we saw in the preceding section, is given by $\lambda t D$. Therefore, equilibrium will occur when the following condition is satisfied:

$$(1 + \lambda t) \, D(1/p_d) = S(1/p), \tag{19.12}$$

where $p = (1 + t)p_d$. Therefore, equation (19.12) is simply a single equation in two variables, namely, p_d and t. Actually, t is a parameter, so equation (19.12) can be interpreted as giving p_d as a function of the parameter t. To find out how p_d changes as t increases from zero, calculate the derivative dp_d/dt and then put $t = 0$. Differentiating equation (19.12) totally with respect to t, we get

$$\lambda D + (1 + \lambda t) \, D' \, \frac{d(1/p_d)}{dt} = S' \, \frac{d(1/p)}{dt}, \tag{19.13}$$

where primes indicate differentiation. From the equation $p = (1 + t)p_d$, we also get

$$\frac{1}{p} = \left(\frac{1}{1 + t}\right)\left(\frac{1}{p_d}\right). \tag{19.14}$$

Thus,

$$\frac{d(1/p)}{dt} = \frac{(1 + t)[d(1/p_d)/dt] - (1/p_d)}{(1 + t)^2}. \tag{19.15}$$

Substituting equation (19.15) into equation (19.13) and solving the latter for $d(1/p_d)/dt$, we get

$$\frac{d(1/p_d)}{dt} = \frac{[\lambda D + (1/p_d)][1/(1 + t)]^2 S'}{[1/(1 + t)]S' - (1 + \lambda t)D'}. \tag{19.16}$$

Putting $t = 0$ and remembering that, at $t = 0$, $p = p_d = \bar{p}$ and $D = S$, we get

$$\left[\frac{d(1/p_d)}{dt}\right]_{t=0} = \frac{\lambda D + (1/p_d)S'}{S' - D'} = \frac{\lambda + (1/\bar{p})(S'/S)}{(S'/S) - (D'/D)} = \frac{\lambda + \eta_B}{\bar{p}(\eta_B - e_A)}, \tag{19.17}$$

where (according to chap. 6, part B)

$$\eta_B \equiv \frac{1}{\bar{p}} \frac{S'}{S} \equiv B\text{'s supply elasticity of exports},$$

$$e_A \equiv \frac{1}{\bar{p}} \frac{D'}{D} \equiv A\text{'s demand elasticity of imports},$$

with both elasticities evaluated at the free-trade equilibrium point.

What is the sign of the right-hand side of equation (19.17)? We know from chapter 6 (see eq. [6.14]) that, for stability, it is required that $\eta_B - e_A > 0$. Therefore, assuming that the free-trade equilibrium is stable, the sign of the right-hand side of equation (19.17) depends on the sign of the numerator, that is, the sign of $(\lambda + \eta_B)$. When $(\lambda + \eta_B) > 0$, the derivative $[d(1/p_d)/dt]_{t=0}$ will be positive and, therefore, $1/p_d$ will tend to rise with the imposition of the trade tax t (or p_d will tend to fall). Commodity Y will become more expensive in the tax-imposing country A, and therefore its output will rise (in A) at the expense of the output of X. On the other hand, when $(\lambda + \eta_B) < 0$, Y will become cheaper in A (after the imposition of the trade tax) and its output will contract, which is the paradoxical outcome referred to earlier. If $\lambda + \eta_B = 0$, $p_d = \bar{p}$ after the tax and the resource allocation in A will remain, after the imposition of the tax, as it was under free-trade conditions.

Making use of equation (6.9), we can rewrite the numerator of equation (19.17) as $\lambda + \eta_B = \lambda - e_B - 1$. Thus, when $(\lambda - e_B) > 1$, p_d falls (i.e., Y becomes more expensive in A) after the imposition of the tax; if $(\lambda - e_B) < 1$, p_d rises; and if $(\lambda - e_B) = 1$, p_d remains the same as before the imposition of the tax. In words, when the sum of the fraction λ, which can be interpreted as the marginal propensity to import in A, and B's elasticity of demand for imports of X (in absolute terms) is greater than unity, the domestic relative price of imports, Y, rises in the tax-imposing country, A; when it is less than unity, the domestic relative price of imports, Y, falls in A; and if it is unity, domestic prices remain the same as before the tax.

The paradox of the imported commodity becoming cheaper in the tax-imposing country after the imposition of the trade tax occurs when $\lambda - e_B < 1$, or $-e_B < 1 - \lambda$. That is, the absolute value of B's elasticity of demand for imports at the free-trade equilibrium position must be less than $1 - \lambda$. Since $0 \leq \lambda \leq 1$, it is required that B's elasticity of demand for imports be less than unity; that is, the free-trade equilibrium must occur somewhere in the backward-bending region of B's offer curve. Thus, when B's demand for imports at the free-trade equilibrium is elastic, the paradox does not arise. But this conclusion is based solely on the assumption that A's government spends the tax revenue on commodities X and Y. The higher the fraction of the tax revenue that A's government spends on the imported commodity, Y (i.e., λ), the less likely it is for Y to become cheaper in A after the imposition of the trade tax. In particular, when $\lambda = 1$, the condition that Y becomes cheaper in A after the tax reduces to $-e_B < 0$, or $e_B > 0$. We can dismiss this as a rather unusual case, because commodity X would have to be not only inferior and a Giffen good but also a Giffen good whose demand, in the region where free-trade equilibrium occurs, falls more sharply than B's production of X as the relative price of X falls. On the other hand, when $\lambda = 0$, the condition that Y become cheaper in A after the tax reduces to $-e_B < 1$; that is, B's demand for imports of X must be inelastic at the free-trade equilibrium.

Let us illustrate the preceding conclusions graphically. This will also enable us to extend the analysis to the case where A's government redistributes the tax revenue among its private residents. Consider figure 19.5. The curve O_A is A's free-trade offer curve. Assume that free-trade equilibrium occurs at E, with the free-trade equilibrium price ratio given by the slope of the vector OE. Now consider the terms-of-trade line OCD; its slope is, by assumption, equal to $(1 + t)$ times the slope of OE. That is, $FD/OF = (1 + t)(FE/OF)$. Country A's domestic price ratio will continue to be given by the ratio FE/OF (i.e., the free-trade price ratio) if, and only if, A's barter terms of trade after the imposition of the trade tax are given by the slope of the terms-of-trade line OCD. If A's barter terms of trade rise above FD/OF, A's domestic price ratio will rise after the imposition of the trade tax; that is, commodity Y will become cheaper in A after the tax. On the other hand, if A's barter terms of trade are lower than FD/OF after the tax, commodity Y will become more expensive in A. Country A's barter terms of trade after the imposition of the trade tax will be higher than, lower than, or equal to the ratio FD/OF depending on whether, at the barter terms of trade FD/OF, the international excess demand for commodity X is positive, negative, or zero, respectively (or the international excess demand for Y is negative, positive, or zero, respectively). Therefore, we have to compare the offers of A and B at $p = FD/OF$. Country A's offer, as we saw earlier, will fall somewhere along the hypotenuse CD. Where will B's offer lie? That depends on the nature of B's offer curve. If B's offer curve is upward sloping (i.e., B's demand for imports is elastic) in the neighborhood of the free-trade equilibrium position (i.e., in the neighborhood of E) as shown by the broken curve

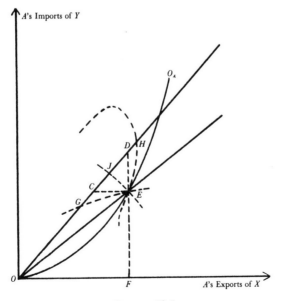

FIGURE 19.5

GE, B's offer will lie somewhere along the straight-line segment OC, as illustrated by point G. In this case, the international excess demand for X at $p = FD/OF$ will be negative, and A's domestic price ratio will definitely be lower than the free-trade price ratio (i.e., FE/OF) after the imposition of the trade tax. Country A will shift resources from the production of X to the production of Y; this reallocation of resources will have the usual effects on factor prices and the distribution of income. This is the normal case where a trade tax enables the import-competing industry of the tax-imposing country to expand at the expense of the export industry.

At the other end of the spectrum is the case where commodity X is a "relatively strong" Giffen good in B such as to cause B's offer curve to behave like the broken curve HE. Note that B's offer curve has a positive slope in this case in the neighborhood of point E. Thus, as X becomes cheaper, B wants to import less and less of X and it offers in exchange less and less of Y. That is, $e_B > 0$. In this case, B's offer for $p = FD/OF$ will lie on the terms-of-trade line OCD but beyond point D, as illustrated by point H. Therefore, at $p = FD/OF$, there will be a positive international excess demand for commodity X, and A's barter terms of trade will be higher than the free-trade international equilibrium price ratio FE/OF. Commodity Y will become cheaper in A after the imposition of the trade tax, and therefore A's import-competing industry, Y, will contract while its export industry, X, will expand, with the usual consequences for factor prices and income distribution.

When B's demand for imports is merely inelastic in the neighborhood of point E, B's offer curve will intersect the terms-of-trade line OCD somewhere along the hypotenuse CD, as illustrated by the broken curve JE. Country B's offer at $p = FD/OF$ will lie somewhere along CD, as illustrated by point J. Whether A's barter terms of trade will be higher or lower than FD/OF after the imposition of the trade tax depends on whether A's offer lies in the region CJ or JD. The precise position of A's offer at $p = FD/OF$ is determined by the way in which A's government spends the tax revenue on X and Y. If all is spent on the imported commodity, Y, that is, if $\lambda = 1$, A's offer will coincide with point D and A's barter terms of trade will definitely be lower than FD/OF after the imposition of the trade tax. (The production of Y will expand at the expense of X.) On the other hand, if A's government spends all the tax revenue on X, A's offer will coincide with point C. Commodity Y will become relatively cheaper in A after the imposition of the trade tax, and resources will shift out of the production of Y into the production of X. What happens when $0 < \lambda < 1$? According to the preceding algebraic analysis, for a sufficiently small trade tax, A's offer at $p = FD/OF$ will coincide with B's when $\lambda - e_B = 1$; it will lie in the region JD when $(\lambda - e_B) > 1$; and it will lie in the region CJ when $(\lambda - e_B) < 1$.

What happens when A's government redistributes the tax revenue among its private citizens? We can use the preceding geometric technique to determine what happens to A's domestic price ratio after the imposition of the trade tax. Consider figure 19.6. The curve O_B is B's offer curve, while the slope of the terms-of-trade line OE shows, as before, A's free-trade equilibrium barter terms of trade. Thus, by assumption, free-trade equilibrium occurs at E. Country A's free-trade offer curve has not been drawn, to avoid cluttering up the diagram. It is not actually needed for the present discussion. Our problem now is the condition under which A's domestic price ratio will remain equal to the free-trade barter terms of trade (i.e., the slope of the vector OE) if country A should impose an infinitesimal trade tax and redistribute the tax revenue among A's citizens. With this information, we shall be able to say when A's domestic price ratio will fall below, and when it will rise above, the free-trade barter terms of trade. First consider the case of a finite trade tax; then, through a limiting process, derive the desired condition.

Suppose that A imposes a trade tax, t, equal to the ratio DF/CD. Country A's domestic price ratio will remain at GE/OG if, and only if, at $p = CF/OC$, A's trade point, after the imposition of the trade tax, coincides with F. What this means is that a subsidy DF (measured in terms of Y at free-trade prices) given by A's government to A's consumers—which is simply the redistri-

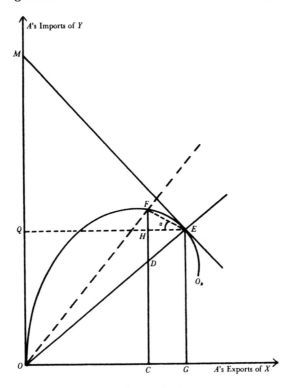

FIGURE 19.6

bution of the tax revenue collected by A's government when A's consumers trade at F at the barter terms of trade CF/OC—induces A's consumers to increase their consumption and, therefore, imports of Y by HF. That is, the ratio HF/DF is simply A's *marginal propensity to import* (m), that is, the fraction of each extra unit of income that A's consumers spend on imports of Y (at the free-trade equilibrium prices). We can express m as a function of the slope (α) of the hypotenuse FE as follows:

$$m \equiv \frac{HF}{DF} = \frac{HF/HE}{DF/HE} = \frac{HF/HE}{(HF/HE) + (DH/HE)} = \frac{\alpha}{\alpha + \bar{p}}. \qquad (19.18)$$

Keeping the domestic price ratio equal to $\bar{p}$ (i.e., the free-trade price ratio), allow the trade tax rate, t, to approach zero continuously. Point F will then travel along B's offer curve toward the free-trade equilibrium point E, and the slope of FE will tend to approach the slope of B's offer curve at E, as shown by the tangent ME. Accordingly, the critical value of m for which an infinitesimal trade tax in A will leave A's domestic price ratio equal to $\bar{p}$ will be given by equation (19.18), where α is simply the slope of B's offer curve at E, that is, $\alpha = QM/QE$. But since $\bar{p} = OQ/QE$, the critical value of m is actually

$$m = \frac{\alpha}{\alpha + \bar{p}} = \frac{QM/QE}{(QM/QE) + (OQ/QE)} = \frac{QM}{QM + OQ} = \frac{QM}{OM}. \qquad (19.19)$$

Recall from chapter 6 that the absolute value of B's elasticity of demand for imports ($|e_B|$) is given by the ratio OQ/OM, that is, $|e_B| = OQ/OM$. Taking the sum $m + e_B$, we get

$$m + |e_B| = \frac{QM}{OM} + \frac{OQ}{OM} = \frac{OM}{OM} = 1. \qquad (19.20)$$

In words, *an infinitesimal trade tax in A with tax revenue redistribution will leave A's domestic price ratio equal to the free-trade price ratio, $\bar{p}$, if, and only if, the sum of A's marginal propensity to import plus the absolute value of B's demand elasticity for imports is equal to unity.* Therefore, A's domestic price ratio will rise above, or fall below, the free-trade price ratio, $\bar{p}$, depending on whether the sum $m + |e_B|$ is less than or greater than unity.

These results coincide with the case where A's goverment spends the fraction λ of the tax revenue on the imported commodity. The parameter λ is now replaced by m. However, there is one difference: whereas λ will ordinarily lie between zero and unity, m can vary over a wider range. Thus, when the imported commodity is inferior, m will assume a negative value; when the exported commodity is inferior, m will assume a value greater than unity. How can our previous conclusion (p. 426) be amended in these two cases? Let us summarize briefly the most important conclusions.

1. When B's demand for imports is elastic at the free-trade equilibrium point and commodity Y is not inferior in A, A's domestic price ratio will always fall (Y will become more expensive) after the imposition of the trade tax. However, if Y is inferior in A, A's domestic price ratio may rise even though $|e_B| > 1$.

2. When B's demand for imports is inelastic at the free-trade equilibrium point and Y is inferior in A, A's domestic price ratio will rise (Y will become cheaper) after the imposition of the trade tax.

3. When commodity X (the commodity imported by B) is a strongly Giffen good in B (see curve HE in fig. 19.5), A's domestic price ratio will always rise provided X is not inferior in A. On the other hand, if X is inferior in A, A's domestic price ratio may fall after the imposition of the trade tax.

SELECTED BIBLIOGRAPHY

The selected bibliography will be found at the end of chapter 20, p. 444.

20

Trade Taxes and Welfare

This chapter is divided into three parts. Part A deals with the welfare effects of trade taxes; part B deals with the effects of import and export subsidies; and finally part C deals briefly with the effects of quantitative restrictions.

A. Trade Taxes and Welfare

What are the effects of trade taxes on the welfare of the world, the welfare of the tax-imposing country, and the welfare of such groups as workers and landlords? These are extremely important questions, and we are now in a position to answer them as efficiently as possible.

1. Trade Taxes and the Welfare of the World

We saw earlier that free trade enables the world to consume along the world production-possibilities frontier; we also saw how the latter can be derived from the production-possibilities frontiers of the individual countries. Before proceeding any further, however, let us clarify the meaning of the world production-possibilities frontier.

In chapter 16, section 5,[1] we derived the world production-possibilities frontier on the assumption that the world consisted of two countries, A and B, whose individual production-possibilities frontiers were given. While the geometrical technique is rather simple, it is important to recall that the frontier we thus derived and shall continue to use shows the maximal quantities of commodities X and Y that the world can produce *under the classical assumption that factors of production do not move internationally*. If this

1. See also chap. 2, section 8.

assumption is dropped and factors of production are allowed to move internationally, the world as a whole will be able to consume, in general, beyond the boundaries of what we have called the world production-possibilities frontier, provided that free commodity trade does not bring about complete equalization of factor prices both relatively and absolutely. For instance, if, after commodity trade equalizes commodity prices, the marginal physical product of labor is lower in B than in A, a migration of labor from B to A will enable the world to produce more of both commodities. In this case, free trade in commodities alone will not permit the world to produce as much as possible of both commodities. In what follows, we shall be interested in the case where factors of production are immobile between countries; therefore, the term "world production-possibilities frontier" will have the narrower meaning we attached to this term earlier. That is, the world production-possibilities frontier, in the narrow sense, shows the maximal quantities of X and Y that the world can produce under the assumption that factors, while perfectly mobile within countries, are completely immobile between countries.

The effect of trade taxes on world output is that they interfere with the international resource allocation in such a way as to make it impossible for the world economy to produce and consume along the world production-possibilities frontier (in the narrow sense). This follows from the observation that the world operates on the world production-possibilities frontier when the two countries are allocating their resources in such a way that their respective marginal rates of transformation are equal. The marginal rate of transformation of a country is in equilibrium equal to its domestic price ratio. Since the existence of trade taxes gives rise to divergence between the domestic price ratios of the two countries, their marginal rates of transformation must necessarily be different. Hence, the world cannot operate on the world production-possibilities frontier in the presence of trade taxes. The cum-tax world production-possibilities frontier necessarily lies inside the free-trade world production-possibilities frontier. But this is by no means the only inefficiency introduced by trade taxes.

Consider two individuals, α a resident of A, and β a resident of B. They both maximize their individual welfares before and after taxes. While, in the absence of trade taxes, the commodity prices paid by consumers are the same everywhere (which implies that the marginal rates of substitution of α and β are identical and, thus, they must be consuming somewhere along their contract curve), the same is not true after the imposition of trade taxes. Country A's domestic price ratio will be different from B's and the marginal rate of substitution in consumption in A will be different from that in B. Therefore, if the same aggregates of X and Y were made available to α and β after the imposition of a trade tax as they were able to consume under free-trade conditions, it would not be possible to make, through lump-sum transfers, both individuals as well off after the trade tax as under free trade.

Because of the divergence between the domestic price ratios of the two countries, the two individuals will not be consuming along the contract curve. This is a second inefficiency introduced by a trade tax (the first being the inability of the world economy to operate along the world production-possibilities frontier).

To summarize, the introduction of a trade tax interferes with the maximization of the potential welfare of the world in two ways: (*a*) the world is forced to produce inside the free-trade world production-possibilities frontier; and (*b*) the allocation of commodities among consumers is inefficient: for the same bundle of commodities before and after the introduction of a trade tax, it is impossible to make all consumers as well off with the trade tax as they were under free-trade conditions. As a result of these inefficiencies, the world as a whole will definitely operate inside the free-trade world utility-possibility frontier. Therefore, from the point of view of potential welfare, the world will be worse off after the introduction of a trade tax. This constitutes, by far, the most important argument against any interference with free international trade.

2. *Trade Taxes and Welfare of the Tax-Imposing Country: The Stolper-Samuelson Theorem*

The *Stolper-Samuelson theorem* purports to determine the effect of trade taxes on the relative and absolute incomes of the tax-imposing country's factors of production.

When a trade tax is imposed, the relative and absolute incomes of the tax-imposing country's factors of production will be affected in two ways: (*a*) through the change of the domestic price ratio and the resultant reallocation of resources, and (*b*) through the redistribution of the tax revenue by the government. The Stolper-Samuelson theorem deals primarily with the first. Its most general formulation within the context of the familiar two-factor, two-commodity model is as follows.

The *Stolper-Samuelson theorem:* The imposition of a trade tax will raise, reduce, or leave unchanged the real wage of factor F used intensively in the production of commodity C (i.e., a trade tax will raise, reduce, or leave unchanged the marginal physical product of factor F in every line of production) as the trade tax raises, lowers, or leaves unchanged the domestic relative price of commodity C.

The truth of the Stolper-Samuelson theorem follows directly from the discussion of the effect of international trade on the welfare of workers and landlords (chap. 15). No further explanation will be given.

This formulation of the Stolper-Samuelson theorem is no doubt correct. But there are those who interpret Stolper and Samuelson differently. They point out that there are several indications that Stolper and Samuelson had in mind a different theorem, namely, "protection raises the real wage of the scarce factor." From the correct formulation of the Stolper-Samuelson theorem, it follows that protection (e.g., the imposition of trade taxes) will raise the real wage of the scarce factor if, and only if, protection raises the domestic relative price of the commodity using intensively the scarce factor (however scarcity is defined). This is not generally true, as we saw earlier in the preceding chapter. However, protection raises the real wage of the scarce factor when the Heckscher-Ohlin theorem is valid (i.e., when a country exports the commodity using intensively its abundant factor) and the imported commodity becomes more expensive in the tax-imposing country after the imposition of a trade tax; or when the Heckscher-Ohlin theorem is invalid and the imported commodity becomes cheaper in the tax-imposing country after the imposition of the trade tax. Since the circumstances under which the Heckscher-Ohlin theorem is valid were analyzed in chapter 9, and since the circumstances under which the imported commodity becomes relatively more expensive or cheaper after the imposition of a trade tax were analyzed earlier in chapter 19, no further refinement of the preceding conclusion (that the statement "protection raises the real wage of the scarce factor" is not generally true) will be given.

3. Trade Taxes and the Welfare of the Tax-Imposing Country: The Optimum Tariff

From the point of view of the world as a whole, free trade is necessarily the best policy. But is it also true that free trade is the best policy from the point of view of a single country?

Chapter 16 introduces the free-trade consumption-possibilities frontier of a country to show the commodity combinations attainable by the country under free trade conditions. Is it possible for a country to consume beyond its free-trade consumption-possibilities frontier by imposing trade taxes? When a country is large (in the sense of being able to affect its barter terms of trade), it will always be possible (in the absence of retaliation by the other country) to impose an appropriate trade tax and consume beyond the free-trade consumption-possibilities frontier. In other words, despite the fact that the imposition of trade taxes implies that the world will be definitely operating inside the world utility-possibility frontier, the tax-imposing country can impose an optimum trade tax and improve its potential welfare, with the other country being penalized, so to speak, both by the tax-imposing country's gain and by the inefficiency introduced by the trade tax.

Consider figure 20.1. The curve *RVS* is *A*'s production-possibilities frontier and the curve *MVN* is *B*'s free-trade offer curve with *V* as origin. In other words, moving from point *V* vertically upward, we measure *B*'s exports of *Y*; moving vertically downward, we measure *B*'s imports of *Y*; moving from *V* to *H* (i.e., leftward), we measure *B*'s imports of *X*; and moving rightward, we measure *B*'s exports of *X*. Point *U* must necessarily lie on *A*'s free-trade

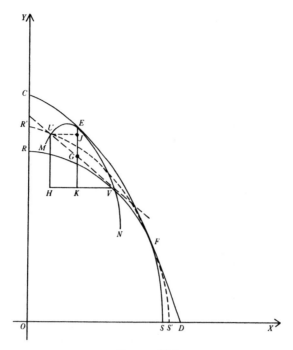

FIGURE 20.1

consumption-possibilities frontier: the tangent to *A*'s production-possibilities frontier at *V* intersects *B*'s offer curve at *U*. Observe that country *A*
can force country *B* to exchange any commodity combination that lies on
the latter's offer curve by simply imposing an appropriate trade tax. Now
slide the origin of *B*'s offer curve along *A*'s production possibilities frontier
and trace out the maximal quantity of each commodity available to country
A for given quantities consumed (by *A*) of the other commodity. By connecting all points so derived by means of a continuous line, we obtain *A*'s
consumption-possibilities frontier that is attainable under an optimum
trade tax scheme, as illustrated by the envelope *CEFD* in figure 20.1. Note
that *A*'s free-trade consumption-possibilities frontier (*R'UFS'*) lies inside the
envelope *CEFD*, except at the singular point *F*. This shows that *A* can
improve its potential welfare by imposing an optimum trade tax and consuming along the envelope *CEFD* instead of consuming on the free-trade
consumption-possibilities frontier *R'UFS'*. Therefore, free trade is *not* the
best policy from the point of view of a single country, assuming away any
retaliatory action by country *B*.

    Observe in figure 20.1 that the slope of the envelope *CEFD* at a point such
as *E* not only is equal to the slope of *B*'s offer curve at *E* but is also equal to
the slope of *A*'s production-possibilities frontier at *V*, the pivot point corresponding to *E*. This follows from the geometrical properties of an envelope,

and it has the important economic interpretation that, at an optimal point (i.e., a point on the envelope *CEFD*), *A*'s marginal rate of transformation is necessarily equal to the *marginal barter terms of trade*. This point requires further clarification.

Assume that under free-trade conditions *A* produces at *V* and consumes at *U* by exchanging *HV* units of *X* for *HU* units of *Y* at the equilibrium terms of trade *HU/HV* (fig. 20.1). Country *A*'s marginal rate of transformation through domestic production (i.e., the slope of *A*'s production-possibilities frontier at *V*) is equal to *A*'s marginal rate of substitution in consumption; however, they are both higher than *A*'s *marginal rate of transformation through trade* (i.e., the number of units of *Y* that *A* will not be able to import from *B* if *A* were to reduce its exports of *X* by 1 unit). Country *A*'s marginal rate of transformation through trade is what we call in the preceding paragraph "marginal barter terms of trade." The average terms of trade at the free-trade equilibrium point are given by the absolute slope of the vector *VU*. How are the marginal terms of trade shown in figure 20.1? For the last *UJ* units of *X* that *A* exported to *B*, it received in exchange *EJ* (negative) units of *Y*. Consider now the ratio *EJ/UJ*, which is simply an approximation of the marginal terms of trade at *U*, and then allow point *E* to approach point *U*. The limit of the ratio *EJ/UJ* as *E* approaches *U* shows the marginal terms of trade at *U*. Graphically, it is given by the slope of the tangent to *B*'s offer curve at *U*. Note that in the case considered in figure 20.1, *A*'s marginal terms of trade are negative. That is, not only did country *A* not receive any positive amount of *Y* from *B* for the last unit of *X* exported to *B*, but, in addition, *A* had to give up some amount of *Y* that it was importing when its exports were a little lower. Therefore, it is to the advantage of *A* to restrict trade and consume more of everything. In general, *A* will maximize the amount of *Y* consumed for any given amount of *X* if, and only if, *A*'s marginal terms of trade are equal to *A*'s marginal rate of transformation (which, in turn, is equal to *A*'s domestic price ratio). Free trade, however, equalizes *A*'s marginal rate of transformation to the average terms of trade. Finally, note that the average terms of trade are equal to the marginal terms only if *B*'s offer curve is a straight line through the origin.

All optimal points on the envelope *CEFD* necessarily correspond to points on *B*'s offer curve where the marginal terms of trade (i.e., the slope) are positive, since *A*'s marginal rate of transformation is always positive. This means that all optimal points on *B*'s offer curve imply that *B*'s demand for imports is elastic.

Where would *A* consume along the envelope *CEFD*? That depends on *A*'s demand conditions as determined both by individual consumer tastes and by optimal transfers to achieve an optimum distribution of income and maximize social welfare. Assuming that the final equilibrium point on the envelope *CEFD* has been determined, can we also determine the optimum tariff (or, in general, the optimum trade tax) that will be required to be

imposed by *A* in order to attain that equilibrium point? Assume that point *E*
in figure 20.1 is the final equilibrium point. Country *A*'s domestic price
ratio (= *A*'s marginal barter terms of trade) will be given by the slope of
VG, while *B*'s domestic price ratio (= *A*'s average barter terms of trade) will
be given by the slope of *VE* (not drawn). The implied trade tax rate is given
by the ratio *GE/KG* (compare with eq. [18.5]), which is the optimum rate.
But the ratio *GE/KG* can be quickly recognized as the reciprocal of *B*'s supply
elasticity of exports (η_B). That is, the optimum tariff, *t*, is equal to the
reciprocal of η_B. Therefore, making use of equations (6.6) and (6.7), we
obtain:

$$t = \frac{1}{\eta_B} = \varepsilon_B - 1 = \frac{-1}{1 + e_B} > 0. \tag{20.1}$$

Note that $t > 0$ because $e_B < -1$. This does not imply that the optimum
trade tax is uniquely determined. The precise value of *B*'s demand elasticity
for imports (e_B) to be used in equation (20.1) depends on the precise equilibrium point along the envelope *CEFD* of figure 20.1. Since, in general, there
is an infinite number of optimal points along the envelope *CEFD*, there will
be an infinite number of optimal tariff rates. Accordingly, very little assistance can be offered in the search for the optimum trade tax: the social
welfare function needs to be completely specified for this purpose.

Assume now that in each of the two countries there exists a completely
specified welfare function and that income is always reallocated among
individuals in such a way as to maximize social welfare. Then, as Samuelson
has shown, there will be a social indifference map in each country, with all
the usual properties of an individual consumer's indifference map, which
will summarize social behavior. A movement from a lower to a higher social
indifference curve will by necessity imply an improvement in social welfare.
Under these conditions, we can be more specific about the optimum trade
tax.

Consider figure 20.2. Free-trade equilibrium occurs at *E*. Country *A*
reaches the broken trade indifference curve I_A^t and *B* the broken curve
I_B^t. Now assume that *B* continues to trade along its free-trade offer curve
irrespective of *A*'s policy. What is the optimum trade tax for country *A*?
We must first determine the point on *B*'s offer curve where *A* would like to
trade and maximize its social welfare. (It is assumed that *A*'s government
redistributes all tax revenue among its private consumers.) The desired
point will be that point on *B*'s offer curve where the latter becomes tangent
to the highest possible trade indifference curve of *A*. In figure 20.2, this
occurs at point *Z*. Now the optimum tax rate can be uniquely determined as
follows. Draw the tangent to *B*'s offer curve at *Z*, as shown by *UZ*; also
draw the horizontal line *RZ* through point *Z*. The implied tax rate is given
by the ratio *OU/UR*, which is simply the reciprocal of *B*'s elasticity of supply
of exports at *Z*. Observe that *A*'s domestic price ratio is given by the slope

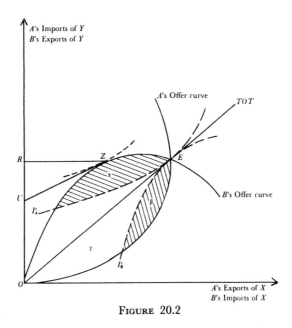

FIGURE 20.2

of UZ, which is also A's marginal barter terms of trade. Therefore, point Z must correspond to a point on A's consumption envelope.

If B's offer curve were a straight line through the origin, as shown by the free-trade equilibrium terms-of-trade line TOT, the optimum trade tax would be zero. Any other point on TOT besides E would put A on a lower trade indifference curve. This confirms our earlier conclusion regarding a small country that takes international prices as given. There, we saw that a trade tax necessarily deteriorates the country's potential welfare, that is, the optimum trade tax is zero.

Up to this point, the discussion has been based on the unrealistic assumption that, while A imposes an optimum trade tax, B continues to maintain a free-trade policy. But both countries can play the game. What happens when B pursues an optimum trade tax policy as well? Beginning from the free-trade position, assume that A imposes an optimum tariff as shown in figure 20.2. Its trade-tax-distorted offer curve (not drawn) will lie to the left of its free-trade offer curve and pass through Z. Country A's welfare improves but B's deteriorates in comparison with the free-trade point E. Country B might then retaliate by imposing an optimum trade tax, which will maximize its own social welfare under the assumption that A will maintain the original trade tax rate. However, B's imposition of a trade tax shifts B's offer curve (below B's free-trade offer curve); therefore, the initial trade tax levied by A is no longer optimal. It would thus be profitable for A to change its initial trade tax rate to some new value. But this in turn shifts A's offer curve further, so B's original trade tax rate will no longer be optimal. Country *B* will be tempted to make a change, and so on in an infinite regression.

Three interesting questions now arise. First, do there exist "equilibrium" trade tax rates which, if they were imposed simultaneously by *A* and *B*, would call for no further change? Second, will the process described in the preceding paragraph lead to the establishment of the equilibrium trade tax rates? Third, is it possible for at least one country to gain from this tariff war? Clearly, both countries cannot gain because of the inefficiencies introduced by the trade taxes. These questions will not be analyzed in detail. Nevertheless, the following comments are worth making.

1. Because a trade tax by *A* shifts *A*'s free-trade offer curve above and to the left, and a trade tax by *B* shifts *B*'s free-trade offer curve below and to the right, any solution will necessarily occur in the region bounded by the two free-trade offer curves, between *O* and *E* (fig. 20.2).

2. If the final equilibrium point lies in the unshaded region γ (fig. 20.2), both countries will definitely lose; if it lies in the shaded region α, *A* will gain but *B* will lose; and if it lies in the shaded area β, *A* will lose but *B* will gain.

3. If the barter terms of trade at the final equilibrium position are equal to the free-trade terms of trade, the final equilibrium point will occur somewhere on the straight line *OE*, and both countries will lose.

4. When both countries lose at the final equilibrium point, they can improve their respective levels of social welfare through bilateral trade liberalization.

5. Even when one country gains, the loser will always be able to bribe the gainer through a direct income transfer to abolish all trade restrictions.

B. Import and Export Subsidies

Trade subsidies are merely negative trade taxes. There is one difference, however, between the analysis of trade subsidies and that of trade taxes. In the latter case, the government has the choice of spending the tax revenue directly on *X* and *Y* in any proportion whatsoever or distributing it among its private citizens. In the case of trade subsidies, we are practically forced to make the assumption that *the government raises the amount used to subsidize trade through a general income tax on its private citizens*. Otherwise, the government would be required to somehow produce positive quantities of *X* and *Y*. While it is always possible for the government to consume positive amounts of *X* and *Y*, as in the case of trade taxes, it is absolutely impossible to produce positive amounts of *X* and *Y* (in the case of trade subsidies) when all productive activity is in the hands of its private citizens. The assumption that the government imposes a general income tax is actually a simplification, because it reduces the number of possibilities.

A detailed analysis of trade subsidies would be redundant. However, an indication of how trade subsidies modify the offer curve of the country paying the subsidies is in order. Assume that the international price ratio (p_x/p_y) is $\bar{p}$. If A's government pays an export subsidy of $s \times 100$ percent to A's exporters of X, A's domestic price ratio (p_d) would be

$$\bar{p} = p_d(1 - s). \tag{20.2}$$

Note that exactly the same relationship between $\bar{p}$ and p_d as given by equation (20.2) will also exist when A's government pays an import subsidy of $s \times 100$ percent to A's importers of Y. Therefore, there is no need to distinguish between an export subsidy and an import subsidy.

Consider now figure 20.3. The terms-of-trade line TOT represents the offer curve of the rest of the world; O_A is A's free-trade offer curve; and the slope of the broken line OE_1 shows A's domestic price ratio under the assumption that the international price ratio is $\bar{p}$ and A's government pays a trade subsidy of $s \times 100$ percent. Free-trade equilibrium occurs at E_0. However, at domestic prices, given by the slope of OE_1, A's consumers would like to trade at E_1 provided the government did not impose any income tax on its citizens. However, A's government will impose a general income tax to finance the trade subsidy. Where would A's private consumers like to trade when $p_d = \bar{p}/(1 - s)$ and A's government imposes the necessary income tax? Imagine the broken line OE_1 shifted in a parallel fashion to the right and trace out all tangencies generated by it with A's trade indifference curves, as shown by the broken line E_1E_2. Since, as we have shown in the

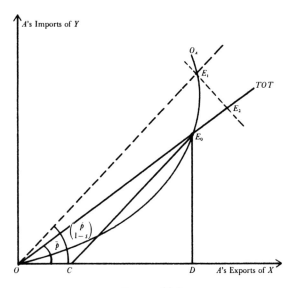

FIGURE 20.3

case of trade taxes, equilibrium can only occur along TOT, the desired trade point must be E_2. Observe that, for reasons explained in the case of trade taxes, point E_2 must lie to the right of A's free-trade offer curve.

How can the rate-of-trade subsidy be shown graphically? Draw a line through E_0 parallel to OE_1, and also draw the vertical line E_0D. Now we have $\bar{p} = DE_0/OD$ and

$$\frac{\bar{p}}{1 - s} = \frac{DE_0}{CD},$$

or

$$\bar{p} = (DE_0/CD)(1 - s),$$

Therefore,

$$DE_0/OD = (DE_0/CD)(1 - s),$$

or

$$CD/OD = 1 - s,$$

or

$$s = 1 - \frac{CD}{OD} = \frac{OD - CD}{OD} = \frac{OC}{OD}. \qquad (20.3)$$

Having determined a point (E_2) on A's subsidy-distorted offer curve, we can repeat the same experiment as many times as we want and produce the whole subsidy-distorted offer curve. This will necessarily lie to the right of the free-trade offer curve. Once the subsidy-distorted offer curve is completely derived, the analysis can proceed along familiar lines.

C. Quantitative Restrictions

Let us consider briefly the second form of trade controls, quantitative restrictions on exports and imports. When the government, for one reason or another, desires to control directly the quantity of imports, it may decree that only a given quantity (import quota) may be imported per unit of time. For this purpose, it may issue import licences that it can either sell to importers at a competitive price or just give away on a first-come, first-served basis. Similarly, the government may desire to control directly the quantity of exports, and it may therefore decree that only a given quantity (export quota) may be exported per unit of time. For this purpose, it may issue export licences that it can either sell or give away.

Consider figure 20.4. Curves O_A and O_B are A's and B's free-trade offer curves, respectively. Free-trade equilibrium occurs at E_1. Country A exports OX_1 units of X to B in exchange for OY_1 units of Y imported from B. Suppose that A's government decides to restrict the imports from B to OY_2 units of Y per unit of time. Assume that it does this by issuing import licences that it sells to A's importers at a competitive price. Assume, further, that it redistributes among its private citizens all revenue collected from the sale

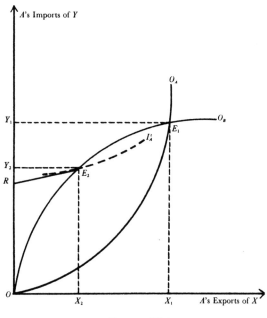

FIGURE 20.4

of the import licences. How would equilibrium be established under these circumstances? Country B will be forced to trade at E_2, and since B remains perfectly competitive, B's domestic price ratio (= barter terms of trade) will be given by the slope of the vector OE_2 (not drawn). What would A's domestic price ratio be? Draw A's trade indifference curve I_A^t through E_2 and then draw the tangent at E_2, as shown by RE_2. Country A's domestic price ratio will necessarily be given by the slope of RE_2.

Several observations can be made. First, A's government, instead of restricting imports to OY_2, could have restricted exports to OX_2. Therefore, there is a symmetry between export and import quotas, as with trade taxes. Second, B could be forced to trade at E_2 with an appropriate trade tax (given by the ratio OR/RY_2). Therefore, the effects of export and import quotas are identical to those of trade taxes. However, there are several fundamental differences between export and import quotas, on the one hand, and trade taxes, on the other. For one thing, the revenue of an import quota, while equal to the tariff revenue of an equivalent tariff, may not accrue to A's government. It may accrue to A's importers (when the government gives the import licences away on a first-come, first-served basis), or it may accrue to B's exporters, when the latter can collude but A's importers cannot. Subsequent shifts in supply and demand in either country will cause the equivalent trade tax rate to change while the country continues to export, or import, as the case may be, the same quantity as before the change took place. Finally, the conversion of a tariff into a quota that admits exactly the same volume of imports may convert a potential into an actual monopoly by eliminating the threat of competition from increased imports. Conversely, the conversion of a quota into an equivalent tariff will eliminate an actual monopoly by threatening it with potential competition from increased imports.

SELECTED BIBLIOGRAPHY

Bhaghwati, J. 1959. Protection, real wages and real incomes. *Economic Journal* 69: 733–48.
Bhaghwati, J., and H. G. Johnson. 1961. A generalized theory of the effects of tariffs on the terms of trade. *Oxford Economic Papers* 13: 225–53.
Bhaghwati, J., and V. K. Ramaswami. 1963. Domestic distortions, tariffs, and the theory of optimum subsidy. *Journal of Political Economy* 71: 44–50; reprinted in A.E.A. *Readings in International Economics*. Homewood, Ill.: R. D. Irwin, Inc., 1968.
Black, J. 1959. Arguments for tariffs. *Oxford Economic Papers* N.S. 11: 191–220.
Haberler, G. 1950. Some problems in the pure theory of international trade. *Economic Journal* 60: 223–40; reprinted in A.E.A. *Readings in International Economics*. Homewood, Ill.: R. D. Irwin, Inc., 1968.
Johnson, H. G. 1965. Optimal trade intervention in the presence of domestic distortions. Published in Baldwin et al. (Editors). *Trade, Growth, and the Balance of Payments*. Chicago, Ill.: Rand McNally & Co., 1965.
———. 1953. Optimum tariffs and retaliation. *Review of Economic Studies* 21: 142–53; reprinted in H. G. Johnson. *International Trade and Economic Growth: Studies in Pure Theory*. Cambridge, Mass.: Harvard University Press, 1958.
Kindleberger, C. P. 1968. *International Economics*, 4th ed. Homewood, Ill.: R. D. Irwin, Inc. Chaps. 7–10.
Meade, J. E. 1955. *The Theory of International Economic Policy. Vol. II: Trade and Welfare*. New York: Oxford University Press.
———. 1961. *A Geometry of International Trade*. London: George Allen & Unwin, Ltd. Chap. VI.
Metzler, L. A. 1949. Tariffs, the terms of trade, and the distribution of national income. *Journal of Political Economy* 57: 1–29; reprinted in A.E.A. *Readings in International Economics*. Homewood, Ill.: R. D. Irwin, Inc., 1968.
Samuelson, P. A. 1962. The gains from international trade once again. *Economic Journal* 72: 820–29; reprinted in J. Stiglitz (Editor). *The Collected Scientific Papers of Paul A. Samuelson*, Vol. 2. Cambridge, Mass.: The M.I.T. Press, 1966.
Scitovsky, T. 1942. A reconsideration of the theory of tariffs. *Review of Economic Studies* 9: 89–110; reprinted in A.E.A. *Readings in the Theory of International Trade*. Homewood, Ill.: R. D. Irwin, Inc., 1950.
Stolper, W. F., and P. A. Samuelson. 1941. Protection and real wages. *Review of Economic Studies* 9: 50–73; reprinted in A.E.A. *Readings in the Theory of International Trade*. Homewood, Ill.: R. D. Irwin, Inc., 1950.
Vanek, J. 1962. *International Trade: Theory and Economic Policy*. Homewood, Ill.: R. D. Irwin. Chap. 16.

Name Index

Subject Index